DATE DUE

			PRINTED IN U.S.A.

SOMETHING ABOUT THE AUTHOR®

Something about
the Author *was named
an "Outstanding
Reference Source"
the highest honor given
by the American
Library Association
Reference and Adult
Services Division.*

ISSN 0276-816X

R

SOMETHING ABOUT THE AUTHOR®

**Facts and Pictures about Authors
and Illustrators of Books for Young People**

EDITED BY
DIANE TELGEN

VOLUME 76

 Gale Research Inc. • *DETROIT* • *WASHINGTON, D.C.* • *LONDON*

STAFF

Editor: Diane Telgen

Associate Editor: Marie Ellavich

Senior Editor: James G. Lesniak

Sketchwriters/Copyeditors: Marilyn K. Basel, Joanna Brod, Cheryl C. Cayce, Robin Cook, Pamela S. Dear, Kathleen J. Edgar, David M. Galens, Ronie-Richele Garcia-Johnson, Mary Gillis, Jeff Hill, David Johnson, Sharyn Kolberg, Margaret Mazurkiewicz, Thomas F. McMahon, Peg McNichol, Michael E. Mueller, Scot Peacock, Tom Pendergast, Wendy Pfeffer, Nancy Rampson, Susan M. Reicha, Terrie M. Rooney, Susan Salter, Mary Lois Sanders, Pamela L. Shelton, Kenneth R. Shepherd, Aarti D. Stephens, Linda Tidrick, Brandon Trenz, Roger M. Valade III, Polly Vedder, Thomas Wiloch, and Lisa A. Wroble

Research Manager: Victoria B. Cariappa
Research Supervisor: Mary Rose Bonk
Editorial Associates: Reginald A. Carlton, Clare Collins, Andrew Guy Malonis, and Norma Sawaya
Editorial Assistants: Patricia Bowen, Rachel A. Dixon, Eva Marie Felts, Shirley Gates, Sharon McGilvray, and Devra M. Sladics

Picture Permissions Supervisor: Margaret A. Chamberlain
Permissions Associates: Pamela A. Hayes, Arlene Johnson, and Keith Reed
Permissions Assistants: Susan Brohman and Barbara Wallace

Production Director: Mary Beth Trimper
External Production Assistant: Shanna Heilveil
Art Director: Cynthia Baldwin
Desktop Publisher/Typesetter: Sherrell Hobbs
Camera Operator: Willie Mathis

Library of Congress Catalog Card Number 72-27107

ISBN 0-8103-2286-2 ISSN 0276-816X

Printed in the United States of America

Published simultaneously in the United Kingdom by Gale Research International Limited
(An affiliated company of Gale Research Inc.)

I(T)P™

The trademark **ITP** is used under license.

10 9 8 7 6 5 4 3 2 1

Contents

Authors in Forthcoming Volumes

Below are some of the authors and illustrators that will be featured in upcoming volumes of *SATA*. These include new entries on the swiftly-rising stars of the field, as well as completely revised and updated entries (indicated with *) on some of the most notable and best-loved creators of books for children.

*Mitsumasa Anno: This Japanese author-illustrator is widely known for picture books that combine visual trickery and humor to create imaginative introductions to scientific and mathematical concepts.

Jennifer Armstrong: Armstrong earned a Golden Kite citation for *Steal Away,* a story of interracial friendship during the nineteenth century.

*Bruce Coville: Author of the bestsellers *Jeremy Thatcher, Dragon Hatcher* and *Jennifer Murdley's Toad,* Coville is popular with middle readers, who enjoy his fast-paced, humorous stories.

Ruby Dee: This famous star of stage and screen recently expanded her career to writing two adaptations of African folktales for children.

Jan Hudson: Before her death at age 35 cut short a promising literary career, this Canadian author penned two historical novels set among the Blackfoot Indian tribe, including the multi-award-winning *Sweetgrass.*

Belinda Hurmence: This North Carolina author has brought the age of slavery to light with both her award-winning novels and her collections of slave narratives. (Entry includes exclusive interview.)

Kit Pearson: Canadian writer Pearson, a former librarian, focuses on the real-life problems of young outsiders in works such as the award-winning trilogy that begins with *The Sky Is Falling.*

Barry Louis Polisar: A former writer for *Sesame Street,* singer-songwriter Polisar has produced numerous children's records and videos in addition to books such as *The Trouble with Ben.*

*Stephen Roos: Roos's works include humorous school stories for middle readers, such as *My Horrible Secret,* and serious novels for young adults, such as *You'll Miss Me When I'm Gone.* (Entry includes exclusive interview).

*Robert Kimmel Smith: Smith uses a humorous approach to write about serious issues, making his work very popular with kids. (Entry includes exclusive interview.)

*Susan Terris: Terris explores turning points in the lives of her protagonists, examining the ways adolescents deal with their fears. (Entry includes exclusive interview.)

William Wegman: Famous for stylized photographs of his Weimaraner dogs, Wegman has recently produced fairy tales featuring his canine models.

Sherley Anne Williams: Noted African-American scholar and poet Williams has also created the best-selling children's book *Working Cotton,* a story of migrant workers based on some of her poems.

*Carol Beach York: York is known both for her amusing "Miss Know It All" stories, which take place in a girls' orphanage, as well as her suspenseful mysteries for young adults. (Entry includes exclusive interview.)

Introduction

Something about the Author (*SATA*) is an ongoing reference series that deals with the lives and works of authors and illustrators of children's books. *SATA* includes not only well-known authors and illustrators whose books are widely read, but also those less prominent people whose works are just coming to be recognized. This series is often the only readily available information source on emerging writers or artists. You'll find *SATA* informative and entertaining whether you are a student, a librarian, an English teacher, a parent, or simply an adult who enjoys children's literature for its own sake.

What's Inside SATA

SATA provides detailed information about authors and illustrators who span the full time range of children's literature, from early figures like John Newbery and L. Frank Baum to contemporary figures like Judy Blume and Richard Peck. Authors in the series represent primarily English-speaking countries, particularly the United States, Canada, and the United Kingdom. Also included, however, are authors from around the world whose works are available in English translation. The writings represented in *SATA* include those created intentionally for children and young adults as well as those written for a general audience and known to interest younger readers. These writings cover the entire spectrum of children's literature, including picture books, humor, folk and fairy tales, animal stories, mystery and adventure, science fiction and fantasy, historical fiction, poetry and nonsense verse, drama, biography, and nonfiction.

Obituaries are also included in *SATA* and are intended not only as death notices but as concise views of people's lives and work. Additionally, each edition features newly revised and updated entries for a selection of *SATA* listees who remain of interest to today's readers and who have been active enough to require extensive revision of their earlier biographies.

Two Convenient Indexes

In response to suggestions from librarians, *SATA* indexes no longer appear in each volume, but are included in alternate (odd-numbered) volumes of the series, beginning with Volume 57.

SATA continues to include two indexes that cumulate with each alternate volume: the Illustrations Index, arranged by the name of the illustrator, gives the number of the volume and page where the illustrator's work appears in the current volume as well as all preceding volumes in the series; the Author Index gives the number of the volume in which a person's Biographical Sketch or Obituary appears in the current volume as well as all preceding volumes in the series.

These indexes also include references to authors and illustrators who appear in Gale's *Yesterday's Authors of Books for Children, Children's Literature Review,* and the *Something about the Author Autobiography Series.*

Easy-to-Use Entry Format

Whether you're already familiar with the *SATA* series or just getting acquainted, you will want to be aware of the kind of information that an entry provides. In every *SATA* entry the editors attempt to give as complete a picture of the person's life and work as possible. A typical entry in *SATA* includes the following clearly labeled information sections:

- *PERSONAL:* date and place of birth and death, parents' names and occupations, name of spouse, date of marriage, and names of children, educational institutions attended, degrees received, religious and political affiliations, hobbies and other interests.

- *ADDRESSES:* complete home, office, and agent's address.

- *CAREER:* name of employer, position, and dates for each career post; military service.

• *MEMBER:* memberships and offices held in professional and civic organizations.

• *AWARDS, HONORS:* literary and professional awards received.

• *WRITINGS:* title-by-title chronological bibliography of books written and/or illustrated, listed by genre when known; lists of other notable publications, such as plays, screenplays, and periodical contributions.

• *ADAPTATIONS:* a list of films, television programs, plays, and other media which have been adapted from the author's work.

• *WORK IN PROGRESS:* description of projects in progress.

• *SIDELIGHTS:* a biographical portrait of the author's development, either directly from the person—and often written specifically for the *SATA* entry—or gathered from diaries, letters, interviews, or other published sources.

• *FOR MORE INFORMATION SEE:* references for further reading.

• *EXTENSIVE ILLUSTRATIONS:* photographs, movie stills, manuscript samples, book covers, and other interesting visual materials supplement the text.

How a SATA Entry Is Compiled

A *SATA* entry progresses through a series of steps. If the biographee is living, the *SATA* editors try to secure information directly from him or her through a questionnaire. From the information that the biographee supplies, the editors prepare an entry, filling in any essential missing details with research and/or telephone interviews. When necessary, the author or illustrator is sent a copy of the entry to check for accuracy and completeness.

If the biographee is deceased or cannot be reached by questionnaire, the *SATA* editors examine a wide variety of published sources to gather information for an entry. Biographical and bibliographic sources are consulted, as are book reviews, feature articles, published interviews, and material sometimes obtained from the biographee's family, publishers, agent, or other associates. Entries compiled entirely from secondary sources are marked with an asterisk (*).

We Welcome Your Suggestions

We invite you to examine the entire *SATA* series, starting with this volume. Please write and tell us if we can make *SATA* even more helpful to you. Send comments and suggestions to: The Editor, *Something about the Author,* Gale Research Inc., 835 Penobscot Bldg., Detroit, Michigan 48226.

Acknowledgments

Grateful acknowledgment is made to the following publishers, authors, and artists whose works appear in this volume.

VIVIEN ALCOCK. Cover of *Travelers by Night,* by Vivien Alcock. Copyright © 1983 by Vivien Alcock. Cover illustration by Vincent Natale. Reprinted by permission of Delacorte Press, a division of Bantam Doubleday Dell Publishing Group, Inc./ Cover of *The Monster Garden,* by Vivien Alcock. Copyright © 1988 by Vivien Alcock. Cover illustration by Frank Morris. Reprinted by permission of Delacorte Press, a division of Bantam Doubleday Dell Publishing Group, Inc./ Cover of *The Trial of Anna Cotman,* by Vivien Alcock. Copyright © 1990 by Vivien Alcock. Cover illustration by Savio. Reprinted by permission of Delacorte Press, a division of Bantam Doubleday Dell Publishing Group, Inc./ Photograph courtesy of Vivien Alcock.

BOB ALLEN. Photograph courtesy of Bob Allen.

EMILY ARNOLD. Illustration by Emily Arnold McCully from *Lulu and the Witch Baby,* by Jane O'Conner. Illustrations copyright © 1986 by Emily Arnold McCully. Reprinted by permission of HarperCollins Publishers, Inc./ Illustration by Emily Arnold from her *The Grandma Mix-Up.* Copyright © 1988 by Emily Arnold McCully. Reprinted by permission of HarperCollins Publishers, Inc./ Illustrations by Emily Arnold McCully from her *Mirette on the High Wire.* Copyright © 1992 by Emily Arnold McCully. Reprinted by permission of G. P. Putnam's Sons, a division of The Putnam & Grosset Book Group./ Photograph by Tom Bloom.

CECILE BERTRAND. Photograph courtesy of Cecile Bertrand.

RAYMOND BIAL. Jacket by Raymond Bial from his *Amish Home.* Houghton Mifflin Company, 1993. Jacket art copyright © 1993 by Raymond Bial. Reprinted by permission of Houghton Mifflin Company./ Photograph courtesy of Raymond Bial.

GRAYCE BOCHAK. Photograph courtesy of Grayce Bochak.

BARBARA BRENNER. Cover of *Lion and Lamb Step Out,* by Barbara Brenner and William H. Hooks. Illustration copyright © 1990 by Bruce Degen and Byron Preiss Visual Publications, Inc. Reprinted by permission of Bantam, a division of Bantam Doubleday Dell Publishing Group, Inc./ Illustration from *The Five Pennies,* by Barbara Brenner. Copyright illustration © 1964 by Erik Blegvad. Copyright renewed 1992 by Erik Blegvad. Reprinted by permission of Random House, Inc.

BILL BRITTAIN. Cover of *Professor Popkin's Prodigious Polish: A Tale of Coven Tree,* by Bill Brittain. Cover art copyright © 1991 by Mike Wimmer. Cover copyright © 1991 by HarperCollins Publishers, Inc. Reprinted by permission of HarperCollins Publishers, Inc./ Cover of *Devil's Donkey,* by Bill Brittain. Cover art copyright © 1990 by Mike Wimmer. Reprinted by permission of HarperCollins Publishers, Inc./ Cover of *The Wish Giver,* by Bill Brittain. Cover art copyright © 1990 by Mike Wimmer. Reprinted by permission of HarperCollins Publishers, Inc.

GEOFFREY BRITTINGHAM. Photograph courtesy of Geoffrey Brittingham.

DICK BRUNA. Cover by Dick Bruna from his *Opa en oma Pluis.* Illustrations Dick Bruna, copyright © Mercis b.v. 1988. Reprinted by permission of Meulenhoff Informatief./ Illustration by Dick Bruna from his *Dick Bruna's Animal Book.* Illustrations copyright © 1972 by Mercis b.v. Reprinted by permission of Methuen Children's Books./ Photograph by Ferry Andre de la Porte.

JIMMY BUFFETT. Photograph by Ray Stanyard, courtesy of Margaritaville Records.

A'LELIA PERRY BUNDLES. Photograph courtesy of A'Lelia Perry Bundles.

DOMINIC CATALANO. Photograph courtesy of Dominic Catalano.

VERA CLEAVER. Jacket of *Where the Lilies Bloom,* by Vera and Bill Cleaver. Copyright © 1969 by Vera and William J. Cleaver. Cover illustration by Jim Spanfeller. Reprinted by permission of HarperCollins Publishers, Inc./ Jacket of *Grover,* by Vera and Bill Cleaver. Copyright © 1970 by Vera and William J. Cleaver. Jacket illustration by Larry Raymond. Reprinted by permission of HarperCollins Publishers, Inc./ Cover of *The Kissimmee Kid,* by Vera and Bill Cleaver. Cover illustration copyright © 1991 by Daniel Mark Duffy. Reprinted by permission of Beech Tree Books, an imprint of William Morrow and Company, Inc./ Cover of *The Whys and Wherefores of Littabelle Lee,* by Bill and Vera Cleaver. Atheneum, New York, 1973. Copyright © 1973 by Vera and Bill Cleaver. Cover by Julie MacRae. Reprinted by permission of Atheneum Publishers, an imprint of Macmillan Publishing Company./ Jacket of *Sugar Blue,* by Vera Cleaver. Jacket illustration copyright © 1984 by Eric Jon Nones. Reprinted by permission of Lothrop, Lee & Shepard Books, a division of William Morrow and Company, Inc./ Photograph courtesy of Vera Cleaver.

JAMES A. CORRICK. Photograph courtesy of James A. Corrick.

MICHELE COXON. Photograph by John Poole, courtesy of Michele Coxon.

DONALD CREWS. Illustration by Donald Crews from his *Bigmama's.* Copyright © 1991 by Donald Crews. Reprinted by permission of Greenwillow Books, a division of William Morrow and Company, Inc./ Illustration by Donald Crews from his *Shortcut.* Copyright © 1992 by Donald Crews. Reprinted by permission of Greenwillow Books, a division of William Morrow and Company, Inc./ Cover by Donald Crews from his *Freight Train.* Copyright © 1978 by Donald Crews. Reprinted by permission of William Morrow and Company, Inc./ Photograph by Chuck Kelton.

FRED H. CRUMP, JR. Photograph courtesy of Fred H. Crump, Jr.

NICHOLAS DALY. Illustration by Niki Daly from his *Papa Lucky's Shadow.* Copyright © 1992 by Niki Daly. Reprinted by permission of Margaret K. McElderry Books, an imprint of Macmillan Publishing Company. Reprinted in Canada and the British Commonwealth by The Bodley Head./ Illustration by Niki Daly from his *Not So Fast Songololo.* Copyright © 1985 by Niki Daly. Reprinted in the United States by permission of Margaret K. McElderry Books, an imprint of Macmillan Publishing Company. Reprinted in Canada and the British Commonwealth by Victor Gollancz Ltd.

ALAN AND LEA DANIEL. Illustration by Alan Daniel from *Rabbit-Cadabra!,* by James Howe. Text copyright © 1993 by James Howe. Illustrations copyright © 1993 by Alan Daniel. Reprinted by permission of Morrow Junior Books, a division of William Morrow and Company, Inc./ Illustration by Alan Daniel from *Down by the Bay.* Copyright © 1990 by Thomas C. Wright, Inc./The Wright Group. Illustrations copyright © 1990 by Alan Daniel. Reprinted by permission of the publisher./ Illustration by Alan and Lea Daniel from *The Ants Go Marching.* Copyright © 1992 by Alan & Lea Daniel. Copyright © 1992 The Wright Group. Reprinted by permission of the publisher./ Illustration by Alan and Lea Daniel from *The Story of Canada,* by Janet Lunn and Christopher Moore. Original illustrations copyright © 1992 by Alan Daniel unless otherwise credited. Reprinted by permission of Alan Daniel./ Photograph courtesy of Alan Daniel.

DAVID DeRAN. Photograph by Cathy DeRan, courtesy of David DeRan.

ARTHUR DIAMOND. Photograph courtesy of Arthur Diamond.

ANGEL DOMINGUEZ. Photograph courtesy of Angel Dominguez.

JOYCE DUNBAR. Jacket of *I Want a Blue Banana!,* by Joyce and James Dunbar. Houghton Mifflin Company, 1991. Text copyright © 1991 by Joyce Dunbar. Jacket art copyright © 1991 by James Dunbar. Reprinted in the United States by permission of Houghton Mifflin Company. Reprinted in the British Commonwealth and Canada by permission of J. M. Dent & Sons Ltd./ Photograph courtesy of Joyce Dunbar.

EILEEN DUNLOP. Cover of *The House on the Hill,* by Eileen Dunlop. Copyright © 1987 by Eileen Dunlop. Reprinted by permission of Troll Associates./ Jacket of *The Valley of the Deer,* by Eileen Dunlop. Copyright © 1989 by Eileen Dunlop. Jacket illustration by Tudor Humphries. Reprinted by permission of Holiday House, Inc./ Photograph by Eric Campbell, courtesy of Eileen Dunlop.

JOHN DYESS. Photograph courtesy of John Dyess.

CLAIRE EWART. Illustration by Claire Ewart from *Time Train,* by Paul Fleischman. Illustrations copyright © 1991 by Claire Ewart. Reprinted by permission of HarperCollins Publishers, Inc./ Photograph by Daniel Nichols, courtesy of Claire Ewart.

MARY ANN FRASER. Photograph courtesy of Mary Ann Fraser.

GYO FUJIKAWA. Illustration by Gyo Fujikawa from her **Oh, What A Busy Day!** Grosset & Dunlap, 1976. Copyright © 1976 by Gyo Fujikawa. Reprinted by permission of Grosset & Dunlap, Inc., a member of The Putnam & Grosset Book Group./ Illustration by Gyo Fujikawa from her *Gyo Fujikawa's A to Z Picture Book.* Copyright © 1974 by Gyo Fujikawa. Reprinted by permission of Grosset & Dunlap, Inc., a member of The Putnam & Grosset Book Group./ Illustration by Gyo Fujikawa from her *Babies.* Grosset & Dunlap, 1963. Copyright © 1963, 1991 by Gyo Fujikawa. Reprinted by permission of Grosset & Dunlap, Inc., a member of The Putnam & Grosset Book Group.

JANE P. FUTCHER. Photograph by Erin Carney, courtesy of Jane Futcher.

LILA GANO. Photograph courtesy of Lila Gano.

JANE GARDAM. Jacket of *The Hollow Land,* by Jane Gardam. Illustration copyright © 1981 by Janet Rawlins. Reprinted in the United States by permission of Greenwillow Books, a division of William Morrow and Company, Inc./ Photograph © Jerry Bauer.

LEON GARFIELD. Cover of *Mr. Corbett's Ghost and Other Stories,* by Leon Garfield. 'Mr. Corbett's Ghost' copyright © 1968 by Leon Garfield. Front cover photograph by David James shows Paul Scofield in Mr. Corbett's Ghost, a VIP Film Production. Reprinted by permission of Penguin Books Limited./ Cover of *Jack Holborn,* by Leon Garfield. Copyright © 1964 by Leon Garfield. The cover shows Patrick Bach in Jack Holborn, a TV60/Georgefilm. Reprinted by permission of Penguin Books Limited./ Cover of *The Apprentices,* by Leon Garfield. Copyright © 1982 by Leon Garfield. Cover illustration by Anthony Kerins. Reprinted by permission of Penguin Books Limited./ Jacket of *The House of Cards,* by Leon Garfield. Copyright © 1982 by Leon Garfield. Jacket painting by Susan Stillman. Reprinted by permission of St. Martin's Press./ Photograph courtesy of Leon Garfield.

SOMETHING ABOUT THE AUTHOR®

AFFABEE, Eric
  See STINE, R(obert) L(awrence)

* * *

ALCOCK, Vivien 1924-

■ Personal

Born September 23, 1924, in Worthing, England; daughter of John Forster (a research engineer and scientist) and Molly (Pulman) Alcock; married Leon Garfield (a writer), October 23, 1947; children: Jane Angela. *Education:* Attended Ruskin School of Drawing and of Fine Arts, Oxford, 1940-42, and Camden Art Centre. *Politics:* Liberal. *Religion:* Church of England. *Hobbies and other interests:* Painting, patchwork, reading.

■ Addresses

Home—59 Wood Lane, London N6 5UD, England. *Agent*—John Johnson Ltd., Clerkenwell House, 45-47 Clerkenwell Green, London EC1R 0HT, England.

■ Career

Writer of books for juveniles and young adults. Artist, Gestetner Ltd. (duplicating firm), London, England, 1947-53; manager of employment bureau, 1953-56; secretary, Whiltington Hospital, London, 1956-64. *Military service:* British Army, ambulance driver, 1942-46. *Member:* Authors Society.

VIVIEN ALCOCK

■ Awards, Honors

Horn Book Honor List citation, and notable book of the year citation, American Library Association (ALA), both 1985, both for *Travelers by Night;* ALA notable

1

book of the year citation, 1986, for *The Cuckoo Sister;*
Voice of Youth Advocate best science fiction/fantasy
book citation, and ALA notable book of the year
citation, both 1988, both for *The Monster Garden.*

■ Writings

FOR YOUNG PEOPLE

The Haunting of Cassie Palmer, Delacorte, 1980.
The Stonewalkers, Delacorte, 1981.
The Sylvia Game: A Novel of the Supernatural, Dela-
corte, 1982.
Travellers by Night, Methuen, 1983, published as *Travel-
ers by Night,* Delacorte, 1985.
Ghostly Companions: A Feast of Chilling Tales (collec-
tion of ten ghost stories), illustrated by Jane Lyd-
bury, Methuen, 1984.
The Cuckoo Sister, Methuen, 1985.
The Mysterious Mr. Ross, Delacorte, 1987.
The Monster Garden, Delacorte, 1988.
The Thing in the Woods, illustrated by Sally Holmes,
Hamish Hamilton, 1989.
The Trial of Anna Cotman, Delacorte, 1990.
Kind of Thief, Delacorte, 1992.
Singer to the Sea God, Delacorte, 1993.

■ Adaptations

The Sylvia Game was adapted for television and broadcast on BBC-TV, 1983; *The Haunting of Cassie Palmer*
was the basis of a television series produced by TVS
(Television South), 1984; *Travellers by Night* was adapted for television and broadcast on BBC-TV, 1984, and
was the basis of a television series produced by TVS,
1985.

■ Sidelights

Vivien Alcock is the author of over ten action-packed
books of mystery and fantasy that are very popular with
teenage readers, especially in Alcock's native country of
England. Reviewers have praised Alcock for creating
gripping and suspenseful tales involving intriguing characters that sensitively reflect many of the emotions and
experiences of her young readers. Alcock is also recognized as an author whose sense of humor is as evident in
her books as her ability to captivate and entertain.
Writing in the *Times Literary Supplement,* Elaine Moss
describes Alcock as a "writer who can command plot,
character, nuance, and dialogue with a precision and
sensitivity that sets her firmly among the elite of English
fantasy authors for the young."

Alcock started writing at a very early age. She found
expressing her thoughts and feelings on paper was an
effective way to deal with such tumultuous events as her
parents' divorce, her mother's illness and eventual death
when Alcock was fourteen years old, and the adjustment
of moving from her home to live with a guardian in
another city. She was thrilled to discover something that
she loved and that was unique to her.

"Our guardian encouraged us to draw and to write,
which my mother being ill never had a chance to do,"
noted Alcock in an interview for *Authors and Artists for
Young Adults* (*AAYA*). "I wrote a lot of verse as a child
and I also made up all kind of stories. It is easy to be the
hero of a story if you write it yourself. I started telling
myself stories in which the heroines were always small
and skinny and dark, like me. It was comforting to find
out how well they got on, facing up to incredible
adventures and danger—as long as I was writing the
script. It was a form of escapism, I suppose, just as
daydreams are. But I think it was a valuable one."

Although she spent much of her childhood and adolescence writing, it wasn't until after she was sparked by
her young daughter's love of original stories that Alcock
considered turning her hobby into a profession. So,
inspired by her daughter's interest in her stories, Alcock
starting writing again, launching what would become a
rewarding career. Alcock once commented: "Careers
often seem to happen almost by accident. When I left
school, I wanted to be either a writer or an artist.
Chance (in the from of an entrance exam needing more
Latin than I possessed), sent me to art school rather than
to the university. Chance (in the form of a small

In Alcock's fantastic story *The Monster Garden,*
**Frankie and David's experiment with a substance from
their father's genetic laboratory yields strange results.**
(Cover illustration by Frank Morris.)

daughter who wanted to be told stories, rather than have them read to her), turned me back to the idea of writing. I like writing for children because I love telling stories of adventure and fantasy. I don't set out to instruct or preach, but it is impossible to write without one's own views showing. I can only hope my heart and my morals are in the right place."

Novels Blend Supernatural and Emotional Elements

Alcock's first book, *The Haunting of Cassie Palmer,* is a tale about the seventh child of a seventh child who has spiritual powers. Cassie Palmer has unhappily inherited her magical abilities from her mother and she longs to be a normal and average teenager—just like her friends. However, one day, on a dare, Cassie conjures up a ghost who refuses to leave her alone. A reviewer for the *Bulletin for the Center of Children's Books* describes Alcock's *The Haunting of Cassie Palmer* as "an impressive first novel from a British writer, with a fusion of realism and fantasy that is remarkably smooth." And Dudley Carlson remarks in *Horn Book* that in *The Haunting of Cassie Palmer* Alcock "achieves a good balance between family tensions and financial worries, on the one hand, and supernatural uncertainties, on the other; the result is a satisfying brew."

As in this first novel, all of Alcock's novels contain elements of fantasy and the supernatural. For example, in Alcock's second novel, *The Stonewalkers,* lonely and friendless Poppy Brown pours her feelings out to a statue that suddenly comes to life. Unfortunately, the statue is mean and destructive and Poppy struggles to stop the statue's trail of terror. Alcock explained her thoughts on writing about fantasy and the supernatural to Amanda Smith in an interview with *Publishers Weekly:* "Oddly enough, I've never had a supernatural experience, and I don't even think I quite believe in them, but I find a ghost or supernatural element is a marvelous catalyst. It can be a sort of an echo of a character, like a shadow thrown out before them, showing back part of their own image. Most ghosts are very pitiful objects, so a child can learn compassion. But it's also fun in a book. It gives a little chill—binds a book together."

In a *School Library Journal* review of *The Stonewalkers,* Anita C. Wilson writes: "The author skillfully creates a sense of escalating horror. The blending of suspenseful fantasy and elements of the contemporary problem novel works remarkably well here, and may appeal to children not ordinarily attracted to fantasy literature."

Writing Lauded by Critics

Critics have continued to praise Alcock's books. Whether it be the suspenseful mystery involving the supernatural and art forgery in *The Sylvia Game: A Novel of the Supernatural,* the exciting attempt of two circus children to save an old elephant from the slaughterhouse in *Travellers by Night,* the thrilling collection of stories found in *Ghostly Companions: A Feast of Chilling Tales,* the fascinating tale of separated sisters in *The Cuckoo*

Two kids from a disbanding circus devise a dangerous plan to save their elephant from the slaughterhouse in this Alcock book. (Cover illustration by Vincent Natale.)

Sister, the untold story dramatically revealed in *The Mysterious Mr. Ross,* the experiments in genetic engineering in *The Monster Garden,* or the evil and secrecy in *The Trial of Anna Cotman,* Alcock's books have been recognized for their intriguing stories and endearing characters. Geoffrey Trease comments in the *Times Literary Supplement* that "Alcock is unsentimental, but there is an unmistakable depth of feeling in her deft handling of her very human and imperfect characters. She is writing of fear and courage, exploring the ambivalent relationships of parent and child, boy and girl, boy and boy. The contemporary juvenile dialogue rings true, and there is felicity in the descriptive phrasing."

"Vivien Alcock has the uncanny ability to create stories of suspense with overtones of fantasy which are firmly grounded in reality," Mary M. Burns similarly observes in *Horn Book.* "Her timing is impeccable; her characters are unforgettable; her imagery is as subtle as it is precise." As George English concludes in *Books for Your Children:* "Vivien Alcock has always been a dramatic writer, with a strong sense of story. Her books begin with a bang almost on page one and they hurtle at breakneck pace to a thundering climax. Where other

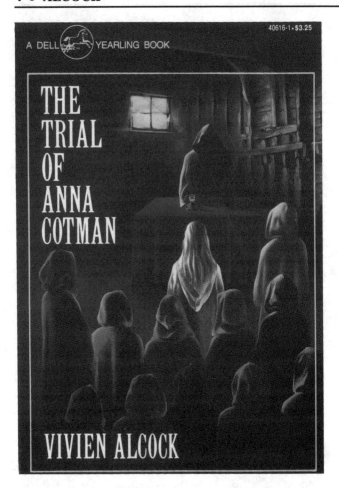

Lindy joins a secret society in order to make friends in a new town, but the group takes on evil tones with the arrival of the Yellow Lord in this suspenseful novel. (Cover illustration by Savio.)

authors linger over physical descriptions of character and setting, Alcock is more concerned with keeping the action moving. Yet at the same time she's very aware of the inner, emotional life that her characters are leading."

Alcock shared with *AAYA* some of her interesting and insightful thoughts on writing in this manner: "Although I have a liking for dramatic and sometimes fantastic plots, I try to make my characters as real as possible, and their relationships true. I suppose, like all writers, I am influenced to some extend by my own experience, though I do not draw on it consciously. My heroines are no longer always small and skinny and dark. I suspect there is a little of me still lurking at the bottom of all the characters I create, blown up out of all recognition. I find I tend to write about children who are facing some great change or difficulty in their lives, and who learn to grow through it to a greater understanding of themselves and other people. I do not apologize for having happy endings. I firmly believe that children are resilient and resourceful, and will make their own happiness somehow if given a chance. The end of childhood is not necessarily when the law decides it shall be."

■ Works Cited

Alcock, Vivien, in an interview for *Authors & Artist for Young Adults,* Volume 8, Gale, 1992, pp. 1-8.
Burns, Mary M., review of *The Monster Garden, Horn Book,* November/December, 1988, p. 781.
Carlson, Dudley, review of *The Haunting of Cassie Palmer, Horn Book,* June, 1982, p. 294.
English, George, "George English Looks at the Work of Vivien Alcock," *Books for Your Children,* Number 1, spring, 1991, p. 22.
Review of *The Haunting of Cassie Palmer, Bulletin for the Center of Children's Books,* May, 1982, p. 161.
Moss, Elaine, "Ghostly Forms," *Times Literary Supplement,* November 20, 1981, p. 1354.
Smith, Amanda, "Of Ghosts and History," *Publishers Weekly,* September 30, 1988, p. 28-30.
Trease, Geoffrey, "Curdling the Blood," *Times Literary Supplement,* July 23, 1982, p. 788.
Wilson, Anita C., *School Library Journal,* May, 1983, p. 68.

■ For More Information See

PERIODICALS

New York Times Book Review, September 11, 1983.
Times Literary Supplement, July 23, 1982; November 8, 1985; September 4, 1987; April 15-21, 1988.*

* * *

ALLEN, Bob 1961-

■ Personal

Full name Robert L. Allen; born May 23, 1961, in Jamestown, ND; son of Eugene O. Allen and Beverly Mae (Joos) Allen. *Education:* Attended Orange Coast College, 1987. *Hobbies and other interests:* Cycling, skiing, travel.

■ Addresses

Home—7919 Thorpe Rd., Bozeman, MT 59715. *Agent*—Pick Marketing, 216 North Third St., Sterling, CO 80751.

■ Career

Freelance photographer and writer. *Military service:* U.S. Navy, 1979-85, served in England and the West Pacific.

■ Awards, Honors

Book of the year nomination, Children's Book Foundation, 1992, for *Mountain Biking.*

BOB ALLEN

■ Writings

JUVENILE

(And photographer with Michelle Dieterich) *Mountain Biking,* Wayland Publishing, 1991, Lerner Publications, 1992.

(And photographer) *Rollin' in the Dirt,* Pick Marketing, 1993.

Also photographer for *Skiing,* Michele M. Dieterich, Wayland Publishing, 1991, Lerner Publications, 1992.

OTHER

Contributor to periodicals, including *Bicycling, Mountain Bike Action, Velo News, Mountain Biker International, Bike, Solo Bici, Velo Tout Terrain, Tuto Mountain Bike,* and *Cycling World.*

■ Work in Progress

Assembling photos and notes for a "coffee table" book featuring photography on mountain biking; printing a fine art portfolio.

■ Sidelights

Upon graduation from high school Bob Allen joined the Navy. "I realized that I wasn't ready to take college seriously and felt the need to travel," he told *SATA.* While stationed in England he bought his first camera and developed a love of photography. "The two years I spent immersed in London's rich culture provided me with a fertile environment to pursue my newfound hobby." Soon he had learned to process and print his own work and a hobby turned into a serious avocation as he visually explored the Far East and Africa during two cruises on the U.S.S. Tarawa.

After his discharge from the Navy in 1985, Allen spent several years racing bikes and skiing in his native Montana. He combined photography with these two sports, taking photos especially of cycling events in which he competed. While at Orange Coast College in California, classes in photography and writing encouraged him to begin selling photographs to cycling magazines. Allen left college before completing his degree and made a career move back to London. "I arrived [in 1989] with a bike, cameras, a handful of transparencies and ... much enthusiasm." The London based magazine, *Mountain Biker,* began publishing his photographs and his career was launched.

In 1991 he wrote and illustrated the book, *Mountain Biking,* which is part of the "All Action" Series. In 1992 he illustrated the companion volume, *Skiing,* for the same publisher. "The 'All Action Series' is geared toward children ages 10-13 and is designed to appeal to kids who might have a reading disability and/or are intimidated by 'traditional' books," Allen told *SATA.* "In my photography, I strive to deliver maximum image impact. My photographs capture the instant where the action and aesthetic collide. I'm fascinated with depicting motion in my work and constantly push for a fresh look."

*   *   *

ALVAREZ, John
See del REY, Lester

*   *   *

ARNOLD, Emily 1939-
(Emily Arnold McCully)

■ Personal

Born July 1, 1939, in Galesburg, IL; daughter of Wade E. (a writer) and Kathryn (a teacher; maiden name, Maher) Arnold; married George E. McCully (a historian), June 3, 1961 (divorced, 1975); children: Nathaniel, Thaddeus. *Education:* Brown University, B.A., 1961; Columbia University, M.A., 1964. *Hobbies and other interests:* Theater, acting, gardening, cooking, travel, tennis.

■ Addresses

Home—3 Washington Sq. Village, New York, NY 10012; and Box 212, Rural District, Chatham, NY 12037. *Agent*—Harriet Wasserman Literary Agency, Inc., 137 East 36th St., New York, NY 10016.

EMILY ARNOLD

■ Career

Worked in advertising and as freelance magazine artist, 1961-67; illustrator of children's books, 1966—; writer, 1975—. Teacher at workshops at Brown University, Boston University, St. Clements, Cummington Community of the Arts, and Rockland Center for the Arts. *Member:* Authors Guild, Authors League of America, Writers Community, PEN American Center, Actors Equity Association, Society of Children's Book Writers and Illustrators.

■ Awards, Honors

Gold medal, Philadelphia Art Directors, 1968; "Showcase Title" citation, Children's Book Council, 1972, for *Hurray for Captain Jane!;* "Art Books for Children" citation, Brooklyn Museum and New York Public Library, for *MA nDA LA;* Juvenile Award, Council of Wisconsin Writers, 1979, for *Edward Troy and the Witch Cat;* National Endowment for the Arts grant in creative writing, 1980; New York State Council on Arts fiction grant, 1982; American Book Award nomination, 1982, for *A Craving;* "Best Books of the Year" citation, *School Library Journal,* 1984, "Notable Book" citation, American Library Association, 1984, Christopher Award, 1985, and inclusion in International Biennale at Bratislava, 1985, all for *Picnic;* Caldecott Medal, and

One of Ten Best Illustrated Books, *New York Times,* both 1993, for *Mirette on the High Wire.*

■ Writings

SELF-ILLUSTRATED; UNDER NAME EMILY ARNOLD McCULLY

Picnic (Junior Literary Guild selection), Harper, 1984.
First Snow (Junior Literary Guild selection), Harper, 1985.
The Show Must Go On, Western, 1987.
School (Junior Literary Guild selection), Harper, 1987.
New Baby, Harper, 1988.
Christmas Gift, Harper, 1988.
You Lucky Duck!, Western, 1988.
The Grandma Mixup, Harper, 1988.
Zaza's Big Break, HarperCollins, 1989.
The Evil Spell, HarperCollins, 1990.
Grandmas at the Lake, HarperCollins, 1990.
Speak Up, Blanche!, HarperCollins, 1991.
Mirette on the High Wire, Putnam, 1992.
Grandmas at Bat, HarperCollins, 1993.
The Amazing Felix, Putnam, 1993.
Crossing the New Bridge, Putnam, 1994.
My Real Family, Harcourt, 1994.

ILLUSTRATOR; UNDER NAME EMILY ARNOLD McCULLY

George Panetta, *Sea Beach Express,* Harper, 1966.
Emily Cheney Neville, *The Seventeenth Street Gang,* Harper, 1966.
Marjorie W. Sharmat, *Rex,* Harper, 1967.
Natalie S. Carlson, *Luigi of the Streets,* Harper, 1967.
Liesel M. Skorpen, *That Mean Man,* Harper, 1968.
Barbara Borack, *Gooney,* Harper, 1968.
Seymour Simon, *Animals in Field and Laboratory: Science Project in Animal Behavior,* McGraw, 1968.
Meindert De Jong, *Journey from Peppermint Street,* Harper, 1968.
Barbara K. Wheeler and Naki Tezel, *The Mouse and the Elephant,* Parents' Magazine Press, 1969.
Jan Wahl, *The Fisherman,* Norton, 1969.
Pierre Gripari, *Tales from the Rue Broca* (translated by Doriane Grutman), Bobbs, 1969.
Virginia O. Baron, editor, *Here I Am!: An Anthology of Poems Written by Young People in Some of America's Minority Groups,* Dutton, 1969.
Janet Louise Swoboda Lunn, *Twin Spell,* Harper, 1969.
Jane H. Yolen, *Hobo Toad and the Motorcycle Gang,* World, 1970.
Jeanne B. Hardendorff, *Slip! Slop! Gobble!,* Lippincott, 1970.
Ruth A. Sonneborn, *Friday Night Is Papa Night* (Junior Literary Guild selection), Viking, 1970.
Mildred Kantrowitz, *Maxie,* Parents' Magazine Press, 1970.
Phyllis M. Hoffman, *Steffie and Me,* Harper, 1970.
Hardendorff, *The Cat and the Parrot,* Lippincott, 1970.
Betsy Byars, *Go and Hush the Baby,* Viking, 1971.
Alix Shulman, *Finders Keepers,* Bradbury Press, 1971.
Arnold Adoff, *MA nDA LA,* Harper, 1971.
Sam Reavin, *Hurray for Captain Jane!,* Parents' Magazine Press, 1971.

Helen E. Buckley, *Michael Is Brave,* Lothrop, 1971.

Seymour Simon, *Finding Out with Your Senses,* McGraw, 1971.

Louise McNamara, *Henry's Pennies,* F. Watts, 1972.

Arthur Miller, *Jane's Blanket,* Viking, 1972.

Lynn Schoettle, *Grandpa's Long Red Underwear,* Lothrop, 1972.

Lee Bennett Hopkins, *Girls Can Too!,* F. Watts, 1972.

Jane Langton, *The Boyhood of Grace Jones,* Harper, 1972.

Adoff, *Black Is Brown Is Tan,* Harper, 1973.

Constance C. Greene, *Isabelle the Itch,* Viking, 1973.

Kantrowitz, *When Violet Died,* Parents' Magazine Press, 1973.

Mary H. Lystad, *That New Boy,* Crown, 1973.

Thomas Rockwell, *How to Eat Fried Worms,* F. Watts, 1973.

Anne Norris Baldwin, *Jenny's Revenge,* Four Winds Press, 1974.

Langton, *Her Majesty, Grace Jones,* Harper, 1974.

Miles, *Tree House Town,* Little, Brown, 1974.

Sharmat, *I Want Mama,* Harper, 1974.

Jean Little, *Stand in the Wind,* Harper, 1975.

Arnold's illustrations express the frustration Lulu Witch feels when her new baby sister gets more attention than she does. (Illustration from *Lulu and the Witch Baby,* written by Jane O'Connor.)

Susan Terris, *Amanda, the Panda and the Redhead,* Doubleday, 1975.

Sylvia Plath, *The Bed Book,* Harper, 1976.

Ianthe Thomas, *My Street's a Morning Cool Street,* Harper, 1976.

Rita Golden Gelman and Joan Richter, *Professor Coconut and the Thief,* Holt, 1977.

Miranda Hapgood, *Martha's Mad Day,* Crown, 1977.

Elizabeth Winthrop, *That's Mine,* Holiday House, 1977.

Adoff, *Where Wild Willie,* Harper, 1978.

Betty Baker, *No Help at All,* Greenwillow, 1978.

Baker, *Partners,* Greenwillow, 1978.

Russell Hoban, *The Twenty-Elephant Restaurant,* Atheneum, 1978.

Glory St. John, *What I Did Last Summer,* Atheneum, 1978.

Nancy Willard, *The Highest Hit,* Harcourt, 1978.

Greene, *I and Sproggy,* Viking, 1978.

Sarah Sargent, *Edward Troy and the Witch Cat,* Follett, 1978.

Kathryn Lasky, *My Island Grandma,* F. Warne, 1979.

Barbara Williams, *Whatever Happened to Beverly Bigler's Birthday?,* Harcourt, 1979.

Clyde Robert Bulla, *Last Look,* Crowell, 1979.

Mirra Ginsburg, *Ookie-Spooky,* Crown, 1979.

Edith Thacher Hurd, *The Black Dog Who Went into the Woods,* Harper, 1980.

Pat Rhoads Mauser, *How I Found Myself at the Fair,* Atheneum, 1980.

Tobi Tobias, *How We Got Our First Cat,* F. Watts, 1980.

Jane Breskin Zalben, *Oliver and Allison's Week,* Farrar, Straus, 1980.

Brooke M. Varnum, *Play and Sing ... It's Christmas! A Piano Book of Easy-to-Play Carols,* Macmillan, 1980.

Vicki Kimmel Artis, *Pajama Walking,* Houghton, 1981.

Alice Schertle, *The April Fool,* Lothrop, 1981.

Kathleen Benson, *Joseph on the Subway Trains,* Addison-Wesley, 1981.

Beatrice Gormley, *Mail-Order Wings,* Dutton, 1981.

Jeannette Everly, *The Seeing Summer,* Lippincott, 1981.

Charlotte Zolotow, *The New Friend,* Harper, 1981.

Gormley, *Fifth Grade Magic,* Dutton, 1982.

Marion M. Markham, *The Halloween Candy Mystery,* Houghton, 1982.

Hurd, *I Dance in My Red Pajamas,* Harper, 1982.

Williams, *Mitzi and the Terrible Tyrannosaurus Rex,* Dutton, 1982.

Williams, *Mitzi's Honeymoon with Nana Potts,* Dutton, 1983.

Laurie Adams and Allison Coudert, *Alice and the Boa Constrictor,* Houghton, 1983.

Corrine Gerson, *Good Dog, Bad Dog,* Macmillan, 1983.

Gormley, *Best Friend Insurance,* Dutton, 1983.

Christopher Smart, *For I Will Consider My Cat Jeoffry,* Atheneum, 1984.

Markham, *The Christmas Present Mystery,* Houghton, 1984.

The Playground, Golden Books, 1984.

Williams, *Mitzi and Frederick the Great,* Dutton, 1984.

Miska Miles, *Gertrude's Pocket,* Smith, Peter, 1984.

Charlotte T. Graeber, *The Thing in Kat's Attic,* Dutton, 1985.

Gormley, *The Ghastly Glasses,* Dutton, 1985.

Williams, *Mitzi and the Elephants,* Dutton, 1985.

Mary Stolz, *The Explorer of Barkham Street,* Harper, 1985.

Barbara M. Joosse, *Fourth of July,* Knopf, 1985.

Jane O'Connor, *Lulu and the Witch Baby,* Harper, 1986.

Jane R. Thomas, *Wheels,* Clarion Books, 1986.

Joosse, *Jam Day,* Harper, 1987.

O'Connor, *Lulu Goes to Witch School,* Harper, 1987.

Ruth Shaw Radlauer, *Molly,* Simon & Schuster, 1987.

Radlauer, *Molly Goes Hiking,* Simon & Schuster, 1987.

Doreen Rappaport, *The Boston Coffee Party,* Harper, 1987.

Mary Stolz, *The Explorer of Barkham Street,* Harper-Collins, 1987.

Radlauer, *Molly Goes Hiking,* Simon & Schuster, 1987.

Marcia Sewall, *Ridin' That Strawberry Roan,* Puffin Books, 1987.

Gormley, *Richard and the Vratch,* Avon, 1988.

Radlauer, *Molly Goes to the Library,* Prentice-Hall, 1988.

Radlauer, *Breakfast by Molly,* Prentice-Hall, 1988.

Rhoda Josephs, *The Baby Bubble Book,* Grosset & Dunlap, 1988.

Juanita Havill, *It Always Happens to Leona,* Crown, 1989.

Joosse, *Dinah's Mad, Bad Wishes,* HarperCollins, 1989.

Joan W. Bloss, *The Grandpa Days,* Simon & Schuster, 1989.

Gormley, *The Magic Mean Machine,* Avon, 1989.

Gormley, *More Fifth Grade Magic,* Dutton, 1989.

Lucy Diggs, *Selene Goes Home,* Macmillan, 1989.

Barbara A. Porte, *The Take-Along Dog,* Greenwillow Books, 1989.

Achim Broger, *The Day Chubby Became Charles* (translated by Renee Vera Cafiero), HarperCollins, 1990.

Sally Wittman, *Stepbrother Sabotage,* HarperCollins, 1990.

Gormley, *Wanted, UFO,* Dutton, 1990.

Havill, *Leona and Ike,* Crown, 1991.

Phyllis Hoffman, *Meatball,* HarperCollins, 1991.

Gormley, *Sky Guys to White Cat,* Dutton, 1991.

Ann Bixby Herold, *The Butterfly Birthday,* Macmillan, 1991.

Marilyn Singer, *In My Tent,* Macmillan, 1992.

Patricia Reilly Giff, *Meet the Lincoln Lions Marching Band* (series), Dell, 1992—.

Crescent Dragonwagon, *Annie's Birthday Bike,* Macmillan, 1993.

OTHER

(Contributor) William Abrahams, editor, *The O. Henry Collection: Best Short Stories,* Doubleday, 1976.

A Craving (novel), Avon, 1982.

Life Drawing, Delacorte, 1986.

Also contributor of short stories to *Massachusetts Review, Dark Horse,* and *Cricket.*

■ Work in Progress

An adult novel, *To the Careless;* several picture books for children; *Little Kit, or: The Industrious Flea Circus Girl,* for Dial, 1995.

■ Sidelights

Emily Arnold is a prolific and award-winning illustrator and author of children's books. Since the mid-1960s, under the name of Emily Arnold McCully, she has illustrated over one hundred works by other authors and has also produced several of her own picture books. In between, Arnold has also achieved success as a fiction writer for adults, been nominated for the American Book Award for her first novel, *A Craving,* and acted in an Off-Broadway play. Arnold's children's books have also earned honors; in 1985 she received the Christopher Award for her first solo picture book, *Picnic,* and she also served as illustrator of Meindert De Jong's 1969 National Book Award-winning *Journey from Peppermint Street.* Arnold was the 1993 recipient of the Caldecott Medal, one of the most prestigious awards for children's illustration, for *Mirette on the High Wire.* In a 1988 interview for *Something about the Author (SATA),* Arnold said she strives for a "spontaneous, sketch-like quality" in her illustrations, and considers characterization the most important aspect of illustrating books, stating, "it is through the characters that the reader enters the story."

Born in Galesburg, Illinois, in 1939, Arnold began drawing around the age of three and by the age of five was already producing "fairly ambitious drawings of men with trouser cuffs, buttons, and pleats," she told *SATA.* "Quickly routed past finger painting and other more personally expressive types of art," Arnold became most concerned with the *subjects* of her drawings. "To this day, I cannot imagine what my work would *look like* if I were a painter or sculptor instead of an illustrator," she told *SATA.* "The need to be linked to something else, to connect with a *subject outside of oneself* is, I think, at the heart of the impulse to illustrate, and is still the inspiration for all of my drawing."

As a child, Arnold began writing and illustrating her own stories, whose characters were usually boys. "I envied ... their freedom and action-packed lives," she told *SATA,* "and my stories and art reflected this with lots of excitement and drama, and no pretty little girls sitting around not getting their dresses dirty." Similarly, Arnold's reading preferences included adventure stories such as *Treasure Island* and *Robin Hood,* in addition to adventure comic strips which she also admired for the "economy of the dramatic techniques employed." She later became very interested in the works of the "Ashcan" group, eight American artists famous for their depictions of everyday life. Arnold began copying their work from a book, while discovering her own preference for, as she told *SATA,* "gritty, significant subject matter."

New York Inspires Artistic Vision

Arnold's family moved to Long Island, New York, where she was raised in a "very conventional" town with "an interesting sense of history," as she told *SATA,* "but ... like a place under glass: there were no blacks, no Jews, no minorities of any stripe." A self-described "maverick" in high school, Arnold stood out because of her drawing talents, and was influenced by an art teacher who encouraged her "naturally quick, spontaneous style of execution." Describing herself as the "only remotely left-wing person" among her peers, Arnold "felt horribly out of sync and isolated" in her community, yet was invigorated by nearby New York City. Arnold often visited her father at his work as a documentary writer and producer in New York's Rockefeller Center, and also became fond of the Museum of Modern Art and of sketching people in Union Square Park. "New York City fueled my ambitions for an active life in the arts, theatre and publishing," she explained to *SATA.* "I had visions of having a glamorous career as an illustrator for the *Saturday Evening Post.*"

Although Arnold attended Brown University in Rhode Island with the intention of becoming an artist, she instead devoted time to her interests in the theater, reading, and art history. "I was tired of the freakishness that seemed to be part of being an artist," she explained to *SATA.* "For years, people stood around me as I drew, marvelling that I could reproduce someone or something. I threw myself into other activities ... which I hadn't done before." Arnold was married after graduation, and attended Columbia University in New York, where she received a master's degree in art history—yet eventually returned to drawing after growing "weary of making so many verbal descriptions of art works." In 1963, she moved to Belgium with her husband, a historian, and again became involved in drawing sketches of people and scenes, and also making collages. "This was very new for me," she told *SATA,* "and I cultivated a freewheeling work style."

Arnold came to illustrating children's books "in a roundabout way," as she described to *SATA.* After returning from Europe, Arnold moved outside of Philadelphia where her husband had a teaching job, and she began doing book review illustrations for the *New York Herald Tribune,* eventually moving into other freelance work. One of Arnold's projects, a series of poster advertisements for a radio station, came to the attention of an editor in New York, who approached Arnold with the idea of illustrating a children's book. "At first, it wasn't easy for me to recapture a child's sensibility," Arnold told *SATA.* "But as I went along, that came more naturally, and then having children of my own certainly helped. I would now say that I illustrate not for 'children' but for myself—the sensibility at work is my own and the story has to be interesting to *me.*" Arnold proved to be very successful; since illustrating her first book in 1966, she has gone on to provide illustrations for over one hundred children's books.

A little boy figures out how to get along with his two very different grandmothers when they both come to babysit him in *The Grandma Mix-Up,* written and illustrated by Arnold.

Arnold branched out on her own in 1984 with *Picnic,* a storybook told entirely in water-color paintings. The tale of a family of mice who go off for a picnic and discover that the youngest mouse has fallen out of their pickup truck, *Picnic* describes both the family's search and the experiences of the little mouse. "The story is ... about the job of coming back after two separate adventures," she explained to Lael Locke in *The Paper: The Monthly Guide to the Berkshires and the Hudson Valley.* "The little mouse who's lost is not utterly miserable—the mouse finds a way of coping with the situation, and I think that's very important." Arnold published a sequel entitled *First Snow,* which recounts the youngest mouse's fear of sledding down a steep hill. "It's another very simple story, but it's funny and has to do with really essential feelings that little kids have—being afraid of sensations, and then experiencing them and loving it," she told Locke. "That's what's so wonderful about children's books ... because they can't be terribly complicated, they get at things that are ... basic and universal."

The next afternoon, when Mirette came for the sheets, there was the stranger, crossing the courtyard on air! Mirette was enchanted. Of all the things a person could do, this must be the most magical. Her feet tingled, as if they wanted to jump up on the wire beside Bellini.

Arnold received a prestigious Caldecott Medal for her self-illustrated book *Mirette on the High Wire*.

Illustrations Earn Caldecott Medal

In 1993 Arnold won the coveted Caldecott Medal for the self-illustrated *Mirette,* which is set in nineteenth-century Paris. The story revolves around a young girl, Mirette, who helps her mother run a boardinghouse for traveling performers. One day a once-famous high-wire artist, Bellini, comes to stay with them and practices walking the high-wire in their courtyard. Mirette is enchanted by the art, and asks Bellini to teach her, but he refuses. She learns that he retired because he has lost his nerve—but Mirette secretly learns to walk the tightrope by herself and eventually helps Bellini to make a triumphant comeback. "Emily Arnold McCully has captured, in admirably few words matched with expressive watercolor paintings, the excitement and stubborn determination of the budding artist," wrote Jean Van Leeuwen in *New York Times Book Review.* A *Horn Book* critic was similarly enthusiastic, calling *Mirette on the High Wire* "a wonderfully exuberant picture book" and a "bravura performance" by Arnold.

Arnold's adult writing explores more complicated subject matter than does her work for children. She began writing fiction in the mid-1970s, telling *Contemporary Authors* that her "first story and then my first book had to wait until I had a story demanding to be told." In the mid-1970s, Arnold divorced and moved to Brooklyn, New York, where she began working on her first novel, *A Craving,* which earned her an American Book Award nomination. The story of an alcoholic artist's struggle with her failing marriage, her alienated children, and the loss of her job, the novel was praised by John Gabree in *Newsday* as "an honest, engaging and moving accomplishment."

Accomplished as both an illustrator and a writer, Arnold described to *SATA* how she divides time between the two interests. "If I am working on a novel or a long story, I write for several hours in the morning and devote the afternoon, and sometimes the evening, to illustration work. I can do art work for many hours at a time. There is something mesmerizing about the physicality of visual work, and of course, knowing that a finished product is just hours away makes it hard for me to stop." Arnold also relayed words of advice to aspiring artists and writers: "Don't worry about what other people are doing. Don't try to emulate. Work from what is inside you, crying out—however softly, however timidly—for expression."

■ Works Cited

Arnold, Emily, interview in *Something about the Author,* Volume 50, Gale, 1988, pp. 29-38.

Contemporary Authors, Volume 109, Gale, 1983, p. 24.

Gabree, John, review of *A Craving, Newsday,* May 16, 1982.

Locke, Lael, "Silent Stories, Moving Pictures," *The Paper: The Monthly Guide to the Berkshires and the Hudson Valley,* April 1984.

Review of *Mirette on the High Wire, Horn Book,* October 1992, p. 577.

Van Leeuwen, Jean, review of *Mirette on the High Wire, New York Times Book Review,* November 8, 1992, p. 38.

■ For More Information See

BOOKS

Contemporary Authors Autobiography Series, Volume 7, Gale, 1988.

de Montreville, Doris, and Elizabeth D. Crawford, editors, *Fourth Book of Junior Authors and Illustrators,* Wilson, 1978.

PERIODICALS

Bulletin of the Center for Children's Books, October 1992, p. 49.

Language Arts, October 1979.

School Library Journal, October 1992, p. 92; June 1993, p. 83.

Time, December 21, 1992, p. 68.

B

BEACH, Lynn
See LANCE, Kathryn

*   *   *

BERTRAND, Cecile 1953-

■ Personal

Born June 20, 1953, in Liege, Belgium; daughter of Andre Bertrand and Pauwen Jeannette Bertrand; married Etienne Bours (a musical adviser), October 26, 1974; children: Antoine. *Education:* Studied painting in Liege at L'Institut Saint Luc. *Hobbies and other interests:* Sculpture, walking in the mountains, jogging, bicycling.

■ Addresses

Home—54 rue de la Magree, 4163 Tavier, Belgium. *Agent*—Rainbow Graphics, 32 rue de la Vallee, 1050 Brussells, Belgium.

■ Career

Contributor of cartoons to a Belgian newspaper; affiliated with a Belgian animation company. *Exhibitions:* Between 1975 and 1980, Bertrand's paintings appeared in exhibits in several cities, including Liege, De Haan, Brussells, and Wenduine; participant in group exhibitions, including Mostra Internazional d'Illustrazione per l'Infanzia in Italy, 1985-90. *Member:* Union Professionnelle des Createurs d'Histoire en Images, d'Illustration, et de Cartoon.

■ Awards, Honors

Prix Jeunesse du Ministere de la Communaute Francaise de Belgique, 1984.

CECILE BERTRAND

■ Writings

(And illustrator) *Mr. and Mrs. Smith Have Only One Child, but What a Child!,* Lothrop, 1992 (originally published as *Monsieur et Madame Smith n'ont qu'une fille, mais quelle fille!*).

■ Work in Progress

A four book set for small children; *Le Bugs,* an animated cartoon.

■ Sidelights

Cecile Bertrand told *SATA:* "Many people have already explained better than I why one loves to create books for children! Simply I can say that I cannot imagine not being able to do this. This takes all my time, my energy, all my life ... I like above all to take serious themes,

13

very serious, and make it a funny story but one which leads into the memory of the reader."

* * *

BIAL, Raymond 1948-

■ Personal

Born November 5, 1948, in Danville, IL; son of Marion (an Air Force officer) and Catherine (a medical secretary) Bial; married Linda LaPuma (a librarian), August 25, 1979; children: Anna, Sarah, Luke. *Education:* University of Illinois, B.S. (with honors), 1970, M.S., 1979. *Politics:* Independent. *Religion:* Catholic. *Hobbies and other interests:* Gardening, fishing, hiking, travel.

■ Addresses

Home—208 West Iowa St., Urbana, IL 61801. *Office*—Parkland College Library, 2400 West Bradley Ave., Champaign, IL 61821. *Agent*—Barbara Kouts, P.O. Box 558, Bellport, NY 11713.

■ Career

Parkland College Library, Champaign, IL, library director, 1988—. *Member:* Children's Reading Roundtable, Society of Children's Book Writers and Illustrators.

■ Awards, Honors

Best Publicity of 1984, Library Public Relations Council, 1984, for "In All My Years" exhibit poster; Historian of the Year, Champaign County, Illinois, 1984; Award of Superior Achievement, Illinois State Historical Society, 1985; First Annual Staff Development Award, Parkland College, 1985, for presentation on print media and computer resources in academic libraries; Certificate of Commendation, American Association for State and Local History, 1986; Writer's Choice selection, National Endowment for the Arts and the Pushcart Foundation, 1986, for *First Frost;* Best Publicity of 1986, Library Public Relations Council, 1987, for poster advertising "Changing Image of Rural and Small Town Life" panel discussion; Staff Development Award, Parkland College, 1990, for presentation entitled "The Language of Photography"; Outstanding Science Trade Book for Children, 1991, for *Corn Belt Harvest.*

■ Writings

NONFICTION FOR CHILDREN; AND PHOTOGRAPHER

Corn Belt Harvest, Houghton Mifflin, 1991.
County Fair, Houghton Mifflin, 1992.
Amish Home, Houghton Mifflin, 1993.
Frontier Home, Houghton Mifflin, 1993.
Shaker Home, Houghton Mifflin, 1994.

OTHER

Ivesdale: A Photographic Essay, Champaign County Historical Archives, 1982.

RAYMOND BIAL

In All My Years: Portraits of Older Blacks in Champaign-Urbana, Champaign County Historical Museum, 1983, revised edition, 1985.
Upon a Quiet Landscape: The Photographs of Frank Sadorus, Champaign County Historical Museum, 1983.
There Is a Season, Champaign County Nursing Home, 1984.
(With Kathryn Kerr) *First Frost,* Stormline Press, 1985.
Common Ground: Photographs of Rural and Small Town Life, Stormline Press, 1986.
Stopping By: Portraits from Small Towns, University of Illinois Press, 1988.
(With wife, Linda LaPuma Bial) *The Carnegie Library in Illinois,* University of Illinois Press, 1988.
From the Heart of the Country: Photographs of the Midwestern Sky, Sagamore Publishing, 1991.
Looking Good: A Guide to Photographing Your Library, American Library Association, 1991.
Champaign: A Pictorial History, Bradley Publishing, 1993.

Also author of introduction to *Beneath an Open Sky,* by Gary Irving, University of Illinois Press, 1990. Contributor of photoessay to *Townships,* University of Iowa Press, 1992.

■ Sidelights

Raymond Bial told *SATA:* "When I was growing up in the 1950s I spent several of the most joyous years of my young life in a small town in Indiana. With my friends, I bicycled around the neighborhood, went swimming at the municipal pool, stopped for ice cream at the local hotspot, and frequently visited our Carnegie public library. Some people might think that such memories are simply nostalgic, but I know that our little town was pleasant, comfortable, and safe—and I will always cherish those years.

"Later, our family moved to a farm in southern Michigan. Although I missed my old friends, as well as the charming atmosphere of my old 'hometown,' I enjoyed taking care of our livestock and running free through the woods, marsh, and fields around our new home. The moment I walked out of the house I was truly outside. The marsh, in particular, was bursting forth with wildlife—turtles, frogs, muskrats, ducks—and I delighted in my explorations and discoveries.

"Not all my childhood was wonderful. At times there were financial difficulties, family arguments, and other painful experiences. Yet for the most part I was simply thrilled to be alive, directly experiencing the world around me, especially when I could be out of doors in the light and weather.

"My work as a writer and photographer first drew upon these early moments of delight. For most of my books I have returned to rural and small town subjects. Just as

Bial uses photographs of everyday objects to convey the spirit of Amish farm life in his *Amish Home*.

when I was a child, I still love to be outside, absolutely free, making photographs. With every photograph I try to recapture that heightened sense of feeling for people, places, and things which meant so much to me as a child. I believe that adults as well as children should live not only in their minds, but through their senses.

"Ever since I was in fourth grade, I wanted to be a writer, but only as an adult in my early twenties did photography happen to me. I say 'happen to me,' because I never consciously decided to become a photographer. I simply loved the experience of making photographs. I've never received any formal training or education in either art form. Rather I have relied upon my own instincts in making photographs which matter to me personally.

"I now live in an old house in a middle-sized town in the Midwest with my wife and three children. Above all else I love being a husband and a father. For me, the only thing better than being a child oneself is to grow up and have children of one's own. In writing and making photographs, I now draw upon my experiences with my family as well as upon the memories of my childhood. I am often able to write my books at home in the midst of my family, which is just wonderful. As far as possible, I also coordinate photography assignments with family vacations so that I can make photographs and have a great time with my wife and children."

* * *

BLACK, Algernon David 1900-1993

OBITUARY NOTICE—See index for *SATA* sketch: Born November 18, 1900, in New York, NY; died after a long illness, May 9, 1993, in Rye, NY. Humanist leader, educator, radio commentator, and writer. Widely known for his affiliation with the New York Society of Ethical Culture, Black was the society's foremost elder statesman for many years and reached emeritus status in 1973. Founded in 1876 by Dr. Felix Adler, the society was conceived as an alternative to established religions and was based on ethics as opposed to creeds and theology. After Dr. Adler's death Black was among those most instrumental in spreading the society's message by developing specific programs to combat the Depression of the 1930s, and following World War II he became known for his views on equal housing opportunities and the issue of health in the ghetto. Beginning in 1940 he was a radio commentator as part of the society's weekly Sunday broadcasts. He was also a teacher in Ethical Culture Schools for more than forty years. Black chaired the board of directors of the New York State and national committees against discrimination in housing and was chair of the civilian complaint review board of the Police Department of the City of New York. In 1963 Black was awarded a citation for distinguished citizenship by the City of New York. Black authored various books, including *The People and the Police, The First Book of Ethics, The Woman of the Wood: A Tale of Old Russia for Children,* and *Without*

Burnt Offerings: Ceremonies of Humanism, as well as numerous articles.

OBITUARIES AND OTHER SOURCES:

PERIODICALS

New York Times, May 11, 1993, p. B6; June 19, 1993, p. 10.

* * *

BLUE, Zachary
See STINE, R(obert) L(awrence)

* * *

BOCHAK, Grayce 1956-

■ Personal

Born April 22, 1956, in Scranton, PA; daughter of Anthony DeNoia and Mrs. James McAuvic; married John Bochak (a therapist), November 7, 1981. *Education:* Temple University, B.S., 1978; Marywood College, M.A., 1981, M.F.A., 1993.

■ Addresses

Home—536 Beech Street, Scranton, PA 18505. *Office*—Laughing Swan Studio, 536 Beech Street, Scranton, PA 18505.

■ Career

Marywood College, Scranton, PA, instructor in children's book illustration, 1989—. Founder of Laughing Swan Studio, Scranton, PA, 1991. *Exhibitions:* Illustrations from *Paper Boat* appeared in the Society of Illustrators of New York City exhibit, "Original Art of 1992." *Member:* Society of Children's Book Writers and Illustrators.

■ Awards, Honors

Dr. Seuss Award finalist, Random House, 1993.

■ Illustrator

Rabindranath Tagore, *Paper Boats* (picture book), Boyds Mills Press, 1992.

■ Work in Progress

The Long Silk Strand for Boyds Mills Press; *The Gamemaster,* a picture book which uses hand-painted marbleized papers; *The Garden Patch Boy,* a picture book which uses hand-painted weathered papers for an antique effect.

■ Sidelights

Grayce Bochak made art the focus of her college studies, but her interest in book illustrating grew when she took a course in that subject as part of a master's degree program. Looking for an inspiring subject, she chose *Paper Boats,* a poem by Rabindranath Tagore. This would become her first children's picture book. "I decided to enhance Tagore's written words with art work that was simple, yet elegant," she recalled. Grayce did extensive research, photographed animals at the Philadelphia Zoo, and compiled photographs and sketches on every detail of the book, including *origami* boats and *shiuli* flowers. She also employed a young boy from India as a model.

Techniques used for the illustrations included the combination of colored paper and hand-painted watercolor papers cut and glued in a collage effect. "Some papers were glued flat, and others were glued loosely, or even a bit raised to create a 3-D look," Grayce commented. "I used a variety of watercolor techniques including flat washes, graded washes, wet-in-wet painting." Reviews of Bochak's *Paper Boats* praised her colorful cut-paper images. A *Kirkus Reviews* contributor called the book an "appealing idyll" for young readers and lauded the illustrator's "promising debut." Carolyn Phelan in her *Booklist* assessment called *Paper Boats* "a simple, satisfying book." Reflecting on her work, Bochak stated, "I hope that in this loud, hustle-bustle world

GRAYCE BOCHAK

children and their parents will enjoy this book as a welcome change of pace."

■ Works Cited

Review of *Paper Boats, Kirkus Reviews,* December 15, 1991.

Phelan, Carolyn, review of *Paper Boats, Booklist,* January 1, 1992.

■ For More Information See

PERIODICALS

Horn Book, March/April, 1992.
School Library Journal, February, 1992.

* * *

BRENNER, Barbara (Johnes) 1925-

■ Personal

Born June 26, 1925, in Brooklyn, NY; daughter of Robert Lawrence (a real estate broker) and Marguerite (Furboter) Johnes; married Fred Brenner (an illustrator), March 16, 1947; children: Mark, Carl. *Education:* Attended Seton Hall College (now University), 1942-43, Rutgers University, 1944-46, New York University, 1953-54, and New School for Social Research, 1960-62. *Politics:* Independent. *Religion:* Jewish.

■ Addresses

Home—Box 1826, Hemlock Farms, Hawley, PA 18428.

■ Career

Prudential Insurance Co., Newark, NJ, copywriter, 1942-46; freelance artist's agent, 1946-52; freelance writer, 1957—; Bank Street College of Education, writer-consultant in Publications Division, became senior editor, 1962-90; college instructor, 1974-80; Parson's School of Design, New York, NY, instructor, 1980-81. Committee for a Sane Nuclear Policy, county chairperson, 1960-61. *Member:* Authors Guild, Authors League of America, PEN, Society of Children's Book Writers and Illustrators, Business and Industry for the Arts in Education, National Audubon Society.

■ Awards, Honors

New York Herald Tribune Children's Spring Book Festival honor book award, 1961, for *Barto Takes the Subway; Washington Post Book World* Children's Spring Book Festival honor book award, 1970, *New York Times* best children's books list, 1970, and American Library Association (ALA) notable book citation, all for *A Snake-Lover's Diary;* Outstanding Science Book awards, National Science Teachers Association and the Children's Book Council, 1974, for *Baltimore Orioles,* 1975, for *Lizard Tails and Cactus Spines,* 1977, for *On the Frontier with Mr. Audubon,* 1979, for *Beware! These Animals Are Poison,* and 1980, for *Have You Heard of a*

BARBARA BRENNER

Kangaroo Bird?: Fascinating Facts about Unusual Birds; On the Frontier with Mr. Audubon was selected one of *School Library Journal*'s Best of the Best Books, 1977; ALA notable book citation, for *Wagon Wheels;* named Outstanding Pennsylvania Author, 1986; Edgar Allan Poe Award nomination, Mystery Writers of America, 1988, for *The Falcon Sting.*

■ Writings

JUVENILE, EXCEPT AS INDICATED

Somebody's Slippers, Somebody's Shoes, W. R. Scott, 1957.

Barto Takes the Subway, photographs by Sy Katzoff, Knopf, 1961.

A Bird in the Family, illustrated by husband, Fred Brenner, W. R. Scott, 1962.

Amy's Doll, photographs by S. Katzoff, Knopf, 1963.

The Five Pennies, illustrated by Erik Blegvad, Knopf, 1963.

Careers and Opportunities in Fashion (for young adults), Dutton, 1964.

Beef Stew, illustrated by John E. Johnson, Knopf, 1965; new edition, 1990.

The Flying Patchwork Quilt, illustrated by F. Brenner, W. R. Scott, 1965.

Mr. Tall and Mr. Small, illustrated by Tomi Ungerer, W. R. Scott, 1966.

Nicky's Sister, illustrated by J. E. Johnson, Knopf, 1966.

Summer of the Houseboat, illustrated by F. Brenner, Knopf, 1968.

Faces, photographs by George Ancona, Dutton, 1970.

A Snake-Lover's Diary, W. R. Scott, 1970.

A Year in the Life of Rosie Bernard, illustrated by Joan Sandin, Harper, 1971.

Is It Bigger than a Sparrow?: A Book for Young Bird Watchers, illustrated by Michael Eagle, Knopf, 1972.

Mystery of the Plumed Serpent, illustrated by Blanche Sims, Houghton, 1972.

Bodies, photographs by G. Ancona, Dutton, 1973.

Hemi, a Mule, illustrated by J. Winslow Higginbottom, Harper, 1973.

If You Were an Ant, illustrated by F. Brenner, Harper, 1973.

(Reteller) *Walt Disney's "The Three Little Pigs,"* Random House, 1973.

(Reteller) *Walt Disney's "The Penguin That Hated the Cold,"* Random House, 1973.

Baltimore Orioles, illustrated by J. W. Higginbottom, Harper, 1974.

Cunningham's Rooster, illustrated by Anne Rockwell, Parents Magazine Press, 1975.

Lizard Tales and Cactus Spines, photographs by Merritt S. Keasey III, Harper, 1975.

Pen Pal from Another Planet, Macmillan, 1975.

Tracks, Macmillan, 1975.

(Editor) Edward Turner and Clive Turner, *Frogs and Toads,* Raintree, 1976.

(Editor) Ralph Whitlock, *Spiders,* Raintree, 1976.

Little One Inch, illustrated by F. Brenner, Coward, 1977.

On the Frontier with Mr. Audubon, Coward, 1977.

We're Off to See the Lizard, illustrated by Shelley Dieterichs, Raintree, 1977.

The Color Bear, Center for Media Development, 1978.

Ostrich Feathers (two-act play; first produced off-Broadway, 1965), illustrated by Vera B. Williams, Parents Magazine Press, 1978.

Wagon Wheels, illustrated by Don Bolognese, Harper, 1978.

Beware! These Animals Are Poison, illustrated by Jim Spanfeller, Coward, 1979.

(With May Garelick) *The Tremendous Tree Book,* illustrated by F. Brenner, Four Winds Press, 1979, new edition, Boyds Mills, 1992.

Have You Ever Heard of a Kangaroo Bird?: Fascinating Facts about Unusual Birds, illustrated by Irene Brady, Coward, 1980.

The Prince and the Pink Blanket, illustrated by Nola Langner, Four Winds Press, 1980.

A Killing Season, Four Winds Press, 1981.

Mystery of the Disappearing Dogs, illustrated by B. Sims, Knopf, 1982.

A Dog I Know, illustrated by F. Brenner, Harper, 1983.

The Gorilla Signs Love, Lothrop, 1984.

The Snow Parade, illustrated by Mary Tara O'Keefe, Crown, 1984.

Saving the President: What If Lincoln Had Lived?, Simon & Schuster, 1987.

The Falcon Sting (for young adults), Bradbury, 1988.

Annie's Pet, Bantam, 1989.

The Color Wizard, Bantam, 1989.

(With William Hooks) *Lion and Lamb,* Bantam, 1989.

(With May Garelick) *Two Orphan Cubs,* Walker, 1989.

(With W. Hooks) *Lion and Lamb Step Out,* Bantam, 1990.

Moon Boy, Bantam, 1990.

(With W. Hooks, Joanne Oppenheim) *No Way, Slippery Slick!,* Harper, 1991.

The Magic Box, Bantam, 1991.

Good News, Bantam, 1991.

If You Were There in 1492, Bradbury, 1991.

Rosa and Marco and the Three Wishes, Bradbury, 1992.

Beavers Beware!, Bantam, 1992.

Noah and the Flood, Bantam, 1992.

Group Soup, illustrated by Lynn Mussinger, Viking, 1992.

Dinosaurium, Bantam, 1993.

(With Bernice Chardiet) *Where's That Insect?* ("Hide and Seek Science" series), illustrated by Carol Schwartz, Scholastic, 1993.

(With Chardiet) *Where's That Reptile?* ("Hide and Seek Science" series), illustrated by Schwartz, Scholastic, 1993.

Planetarium, Bantam, 1993.

If You Were There in 1776, Macmillan, 1994.

(Editor) *The Earth Is Painted Green* (poetry), Scholastic, 1994.

Also the author of *Too Many Mice,* Bantam. Contributor to *Cricket* magazine.

FOR ADULTS

Love and Discipline, Ballantine, 1983.

Bank Street's Family Guide to Home Computers, Ballantine, 1984.

(With Betty Boegehold and Joanne Oppenheim) *Raising a Confident Child,* Pantheon, 1985.

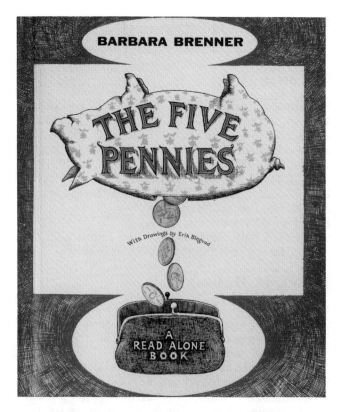

Although Brenner initially found writing children's books to be difficult, she soon became an established author of works geared toward young readers. (Cover illustration by Erik Blegvad.)

(Co-author) *Choosing Books for Kids: How to Choose the Right Book for the Right Child at the Right Time,* Ballantine, 1986.
The Preschool Handbook, Pantheon, 1990.

Contributor of articles to periodicals, including *Good Housekeeping, Newsweek,* and *Sierra.*

■ Adaptations

Wagon Wheels was adapted for the "Reading Rainbow" television series, Public Broadcasting System.

■ Sidelights

Barbara Brenner's books encompass a wide variety of genres and are geared toward a range of readers, from preschool to adult. A respected and prolific writer, she has produced more than fifty titles for children, both fiction and nonfiction, and is known for her focus on animals, nature, and ecology. Many of Brenner's books have been illustrated by her husband, Fred Brenner.

Brenner became interested in writing at age nine. "All the circumstances of my life conspired to make me a writer," she told *Contemporary Authors New Revision Series (CANR).* "I grew up in Brooklyn, which supplied the color, and my mother died when I was a year old, which supplied the sensitivity. We were poor, which gave me the social outlook, and my father was ambitious for me, which developed the intellectual curiosity."

Encouraged by a grade-school teacher, Brenner, already an avid reader, became a writer of short stories. She recalled to *SATA* how four books from her youth—*The Tale of Peter Rabbit, When We Were Very Young, Pinocchio,* and *Blackie's Children's Annual*—enhanced her life. "I still remember those books vividly. I wish I still had them. They taught me to fantasize. They taught me to read. They taught me how wonderful books can be. I think they may have been somewhat responsible for my becoming a writer of children's books. Anyway, I know that books can make a difference in your life."

After graduating from high school, Brenner worked as a salesperson and then for an insurance company before finally finding a position as copywriter for an advertising agency. In 1946 she met illustrator Fred Brenner, and they married the following year. Even before her marriage, her career took a new direction as she began representing Fred and other artists as an illustrator's agent. During these years, Brenner continued her education by taking courses at Seton Hall College, Rutgers University, New York University, and Manhattan's New School for Social Research.

Books Involve Children and Nature

The Brenners settled in New York City and eventually had two sons, Mark and Carl. It was when Mark was old enough to attend nursery school that Brenner once again turned to writing, beginning with freelance assignments. She soon found that reading to her young son gave her the urge to try her hand at children's books. As she

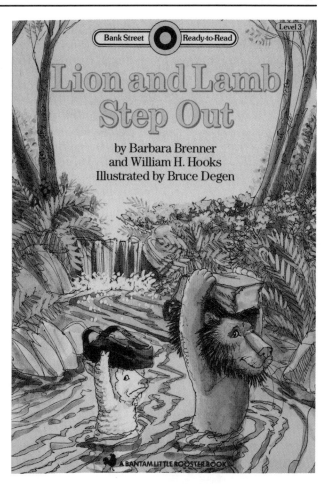

The adventures of Lion and Lamb are easily read and enjoyed by beginning readers in this collaboration by Brenner and William Hooks. (Cover illustration by Bruce Degen.)

recalled in *Something about the Author Autobiography Series,* the transition turned out to be much more difficult that she had anticipated: "These children's books. They seemed easy to do. I thought to myself, *So few words! Such simple ideas! I can write one of these during Mark's naptime.* Was I ever wrong!" Her first published children's book, *Somebody's Slippers, Somebody's Shoes,* appeared in 1957, the same year her second son was born. Her second published work, *Barto Takes the Subway,* garnered the fledgling writer a Children's Spring Book Festival honor award from the *New York Herald Tribune.*

With titles like *A Bird in the Family, A Snake-Lover's Diary,* and *Lizard Tails and Cactus Spines,* Brenner's works began to lean toward subjects connected with nature and animals. One of these is her book on the life of the great ornithologist John James Audubon, *On the Frontier with John James Audubon.* Paul Showers noted in the *New York Times Book Review* that with this book Brenner "again demonstrates her gift for invention and respect for facts. This is a combination of fiction and fact that works so well it might almost be the thing it imitates." Showers went on to explain that the book is "written in the polite but colloquial language of the frontier, sketching in Audubon's biographical background and recording events of the journey as they might have been observed by a serious, very perceptive 13-year-old."

During the 1960s Brenner joined the staff of the Bank Street College of Education as a writer-consultant, later becoming a senior editor. That job, she explained to *SATA,* "enabled me to get another perspective on children, parents, and on children's learning, as well as on some of the new forms of communication available to kids."

One title that holds particularly fond memories for Brenner is her 1965 work *The Flying Patchwork Quilt.* The idea for this lighthearted tale—about a little girl named Ellen who learns to fly on a magic quilt—"took shape when my son Carl went through what is referred to in our house as a 'flying stage,'" she told *SATA.* "During this time he tried constantly and unsuccessfully to become airborne. Since this was the second time I had encountered this phase (my older boy, too, had a flying stage), I decided there must be something fairly typical in it." The quilt "is modeled after an old patchwork quilt that I bought several years ago," she continued. "The children have always been fond of it, and for that reason I thought it would be interesting to use it as the focal point of a fantasy."

The Flying Patchwork Quilt was not the only story that was inspired by real experience. As the author told *SATA,* many of her book ideas come from such sources as "my own reading and my hobbies and interests. I read a couple of books a week. My children's interests very often spark an idea, and I also have a group of young friends who can usually be depended upon to contribute ideas." Even after her sons had grown and moved away, Brenner continued to draw upon their lives for her books. To one son, now a biologist, she owes her interest in reptiles; and to the other, a musician, her interest in music.

But Brenner knows that sometimes inspiration is not enough. "I consider writing books for children a very difficult and challenging art form," she observed in *SATA.* "Amateur or professional, you're still faced with that blank page and the need to put your thoughts in order."

■ Works Cited

Brenner, Barbara, essay in *Something about the Author Autobiography Series,* Volume 14, Gale, 1991.
Contemporary Authors New Revision Series, Gale, Volume 31, 1990.
New York Times Book Review, March 27, 1977.
Something about the Author, Volume 42, Gale, 1986.

■ For More Information See

BOOKS

De Montreville, Doris, and Elizabeth D. Crawford, editors, *Fourth Book of Junior Authors and Illustrators,* H. W. Wilson, 1978.

PERIODICALS

Horn Book, August 1970.
Library Journal, July 1968; May 15, 1970.
New York Times Book Review, August 2, 1981.

*   *   *

BRITTAIN, Bill
See BRITTAIN, William (E.)

*   *   *

BRITTAIN, William (E.) 1930-
(Bill Brittain; James Knox, a
pseudonym)

■ Personal

Born December 16, 1930, in Rochester, NY; son of Knox (a medical doctor) and Dorothy (a nurse; maiden name, Sunderlin) Brittain; married Virginia Ann Connorton (a teacher), February 6, 1954; children: James, Susan. *Education:* Attended Colgate University, 1948-

BILL BRITTAIN

50; State Teachers College at Brockport (now New York State University at Brockport), B.S., 1952; Hofstra University, M.S., 1958.

■ Addresses

Home—17 Wisteria Dr., Asheville, NC 28804.

■ Career

Writer. English teacher in LeRoy, NY, 1952-54; elementary teacher in Lawrence, NY, 1954-60; Lawrence Junior High School, Lawrence, remedial reading teacher, 1960-86. *Member:* Mystery Writers of America, Society of Children's Book Writers and Illustrators.

■ Awards, Honors

Children's Choice citation, International Reading Association/Children's Book Council, 1980, and Charlie May Simon Award, 1982, both for *All the Money in the World;* Notable Children's Book citation, American Library Association, 1981, for *Devil's Donkey;* Newbery Award Honor Book, 1984, for *The Wish Giver: Three Tales of Coven Tree.*

■ Writings

UNDER NAME BILL BRITTAIN

All the Money in the World, illustrated by Charles Robinson, Harper, 1979.
Who Knew There'd Be Ghosts?, illustrated by Michele Chessare, Harper, 1985.
The Fantastic Freshman, Harper, 1988.
My Buddy, the King, Harper, 1989.
Wings, Harper, 1991.
The Ghost from Beneath the Sea, illustrated by Michele Chessare, Harper, 1992.
Shape Changer, Harper, 1994.

"COVEN TREE" SERIES

Devil's Donkey, illustrated by Andrew Glass, Harper, 1981.
The Wish Giver: Three Tales of Coven Tree, illustrated by Glass, Harper, 1983.
Dr. Dredd's Wagon of Wonders, illustrated by Glass, Harper, 1987.
Professor Popkin's Prodigious Polish: A Tale of Coven Tree, illustrated by Glass, Harper, 1991.

OTHER

Survival Outdoors, Monarch, 1977.

Contributor of short mystery stories to *Ellery Queen's Mystery Magazine, Alfred Hitchcock's Mystery Magazine,* and *Antaeus,* sometimes under the pseudonym James Knox. Many of these stories have been anthologized in books for children and adults.

■ Sidelights

William Brittain's writing career has been a long and successful one. Over the years, he has had many of his

The characters in Brittain's "Coven Tree" series are based on people the author knows from his hometown of Spencerport, New York. (Cover illustration by Mike Wimmer.)

short mystery stories published in periodicals such as *Ellery Queen's Mystery Magazine* and *Alfred Hitchcock's Mystery Magazine.* Brittain has also written novels for children, and to this audience he is perhaps best known as the author of the Coven Tree books, including *Devil's Donkey, The Wish Giver,* and *Professor Popkin's Prodigious Polish.* Prior to 1986, Brittain was only a part-time writer, teaching remedial English as his full-time profession. Since his retirement, though, he has had more time to devote to writing.

From early childhood, Brittain felt that he had grown up in the shadow of his older brother. He recalls in an essay for *Something about the Author Autobiography Series* (*SAAS*): "As a boy I felt Bob had been put on this earth with no other mission than to make me feel inferior. He was ... outstandingly handsome. His conversation was witty and urbane, and he made friends at the drop of a hat. He excelled in all sports.... I, on the other hand, was endowed with a pudgy baby face. 'Hello' and 'goodbye' constituted the major part of my discussions. I was a complete klutz at sports, I cried easily, and I was terrified at the idea of getting into a fight with anyone. This made for a somewhat lonely childhood." So,

Brittain took refuge in his imagination, where he could be the hero. He was aided in this escape by the books he read, most of which he acquired from the local public library. "When I first went there—in about third grade—I was terrified by Mrs. Lapp, the librarian, who, with a pencil stuck in her bun of hair and glasses suspended around her neck on a silver chain, seemed more formidable than Darth Vader," remembers Brittain in his autobiographical essay. "As the years passed, however, she introduced me to the glorious characters in her small stock of books. King Arthur and his knights ... Booth Tarkington's Penrod ... Tom and Huck ... and above all, Sherlock Holmes and Doctor Watson." But Brittain was not so involved in his books that he did not make friends and acquaintances in the small town of Spencerport, New York, where he grew up. Later he would use these people as models for the characters in his Coven Tree stories.

But at first Brittain did not think of becoming a writer. His father, a doctor, wished that both Brittain and his brother Bob would follow in his footsteps. But Brittain declares in *SAAS:* "I ... had peeked into my father's small laboratory in the basement of our house where he kept tubs of calf organs in a preservative solution to aid his proctological studies. Having once experienced the sight—and smell—of these ghastly objects, I knew that being a doctor was not for me." Instead he tried to please his father by becoming a lawyer. He followed his elder brother to Colgate University in 1948 with that intent, but explains in his autobiographical essay: "My two years at Colgate were a study in unhappiness. The instructors and professors there insisted that their students constantly discuss, debate, and challenge their remarks. I was used to simple acceptance of whatever the teacher said. I also had the feeling I was rejected socially and couldn't live up to what Bob, a year ahead, was achieving. I managed to maintain a *C* average and that was about it. Perhaps the only good thing to come out of that time was my realization that the law was not for me."

Brittain next transferred to Brockport State Teacher's College (now part of the New York University system) with the intent of becoming a teacher. As he puts it in *SAAS:* "I had no burning desire to become a teacher, but on the other hand, I had no great yearning to be anything else." While earning his degree at Brockport, Brittain met Dr. James Edmunds, an English professor who eventually became the inspiration for his "Mr. Strang" mysteries. He also met fellow student Virginia Connorton, whom he married after he had graduated and been teaching for about a year.

Mystery Stories Begin Writing Career

At first he taught fifth graders in LeRoy, New York, but eventually Brittain was transferred to the junior high, which he found more satisfying. He also directed some of the students' dramatic efforts. After his marriage, he got a better-paying teaching position on Long Island, where he taught remedial reading. It wasn't until after Brittain's children were born during the late 1950s that

HARPER TROPHY
$3.95 US
$5.25 CDN

BILL BRITTAIN
DEVIL'S DONKEY

A Tale of Coven Tree

"Delightfully spooky." —*The New York Times*

A skeptical teenager learns the power of the superstitions of Coven Tree residents when he is turned into a donkey by a witch. (Cover illustration by Wimmer.)

he decided to try writing as a means of supplementing his income. Because Brittain enjoyed the stories he read in the *Ellery Queen* and *Alfred Hitchcock* mystery magazines, he first tried submitting to them. He didn't make a sale for five years, but then, in 1964, he sold "Joshua" to *Alfred Hitchcock's Mystery Magazine.* Another dry period, lasting about a year, followed this publication before Brittain managed to attract the attention of *Ellery Queen*'s editor Frederic Dannay. Dannay helped him edit some of his other stories, starting with "The Man Who Read John Dickson Carr," which began Brittain's "The Man Who Read" series. Dannay also suggested that Brittain create a school-teacher detective, which led to the writing of the "Mr. Strang" series. Brittain recalls in *SAAS:* "If ever anyone had expert guidance in his first attempts at writing, I was that person. To be tutored in the craft of mystery writing by [Dannay], one of the finest detective-story writers ever known, was far more than I could ever hope for. I wasn't, however, one of a small number of lucky souls. Frederic Dannay, in his lifetime, assisted more than five hundred beginning writers!"

"By the mid-1970s," Brittain continued in his autobiographical essay, "having had some fifty or sixty mystery short stories published, I began getting the itch to do a book." He first helped an illustrator friend by writing the text of a nature book, *Survival Outdoors*. Then he wrote a mystery novel featuring Mr. Strang, but was never able to find a publisher for it—he was told that it fell between the juvenile and adult categories. One day he overheard one of his remedial students wish for "all the money in the world," and, as he notes in *SAAS*, "I couldn't help wondering what would happen if he got it . . . . I began outlining all the problems that might arise if all the money in the world were concentrated in the hands of one boy. My scribbled notes slowly arranged themselves into chapters." The result, *All the Money in the World*, was rejected by five publishers before it attracted the attention of Elaine Edelman at Harper and Row. She guided Brittain through a few revisions, and the book was published in 1979.

All the Money in the World is a story in the tradition of the legend of King Midas, whose touch turned all material into gold. In Brittain's story, a young boy named Quentin Stowe captures a leprechaun and wishes for all the money in the world. His wish is granted, and all of the world's money, in all currencies and denominations, is piled unceremoniously onto his family's farm, killing the crops. A further problem is that the money cannot be spent: the moment it changes hands it vanishes, transported back to the pile. Worldwide commerce grinds to a halt, and several foreign powers threaten to go to war for Quentin's money. Though *All the Money in the World* contains a thinly veiled economics lesson, *School Library Journal* reviewer Mary I. Purucker insists: "Children will love this exaggerated, funny tale."

Like *All the Money in the World*, the first of Brittain's Coven Tree books was also inspired by one of his students. He explains in *SAAS:* "There was an eighth-grade girl in one of my reading classes who simply would not read, no matter what motivation I used or what ruses I tried. To her, a book held all the charm of a rattlesnake. One Monday, however, she met me at the door, bursting with enthusiasm. 'Oh, Mr. Brittain,' she cried, 'I just read the greatest book this weekend. Lemme tell you all about it!' The book she'd read . . . was *The Shaggy D.A.* It was the story of a detective who, on odd occasions, turned into an English sheepdog. Over the next several days, it occurred to me that if the story of a human who changes into an animal could create such interest, maybe I should try working with the idea myself." The result, after a few false starts, became *Devil's Donkey*.

"Coven Tree" Books Provide Lessons

"Witchy and devilish things happen in Coven Tree, New England," warns George Gleason in the *School Library Journal*, and it is in this rustic village that *Devil's Donkey* is set. It is the story of a young boy, Dan'l Pitt, who has an unfortunate run-in with Old Magda, the last witch in New England. When Dan'l doubts the authenticity of her powers, Old Magda casts a spell on him—a spell that slowly transforms the boy into a donkey. With the help of his friend, Jenny Bingham, and his guardian, Stewart Meade (known to the villagers as Stew Meat), Dan'l battles against Old Magda and, ultimately, the devil himself to break the evil spell. "I can't imagine how any young child could remain unmoved by this story's pleasurable chills," writes Merri Rosenberg in the *New York Times Book Review*, "and older children should derive even more enjoyment from this sometime tongue-in-cheek, always well-crafted, entertainment."

The popularity of *Devil's Donkey* warranted a second visit to Coven Tree, which Brittain provided in 1986's *The Wish Giver: Three Tales of Coven Tree*, a Newbery Award Honor Book. As with the first book, storekeeper and historian Stew Meat spins the tale, this time of three children who are granted one wish each by a funny little man at the church social. Much like Quentin Stowe, they soon learn that wishes shouldn't always come true: when Polly Kemp, who wants only to be popular, wishes for people to "pay attention to me" and "smile when they see me," her voice is stolen, replaced by the hoarse croak of a frog; when Rowena Jervis wishes for the man of her dreams to "put down roots here in Coven Tree,"

A granted wish may do more harm than good, as is demonstrated in this suspenseful Newbery Honor book by Brittain. (Cover illustration by Wimmer.)

the poor fellow is turned into a tree, himself; and when Adam Fiske wishes for his family's parched farm to have "water all over," the ensuing flood drives the Fiskes out of their home. Natalie Babbitt of the *New York Times Book Review* hails *The Wish Giver* as "an eerie delight, told in a homey, back-country voice."

Brittain has since written two more Coven Tree books, 1987's *Dr. Dredd's Wagon of Wonders* and 1990's *Professor Popkin's Prodigious Polish.* Each is rife with the author's "distinctive mix of comedy and horror," according to one *Publishers Weekly* reviewer, delivering its moral through drama, tension, and, above all, humor. Of his stories, Brittain says in *SAAS:* "I don't try to teach any enduring lessons. If my audience considers what I've written to be 'a good read,' that's enough for me."

■ Works Cited

Babbitt, Natalie, review of *The Wish Giver: Three Tales of Coven Tree, New York Times Book Review,* May 5, 1983, p. 34.
Brittain, Bill, essay in *Something about the Author Autobiography Series,* Volume 7, Gale, 1989, pp. 17-30.
Gleason, George, review of *The Devil's Donkey, School Library Journal,* April, 1983, p. 110.
Publishers Weekly, June 26, 1987, p. 72.
Purucker, Mary I., review of *All the Money in the World, School Library Journal,* March, 1979, p. 135.
Rosenberg, Merri, review of *The Devil's Donkey, New York Times Book Review,* May 3, 1981, p. 41.

■ For More Information See

PERIODICALS

Bulletin of the Center for Children's Books, June, 1979, p. 170; April, 1983, p. 144; June, 1987.
Horn Book, June, 1983, p. 300; July, 1985, p. 448; October, 1987, p. 609; November, 1989, p. 768; January, 1991, p. 66.
Los Angeles Times Book Review, November 20, 1988, p. 6.
New Yorker, December 7, 1981, p. 236; November 30, 1987, p. 144.
New York Times Book Review, May 3, 1981, p. 41.
Publishers Weekly, June 27, 1986, p. 98; July 29, 1988, p. 234; October 27, 1989, p. 70; October 12, 1990, p. 64; November 2, 1990, p. 75.
School Library Journal, March, 1979, p. 135; March, 1981, p. 141; May, 1985, p. 108; August, 1987, p. 78; September, 1988, p. 182; March, 1989, p. 123; September, 1989, p. 249; October, 1990, p. 113.
Voice of Youth Advocates, December, 1988, p. 235.

GEOFFREY BRITTINGHAM

BRITTINGHAM, Geoffrey (Hugh) 1959-

■ Personal

Born May 5, 1959, in Doylestown, PA; son of Stan Brittingham and Jean Mackay Scott Brittingham; married Amy Brown (a neon glass artist), January 9, 1985. *Education:* Ringling School of Art, B.A., 1983. *Hobbies and other interests:* Cycling, repairing old radios, collecting old radio shows on tape. Brittingham and his wife share their home with two dogs, four cats, and a rat.

■ Addresses

Home—1603 North Observatory, Nashville, TN 37215.

■ Career

Children's book illustrator. T-Screens, Inc., Sarasota, FL, artist, 1983-85; CatPak, Dallas, TX, airbrush illustrator, 1985-89; freelance illustrator, 1989—. *Member:* The Society to Preserve and Encourage Radio Drama, Variety, and Comedy.

■ Illustrator

The Killer Brussel Sprouts, JTG of Nashville, 1990.

Mimi Petroske, *Boy, My Very Special Friend,* Winston-Derek, 1991.

Composition and Creative Writing, Incentive Publishers, 1991.

Fun with Words, The South Western Co., 1991.

Kerry Mendell, *On Grandma's Porch,* Winston-Derek, 1991.

Richard Andersen, *The Reluctant Hero,* Winston-Derek, 1991.

Judith McKenzie, *Two Mothers Speak,* Winston-Derek, 1991.

Writing Survival Skills, Incentive Publishers, 1991.

Thelma Osborne, *The Adventures of Speedy,* Winston-Derek, 1992.

The Cooperative Learning Companion, Incentive Publishers, 1992.

Susan Borrely, *Freedom in the Sun,* Winston-Derek, 1992.

Phyllis Johnson, *The Greater Traders,* Winston-Derek, 1992.

Eva Phillips, *Nodley, the Duck Who Paddled Backward,* Winston-Derek, 1992.

Ann Drake, *Quigby Captures His Dreams,* Winston-Derek, 1992.

Richard Conant, *The Race to Save Christmas,* Winston-Derek, 1992.

D.W. Hayes, *Shorty Gordy,* Winston-Derek, 1992.

Beverly Hoffman, *Skipper and Jade,* Winston-Derek, 1992.

Lynda Holland, *The Snicker-Snees,* Winston-Derek, 1992.

Darleen Carter, *Uh-Uh Not Me!,* Winston-Derek, 1992.

Walter Manon, *The Unveiling,* Winston-Derek, 1992.

Stewart the Stegasaurus, JTG of Nashville, 1993.

■ Sidelights

"I've always liked to draw," Geoffrey Brittingham told *SATA.* "When my family moved to Florida in 1971, drawing took on a whole new importance in my life. Making friends was hard for me and drawing helped.

"I bought my first airbrush in 1975," Brittingham recalled, "and got a job spraying surfboards. It was great because when the waves were up no one worked! Through the years the airbrush has been my chief money-making tool. The funny thing is, slick airbrush illustration is my least favorite. Since going freelance I've used the airbrush for laying down my primary colors, shapes, and shadows and then going back over it all with brushwork. I'm indebted to my former boss at the CatPak advertising and illustration studio, Bill Jenkins, for showing me the ropes that prepared me for my freelance career. There are so many artists I admire in the commercial and fine arts. My first big art hero was Frank Frazetta."

BRUNA, Dick 1927-

■ Personal

Born August 23, 1927, in Utrecht, Netherlands; son of Albert Willem (a publisher) and Johanna Clara Charlotte (Erdbrink) Bruna; married Irene de Jongh, 1953; children: Sierk, Marc, Madelon. *Education:* Attended Art Academy, Amsterdam, Netherlands. *Religion:* Protestant.

■ Addresses

Home—Gabrieallaan 10, Utrecht, Netherlands 3582 HC. *Office*— Jeruzalemstraat 3, Utrecht, Netherlands 3512 KW.

■ Career

Designer of book jackets, 1945—, and posters, 1947—; author and illustrator of books for children, 1953—. Also designer of postage stamps, murals, greeting cards, and picture postcards. *Exhibitions:* Central Museum, Utrecht, 1966-67; Gemeentemuseum, Arnhem, Netherlands, 1977; Dutch National Museum of Book and Typography, The Hague, Netherlands, 1985; Parco Gallery, Kechijoji Department Store, Tokyo, Japan, 1988; Frans Halsmuseum, Haarlem, Netherlands, 1989. *Member:* Alliance Graphique Internationale, PEN International, Netherlands Graphique Internationale, Authors League of America, Netherlands Graphic Designers, Art Directors Club (Netherlands).

DICK BRUNA

■ Awards, Honors

Recipient of various awards for the design of posters, including the Poster Prize, 1958, 1960, 1967, and the Benelux Prize, 1960; created Knight of the Order of Orange Nassau; recipient of a silver medal from the city of Utrecht, Netherlands, 1987, because "his illustrious imagination lifted the city to a higher level"; D.A. Thiemeprize, Netherlands, 1990.

■ Writings

SELF-ILLUSTRATED; IN ENGLISH TRANSLATION

The Apple: A Toy Box Tale, translation by Sandra Greifenstein, Follett, 1963, revised edition with Judith Klugmann published as *The Happy Apple,* Hart Publishing, 1959 (originally published as *De appel,* Bruna & Zoon [Utrecht, Netherlands], 1953).

The King, Methuen, 1964, Follett, 1968 (originally published as *De kleine koning,* Bruna & Zoon, 1955, revised edition published as *De koning,* 1962).

Tilly and Tessa, Methuen, 1962, translation by Greifenstein published as *Tilly and Tess: A Toy Box Tale,* Follett, 1963 (originally published as *Fien en Pien,* Bruna & Zoon, 1959).

The Little Bird, Methuen, 1962, Two Continents, 1975, translation by Greifenstein published as *Little Bird Tweet: A Toy Box Tale,* Follett, 1963 (originally published as *Het vogeltje,* Bruna & Zoon, 1959).

Kitten Nell: A Toy Box Tale, translation by Greifenstein, Follett, 1963, published in England as *Pussy Nell,* Methuen, 1966 (originally published as *Poesje Nel,* Bruna & Zoon, 1959).

The Circus: A Toy Box Tale, translation by Greifenstein, Follett, 1963 (originally published as *Circus,* Bruna & Zoon, 1962).

The Egg, Methuen, 1964, translation by Greifenstein published as *The Egg,* Follett, 1968 (originally published as *Het ei,* Bruna & Zoon, 1962).

The Fish, Methuen, 1962, translation by Greifenstein published as *The Fish: A Toy Box Tale,* Follett, 1963 (originally published as *De vis,* Bruna & Zoon, 1962).

The Christmas Book, Methuen, 1964, new edition, Two Continents, 1976, translation into verse by Eve Merriam published as *Christmas,* Doubleday, 1969 (originally published as *Kerstmis,* Bruna & Zoon, 1963).

The Sailor, Methuen, 1966, translation by Greifenstein published as *The Sailor,* Follett, 1968 (originally published as *De matroos,* Bruna & Zoon, 1964).

The School, Methuen, 1966, Follett, 1968 (originally published as *De school,* Bruna & Zoon, 1964).

(Adapter) *Tom Thumb,* Methuen, 1966 (originally published as *Klein duimpje,* Bruna & Zoon, 1965).

I Can Read (also see below), Methuen, 1968, Two Continents, 1975 (originally published as *Ik kan lezen,* Bruna & Zoon, 1965).

I Can Read More, Methuen, 1969, Two Continents, 1976 (originally published as *Ik kan nog meer lezen,* Bruna & Zoon, 1965).

(Adapter) *Cinderella,* Follett, 1966 (originally published as *Assepoester,* Bruna & Zoon, 1966).

(Adapter) *Snow White and the Seven Dwarfs,* Follett, 1966 (originally published as *Sneeuwwitje,* Bruna & Zoon, 1966).

(Adapter) *Little Red Riding Hood,* Follett, 1966 (originally published as *Roodkapje,* Bruna & Zoon, 1966).

B Is for Bear: An ABC, Methuen, 1967, 2nd edition, 1971 (originally published as *B is een beer,* Bruna & Zoon, 1967).

I Can Count (also see below), Methuen, 1968, Two Continents, 1975 (originally published as *Telboek,* Bruna & Zoon, 1968).

A Story to Tell (also see below), Methuen, 1968, Two Continents, 1975 (originally published as *Boek zonder woorden,* Bruna & Zoon, 1968).

Snuffy, Methuen, 1970, Two Continents, 1975 (originally published as *Snuffie,* Bruna & Zoon, 1969).

Snuffy and the Fire, Methuen, 1970, Two Continents, 1975 (originally published as *Snuffie en de brand,* Bruna & Zoon, 1969).

ABC Frieze (four foldout panels), Methuen, 1971, Methuen (U.S.), 1976.

Dick Bruna's Animal Book, Methuen, 1974, Two Continents, 1976 (originally published as *Dierenboek,* Bruna & Zoon, 1972).

I Can Count More 13-24, Methuen, 1973, Two Continents, 1976 (originally published as *Telboek 2,* Bruna & Zoon, 1972).

My Vest Is White (also see below), Methuen, 1973, published as *My Shirt Is White,* Two Continents, 1975 (originally published as *Mijn hemd is wit,* Bruna & Zoon).

Another Story to Tell, Methuen, 1974 (originally published as *Boek zonder woorden 2,* Bruna & Zoon, 1974).

I Am a Clown, Methuen (originally published as *Ik ben een clown,* Bruna & Zoon, 1974).

Christmas Crib Print-Outs, Methuen (U.S.), 1974.

Lisa and Lynn, Two Continents, 1975.

Dick Bruna's Animal Frieze (four foldout paper panels), Methuen, 1975.

One-Two-Three Frieze (four foldout paper panels), Two Continents, 1976.

I Can Read Difficult Words, Methuen, 1977, Methuen (U.S.), 1978 (originally published as *Ik kan moeilijke woorden lezen,* Bruna & Zoon, 1976).

I Can Dress Myself, Methuen, 1977, Methuen (U.S.), 1978 (originally published as *Ik kan nog weel meer lezen,* Bruna & Zoon, 1976).

Poppy Pig, Methuen, 1978 (originally published as *Betje big,* Bruna & Zoon, 1977).

Poppy Pig's Garden, Methuen, 1978 (originally published as *De tuin van betje big,* Bruna & Zoon, 1977).

The Dick Bruna Calendar 1979, Methuen, 1978.

Dick Bruna's Nature Frieze, Methuen, 1978, published as *The Nature Frieze* (four foldout paper panels), Methuen (U.S.), 1979.

A Child's First Books (contains *I Can Read, I Can Count, A Story to Tell,* and *My Vest Is White*), Methuen, 1979.

My Meals, Methuen, 1980 (originally published as *Eten,* Bruna & Zoon, 1979).

My Toys, Methuen, 1980 (originally published as *Spelen,* Bruna & Zoon, 1979).

Out and About, Methuen, 1980 (originally published as *Naar buiten,* Bruna & Zoon, 1979).

Poppy Pig Goes to Market, Methuen, 1981 (originally published as *Betje big gaat naar de markt,* Bruna & Zoon, 1980).

When I'm Big?, Methuen, 1981 (originally published as *Heb jij een hobbie?,* Bruna & Zoon, 1980).

I Know about Numbers, Methuen, 1981 (originally published as *Ik kan sommen maken,* Bruna & Zoon, 1980).

I Know More about Numbers, Methuen, 1981 (originally published as *Ik kan nog meer sommen maken,* Bruna & Zoon, 1980).

Dick Bruna's Word Book, Methuen, 1982.

Farmer John, Price Stern, 1984 (originally published as *Jan,* De Harmonie, 1982).

I Know about Shapes, Price Stern, 1984 (originally published as *Rond, vierkant, driehoekig,* De Harmonie, 1982).

The Orchestra, Price Stern, 1984 (originally published as *Wij hebben een orkest,* De Harmonie, 1984).

The Rescue, Price Stern, 1984 (originally published as *De redding,* De Harmonie, 1984).

Blue Boat, Methuen, 1984.

Through the Year with Boris Bear, Methuen, 1986 (originally published as *Lente, zomer, herfst en winter,* De Harmonie, 1986).

Poppy Pig's Birthday, Methuen, 1986 (originally published as *De verjaardag van Betje Big,* De Harmonie, 1986).

Snuffy's Puppies, Methuen, 1986 (originally published as *De Puppies van Snuffie,* De Harmonie, 1986).

Sophie's Toys, Collins, 1989 (originally published as *Boek zonder woorden 3,* Van Goor, 1988).

Boris Bear, Methuen, 1990 (originally published as *Boris beer,* Van Goor, 1989).

Boris and Barbara, Methuen, 1990 (originally published as *Boris en Barbara,* Van Goor, 1989).

Boris on the Mountain, Methuen, 1990 (originally published as *Boris op de berg,* Van Goor, 1989).

Also author of *Children's Haemophilia Book.*

SELF-ILLUSTRATED; UNTRANSLATED WORKS

Toto in volendam, Bruna & Zoon, 1953.

De auto (title means "The Car"), Bruna & Zoon, 1957.

Tijs, Bruna & Zoon, 1957.

Moeder, moeder de beer is los, Bruda & Zoon, 1962.

Bloemenboek (title means "Flower Book"), Bruna & Zoon, 1975.

(With Edith Brinkers) *Verjaardagboekje t.b.v. unicef* (title means "Birthday Book in Support of UNICEF), Bruna & Zoon, 1979.

Sportboek (title means "Sport Book"), De Harmonie, 1985.

Wie zijn rug is dat? (riddle book), De Harmonie, 1985.

Wie zijn hoed is dat? (riddle book), De Harmonie, 1985.

"MIFFY" SERIES

Miffy, Methuen, 1964, Follett, 1970 (originally published as *Nijntje,* Bruna & Zoon, 1955, revised edition, 1963).

Miffy at the Zoo, Methuen, 1965, Follett, 1970 (originally published as *Nijntje in de dierentuin,* Bruna & Zoon, 1955, revised edition, 1963).

Miffy in the Snow, Methuen, 1965, Follett, 1970 (originally published as *Nijntje in de sneeuw,* Bruna & Zoon, 1963).

Miffy at the Seaside, Methuen, 1964, Follett, 1970, also published as *Miffy at the Beach,* Methuen, 1979 (originally published as *Nijntje aan see,* Bruna & Zoon, 1963).

Miffy's Birthday (also see below), Methuen, 1971, Two Continents, 1976 (originally published as *Het feest van Nijntje,* Bruna & Zoon, 1970).

Miffy Goes Flying (also see below), Methuen, 1971, Two Continents, 1976 (originally published as *Nijntje vliegt,* Bruna & Zoon, 1970).

Miffy Painting Book (activity book), Methuen, 1974.

Miffy at the Playground, Methuen, 1976 (originally published as *Nijntje in de speeltuin,* Bruna & Zoon, 1975).

Miffy in Hospital (also see below), Methuen, 1976, also published as *Miffy in the Hospital,* Methuen (U.S.), 1978 (originally published as *Nijntje in het ziekenhuis,* Bruna & Zoon, 1975).

Miffy Books, (contains *Miffy's Birthday, Miffy Goes Flying,* and *Miffy in the Hospital*) Methuen (U.S.), 1978.

Miffy's Dream, Methuen, 1979, Methuen (U.S.), 1980 (originally published as *Nijntje's droom,* Bruna & Zoon, 1979).

Read-with-Miffy Frieze, Methuen, 1980.

Bruna's Miffy Calendar 1980, Methuen, 1980.

Bruna's self-illustrated tales are populated with animal characters such as Poppy Pig, Boris Bear, and Miffy's rabbit family.

Miffy's Bicycle, Price Stern, 1984 (originally published as *Nijntje op de fiets,* De Harmonie, 1982).

Miffy Goes to School, Price Stern, 1984 (originally published as *Nijntje op school,* De Harmonie, 1984).

Miffy and Her Friend, Collins, 1989 (originally published as *Nijntje gaat logeren,* Van Goor, 1988).

Miffy Goes to Stay, Collins, 1989 (originally published as *Opa en oma Pluis,* Van Goor, 1988).

ILLUSTRATOR

Vera Cerutti, *Kind Little Joe,* Hart Publishing, 1959.

Cover illustrator of adult book, *Moeder, moeder de beer is los.*

■ Sidelights

Dick Bruna, author and illustrator of over seventy books, is internationally recognized for introducing the youngest of children to their first books. His books, which have been translated into twenty-eight languages, range from interpretations of classic fairy tales such as *Snow White and the Seven Dwarfs* to original stories about animal characters to books that help young children learn to count and recognize colors. Bruna began his career as an illustrator at the age of sixteen, when he produced a book jacket for the A. W. Bruna publishing firm, a firm founded by his great-grandfather. Although Bruna attended Art Academy in Amsterdam, he left after six months; and since 1945 he has worked as an artist, designing book jackets and posters, and creating his own picture books.

Simply drawn pictures are used to teach very young children about the animal world in *Dick Bruna's Animal Book.*

Bruna's success in the field of children's literature occurred after his own three children were old enough to read. His wife, Irene, plays an important role in the creation of his books, providing critical commentary on his designs. Although Bruna's books have been lauded for their appeal to small children, he comments: "I don't sit down and think: this is meant for children. I design a book that I like myself and if that happens to get across to children, then that's my good luck." Nor does Bruna test his books out on children; instead he works on them for months until he feels that he is finished, then shows them only to his wife. "It's really strange," says Bruna, "some of my books turn out to be suitable for four-year-olds, and others for two-year-olds. Sometimes I can understand why, but I didn't work on them with that conscious goal." In fact, Bruna's conscious goal is simply to turn out the most sincere and honest portrayal of the story he is trying to tell. Bruna is a perfectionist, creating a hundred drawings for a book that will only contain twelve. "I go on writing texts endlessly too," he admits. "I type pages and pages of them, much too much, and then suddenly see what's right."

Though many critics have complimented Bruna for his books' educational value, Bruna claims that he doesn't "try to educate children one way or another. Of course, when it's a counting-book, then some kind of teaching is automatically involved. But even then, the most important thing is for the child to have nice pictures." Nevertheless, the books are helpful for teaching very young children to recognize words, colors, and objects, because Bruna is always careful to identify the colors and the objects on the same page as their corresponding words.

Simple Drawings Appeal to Children

Bruna usually starts his works off with a simple image: "As soon as I have an image, . . . I start to make up a story. . . . But it quite often happens that I change [the story] when I'm about halfway through, and then the story goes off in a completely different direction. The whole process takes quite a long time." He always works with brushes and poster paints, and takes care that the imperfections in the brush strokes show up in the printed work, for he feels that it is important for children to see that the figures have been drawn by someone just like them. Bruna strives to maintain simplicity in his work, in part because he is irritated by the complexity that many children's books offer. "They sometimes seemed to be written for parents more than for children of a particular age. My books are definitely intended for children." Simplification, according to Bruna, appeals to young children. "If you make it that simple, you leave the children a lot of room for their own imagination." For these reasons, Bruna's drawings are often of single characters alone on the page, rendered in just a few primary colors like red, yellow, and blue.

Bruna is perhaps best known for the simplicity and honesty of the characters in his books. Animal characters like Poppy Pig, Miffy, and Snuffy look directly from page to the child. Bruna says "It's a matter of directness.... It's just like talking to someone, you look straight at them, don't you?" Gedolph Adriaan Kohnstamm, in his *The Extra in the Ordinary: Children's Books by Dick Bruna,* writes that this is "the most outstanding characteristic of all in Bruna's work: the characters look at the observer." This direct gaze from open friendly eyes not only invites the child to feel a part of the story, it also conveys to them the honesty of the character.

Some critics, however, feel that the simplicity of Bruna's work shelters children from experiencing the reality of more complex and more realistic emotions. "By emphasizing the upturned corners of the mouth for happiness and the downturned for distress," notes Kohnstamm, Bruna and other children's authors have developed a symbolism for facial expression which they "spoonfeed to our children." Liam Hudson, writing in the *Times Literary Supplement,* also faults Bruna for oversimplification, arguing that "if we impose on ourselves a reign of niceness and good taste, the everyday life we grow up to lead may well turn out to be suffused with a sense of artifice, of inauthenticity." In contrast, another *Times Literary Supplement* reviewer thinks that the simplicity is appropriate: "In *Miffy's Birthday* and *Miffy Goes Flying,* the heroine's expression remains deadpan and her reactions are predictable in the face of all kinds of excitements, but to the inexperienced two-year-old, whose chief pleasure in literature has always been the spotting and naming of objects he recognizes, the unchanging world of Miffy is stimulating stuff."

To Bruna, simplification is just part of the process of creation. "Everything starts out complicated," he says. "Then, I take out more and more that seems to me unnecessary." He continued: "I just draw what I think is good and I try to do that to the best of my ability. I wouldn't know how to do it any other way." For the millions of children who have read Bruna's books, his method is fine, for Bruna's characters seem to invite the child into a world of bright colors, smiling faces, and discovery. "Bruna's [books] are not aimed at the adult who presents them," writes J. H. Dohm in *Junior Bookshelf,* "but direct at the child they are bought for—they aren't books to be kept on a 'clean-hands' shelf, but books to be lived with and slept with, and, very likely, chewed at the owner's discretion. As an introduction to book ownership they probably can't be bettered."

■ Works Cited

Dohm, J. H., "D is for Dutch—and Dick," *Junior Bookshelf,* August, 1967, pp. 225-28.
Hudson, Liam, "Ghastly Good Taste," *Times Literary Supplement,* April 2, 1976, p. 385.
"Keeping It Small," *Times Literary Supplement,* July 2, 1971, p. 771.
Kohnstamm, Gedolph Adriaan, *The Extra in the Ordinary: Children's Books by Dick Bruna,* translated by Patricia Crampton, Mercis, 1979.

■ For More Information See

BOOKS

Children's Literature Review, Volume 7, Gale, 1984.
Huerlimann, Bettina, *Picture-Book World,* World Publishing, 1969.
Kingman, Lee, and others, editors, *Illustrators of Children's Books: 1967-76,* Horn Book, 1978.
Tucker, Nicholas, *The Child and the Book: A Psychological and Literary Exploration,* Cambridge University Press, 1981, pp. 23-45.

PERIODICALS

Books for Your Children, summer, 1978, pp. 12-13; autumn-winter, 1980, p. 35.
Children's Book Review, April, 1971, p. 50.
Growing Point, July, 1966, p. 735; July, 1981, p. 3918.
Publishers Weekly, September 18, 2982, p. 254.
Times Literary Supplement, December 9, 1965, p. 1149.*

*   *   *

BUFFETT, Jimmy 1946-

■ Personal

Born December 25, 1946, in Pascogoula, MS; son of James Delaney (a shipwright) and Lorraine (Peets) Buffett; married second wife, Jane Slagsvol, August 27, 1977; children: Savannah Jane, Sarah Delaney. *Education:* Attended Auburn University, 1964; University of Southern Mississippi, B.S., 1969. *Politics:* Democrat. *Religion:* Roman Catholic.

JIMMY BUFFETT

■ Addresses

Home—Key West, FL; Sag Harbor, NY; and Nashville, TN. *Office*—Margaritaville Records, 54 Music Sq. E., Suite 303, Nashville, TN 37203; and 1880 Century Park E., Suite 900, Los Angeles, CA 90067. *Agent*—Morton Janklow, 598 Madison Ave., New York, NY 10022.

■ Career

Songwriter and performer, beginning in the 1960s; *Billboard* Publications, Nashville, TN, writer, 1971-73; writer. *Member:* Greenpeace Foundation (honorary director), Cousteau Society, Save the Manatee Commission of Florida (chair).

■ Writings

(With daughter Savannah Jane Buffett) *The Jolly Mon* (juvenile), illustrated by Lambert Davis, Harcourt, 1988.

Tales from Margaritaville: Fictional Facts and Factual Fictions (short story and autobiographical sketch collection), Harcourt, 1989.

(With Savannah Jane Buffett) *Trouble Dolls* (juvenile), Harcourt, 1991.

Where Is Joe Merchant? A Novel Tale (novel), Harcourt, 1992.

Contributor to *Inside Sports, Outside, Miami Herald,* and *Smart.*

RECORD ALBUMS, LYRICS AND MUSIC

Down to Earth, Barnaby, 1972.

A White Sport Coat and a Pink Crustacean, Dunhill, 1973.

Living and Dying in 3/4 Time, Dunhill, 1974.

A-1-A, Dunhill, 1974.

Rancho Deluxe (soundtrack), United Artists, 1975.

High Cumberland Jamboree, Barnaby, 1976.

Havana Daydreamin', ABC, 1976.

Changes in Latitudes, Changes in Attitudes, ABC, 1977.

Son of a Son of a Sailor, ABC, 1978,

Jimmy Buffett Live, You Had to Be There, MCA, 1978.

Volcano, MCA, 1979.

Somewhere over China, MCA, 1981.

Coconut Telegraph, MCA, 1981.

One Particular Harbor, MCA, 1983.

Riddles in the Sand, MCA, 1984.

Last Mango in Paris, MCA, 1985.

Songs You Know by Heart: Jimmy Buffett's Greatest Hits, MCA, 1986.

Floridays, MCA, 1986.

Hot Water, MCA, 1988.

Off to See the Lizard, MCA, 1989.

Boats, Beaches, Bars, and Ballads, MCA, 1992.

Before the Beach (reissue of *Down to Earth* and *High Cumberland Jamboree*), Margaritaville Records, 1993.

■ Work in Progress

An album of new songs, release expected in 1994.

■ Sidelights

Jimmy Buffett is known to millions of music and mixed drink fans as the writer and performer of "Margaritaville," a humorous song about alcohol-inspired melancholy and lost love. The musician is famous for his trademark humor and laid-back style, and both music critics and record buyers have remarked on the narrative quality of his songwriting. So it came as no surprise to his legions of devoted fans, affectionately dubbed "parrotheads" for their colorful concert-going garb, when Buffett published *Tales from Margaritaville,* a collection of humorous short stories and personal anecdotes. Buffett had previously written a short children's book, *The Jolly Mon,* with his daughter Savannah Jane, but *Tales from Margaritaville* marked his first full-length book. He followed it with the novel *Where Is Joe Merchant?* in 1992. The books achieved considerable popular success, thanks in part to the parrotheads' voracious appetite for all things Buffett. It is the singer's growing popularity among readers unfamiliar with his music, however, that has led critics to suggest that Buffett is not only an engaging musician but a capable writer of fiction.

Born on Christmas Day, 1946, Buffett was raised a Southerner. He spent much of his formative years on the shores of the Gulf of Mexico in Alabama, where his father was a naval architect. Life on the water ran in the Buffett family; his grandfather was a sailor, and it was from the paternal side of his family that he inherited his lifelong love of the sea. Growing to adulthood, Buffett attended Auburn University and eventually earned a degree from the University of Mississippi. Despite his love for the ocean, Buffett decided to travel inland and seek his fortune.

After traveling throughout America for a number of years and working as a freelance writer, Buffett briefly lived in Nashville, Tennessee, where he recorded his first album, *Down to Earth.* The album sold modestly and Buffett soon began his travels anew. He moved to various locations, including Los Angeles, California, before settling in Key West, Florida. Once again on the Gulf of Mexico, Buffett found his true home in Key West and began writing and recording the music that would bring him his greatest fame. In 1977 he released *Changes in Latitudes, Changes in Attitudes,* which features the song "Margaritaville." The album proved to be his breakthrough recording. Enchanted by Buffett's idealized world of idyllic sun worship, sea travel, and carefree partying, listeners embraced the singer's music. Since that time, a growing host of parrotheads have flocked to Buffett concerts, events that have been described by the faithful as more like a party for five thousand close friends than a big, impersonal show.

With his increasing financial stability, Buffett was able to pursue the love of his life. He purchased a boat and became a frequent traveler along the Gulf Stream, often making trips to the Caribbean. Describing the attraction the region held for him, he told *Time,* "There are a lot of incredible characters down there, as migratory and gypsy-souled as I am." By the late 1980s, Buffett's concert tours and various journeys had exposed him to an often unseen world of unusual characters and colorful locations. He realized that descriptions of these elements need not be confined to his songwriting, and he decided to write a book.

Encounters on the Road Inspire Book

This inspiration to write fiction came to Buffett in the late 1980s, following a concert tour of Australia. While in that country, Buffett happened across author Bruce Chatwin's book *The Songlines*. That book, along with mythologist Joseph Campbell's *The Power of Myth,* so affected Buffett that—as he wrote in *Tales from Margaritaville*—he made a "New Year's resolution to start my own book." Buffett adopted American folklorist Mark Twain's statement "Write what you know about" as his book's epigraph and, working on the island of South Bimini, began writing tales inspired by his travels.

The stories in *Tales from Margaritaville* are broken down into four sections and all center on life on the ocean, in particular the Gulf Stream, a current of warm water that flows from the Gulf of Mexico to as far away as the Scandinavian country of Norway. With the exception of the four stories in the section titled "Son of a Son of a Sailor" (also the title of one of Buffett's better-known albums), the stories are all fictional. The "Son of a Son of a Sailor" stories are autobiographical and relate events from Buffett's childhood through his adult life as an entertainer.

Among the fictional tales in the book is "Take Another Road," the story of Wyoming cattle hand Tully Mars. When the new owner of the ranch Tully works on decides to switch from cattle raising to poodle breeding, Tully decides to seek his fortune elsewhere. He takes his horse, Mr. Twain, and fulfills a lifelong dream to live on the ocean. On the way to his final destination in Key West, the cowboy encounters a sage diner waitress, the hometown of his hero Mark Twain, and the ghosts of a famous Native American battle. Tully also meets two sisters, Aurora and Bora Alice Porter, proprietors of a cafe in Heat Wave, Alabama. The Porter sisters figure prominently in another story, "Off to See the Lizard," which is an account of a local high school football team's unconventional triumph over adversity. Other stories in the collection include "Boomerang Love," in which a young woman returns to her hometown to encounter a horrendous hurricane and the one true love of her life, and a collection of tales that center around the inhabitants of the imaginary island of Snake Bite Key.

In the introduction to *Tales from Margaritaville*, Buffett provides some clues for his readers regarding the location of the fictional Margaritaville. As he writes: "Ever since I was a child, I have had a recurring dream of visiting an island; it appears at different locations on the perimeter of the Gulf of Mexico—west of Tortuga, south of Ship Island, or in the middle of Perdido Bay. Somewhere and everywhere, Margaritaville has its origins." Critics responded favorably to Buffett's imaginary landscapes, with a *Library Journal* reviewer remarking that the collection creates a "vivid image of time and place." Reviewing *Tales from Margaritaville* in the *New York Times Book Review*, Janet Kaye commented on the book's collection of "good-natured tales" and "exuberant antics." Kaye concluded her review by stating that "Mr Buffett's lighthearted endorsement of adventure is so persuasive that, upon finishing the book, many readers will be tempted to get out their maps."

Margaritaville Success Followed by Novel

Tales from Margaritaville became so popular that it stayed on the *New York Times* best-seller list for seven months. Buffett followed the book's success with another best-seller in 1992, his first novel, *Where Is Joe Merchant?* The Joe Merchant of the title is a famous rock star. At the height of his popularity, Joe disappeared and is now believed to be dead. As the novel begins, there have been repeated Caribbean sightings of a man who bears a striking resemblance to the missing rocker. Joe's sister, Trevor Kane, decides to track this man down and see if he truly is her long lost brother. She enlists the aid of her former boyfriend, a seaplane pilot named Frank Bama, and along with a pushy, obnoxious journalist, they go in search of Joe. Frank and Trevor hop from island to island in pursuit of the elusive man. During their trek, they encounter modern-day pirates and other violence-happy personalities—in addition to the beauty and mystery of the tropics. While he found the plot "slender," *New York Times Book Review* contributor Richard E. Nicholls did praise the novel's "gentle charm" and stated that Buffett "does know how to keep a story moving." Describing his intentions in writing the novel, Buffett told the *New York Times:* "I think it's human nature to love romantic tales and exotic places.... So I didn't set out to write *War and Peace.* My goal was to write about what I knew and was told, an escapist adventure that book people would bring to the beach."

"I never wanted to be one-dimensional," Buffett told the *Washington Post* while describing his career. "If you're in charge of yourself and know what you want to do, there's plenty of things out there." Buffett has used this ethic to forge two successful careers and has managed to effectively balance both. In addition to the literary popularity of his books, Buffett's tour was the third most attended of the 1992 summer concert season—*New York Times* contributor Thomas Clavin called him "one of a few recession-proof performers." Despite the pride he takes in his music, the success of his books is the culmination of a dream for Buffett, as he told Clavin in the *New York Times:* "I was a journalism major in college and wanted to be a writer. But then what happened was my music career sort of got in the way for over twenty years." When Buffett finally did get to writing, he found it a new experience compared to his musical profession. Describing his situation in the introduction to *Tales from Margaritaville*, Buffett writes: "There seem to be a lot of responsibilities that I didn't comprehend when I decided to pursue this new career, but in the words of Tully Mars ... 'Hell,

Columbus thought Cuba was China.' But that seems true of life in general, at least on this planet and in this lifetime, which in the only one I am halfway familiar with."

■ Works Cited

Buffett, Jimmy, *Tales from Margaritaville: Fictional Facts and Factual Fictions,* Harcourt, 1989.

Clavin, Thomas, article in *New York Times,* October 4, 1992, p. L11.

Kaye, Janet, review of *Tales from Margaritaville, New York Times Book Review,* November 26, 1989, p. 30.

Nicholls, Richard E., review of *Where Is Joe Merchant?, New York Times Book Review,* October 11, 1992, p. 22.

Review of *Tales from Margaritaville, Library Journal,* October 1, 1989, p. 95.

Time, April 18, 1977.

Washington Post, December 17, 1989.

■ For More Information See

BOOKS

Contemporary Musicians, Volume 4, Gale, 1991, pp. 27-28.

PERIODICALS

Booklist, August, 1990, p. 2195.

School Library Journal, October, 1990, p. 78.

—*Sketch by David M. Galens*

*   *   *

BUNDLES, A'Lelia Perry 1952-

■ Personal

Born June 7, 1952, in Chicago, IL; daughter of S. Henry Bundles, Jr. (a business executive) and A'Lelia Mae (Perry) Bundles (a business executive). *Education:* Harvard & Radcliffe, A.B., 1974; Columbia University Graduate School of Journalism, M.S.J., 1976. *Hobbies and other interests:* Collecting kaleidoscopes and black memorabilia.

■ Addresses

Home—3566 South George Mason Drive, Alexandria, VA 22302. *Office*—ABC News, 1717 DeSales Street, N.W., Washington, DC 20036.

■ Career

Producer for NBC News in Washington, DC, Atlanta, GA, Houston, TX, and New York, NY, 1976-89; ABC News, Washington, DC, producer for *World News Tonight,* 1989—. Radcliffe College, trustee, 1985-89; Schlesinger Library on the History of Women in America, member of advisory board, 1987-94. *Member:* Metropolitan D.C. Links, Alpha Kappa Alpha.

■ Awards, Honors

National Association of Black Journalists Feature Award, 1987, for "Paradise Lost: Daufuskie Island, South Carolina"; Emmy Award, 1989, for documentary; American Book Award and New York Public Library Best Books for the Teenage citation, both 1992, for *Madam C. J. Walker: Entrepreneur;* American Women in Radio and TV News Feature Award, 1992.

■ Writings

Madam C. J. Walker: Entrepreneur, Chelsea House, 1991.

Contributor to books, including *Black Women in the United States: An Historical Encyclopedia,* Carlson Publishers, 1993; *Encyclopedia of African American Culture and History,* Macmillan, 1994; and *Encyclopedia of Indianapolis,* Indiana University Press, 1994. Contributor to periodicals, including *Parade, Essence, Ms., Radcliffe Quarterly, Sage, Harvard Gazette, Ebony, Jr., Seventeen, Washington View, NABJ News,* and *One.*

■ Work in Progress

"*The Walker Women,* is the working title for a biography of Madam C. J. Walker, A'Lelia Walker, and Mae Walker Perry (my great-great-grandmother, great-grandmother, and grandmother)—this work is still in an early writing stage. I am also researching for the long term—a novel based on the lives of family members who traveled the Underground Railroad, held political office during Reconstruction, and sent their children to Oberlin College and Lincoln University in the 1880s."

A'LELIA PERRY BUNDLES

■ Sidelights

A'Lelia Bundles is a producer for the "American Agenda" series on the ABC News program *World News Tonight.* "Magazine and book writing for me ... is still largely a part-time, weekend pursuit," she told *SATA.* But even so, she loves to write and feels most content in her office at home, where she surrounds herself with "piles of research and pending projects," types on her computer, and communicates with her muse.

"I sensed I might be a writer in third grade when the act of creating one of my first short stories gave me sweaty palms and heart palpitations," Bundles remembers. "The thrill of seeing a byline some years later added to the exhilaration I rediscover each time I start, struggle through, then complete a project."

Her first book, *Madam C. J. Walker: Entrepreneur,* is the result of a combination of influences, not the least of which were the stories of her family. "The topic of the life of entrepreneur and social activist Madam C. J. Walker found me," she told *SATA.* "In fact, it might be more accurate to say that it followed me, grabbed me, and forced me to take it on." Bundles grew up hearing stories about her great-great-grandmother, Madam C. J. Walker, and her daughter, A'Lelia Walker (whom author Langston Hughes called the "Joy Goddess of Harlem"), Bundles' great-grandmother. "But it was up to me to try to make sense of their lives and the history and people surrounding them from the thousands of pages of letters, articles and documents they left."

Another great influence on Bundles' writing was *Roots* author Alex Haley. "For several years I prepared research for a project he planned, but never completed, on Madam Walker," she remembers. "In the process he became a pivotal mentor for me. I learned invaluable lessons from him about friendship, research, and the art of storytelling." In 1990 Haley invited Bundles and two other writers to join him on a freighter cruise from California to Ecuador. "The total calm and solitude gave me exactly the atmosphere I needed to finish the rough draft of my manuscript for *Madam C. J. Walker: Entrepreneur.*"

Bundles further commented: "I am delighted that my first book is part of Chelsea House's 'Black Americans of Achievement' series, a wonderful group of biographies for young adult readers. I only wish I had had such a series to read when I was in junior high school in the mid-1960s when it seemed the only women we learned about in school were Louisa May Alcott and Florence Nightingale, and the only African Americans on the library shelves of my predominantly white elementary school were *Little Black Sambo* and, sometimes, George Washington Carver.

"Now that my first book is finished I especially enjoy speaking about the Walker women because their lives are so relevant today. Madam Walker's struggles to overcome the obstacles in her life are some of the same struggles women still face. Despite being a poor, single mother with little education, she persevered, established her own business, and became economically independent. Even more important, she provided jobs and hope for thousands of other women and used her wealth to support educational and political causes that benefitted her community.

"For young readers, Madam Walker's rags to riches rise shows that almost anything is possible, that dreams do come true. For adults—especially women—her story provides inspiration that life's hard knocks are only the beginning of achieving success."

C

CATALANO, Dominic 1956-

■ Personal

Born January 9, 1956, in Syracuse, NY; son of Dominic (a blue-collar manager) and Virginia Mayer (a blue-collar worker; maiden name, Strong) Catalano; married Virginia Hullings (a doctoral candidate in human development), April 15, 1989; children: Sara Elizabeth, Grant Haskell (stepson). *Education:* State University of New York at Buffalo, B.S., 1978; State University of New York at Oswego, M.A., 1988; Syracuse University, M.F.A., 1991. *Hobbies and other interests:* Reading, camping, canoeing, cooking, woodworking, toy making.

■ Addresses

Home and office—106 Terrace Drive, Syracuse, NY 13219.

DOMINIC CATALANO

■ Career

Children's book illustrator and author. Cat Graphics Design and Illustration, Syracuse, NY, owner, art and creative director, 1978—; art and music teacher for various schools in New York State, 1978-87; *Herald Journal* and *Post Standard* (newspapers), Syracuse, art director and graphic artist, 1982-86; Cazenovia College, Cazenovia, NY, design, drawing, and illustration teacher, 1988—; State College of New York at Oswego, Syracuse, assistant professor of illustration, 1989-91; Onondaga County Board of Cooperative Educational Services, Syracuse, graphic design teacher, 1991-93. *Exhibitions:* Society of Illustrators "Original Art Show" of children's book illustration, 1992. Catalano has also exhibited at the Tyler Gallery of the State University of New York at Oswego, the New York State Fair, the Everson Museum in New York, and the Limestone Gallery in Fayetteville, NY. *Member:* National Wildlife Federation, Nature Conservancy.

■ Awards, Honors

First prize in graphics, New York State Fair; second prize in WCNY art invitational at the Everson Museum.

■ Writings

SELF-ILLUSTRATED

Wolf Plays Alone, Philomel, 1992.

ILLUSTRATOR

Arnold Sungaard, *The Bear Who Loved Puccini,* Philomel, 1992.
Nancy W. Carlstrom, *Rise and Shine,* HarperCollins, 1993.
Eric L. Houck, Jr., *Rabbit Surprise,* Crown, 1993.
Roni Schotter, *Monsieur Cochon,* Philomel, 1993.

■ Work in Progress

Writing and illustrating picture books, including *The Blue's Heron,* about "a sax-playing jazz bird who searches for his fame and fortune"; *Waterbury's Land-*

ing, about "a water buffalo who wants to fly"; and *Coyote Magic.* Retelling and illustrating *Frog Went A-Courting,* and the Breman Town Musicians story, retitled *Breman Town Dixie.* Researching species of flora and fauna native to the Indochina rainforest for *Tiger in the Rain,* a picture book.

■ Sidelights

"As a junior high school student," Dominic Catalano reminisced to *SATA,* "I 'rediscovered' picture books. The class, a creative writing course, was taught by a man who just sparkled when he read to us. *Where the Wild Things Are* by Maurice Sendak was a motivational 'read' and each of us wrote our own stories a la Max's adventure. I illustrated mine as well. Needless to say I was bitten by the bug. Now, some twenty-three years later, my dreams have finally become a reality.

"I feel so lucky to be writing and illustrating children's books now," Catalano added. "This is an exciting time in books, and a very competitive one. I know my most valuable trait will be my persistence. I believe in myself—one has to! I know I have a contribution to make to our children. In some ways I just can't believe it's all happening! If my junior high teacher could see me now."

*   *   *

CAVE, Kathryn 1948-

■ Personal

Born June 22, 1948, in Aldershot, Hampshire, England; daughter of Henry (a research scientist) and Eve (a teacher; maiden name, Wilson) Wilson; married Martin Cave (a professor) July, 1972; children: Eleanor, Joseph, Alice. *Education:* Oxford University, B.A., 1969; graduate studies at Massachusetts Institute of Technology, 1969-70, and Birmingham University, 1972-73. *Hobbies and other interests:* Teaching tennis, coaching athletes, walking, poetry, theater, travel.

■ Addresses

Home—11 West Common Road, Uxbridge, Middlesex UB8 IN2, England. *Office*—Frances Lincoln Ltd., Apollo Works, 5 Charlton King's Road, London N5, England. *Agent*—Gina Pollinger, 222 Old Brompton Road, London SW5 OBZ, England.

■ Career

Penguin Publishing, London, England, editor, 1970-71; Blackwell (publishers), Oxford, England, editor, 1971-72; Metier (publishers), Hayes, England, technical editor, 1987-88; Frances Lincoln Ltd., London, England, editorial director for children's nonfiction, 1990-92.

■ Awards, Honors

Many Happy Returns was named one of the best ten books of the year by the Federation of Children's Book Group, 1986.

■ Writings

Dragonrise, Penguin, 1984.
Many Happy Returns, Transworld, 1986.
Just in Time, illustrated by Terry McKenna, Potter, 1988.
Poor Little Mary, Penguin, 1988.
Henry Hobbs, Alien, illustrated by Chris Riddell, Penguin, 1990.
Jumble, illustrated by Riddell, Blackie, 1990.
William and the Wolves, Penguin, 1991.
Out for the Count, illustrated by Riddell, Simon & Schuster, 1991.
Running Battles, Penguin, 1992.
Something Else, illustrated by Riddell, Viking/Penguin, in press.

■ Sidelights

"Most of my stories are concerned with the gap between our own perceptions of reality and those of other people," Cave told *SATA.* "I like the borderline where logic turns into madness." When Cave's oldest daughter, Eleanor, became involved in sports, the author "had plenty of chances to watch children, parents and coaches cross that borderline, under the influence of sheer obsession—it's always fascinating to see single-minded pursuit of any objective (sometimes it's horrifying too, of course)." Cave explores the humorous side of this theme in her book *Running Battles.* "I hope it is funny, although the issues involved are really no joke," she commented.

Cave's counting book, appropriately named *Out for the Count: A Counting Adventure,* is about Tom, a sleepless young boy who tries counting sheep at bedtime and ends up pursuing one into the woods. Tom and his stuffed bunny then encounter wild animals, pirates, and ghosts, counting the members of various scary groups even as they elude them. A critic in *Publishers Weekly* stated that the author's "bouncy verse carries Tom through his caper at a bracing clip." All of Cave's books are fantasies, she explained, "where a different world (either imaginary or real) obtrudes itself upon ordinary life. That no man's land between the ordinary and the fantastic is an interesting place to be."

■ Works Cited

Review of *Out for the Count: A Counting Adventure, Publishers Weekly,* June 1, 1992, p. 61.

■ For More Information See

PERIODICALS

School Library Journal, May, 1992, p. 86.

VERA CLEAVER

CLEAVER, Vera 1919-1992

■ Personal

Born January 6, 1919, in Virgil, SD; died after a long illness, August 11, 1992, in Winter Haven, FL; daughter of Fortis Alonzo and Beryl Naiome (Reininger) Allen; married William Joseph Cleaver (an author), October 4, 1945 (died, 1981). *Education:* Educated at schools in Kennebeck, SD, and Perry and Tallahassee, FL.

■ Career

Author of books for children with husband, Bill Cleaver. Freelance accountant, 1945-54; United States Air Force, accountant (civilian) in Tachikawa, Japan, 1954-56, and Chaumont, France, 1956-58.

■ Awards, Honors

Horn Book Honor List, 1967, for *Ellen Grae; Horn Book* Honor List, 1969, American Library Association (ALA) notable book, 1970, Newbery Honor Book, and National Book Award nomination, all for *Where the Lilies Bloom;* National Book Award nomination, 1971, for *Grover; New York Times* outstanding book, and ALA notable book, both 1973, for *Me Too;* National Book Award nomination, 1974, for *The Whys and Wherefores of Littabelle Lee;* Golden Spur Award, Western Writers of America, Lewis Carroll Shelf award, and *New York Times* outstanding book citation, all 1975, for *Dust of the Earth;* National Book Award nomination, 1979, for *Queen of Hearts;* Children's Choice Award, 1986, for *Sweetly Sings the Donkey.*

■ Writings

CHILDREN'S FICTION; WITH HUSBAND, BILL CLEAVER

Ellen Grae, illustrated by Ellen Raskin, Lippincott, 1967.
Lady Ellen Grae, illustrated by E. Raskin, Lippincott, 1968.
Where the Lilies Bloom, illustrated by Jim Spanfeller, Lippincott, 1969.
Grover, illustrated by Frederic Marvin, Lippincott, 1970.
The Mimosa Tree, Lippincott, 1970.
I Would Rather Be a Turnip, Lippincott, 1971.
The Mock Revolt, Lippincott, 1971.
Delpha Green and Company, Lippincott, 1972.
The Whys and Wherefores of Littabelle Lee, Atheneum, 1973.
Me Too, Lippincott, 1973.
Ellen Grae [and] *Lady Ellen Grae,* Hamish Hamilton, 1973.
Dust of the Earth, Lippincott, 1975.
Trial Valley, Lippincott, 1977.
Queen of Hearts, Lippincott, 1978.
A Little Destiny, Lothrop, 1979.
The Kissimmee Kid, Lothrop, 1981.
Hazel Rye, Lippincott, 1983.

CHILDREN'S FICTION

Sugar Blue, illustrated by Eric Nones, Lothrop, 1984.
Sweetly Sings the Donkey, Lippincott, 1985.
Moon Lake Angel, Lothrop, 1987.
Belle Pruitt (Junior Library Guild selection), Lippincott, 1988.

OTHER

The Nurse's Dilemma (adult fiction), Avalon Books, 1966.

Contributor of stories to numerous periodicals, including *McCall's* and *Woman's Day.* Collections of Cleaver's manuscripts are at the Kerlan Collection, University of Minnesota, Minneapolis, and at the University of North Carolina, Chapel Hill.

■ Adaptations

Where the Lilies Bloom was filmed by United Artists, 1974.

■ Sidelights

For almost twenty-five years, Vera and Bill Cleaver wrote as a team—one developing and researching the ideas, the other doing the actual writing. After her husband's death in 1981, Vera continued to write the type of novels that she and her husband had jointly produced—novels that depict young people accepting responsibility beyond their years and coming to terms with the harsh circumstances of life. "Despite what for many would be overwhelming circumstances, they preserve and exert their newly found individuality with uncommon, but not unbelievable, resourcefulness and intelligence," wrote Jane Harper Yarbrough in an essay

Together with her husband, Bill, Cleaver produced numerous acclaimed novels in which young people deal with responsibilities and problems beyond their years. (Cover illustration by Daniel Mark Duffy.)

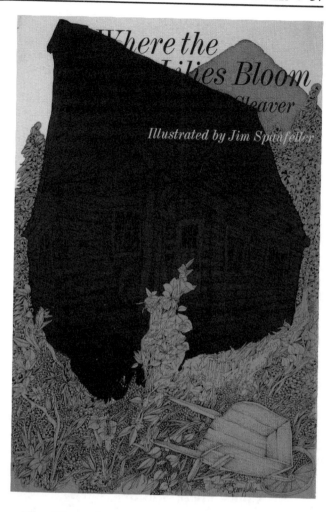

The Cleavers' story of a fourteen-year-old girl's attempts to keep her mountain family together after their father's death earned a Newbery Honor citation. (Cover illustration by Jim Spanfeller.)

in *Dictionary of Literary Biography.* "The Cleavers offer young adult readers sensitive, insightful characters with whom to identify, with whom to join on the turbulent voyage of growing up responsible."

Born in Virgil, South Dakota, Vera began writing at the early age of six under the influence of her maternal grandfather, who published a newspaper at the time; she received her education in schools in South Dakota and Florida and eventually worked as a freelance accountant. She met Bill during World War II. A native of Seattle, Washington, Bill had been educated in private schools in British Columbia before joining the United States Air Force. In 1945 they married, and Vera worked as an accountant for the Air Force in Tachikawa, Japan, and Chaumont, France. Unable to complete their formal education, the Cleavers taught themselves in public libraries and got their literary start by publishing almost three hundred stories about children for adults in various pulp magazines. Later, they wrote for periodicals such as *McCall's* and *Woman's Day,* and in the late 1960s, they turned to writing for young adult readers. Yarborough reported that the Cleavers worked as a team. Bill would usually generate the ideas and

work on developing them with Vera. Later, he would do the research, and Vera would incorporate this in the writing. Their work was popular and well received critically, regularly earning American Library Association notable book citations; four of their novels were finalists in the National Book Award competition: *Where the Lilies Bloom, Grover, The Whys and Wherefores of Littabelle Lee,* and *Queen of Hearts.*

In *Where the Lilies Bloom,* which was also named a Newbery Honor Book, fourteen-year-old Mary Call Luther's father dies, leaving her with the responsibility of holding together her impoverished and parentless family, of guiding and providing for herself and her siblings in the mountains of Appalachia. Yarbrough praised the heroine, "whose inner strength, love of family, irrepressible dignity, pragmatic resourcefulness, indomitable will, and joy for life combine to provide readers with a vividly memorable character whose uplifting story is of one young woman's victories over the oppressive forces of nature and society." Compelled to keep their father's death a secret lest they be dispatched to separate foster homes, the children bury him in a mountainside grave and sustain themselves by "wildcrafting," or collecting medicinal herbs that grow wild. Calling it "a story of good people, with real natures, living under conditions of hardship, in poverty, in the midst of bereavement, maintaining their independence, wit and dignity," William Saroyan, in a *New York Times Book Review* critique of the novel, concluded: "Reading the book has been like eating a good meal of bread, cheese, onion and cold water. I tend to have this feeling of hunger satisfied when I read very good writing."

Grover is the story of Grover Ezell, an eleven-year-old boy who struggles with his mother's suicide and his father's emotional instability. Although he had not been told that his mother was dying, Grover somehow knew. When his mother's surgery was followed by his father's sudden attentive attempts to provide her with the things she had long wanted, Grover suspected that his mother's health would not improve; however, he was unprepared for her death by a self-inflicted gunshot wound. Grover does not believe his father when he tells him that his mother's death was accidental; he struggles to understand the meaning of death, eventually gaining insight into the incident. Calling it "a sad, but not a somber story, in which there is humor to counterbalance sorrow, and action as well as introspection," Diane Farrell remarked in her *Horn Book* review that it was also "a profoundly wise and real tale." Although she deemed it "a raw book," Joan Murphy remarked in *School Librarian* that it "is much nearer to everyman's, or every child's, experience than we care to think."

Critics Praise Sensitive Novels

The Whys and Wherefores of Littabelle Lee tells the story of a sixteen-year-old girl who lives in the Ozark Mountains with her elderly grandparents and her Aunt Sorrow, whose income as a doctor of natural medicine supports them all. When her aunt falls from a horse and injuries prevent her from maintaining her practice, she marries her longtime suitor, and Littabelle Lee is left with the responsibility of caring for herself and her grandparents. "To read this book, full of truth and the natural life of the country, is a rewarding experience," remarked M. H. Miller in the *Children's Book Review*. "It contains much eventful incident, and much simple, wise reflection." Although Ruth Pegau, in a *Library Journal* review, found the story "predictable, talky, and dull," Jonathan Yardley believed that the Cleavers offered "morals without belaboring them," and he suggested in the *New York Times Book Review* that the book was more "about the dignity of poor people who struggle to live on a demanding mountain land that they love.... It is about children who are faithful to family, and children who are not. It is about a law in which there is mercy and true justice. Most of all, it is about growing up, about meeting the responsibilities that are one's 'whys and wherefores.'"

In *Queen of Hearts,* twelve-year-old Wilma Lincoln agrees to stay with her seventy-nine-year-old grandmother who is recovering from a mild stroke. Granny Lincoln, who has gone through three hired women

The love of an enthusiastic four-year-old draws a reclusive girl out of her private world in this novel by Cleaver. (Cover illustration by Eric Jon Nones.)

before Wilma arrives and resents depending upon others, tries to humiliate Wilma, who responds in anger; however, wrote Jean Fritz in the *New York Times Book Review,* "Wilma learns to stand up to the cantankerous old soul, to follow her into her past, and she even finds a way to make her grandmother feel useful." Referring to it as "a devastatingly honest tragicomedy," Ethel Heins, in a *Horn Book* review, praised the novel as "a brave, humane book, wholly individual in conception and style."

"The Cleavers know human nature and they portray many facets of it in a truly believable and arousing manner," wrote Patricia J. Cianciolo in *Top of the News.* "Their stories highlight the humor as well as the pathos characteristic of the human experience.... The human experiences they portray are done with an honesty, a sensitivity, and a realism that are unique in children's literature today." Critics agreed that although the Cleaver novels were relentlessly realistic, they were not depressing. "The fight must be fought, but if the end is defeat, very well then, the end is defeat and there is no disgrace in it," observed John Rowe Townsend in his *A Sounding of Storytellers.* "It is better to have fought and lost than not to have fought.... This sense of the indomitability of the human spirit is undoubtedly the major reason why in the end the Cleaver books are more likely to lift up than cast down the reader, to offer an astringent yet stimulating experience."

■ Works Cited

Cianciolo, Patricia J., "Vera and Bill Cleaver Know Their Whys and Wherefores," *Top of the News,* June, 1976, pp. 338-50.

Farrell, Diane, review of *Grover, Horn Book,* April, 1970, pp. 158-59.

Fritz, Jean, review of *Queen of Hearts, New York Times Book Review,* April 30, 1978, p. 51.

Heins, Ethel, review of *Queen of Hearts, Horn Book,* June, 1978, p. 275.

Miller, M. H., review of *The Whys and Wherefores of Littabelle Lee, Children's Book Review,* summer, 1974, p. 64.

Murphy, Joan, review of *Grover, School Librarian,* December, 1971, p. 370.

Pegau, Ruth, review of *The Whys and Wherefores of Littabelle Lee, Library Journal,* June 15, 1973, p. 2000.

Saroyan, William, review of *Where the Lilies Bloom, New York Times Book Review,* September 28, 1969, p. 34.

Townsend, John Rowe, *A Sounding of Storytellers: New and Revised Essays on Contemporary Writers for Children,* Harper, 1979, pp. 30-40.

Yarbrough, Jane Harper, essay in *Dictionary of Literary Biography,* Gale, Volume 52: *American Writers for Children since 1960: Fiction,* Gale, 1986, pp. 91-97.

Yardley, Jonathan, review of *The Whys and Wherefores of Littabelle Lee, New York Times Book Review,* March 4, 1973, pp. 6-7.

■ For More Information See

BOOKS

Children's Literature Review, Volume 6, Gale, 1984.
Twentieth-Century Children's Writers, 3rd edition, St. James Press, 1989.

PERIODICALS

Horn Book, October, 1979.

OBITUARIES:

Death information provided by sister, Kathryn Malone.

*　　*　　*

COOPER, Melrose
See KROLL, Virginia L(ouise)

*　　*　　*

CORRICK, James A. 1945-

■ Personal

Born September 12, 1945, in Astoria, OR; son of James (a captain in the United States Navy and a college professor) and Harriet (a food technologist; maiden name, Perry) Corrick; married Gay Miller (a naturalist and sculptor), November 26, 1982. *Education:* University of Tennessee, B.S., 1967, M.S., 1969, M.A., 1971; University of Arizona, Ph.D., 1981. *Politics:* Independent. *Religion:* "None."

■ Addresses

Home and office—4402 East Cooper Circle, Tucson, AZ 85711-4260. *Agent*—Henry Rasof, 4800 Osage Dr., No. 24, Boulder, CO 80303.

■ Career

Writer and editor, Tucson, AZ, 1979—; University of Arizona, Tucson, tutor, 1981-82; L5 Society, Tucson, editor, 1985-87; National Space Society, Washington, DC, editor, 1987; Muscular Dystrophy Association, Tucson, science writer, 1991-92. *Member:* Tucson Book Publishers Association, Arizona Sonora Desert Museum, Southern Arizona Arthropod Association, Tucson Zoological Society, Arizona Historical Society.

■ Awards, Honors

National Defense Education Act fellow, 1967 and 1968.

■ Writings

The Human Brain: Mind and Matter, Arco, 1983.
Recent Revolutions in Chemistry, Franklin Watts, 1986.
Recent Revolutions in Biology, Franklin Watts, 1987.
Career Preparation, Chaparral, 1988.
Double Your Pleasure: The Ace SF Double, Gryphon, 1989.
The World of Nature: Farm Animals, W. H. Smith, 1991.
Mars, Franklin Watts, 1991.

JAMES A. CORRICK

Muscular Dystrophy, Franklin Watts, 1992.
Science People, Profiling the Men and Women of Science, Vol. 1, WP Press, 1993.

Contributor to books, including *Earthwise: Energy,* WP Press, 1993. Has also published over 175 articles and short stories. Editor of journals, including *L5 News,* 1985-87; *Space Frontier,* 1986-87; and *Space Advocate,* 1987.

■ Work in Progress

The Low Middle Ages and *The High Middle Ages,* for Lucent Books, publication expected 1994; *The DNA Scalpel: Human Genetic Engineering,* for Enslow, publication expected 1995; *The Planet Seekers; Creation Station,* a novel; and research for *The Bone Warriors.*

■ Sidelights

James A. Corrick told *SATA:* "My father's reading of the *Oz* books to my sister and me certainly put me on the road to becoming a writer. First, I became an omnivorous reader and avid book collector (I bought my first book, which I still have, when I was eleven). Because my father and mother had technical backgrounds, I also became interested in science, and for a time, I seriously thought I would be a scientist who wrote. However, two years of graduate studies in biochemistry made me realize that writing was much more important. The science, of course, would eventually come back into my life when I became the author of several popular science books.

"I spent a decade as a graduate student in English, reading and studying as wide a variety as I could: nothing from classical poetry to modern journalism escaped me. In the end, I found that education useful, even though the practical craft of being a writer forced me to set aside most of the more esoteric lore I had picked up.

"I believe that all good nonfiction rests squarely on good, thorough research. The writer's job then is to take that research and present it in a clear, concise, organized manner. Personally, I like facts, and so tend to pack my books with as many facts as they can comfortably hold, but never so many that they get in the reader's way."

Corrick's first book, *The Human Brain: Mind and Matter,* is a basic text covering the brain and its functions. Topics discussed include parts of the brain, chemical and electrical reactions, memory, and sleep. Illustrations and pictures complement the text. A reviewer in *Choice* noted that the book is written "in a very simple, easy-to-follow format and style," although "rather limited" in content and depth. *School Library Journal* contributor Kathryn Weisman judged *The Human Brain* to be a "succinct yet broad overview of the human brain." And Stephen Cox, writing in *Book Report,* commented in his conclusion that "Corrick's book is an excellent, concise work. The material is current, thought-provoking and readable."

■ Works Cited

Cox, Stephen, review of *The Human Brain: Mind and Matter, Book Report,* May/June, 1984.
Review of *The Human Brain: Mind and Matter, Choice,* January, 1984.
Weisman, Kathryn, review of *The Human Brain: Mind and Matter, School Library Journal,* January, 1984.

■ For More Information See

PERIODICALS

Analog, December, 1989, p. 185.
School Library Journal, December, 1986, p. 114; August, 1987, p. 91; September, 1991, p. 263.
Voice of Youth Advocates, April, 1987, p. 43; August, 1987, p. 135; December, 1991, p. 333.

*　　*　　*

COXON, Michele 1950-

■ Personal

Born July 20, 1950, in Kent, England; daughter of Stan Kelly Bootle (a mathematician and writer) and Margaret (Jones) Bootle (a homemaker); married Philip Stanley Coxon (a poet, writer, and wildlife warden), April 27, 1976 (died May 25, 1987); children: Crispin, Sam. *Education:* Royal Leamington Art School. *Hobbies and other interests:* Completing triathalons (swimming, biking, and running).

MICHELE COXON

■ Addresses

Home—Sunny Lea, Meifod, Powys, Wales, United Kingdom.

■ Career

Children's book illustrator. Coxon has worked for the Royal Society for the Protection of Birds and the Seal Research Unit as a muralist and cartoonist. She is also a homemaker and mother.

■ Writings

SELF-ILLUSTRATED

The Cat Who Lost His Purr, Blackie and Son, 1991.
Who Will Play with Me?, Blackie and Son, 1992.

ILLUSTRATOR

Philip Coxon, *The World of an Island,* Faber, 1977.

■ Work in Progress

The Tale of the Tatty Cat.

■ Sidelights

"I started writing children's stories after I picked up my cat and there was silence!" Michele Coxon told *SATA.* "My cat normally purrs like a pneumatic drill and that day there was nothing. My children were there and I asked them if they had seen the cat's purr. So *The Cat Who Lost His Purr* was born. That was three years ago and I am on my third book. All the stories so far are developed from ideas that my cats give me. I have six cats, one rat, and recently a stray dog walked into my life and took over my sofa.

"I have always painted and I have had several wildlife exhibitions. I love the countryside and animals and hope to give more of my time to conservation. I enjoy traveling and going to schools. I talk to the children about books and stories and encourage them to illustrate their own stories."

*　　*　　*

CREWS, Donald 1938-

■ Personal

Born August 30, 1938, in Newark, NJ; son of Asa (a railroad trackman) and Marshanna (a dressmaker; maiden name, White) Crews; married Ann Jonas (an author, artist, and designer), January 28, 1964; children: Nina Melissa, Amy Marshanna. *Education:* Graduated from Cooper Union for the Advancement of Science and Art, 1959.

DONALD CREWS

■ Addresses

Home—New York, NY. *Office*—c/o Greenwillow Books, 1350 Avenue of the Americas, New York, NY 10019.

■ Career

Illustrator and author; freelance artist, photographer, and designer. *Dance* (magazine), New York City, assistant art director, 1959-60; Will Burton Studios, New York City, staff designer, 1961-62. *Military service:* U.S. Army, 1962-64.

■ Awards, Honors

One of Fifty Books of the Year, American Institute of Graphic Arts, 1968, for *We Read: A to Z;* Children's Book Showcase selection, Children's Book Council, 1974, for *Eclipse: Darkness in Daytime;* Notable Book citation, American Library Association (ALA), 1978, and Caldecott Honor Book, 1979, both for *Freight Train;* American Institute of Graphic Arts Book Show selection, 1979, for *Rain;* Notable Book citation, ALA, 1980, and Caldecott Honor Book, 1981, both for *Truck;* one of the ten best illustrated books, *New York Times,* 1986, for *Flying.*

■ Writings

CHILDREN'S PICTURE BOOKS; SELF-ILLUSTRATED

We Read: A to Z, Harper, 1967.
Ten Black Dots, Scribner, 1968, revised edition, Greenwillow, 1986.

Crews's childhood fascination with trains is apparent in this Caldecott Honor book.

Freight Train, Greenwillow, 1978, big book edition, Morrow, 1993.

Truck, Greenwillow, 1980, big book edition, Morrow, 1993.

Light, Greenwillow, 1981.

Harbor, Greenwillow, 1982.

Carousel, Greenwillow, 1982.

Parade, Greenwillow, 1982.

School Bus, Greenwillow, 1984.

Bicycle Race, Greenwillow, 1985.

Flying, Greenwillow, 1986.

Bigmama's, Greenwillow, 1991.

Shortcut, Greenwillow, 1992.

ILLUSTRATOR

Harry Milgrom, *ABC Science Experiments,* Crowell, 1970.

J. Richard Dennis, *Fractions Are Parts of Things,* Crowell, 1971.

Milgrom, *ABC of Ecology,* Macmillan, 1972.

Franklyn M. Branley, *Eclipse: Darkness in Daytime,* Crowell, 1973, revised edition, HarperCollins, 1988.

Robert Kalan, *Rain,* Greenwillow, 1978.

Kalan, *Blue Sea,* Greenwillow, 1979.

Dorothy de Wit, editor, *The Talking Stone: An Anthology of Native American Tales and Legends,* Greenwillow, 1979.

Paul Giganti, Jr., *How Many Snails?: A Counting Book,* Greenwillow, 1988.

Giganti, *Each Orange Had Eight Slices,* Greenwillow, 1991.

Patricia Lillie, *When This Box Is Full,* Greenwillow, 1993.

OTHER

Works included in the Kerlan Collection, University of Minnesota.

■ Adaptations

Freight Train (sound filmscript), Educational Enrichment Material, 1980; *Truck* (sound filmscript), Live Oak Media, 1981.

■ Sidelights

Donald Crews is a respected and award-winning author-illustrator of children's picture books. Blending sparse text with innovative uses of color, space, and perspective, Crews's picture books depict such diverse subjects as language arts, counting, and various modes of modern transportation. His first book, *We Read: A to Z,* was noted as a sophisticated and fresh approach to illuminating language arts for children, while his Caldecott Honor Book-designated *Freight Train* and *Truck* showed his ability to both inform readers and tell powerful stories through images of everyday objects and activities. Featuring poster-style illustrations which connect from page to page, *Freight Train* and *Truck* are noteworthy in that they "allow the child [reader] to conjure up visual images, thereby offering him/her an enjoyable tumble into the abyss of literary imagination," writes Marjorie Reinwald Romanoff in *Children's Literature Association Quarterly.* Since *Freight Train* and *Truck,* Crews has established himself as a distinctive picture book artist—popular among both readers and critics—and has expanded into a whole series of books which imaginatively depict transportation, motion, and energy in everyday life.

Crews was born in 1938 in Newark, New Jersey, the third of four children of Asa and Marshanna Crews. "I've drawn and sketched for as long as I can remember," he once told *SATA.* Particularly influenced by Marshanna Crews, an accomplished craftswoman and dressmaker, Crews and his siblings "were all involved in art-related projects," he stated in *Fifth Book of Junior Authors and Illustrators.* Also important during his childhood were annual summer trips to his mother's hometown of Cottondale, Florida, where his grandparents owned and operated a small farm. Working on the farm was exciting for Crews, yet he especially enjoyed the steam engine trains that passed nearby. "My grandparents' porch is about 150 yards from the rail line," he continued. "It was from there that for the next three months we watched trains pass. Freights were frequent and long, counting them a favorite activity. It is from this memory of the summers in Cottondale that *Freight Train* comes."

Crews studied art at Arts High School in Newark, and later at New York City's Cooper Union for the Advancement of Science and Art. Trained as a designer in college, he found work on the staff of *Dance* magazine, and later at Will Burton Studios in New York City. In 1962, he was drafted into the U.S. Army and was stationed in Germany for eighteen months. There, he was joined by his wife, Ann, who had been a fellow student at Cooper Union. While in Germany, Crews produced his first book, *We Read: A to Z*—not for publication, but as an addition to his work portfolio.

"Portfolios are such a brief experience for art directors," he told Jim Roginski in *Behind the Covers.* " . . . . So I designed a children's book as a 'freshener' and a 'pacer.'" When he returned to the United States in 1964, Crews was employed as a freelance artist and designer, working on book jackets, book illustrations, and as a technical illustrator.

In 1967, Harper and Row published *We Read,* which earned praise for its innovative approach to the standard children's "ABC" book, and for its high artistic quality. Crews's book matched concept words to the letters of the alphabet, such as "middle" for "m," which were then depicted through abstract illustrations. The drawing for "middle," for example, which Crews states as meaning "the center from any direction," features a square (in the middle of a larger square) whose four sides are bisected by the tips of four different arrows. Another example, "e" meaning "equal," is represented by a checkerboard design in equal numbers of black and yellow squares. *We Read* "is primary communication stunningly presented," writes a contributor to *Kirkus Reviews,* "with ... a bright future in introducing children to abstract concepts and aesthetic quality, in addition to letters and words." Crews followed with a book that similarly depicted numbers and counting through abstract illustrations, *Ten Black Dots,* published in 1968.

Turns to Career in Children's Books

Although Crews's first two solo efforts received critical praise, "many years passed," he stated in *Fifth Book of Junior Authors and Illustrators,* "before I once again tested my abilities with a complete project." During the first half of the 1970s, Crews concentrated on illustrating books by other authors, and his output included two

Taking a shortcut down the railroad tracks leads to a close call for the children in Crews's self-illustrated *Shortcut*.

In this autobiographical picture book, Crews captures the joy of spending the summer on his grandparents' farm. (Illustration from *Bigmama's.*)

other "ABC" books, as well as a book describing mathematical fractions. Then, in 1978, he achieved national recognition for his picture book *Freight Train,* which successfully combined Crews's illustrative talents with a subject that he was particularly close to: the old-fashioned steam locomotives which passed by his grandparents' farm in Florida. The book also marked a new realization by Crews of being a picture book "artist." Commenting to Roginski on the roots of his artistic impetus, he stated that "you have to find something that interests you, and create a visual interpretation that will excite people. . . . [Books] should each be something different and filled with your full creative range."

Freight Train follows the progress of a locomotive as it travels, from page to page, through day and night, on a journey across city and country landscapes. *Freight Train,* according to Romanoff, provides the reader "with a visual experience in the illustrations that both inform and move vibrantly across the page. . . . In the beginning of this very attractive book, the reader views

five white background pages of track as he/she waits for the train to pass. . . . The author/illustrator continues to propel the reader along through the adventure of the train." Crews was widely praised for the high quality of his illustrations, which feature bold, solid colors (as in the individual train cars), and strong, definite shapes and forms. He supplemented his illustrations with brief, descriptive phrases, creating a poster-like quality to each of the pictures.

Freight Train, which earned Crews a Caldecott Honor Book Award, introduces "a superb, beautifully designed book by a new talent to the children's book scene," writes a *Books for Your Children* reviewer. "Everything," the reviewer adds, " . . . is integrated for a child to discover the feel of a good book as the train moves through the pages in light and darkness in perfect rhythm." Crews's next book, *Truck*—which depicts the journey of a truck as it travels across the country—offers similar enchantments. "Readers will feel they are traveling the superhighways, fighting the traffic, handling the monster vehicle as their pulses leap with the excitement of the trip," writes a reviewer in *Publishers Weekly. Truck* earned Crews his second Caldecott Honor Book citation.

Following the success of *Freight Train* and *Truck,* Crews produced a whole series of picture books depicting various subjects of motion, energy, and transportation. Throughout he confirms his stature as a picture book artist of distinctive gifts. *Light* (1981) shows different representations of light in both the city and country and, according to Denise M. Wilms in *Booklist,* is "a kind of visual poem that translates an everyday phenomenon into something to be especially appreciated." *Harbor* (1982) illustrates the activities of a busy harbor, tracing the movement of ships of different shapes and sizes as they travel to a big city port. In *Carousel* (1982), according to Amy L. Cohn in *Horn Book,* Crews "celebrates the up-and-down, 'round-and-'round exhilaration of a merry-go-round ride in a narrative study of light, shape, and movement combining collage, graphics, and photography to reveal the inherent drama contained within the captive energy of the carousel itself." And *Parade* (1982) traces the movement of a parade—marching bands, floats, fire engines, confetti, excited bystanders—from start to finish, while *Flying* (1986), a *New York Times* Best Illustrated Book, presents images that one experiences when flying in an airplane.

Each of Crews's picture books, although often using similar illustrative techniques, comes from his own unique feelings about a particular subject. "My training and the process of development is from a designer's point of view," he told *SATA.* "I attempt to isolate an area of interest and to involve my readers in my excitement about that area. Style is less important than effect." For each book, Crews explores a distinct perspective. "Both *Freight Train* and *Truck* for instance are involved primarily with movement. The visualization of that idea is quite different in each. I've even utilized photography in one picture book. The photographs are taken from the same simple, stylized point of view as my graphic images." He elaborated to Roginski that he is interested in only exploring ideas that are "serious" to him, meaning: "Something that means something. Some real thing: some tangible thing. When you walk down the street and see a truck or fire engine, what's the importance of that natural event? Can you make a statement about that experience? What's special about it? It's taking a piece of something and seeing if it's special and making it important through a visual medium that can excite you and the children you're working for."

■ Works Cited

Cohn, Amy L., review of *Carousel, Horn Book,* December, 1982, pp. 639-40.

Crews, Donald, *We Read: From A to Z,* Harper, 1967.

Crews, Donald, comments in *Fifth Book of Junior Authors and Illustrators,* edited by Sally Holmes Holtze, H. W. Wilson, 1983, pp. 88-90.

Review of *Freight Train, Books for Your Children,* summer, 1979, p. 3.

Roginski, Jim, interview with Donald Crews, *Behind the Covers: Interviews with Authors and Illustrators of Books for Children and Young Adults,* Libraries Unlimited, 1985, pp. 42-50.

Romanoff, Marjorie Reinwald, "'Freight Train' and 'Truck': A New Trend in Children's Literature?," *Children's Literature Association Quarterly,* fall, 1981, pp. 19-21.

Something about the Author, Volume 32, Gale, 1983, pp. 59-60.

Review of *Truck, Publishers Weekly,* February 15, 1980, p. 110.

Review of *We Read: From A to Z, Kirkus Reviews,* February 1, 1967, p. 125.

Wilms, Denise M., review of *Light, Booklist,* April 1, 1981, p. 1097.

■ For More Information See

BOOKS

Children's Literature Review, Volume 7, Gale, 1984.

PERIODICALS

Bulletin of the Center for Children's Books, October, 1982; March, 1983; October, 1984.

New York Times Book Review, January 29, 1989.

Publishers Weekly, July 22, 1983.

Yellow Brick Road, January/February, 1987.*

* * *

CRUMP, Fred H., Jr. 1931-

■ Personal

Born June 7, 1931, in Houston, TX; son of Fred H. and Carol Crump. *Education:* Sam Houston State Teachers College (now Sam Houston State University), B.S., 1953, M.S., 1961.

■ Addresses

Home—94 Santa Anita, Rancho Mirage, CA 92270.

■ Career

Junior high school art teacher, Orange, TX, and Palm Springs, CA, 1960-90; author and illustrator of children's books.

■ Writings

SELF-ILLUSTRATED JUVENILES

Marigold and the Dragon, Steck, 1964.

The Teeny Weeny Genie, Steck, 1966.

Missy and the Duke/Missy y el duque (in English and Spanish), translation by Horst Woyde, Blaine Ethridge, 1977.

Ringo the Raccoon, Children's Press, 1982.

Petipois le panda, Harlequin Publishers (Paris), 1982.

Doc le coq, Harlequin Publishers, 1982.

FRED H. CRUMP, JR.

Tetenlair le ver, Harlequin Publishers, 1982.
Pluche LaTruche, Harlequin Publishers, 1982.
Fripon le raton-laveur, Harlequin Publishers, 1982.
Floc le phoque, Harlequin Publishers, 1982.
Sacha le petit rat, Harlequin Publishers, 1982.
Trigger the Trucker Mouse, Curtis, 1982.
A Rose for Zemira, Winston-Derek, 1987.
Thumbelina: A Retold Story, Winston-Derek, 1988.
Little Red Riding Hood, Winston-Derek, 1989.
Mother Goose: A Retold Story, Winston-Derek, 1989,
     published as *Mother Goose Nursery Rhymes,* 1990.

Cinderella, Winston-Derek, 1990.
Jamako and the Beanstalk, Winston-Derek, 1990.
Afrotina and the Three Bears, Winston-Derek, 1991.
Hakim and Grenita, Winston-Derek, 1991.
Rapunzel, Winston-Derek, 1991.
Beauty and the Beast, Winston-Derek, 1991.
The Ebony Duckling, Winston-Derek, 1991.
Mgambo and the Tigers, Winston-Derek, 1991.
Sleeping Beauty: A Retold Story, Winston-Derek, 1991.
Rumpelstiltskin, Winston-Derek, 1991.
The Mouse Opera House, Winston-Derek, 1992.
The Mouse Ballet, Winston-Derek, 1993.

*ILLUSTRATOR OF JUVENILES BY GARRY SMITH AND
     VESTA SMITH*

Creepy Caterpillar, Steck, 1961.
Flagon the Dragon, Steck, 1962.
Mitzi, Steck, 1963.
Jumping Julius, Steck, 1964.
Leander Lion, Steck, 1966.
Florabelle, Steck, 1968.
Clickety Cricket, Steck, 1969.
Poco (in English and Spanish), translation by Leticia
     Guerrero, Blaine Ethridge, 1975.

OTHER

Contributor to periodicals, including *Humpty-Dumpty,
Playmate,* and *Turtle.*

■ Work in Progress

A Reluctant Black Angel; A Stubborn Hippo; cartoon
"mouse musicals."

■ Sidelights

Fred H. Crump, Jr., told *SATA:* "I'm retired from
teaching art but still writing and drawing for children's
books. I visit a dog named Blue, go to lots of movies,
take naps, eat pizza, and, so far, am living 'happily ever
after.'"

D

DALMAS, John
    See JONES, John R(obert)

*   *   *

DALY, Nicholas 1946-
    (Niki Daly)

■ Personal

Born June 13, 1946, in Cape Town, South Africa; son of George (a carpenter) and Sarah (Mathusen) Daly; married Judith Mary Kenny (an artist), July 7, 1973; children: Joseph, Leo. *Education:* Cape Town Technikon, diploma, 1970.

■ Addresses

Home and office—36 Strubens Rd., Cape Town, South Africa. *Agent*—Laura Cecil, 17 Alwyne Villas, London N1 2HG, England.

■ Career

C.B.S. Record Company, London, England, singer and songwriter, 1971-73; Advertising Agency, Cape Town, South Africa, and London, junior art director, 1973-75; freelance illustrator, London, 1975-79; East Ham Technical College, London, graphics teacher, 1976-79; Stellenbosch University, head of graphic design, 1983-89; David Philip Publishers, head of Songololo Books, 1989—; The Inkman Company, facilitator of children's picture books, 1993—; author and illustrator.

■ Awards, Honors

Award for Illustration from the British Arts Council and Provincial Booksellers, 1978; Parents' Choice Book Award for Literature, Parents' Choice Foundation, 1986, *Horn Book* Honor List, 1987, and Katrien Harries Award (South Africa) for illustration, all for *Not So Fast, Songololo.*

■ Writings

FICTION FOR CHILDREN; SELF-ILLUSTRATED UNDER NAME NIKI DALY

The Little Girl Who Lived down the Road, Collins, 1978.
Vim the Rag Mouse, McElderry, 1979.
Joseph's Other Red Sock, McElderry, 1982.
Leo's Christmas Surprise, Gollancz, 1983.
Ben's Gingerbread Man, Walker Books, 1985.
Teddy's Ear, Viking, 1985.
Monsters Are Like That, Viking Kestrel, 1985.
Not So Fast, Songololo, Gollancz, 1985, Atheneum, 1986.
Just Like Archie, Viking Kestrel, 1986.

NIKI DALY

Look at Me!, Viking Kestrel, 1986.

Thank You Henrietta, Viking Kestrel, 1986.

Mama, Papa and Baby Joe, Viking Kestrel, 1991.

Papa Lucky's Shadow, McElderry, 1991.

(With Ingrid Mennen), *Somewhere in Africa,* illustrated by Nicolaas Maritz), Dutton Children's Books, 1992.

Mary Malloy and the Baby Who Wouldn't Sleep, Golden Books, 1993.

Why the Sun and Moon Live in the Sky, Lothrop, Shepherd & Lee, 1994.

ILLUSTRATOR; UNDER NAME NIKI DALY

Kathleen Hersom, *Maybe It's a Tiger,* Macmillan (London), 1981.

Louis Baum, *I Want to See the Moon,* Bodley Head, 1984, Overlook Press, 1989.

Ruth Craft, *The Day of the Rainbow,* Viking Kestrel, 1989.

Reviva Schembrucker, *Charlie's House,* Viking Kestrel, 1991.

Wendy Hartmann, *All the Magic in the World,* Dutton Children's Books, 1993.

Ingrid Mennen, *One Round Moon and a Star for Me,* Orchard Books, 1994.

■ Adaptations

With Weston Woods, produced a video presentation of *Not So Fast, Songololo,* 1990.

Malusi enjoys a day shopping in the city with his grandmother in Daly's self-illustrated *Not So Fast, Songololo.*

■ Sidelights

Nicholas Daly first became involved in drawing by using pencil stubs handed down from an uncle who painted watercolor pictures. Born in South Africa, Daly travelled to London at the age of twenty-four in order to pursue a career in singing and songwriting. However, economic difficulties ended his music career after two years, and Daly found work as a commercial artist. Daly is known for illustrations of children's books that depict incidents—sometimes realistically, and at other times fantastically—from everyday life.

Daly once commented: "My interest in illustrating for children started after I settled in London. My first book, *The Little Girl Who Lived down the Road,* was written by myself simply as an excuse to draw the pictures, after realizing that a completed product was more useful to a publisher than trying an unknown illustrator on the work of an established writer. I was very encouraged by the favorable reviews I received concerning the writing of *The Little Girl Who Lived down the Road*—which spurred me on to further books.

"This first book was influenced by the technique and certain simplifying of form in the work of Maurice Sendak. I was also drawn to his work because of its emotional content. Nevertheless, I enjoyed working on my first book, very aware that I was using it to cut my teeth on. I do not think it at all a bad thing to allow influences to help you find your way—some illustrators don't need it, perhaps they have a clearer view to start off with. My drawings (that is, my natural drawing) had been interfered with by the training I had as a graphic designer, where effects become paramount. Truth and emotion are of no consequence when drawing for advertising. The work I admire most is the work of illustrators who have these qualities—[Edward] Ardizonne and Harold Jones, and also the artists who left such a rich heritage to British illustration, for example, Tenniel, the various *Punch* artists, and Ernest Shepard.

Unique Illustration Style Develops

"It took about four years for me to pull out of the shadow of people like Edward Ardizonne and Harold Jones. Sendak's [influence] was much shorter-lived. The very mechanical look of cross-hatched drawing seemed to be less appealing or suitable to my temperament, which is more at home with a sketchy style—started in *Joseph's Other Red Sock* and further resolved in *Leo's Christmas Surprise.* I now feel that I'm working from my own source rather than other artists. I'm growing up as an illustrator."

Joseph's Other Red Sock, one of Daly's early works, is a read-aloud story for young children where the hunt for a missing sock, from one room to another, turns into imaginative play. The clutter in Joseph's closet becomes a monster who has the sock perched on his ear. In *Leo's Christmas Surprise* Daly explores the relationship between a young boy and a grandparent, a theme he used later in *Papa Lucky's Shadow* and *Not So Fast, Songololo.* Here Daly relates the Christmas activities of Leo and

Papa Lucky and his granddaughter, Sugar, share a love of dancing in Daly's *Papa Lucky's Shadow.*

his family as they blow up balloons, decorate the tree, and ice the cake while Grandpa Bob is making Leo a surprise gift in the shed.

Daly said: "My work is based on drawing rather than painting. Because I love change I might like to discover a way in which I could illustrate work in a more painterly way. I find that there are two needs to fulfill as an illustrator: one is to develop as an artist and one is to always serve the needs of the text you're illustrating."

"As a writer/illustrator, I'm interested in themes that evolve around young children (one to six years) as they play around the home and on little excursions outside their home, the usual way children observe and interpret things which hold no charm to the adult eye—bath plugs which become telephones when held to the ear, or steering wheels when held firmly between fingers. I'm fascinated by the dual reality children have when playing games. On one level they know the bath plug is 'just a plug,' but on another they can transform it into other things by their belief. As my children grow up, I return to my own childhood and discover a pool of fantasy waiting to be resurrected.

South African Themes Appear in Books

In 1980, shortly after Daly's first son, Joseph, was born, the family returned to South Africa. "We returned home at a time of great unrest and growing change," Daly told *SATA*. "During the years that followed, I wrote and illustrated a number of books which reflected the lives of the children on the other side of the racial divide. In retrospect, I see these books (*Not so Fast Songololo, Charlie's House, Papa Lucky's Shadow,* and *All the Magic in the World*) as half-way bridges between white and black children who live separate and unequal lives determined by the appaling apartheid system. In order to do these books I ignored the myth propogated through apartheid and some political activists who said that there are differences between people.

"Despite exposure to crude racist and sexist propaganda during my 'white working-class' South African child-hood, I have remained unconvinced by any belief or fear that sets people apart. Indeed, I suspect that many of my books have been prompted by a delayed reaction to the 'whites vs. black' and 'boys vs. girls' propaganda which at times seemed to threaten my spirit in the most vicious way.

"'Hope' is the word that all peace-loving South Africans carry in their hearts. I hope the issues of race and gender will soon become ghosts of our past. I hope that my books, which I have done with joy and love, will have helped to support human kindness, individual rights, and a sense of infinite possibilities in this extraordinary world."

■ For More Information See

PERIODICALS

New York Times Book Review, June 1, 1986, p. 48.

Times Literary Supplement, October 25, 1985, p. 1218.

* * *

DALY, Niki
See DALY, Nicholas

* * *

DANIEL, Alan 1939-

■ Personal

Born June 12, 1939, in Ottawa, Canada; son of Lyman Keith (a Baptist minister) and Grace Edna Daniel; married Donna Lea Smith (an illustrator), February 2, 1963; children: Timolin Lea (Daniel) Way, Melissa Lea, Jeffrey Alan. *Education:* Attended Belleville Collegiate Institute, University of Toronto, and McMaster University. *Hobbies and other interests:* Canoeing in Northern Ontario, long-distance walking.

■ Career

Freelance illustrator. Has illustrated book jackets for American and Canadian publishers, annual report covers and videos for businesses, including Imperial Oil and Mutual Life, and poster art for the Canadian government, Canadian sports organizations, and The Children's Book Centre. Created official promotional posters for the 1984 Olympics, the 1984 and 1985 Canada Day celebrations, and the National Ski Council,

Alan Daniel illustrates the lyrics of a popular song with colorful collages in *Down by the Bay*.

1984-87. Commissioned to paint a series of maritime paintings for the movie *The Sea Is at Our Gates*. Work has been exhibited in galleries.

■ Awards, Honors

The Orchestra Book was named an Our Choice/Your Choice book by The Children's Book Centre in Toronto, 1985-86; selected work has been included in *Treasures*, 1986, and Canada at Bologna show of children's illustration, 1990; Directors' Choice Award (co-winner with wife Lea Daniel), Early Childhood News, 1992, for "Song Box" series; IODE Book Award, 1993, for *The Story of Canada*.

■ Illustrator

Eileen Piper, *The Magician's Trap*, Scholastic Book Services, 1976.
James Howe, *Bunnicula: A Rabbit Tale of Mystery*, Atheneum, 1979.
Phyllis Reynolds Naylor, *How Lazy Can You Get?*, Atheneum, 1979.
Erna Dirks Rowe, *Flying and Swimming Creatures from the Time of the Dinosaurs*, North Winds Press, 1980.
Rowe, *Strange Creatures from the Time of the Dinosaurs*, Scholastic Book Services, 1981.
Silver Donald Cameron, *The Baitchopper*, Lorimer, 1982.
Beatrice Schenk de Regniers, *This Big Cat and Other Cats I've Known*, Crown, 1985.
Mark Rubin, *The Orchestra*, Groundwood Books, 1984.
Dennis Lee, *The Difficulty of Living on Other Planets*, Macmillan (Toronto), 1987.
Robert Munsch, *Good Families Don't*, Dell Publishing, 1990.
Howe, *Return to Howliday Inn*, Atheneum, 1992.
(With wife, Lea Daniel) Janet Lunn and Christopher Moore, *The Story of Canada*, Key Porter Books, 1992.
Phyllis Reynolds Naylor, *The Grand Escape*, Atheneum, 1993.
Howe, *Rabbit-Cadabra*, Morrow, 1993.
Howe, *The Bunnicula Fun Book*, Morrow, 1993.
(With L. Daniel) *Bunnicula Escapes! A Pop-Up Adventure*, Morrow, in press.

Also illustrator of numerous other trade and educational books. Contributor of illustrations to *Chickadee* and *Owl* magazines.

"SONG BOX" SERIES

Down by the Bay, Wright Group, 1990.
The Eensy Weensy Spider, Wright Group, 1990.
Yankee Doodle, Wright Group, 1991.
I've Been Working on the Railroad, Wright Group, 1992.

"SONG BOX" SERIES; WITH WIFE, LEA DANIEL

She'll Be Comin' 'Round the Mountain, Wright Group, 1990.
The More We Get Together, Wright Group, 1990.

Cricket Rohman, *The Monster Party*, Wright Group, 1991.
Rohman, *Fee-Fie-Foe-Fum*, Wright Group, 1991.
The Animal Fair, Wright Group, 1991.
Old MacDonald Had a Farm, Wright Group, 1991.
The Ants Go Marching, Wright Group, 1991.
Father's Old Grey Whiskers, Wright Group, 1992.
This Old Man, Wright Group, 1992.
And the Sidewalk Went All Around, Wright Group, 1992.
Goober Peas, Wright Group, 1992.
Rohman, *Gary the Ghost*, Wright Group, 1992.
Miss Mary Mack, Wright Group, 1993.
An Austrian Went Yodeling, Wright Group, 1993.

■ Work in Progress

Illustrating *Bo-Wo-Wones!*, *Down in the Meadow*, and *There's a Hole in My Bucket*, all for the Wright Group; *Big David, Little David*, a book for young children by S. E. Hinton, for Dell.

■ Sidelights

Alan Daniel told *SATA:* "Books and book illustration are a passion with me. I have made excursions, often enjoyable, into other areas of the art world, but I always return to books." Please see Lea Daniel's essay in this volume for a *SIDELIGHTS* interview with Alan and Lea Daniel.

*   *   *

DANIEL, (Donna) Lea 1944-

■ Personal

Born July 15, 1944, in Brampton, Ontario, Canada; daughter of John Merle (an illustrator) and Norma Jean Smith; married Alan Keith Daniel (an illustrator), February 2, 1963; children: Timolin Lea (Daniel) Way, Melissa Lea, Jeffrey Alan. *Education:* McMaster University, B.A., 1971. *Hobbies and other interests:* Reading, attending public lectures and readings, politics, aerobics, walking, biking, gardening.

■ Career

Freelance illustrator. Has illustrated educational textbook series, including "Supermath," Rand McNally, 1976, "Impressions," Holt, Rinehart and Winston of Canada, 1978, and "Le Francais en action," D.C. Heath Canada, 1985-89; contributing illustrator to *Canadian Book of the Road*, Reader's Digest Association (Canada) Ltd., and Canadian Automobile Association, 1979; has done commercial illustration and design for Equitable Life of Canada; has illustrated posters for sports organizations and National YMCA; work has been exhibited in galleries.

■ Awards, Honors

Directors' Choice Award (co-winner with husband Alan Daniel), Early Childhood News, 1992, for "Song Box" series.

■ Illustrator

JUVENILE

Martyn Godfrey, *Fire! Fire!*, Collier Books (Canada), 1985.

(With husband, Alan Daniel) Janet Lunn and Christopher Moore, *The Story of Canada*, Key Porter Books, 1992.

(With A. Daniel) *Bunnicula Escapes! A Pop-Up Adventure*, Morrow, in press.

Also contributor of illustrations to *Chickadee* and *Owl* magazines.

"SONG BOX" SERIES; WITH HUSBAND, ALAN DANIEL

She'll Be Comin' 'Round the Mountain, Wright Group, 1990.

The More We Get Together, Wright Group, 1990.

Cricket Rohman, *The Monster Party*, Wright Group, 1991.

Rohman, *Fee-Fie-Foe-Fum*, Wright Group, 1991.

The Animal Fair, Wright Group, 1991.

Old MacDonald Had a Farm, Wright Group, 1991.

The Ants Go Marching, Wright Group, 1991.

Father's Old Grey Whiskers, Wright Group, 1992.

This Old Man, Wright Group, 1992.

And the Sidewalk Went All Around, Wright Group, 1992.

Goober Peas, Wright Group, 1992.

Rohman, *Gary the Ghost*, Wright Group, 1992.

Miss Mary Mack, Wright Group, 1993.

An Austrian Went Yodeling, Wright Group, 1993.

■ Work in Progress

Down in the Meadow and *There's a Hole in My Bucket*, both for Wright Group.

■ Sidelights

Alan and Lea Daniel, a husband and wife illustrating team from Canada, have established a reputation for producing lively, colorful artwork for children's books. Whether pursuing solo projects or combining their talents on works such as the award-winning *The Story of Canada*, the Daniels strive to create illustrations that, according to Alan, "say something beyond what is naturally appearing in the text."

Both Alan and Lea believe that their interest in children's books stems in part from their regard for all types of literature, which can be traced to their childhoods. In an interview with *SATA*, Alan recalled taking frequent trips to the library and reminisced about Sunday gatherings when his father would sit down and read aloud to the family. "I think that's where my love of books began," Alan said. "I can remember all the really early Dr. Seuss books and being incredibly excited by

LEA AND ALAN DANIEL

The Daniels have often explored historical topics in their work, as in the book *The Story of Canada*. (Text by Janet Lunn and Christopher Moore.)

those, as well as some of the old classics." Lea, who described herself during the interview as an "extremely quiet and shy" child who was "always a reader," recalled that English was among her favorite subjects in school. "I loved English," she remarked. "I still love it. I love to read. After I graduated from McMaster University, I often would go back and audit courses just for the pleasure of it."

The Daniels also began to develop their artistic talents when they were children, especially Alan, who was drawing and painting at an early age. In the interview, Alan recalled a boyhood experiment with costume design that proved disastrous: "I had a bicycle group called the Golden Hawks, and we used to all roar down through the big, swampy areas that were behind the university we were near in Hamilton. I can remember I made up a uniform for myself from my grandfather's long underwear, dyed black. I sewed on a black cape with a golden eagle painted on it. It was really great until one day we were away, probably five or six miles from home, and it began to rain. I found out that the dye was water-soluble; I came home black from head to toe!" As Alan and Lea grew older and attended junior high and high school, art took a backseat to other activities. Lea, a bright, motivated student who excelled in the classroom, also found success as a model, while Alan concentrated

on science and math courses. Neither one seriously considered art as a career during this time, and in fact, the Daniels almost didn't become professional illustrators at all, both having chosen this line of work seemingly by accident.

For years, Lea struggled with the thought of becoming an artist, even though her father, J. Merle Smith, worked as an illustrator. "My idea was always that I would stay as far away from it as I could," she admitted, "but I did draw; everybody sort of sits and draws. My dad gave me an oil painting set when I was quite young, so it was always there, and I took lessons here and there through my teen years. But I didn't go to a formal art school." Lea believes she started drawing seriously after she married, helping Alan to meet deadlines on his projects. Lea enjoyed the work, but it took some time before she could think of herself as an artist. As she explained during the interview: "I think the big turning point for me was early on when I was illustrating. I did a portrait just for myself of my daughter. Up until then I had been really fighting getting involved in the arts. But while I was painting this portrait, something just clicked, and I was totally hooked. Ever since then I never really considered doing anything else."

Like Lea, Alan dabbled in art throughout his teenage years, but after graduating from high school, he enrolled at McMaster University to pursue his interests in physics and chemistry. He left McMaster after one year to work at the Ontario School for the Deaf, and after a year there, he decided to attend the University of Toronto to study philosophy and the social sciences. As time went on, however, he found himself increasingly dissatisfied with his chosen path and began spending time in art museums "doing a lot of drawing instead of studying." Interestingly, Alan credits Lea's father with helping him find an outlet for his creative instincts. In fact, Smith, who headed a studio of freelance artists in Ontario, gave Alan his first illustrating job. Discussing the influence Smith had on his life, Alan declared: "If it hadn't been for Merle, I think I probably never would have gotten into art."

Alan's association with Smith began after Alan arrived home from Toronto one weekend with some artwork he had done. Alan's mother showed the drawings to Smith, who liked the work and invited Alan to visit the art studio. "It was an incredible shock," Alan recalled, "when I suddenly walked into the studio on one weekend and Merle said, 'Take off your shoes. Now draw them.' I did and found out how hard shoes are to draw. I then looked around at what everybody was doing and said, 'This is what I've been looking for.'" After finishing the school year at the university, Alan moved into the studio to work full-time.

Alan's decision to work with Smith proved to be significant for another reason; it helped to bring Alan and Lea together. The two had actually met even before Alan joined the studio; Alan's father was a Baptist minister in Brampton, Ontario, where Lea grew up, and Lea attended services at his congregation. One weekend when Alan returned home from the University of Toronto, he noticed Lea among the members of the congregation. Though Alan was instantly attracted to Lea, he knew that she was about five years younger than he was and still in high school, and he felt that it would be improper to ask her out. However, as his relationship with Smith and his wife, Norma Jean, grew, Alan "spent a lot of time at their house and, of course, met Lea often," he recalled. They began dating, and a couple of years after he started work at the studio, Alan was invited to spend a summer at the Smith's family cottage. It was during that time that Alan and Lea realized they were in love. "We just knew," Alan said. "That summer sealed it." The pair were married the next year.

The couple now not only live together but work together, too. A large part of the Daniels' success is due to a shared belief in the nature and purpose of their work. Neither Alan or Lea particularly enjoys commercial illustration, and they both feel strongly that their drawings for children's books should serve as more than mere decoration for the page. Authors and publishers respect their wishes, and so, Alan stated, "We tend to get offered things that we can take a step further." Taking things a step further is the trademark of the Daniels' style; their illustrations "tell their own story,

independent of, although complementary to, the written narrative," according to a reviewer for *Books in Canada.*

An example of this is seen in *The Orchestra,* a work illustrated by Alan. Originally envisioned as an easy-to-read picture book featuring a description and illustration of each instrument in an orchestra, the book evolved into something completely different in Alan's hands. The idea for *The Orchestra's* illustrative story-within-a-story "came as a daydream," he recalled. "Quite literally, in my daydream, a cat came into my vision and was followed by a couple of kids. They went into a building and there was an orchestra practicing. The cat went in among the players' legs and the kids followed. Then they met people in the orchestra. That was the start in my head."

Later, Alan adapted his vision to better suit the text. In the finished book, a pair of children are invited to view an orchestra rehearsal, meet several musicians, and learn about the different instruments. That night, the children and their mother attend the orchestra's grand performance. While Alan admits that his version of the book strays far from the original plan, "I think it made the book a lot richer for me to do, anyhow, and I think, obviously, for kids who read it." Several critics agreed with Alan's assessment; a reviewer in *Children's Book News* complimented Alan's "marvelously imaginative work," and a Toronto *Globe and Mail* critic praised the "lively, sometimes amusing drawings."

Though *The Orchestra* was strictly Alan's project, other books are done in tandem with Lea, the drawings being passed back and forth between the two in the separate studios they keep at their Ontario home. Discussing how that process works, Alan remarked: "In general terms, when we get a new project in, we usually talk about it together and try to decide what direction we want it to take. Then I usually do the internal concept work, the little picture-story-within-the-story, and I usually do the drawings." He continued, "Sometimes I paint, but ... in most cases Lea does the painting and I tend to do the drawing."

The couple believes that their partnership is a case of two heads being better than one. Alan noted that "we can paint very, very closely together when we want to, but then Lea often takes over at a certain point; she often gives something to it, in the technique or the approach she uses, that I had not even considered." Of the partnership, Lea noted: "I think it's a very efficient way for us to work because it's hard to do the volume of work that you do as an illustrator all on your own." She also mentioned that on lengthier projects, like the four-year commitment to *The Story of Canada,* their collaboration helps them sustain interest in the work, resulting in a better finished product.

Alan admitted that he had certain misgivings about the partnership at first, stating, "I thought when we started to do this it would be just too difficult, to tell the truth, because like most artists we're really devoted to what we

Alan and Lea Daniel combined their artistic talents to produce the imaginative pictures of *The Ants Go Marching*.

do and sensitive. But over the years now we really have got to the point where we trust one another implicitly, so that we can work on the same piece and be happy with what the other person does with it, or let it go at a certain point and let the other person just fly with it. It's great."

The Daniels have collaborated on a variety of books over the years. When asked which type of project she finds most fulfilling, Lea responded, "I have done a lot of educational work over the years, and I've really enjoyed it. It appeals to me to think of how a child could learn, how you could show something to them in a way that helps them to learn." Alan commented that "historical illustration is a particular love of mine." He went on to state that he enjoys doing the research for historical works almost as much as he enjoys illustrating them

"because it takes me way beyond where I am into areas that I would not otherwise go, and many times there is an expert leading me along the way that makes it incredibly interesting." He added, "I find it really worthwhile to give kids the opportunity to see their history before their eyes."

A project which allowed the Daniels to merge their interests is *The Story of Canada*. Hailed by *Quill & Quire* contributor Elizabeth Abbott as "a visual treat," *The Story of Canada* chronicles the history of that nation from prehistoric times to the present and includes the Daniel's renderings of such dramatic scenes as tribesmen hunting a wooly mammoth and a soldier returning from World War I to meet his family at a small-town train depot. Alan noted that the book involved a true team effort: "The authors and I worked

Alan Daniel's lively illustrations have appeared in a number of books by author James Howe, including *Rabbit-Cadabra!*

very closely together and in fact sometimes decided what stories would be best done in the pictures and what stories would be best done in the text. And we supplied each other with information, contacts, and ideas lots of times." He concluded, "It was a really collaborative effort for all of us."

The Daniels' combined talents are also on display in the set of big books published by The Song Box. Each book in the series, which is intended for classroom use, includes a pictorial representation of a well-known children's song; the song's lyrics comprise the book's text. Among the titles in the series are *She'll Be Comin' 'Round the Mountain, Old MacDonald Had a Farm,* and *This Old Man.* Lea mentioned one book, *The Ants Go Marching,* as a favorite of hers. She commented that it was fun "to paint very realistic ants at a large scale so children can see how they are constructed and their rather scary mouthparts, while at the same time keeping all the humor and lightness which is implicit in the song."

Asked if she had any advice for aspiring young artists, Lea commented, "I think that you need to learn the basics and build on that. I think one of the advantages for both of us is that we've had to make our living at it right from the start. We could never avoid learning anything; I've drawn many moon landings and things like that because that was what I was given to do, and so I just had to learn it. We had to learn everything, and it really stands us in good stead now." Alan harkened back to the words of his mentor, Smith, who advised him to "draw, draw, draw." Finally, he had this to say to youngsters thinking of going into art: "Don't do it unless you love it. But if you do love it, it's very rewarding."

■ Works Cited

Abbott, Elizabeth, review of *The Story of Canada, Quill & Quire,* November, 1992.
Daniel, Alan, and Lea Daniel, telephone interview for *Something about the Author* with Thomas F. McMahon, April 13, 1993.
Review of *The Orchestra, Books in Canada,* December, 1984.
Review of *The Orchestra, Children's Book News,* December, 1984.
Review of *The Orchestra, Globe and Mail* (Toronto), February 10, 1985.

■ For More Information See

PERIODICALS

Bulletin of the Center for Children's Books, November, 1985.
Horn Book, December, 1985.
New York Times Book Review, September 30, 1979.
Quill & Quire, December, 1984.

*   *   *

del REY, Lester 1915-1993 (John Alvarez, Cameron Hall, Marion Henry, Philip James, Wade Kaempfert, Henry Marion, Philip St. John, Erik van Lhin, Kenneth Wright; joint pseudonyms: Edson McCann, Charles Satterfield)

OBITUARY NOTICE—See index for *SATA* sketch: Name originally Ramon Felipe San Juan Mario Silvo Enrico Alvarez del Rey; born June 2, 1915, in Clydesdale, MN; died after a brief illness, May 10, 1993, in New York, NY. Publisher, editor, and science fiction writer. The author of numerous fiction and nonfiction books, del Rey is best remembered as cofounder of Del Rey Books, one of the foremost science fiction publishers in the United States. del Rey started writing in the 1930s and published numerous short stories in the periodical *Astounding Science Fiction.* A prolific writer, he used various pseudonyms in addition to his own name. In 1952 he turned his hand to juvenile science fiction, producing such titles as *Marooned on Mars* and *The Cave of Spears.* Two of his most successful books were *Nerves* and *The Eleventh Commandment,* both science fiction novels set on Earth. In 1975 del Rey began working as a fantasy editor for Ballantine Books, and in 1977 he went on to form the Del Rey Books imprint with his wife, Judy-Lynn. Besides working as a writer and publisher, del Rey also edited such books as *Best Science Fiction Stories of the Year* and *Fantastic Science Fiction Art* and was editor of various science fiction magazines for a period of twenty years.

OBITUARIES AND OTHER SOURCES:

BOOKS

The Writers Directory: 1992-1994, St. James Press, 1991, pp. 245-246.

PERIODICALS

Los Angeles Times, May 14, 1993, p. A26.
New York Times, May 12, 1993, p. B7; May 21, 1993, p. 19.
Times (London), May 21, 1993, p. 19.

*   *   *

DeRAN, David 1946-

■ Personal

Born December 21, 1946, in Maryland; son of James J. (an insurance agent) and Helen (a teacher and postal worker; maiden name, Harry) DeRan; married Roxanne Welch (a teacher), December 13, 1974.

■ Addresses

Home—Rural Route 2, Box 74, Delta, PA 17314.

DAVE DeRAN

■ Career

Self-employed artist, 1968—; children's book illustrator.

■ Illustrator

Linda L. Morris, *Morning Milking,* Picture Book Studio, 1991.

Contributor of illustrations to the *Baltimore Sun* Sunday magazine.

■ Work in Progress

Illustrating another picture book by Linda L. Morris.

■ Sidelights

David DeRan told *SATA:* "I've been making my living as an artist since 1968 through sales of my paintings of farm and woodland realism. *Morning Milking* is my first illustrating project, and the author had to talk me into it. The importance of my illustrations lies in their ability to encourage children to read the book."

■ For More Information See

PERIODICALS

New York Times, December 7, 1991.
Smithsonian, November, 1992.

*   *   *

DEUTSCH, Helen 1906-1992

■ Personal

Born March 21, 1906, in New York, NY; died March 15, 1992, in Manhattan, NY; daughter of Heyman (a furniture manufacturer) and Ann (Freeman) Deutsch. *Education:* Barnard College, B.A., 1927; attended Columbia University. *Hobbies and other interests:* The twelfth century, reading Middle Latin, Middle French, Middle English, French, and German.

■ Career

Provincetown Playhouse, New York City, play reader and general executive, 1927-29; freelance writer, New York City, 1929-42; Metro-Goldwyn-Mayer (MGM), Hollywood, CA, screenwriter, 1942-56; freelance television writer and screenwriter. Founder and secretary of New York Drama Critics Circle, 1934-39; assistant to executive director of New York Theatre Guild, 1937-38. Consultant on motion picture, television, and Broadway productions. *Member:* American Society of Composers, Authors, and Publishers, Writers Guild of America, Academy of Motion Picture Arts and Sciences, Dramatists Guild.

■ Awards, Honors

National Velvet was named one of the year's ten best films, *New York Times,* 1944; Academy Award nomination for best screenplay, Academy of Motion Picture Arts and Sciences, screen award for best musical, Writers Guild of America, Cannes International Film Festival award for screen writing, Association Francaise du Festival International du Film, and Golden Globe Award for best screenplay, Hollywood Foreign Press Association, all 1953, and Exhibitor Laurel Award, Film Buyers Association, 1953-54, all for *Lili; Lili* was named one of the year's ten best films by *New York Times, Film Daily,* National Board of Review of Motion Pictures, and numerous others, all 1953; Books and Authors Award, Books and Authors Association, 1955, for *I'll Cry Tomorrow;* All-American Award of the Year, *Radio Daily,* 1956, for *Jack and the Beanstalk;* seven awards for *The General Motors Fiftieth Anniversary Show,* all 1957; Gold Medal Award, *Photoplay,* 1964, for *The Unsinkable Molly Brown;* Certificate of Recognition, American Film Institute, 1982.

■ Writings

SCREENPLAYS

(With Theodore Reeves) *National Velvet* (adapted from the novel of the same title by Enid Bagnold), Metro-Goldwyn-Mayer (MGM), 1944.
The Seventh Cross, MGM, 1944.
Golden Earrings, MGM, 1947.
The Loves of Carmen, MGM, 1948.
Kim (adapted from the novel of the same title by Rudyard Kipling), MGM, 1950.
King Solomon's Mines (adapted from the novel of the same title by H. Rider Haggard), MGM, 1950.
(With William Ludwig, Ray Chordes, and others) *It's a Big Country,* MGM, 1952.
Plymouth Adventure (adaptation from the novel of the same title by Ernest Gebler), MGM, 1952.
Lili (adapted from "The Man Who Hated People," a short story by Paul Gallico), MGM, 1953.
The Glass Slipper, MGM, 1955.
I'll Cry Tomorrow (adapted from the book of the same title by Lillian Roth, Mike Connolly, and Gerold Frank), MGM, 1956.
The Unsinkable Molly Brown (adapted from the musical play of the same title by Richard Morris and Meredith Willson), MGM, 1964.
(With Dorothy Kingsley) *Valley of the Dolls* (adapted from the novel of the same title by Jacqueline Susann), Twentieth Century-Fox, 1967.

OTHER

(With Stella B. Hanau) *The Provincetown: A Story of the Theatre* (history), Farrar & Rinehart, 1931, reprinted, Russell & Russell, 1972.
Love on an Island (play), first produced in Connecticut at Westport County Playhouse, 1934.
Jack and the Beanstalk (television script), National Broadcasting Co. (NBC-TV), 1956.
The General Motors Fiftieth Anniversary Show (television script), NBC-TV, 1957.

The Hallmark Christmas Tree (television script), NBC-TV, 1958.

Author of narrative verse "The White Magnolia Tree"; lyricist for songs, including: "Hi-Lili-Hi-Lo," "Take My Love," "The Ballad of Jack and the Beanstalk," "Twelve Feet Tall," "Sweet World," "I'll Go Along with You," "Looka Me," "He Never Looks My Way," and "March of the Ill-Assorted Guards." Contributor of short stories and articles to periodicals, including *Saturday Evening Post, McCall's, Ladies' Home Journal, Cosmopolitan,* and *Redbook.*

■ Sidelights

Helen Deutsch was most famous for her popular screenplays, though she began her career in theatre and journalism in the 1930s. She began her screenwriting career collaborating on the film adaptation of Enid Bagnold's novel *National Velvet.* The highly successful 1944 production starring Elizabeth Taylor launched Deutsch's Hollywood career. Among her screenplay hits of the 1950s and 1960s were the Academy Award-nominated *Lili, The Seventh Cross, I'll Cry Tomorrow,* and *The Unsinkable Molly Brown,* which received six Academy Award nominations.

Set in pre-World War II England, *National Velvet* revolves around Velvet Brown, a young girl who, with the help of an ex-jockey, trains her horse for England's most important jumping race, the Grand National Steeplechase. Just prior to the race, the jockey hired to ride Velvet's horse in the competition admits that he doesn't believe the horse can win. Velvet dismisses him, deciding she will ride the horse herself, and triumphantly wins the Grand National. The film continues to be popular in the genre of family entertainment.

Deutsch scored another success with her screenplay for the 1953 movie-musical *Lili.* The film's title character is an innocent orphan girl who finds work as a waitress with a French carnival, only to lose her job when she falls in love with the carnival magician and begins to neglect her customers. A crippled puppeteer in the carnival uses his puppets to comfort and cheer Lili and persuades her to join the puppet act. The movie ends happily as Lili and the puppeteer discover their love for one another.

Deutsch also wrote the screenplay for *The Unsinkable Molly Brown,* a highly popular musical based on the hit Broadway production of the same name. The film is loosely based on the true story of a woman who became a celebrated heroine as a survivor of the sinking of the *Titanic.* When the ship hits an iceberg and sinks, Molly's "unsinkable" spirit enables her to save her own life and those of her fellow lifeboat passengers. Molly then becomes an internationally acknowledged heroine and is tearfully reunited with her estranged husband.

Deutsch's other notable achievements in screenwriting include the 1950 film *Kim,* the story of an orphan boy who learns about the world of espionage while growing up in India. The 1950 screenplay *King Solomon's Mines* takes place on a safari in Africa. *The Glass Slipper,* released in 1955, is Deutsch's adaptation of the Cinderella story. Her 1956 screenplay adaptation, *I'll Cry Tomorrow,* was a departure from the fanciful, romantic films of her earlier career, being a frank treatment of the theme of alcoholism.

■ For More Information See

PERIODICALS

Chicago Tribune, March 22, 1992, section 2, p. 6.
Detroit Free Press, March 16, 1992.
Los Angeles Times, March 17, 1992, p. A18.
New York Times, March 17, 1992, p. B6.*

*   *   *

DIAMOND, Arthur 1957-

■ Personal

Born February 18, 1957, in New York, NY; son of Charles (in business) and Thelma (a homemaker; maiden name, Shulman) Diamond; married Irene Kaufmann (a hospital administrator), June 19, 1988; children: Benjamin Thomas, Jessica Ann. *Education:* University of Oregon, B.A., 1984; Queens College, M.A., 1990. *Religion:* Jewish.

■ Addresses

Home—80-17 209th Street, Queens Village, NY 11427.

■ Career

Writer. St. John's University, Queens, NY, adjunct professor of English, 1990-91; high school English teacher in Queens. *Member:* Society of Children's Book Writers and Illustrators.

■ Writings

The Romanian Americans, Chelsea House Publishers, 1988.
Paul Cuffe, Chelsea House Publishers, 1989.
The Bhopal Chemical Leak, illustrated by Brian McGovern, Lucent Books, 1990.
Smallpox and the American Indian, Lucent Books, 1991.
Alcoholism, Lucent Books, 1992.
Jackie Robinson, Lucent Books, 1992.
Egypt: Gift of the Nile, Dillon Press, 1992.
Prince Hall: Social Reformer, Chelsea House Publishers, 1992.
Malcolm X, Enslow Publishers, 1993.

■ Work in Progress

A biography on Anwar Sadat for Lucent Books.

Arthur Diamond and his children.

■ Sidelights

Arthur Diamond writes nonfiction books about various places and people. He sold his first book, *The Romanian Americans,* in 1988. *The Romanian Americans* is part of the Chelsea House Publishers "The People of North America" series. Diamond details Romania's history, culture, and emigration practices as well as depicting the contemporary lives of Romanian Americans. Noting that the book provides information on a widely ignored area, Alice F. Stern in her *Voice of Youth Advocates* review praised Diamond's "straightforward and readable" style.

Writing for another Chelsea House series, the "Black Americans of Achievement" series, Diamond focuses on the life of an individual in *Paul Cuffe.* Paul Cuffe was a half black, half Wampanoag Indian who began his career as a seaman and ended owning his own fleet of ships. Alice Cronin, in a *School Library Journal* review, pegged the book as something more than a shelf filler on black history. Cronin added that Diamond illustrates through *Paul Cuffe* "that courage, intelligence, and determination transcend ethnic and racial boundaries."

Diamond's other books also introduce the reader to historical people and events. In *Prince Hall: Social Reformer,* the focus is not just on the man who organized the first black chapter of the Masons, but on the period in which he lived and how it affected blacks. In *Smallpox and the American Indian,* a specific time period is the focus. "The disease is placed in the larger perspective as one of numerous factors leading to the demise of the once-powerful Indian nations," according to Rosie Peasley in a review of the book in *School Library Journal.*

Diamond told *SATA:* "I hope that the books I write now will serve young people in the same manner they served me when I was young—as rooms. They are generally rooms of refuge, where the din of this very busy society we inhabit is left outside, at least for a short time, allowing for a thought or two to gather and grow. And they are rooms where one might even open up to new ways of seeing and thinking and feeling, and emerged changed, in some subtle fashion. My goal, in writing, is to make houses, even buildings.

"While the writer's financial status—or lack of it—is always an anxiety for me, writing books has always afforded me certain advantages, adventures, and satisfactions. I am glad for advantages like avoiding rush-hour commutes and being in proximity to my children during the day as I work. There have been and continue to be adventures, too, like personal and telephone interviews, photo research, and apprehending a purse snatcher in the New York Public Library. And the satisfaction comes when I get my complimentary copies in the mail, and when I visit the local library and grab a copy of my book and find that it has actually been checked out."

■ Works Cited

Cronin, Alice, review of *Paul Cuffe, School Library Journal,* January, 1990, p. 111.
Peasley, Rosie, review of *Smallpox and the American Indian, School Library Journal,* June, 1992, p. 131.
Stern, Alice F., review of *The Romanian Americans, Voice of Youth Advocates,* October, 1988, p. 198.

* * *

DOMINGUEZ, Angel 1953-

■ Personal

Full name, Angel Dominguez Gazpio; born March 1, 1953, in Galdacano, Vizcaya, Spain; son of Magencio Dominguez (a turner) and Santa Gazpio (a homemaker); married Mari Carmen Pazo (a homemaker), July, 1983; children: Raul, Oscar. *Religion:* Catholic. *Hobbies and other interests:* Drawing whales, walking in the countryside and by the sea, collecting stamps, reading Ray Bradbury and books about the sea, listening to music.

■ Addresses

Home—Ctra. Basurto-Castrejana, No. 67-3H, 48002 Bilbao, Vizcaya, Spain.

■ Career

Free-lance illustrator, 1971-82; G & E (publicity agency), Bilbao, Spain, designer and illustrator, 1982-88; free-lance illustrator, 1989—. *Exhibitions:* Illustrations from *The Diary of a Victorian Mouse* were shown at the Chris Beetles Gallery in 1991. *Military service:* Served as army engineer for approximately one year. *Member:* Greenpeace.

ANGEL DOMINGUEZ

■ Awards, Honors

Artistic award, calligraphy competition, Basque Government, 1991.

■ Writings

Fedra, Toutain, 1982.

ILLUSTRATOR

Aitor Galarza and Alberto Fernandez, *Nuestras aves* (title means "Our Birds"), Petronor, 1980.
X. Mendiguren, *Iparragirre,* Elkar, 1981.
Mark Twain, *Printzea eta eskalea* (title means "Prince and Beggar"), Elkar, 1981.
Aitor Galarza, *Mamiferos salvajes de euskalherria* (title means "Wild Mammals from Basque Country"), Bilbao Savings Bank, 1983.
Aitor Galarza, *Urdaibai,* Biscay County Council, 1989.
Arboles singulares (title means "Singular Trees"), Basque Government, 1990.
Michael Cole, *Diary of a Victorian Mouse,* Arcade, 1991.
Lesley O'Mara, editor, *Classic Animal Stories,* Arcade, 1991.
Cuentos hispanoamericanos, Elkar, 1991.
Seve Calleja, *Dos hamsters en una jaula* (title means "Two Hamsters in a Cage"), Bruno, 1991.
Seve Calleja, *Polypuy,* Elkar, 1991.

Inaki Zubeldia, *Tximu bat klinikan* (title means "A Monkey inside a Clinic"), Elkar, 1991.

Marie Leprince de Beaumont and Marie-Catherine le Jumel de Barneville de la Motte, *La bella y la bestia y otros cuentos* (title means "Beauty and the Beast and Other Stories"), Gaviota, 1992.

Kuki, Ibaizabal, 1992.

Enrique Ordiales and others, *Castillo de Butron,* Estudios Arriaga, 1993.

Emma Orive and Ana Rallo, *Los rios,* Biscay County Council, 1993.

Ciencias naturales (natural science textbooks), Ibaizabal, 1993.

■ Work in Progress

Illustrations for a book about whales, a volume of Aesop's fables, a volume of nursery rhymes, and Lewis Carroll's *Alice in Wonderland.*

■ Sidelights

Angel Dominguez told *SATA:* "My profession was born when I discovered the artwork of my most venerated master, Arthur Rackham. I only saw one illustration, and I thought, I want to do wonderful pictures like that. The illustration was 'The Mad Tea Party' from *Alice in Wonderland* by Lewis Carroll. I have done two tales with the same flavor of the old books by Rackham with much success. My style is a mixture of Edmund Dulac, Charles and William Heath Robinson, Beatrix Potter, and many other good artists from the past, including Rackham, of course."

■ For More Information See

PERIODICALS

CLIJ (Barcelona), November 25, 1991.

* * *

DONALDSON, Gordon 1913-1993

OBITUARY NOTICE—See index for *SATA* sketch: Born April 13, 1913, in Edinburgh, Scotland; died March 16, 1993. Historian, educator, editor, and writer. A specialist in Scottish church history, Donaldson taught history at the University of Edinburgh from 1947 to 1979 and served as the Queen's historiographer in Scotland from 1979 onward. He was also a member of the Royal Commission on the Ancient and Historical Monuments of Scotland and the Scottish Records Advisory Council for approximately twenty years. Donaldson was president of the Scottish Ecclesiological Society between 1963 and 1965 and of the Scottish Record Society from 1981 on. Named Commander of the British Empire in 1988, he was also author of various books on the history of Scotland and its churches, including *The Making of the Scottish Prayer Book of 1637, Scottish Church History, Reformed by Bishops, The Faith of the Scots,* and *A Northern Commonwealth: Scotland and Norway.* In addition, he wrote *Northwards by Sea,* a book appealing to young readers.

He was editor of the *Scottish Historical Review* for five years.

OBITUARIES AND OTHER SOURCES:

BOOKS

Who's Who, 145th edition, St. Martin's, 1993, p. 523

PERIODICALS

Times (London), March 23, 1993, p. 21.

* * *

DUNBAR, Joyce 1944-

■ Personal

Born June 1, 1944, in Scunthorpe, England; daughter of Russell (a steel worker) and Marjorie (a homemaker; maiden name, Reed) Miles; married James Dunbar-Brunton (an illustrator), January 27, 1972; children: Ben, Polly. *Education:* Goldsmiths College, London University, B.A. (with honors). *Hobbies and other interests:* Gardening, walking, theatre, art, building.

■ Addresses

Agent—Murray Pollinger, 222 Old Brompton Rd., London SW5 0B2, England.

JOYCE DUNBAR

Career

Writer. Worked as an English teacher, 1968-89, the last ten years in the drama department at the college at Stratford-on-Avon; teaches part-time, including workshops for deaf playwrights at the Unicorn Theatre; visits numerous schools, often with husband, James Dunbar. Secretary of the East Anglian Society of Authors. *Member:* Society of Authors, Norfolk Contemporary Art Society.

Awards, Honors

Guardian Children's Fiction Award runner-up, 1985, for *Mundo and the Weather-Child; A Bun for Barney* was shortlisted for *Parents* Best Books for Babies Award, 1987; *Software Superslug* was listed on *Smarties* Guide to Children's Reading, 1991.

Writings

Jugg, illustrated by husband, James Dunbar, Scolar Press, 1980.

The Magic Rose Bough, illustrated by James Dunbar, Hodder & Stoughton, 1984.

Mundo and the Weather-Child, Heinemann, 1985, Dell, 1993.

A Bun for Barney, illustrated by Emilie Boon, Orchard Books (London), 1987, Orchard Books (New York), 1988.

The Raggy Taggy Toys, illustrated by P. J. Lynch, Orchard Books, 1987, Barrons, 1988.

Software Superslug, illustrated by James Dunbar, Macdonald, 1987.

Tomatoes and Potatoes, illustrated by Lynn Breeze, Ginn, 1988.

Billy and the Brolly Boy, illustrated by Nick Ward, Ginn, 1988.

Mouse Mad Madeline, illustrated by James Dunbar, Hamish Hamilton, 1988.

One Frosty Friday Morning, illustrated by John Dyke, Ginn, 1989.

Joanna and the Bean-Bag Beastie, illustrated by Francis Blake, Ginn, 1989.

Software Superslug and the Great Computer Stupor, illustrated by James Dunbar, Simon & Schuster, 1989.

Ollie Oddbin's Skylark, illustrated by James Dunbar, Heinemann, 1989.

I Wish I Liked Rice Pudding, illustrated by Carol Thompson, Simon & Schuster, 1989.

Software Superslug and the Nutty Novelty Knitting, illustrated by James Dunbar, Simon & Schuster, 1990.

Ten Little Mice, illustrated by Maria Majewska, Methuen, 1990.

Five Mice and the Moon, illustrated by James Mayhew, Orchard Books, 1990.

The Scarecrow, illustrated by James Dunbar, Collins Educational, 1991.

Giant Jim and Tiny Tim, illustrated by James Dunbar, Collins Educational, 1991.

I Want a Blue Banana, illustrated by James Dunbar, Houghton, 1991.

Why Is the Sky Up?, illustrated by James Dunbar, Houghton, 1991.

Lollopy, illustrated by Susan Varley, Anderson Press, 1991, Macmillan, 1992.

Four Fierce Kittens, illustrated by Jakki Wood, Orchard Books, 1991.

Can Do, illustrated by Thompson, Simon & Schuster, 1992.

Mouse and Mole, illustrated by Mayhew, Transworld, 1993.

Mouse and Mole Have a Party, illustrated by Mayhew, Transworld, 1993.

Seven Sillies, illustrated by Chris Downing, Anderson Press, 1993.

My First Read Aloud Story Book, illustrated by Colin and Moira Maclean, Kingfisher, 1993.

The Spring Rabbit, illustrated by Varley, Anderson Press, 1993.

The Wishing Fish Tree, Ginn, in press.

Also author of many stories for children's educational series. Contributor of stories to anthologies, including "The Wishing Fish Clock," *Tobie and the Face Merchant,* edited by Julia Eccleshare, Collins, 1991; "The Fly," *The Trick of the Tale,* edited by Eccleshare, Viking, 1991; "The Way Out," *Bedtime Stories for the Very Young,* edited by Sally Grindley, Kingfisher, 1991; and "Hilda Mathilda," *Fairy Tales,* edited by Grindley, Little, Brown, 1993. Stories have been broadcast on the BBC Radio show *Listening Corner,* including "Jim Sparrow," 1982, "Sally and the Magic Rattle," 1983, "Doomuch and Doolittle," 1983, and "Shapes and Sounds," 1983 and 1984. *A Bun for Barney* was made into an inter-active video game by the Multi-Media Corporation of the BBC, 1990.

Work in Progress

Television storylines; picture books; a novel; a play.

Adaptations

A Bun for Barney was adapted into a musical play and performed by the Royal Shakespeare Company for their children's Christmas Pantomime, 1988 and 1989; *Software Superslug* was adapted into a musical play performed at the Angel Road School, Norwich, England, 1990.

Sidelights

Joyce Dunbar told *SATA:* "I'd been writing for some time before a strange combination of circumstances turned me into a writer for children: First, I found myself married to an illustrator. A barrister by training, he used to draw a character called Jugg who was his alter-ego. I liked this character so much that I thought he should have a story. *Jugg* became our first book. Secondly, my children. Writing children's stories was a way of entering into and sharing their world. Third,

Joyce and James Dunbar

During a lively trip to the grocery store, a boy learns about colors and the names of common fruits in this comical story by Dunbar. (Cover illustration by James Dunbar.)

desperation. The house was falling down round my ears and I needed to do something to cheer myself up.

"The great thing about writing is that it makes almost every experience worthwhile because you can make a story out of it. The other great thing is that you can live two lives at once: one in the so called 'real' world (which is never quite what we ordered), and one inside your head, which you can order in whatever way you like. This inner world is as full of possibilities as your imagination can make it, and gives one a wonderful excuse for daydreaming.

"I like to write in the mornings, and do something physical in the afternoons, like gardening. Even then I'm working, revising and developing in my head. A lot of a writer's work goes on in the subconscious, even while they are sleeping and dreaming. When it is 'real' writing, and not what I call 'made-up,' it seems a very mysterious process. Like lots of things in life, it is sometimes painful, sometimes exhilarating.

"My favourite contemporary children's authors are Maurice Sendak, Arnold Lobel, and Russell Hoban. Two of them are also illustrators. They all write books that are just as interesting to adults as to children, and they all ask the same fundamental questions that children, relative newcomers in the world, also ask themselves: Goodness! The world! How did it get here and how did I come to be in it?

"I used to be a teacher and loved it, but deafness put an end to that career. I'm glad in a way, because it gave me a very strong motive to survive the early difficult stages of writing, when you are very unsure of yourself, and

can't believe that anyone will want to read what you write, never mind publish it!"

* * *

DUNLOP, Eileen (Rhona) 1938-

■ Personal

Born October 13, 1938, in Alloa, Scotland; daughter of James and Grace (Love) Dunlop; married Antony Kamm (an editor and writer), October 27, 1979. *Education:* Moray House College of Edinburgh, teacher's diploma, 1959. *Religion:* Presbyterian. *Hobbies and other interests:* Reading, going to the theatre.

■ Addresses

Home—46 Tarmangie Dr., Dollar, Clackmannanshire FK14 7BP, Scotland.

■ Career

Writer. Eastfield Primary School, Penicuik, Scotland, assistant mistress, 1959-62; Abercromby Primary School, Tullibody, Scotland, assistant mistress, 1962-64; Sunnyside School, Alloa, Scotland, assistant mistress, 1964-70, assistant headmistress, 1970-79; Dollar Academy, Dollar, Scotland, headmistress of preparatory school, 1980-90. *Member:* International PEN (Scottish Centre), Society of Authors.

■ Awards, Honors

Edgar Allan Poe Award nomination, 1983, for *The Maze Stone;* Scottish Arts Council Book Awards, 1983, for *The Maze Stone,* and 1986, for *Clementina;* American Library Association Notable Book citation, and Carnegie Medal commendation, both 1987, both for *The House on the Hill;* McVitie's Scottish Writer of the Year Prize, 1991, for *Finn's Island;* best novel of the year citation, National Book League, for *Robinsheugh.*

■ Writings

NOVELS FOR CHILDREN

Robinsheugh, illustrated by Peter Farmer, Oxford University Press, 1975, published as *Elizabeth Elizabeth,* Holt, 1976.

A Flute in Mayferry Street, illustrated by Phillida Gili, Oxford University Press, 1976, published as *The House on Mayferry Street,* Holt, 1977.

Fox Farm, Oxford University Press, 1978, Holt, 1979.

The Maze Stone, Oxford University Press, 1982, Coward, McCann & Geohegan, 1983.

Clementina, Oxford University Press, 1985, Holiday House, 1987.

The House on the Hill, Holiday House, 1987.

The Valley of Deer, Holiday House, 1989.

The Chip Shop Ghost, Blackie & Son, 1991.

Finn's Island, Blackie & Son, 1991.

Green Willow's Secret, Blackie Children's Books, 1993.

Red Herring, Blackie Children's Books, 1993.

WITH HUSBAND, ANTONY KAMM

Edinburgh, illustrated by Helen Herbert, Cambridge University Press, 1982.

The Story of Glasgow, illustrated by Maureen and Gordon Gray, Drew Publishing, 1983.

Kings and Queens of Scotland, illustrated by M. and G. Gray, Drew Publishing, 1984.

Scottish Heroes and Heroines of Long Ago, illustrated by M. and G. Gray, Drew Publishing, 1984.

(Editor) *A Book of Old Edinburgh,* Macdonald Publishers, 1984.

Scottish Homes through the Ages, illustrated by John Harrold, Drew Publishing, 1985.

(Editor) *The Scottish Collection of Verse to 1800,* Drew Publishing, 1985.

(Editor) *Scottish Traditional Rhymes for Children,* Drew Publishing, 1985.

■ Sidelights

"Eileen Dunlop is haunted by the past—the dark, sinister, yet compellingly romantic past of her native Scotland," Angela Bull notes in *Twentieth-Century Children's Writers.* The characters in her novels "become possessed by the past, sometimes drawn into it by magic talismans, sometimes just by being in the right place at the right time; and once there, they experience for themselves its glamour and terror." In works such as *Robinsheugh, The Maze Stone, Clementina,* and *The House on the Hill,* a supernatural event not only "provides considerable excitement in its own right," according to J. K. L. Walker in the *Times Literary Supplement,* but also "acts as a catalyst" in helping the young protagonist mature.

Born in 1938, Dunlop's life was affected by the events of World War II. She was eleven months old when Germany invaded Poland and Britain entered the war. Her father was called into military service in 1942. Dunlop recalled that time in her *Something about the Author Autobiography Series* (*SAAS*) essay: "The day of his departure is the first day of my life which I remember really vividly. After he had gone, I went and stood behind the front door, and there, despite all my mother's attempts to divert me, I spent most of the day, peeping through the letter-box, and tracing with my finger the grain of the dark brown, varnished wood. Gradually, I suppose, it dawned on me that he was not coming back—at least, not yet—and so began a life of waiting, waiting for a letter, waiting for the next leave, waiting for the war to end."

The war even affected simple, everyday aspects of life, as Dunlop wrote in her essay. "We children heard adults talk of things like streetlights and bananas, but such talk meant nothing to us, who had never seen a streetlight nor tasted a banana. Everything was simple, because all actions were, or ought to be, directed to one end—winning the war. Hitler was bad. We were good. God was on our side. Never did it occur to me that we could lose."

EILEEN DUNLOP

In 1943, Dunlop enrolled in the Alloa Academy. It was to be the only school she ever attended. In *SAAS,* Dunlop recalled mandatory gas mask drills: "For half an hour I sat in the classroom wearing mine, along with thirty other small 'Mickey Mice.' While our teacher, Miss Keir, read us a story, the little Perspex windows before my eyes misted over, and my face sweated blindly in the damp, rubbery space."

Classic Tales Brighten Childhood

Dunlop was a sickly child and missed much school as a result. It was during a bout with diphtheria that she first learned the delight of reading for herself. She remembers enjoying "*Alice in Wonderland, The Wind in the Willows,* Hans Andersen's fairy tales, *Anne of Green Gables, A Girl of the Limberlost,* Andrew Lang's *Tales of Troy and Greece.* I had also read, before I was ten, most of the novels of Charles Dickens, books which engrossed and repelled me."

When Dunlop was twelve, with the war over and her father home for good, her family moved to a new house. Dunlop describes this as the first time in her life when she felt happy and secure. Her teenage years were busy, with school activities such as athletics and acting; she also enjoyed reading and imagining about history. But at the age of seventeen, Dunlop left school "with a great disappointment," she recalled in *SAAS.* "I failed—not surprisingly, I suppose—to get the examination pass in mathematics, which I needed to secure a place at a Scottish university." Her father strongly discouraged her from professional acting, considering it a profession too difficult to earn a living in. "So, in October of 1956,

I drifted from school to Teacher Training College, with no sense of vocation, and seeing my course as little more than a way of passing the time while I waited for marriage to overtake me."

The early sixties were "a flat, unprofitable time. I seemed to have no purpose, and no sense of direction. I had a few boyfriends, ... and I went on teaching, neither loving nor hating the job. My friends married, and had children, and lived lives which seemed much more fulfilled and interesting than mine." In 1966, however, Dunlop wrote her first children's book, which she called *The Nard in the Fire.* The first publisher she submitted it to rejected it; Dunlop set it aside and got on with her life.

Eight years later Dunlop decided she would try again to find a publisher for her novel; this time she sent her work to Oxford University Press. The editor there who read the manuscript, Mabel George, decided not to publish it. "She told me frankly what was wrong with my writing, and made some suggestions as to how its flaws might be overcome. I left inspired, and determined to try again." This association resulted in the book *Robinsheugh.*

First Book Links Past and Present

Robinsheugh is a story of Elizabeth, a spoiled girl, who has been sent to her Aunt Kate's for the summer. Aunt Kate, busy working on a research project of the historic Melville family, distances herself from her young niece. Elizabeth, feeling lonely and rejected, searches for ways to entertain herself and finds an enchanted mirror that transports her back into the eighteenth century. In this world of the past, she becomes the daughter of the same Melville family her aunt is researching. Elizabeth enjoys the closeness of the family life she experiences during her stays, especially with her eighteenth-century brother Robin, while she becomes increasingly resentful of her aunt's neglect and distance in her contemporary life. Indulging in self-pity, Elizabeth spends greater amounts of time in her eighteenth-century life. Gradually, however, Elizabeth begins to realize the disadvantages of life in the 1700s and the danger she is in from her charming but evil eighteenth-century brother. No longer able to control her passage to and from the eighteenth century, Elizabeth is held by Robin's malicious powers. Her aunt risks her own life to rescue Elizabeth and they both discover the true concern they have for one another.

Robinsheugh met with many good reviews. "Eileen Dunlop's ... vivid re-creation of the perverse and uncontrollable passions of early adolescence make this an impressive first book," writes Julia Briggs in the *Times Literary Supplement.* A reviewer for the *Bulletin of the Center for Children's Books* praises Dunlop's portrayal of relationships and characters, her use of suspense, and her skill in the "merging of fantasy and realism." *Robinsheugh* "can convince almost anybody that ghosts exist," asserts a *Publishers Weekly* contributor.

After this success, Dunlop continued to write, turning out more stories of children and the supernatural. When asked why she writes this type of book, Dunlop related in her autobiographical essay: "Children love a ghost story. Whether or not they admit to a belief in ghosts, they enjoy being scared within the secure environment of a story about other people. Any of my books can be read simply on the level of a weird tale. But there is more to it than that." Dunlop believes that the key to writing a fantasy is to "create a strong, credible background.... So I try to describe my places convincingly, then let strange happenings unfold against a background of apparent normality. The intertwining of fantasy and humdrum reality is common in Scottish folklore and literature, and can be very chilling!" This combination of fantasy and reality is evident in Dunlop's later books, including *The House on the Hill.*

Novels Combine Fantasy and Reality

The House on the Hill tells a realistic story of relationships and prejudices. Shortly after Philip's father dies, his mother registers for nursing school and sends Philip to spend a few months with his spinster great-aunt Jane and cousin Susan in their dilapidated mansion. Philip,

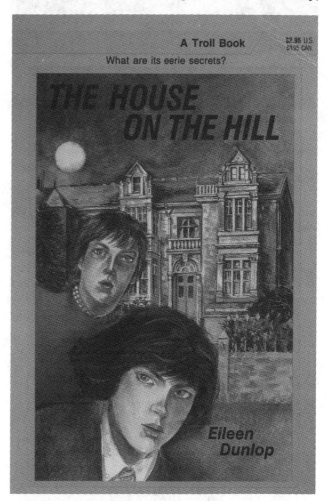

Philip and Susan set out to solve the mystery of an empty room where ghostly lights and images appear in *The House on the Hill.*

Anne investigates a seventeenth-century tale of witchcraft and murder when a family heirloom is discovered in her bedroom wall in this novel by Dunlop. (Cover illustration by Tudor Humphries.)

filled with family prejudices about social classes, arrives at the mansion with many misconceptions of his relatives and expects great-aunt Jane and Susan to behave like upper-class snobs. He is surprised when he realizes he is more class conscious than his great-aunt or cousin. The fantasy aspect of *House on the Hill* emerges when mysterious happenings in the mansion, such as an empty room that lights up at night, recent photographs that reveal hazy outlines of nonexistent furniture, and a painting that emerges from a spot on a wall, bring Philip and Susan together. The adventure to uncover the puzzling occurrences leads to an understanding of great-aunt Jane's loneliness and Philip's mixed emotions about his father's death and serves to heal his aunt's grief with her past, as well as Philip's grief with the present.

Dunlop received much praise for her well developed characters and deftly written story of relationships. "Drawn in by the entrancing mystery, readers will be enriched by the forcefully drawn characters," asserts *Kirkus Review*'s contributor. A contributor to *Publishers Weekly* hails the "finely wrought emotions and relationships of the book's living characters," but also points

out that the ghost story is "almost too pat." *Times Literary Supplement's* J. K. L. Walker, however, finds "the ghost story, acts as a catalyst for ... sentiments, and provides considerable excitement in its own right." Walker summarizes *House on the Hill* as "a classic, near-Victorian, moral tale, in which ignorance, obstinacy and selfishness are conquered by the forces of love, understanding and reason."

In 1978 Dunlop met Antony Kamm, Mabel George's successor at Oxford University Press. Kamm and Dunlop were married in 1979 and moved to Dollar, Scotland, where Dunlop taught at the Dollar Academy. Although she was enjoying success as a writer, she had discovered a new joy in teaching. She related in her essay that when teaching curriculum became less strict, allowing teachers more freedom to design their lessons, "this suited me perfectly .... To be able to plan my own work, choose the literature I wanted to teach, and encourage children to express their feelings creatively— these were great responsibilities, but the freedom was wonderful." In 1990, however, Dunlop decided to devote herself completely to her writing and resigned her position as headmistress. She pointed out in *SAAS:* "This was not an easy decision, since I knew I would miss the children, and, after almost thirty years, teaching had become a way of life. It was made easier by the knowledge that I had given the job all I had to give, and that the future belonged—as it always does—to the young. And I have books still to write."

■ Works Cited

Bull, Angela, *Twentieth-Century Children's Writers,* 3rd edition, St. James Press, 1989, pp. 305-306.

Briggs, Julia, "Intrusive Past," *Times Literary Supplement,* July 11, 1975.

Dunlop, Eileen, *Something about the Author Autobiography Series,* Volume 12, Gale, 1991, pp. 58-69.

Review of *Elizabeth Elizabeth, Bulletin of the Center for Children's Books,* July, 1977, p. 174.

Review of *Elizabeth Elizabeth, Publishers Weekly,* April 4, 1977, p. 89.

Review of *House on the Hill, Kirkus Review,* October 1, 1987.

Review of *House on the Hill, Publishers Weekly,* November 13, 1987, p. 71.

Walker, J. K. L., "Through the Proper Channels," *Times Literary Supplement,* May 15, 1987, p. 529.

■ For More Information See

PERIODICALS

Times Literary Supplement, November 11, 1982; November 8, 1985; May 19-25, 1989.

DYESS, John (Foster) 1939-

■ Personal

Born April 10, 1939, in St. Louis, MO; son of Ezekiel B. (a radio engineer) and Adele (a homemaker; maiden name, Kestler) Dyess; married Carolyn R. Dixon (a graphic artist), August 8, 1980; children: (first marriage) Christine, Mark, Michael; (second marriage) Audrey. *Education:* Washington University, B.F.A., 1961. *Politics:* Independent. *Religion:* Christian. *Hobbies and other interests:* Listening to recorded books, reading about American history, painting.

■ Addresses

Home and office—703 Josephine Ave., Glendale, MO 63122. *Member:* St. Louis Artist Guild (member of board of governors of art section, 1993-94).

■ Career

Self-employed illustrator, 1980—. Maritz Motivation Company, St. Louis, MO, illustrator, 1969-80; Washington University, St. Louis, part-time instructor in illustration, 1977-80; Meramec Community College, part-time instructor, 1982; Webster University, adjunct professor, 1993. *Military service:* U.S. Army Reserve, 1961-67.

■ Illustrator

(With John Michael Bailey) James Clark, *Cars,* Raintree Publishers, 1981.
Alice Delacroix, *Mattie's Whisper,* Boyds Mills Press, 1992.

Contributor of illustrations to textbooks for Harcourt Brace Jovanovich, Silver Burdett, and Macmillan. Contributor of illustrations to periodicals, including *Highlights for Children, T.V. Guide, Popular Mechanics, Field and Stream, Sports Afield,* and *Alaska Magazine.*

JOHN FOSTER DYESS

■ Sidelights

John Dyess told *SATA:* "An early influence on my work came in the newspaper comics, especially 'Prince Valiant,' drawn by Hal Foster and 'Rip Kirby,' drawn by Alex Raymond. I enjoyed looking at the illustrations in the *Saturday Evening Post,* and I enjoyed the drawings of Jack Davis and Wallace Wood, whose work appeared during the 1950s.

"I began drawing at an early age, and by the time I entered high school I knew I wanted to be an illustrator. During high school I became aware of the 'old masters,' such as Rembrandt, Vermeer, Valazquez, and Van Gogh."

E–F

EWART, Claire 1958-

■ Personal

Born June 15, 1958, in Holland, MI; daughter of John A. Ewart (a business owner) and Caryl J. Van Houten (a homemaker; maiden name Curtis); married Thomas A. Herr (a trial attorney), August 31, 1985. *Education:* attended Oberlin College, 1976-77; Rhode Island School of Design, B.F.A., 1980. *Hobbies and other interests:* Travel and travel writing, swimming, canoeing, horseback riding, cross-country skiing, gardening.

■ Addresses

Home—Northern Indiana.

■ Career

Animator and acting art director for television stations in South Bend, IN, area; Computer Creations Inc., South Bend, art director, 1981-85; free-lance courtroom illustrator for WSJV-TV, South Bend, 1981-85, and for WKJG-TV and the *Fort Wayne News Sentinel*, Fort Wayne, IN, 1985—; free-lance author and illustrator of children's books, 1989—. Member of Artists Panel, Artlink Gallery, 1986—. *Member:* Designer/Craftsmen Guild (vice president, 1990-91), Society of Children's Book Writers and Illustrators, Greenpeace, World Wildlife Fund, Natural Resources Defense Council, Nature Conservancy.

■ Awards, Honors

Time Train was named one of the best books of 1991 by *School Library Journal* and *Parent's Magazine*, named one of the best books of the season by *The Chicago Tribune* and *New Yorker*, and was selected for the Original Art Show at the Society of Illustrators, 1991; International Reading Association Celebrate Literacy Award, 1992; Best Children's Science Fiction Picture Book Award, DucKon, 1992, for *Time Train; Time Train* was selected for Indiana State READ ALOUD list, 1993-94.

■ Writings

SELF-ILLUSTRATED

One Cold Night, Putnam, 1992.

ILLUSTRATOR

Paul Fleischman, *Time Train,* HarperCollins, 1991.
Karen Greenfield, *Sister Yessa's Story,* HarperCollins, 1992.

CLAIRE EWART

Ewart's illustrations bring to life a class trip to get a first-hand look at real dinosaurs in Paul Fleischman's *Time Train*.

Tomie dePaola, *The Legend of the Persian Carpet*, Whitebird Books, 1993.

Susan Arkin Couture, *The Biggest Horse I Ever Did See*, HarperCollins, 1994.

■ Work in Progress

Writing and illustrating *In the Wild Place*, a book about a child and a horse, for G. P. Putnam's Sons, 1995.

■ Sidelights

When Claire Ewart was a child, her family moved several times. However, her parents always made sure that they lived on a lake. They traveled cross country, saw great paintings, visited national parks, rode horses and hiked, often seeing remote areas still as untouched as when the Native Americans had traveled the land. "My parents not only exposed us to everything they could," Ewart told *SATA*, "but they encouraged us in our interests. They taught us to persevere, and to believe that we could do what we set out to do."

Ewart's self-illustrated book *One Cold Night* came about as a result of paintings she saw on a trip she and her husband took to New Mexico. Months later, she woke up on a cold October morning with the first sentence of the story in her head: "One cold night the cloud coyotes howled in the moonlight, and Snow Woman came to tuck us in."

"Having been trained as an animator," Ewart reported to *SATA*, "I approach the process of illustrating the way a director might plan the shots for a film. Essentially, having read the manuscript, I see the imagery moving through my head, and choose the most important moments of the story to focus in on. I learn a lot from

looking at the work of others, whether that be books, film, or paintings in a museum.

"In illustrating *Sister Yessa's Story* written by Karen Greenfield, I purposely included many endangered animals, as well as animals that children might not be familiar with. Paul Fleischman's *Time Train* gave me the opportunity to learn more about dinosaurs and trains and to create a mood befitting this story of time travel." For the manuscript of *The Legend of the Persian Carpet*, the retelling of a Persian folktale by Tomie dePaola, Ewart traveled to places where carpets are made, visited places like the palace the king might have lived in, and tried to translate that imagery into the illustrations.

Ewart feels that with encouragement and hard work, she has been able to make her dreams come true. "When I travel to a destination on the other side of the world ... I feel a responsibility to share some of that experience with children upon returning. I hope that by widening my world, I am also expanding the parameters of theirs."

■ For More Information See

BOOKS

Children's Writers and Illustrators Market, Writer's Digest Books, 1992.

PERIODICALS

Kirkus Review, November 15, 1992, p. 1441.

*　　*　　*

FRASER, Mary Ann 1959-

■ Personal

Born March 6, 1959, in Santa Monica, CA; daughter of Noel (an electrical engineer) and Genevieve (a registered nurse) Damon; married Todd C. Fraser (a certified public accountant); children: Ian, Alex, Brett. *Education:* University of California at Los Angeles, B.A. (summa cum laude), 1981; College of Art and Design, Exeter, England, postgraduate diploma, 1983. *Hobbies and other interests:* Hiking, marble collecting, cooking, camping, nature study, travel.

■ Addresses

Home and office—2270 Rockdale Ave., Simi Valley, CA 93063.

■ Career

Graphic artist, 1982-90; fine artist, 1983—. *Member:* Society of Children's Book Writers and Illustrators, Sierra Club, National Wildlife Federation, Southern California Council on Literature for Children and Young People.

MARY ANN FRASER

■ Awards, Honors

On Top of the World: The Conquest of Mount Everest was named a Young Reader's Choice, International Reading Association, and a Notable Children's Trade Book in the Field of Social Studies, NCSS-CBC, both 1991; Rotary International fellowship; *Ten Mile Day and the Building of the Transcontinental Railroad* was named a Pick of the List, American Booksellers.

■ Writings

On Top of the World: The Conquest of Mount Everest, Henry Holt, 1991.
Ten Mile Day and the Building of the Transcontinental Railroad, Henry Holt, 1993.
One Giant Leap, Henry Holt, 1993.

iLLUSTRATOR

Betsy Bunny's Birthday, Macmillan, 1988.
Bobby Bear's Three Wishes, Macmillan, 1988.
The Night before Christmas, Macmillan, 1988.
The Nutcracker, Macmillan, 1988.
Randy Raccoon's Big Mess, Macmillan, 1988.
Sally Squirrel's Late Day, Macmillan, 1988.
The Dutchess Sees Double, Tor Books, 1989.
If Wishes Were Horses, Tor Books, 1989.
A Leg up for Lucinda, Tor Books, 1989.
The Only Boy in the Ring, Tor Books, 1989.

Armadillos and Other Unusual Animals, Julian Messner, 1989.
Lightning and Other Wonders of the Sky, Julian Messner, 1989.
Quicksand and Other Earthly Wonders, Julian Messner, 1989.
Tidal Waves and Other Ocean Wonders, Julian Messner, 1989.
Little Kids at Home, Modern, 1989.
Little Kids at Play, Modern, 1989.
Little Kids at School, Modern, 1989.
Little Kids in the Neighborhood, Modern, 1989.
Patty for President, Modern, 1990.
Tell Me about Nature Dictionary, Derrydale Books, 1990.
Killer Whales and Other Wonders of the Frozen World, Julian Messner, 1991.
Piranhas and Other Wonders of the Jungle, Julian Messner, 1991.
Saber-toothed Cats and Other Prehistoric Wonders, Julian Messner, 1991.
Tyrannosaurus Rex and Other Dinosaur Wonders, Julian Messner, 1991.
The Stargazer's Guide to the Galaxy, Tor Books, 1991.
My Favorite Dinosaur: Tyrannosaurus rex, Lowell House, 1993.

Also illustrated Mix and Match Tracing Books, a series of six books, and Science Activity Crossword Puzzles, a series of four books, both for Price, Stern, 1988; Science Activity Flashcards, a series of four books, for ERS, 1988; and Make Your Own Pop-ups, a series of four books, for Price, Stern, 1990. Cover illustrations for four Word Search Adventures, for Price, Stern, 1988.

■ Work in Progress

Sanctuary, the story of Three Arch Rocks, completion expected in 1994.

■ Sidelights

Mary Ann Fraser told *SATA:* "When I was growing up I always imagined I would be an artist, probably because I was drawing or painting from the time I was three years old. Although I thought writing was a wonderful occupation, I never believed it was something I could do professionally. It wasn't until I fell into illustrating children's books that I even dared to consider writing them. English composition had always been my most challenging subject in school. Then I remembered my second grade teacher, Mrs. Floberg. If anyone deserves credit for giving me the courage to try writing as a career, it would have to be her. I used to finish my in-class assignments early. To keep me busy while the others finished she would have me work on a story of my own, complete with illustrations. I will never forget the pleasure those stories gave me and the thrill it was to share them with my classmates. In many ways that is what I am still doing today. Nothing is more exciting than discovering a terrific story to share with others. Not only do I love to write and illustrate, but I have been surprised by how much I relish the research. If I can turn history into an adventure for the reader, then I feel I have done my job well.

"I work at home in a studio in my garage. I love children's books and probably read at least ten a day to my children. When they are not around I can often be found sneaking in a few more."

*   *   *

FUJIKAWA, Gyo 1908-

■ Personal

Born November 3, 1908, in Berkeley, CA; daughter of Hikozo (an interpreter) and Yu (a journalist and poet) Fujikawa. *Education:* Attended Chouinard Art Institute.

■ Addresses

Home—New York, NY. *Office*—c/o Random House, Inc., Publicity Offices, 225 Park Ave. S., New York, NY 10003.

■ Career

Free-lance commercial illustrator and author/illustrator of books for children. Instructor in color and design, Chouinard Art Institute, 1933-39; Walt Disney Studios,

GYO FUJIKAWA

Anaheim, CA, artist in the promotion department, 1939-41; Fox Film Co., New York, NY, designer of movie advertisements, 1942; William Douglas McAdams (pharmaceutical advertising agency), New York, NY, art director, 1943-51. Work includes U.S. postage stamps commemorating Lady Bird Johnson's beautification program, Eskimo Pies advertisements, Beechnut Baby foods advertisements, the centennial of golden anniversary of the International Peace Garden, illustrations in *Family Circle, Ladies' Home Journal,* and *McCall's,* and cover illustrations for *Saturday Evening Post.*

■ Awards, Honors

Gyo Fujikawa's Oh, What a Busy Day! was chosen for inclusion in the American Institute of Graphic Arts Book Show, 1976.

■ Writings

SELF-ILLUSTRATED; FOR CHILDREN

Babies, Grosset, 1963.
Baby Animals, Grosset, 1963.
A to Z Picture Book, Grosset, 1974.
Let's Eat, Grosset, 1975.
Let's Play, Grosset, 1975.
Puppies, Pussycats, and Other Friends, Grosset, 1975.
Sleepy Time, Grosset, 1975.
Gyo Fujikawa's Oh, What a Busy Day!, Grosset, 1976.
Babies of the Wild, Grosset, 1977.
Betty Bear's Birthday, Grosset, 1977.
Can You Count?, Grosset, 1977.
Our Best Friends, Grosset, 1977.
Millie's Secret, Grosset, 1978.
Let's Grow a Garden, Grosset, 1978.
My Favorite Thing, Grosset, 1978.
Surprise! Surprise!, Grosset, 1978.
Come Follow Me ... to the Secret World of Elves and Fairies and Gnomes and Trolls, Grosset, 1979.
Jenny Learns a Lesson, Grosset, 1980.
Welcome Is a Wonderful Word, Grosset, 1980.
Come Out and Play, Grosset, 1981.
Dreamland, Grosset, 1981.
Fairyland, Grosset, 1981.
Faraway Friends, Grosset, 1981.
The Flyaway Kite, Grosset, 1981.
Good Morning!, Grosset, 1981.
Here I Am, Grosset, 1981.
Jenny and Jupie, Grosset, 1981.
The Magic Show, Grosset, 1981.
Make-Believe, Grosset, 1981.
My Animal Friends, Grosset, 1981.
One, Two, Three, A Counting Book, Grosset, 1981.
Shags Has a Dream, Grosset, 1981.
Mother Goose, Grosset, 1981.
A Tiny Word Book, Grosset, 1981.
Year In, Year Out, Grosset, 1981.
Jenny and Jupie to the Rescue, Grosset, 1982.
Fraidy Cat, Grosset, 1982.
Me Too!, Grosset, 1982.
Sam's All-Wrong Day, Grosset, 1982.
Shags Finds a Kitten, Grosset, 1983.

That's Not Fair, Grosset, 1983.
Are You My Friend Today?, Random House, 1988.
Sunny Books: Four Favorite Tales, J. B. Communications, 1989.
Ten Little Babies, Random House, 1989.
See What I Can Be!, Putnam, 1990.
Good Night, Sleep Tight, Shh, Random House, 1990.

ILLUSTRATOR

Robert Louis Stevenson, *A Child's Garden of Verses,* Grosset, 1957.
Clement C. Moore, *The Night before Christmas,* Grosset, 1961.
Mother Goose, Grosset, 1968.
A Child's Book of Poems, Grosset, 1969.
Eve Morel, editor, *Fairy Tales and Fables,* Grosset, 1970.
Poems for Children, Platt, 1980.
Baby Mother Goose, Random House, 1989.
Bobbi Katz, *Poems for Small Friends,* Random House, 1989.
Gyo Fujikawa's A Child's Book of Poems, Grosset, 1989.

■ Sidelights

Gyo Fujikawa is best known for her enchanting illustrations of popular children's classics as well as her own books for children. A prolific writer and illustrator of children's books, having completed over fifty in her career, Fujikawa is motivated by being able to entertain children with her work. With attention to detail she learned while working under the late Walt Disney, Fujikawa brings to her illustrations an interconnectedness with the text that delights her young readers.

Born in California, Fujikawa knew she wanted to be an artist while in high school. After winning a poster contest in high school, Fujikawa decided that she "wanted to do artwork FOR children ABOUT children," she related in *Something about the Author Autobiography Series (SAAS)*. "I felt most comfortable with that side of artwork, though I didn't know whether I would ever be able to do it." Although Fujikawa grew up in a Japanese household, she received traditional American schooling, and one of her teachers encouraged her and helped her apply for scholarships to art school. Fujikawa was accepted at several places, and eventually chose to go to Chouinard Art Institute in Los Angeles. Although she attended the school for several years, Fujikawa told *Something about the Author (SATA)* that "I have no degrees from Chouinard. In my day ... degrees were not given." After attending for several years, she became an instructor there.

In the 1930s, Fujikawa supported herself through freelance drawing and took a trip to Tokyo to get in touch with her cultural heritage. Japan "was really a most wonderful experience," recounts Fujikawa in *SAAS*. "Without it, I would never have known what it was like to be Japanese." Later Fujikawa adds that "my Japanese connections greatly affected my work because I have always LOVED Japanese art.... I love the work of people like Utamaro, Hiroshige, and Sesshu; they were

Fujikawa includes many details in her drawings for *Gyo Fujikawa's A to Z Picture Book* so even non-readers will be rewarded for paying attention to the page.

all wonderful designers as well as artists. I especially like the work of Korin who did marvelous things with nature.... A lot of the influence is in my system." Then, in 1939, she got a job with Walt Disney Studios designing promotional material for *Fantasia*. Through the nudgings of a perfectionistic Walt Disney, Fujikawa learned to be quite detail-oriented in her work. In 1941, she was sent to New York to work on merchandising Disney material, including books. "I designed a lot of those little twenty-five-cent Golden-type books," Fujikawa told *SAAS*. "And that led me eventually to children's books." While in that office she also met several people who were creating excellent children's books. She wanted to get involved with them but was soon offered a job in advertising, which she took. A job with a pharmaceutical advertising agency soon followed.

During the time that Fujikawa was working in New York, Pearl Harbor was attacked. Since she was on the East Coast, she was not interred in the American prison camps for Asian and Asian-Americans like her parents and brother who lived on the West Coast. "I went to visit them [her family] while they were still in camp." Fujikawa states in *SAAS*. "I was free to do that because as an American citizen I could travel freely. If strangers asked questions, I lied a lot. I would say I was part Chinese and part Japanese and have lots of fun making up stories." Disney, displaying concern about her well being, questioned Fujikawa about how others treated her. When Fujikawa explained that she often had to lie, Disney asserted "'You're an American citizen! If that happens again, you just tell them you're an American citizen.' From that moment on, that's exactly what I did tell them," Fujikawa notes in *SAAS*.

Embarks on Writing Career

In 1951 Fujikawa left the advertising world to become a full-time free-lance writer. "I was doing art for advertising, I was also doing a great deal of work for magazines," Fujikawa recalls in *SAAS*. "Each magazine used different phases of my work. For example, *Reader's Digest* used me for animals and nature stories. I loved to do animals and birds and flowers. And then I would turn around and do children's things for magazines like *Family Circle*. Then I would do food art for *McCall's* magazine and *Ladies Home Journal*." About five years later, she was asked by Doris Duenewald, juvenile editor at Grosset & Dunlap, to illustrate the classic *A*

Child's Garden of Verses. Doris had noticed an ad Fujikawa had illustrated for *McCall's*. The opportunity "was my chance to see if there was a market for my kind of art in children's books," points out Fujikawa in *SAAS*. Working on the between her commercial assignments, Fujikawa completed the illustrations in 1957. "For a long time I thought I would like to draw pictures for children about children.... It was fun to illustrate a good book," Fujikawa told *SATA*.

As a commercial artist, Fujikawa had done some notable illustrations. She designed the round-faced Eskimo child for Eskimo Pies and the babies for Beech-Nut Baby Foods. It was during these assignments that her ethnic background almost cost her a job. Management from both Eskimo Pie and Beech-Nut thought that since she was Japanese, her illustrations would be too "oriental." The Eskimo Pie advertising agency, however, took the proposed artwork out onto Fifth Avenue in New York City to poll passersby, and Fujikawa's logo won.

Fujikawa's bestselling work *Babies,* published in 1963, defied racial prejudices by presenting children of different ethnic origins engaged in typical infant activities.

Fujikawa turned this kind of discrimination around in her book *Babies.* Published in 1963, it was one of the first children's books to use multi-racial characters; babies of African, Oriental, and European descent are seen on its pages. Initially the publishers were concerned that the book would not sell well because of the multiracial characters and because no one had ever done a book just on babies. "The man in charge of sales said that the books wouldn't sell down South. He told me to take the black babies out. I said I didn't care if the books didn't sell; the black babies must stay," asserts Fujikawa in *SAAS.* "The black babies stayed, and the book ended up being a best-seller. I am grateful and happy it is still selling today!" Since the publication of this book, the artist's work has been translated into seventeen languages and read in more than twenty-two countries.

Detailed Illustrations Entertain Young Readers

After Fujikawa illustrated the classic works of other authors, including *Mother Goose* and *Fairy Tales and Fables,* she decided to develop her own original stories and concentrate on a young audience—from two- to six-year olds. "To complete one little book takes months of engrossing work; sometimes I don't go out of my apartment studio for days on end," she commented in *SATA.* "But it is so rewarding to think that I can reach out and touch small children through words and pictures and make friends with them." By 1974, Fujikawa had decided to devote herself entirely to children's books. Some of her most popular books include: *A to Z Picture Book, Oh, What a Busy Day!, Come Follow Me,* and *Jennie and Jupie.* When working, she pores over the text to find the smallest details, and makes sure to put them in her illustrations. "I like to include lots of details, small objects and variety that make children give a lot of attention to the illustrations," she remarked in *Publisher's Weekly.* She owes some of this attention to detail to her work at the Disney Studios. And she also gives credit for this habit to the popularity she has won with children: "I include [details] in the art because I know children sit and look for them when the stories are read to them."

Fujikawa uses two primary artistic styles in her work: watercolor paintings and black-and-white line drawings. Her watercolors include "hazy washes of color that set the mood for richly detailed pictures ... which are a pleasant balance between realistic renderings and stylized fancy," noted a *Publisher's Weekly* contributor. Her line drawings are similarly detailed; Fujikawa "uses many strokes to build forms and shades and textures, often using the cross-hatch technique." Her trademark is painting children and adults with round, happy faces, black dots for their eyes, and a light blush on their cheeks.

After having completed more than fifty books for children, Fujikawa has won a devoted following. "I am flattered when people ask me how I know so much about how children think and feel," Fujikawa admits in *SAAS.* "Although I have never had children of my own and cannot say I had a particularly marvelous childhood,

Fujikawa explores all the fun things that one day can hold in this popular picture book. (Illustration from *Oh, What a Busy Day!*)

perhaps I can say I am still like a child myself. Part of me, I guess, never grew up." In writing to *SATA* about her work, she tells her motivation for illustrating for children: "What I relish the most is trying to satisfy the constant questions in the back of my mind—will this picture capture a child's imagination? What can I do to enhance it further? Does it help to tell a story?" Although she claims not to be successful, she has achieved her purpose in writing these books—"To entertain children from the printed page."

■ Works Cited

Publishers Weekly, January 4, 1971, pp. 45-48.
Something about the Author, Volume 39, Gale, 1985, pp. 76-77.
Fujikawa, Gyo, essay in *Something about the Author Autobiography Series,* Volume 16, Gale, 1993, pp. 5-9, 14.

■ For More Information See

BOOKS

Illustrators of Books for Young People, 2nd edition, Scarecrow, 1975.
Illustrators of Children's Books: 1957-66, Horn Book, 1968.
Klemin, Diana, *The Art of Art for Children's Books,* Clarkson Potter, 1966.
Lanes, Selma C., *Down the Rabbit Hole,* Atheneum, 1971.

PERIODICALS

American Artist, May, 1954.
Publishers Weekly, September 24, 1982.

*   *   *

FUTCHER, Jane P. 1947-

■ Personal

Born February 27, 1947, in St. Louis, MO; daughter of Palmer H. (a physician) and Mary (a social worker and homemaker; maiden name, Rightor) Futcher; companion of Erin Carney (a midwife). *Education:* Dickinson College, B.A., 1969; Boston University, M.A., 1971. *Politics:* Democrat. *Religion:* Wiccan.

■ Addresses

Home—235 Shelvin Road, Novato, CA 94947.

■ Career

Writer. Philadelphia Public School System, substitute teacher in junior high classrooms, 1972-73; Harper & Row Media, New York City, staff project editor, producer, and writer, 1973-77; Guidance Associates, New York City, scriptwriter, 1977-80; World College West, Petaluma, CA, adjunct faculty member and writing tutor, 1990-92.

JANE P. FUTCHER

■ Writings

NOVELS

Crush, Little, Brown, 1981.
Promise Not to Tell, Avon, 1991.

NONFICTION

(With Robert Conover) *Marin: The Place, the People,* Holt, 1981.

OTHER

Also author of educational filmstrips and teaching guides for Concept Media, University of Mid-America, and Guidance Associates. Contributor to articles to periodicals, including *San Francisco Chronicle, Plexus,* and *Drummer.*

■ Work in Progress

Come Home with Me Tonight, a novel about a lesbian love affair; *Don't Catch Me, I'm Falling,* a young adult novel about a teenage suicide in an affluent California county.

■ Sidelights

Jane Futcher writes novels that deal with issues that are of concern to teens but are considered controversial by adults—teenage suicide, abuse, and sexuality. Futcher told *SATA* that writing had always been a difficult process for her, with composition assignments causing much frustration. "But over time, this thorny, awkward, lonesome process I now know as writing became my way of dealing with the world, with contradictions, with beauty, with love, with all the aspects of life which are so confusing and intriguing. By the age of sixteen, after attending a summer six week writing workshop at Exeter Summer School in New Hampshire, I knew I wanted to be a writer."

Futcher attended Dickinson College in Carlisle, Pennsylvania, majoring in English. After earning her bachelor of arts degree in 1969 she worked for the summer as a counselor in the Language Arts Reading camp at the Lighthouse Settlement in Philadelphia. She then attended Boston University and received her master's degree in creative writing in 1971. Returning to the Philadelphia area, she supported herself by substitute teaching at the junior high school level and writing features for a weekly newspaper. In 1973 she joined the staff at Harper and Row Media in New York and worked her way from staff project editor to writer and producer, creating high school and college programs on science and social issues.

Futcher continued to write educational filmstrips and teaching guides while working on her first novel and writing feature stories and book reviews. In 1990 she joined the staff of World College West in Petaluma, California as an adjunct faculty member and writing tutor. She continues to write novels while working on her teacher certification in English as a Second Language through the University of California Extension, Berkeley.

"I have always used my writing to help remember and understand life experiences that have affected me deeply," Futcher related to *SATA*. "At age 30, I began my first novel, *Crush*, in an attempt to describe and explain the feelings of attraction I'd had for other girls at school during the 1960s. Because so little had been written at the time on lesbian relationships, I was breaking a personal and social taboo by describing my own homosexual feelings. But the process was an important one for me, and my book, I believe, touched other lesbians who had struggled silently in school with their lesbianism." *Crush*, Futcher's first novel, is described by Marsha Hartos in the *School Library Journal* as addressing "the fear that one may be too far along on the sliding scale of hetero-, bi-, and homosexuality." According to reviewers Rebecca Sue Taylor and Gayle Keresey in *Voice of Youth Advocates*, "the book's strength is the depth in which the emotions of the girls is explored."

In Futcher's second young adult novel, *Promise Not to Tell*, the issue of sexuality centers around sexual abuse and harassment. Simon is a fifteen-year-old troubled youth, struggling to come to grips with responsibility and integrity. His problems are compounded when his new friend, Laura, confides to him she is being sexually molested by her boss. Simon wants to help her though he has promised to tell no one. The reviews for *Promise Not to Tell* were mixed. Randy Meyer stated in *Booklist* that although the author writes with "honest characters and frank dialogue, . . . her depiction of Laura's situation is poor." Meyer finds fault with Futcher's treatment of the sensitive topic because Laura does not fight back. The story is about Simon, however, and reviewer Dorothy M. Broderick in *Voice of Youth Advocates*

focuses on Simon's deeply ingrained problems. "By the end of the book, he's come a long way, but he still needs therapy. I hope he gets it."

The topics Futcher chooses to write about are issues of true concern to adolescents. Her readers are just beginning to deal with personal growth and relationships, and Futcher offers them awareness developed through her creative process. "Writing is a chance for me to be alone, to distill and think, slowly, painstakingly, about human relationships and my own growth as a human being. I have written some of my best work as a member of a woman's writing group that meets monthly. I find the group gives me a chance to commiserate and celebrate with other writers, and to receive feedback on work that I've not shared with anyone. This community of writers helps to offset the isolation of the writing process. My own process involves a deep commitment to honesty, to telling the truth, as I see it, no matter how upsetting it might be to others. This commitment to honesty comes directly from my own experience of secrecy, shame, and repression regarding my early sexual attractions to women. I will never go back in the closet, as a writer, as a lesbian."

■ Works Cited

Broderick, Dorothy M., review of *Promise Not to Tell*, *Voice of Youth Advocates*, December, 1991, p. 310.

Hartos, Marsha, review of *Crush*, *School Library Journal*, December, 1981, p. 70.

Meyer, Randy, review of *Promise Not to Tell*, *Booklist*, August, 1991, p. 2140.

Taylor, Rebecca Sue and Gayle Keresey, review of *Crush*, *Voice of Youth Advocates*, December, 1981, p. 29.

G

GANO, Lila 1949-

■ Personal

Born September 25, 1949, in Fort Benning, GA; daughter of Tenton Nelson Horton (a retired civil servant) and Maria Gloria Horton (an entrepreneur); married Richard Dale Gano (an engineer), December 30, 1977. *Education:* University of South Carolina, B.A., 1971; University of Northern Colorado, M.A., 1975. *Hobbies and other interests:* Racquetball, gardening, boating.

■ Addresses

Home and office—2528 Pretty Bayou Island Dr., Panama City, FL 32405.

■ Career

CACI, Rosslyn, VA, project manager, 1980-81; Integrated Systems Analysts, Inc., Chula Vista, CA, analyst, 1987-90; Analysis and Technology, Panama City, FL, technical writer, 1990-92. Also works as a free-lance editor, technical writer, and promoter. *Military service:* U.S. Navy, 1971-77, served as a maintenance officer in San Diego, CA, became lieutenant. *Member:* Panhandle Writer's Guild, Society of Children's Book Writers and Illustrators.

■ Writings

Smoking, Lucent Books, 1989.
Television—Electronic Pictures, Lucent Books, 1990.
Hazardous Waste, Lucent Books, 1991.

Contributor of nonfiction to periodicals, including *San Diego Woman, Network Newsletter, Housewife-Writer's Forum, TACTALK, Wifeline.*

■ Work in Progress

The Sinking of the U.S.S. Indianapolis, a book for young readers; *Bottom Line Living,* a book for adults.

LILA GANO

■ Sidelights

Lila Gano, who was a shy child and teenager, found verbal communication difficult, but putting words on paper flowed easily for her. "Thoughts spilled from my pencil and even seemed to make sense," she told *SATA.* Lila enjoys research and will spend hours finding the most useful materials for whatever project she is working on. "For my book *Television—Electronic Pictures* I consulted over twenty references. Surprisingly, some of the most useful material came from other children's books."

It is not unexpected that Lila's interest and success in nonfiction is in technical fields. Technical projects and report writing while in the Navy provided her with a solid background and understanding of researching a variety of technical subjects. Since leaving the Navy she has put this experience to good use writing lecture guides, research studies, maintenance and operation manuals, management plans, user guides, and booklets.

In 1988 Lila's interest in writing prompted her to attend a local writers' workshop in San Diego where she heard that Lucent Books, recently moved to San Diego, needed writers of nonfiction books for young readers. When she contacted the company, she found the editors willing to work with new writers and interested in her book ideas. Her first book, *Smoking,* was published in 1989. The book examines the history of tobacco in America, its use and abuse, the medical effects of this habit and ways of overcoming tobacco addiction.

Lila's next book for Lucent, *Television—Electronic Pictures,* was written to be part of a series on inventions that changed the world. It took her into research about the electronics, history, and psychological effects of television. Later she produced the book *Hazardous Waste,* again for young readers. Her goals for the future include writing nonfiction for adults.

■ For More Information See

PERIODICALS

Booklist, February 1, 1990, p. 1088.

*   *   *

GARDAM, Jane 1928-

■ Personal

Born July 11, 1928, in Coatham, Yorkshire, England; daughter of William (a schoolmaster) and Kathleen Mary (Helm) Pearson; married David Hill Gardam (a Queen's counsel), April 20, 1952; children: Timothy, Mary, Thomas. *Education:* Bedford College, London, B.A. (honors), 1949, graduate study, 1949-52. *Politics:* Liberal. *Religion:* Anglo-Catholic. *Hobbies and other interests:* Growing roses.

■ Addresses

Home—Haven House, Sandwich, Kent, England. *Agent*—Bruce Hunter, David Higham Associates, 5-8 Lower John Street, London W1R 4HA England.

■ Career

Weldons Ladies Journal, London, England, sub-editor, 1952-53; *Time and Tide,* London, assistant literary editor, 1953-55, author, 1971—. Organizer of hospital libraries for Red Cross, 1950. *Member:* Royal Society of Literature (fellow), University Women's Club, Arts Club, PEN.

■ Awards, Honors

A Long Way from Verona received special mention from the Guardian Award for children's fiction, and was selected an honor book by *Book World's* Spring Book Festival award, both 1972, and won the Phoenix Award,

JANE GARDAM

1991; *Boston Globe-Horn Book* honor book for text, 1974, for *The Summer after the Funeral;* David Higham Prize for fiction and Winifred Holtby Memorial prize for fiction, both 1977, for *Black Faces, White Faces;* runner-up citation, Booker Prize, 1978, for *God on the Rocks;* Whitbread Literary Award, 1981, for *The Hollow Land;* Carnegie Medal "highly recommended" award, for *The Hollow Land* and "commended" award, for *Bridget and William,* both 1983; Katherine Mansfield Award, 1984, for *The Pangs of Love.*

■ Writings

A Few Fair Days, illustrated by Peggy Fortnum, Macmillan, 1971.

A Long Way from Verona, Macmillan, 1971.

The Summer after the Funeral, Macmillan, 1973.

Black Faces, White Faces, Hamish Hamilton, 1975, published as *The Pineapple Bay Hotel,* Morrow, 1976.

Bilgewater, Hamish Hamilton, 1976, Greenwillow, 1977.

God on the Rocks, Morrow, 1978.

The Sidmouth Letters, Hamish Hamilton, 1980.

Bridget and William, illustrated by Janet Rawlings, MacRae, 1981, F. Watts, 1983.

The Hollow Land, illustrated by J. Rawlings, MacRae, 1981, Greenwillow, 1982.

Horse, F. Watts, 1982.

The Pangs of Love, Hamish Hamilton, 1982.

Kit, MacRae, 1983.

Kit in Boots, MacRae, 1986.

Crusoe's Daughter, Atheneum, 1986.

Swan, MacRae, 1986.

Through the Doll's House Door, MacRae, 1987.

Showing the Flag, Penguin, 1989.

Also author of *The Queen of the Tambourine,* 1990. Contributor of short stories to magazines.

■ Sidelights

Regarded as a talented and original writer, British author Jane Gardam has been successful with children's fiction as well as with short stories and novels for adults. "All of Gardam's work," asserts *Dictionary of Literary Biography* contributor Patricia Craig, "is marked by certain admirable characteristics: economy of style, exuberance and humor, a special relish for the startling and the unexpected." In an article for *Horn Book,* Gardam declares, "[T]he best sound in the world is a child by himself laughing out loud at a book."

Gardam was born July 11, 1928 in Coatham, Yorkshire, England. Her father, William Pearson, had come to Coatham to teach math and physics at Sir William Turner's school and remained there all his life. Each year, Jane and her family spent three months at Thornby End, her paternal grandparents' farm in the Lake District. Her mother was "horrified" by this environment but Gardam enjoyed the change.

At the age of five, Gardam entered her first school, and it was at this time that she began to write. However, all her early manuscripts were accidentally burned in her bedroom chimney. She states in *Something about the Author Autobiography Series* (*SAAS*): "I remember not minding much. Thinking—oh well, I'll write it again. How easy it is to write, before the age of ten."

With the assistance of her father, Gardam passed the entrance examinations necessary to attend high school at Saltburn-by-the-Sea. He also insured that she would be able to attend the university by hiring the classics master to tutor her in Latin. Not only did she achieve the required score, but she also continued to study Latin for her first year at Bedford College for Women in the University of London.

Gardam arrived in London immediately after World War II. Despite the desolate conditions, she was very happy. It was here that Gardam developed her love for the theatre. She recalls in *SAAS,* "I did very little work but went day after day (sometimes twice a day) to the theatre and the ballet and to foreign films for the first time." Gardam received her B.A. with honors in 1949 and immediately began postgraduate work. After her grant ran out, Gardam returned home to complete her studies but was unable to do so.

In need of employment, Gardam returned to London and began proofreading at *Weldons Ladies Journal.* "I found it difficult," she writes in *SAAS.* "I couldn't take the articles on flower arranging seriously enough and was sacked." After drifting, the author met David Gardam, and married him in 1952. She began work on *Time and Tide,* a literary weekly, and enjoyed her work there until her first child was born in 1954. She left just prior to his birth, planning to return in six weeks. "Instead, I found myself amazed by my baby and totally absorbed by him," Gardam declares in her *SAAS* essay. "Nothing else seemed to be anywhere near as interesting." It was ten years before Gardam attempted to write again.

History Relived through Young Protagonists

Several of Gardam's books are considered classics, especially *A Few Fair Days, A Long Way from Verona, Bilgewater,* and *The Hollow Land. A Few Fair Days* relates nine episodes from a girl's life in pre-war England. In *Growing Point,* Margery Fisher describes *A Few Fair Days* as "Supremely well-planned, crisply and deftly written ... a book of exceptional literary value." *A Long Way from Verona* is a first-person narrative of thirteen-year-old Jessica's year as a student in Cleveland Spa during World War II. Gardam describes with great humor the trials and tribulations of a thirteen-year-old witnessing the destruction wrought by the war. Her next children's novel was *Bilgewater,* an imaginative narrative about a seventeen-year-old girl whose parents have died. Craig asserts that "Gardam makes high comedy of the fidgets and fancies of adolescence, with her heroine constantly on the brink of some contretemps or social

In this set of related stories, a family in the English countryside learns to accept their new neighbors from London. (Cover illustration by Janet Rawlins.)

disaster; but the narrative is charged as well with a kind of muted fairy-tale glamour. The effect is striking."

The Hollow Land, about the evolving relationship between two families, is written in a linked stories format. The connecting theme is "the gradual and mutual acceptance by the 'incomers' and the local inhabitants of each other," according to *Twentieth-Century Children's Writers* contributor Kit Pearson. It is set in the Cumbrian moors and ventures from the present to 1999, when a total eclipse of the sun is expected. Craig comments, "This is a story of domestic, country life felicity; summer sultriness and winter frost; the interesting peculiarities of neighbors; boys' escapades in the open air."

Perhaps the most perceptive comment about Gardam's talent appears in a *Times Literary Supplement* review of *A Long Way from Verona:* "Jane Gardam is a writer of such humorous intensity—glorious dialogue, hilarious set-pieces—that when one reads her for the first time one laughs aloud and when rereading her, the acid test for funny books, one's admiration increases a hundred-fold." Since Gardam has been writing fiction, Craig concludes, she "has shown herself to be a novelist of rare invention."

■ Works Cited

Dictionary of Literary Biography, Volume 14: *British Novelists since 1960,* Gale, 1983.

Fisher, Margery, review of *A Few Fair Days, Growing Point,* October, 1971, pp. 1798-99.

Gardam, Jane, "On Writing for Children: Some Wasps in the Marmalade, Part II," *Horn Book,* December, 1978, pp. 672-79.

Something about the Author Autobiography Series, Volume 9, Gale, 1990.

Times Literary Supplement, November 22, 1971; December 3, 1971.

Twentieth-Century Children's Writers, 3rd edition, St. James Press, 1989, pp. 372-74.

■ For More Information See

BOOKS

Children's Literature Review, Volume 12, Gale, 1987, pp. 156-71.

Gardam, "Mrs. Hookaneye and I," in *The Thorny Paradise: Writers on Writing for Children,* edited by Edward Blishen, Kestrel, 1975, pp. 77-80.

PERIODICALS

Horn Book, October, 1978, pp. 489-96.

* * *

GARFIELD, Leon 1921-

■ Personal

Born July 14, 1921, in Brighton, Sussex, England; son of David Kalman (in business) and Rose (Blaustein) Gar-

LEON GARFIELD

field; married Vivien Dolores Alcock (an artist), October 23, 1948; children: Jane Angela. *Education:* Attended grammar school in Brighton, England. *Politics:* "Somewhere between Labour and Liberal." *Religion:* Jewish. *Hobbies and other interests:* Eighteenth-century music, collecting paintings and china, films, theatre (mainly Shakespeare).

■ Addresses

Home—59 Wood Lane, Highgate, London N6 5UD, England. *Agent*—The Ellen Levine Literary Agency Inc., Suite 906, 370 Lexington Ave., New York, NY 10017; Jo Stewart, 201 East 66th St., New York, NY 10021; and Winant, Towers, Ltd., Clerkenwell House, 45-47 Clerkenwell Green, London EC1R 0HT, England.

■ Career

Whittington Hospital, London, England, biochemical technician, 1946-66; part-time biochemical technician in a hospital in London, England, 1966; novelist, 1966—. *Military service:* British Army, Medical Corps, 1940-46; served in Belgium and Germany. *Member:* International PEN.

■ Awards, Honors

Gold Medal, Boys' Clubs of America, 1966, for *Jack Holborn;* first *Guardian* Award for children's fiction, 1967, for *Devil-in-the-Fog;* Arts Council of Great Britain Award for the best book for older children, and American Library Association (ALA) Notable Book citation, both 1967, *Boston Globe-Horn Book* honor book citation, 1968, and Phoenix award, 1987, all for *Smith;* Carnegie Medal runner-up, 1967, for *Smith,* 1968, for *Black Jack,* and 1970, for *The Drummer Boy; New York Times* Best Illustrated Book citation, 1968, for *Mister Corbett's Ghost;* Carnegie Medal for the most outstanding book of the year, 1970, for *The God beneath the Sea;* ALA Notable Book citation, 1972, for *The Ghost Downstairs;* Child Study Association of America's Children's Books of the Year citation, 1976, for *The House of Hanover: England in the Eighteenth Century;* Whitbread Literary Award, 1980, for *John Diamond; Boston Globe-Horn Book* Fiction Honor citation, 1981, for *Footsteps;* Federation of Children's Book Groups award, 1981, for *Fair's Fair;* Hans Christian Andersen Award nomination, 1981; Golden Cat Award, 1985; runner-up for Maschler awards, 1985, for *Shakespeare Stories* and *The Wedding Ghost.*

■ Writings

JUVENILE NOVELS

Jack Holborn, illustrated by Antony Maitland, Constable, 1964, Pantheon, 1965.
Devil-in-the-Fog, illustrated by Maitland, Pantheon, 1966.
Smith, illustrated by Maitland, Pantheon, 1967.
Mr. Corbett's Ghost, illustrated by Alan E. Cober, Pantheon, 1968.
Black Jack, illustrated by Maitland, Longman, 1968, Pantheon, 1969.
The Drummer Boy, illustrated by Maitland, Pantheon, 1969.
The Ghost Downstairs, illustrated by Maitland, Longman, 1970, Pantheon, 1972.
The Strange Affair of Adelaide Harris, illustrated by Fritz Wegner, Pantheon, 1971.
The Captain's Watch, illustrated by Trevor Ridley, Heinemann, 1971.
Lucifer Wilkins, illustrated by Ridley, Heinemann, 1973.
(With Edward Blishen) *The Sound of Coaches,* illustrated by John Lawrence, Viking, 1974.
The Prisoners of September, Viking, 1975.
The Pleasure Garden, illustrated by Wegner, Viking, 1976.
An Adelaide Ghost, Ward, Lock, 1977.
The Confidence Man, Kestrel, 1978, Viking, 1979.
The Night of the Comet: A Comedy of Courtship Featuring Bostock and Harris, Delacorte, 1979.
Footsteps: A Novel, illustrated by Maitland, Delacorte, 1980, published in England as *John Diamond,* Kestrel, 1980.
Fair's Fair, illustrated by Margaret Chamberlain, Macdonald, 1981, American edition illustrated by S. D. Schindler, Doubleday, 1983.
Guilt and Gingerbread, illustrated by Wegner, Kestrel, 1984.
The Wedding Ghost, illustrated by Charles Keeping, Oxford University Press (Oxford), 1985, (New York), 1987.
The December Rose, Kestrel, 1986.
The Empty Sleeve, Delacorte, 1988.

Blewcoat Boy, Gollancz, 1988, published as *Young Nick and Jubilee,* illustrated by Ted Lewin, Delacorte, 1989.
Revolution!, Collins, 1989.

"APPRENTICES" SERIES

The Lamplighter's Funeral, illustrated by Maitland, Heinemann, 1976.
Mirror, Mirror, illustrated by Maitland, Heinemann, 1976.
Moss and Blister, illustrated by Faith Jaques, Heinemann, 1976.
The Cloak, illustrated by Jaques, Heinemann, 1977.
The Valentine, illustrated by Jaques, Heinemann, 1977.
Labour in Vain, illustrated by Jaques, Heinemann, 1977.
The Fool, illustrated by Jaques, Heinemann, 1977.
Rosy Starling, illustrated by Jaques, Heinemann, 1977.
The Dumb Cake, illustrated by Jaques, Heinemann, 1977.
Tom Titmarsh's Devil, illustrated by Jaques, Heinemann, 1977.
The Enemy, illustrated by Jaques, Heinemann, 1978.
The Filthy Beast, illustrated by Jaques, Heinemann, 1978.
The Apprentices (collection of series titles), Viking, 1978.

JUVENILE SHORT STORIES

The Restless Ghost: Three Stories by Leon Garfield, illustrated by Saul Lambert, Pantheon, 1969.
Mister Corbett's Ghost, and Other Stories, illustrated by Maitland, Longman, 1969.
The Boy and the Monkey, illustrated by Ridley, Heinemann, 1969, F. Watts, 1970.
(Reteller with Blishen) *The God beneath the Sea,* illustrated by Keeping, Longman, 1970, American edition illustrated by Zevi Blum, Pantheon, 1971.
(Reteller with Blishen) *The Golden Shadow,* illustrated by Keeping, Pantheon, 1973.
(Reteller) *King Nimrod's Tower,* illustrated by Michael Bragg, Lothrop, 1982.
(Reteller) *The Writing on the Wall,* illustrated by Bragg, Methuen, 1982, Lothrop, 1983.
(Reteller) *The King in the Garden,* illustrated by Bragg, Methuen, 1984, Lothrop, 1985.

Author of short stories, "The Questioners" in *Winter's Tales for Children, 4,* Macmillan, 1968, and the title story in *The Restless Ghost and Other Encounters and Experiences,* edited by Susan Dickinson, Collins, 1970.

ADAPTOR OF WORKS BY WILLIAM SHAKESPEARE

Tales from Shakespeare, illustrated by Michael Foreman, Schocken, 1985.
Shakespeare Stories, illustrated by Foreman, Houghton, 1991.
Hamlet, illustrated by Natalia Orlova, Peter Kotov, and Natasha Demidova, Knopf, 1993.
Macbeth, illustrated by Nikolai Serebriakov, Knopf, 1993.
A Midsummer Night's Dream, illustrated by Elena Prorokova, Knopf, 1993.

Romeo and Juliet, illustrated by Igor Makarov, Knopf, 1993.

The Tempest, illustrated by Elena Livanova, Knopf, 1993.

Twelfth Night, illustrated by Ksenia Prytkova, Knopf, 1993.

NOVELS FOR ADULTS

The Mystery of Edwin Drood (completion of the novel begun by Charles Dickens), Deutsch, 1980, Pantheon, 1981.

The House of Cards, Bodley Head, 1982, St. Martin's, 1983.

EDITOR

Baker's Dozen: A Collection of Stories, Ward, Lock, 1973, published as *Strange Fish and Other Stories,* Lothrop, 1974.

The Book Lovers: A Sequence of Love-Scenes, Ward, Lock, 1977, Avon, 1978.

A Swag of Stories: Australian Stories, illustrated by Caroline Harrison, Ward, Lock, 1977.

(With Mervyn Peake and Blishen) *Sketches from Bleak House,* Methuen, 1983.

OTHER

(With David Proctor) *Child O'War: The True Story of a Sailor Boy in Nelson's Navy,* illustrated by Maitland, Holt, 1972.

The House of Hanover: England in the Eighteenth Century (nonfiction), Seabury, 1976, Houghton, 1979.

Also author, with Patrick Hardy, of the play *The Cabbage and the Rose,* published in *Miscellany Four,* edited by Blishen, Oxford University Press, 1967.

■ **Adaptations**

John Diamond was filmed for BBC-TV, 1981; *Jack Holborn* was made into a Taurus Film (shown on German television), 1982; *The Ghost Downstairs* and *The Restless Ghost* were dramatized for television in 1982 and 1983, respectively; a six-part series based on *The December Rose* was shown on BBC-TV, 1986-87; *Mr. Corbett's Ghost* was filmed in 1987. Several of Garfield's other books have been dramatized for film and television. *Devil-in-the Fog, Smith* and *The Strange Affair of Adelaide Harris* have been adapted as television serials for British television, and *Black Jack* was made into a film produced by Tony Garnett and directed by Ken Loach.

■ **Sidelights**

Leon Garfield's works are categorized as books for children, but he writes for readers of all ages. Inspired by Greek myths, Bible stories, and Victorian novels like Charles Dickens's *Great Expectations,* his fiction recalls the mystery associated with the long-ago past. His retellings of old stories take readers back to ancient Greece, Babylon, and the scenes of Shakespeare's plays; his novels are most often set in Britain during the 1700s

and 1800s. Readers find memorable characters in easy-to-picture settings in his historical novels and in his retellings of myths and parables.

Garfield was born and grew up in the seaside town of Brighton, on the south coast of England. Although he had an older brother, the difference in their ages and temperaments made it "virtually the same as being an only child," the author told *Publishers Weekly* interviewer Amanda Smith. His interests turned to writing, as he recalled in John Rowe Townsend's *A Sense of Story:* "I always wanted to write. I do recall soggy stories a la Tolstoy ... weird tales a la Poe ... and then drifting toward farcical thrillers. Then to Lewis Carroll-like efforts, then to Hans Andersen."

Despite his interest in writing, Garfield took art classes as a young man, before World War II interrupted his studies. Garfield joined the British Army Medical Corps and served in Germany and Belgium, where he met his future wife, Vivien Alcock, who also writes children's

Determined to find a better life for himself, a boy stows away on a ship bound for Africa—only to discover he is aboard a pirate vessel. (Cover design by Antony Maitland.)

books. The two found common interests in writing and painting but, as Garfield told Smith, "Vivien ... took one look at my drawings and said I ought to be a writer. We've been together ever since." Garfield returned to England and after the war took a job in a hospital as a medical technician. He married Alcock soon after, and her support was instrumental in getting his writing career started, as he related to Smith: "I was writing early in the morning, lunch time, late at night, on holidays.... Vivien helped enormously, and I realize now that she could have been writing her own books at that time."

Garfield's first published novel was *Jack Holborn,* a tale of adventure and piracy set in the eighteenth century. The result of years of careful research and writing, the novel hadn't originally been intended for children; but when he was offered publication if he cut the lengthy manuscript for a younger audience, Garfield agreed. Other novels followed, many set during the eighteenth and nineteenth centuries as well. As the author explained to Smith, that period of history lends itself well to children's fiction: "It is a period in which the division between childhood and adulthood is very sharp: the time of apprenticeships when, literally, one day a child was at home and the next day would be sent out to live with master ... [in] a very adult world and the child was alone in it and was expected to make a living."

Historic London Seen in *The Apprentices*

This situation comes to life in *The Apprentices,* which was first published as separate titles in England. The stories, none of which are longer than thirty pages, show young adults learning all-but-forgotten skills such as lamplighting and mirror-silvering in historic London. The city's history is woven into the books, which explain the origins of street names and describe alleyways and buildings that give London its distinctive atmosphere. Nicholas Tucker writes in the *Times Literary Supplement* that "as parables, the stories certainly have power." Though Garfield's heroes confront problems that belong to London's past, Tucker suggests, "our own age should always be grateful for effective moral tales illustrating the need for greater love and understanding."

The Drummer Boy looks at the aftermath of a massacre during the Napoleonic Wars from the viewpoint of a boy who leads thousands of men to their deaths on the battlefield. Love figures importantly in the boy's future encounters with a general's daughter and her maid. More important is the boy's discovery of a role model in the person of a brave and kind surgeon. In the *New York Times Book Review* Robert Hood writes that this insightful novel teaches children about fame, love, and dreams in conflict with death and other realities. And a *Times Literary Supplement* reviewer recommends it to readers of all ages for its memorable themes and scenes.

House of Cards, written specifically for adults, can be appreciated by younger readers who have a taste for elaborate suspense novels that were popular in England

during the Victorian era. "A good Victorian novel is like a suite of rooms deliciously furnished for our comfort; they open into each other—the plots and subplots—and are each decorated with all manner of captivating objects, that is, the descriptions and flourishes of the text. Virtue is rewarded, evil is banished and the merely unpleasant are made to slink away," Michele Slung explains in a *Washington Post* review. With its gradually revealed secrets about a beautiful young girl's past, including her hasty exit from Poland in 1847, *House of Cards* promises to be a satisfying reading experience even for those "who think they don't like Dickens," Bruce Allen writes in the *Christian Science Monitor.* *Times Literary Supplement* contributor Peter Lewis recommends it to readers who wish Dickens had penned a few more suspense novels before his death in 1870. Says Lewis, "It is an entertainment, plotted with great skill and ingenuity, peopled by vivid, boldly drawn and memorable characters, and narrated by a master storyteller with verve, wit, and a delight in the well-turned phrase."

The plot of *John Diamond* is not as complicated as the plot of *House of Cards,* yet at every turn it displays the author's craftiness. A boy seeking to make amends for

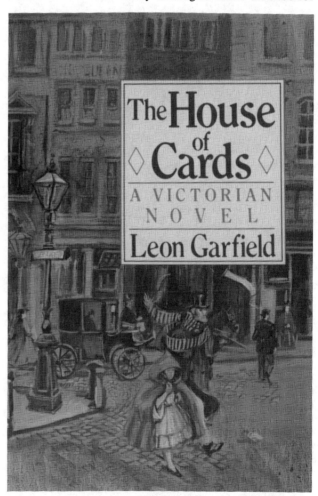

Set in Victorian London, this novel by Garfield has been compared to the writing of author Charles Dickens. (Cover illustration by Susan Stillman.)

his late father's sins finds he must also evade a gang of violent street urchins. By the time these mysteries unravel, "something more than tale-telling has been accomplished. A deeper reassurance is delivered," Jacky Gillott declares in the London *Times.* Like the works of Dickens, the story of the boy's quest sheds light on guilt and love in the context of an exciting adventure story. As Garfield noted in Townsend's book, "I use the quest for identity, which seems to occur pretty often, because I have a passion for secrets and mystery. And the secret and mystery of another individual seems to me the only mystery one can unravel endlessly—and still be uncertain."

Brings Classic Tales to Children

Garfield ventures outside historical England to retell Greek myths in a manner which appeals to both younger and older readers. According to *New York Times Book Review* contributor Barbara Wersba, *The God beneath the Sea* is "like a mosaic of fiery, precious jewels," keeping all the excitement of the original myths. Speaking of *The Golden Shadow,* a collection of mythical tales from the life of Heracles, *New Statesman* contributor Gerard Benson writes that Garfield turns the myths

Garfield explores the hopes of twelve eighteenth-century English laborers in this book of stories. (Cover illustration by Anthony Kerins.)

"into something new: utterly modern in its writing and still Greek in feeling."

Garfield's retellings of Bible stories are also masterful. In *The King in the Garden,* a little girl helps the cursed Old Testament King Nebuchadnezzar regain his bearings after a season of madness. He returns to Babylon to find out he hasn't even been missed, and all is well. This parable of the theme that "people can get along just fine without a king, but neither people nor a king can get along without the help of God" is told in language that sounds beautiful when read aloud, Elizabeth Crow relates in the *New York Times Book Review.* Garfield gives the Old Testament story of the Tower of Babel a new angle in *King Nimrod's Tower.* While crowds of people bicker about the building of the Tower of Babel, a "ladder" they hope will help them to reach God, God's attention centers on a boy who is trying to understand his stray puppy. At the point in the story when the languages become confused and work on the tower stops, suddenly the boy and the dog can understand each other.

Similarly, *Shakespeare Stories* retells the stories of twelve famous plays in a way that both young readers and adults can enjoy. Pared down to their main actions, the plays in this form preserve a sense of what it is like to see the plays acted on stage. When relating what the characters say, Garfield uses the playwright's original words. Because of this, says D. J. R. Bruckner of the *New York Times Book Review,* readers can enjoy the dramatic power of the plays "and learn something new about English at the same time." Garfield has since adapted several of Shakespeare's plays, including *Hamlet* and *Macbeth,* for use by young students.

Many critics praise Garfield's achievements as a writer. Carolyn See concludes in the *Los Angeles Times:* "Garfield has written award-winning children's books and possesses that priceless ability to create a make-believe picture and let you walk into it, to let you be there, and he makes that world so sweetly inviting that you put down the book with a sigh of regret, sorry to be back in this real world." As the author himself explained in *Horn Book:* "One does not write *for* children. One writes so that children can understand. Which means writing as clearly, vividly, and truthfully as possible. Adults might put up with occasional lapses; children are far less tolerant. They must never be bored; not for an instant. Words must live for them; so must people. That is what really matters, and it entails believing entirely in what one writes and having a real urgency to convince the reader that it is absolutely, utterly true."

■ Works Cited

Allen, Bruce, review of *The House of Cards, Christian Science Monitor,* February 9, 1983, p. 15.

Benson, Gerard, review of *The Golden Shadow, New Statesman,* May 25, 1973, p. 782.

Bruckner, D. J. R., "Children's Books: *Shakespeare Stories* by Leon Garfield," *New York Times Book Review,* January 26, 1986, p. 32.

A ghost accuses a boy of murdering him in the title story of this collection by Garfield. (Cover photograph by David James.)

Crow, Elizabeth, "Children's Books: *The King in the Garden* by Leon Garfield," *New York Times Book Review,* April 14, 1985, p. 43.

Review of *The Drummer Boy, Times Literary Supplement,* April 16, 1970, p. 411.

Garfield, Leon, "And So It Grows," *Horn Book,* December, 1968.

Gillott, Jacky, "Jacks and Knaves," *Times* (London), July 2, 1980.

Hood, Robert, review of *The Drummer Boy, New York Times Book Review,* May 17, 1970, p. 26.

Lewis, Peter, "In the Dickens Mould," *Times Literary Supplement,* May 21, 1982, p. 566.

See, Carolyn, "A Confection of Dickensian Doings," *Los Angeles Times,* February 24, 1983, pp. 2, 20.

Slung, Michele, "Book World: *The House of Cards,* by Leon Garfield," *Washington Post,* March 26, 1983.

Smith, Amanda, "Of Ghosts and History," *Publishers Weekly,* September 30, 1988, pp. 28-30.

Townsend, John Rowe, *A Sense of Story,* Lippincott, 1971.

Tucker, Nicholas, "Powerful Parables," *Times Literary Supplement,* November 26, 1982, p. 1301.

Wersba, Barbara, review of *The God beneath the Sea, New York Times Book Review,* May 2, 1971, p. 46.

■ **For More Information See**

BOOKS

Blishen, Edward, editor, *The Thorny Paradise,* Kestrel Books, 1975.

Children's Literature Review, Volume 21, Gale, 1990.

Contemporary Literary Criticism, Volume 12, Gale, 1980.

Twentieth-Century Children's Writers, 3rd edition, St. James Press, 1989, pp. 374-376.

Wintle, Justin, and Emma Fisher, *The Pied Pipers,* Paddington, 1974.

PERIODICALS

Children's Literature in Education, winter, 1978.

Christian Science Monitor, November 2, 1967.

Contemporary Children's Literature, Number 54, 1989.

Horn Book, February, 1971; February, 1972; October, 1974; March, 1990.

New Statesman, May 26, 1967; November, 1968.

New York Times Book Review, November 26, 1967; March 1, 1981, p. 7.

Time, October 27, 1980.

Times Literary Supplement, May 25, 1967; March 28, 1980, p. 355; July 20, 1980.

Washington Post Book World, October 3, 1980, p. 1087; March 15, 1981, p. 7; December 1, 1985, p. 11; June 24, 1988, p. 716.

OTHER

Leon Garfield, Conn Films, Inc., 1969.*

*   *   *

GIFALDI, David 1950-

Personal: Born February 24, 1950, in Brockport, NY; son of Americo and Angie (maiden name, DiNicola) Gifaldi; married Marita Keys, November 25, 1989. *Education:* Duquesne University, B.A., 1972; Western Washington University, elementary and secondary teaching credentials. *Hobbies and other interests:* Reading, swimming, backpacking, gardening, baseball.

■ **Addresses**

Home—4305 Northeast Skidmore Street, Portland, OR 97218.

■ **Career**

Bellingham School District, Bellingham, WA, and Vancouver School District, Vancouver, WA, substitute teacher, 1980-83; Vancouver School District, teacher, 1985—. *Member:* Society of Children's Book Writers and Illustrators, National Educational Association.

DAVID GIFALDI

■ Awards, Honors

Nomination to the Mark Twain Award Master List, Missouri Association of School Librarians, 1988-89, for *One Thing for Sure;* Best Book for Reluctant Young Adult Readers, American Library Association, 1990, and Michigan Library Association Young Adult Forum Award nominee, both for *Yours till Forever;* Junior Literary Guild selection (now Junior Library Guild), for *One Thing for Sure.*

■ Writings

NOVELS

One Thing for Sure, Clarion Books, 1986.
Yours till Forever, Lippincott/HarperCollins, 1989.
Gregory, Maw, and the Mean One, Clarion Books, 1992.
Toby Scudder, Ultimate Warrior, Clarion Books, 1993.

OTHER

The Boy Who Spoke Colors (an original folktale), illustrated by Carol Greger, Houghton Mifflin, 1993.

Also contributor to periodicals, including *Cricket, Teen, Highlights for Children, Alive! for Young Teens, Children's Digest* and *Jack and Jill.*

■ Work in Progress

A book of poems for middle grade readers.

■ Sidelights

David Gifaldi grew up in a small town near Lake Ontario named Holley, New York. "Summers in Holley were filled with baseball, band concerts, carnivals, and playing Tarzan off the rope swings at various swimming holes," he told *SATA.* "Winters were for ice skating and sledding. The town had an outdoor rink, really just a scooped out pond that the firemen would fill when the cold came down from Canada. There was a little shed for changing and taking a breather after playing hockey or trying out some of the figure skating moves we kids saw on TV. The best was skating at night with the floodlights on and stars shivering in the dark overhead ... the cold sucking your breath. I recall the sound of skate blades on ice, the cries of children and adults at play, and the warm feeling inside knowing that Christmas was just a week away." It was during his childhood that the magic of books opened up for Gifaldi. In fact, he credits his third grade teacher with introducing him to literature. She read books such as *Tom Sawyer* daily after recess, and Gifaldi said he looked forward to being carried away to visit with characters from these books.

Young Felix, who has the unusual gift of speaking in colors, must use all his powers to escape when an evil king abducts him. (Illustration by Carol Greger from *The Boy Who Spoke Colors.*)

Though Gifaldi began writing poetry and keeping a journal after college, he said he did not get serious about writing until he met Richard Peck at a summer workshop, who greatly encouraged Gifaldi to write. While completing a teacher certification program at Western Washington University, Gifaldi also took a correspondence writing course. His persistence in writing stories for children led to his first sale of a short story to *Children's Digest.* He continued to write while supporting himself as a substitute teacher.

It was while substitute teaching for a fifth grade class that Gifaldi got the idea for his first novel, *One Thing for Sure.* He described this experience to *Junior Literary Guild:* "A boy got up during sharing time, and said, 'My father's in jail.' This statement was followed by an uneasy quiet. The other students didn't know how to respond. It was as if everyone was wondering what it would be like if their own father was in prison." In the novel, twelve-year old Dylan is shocked and disillusioned when his father is arrested. Since he lives in a small town, he must deal with being labeled a thief himself and defend his father at the same time he resents him. A review in *Publishers Weekly* noted "Gifaldi has great flair for figurative language" and uses it to demonstrate Dylan's perception of the world.

Reincarnation Featured in *Yours till Forever*

Gifaldi's next novel, *Yours till Forever,* was named a 1990 American Library Association Best Book for Reluctant Young Adult Readers. Rick, a high school senior, notices his two friends were born the same day his parents were killed in a car accident. As the young couple falls in love, Rick suspects they are the reincarnation of his parents and will die the same tragic death. Through the combination of Eastern religion and American high-school life "the concept of forever takes on special meaning ... in a competently sketched tale," noted Margaret A. Bush in *Horn Book.* Carolyn Cushman described the book as "an involving and intelligent tale of teenagers just starting out in life" in her *Locus* review. She also commented on the book's educational exploration of the topic of reincarnation.

Gifaldi's more recent books mimic the style of folktales and tall tales. *Gregory, Maw, and the Mean One* is a tall tale in which the Mean One goes back into the past to reclaim his lost heart, so he will not have to continue to be so mean. A review in *Publishers Weekly* stated Gifaldi's "clever writing bears a subtle though worthwhile message about the potential good in everyone."

Gifaldi said he enjoys both teaching and writing because the two go together. The teaching experiences and the students themselves give him numerous ideas to write about. "I like writing for young people because I enjoy looking at the world through the eyes of a ten or twelve or sixteen-year old. Things always seem fresher that way. Growing up is hard. But it's also a time of wonder and discovery. Writing keeps me on my toes, wondering and discovering."

In this young adult novel, Rick fears that two of his friends are reincarnations of his deceased parents and are doomed to reenact their tragic deaths. (Cover illustration by George Wilson.)

■ Works Cited

Bush, Margaret A., review of *Yours till Forever, Horn Book,* September/October, 1989, p. 627.

Cushman, Carolyn, review of *Yours till Forever, Locus,* July, 1989, p. 50.

Review of *Gregory, Maw, and the Mean One, Publishers Weekly,* August 3, 1992, p. 72.

Review of *One Thing for Sure, Junior Literary Guild,* October, 1986.

Review of *One Thing for Sure, Publishers Weekly,* August 22, 1986, p. 99.

■ For More Information See

PERIODICALS

School Library Journal, October, 1993, p. 124.

GIRZONE, Joseph F(rancis) 1930-

■ Personal

Born May 15, 1930, in Albany, NY; son of Peter Joseph (a meat cutter) and Margaret Rita (a homemaker; maiden name, Campbell) Girzone. *Education:* St. Bonaventure University, B.A., 1951; received theology degree from Catholic University of America, 1955; graduate study at Fordham University. *Politics:* Independent. *Religion:* Roman Catholic. *Hobbies and other interests:* Painting, gardening.

■ Addresses

Home—39 St. John St., Amsterdam, NY 12010. *Office*—8 Leesome Ln., Altamont, NY 12009. *Agent*—Peter Ginsberg, Curtis Brown, Ltd., 10 Astor Pl., New York, NY 10003.

■ Career

Entered Carmelite Order, 1948; ordained Catholic priest, 1955; high school teacher in New York and Pennsylvania, 1955-64; St. Albert's Seminary, Middletown, NY, faculty member, 1960-61; pastor at churches in New York, 1964-74; Our Lady of Mt. Carmel Church, Amsterdam, NY, pastor, 1974-81; writer, 1981—. Worked as computer salesperson for Olivetti Corporation. Director of Dominican Third Order of Religious Lay People, 1964-76; member of New York State Bishops' Advisory Commission for Criminal Justice, beginning in 1973; chair of Schenectady County, NY, Human Rights Commission, 1973-74; vice-chair of Title III advisory board for New York State Office of Aging, 1974-76; member of Roman Catholic Diocesan Peace and Justice Commission, beginning in 1976; member of board of directors of Schenectady Joint Commission of Christians and Jews; president of Amsterdam Community Concerts. Co-owner of senior citizens newspaper *Golden Age Sentinel.* Public speaker and retreat organizer.

■ Awards, Honors

Liberty Bell Award, American Bar Association, 1974; Citizen of the Age of Enlightenment Award, Society for Creative Intelligence, 1976.

■ Writings

NOVELS

Kara, the Lonely Falcon, Vantage, 1977.
Gloria: Diary of a Teenage Girl, Richelieu Court, 1982.
Joshua, Richelieu Court, 1983, Macmillan, 1986.
Joshua and the Children, Macmillan, 1988.
The Shepherd, Macmillan, 1990.
Joshua in the Holy Land, Macmillan, 1992.

NONFICTION

Who Will Teach Me?, Richelieu Court, 1982.

■ Work in Progress

Joshua in the City, The Life of Christ, and *Never Alone: A Personal Way to God.*

■ Sidelights

Joseph Girzone was ordained a Carmelite Monk in 1955. When a serious illness forced him to retreat from his parish work in 1981, he turned to writing. He had already written and published an allegory, *Kara, The Lonely Falcon,* in 1977. Since he had refused to accept a pension before his official retirement age, Girzone made arrangements with his diocese to support himself through writing and lecturing.

While traveling the country giving lectures, Girzone developed the idea for *Joshua,* a story based on what Girzone imagined would happen if Jesus Christ were to return to present-day Earth. "I am shocked by how few Christians, even clergy, know Jesus, and I'm dismayed by the confusion among Christians over the message of Jesus," Girzone told *SATA.* "I decided, after years of working in parishes and studying the scriptures, to draw a portrait of Jesus, faithful to the gospels, that people could use in putting the message of Jesus into proper focus in their lives."

In the novel *Joshua,* a simple woodcarver moves to a small cabin on the edge of the fictional town of Auburn, NY. "He was just a healthy person who had a supremely

JOSEPH F. GIRZONE

well-balanced view of life and whose relationship with God was well integrated into the fabric of his personality," Girzone wrote. "To Joshua, God was like the air he breathed." Joshua mesmerizes the town with his kind and quiet manner. He also causes many people to wonder about him and the seeming miracles they have heard he has performed.

Girzone not only creates a modern-day Jesus, but uses Joshua's philosophy to explain where religion today deviates from Christ's teachings. When asked to express his thoughts on God and religion, Joshua complies: "Over the centuries religious leaders have twisted the law into a code that is irrelevant to man's nature and thereby restricts the natural freedom people should enjoy. This is what makes religion seem like a burden to people rather than something they should find joy and comfort in."

After finishing the novel, Girzone's funds were getting low and he was unable to find an interested publisher. Looking into self-publishing, he learned the cost would be drastically reduced if the manuscript was put onto computer disk. He convinced the Olivetti Corporation to hire him as a computer dealer, allowing him to acquire both the skills and resources to produce his book electronically. By 1983 his novel was self-published and he had also become one of the firm's top salesmen.

Solo Efforts Reap Publishing Success

Girzone's next obstacle was in marketing *Joshua.* Since book stores were reluctant to stock self-published titles, many of his sales were to leaders of religious retreats. The demand grew as word-of-mouth recommendations spread. He finally persuaded Gary Mele, a Waldenbooks district sales manager, to read *Joshua.* Mele was moved and placed several copies in his district's stores; they immediately sold, and more were distributed. As the book grew from a regional into a national best-seller, solely through word-of-mouth advertising, it attracted the attention of Collier, a Macmillan subsidiary. Collier published *Joshua* in 1987 as a paperback, and more than half a million copies have been sold since.

Girzone commented to William Griffin in an interview for *Publishers Weekly* on his purpose in writing: "It seems to me almost as if God wanted *Joshua* to be written. To get it done, He had to kick me out of the mainstream of the Church, keep me away from ecclesiastical structure, and give me the freedom to do it."

Having tackled the notion of what would happen to Jesus Christ if he were to return to modern times, teaching the things he originally taught, Girzone wrote a sequel, *Joshua and the Children,* which addresses the violence and religious conflicts enacted in the name of God. In this second novel, Joshua returns again, this time to a community torn apart by political turmoil. Though many readers have drawn similarities between the setting of the book and Northern Ireland, the location could be anywhere children are caught in the midst of violence and turmoil.

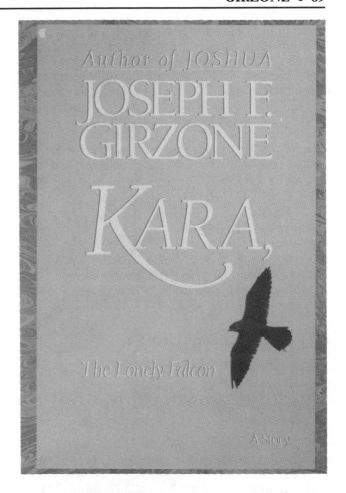

In Girzone's first novel, Kara, a falcon who gives up killing, becomes an example of those who are rewarded for putting others first. (Cover photo by Marty Stouffer/Animals Animals.)

Realizing the adults in the village are too emotionally involved in the destructive conflict, Joshua befriends the children. He "immediately captures the hearts of the children, enchanting them with gentle stories," according a reviewer for *Publishers Weekly.* Through his message of peace, Joshua shows the children how to trust and love each other and to face their fears. Though Joshua is killed in the end, his legacy flourishes in the children, who are able to bring about peace in their country once more.

The third book in the series is *The Shepherd.* In this story, Joshua first appears in a dream of a newly anointed bishop, David Campbell. Moved by the dream and an actual meeting with Joshua, Campbell makes drastic changes in how the message of Jesus is dispersed—changes which anger his fellow clergymen. Through Campbell's spiritual campaign, Girzone again voices the philosophy he began in *Joshua:* that structured religion has somehow moved away from what God intended, becoming a network of laws and rules that give religious leaders the power to dominate their followers.

Joshua in the Holy Land continues the saga of the modern messiah. In this novel Joshua wanders the desert in the Middle East, entering into the good graces of a prominent sheik when he finds a lost lamb and cures a sick little girl. Joshua's friendship with the sheik opens the door for his true mission: to bring peace to this turbulent area of the world by uniting Jews, Arabs and Christians as the "Children of Peace." The Children of Peace movement continues to grow until governments topple and the foundation for lasting peace is established. Though his mission is accomplished, and Joshua has disappeared from the Middle East, the story of Joshua does not stop here; Girzone is currently penning *Joshua in South America.*

■ Works Cited

Girzone, Joseph, *Joshua,* Collier, 1987.
Griffin, William, interview with Joseph Girzone, *Publishers Weekly,* October 6, 1989.
Publishers Weekly, June 23, 1989, p. 48.

■ For More Information See

BOOKS

Bestsellers 90, Issue 1, Gale, 1990, pp. 29-31.
Contemporary Authors, Volume 130, Gale, pp. 160-161.

PERIODICALS

Booklist, October 1, 1989, p. 261; September 15, 1990, p. 102.
Kirkus Reviews, July 1, 1987, p. 948; June 15, 1989, p. 858; September 15, 1990, p. 1271; July 15, 1992, p. 868.
Library Journal, August, 1989, p. 163; October 15, 1989, p. 50; November 1, 1990, p. 124; November 1, 1991, p. 67; September 15, 1992, p. 111.
Publishers Weekly, August 3, 1990, p. 50; August 31, 1990, p. 49; September 27, 1991, p. 56; August 10, 1992, p. 50.
Voice Literary Supplement, July, 1990, p. 15.
Voice of Youth Advocates, August, 1991, p. 170.
WB, November/December, 1989.

—Sketch by Lisa A. Wroble

*   *   *

GLASSMAN, Bruce 1961-

■ Personal

Born September 15, 1961, in San Francisco, CA; son of Richard (a publisher) and Sonja (a homemaker) Glassman; married Tracy Hughes (a clinical social worker), June 23, 1985. *Education:* Wesleyan University, B.A.

■ Addresses

Office—Blackbirch Press, 1 Bradley Rd., Woodbridge, CT 06525.

■ Career

Blackbirch Press, Inc., Woodbridge, CT, editorial director, 1985—.

■ Writings

YOUNG ADULT FICTION

The Marathon Race Mystery, illustrated by Jackie Rogers, Troll, 1985.

NONFICTION

The Crash of '29 and the New Deal, Silver Burdett, 1986.
Everything You Need to Know about Step-Families, Rosen Publishing, 1988.
Everything You Need to Know about Growing up Male, Rosen Publishing, 1991.
New York: Gateway to the New World, Blackbirch Press, 1991.

BIOGRAPHY

J. Paul Getty: Oil Billionaire, edited by Nancy Furstinger, Silver Burdett, 1989.
Mikhail Baryshnikov, Silver Burdett, 1990.
Arthur Miller, Silver Burdett, 1990.
Wilma Mankiller: Chief of the Cherokee Nation, Blackbirch Press, 1992.

■ Work in Progress

A full length romantic comedy for the theater; television screenplays for HBO.

■ Sidelights

Bruce Glassman concentrates his creative efforts on nonfiction for children. His nonfiction debut was a book for Silver Burdett's "Turning Points in American History" series entitled *The Crash of '29 and the New Deal,* which discusses the stock market crash and the Great Depression that followed it. According to a reviewer in *Booklist:* "Glassman does a good job of crisply explaining how these disasters occurred and the impact they had on American society, beginning with the panic on Wall Street in October, 1929."

Glassman continues to write nonfiction, particularly biographies of influential historical figures. His 1992 book *Wilma Mankiller: Chief of the Cherokee Nation* describes not only the life of Mankiller, but introduces some of the events and people important to the Cherokee at this time: Sequoyah, the Cherokee alphabet, and the Trail of Tears. "Extensive coverage is given to Mankiller's accomplishments and struggles for the Cherokee," writes Lisa Mitten in the *School Library Journal,* "but Glassman also discusses the chief's efforts to counter Cherokee and Indian stereotypes in the United States."

Glassman has also written a book about New York and several titles in Rosen Publishing's "Need to Know" series. The first, *Everything You Need to Know about Step-Families* is written in a conversational style and is designed to be appealing to even the most reluctant readers. Says Karen K. Radtke in *School Library Journal:* "Glassman is very supportive of readers and tries to explain in real terms how everyone's feelings are valid."

In *Everything You Need to Know about Growing up Male,* Glassman again uses a conversational tone to present both the facts and feelings connected to puberty. "Glassman's text for boys is a straightforward, clearly written summary," observes Stephanie Zvirin in *Booklist.* "Aimed at reluctant readers, it is easy to read and filled with teen-appealing photographs and helpful diagrams."

■ Works Cited

Booklist, August, 1986, p. 1687.
Mitten, Lisa, review of *Wilma Mankiller: Chief of the Cherokee Nation, School Library Journal,* April, 1992, p. 132.
Radtke, Karen K., review of *Everything You Need to Know about Step-Families, School Library Journal,* April, 1989, p. 112.
Zvirin, Stephanie, review of *Everything You Need to Know about Growing up Male, Booklist,* October 15, 1991, p. 426.

■ For More Information See

PERIODICALS

Booklist, January 1, 1990, p. 908; September 15, 1990, p. 154; July, 1991, p. 2044.
Bulletin of the Center for Children's Books, November, 1986.
School Library Journal, December, 1986, p. 116; March, 1990, p. 243; August, 1991, p. 202.
Voice of Youth Advocates, April, 1991, p. 56; December, 1991, p. 336.

*   *   *

GOULD, Marilyn 1928-

■ Personal

Born February 12, 1928, in Cleveland, OH; daughter of Seymour Irving (an executive) and Edith (Eisner) Amster; married Paul Irving Gould (in real estate and building management), January 29, 1950; children: Sheri Ellen Sindell, Melanie Jane Adams, George Marshall. *Education:* University of California at Los Angeles, Associate of Arts, 1948; attended Columbia University, summer, 1948; University of Southern California, B.S., 1950; California State University, teaching credential, 1956. *Hobbies and other interests:* Tennis, skiing, travel.

■ Addresses

Home—726 Bison Avenue, Newport Beach, CA 92260.
Office—407 East Pico Boulevard, Los Angeles, CA

MARILYN GOULD

90015. *Agent*—Rhodes Literary Agency, 140 West End Ave., New York, NY 10023.

■ Career

Los Angeles City Schools, Los Angeles, CA, teacher, 1965-75; Allied Crafts Building, Los Angeles, in building management, 1977-78; writer. Lectures in classrooms on writing. Newport Harbor Art Museum docent. *Member:* PEN, Society of Children's Book Writers and Illustrators, Southern California Conference on Literature for Children and Young People, Southern California Children's Booksellers Association, Orange County Philharmonic Society.

■ Writings

NONFICTION

(With son, George Gould) *Skateboards, Scooterboards, and Seatboards You Can Make,* illustrated by Loring Eutemey, photographs by Lou Jacobs, Jr., Lothrop, 1977.
Playground Sports: A Book of Ball Games, illustrated by Rita Floden Leydon, photographs by Jacobs, Lothrop, 1978.
Skateboarding, Capstone Press, Inc., 1991.

NOVELS

Golden Daffodils, Allied Crafts Press, 1982.
The Twelfth of June, Allied Crafts Press, 1986.
Graffiti Wipeout, Allied Crafts Press, 1992.
Friends True and Periwinkle Blue, Avon Books, 1992.

OTHER

Contributor to *Cars, Cars, Cars,* Random House, 1977. Contributor to periodicals, including *Highlights for Children, Bike World, Cricket,* and *Family Circle.*

■ Work in Progress

An untitled novel.

■ Sidelights

As a girl growing up in Shaker Heights, Ohio, Marilyn Gould had a friend who had cerebral palsy. "Though she was quite disabled, she was a terrific gal and had a great influence on me," Gould told *SATA.* The author ultimately lost touch with her friend, and it would be years before either of them knew how deep an influence it was.

When Gould started college, she chose occupational therapy as her major. She wanted to work with children who had cerebral palsy. She later changed her major and became an educator while raising a family with her husband, Paul. Her writing career actually started in her own classroom, where Gould found it easier to create her own teaching material. Eventually, she collaborated on a how-to book on skateboarding, *Skateboards, Scoot-*

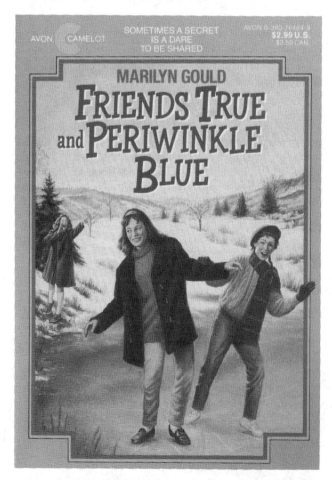

Three unlikely friends are drawn closer together when they each share a difficult secret in this novel by Gould.

erboards, and Seatboards You Can Make, with her son, George.

That book was published by Lothrop in 1977 and again, in Spanish, by Ediciones Altea in 1980. Gould contributed to *Cars, Cars, Cars,* a 1977 compilation published by Random House, writing a section about "bugmobiles." After that, there was another how-to book. Then a television producer asked Gould for a script dealing with a child who had overcome a difficulty. "I thought about a friend I knew in third grade, someone I knew and loved very much," Gould remembered. She named her character Janis, after her long-lost friend. The resulting book, *Golden Daffodils,* is the story of a fifth grader who must make the transition from a special school to the public school in her neighborhood. Her challenges include harder schoolwork and dealing with children who don't always understand her facial tics and occasional seizures.

"It's not [my friend's] story, but the character, the sense of humor and honesty is the same," Gould said. The author was delighted to be reacquainted with the original Janis after the first book was published. In fact, it turned out that her friend was very knowledgeable about children's literature and an expert on the history of the Shakers as well. "She helped me with the editing of the second book about Janis, *The Twelfth of June,*" Gould said. "And I used some of her information on Shaker history for my most recent novel, *Friends True and Periwinkle Blue.*"

That book, not surprisingly, is informed by Gould's childhood in Shaker Heights. Though she continued her correspondence with Janis, Gould turned to new projects—another how-to book, *Skateboarding,* and her third novel, *Graffiti Wipeout.* The novel follows two teens as they scour Los Angeles' garment district to catch a graffiti tagger.

That novel led to her current work in progress. It's an untitled piece about a young boy, 13-year-old Xavier, who travels from his Tijuana home, where he cared for his grandmother, to live with his housekeeper mother in California. The story weaves elements of graffiti, border crossing, homing pigeons, and Mexican history and folklore into a boy's search for his true identity in a new country. The author has kept busy doing extensive research into all those areas. Gould isn't sure when this book will be published, because, she said, "I'm an awfully slow writer." Writing for children seems natural to this former teacher, Gould once told *SATA.* "I remember how I felt as a child and I remember the important part books played in my life," she said. "I don't feel much different, now that I've grown up."

■ Works Cited

Gould, Marilyn, telephone interview with Peg McNichol for *Something about the Author,* conducted August 4, 1993.

■ For More Information See

PERIODICALS

Booklist, June 15, 1977, p. 1575; April 1, 1979, p. 1223; March 15, 1983, p. 969.
Kirkus Reviews, April 15, 1977, p. 430; January 15, 1979, p. 68.
Los Angeles Times Book Review, November 9, 1986, p. 13.
Publishers Weekly, December 12, 1986, p. 55.
School Library Journal, September, 1977, p. 128; March, 1979, p. 139; April, 1983, p. 114; November 13, 1986, p. 88.
Small Press, summer, 1992, p.61.
Voice of Youth Advocates, December, 1986, p. 216.

*   *   *

GREENE, Jacqueline Dembar 1946-

■ Personal

Born May 21, 1946, in Hartford, CT; married Malcolm R. Greene (an optometrist), in 1967; children: Matthew, Kenneth. *Education:* University of Connecticut, B.A. (with honors), 1967; Central Missouri University, M.A. (with special distinction), 1970. *Hobbies and other interests:* Gardening, cross-country skiing, travel (has traveled extensively in the American Southwest, Mexico, and Europe), photography.

■ Addresses

Home and office—21 Sunnyside Ave., Wellesley, MA 02181. *Agent*—Ginger Knowlton, Curtis Brown Ltd., 10 Astor Place, New York, NY 10003.

■ Career

French teacher in and near Boston, MA, 1967-71; worked variously as reporter, columnist, and feature writer for newspapers, including *Middlesex News,* Framingham, MA, and *Wellesley Townsman,* Wellesley, MA, 1971-80; writer, 1980—. *Member:* Pi Delta Phi, Kappa Delta Pi.

■ Awards, Honors

Pick of the List citation, *American Bookseller,* 1984, for *The Leveller;* National Jewish Book Award finalist, 1984, for *Butchers and Bakers, Rabbis and Kings;* Sydney Taylor Honor Book citation, Association of Jewish Libraries, and Book for the Teen Age citation, New York Public Libraries, both 1988, for *Out of Many Waters.*

■ Writings

A Classroom Hanukah, illustrations by Debra G. Butler, Pascal Publishers, 1980.
The Hanukah Tooth, illustrations by Pauline A. Ouellet, Pascal Publishers, 1981.

JACQUELINE DEMBAR GREENE

Butchers and Bakers, Rabbis and Kings, Kar-Ben Copies, 1984.
The Leveller, Walker & Co., 1984.
Nathan's Hanukkah Bargain, illustrations by Steffi Karen Rubin, Kar-Ben Copies, 1986.
Out of Many Waters, Walker & Co., 1988.
The Maya, edited by Iris Rosoff, F. Watts, 1992.
What His Father Did, illustrations by John O'Brien, Houghton, 1992.
The Chippewa, edited by Russell Primm, F. Watts, 1993.
One Foot Ashore, Walker & Co., 1994.
Manabozho's Gifts, Houghton, 1994.

Contributor to periodicals, including *Boston Globe, Day Care, Highlights for Children, Lollipops, Ladybugs and Lucky Stars, Nitty Gritty City, Parenting, Parents' Choice, Small Talk,* and *Wellesley.*

■ Work in Progress

The Abenaki, "a nonfiction book about a native American group that lives in Maine and Vermont."

■ Sidelights

Jacqueline Dembar Greene told *SATA:* "I have been interested in writing for young people since a college course in children's literature initiated me to the power and depth of this genre. All through my journalism career, my former professor continued to encourage me to write for children. With the publication of my first book, I left the bustle of the news office for the quiet of my own imagination. I have continued to use the research skills from my former career to find the facts and history that I feel make a story relevant and alive.

"I always remember that we are never very far from childhood. All the things we have done, the friends we have made, the embarrassments and successes we felt, are part of us and make us the people we are. When I write a book, it is not just written with children in mind. It reflects my feelings and should strike a responsive chord in every reader, regardless of age. I hope my characters speak to everyone, expressing the ageless and human emotions we all share, and making readers feel as if they have met someone they never knew before, and will remember for a long time."

Greene's third book for children, *Butchers and Bakers, Rabbis and Kings,* tells of the seemingly all-powerful King Alfonso the Warrior, who strides into Tudela, Spain, in 1114 thinking he needs no one. Concerned about their safety in the new kingdom, the Jews of the city devise a plan to convince the king that without his subjects, he is just an ordinary man.

Greene's book *The Leveller* was chosen a Pick of the List by the *American Bookseller* in 1984. The protagonist, Tom Cook, was a real person who was shunned by townsfolk in eighteenth-century Massachusetts because they thought he was in league with the devil. Using the people's superstitions to avoid capture, Tom set out to secretly "level" the fortunes of the poor farmers with those who had an abundance of food and wealthy, all the while trying to outwit the devil, who coveted his soul.

Greene's historical novel *Out of Many Waters* relates the fictional saga of two sisters who escape from a monastery in Brazil in 1654 in search of their parents. Forced to stow away on a ship without her sister, twelve-year-old Isobel is rescued by a small group of Jewish colonists who founded the first Jewish settlement in America. Susan Levine, writing for the *Voice of Youth Advocates,* notes that Greene's characterization of Isobel helps the reader "sympathize with her and be interested in her success." The critic adds, "It is a good story with a memorable character and an easy way to learn a little history." Storms, pirates, kidnapping, first love, landing in New Amsterdam, and Isobel's hopes of finding her family move the plot along. Eli N. Evans in the *New York Times Book Review* writes, "Greene has done a relatively smooth job of weaving history, drama and narrative into an arresting story."

One of Greene's picture books, *What His Father Did,* is a humorous story of the trickster Hershel, who figures prominently in Jewish folklore. Traveling on a long journey with little money, Herschel stops at an isolated inn and tricks an innkeeper into giving him supper by vaguely threatening to "do what his father did" if he is

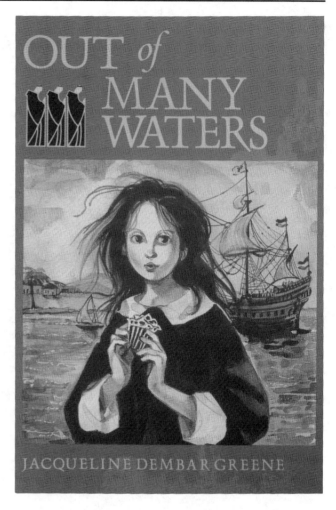

Greene researched the days of the Portuguese Inquisition in order to accurately portray her story of two children kidnapped from their homes and sent to work as slaves in Brazil. (Cover illustration by Norma Welliver.)

left hungry. The frightened innkeeper gathers food from nearby merchants, imagining all manner of horrible things the father could have done, and gets a surprise when Herschel reveals what his father really did. A *Kirkus Reviews* writer noted that Greene's writing is "lively and economical, fine for sharing aloud."

■ Works Cited

Evans, Eli, N., "Children's Books," *New York Times Book Review,* March 19, 1989, p. 24.

Review of *The Leveller* in *Horn Book,* August, 1984, p. 474.

Levine, Susan, review of *Out of Many Waters* in *Voice of Youth Advocates,* December, 1988, p. 238.

Review of *What His Father Did* in *Kirkus Reviews,* February 1, 1992, p. 183.

■ For More Information See

PERIODICALS

Booklist, July, 1984; February 1, 1987, p. 843; June 15, 1992, pp. 1829-30.

Boston Globe, July 8, 1984.
Bulletin of the Center for Children's Books, April, 1984,
    p. 146; January, 1989, p. 121.
Horn Book, May/June, 1992.
Kirkus Reviews, August 15, 1988, pp. 1240-41.
Publishers Weekly, February 10, 1992.
School Library Journal, April, 1984, pp. 114-15; No-
    vember, 1984, p. 108; October, 1988, p. 144;
    August, 1992, pp. 151-52, 164.
Voice of Youth Advocates, August, 1992, p. 187.

*   *   *

GREENSPUN, Adele Aron 1938-
(Adele Aron Schwarz)

■ Personal

Born December 22, 1938, in Philadelphia, PA; daughter of Samuel and Eva (maiden name Stern) Aron; married Steven Schwarz (divorced); married Bertram Greenspun (physician), January 18, 1987; children: (first marriage) Erica, Joanie. *Education:* Attended University of Arts, International Center for Photography, The New School, and Wilkes College; University of Pennsylvania, B.S., 1960.

■ Addresses

Home and Office—1900 Rittenhouse Square #9, Philadelphia, PA 19103. *Agent*—Regina Ryan, 251 Central Park West, New York, NY 10024.

■ Career

Freelance and portrait photographer. Financial account executive, Fuhrman-Matt Securities Inc. *Exhibitions:* Under the Northeastern Pennsylvania Art Alliance photographs toured twelve towns, colleges and art museums, 1979-81; The Art Gallery, College Miseracordia, Dallas, PA, 1981; The Art Institute, Philadelphia, PA, 1990; American Society of Media Photographers and University of the Arts, both 1992-93. *Member:* Authors Guild, American Association of Media Photographers, Society of Children's Book Writers and Illustrators.

■ Awards, Honors

Wilkes College poetry prize, 1977; Silver Award for the best book, Art Directors Club, 1992; Philadelphia Children's Reading Round Tablebook of the Month Selection, Free Library of Philadelphia, 1992.

■ Writings

(And photographer) *Daddies,* Philomel Books, 1992.

Also contributor of fiction and nonfiction to books, including *Encounter with Family Realities,* West Publishing, 1977, and *Stories for Free Children,* McGraw, 1985. Contributor of photographs to books including *Ten Thousand Eyes: ASMP's Celebration of the 150th*

ADELE ARON GREENSPUN

Anniversary of Photography, 1991, and *Philadelphia Images,* University of the Art Press, 1990. Contributor of fiction and nonfiction to periodicals, including *Ladies Home Journal, McCall's,* and *Ms.* Contributor of photographs to periodicals, including *Parents, U.S. News and World Report, Moment,* and *Self.* Contributor to periodicals under the name Adele Aron Schwarz ending 1991.

■ Work in Progress

Is My Family Normal?, includes interviews and photographs, *The Grandmas & the Grandpas, Baby & Bunny, Ariel & Emily, What Color Is the Sky, Just Like Everything Else, Old Rink Rank.*

■ Sidelights

When Adele Aron Greenspun was nine years old, her father gave her a Kodak Brownie Box camera, and she took pictures of all her family and friends. When Greenspun was eleven, her father, to whom she was devoted, died. Greenspun was on her way to summer camp the day he died, and her mother did not tell her. She spent the summer writing letters to her father, and crafting a beautiful blue box she planned to give him at summer's end.

More than 50 black and white photographs of fathers with children under the age of 12 capture what Greenspun in a publicity release has called "emotional, dramatic, loving and joyous moments" of daddies and their sons and daughters sharing everyday occasions such as a visit to the zoo, a piano lesson, and the disappointment of a lost baseball game. She traveled to places as far away as St. Croix and as nearby as the house next door in Philadelphia, and took over 10,000 photographs before the book was done.

Although she is a practicing financial consultant, as well as a portrait photographer who specializes in families, children and teenagers, Greenspun elaborates in the publicity release that all along "the voice inside me to do a book never was quieted.... By the end of 1988 ... the book *Daddies* took hold as an idea and catapulted me throughout the United States to witness and document children and their fathers."

"The book has settled things for me in a lot of ways," Greenspun told Ruth Rovner of the *Jewish Times*. "The blue box I could never give to my own father I'm finally giving to my readers and their fathers."

■ Works Cited

Greenspun, Adele, publicity packet from Putnam and Grosset.
Rovner, Ruth, "Greenspun No Longer Finds Father's Day Depressing," *Jewish Times,* June 18, 1992.

*   *   *

GURNEY, James 1958-

■ Personal

Born June 14, 1958; son of Robert Denison (an engineer) and Joanna (Mackay) Gurney; married Jeanette Lendino (an artist), April 24, 1983; children: Daniel, Franklin. *Education:* University of California, Berkeley, B.A., 1979; attended Art Center College of Design, 1980.

■ Career

Writer and illustrator. Ralph Bakshi Productions, Burbank, CA, animation background artist, 1981; National Geographic Society, Washington, DC, historical and archaeological illustrator, 1983-90; freelance illustrator for paperback science fiction and fantasy books, 1982-91. *Member:* Association of Science Fiction Artists, Authors Guild, Phi Beta Kappa.

■ Awards, Honors

Chesley Award, Association of Science Fiction and Fantasy Artists, 1991, 1992; Abby Award nomination, World Science Fiction Convention, 1992, for *Dinotopia;* Hugo Award for best original artwork, World Science Fiction Convention, 1993, for *Dinotopia;* Judges' Art Award, World Science Fiction Convention, 1993, for

painting *Garden of Hope;* Locus Award, *Locus* magazine, 1993.

■ Writings

(With Thomas Kinkade) *The Artist's Guide to Sketching,* Watson-Guptill Publications, 1982.
(And illustrator) *Dinotopia,* Turner Publishing, 1992.

■ Work in Progress

Writing a sequel to *Dinotopia,* publication expected in 1995.

■ Sidelights

Set in 1862, James Gurney's book *Dinotopia* is the tale of Arthur Denison and his young son, Will, who are saved by dolphins from being shipwrecked. The dolphins bring them to the island of Dinotopia, where dinosaurs, mammoths, and other prehistoric creatures have developed their own civilization, language, and culture. On Dinotopia, human beings—all shipwreck survivors like Arthur and Will Denison—and dinosaurs peacefully co-exist. With a dinosaur named Bix as their guide, Arthur and Will explore the island. The book has been a popular success. Montgomery Ward has begun selling *Dinotopia* memorabilia, including mugs and stuffed toys. A calendar and a pop-up book will also be published, and Gurney has been approached by film studios about live-action version of the book.

The inspiration for *Dinotopia* came from two of Gurney's paintings, *Dinosaur Parade* and *Waterfall City.* He drew a map of Dinotopia, and then began to develop characters and a story line. Gurney wanted both the story and the artwork to be as realistic as possible. He read nineteenth-century travel journals, studied current scientific literature about dinosaurs, traveled to the Smithsonian, and consulted such noted paleontologists as Michael Brett-Surman.

Creating the artwork was an equally painstaking endeavor. "The process for doing the paintings is very much like doing a frame for a big-budget movie," Gurney told *Something about the Author.* He built models of dinosaurs and then brought them outside, onto the lawn of his Hudson Valley home. His wife Jeanette—who is also an artist—designed period costumes. Neighborhood children then put on the costumes and acted out scenes from the book. Sometimes, Gurney's own two sons, Daniel and Franklin, would join them on the lawn. "They're the cheapest models," he joked. Gurney photographed the scenes, and then used the photographs as the basis for his paintings. "I ... wanted the pictures to dominate each page spread," he told *SATA.* "I really wanted it to hinge on all the visuals."

Critics have reacted favorably to *Dinotopia.* Cathryn A. Camper wrote in the *School Library Journal,* "Younger readers ... will be enticed by the dramatic, full-color illustrations, which include both panoramic sweeps of

After being shipwrecked, a boy and his father take refuge on a strange island where dinosaurs and other prehistoric creatures live in harmony with human beings. (Illustration from *Dinotopia,* written and illustrated by James Gurney.)

the utopian cities and detailed sketches of Dinotopian contraptions." A reviewer for *Kirkus Reviews* called the book "a sweet, visually attractive utopian fantasy" and added, "some adults—and children—will love it dearly."

"We are in the midst of a major renaissance of new thinking about dinosaurs," Gurney believes. He explains that paleontologists (scientists who study prehistoric life) have discovered new evidence that dinosaurs were "birdlike and colorful, not dumb." In an interview with *People* magazine, Gurney stated, "We all grew up with the view of the sluggish monster of the swamp, the predators tearing each other limb from limb. But in the last twenty years, we found out dinosaurs were warm-blooded, nimble, and active. Some were caring parents who looked after their young."

The reaction to *Dinotopia* has pleased Gurney. "I've been absolutely delighted ... as a new author to have this incredible response," Gurney told *SATA*. He has already begun work on a sequel. "I don't think of

[Dinotopia] as a fantasy world to escape to, but rather as a real world to participate in," Gurney says. "I try to make each painting so real that you feel you can step through the frame and disappear into it.

"I don't see myself as having created Dinotopia, because it feels like it existed before I discovered it. I'm just an explorer. Every morning I put on my safari hat, head upstairs to the studio, and take a little adventure. I straddle two worlds. One foot is squarely in my little village in the Hudson Valley. The other is in Dinotopia."

■ Works Cited

Camper, Cathryn A., review of *Dinotopia, School Library Journal,* December, 1992.

Chin, Paula, and Tony Kahn, "Prehistoric Pals: In James Gurney's New Illustrated Fantasy, Dinosaurs Are Man's Best Friends," *People,* December 14, 1992.

Review of *Dinotopia, Kirkus Reviews,* July 15, 1992.

H

HAEFFELE, Deborah 1954-

■ Personal

Born June 22, 1954, in Gary, Indiana; daughter of Charles F. (a manager) and Bette J. (a homemaker) Wunschel; married Steven Haeffele (a senior manager), August 10, 1974; children: Christiane, Cathryn. *Education:* Attended University of Georgia, 1970-72; University of North Carolina, B.A., 1974; North Carolina State University, M.Des., 1987. *Religion:* Episcopal. *Hobbies and other interests:* Playing the cello, singing, gardening.

■ Addresses

Home and Office—920 Northwoods Dr., Cary, NC 27513. *Agent*—Cornell & McCarthy, 2-D Cross Highway, Westport, CT 06880.

■ Career

University of North Carolina Alumni Publications, Chapel Hill, NC, assistant editor and advertising manager, 1974-75; Wills, Pennington, and Associates, Raleigh, NC, account executive and writer, 1975-79; Deborah Haeffele Communications, Cary, NC, president, 1979-82; Sand Communications, Inc., Cary, NC, president, 1983—.

EXHIBITIONS: North Carolina Museum of Art, Raleigh, NC, exhibition of original paintings for *The Ring and the Window Seat,* 1990, and *Harvest Song,* 1991; Artspace, Raleigh, NC, exhibition of original paintings for *The Ring and the Window Seat,* 1990; Jill Flink's Gallery, exhibition of original paintings for *Harvest Song,* 1991; Janice Charach Epstein Museum, Bloomfield Hills, MI, 1992; Page-Walker Arts Center, Cary, NC, exhibition of original paintings for *Island Child,* 1992; Elizabeth Stone Gallery, Birmingham, MI, exhibition of original paintings for *Island Child,* 1992. *Member:* North Carolina Association of Designers and Illustrators (vice president, 1989-90).

■ Awards, Honors

Merit award from Society of Illustrators, 1986; *Harvest Song* was included on the *Smithsonian* magazine list of books and the National Booksellers list of books, both 1991, and on the Bank Street College Children's Book List, 1992.

■ Illustrator

CHILDREN'S BOOKS

Amy Hest, *The Ring and the Window Seat,* Scholastic, 1990.
Ron Hirschi, *Harvest Song,* Cobblehill Books, 1991.
Lisa Wallis, *Island Child,* Lodestar, 1992.
Joanne Ryder, *The Goodbye Walk,* Lodestar, 1993.
Janice Johnson, *Rosamond,* Simon & Schuster, 1994.

DEBORAH HAEFFELE

Much of Haeffele's art is modeled after her own family members, as is seen in her illustrations for Ron Hirschi's book *Harvest Song*.

OTHER

Work included in *Illustrators 29,* Madison Square Press, 1988.

■ Sidelights

Deborah Haeffele told *SATA:* "Before I could read, I remember telling myself stories by drawing them. My father would bring home small pads of paper from work, and I would fill them in with stories, in picture form, of course. There is something provocative about telling stories with pictures. Even now, when I get a wonderful magazine or a pick up another's picture book, I always look at the pictures first. Maybe that maxim, 'you can't tell a book by its cover,' is true some of the time, but not always. In picture books, the illustrations become more of the story than the story itself. When I illustrate a book, I always add to the story: characters, animals, and elements in the setting which go well beyond the bare bones story line.

"When I create a character for a story, I begin to *know* them. I imagine them at off hours, dream about their personalities. They become a part of my life. Which, of course, makes it a mixed blessing to finish a book. I feel relieved at having completed sixteen to twenty large drawings (my drawings are much larger than they appear printed), but I also feel a bit sad, a little empty at

having completed the book, especially one that I love. *Island Child* was such a book. Starting work on paintings for another story helps relieve the sadness.

"My current project, *Rosamond,* begins during the reign of King Henry II of England and continues forward to contemporary times. I have had to research costumes and settings amongst castles and walled gardens—elements that I have never drawn before. (To draw something is to know it.) This book is truly an adventure. I've borrowed about twenty costumes from the Raleigh Little Theatre, and my family and friends will be helping me by modeling for the book. I will take photos of them that will help me see what I need to see to create the drawings.

"My family has been a part of every book so far, in some capacity. In *Island Child,* both my daughters were in the book as characters, with my youngest as the main character. I think that's partly why I love *Island Child* so much, maybe even more than the other books.

"I have several manuscripts and story ideas. My next goal is to write books in addition to illustrating them, as well as continuing my portraiture and fine arts work. I may also teach college-level illustration.

"I have worked as a writer, been trained in marketing and psychology, learned about printing, photography, typography, and design. I use all of this in illustrating picture books—and I still keep learning more everyday. Picture book illustrating pushes you to use all your resources and sharpens your imagination."

*   *   *

HALL, Cameron
See del REY, Lester

*   *   *

HANNELE, Pirkko
See VAINIO, Pirkko

*   *   *

HEAGY, William D. 1964-

■ Personal

Born May 2, 1964, in Belton, TX; son of Otis L. (in the military) and Susan E. (Motson) Heagy; married Marsha A. Flom (an insurance coordinator), July 11, 1987; children: Zackery David.

■ Addresses

Home and office—7380 143rd St. Court, Apple Valley, MN 55124.

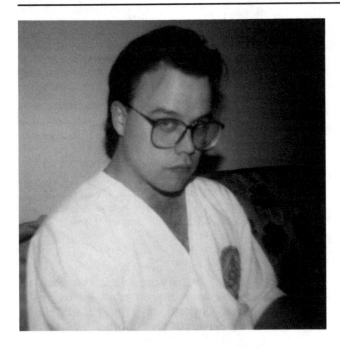

WILLIAM D. HEAGY

■ Career

Children's book illustrator.

■ Illustrator

David R. Collins, *J. R. R. Tolkien: Master of Fantasy*, Lerner Publications, 1992.

Contributor of cover illustration to *L. Frank Baum: Royal Historian of Oz*, by Angelica S. Carpenter and Jean Shirley, Lerner Publications, 1991.

■ Work in Progress

Writing and illustrating a children's book, *There's a Monster under My Bed*.

* * *

HENKES, Kevin 1960-

■ Personal

Born November 27, 1960, in Racine, WI; son of Bernard E. and Beatrice (Sieger) Henkes; married Laura Dronzek, May 18, 1985. *Education:* Attended University of Wisconsin—Madison.

■ Addresses

Home—Madison, WI.

■ Career

Writer and illustrator.

■ Awards, Honors

A Weekend with Wendell was named a Children's Choice Book by the Children's Book Council and the International Reading Association, 1986; *Chester's Way* was named a notable book by the American Library Association, 1988; Elizabeth Burr Award, Wisconsin Library Association, 1993, for *Words of Stone*.

■ Writings

Once around the Block, illustrated by Victoria Chess, Greenwillow, 1987.

SELF-ILLUSTRATED

All Alone, Greenwillow, 1981.
Clean Enough, Greenwillow, 1982.
Margaret and Taylor, Greenwillow, 1983.
Bailey Goes Camping, Greenwillow, 1985.
Grandpa and Bo, Greenwillow, 1986.
Sheila Rae, the Brave, Greenwillow, 1987.
A Weekend with Wendell, Greenwillow, 1987.
Chester's Way, Greenwillow, 1988.
Jessica, Greenwillow, 1989.
Shhhh, Greenwillow, 1989.
Julius, the Baby of the World, Greenwillow, 1990.
Chrysanthemum, Greenwillow, 1991.
Owen, Greenwillow, 1993.

KEVIN HENKES

NOVELS

Return to Sender, Greenwillow, 1984.
Two under Par, Greenwillow, 1987.
The Zebra Wall, Greenwillow, 1988.
Words of Stone, Greenwillow, 1992.

■ **Adaptations**

A Weekend with Wendell was made into a filmstrip and a read-along audio cassette, both by Weston Woods, both 1988.

■ **Sidelights**

The books of Kevin Henkes have been consistently praised for the funny and, above all, realistic way they portray children and the relationships they have with their parents and peers. A reviewer for the *Bulletin of the Center for Children's Books* observes that Henkes's writing "sounds as if the author has been eavesdropping on children at play," while *Tribune Books* critic Mary Harris Veeder writes: "Henkes's children are full of the imperfections and emotions which mark real life."

Many of Henkes's most popular books feature a group of young mice whose adventures and concerns mirror those of children worldwide. Among these is the Children's Choice Book *A Weekend with Wendell*. Wendell's parents have gone out of town, leaving Wendell to stay with Sophie's family for the weekend. Wendell, however, is a difficult houseguest, in spite of Sophie's attempts to be a good host. When the two play house, for example, Wendell is the father, mother, and children, leaving Sophie to be the dog; when they play hospital, Wendell makes himself the doctor, the patient, and the nurse, allowing Sophie to act as a desk clerk; and, while playing bakery, Wendell is the baker—Sophie is a sweet roll. In the end she can bear it no longer; Wendell gets his comeuppance, and the two mice ultimately become close friends.

Another of Henkes's mouse books, *Julius, the Baby of the World*, has received high praise from reviewers. In this story, young Lilly (who is also the star of Henkes's *Chester's Way*) is about to become a sister—much to her displeasure. Her jealousy rises up even before the baby is born, as she watches her parents buy toys for it and talk to it through her mother's swollen belly. When little Julius is born, Lilly is disgusted by the attention he commands—attention that was, until recently, reserved for Lilly alone. She wishes Julius away. She pinches his tender flesh. She recites to him a mixed-up alphabet, to undo the lessons of her parents. However, when a visiting cousin voices *his* disapproval, big sister comes to Julius's defense. "There is much to admire, giggle over and learn from *Julius, the Baby of the World*," writes Ann Pleshette Murphy in the *New York Times Book Review*. "No matter how vitriolic a big sister may become, she really does love her little brother after all." Veeder concurs, admitting: "I've read this one over and over just for fun."

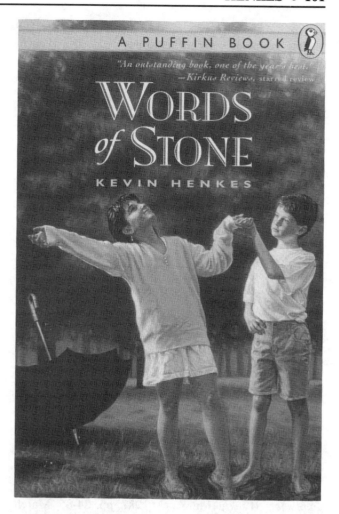

Henkes's ability to capture the emotional tone of young people is shown in this story of a boy who is afraid a new friendship will ultimately hurt him. (Cover illustration by Diana Zelvin.)

In addition to his shorter works, Henkes has written three novels—*Return to Sender, Two under Par,* and *The Zebra Wall*—that continue to address the issues that confront children everywhere. *Two under Par* is the story of a boy, Wedge, as he tries to adapt to his new step-father and -brother. When his mother becomes pregnant, Wedge feels more isolated than ever. One *Publishers Weekly* reviewer applauded *Two under Par,* in particular the "complicated process of learning acceptance and being accepted ... [which] Henkes explores with confidence and care." A new baby is also arriving in *The Zebra Wall*, prompting a visit by the eccentric and slightly annoying Aunt Irene. Adine, the young girl who must share her room with Aunt Irene during her stay, is none too pleased—about either new arrival. "This is not [just] another new baby story," claims a reviewer for *Publishers Weekly*. "Henkes knows that every worry in a child's life has many layers."

An artist as well as an author, Henkes has also received praise for his books' illustrations. His childlike mice, depicted in warm watercolors, are "cheerful and amusing," says Kathy Piehl in the *School Library Journal*, while the broad-stroked acrylic paintings in *Shhh* are perfect for conveying "the hushed world of a child's first waking moments," according to one *Publishers Weekly* critic. "How rewarding to watch an artist stretch, and achieve another perfect fit."

Henkes explains in his autobiographical sketch for *Sixth Book of Junior Authors and Illustrators* his feelings on being an author of children's books: "I'm a very lucky person. I've known for a very long time that I wanted to be an artist and a writer—and that's exactly what I do for a living. Making books is my job, but more importantly, it is what I love doing more than anything else.

"My first book—*All Alone*—was published in 1981. Since then, I've tried to create different kinds of books, even novels. I like trying new ways to fill the pages between two covers. Experimenting with words and paint and ink keeps my job interesting."

■ Works Cited

Bulletin of the Center for Children's Books, October, 1986.
Henkes, Kevin, autobiographical sketch, *Sixth Book of Junior Authors and Illustrators,* Wilson, 1989, pp. 123-24.
Murphy, Ann Pleshette, review of *Julius, the Baby of the World, New York Times Book Review,* April 28, 1991, p. 22.
Piehl, Kathy, review of *A Weekend with Wendell, School Library Journal,* November, 1986, p. 78.
Publishers Weekly, March 13, 1987, pp. 84-85; March 11, 1988, pp. 104-05; June 9, 1989, p. 65.
Veeder, Mary Harris, review of *Jessica, Tribune Books* (Chicago), May 14, 1989, p. 5.
Veeder, review of *Julius, the Baby of the World, Tribune Books* (Chicago), August 12, 1990, p. 5.

■ For More Information See

PERIODICALS

Bulletin of the Center for Children's Books, September, 1984; May, 1986; March, 1987; April, 1988.
Horn Book, November, 1986, p. 734; November, 1987, p. 781; May, 1988, p. 352; May, 1989, p. 357.
Junior Bookshelf, October, 1985, p. 218.
New York Times, December 3, 1990.
New York Times Book Review, January 11, 1987, p. 38.
Publishers Weekly, December 18, 1981; April 24, 1987, p. 69; June 26, 1987, p. 71; July 25, 1987, p. 187; July 8, 1988, p. 53; July 27, 1990, p. 233; September 20, 1993, p. 71.
School Library Journal, December, 1985, p. 74; September, 1986, p. 122; June, 1987, pp. 83, 96; September, 1987, p. 164; January 13, 1989, p. 90; November, 1993, p. 82.
Times Educational Supplement, October 24, 1986, p. 24.
Tribune Books (Chicago), July 19, 1987, p. 6; April 24, 1988, p. 6.*

HENRY, Marion
See del REY, Lester

*   *   *

HERSEY, John (Richard) 1914-1993

OBITUARY NOTICE—See index for *SATA* sketch: Born June 17, 1914, in Tientsin, China; died March 23, 1993, in Key West, FL. Educator, journalist, novelist, and author. Hersey began his writing career as a journalist, first as an editor at *Time* magazine, then as a foreign correspondent during World War II. He came to teaching in 1971, spending 18 years as a professor of writing at Yale University and the Massachusetts Institute of Technology. Hersey wrote numerous books and novels, a number of which hold interest for young adult as well as adult readers. He won a Pulitzer Prize in 1945 for *A Bell for Adano,* which recounts the effect of an American military presence in World War II Italy. Although also a novelist, Hersey was most admired for his nonfiction work, particularly his coverage of the atomic bombing of Hiroshima, Japan, in the book *Hiroshima* and, in *The Algiers Motel Incident,* events stemming from the race riots in Detroit. Hersey was well respected for his examinations of World War II events. As author James Michener stated in the *Detroit Free Press,* "John Hersey's writing about the moral problems in World War II was of the highest quality.... Those of us who participated in that war at any level recognize the gravity of what he was attempting." Among Hersey's other successful publications are *Men on Bataan, Blues, Life Sketches,* and *Antonietta.*

OBITUARIES AND OTHER SOURCES:

BOOKS

Who's Who, 145th edition, St. Martin's, 1993.

PERIODICALS

Detroit Free Press, March 25, 1993, p. 6B.

*   *   *

HONG, Lily Toy 1958-

■ Personal

Born May 3, 1958, in Salt Lake City, Utah; daughter of Raymond Hee (a restaurant owner) and Heng Tsoi (a homemaker) Hong; married Kellan Hatch (a software engineer), September 8, 1990; children: Evan Leung Hatch. *Education:* Attended University of Utah; Utah Technical College, A.A.S., 1981; Utah State University, B.F.A., 1983. *Hobbies and other interests:* Getting together with the family, eating Chinese food, learning about her heritage, camping in the mountains or the desert.

LILY TOY HONG

Addresses

Office—c/o Albert Whitman & Co., 6340 Oakton St., Morton Grove, IL 60053-2723.

Career

Hallmark Cards, Inc., artist-designer and production artist, 1983-86; freelance author and illustrator, 1988—. Participant in Overseas Chinese Youth Language Training and Study Tour, summers, 1980 and 1981; Missionary in the Republic of China (Taiwan) for the Church of Jesus Christ of Latter-Day Saints, 1986-88.

Awards, Honors

Don Freeman Memorial Grant-in-Aid (honorable mention), Society of Children's Book Writers and Illustrators, 1989; *How the Ox Star Fell from Heaven* was named one of the year's ten best books, *Parenting Magazine,* and received a picture book honor seal, *Parent's Choice,* both 1991.

Writings

(And illustrator) *How the Ox Star Fell from Heaven,* Albert Whitman, 1991.
(And illustrator) *The Moon in the Well,* Fables from around the World, Scott Foresman, 1992.
(Co-author with husband, Kellan Hatch) *Marco Polo and Kublai Khan: A Great Friendship,* Macmillan McGraw-Hill, 1993.
(And illustrator) *Two of Everything,* Albert Whitman, 1993.

Also illustrator of *Mr. Sun and Mr. Sea,* Scott Foresman, 1992.

Sidelights

Author and illustrator Lily Toy Hong grew up in a large Chinese-American family with seven sisters and one younger brother. Her parents and grandparents emigrated from Kwangtung, China, to the United States ten years before Lily was born. She told *SATA:* "Sometimes I wonder what my life would have been like if my parents did not leave their country and I was born behind the bamboo curtain. I love my heritage but I am so glad they had the courage to flee. One day I would love to visit China and explore the land of my forefathers, bask in all her splendors, and maybe discover more folktales."

Hong's first picture book, *How the Ox Star Fell from Heaven,* is based on an ancient Chinese folktale. The idea for the book came to her when she was in college studying art and her class was assigned to illustrate the term "water." Hong did a painting of oxen, or water buffalo. During her research she discovered an ancient folktale about how oxen came to Earth. She was delighted with the story and expanded the illustration into a picture book, which she considered crude. For the next several years she lived in Taiwan and witnessed "the farmers sweating in the rice paddies and oxen pulling plows in the sun-bleached fields." It was more than six years after her art work and research in college that she began to rework the book, incorporating the scenes she had witnessed in Taiwan. The following year, 1991, the book was published. Hong told *SATA:* "It was well worth the wait. My childhood memories, my studies in art, and my overseas experiences seemed to all come together."

Of *How the Ox Star Fell from Heaven,* John Philbrook wrote in a *School Library Journal* review, "The whimsical characters satisfy the needs of the story and the eye; the blase expressions on the oxen's faces tickle the funnybone, yet add a depth to their resignation. In short, an impressive debut and a delight fallen from heaven." *Two of Everything,* Hong's second picture book, is also based on a Chinese folktale.

Hong noted that she has always loved books, especially picture books, and admitted, "It has always been my secret desire to write and illustrate children's books." She added, "Now that I'm almost grown up, I can't believe my dream has come true."

Works Cited

Philbrook, John, review of *How the Ox Star Fell from Heaven, School Library Journal,* July, 1991, p. 69.

For More Information See

PERIODICALS

Booklist, March 15, 1993, p. 1320.
Horn Book, July/August, 1993, pp. 469-70.
New York Times Book Review, August 11, 1991, p. 17.
Publishers Weekly, April 26, 1991, pp. 59-60.
School Library Journal, June, 1993, p. 101.

The gods send Ox Star to the humans with a message, but when he gets the announcement wrong, he is doomed to a life of labor in Hong's self-illustrated retelling of a Chinese tale.

HOOPER, Maureen Brett 1927-

■ Personal

Born August 5, 1927, in Chino, CA; daughter of Herbert E. (a minister) and Adelaide A. (a homemaker) Hooper. *Education:* University of California, Los Angeles, B.A., 1949; California State University, Northridge, M.A., 1960; University of Southern California, Ed.D., 1969. *Hobbies and other interests:* Travel, concerts and plays, reading.

■ Addresses

Home—1635 Hilts Ave., Los Angeles, CA 90024. *Office*—c/o University of California, Los Angeles, Department of Music, 405 Hilgard Ave., Los Angeles, CA 90024-1616.

■ Career

Los Angeles Unified School District, Los Angeles, CA, music teacher, 1949-62; University of California, Los Angeles, senior lecturer of music education, 1962-91, emeritus lecturer, 1991—. Curriculum consultant and music textbook consultant; speaker and clinician for gifted and talented programs; director of the American Suzuki Institute West. *Member:* Society of Children's Book Writers and Illustrators, Golden Key Fraternity (honorary member), Los Angeles City Elementary Schools Music Teachers' Association, Inc. (lifetime member).

■ Writings

The Violin Man (middle grade novel), Boyds Mills Press, 1991.
The Christmas Drum (picture book), Boyds Mills Press, in press.

MAUREEN BRETT HOOPER

Also author of professional articles and curriculum guides.

■ Work in Progress

The Orange Clarinet (picture book), *The Year the Rabbit Dance Began* (picture book), *Mrs. Periwether's Piano* (middle grade novel), *The Almost Terrible Tuba Tragedy* (picture book).

■ Sidelights

Maureen Brett Hooper told *SATA:* "A few years ago I became an admirer of Suzuki string students. I admired not only their skills but the joy with which they made music. I wanted somehow to be a part of it. My cello had stood dormant in a corner of my closet for many years, so I knew teaching would not do. Then one day I surprised myself by deciding to write a book for these students. It would not be a book about the facts of music, although those books are important, but a book about the wonders of making music. From that decision came my first book. Now I spend much of my time writing other stories on this theme. And as I write, I learn more and more about this mystical power we call music."

*   *   *

HOPKINSON, Deborah 1952-

■ Personal

Born February 4, 1952, in Lowell, MA; daughter of Russell W. (a machinist) and Gloria D. Hopkinson; married Andrew D. Thomas (a teacher); children: Rebekah, Dimitri. *Education:* University of Massachusetts—Amherst, B.A., 1973; University of Hawaii,

M.A., 1978. *Hobbies and other interests:* Reading, hiking, swimming, history.

■ Addresses

Home—3561-D Pinao St., Honolulu, HI 96822. *Office*—East-West Center, 1777 East-West Rd., Honolulu, HI 96848.

■ Career

Manoa Valley Theater, Honolulu, HI, marketing director, 1981-84; University of Hawaii Foundation, Honolulu, development director, 1985-89; East-West Center, Honolulu, development director, 1989—. Creative Fund Raising Associates, Honolulu, consultant, 1991—. Board member of the National Society of Fund Raising Executives, Aloha Chapter, 1985-91. *Member:* Society of Children's Book Writers and Illustrators, National League of American Pen Women.

■ Awards, Honors

Merit award, Society of Children's Book Writers and Illustrators, 1991; work-in-progress grant recipient, Society of Children's Book Writers and Illustrators, 1993.

■ Writings

Pearl Harbor, Dillon Press/Macmillan, 1991.
Sweet Clara and the Freedom Quilt, illustrated by James Ransome, Knopf, 1993.

■ Work in Progress

Stories about the settling of the West, lighthouses, and a book about the Civil War.

■ Sidelights

"As a girl, I always wanted to be a writer," Deborah Hopkinson told *SATA.* "But I never knew what I wanted to write. Then, when my daughter Rebekah was about three, we were reading a lot of children's books. Having a full-time career and a child, I was very busy. But I thought, 'Maybe I'll try writing for children. At least the books are short!' I have since found out that simply because a story is short, that doesn't mean that it is easy to write!"

Hopkinson's first book, *Pearl Harbor,* was published in 1991 as part of Dillon Press's "Places in American History" series. Aimed at older children, the book tells the story of the bombing of Pearl Harbor during World War II and includes photographs showing Pearl Harbor both during the war and today.

For her second book, Hopkinson decided to try her hand at fiction. *Sweet Clara and the Freedom Quilt* is about a slave girl who is separated from her mother and sent to work in the fields. She lives with an elderly woman named Aunt Rachel, who teaches her to sew. Clara becomes a seamstress, but she is always preoccu-

DEBORAH HOPKINSON

pied with thoughts of her mother and freedom. Clara overhears other slaves discussing the "underground railroad," and decides to use her sewing skills to help herself and other slaves escape. In her spare time, she sews a quilt; but instead of patchwork, Clara's quilt is a map detailing an escape route. When she finally does escape the plantation, she leaves the quilt for other slaves.

Hopkinson told *SATA:* "The idea for *Sweet Clara and the Freedom Quilt* came to me while listening to a radio story about African-American quilts. I consider this story a wonderful gift, and feel very happy that I was able to tell it." The story "brings power and substance to this noteworthy picture book," writes a contributor for *Publishers Weekly.* The contributor concludes: "This first-rate book is a triumph of the heart."

In addition to her books, Hopkinson also writes short stories, especially for *Cricket* magazine. While her main interest "is stories that also tell about history," she adds, "I also like to write about girls, because when I was a girl, there weren't many stories about the exciting things that girls can do!"

■ Works Cited

Publishers Weekly, review of *Sweet Clara and the Freedom Quilt,* February 8, 1993, p. 87.

■ For More Information See

PERIODICALS

Bulletin of the Center for Children's Books, July/August 1993, p. 346.
Publishers Weekly, July 12, 1993, pp. 25-26.
School Library Journal, June 1993, p. 76.

* * *

HOPPE, Matthias 1952-

■ Personal

Born December 5, 1952, in Schluechtern, Germany; son of Bodo (a preacher) and Gisela (a musician and homemaker) Hoppe; children: Aniela. *Education:* Attended University of Erlangen (Germany), 1971-74, and University of Munich, 1974-78. *Hobbies and other interests:* Playing piano, composing music, painting, photography.

■ Addresses

Home and office— Bucheckernweg 3, D-81547, Muenchen, Germany.

■ Career

Journalist and author, 1981—. Television journalist, 1985-87; *Ambiente* magazine, editor, 1990-92. Press speaker for the German peace movement, 1983, and for *Die Gruenen,* 1984-85. *Member:* IG Medien (German Writers Association).

■ Awards, Honors

Fourth prize in a writing contest, *Eltern* magazine, 1991.

■ Writings

IN ENGLISH TRANSLATION

Mouse and Elephant, illustrated by Jan Lenica, Little, Brown, 1991 (originally published as *Die Maus und der Elefant,* Bohem Press, 1990).

UNTRANSLATED WORKS

(With Klaus Gerosa, Beate Kuhn, and Ursula Kopp) *Lexikon fuer Waldfreunde* (dictionary; title means "All about the Forest"), Bucher Verlag, 1982.
Muenchen April '82: Ostermaersche, SPD-Parteitag, Demonstrationen (documentary), SBV-Verlag, 1982.
Was macht Arno im Sommer oder Ein Schneemann hat Heimweh (picture book; title means "What Does Arno Do in Summer; or, A Snowman Is Homesick"), illustrated by Rolf Faenger, Coppenrath Verlag, 1989.
Das kleine Buch der grossen Wunder (aphorisms; title means "Little Book about Great Miracles"), ars edition, 1990.

Contributor to periodicals, including *Stern, Die Zeit, Abendzeitung, Frankfurter Rundschau,* and *Ambiente.* Also contributor to German television.

■ Work in Progress

A sequel to *Mouse and Elephant;* other children's books; a novel, tentatively titled *Havana in Dresden;* a stage play, tentatively titled *Mosquitos under the Bridge,* about people who live under a bridge.

■ Sidelights

Matthias Hoppe told *SATA:* "When my daughter Aniela was five years old, she wanted me to tell her my own stories before going to bed—no more reading any book stories. So I had to find new stories for children, another one each day. One day I began to note down my ideas. With a friend of mine, a talented illustrator, I developed my first children's book in 1989: *Was macht Arno im Sommer oder Ein Schneemann hat Heimweh,* a story about a snowman. So it began.

"Writing is my hobby and business. To express what you have seen, your experiences, your thoughts, together with imagination and the will to do something for this world—that's what I want. Not only for children but also for adults, politically, psychologically, ecologically."

MATTHIAS HOPPE

HUNT, Peter 1945-

■ Personal

Born September 2, 1945, in Rugby, Warwickshire, England; son of Walter Henry (an engineer) and Lillian (a homemaker; maiden name, McPherson) Hunt; married Sarah Wilkinson, October 24, 1981; children: Felicity, Amy, Abigail, Chloe. *Education:* University of Wales, B.A., 1966, M.A., 1970, Ph.D., 1981.

■ Addresses

Home—West Sundial Cottage, Downend, Horsley, Gloucestershire GL6 0PF, England. *Office*—School of English, University of Wales, Cardiff CF9 3XE, Wales.

■ Career

University of Wales, Cardiff, Wales, senior lecturer in English and children's literature, 1968—; John Kirkman Communication Consultancy, Marlborough, England, principal associate, 1986—. Visiting professor at University of Michigan, 1977, Massachusetts Institute of Technology, 1984-89, and San Diego State University, 1991; visiting fellow, University of Wollongong, Australia, 1991.

■ Writings

JUVENILE

The Maps of Time, Julia MacRae, 1983.
A Step off the Path, Julia MacRae, 1985.
Backtrack, Julia MacRae, 1986.
Going Up, Julia MacRae, 1989.
Sue and the Honey Machine, Julia MacRae, 1989.
Fay Cow and the Missing Milk, Julia MacRae, 1989, published as *Fay Cow and the Honey Machine,* Walker Doubles, 1992.

OTHER

(Editor) Richard Jeffries, *Bevis,* Oxford University Press, 1989.
(Editor) *Children's Literature: The Development of Criticism,* Routledge, 1990.
Criticism, Theory, and Children's Literature, Basil Blackwell, 1991.
Arthur Ransome, Twayne, 1991, revised edition published as *Approaching Arthur Ransome,* Cape, 1992.
(Editor) *Literature for Children: Contemporary Criticism,* Routledge, 1992.
Children's Literature: An Introduction, Oxford University Press, in press.
Masterworks: The Wind in the Willows, Twayne, in press.

Also author of numerous articles and book chapters on children's literature.

■ Work in Progress

Editing *An Illustrated History of Children's Literature,* for Oxford University Press, 1995; *The Routledge*

PETER HUNT

Encyclopedia of Children's Literature, for Routledge, 1996.

■ Sidelights

Peter Hunt told *SATA:* "I've been writing books since the age of four, and although I've had to make a living as an academic and a consultant (on technical writing), I've always been a writer. Even now, when writing brings in the least money and gets pushed to the bottom of the pile, I'm still a writer."

Hunt's first attempts at writing children's books proved frustrating, so he turned instead to the study of children's literature. Later, at his wife Sarah's urging, Hunt resubmitted *The Maps of Time* to British publishers and subsequently sold the work. Since then, Hunt has successfully rewritten and published two other early efforts.

Hunt admitted to *SATA* that he is "interested in out-of-the-way things;" he combined two of his interests—old railroads and detective novels—for *Backtrack,* the fictional story of a 1912 train crash in Britain that kills two brothers. A strange coincidence occurred with that work, Hunt recalled: "I invented a railway company, with a route map; designed a steam locomotive; faked up newspaper cuttings and guidebooks, and laid it all in an invented square mile of country, which I slotted in near a real-life town called Ledbury. In the book,

students at the local school have a history project concerning the rail crash. Two years after the book came out, I was invited to give a talk at the real-life Ledbury school. I told the story of the book, and I thought the librarian was going to faint—there really had been a rail crash, and two brothers had been killed, and the school had done a project!"

Other Hunt stories are based on situations he and his wife face at their country home. Those works got their start, Hunt said, because "Sarah was keeping a cow and bees and sheep and pigs. And so I wrote two short books, *Fay Cow and the Missing Milk* and *Sue and the Honey Machine.* I hope there will be a series one day; they're really Sarah's books. She did almost everything in them—milking, making butter and cheese, spinning out the honey; I just wrote it down. She now keeps ponies, so the next book is about ponies."

"Meanwhile," the author concluded, "I'm writing big books about children's books, and wishing I had more time to write children's books. I don't plan to get any less 'clever' in the books for children—because I just happen to think that children are a lot cleverer than grown-ups give them credit for. And having four daughters has merely proved it!"

*   *   *

HYDE, Margaret O(ldroyd) 1917-

■ Personal

Born February 18, 1917, in Philadelphia, PA; daughter of Gerald James and Helen (Lerch) Oldroyd; married Edwin Y. Hyde, Jr., 1941; children: Lawrence Edwin, Bruce Geoffrey. *Education:* Beaver College, A.B., 1938; Columbia University, M.A., 1939; Temple University, 1942-43.

■ Addresses

Home—336 Essex Meadows, Essex, CT 06426.

■ Career

Columbia University, Teachers College, New York City, science consultant, 1941-42; Shipley School, Bryn Mawr, PA, teacher, 1942-48. Lecturer in elementary education, Temple University, Philadelphia, PA, part-time and summers, 1942-43; writer for young people, 1944—. Member of board of directors, Northeast Mental Health Clinic, 1963-67. *Member:* Authors League of America, Authors Guild, Society of Children's Book Writers and Illustrators.

■ Awards, Honors

Thomas Alva Edison Foundation National Mass Media Award, best children's science book, 1961, for *Animal Clocks and Compasses;* honorary doctor of letters from Beaver College, 1971.

■ Writings

(With Gerald S. Craig) *New Ideas in Science,* Ginn, 1947.

Playtime for Nancy (fiction), Grosset, 1951.

(With Frances W. Keene) *Hobby Fun Book for Grade School Boys and Girls: A Collection of Carefully Chosen Creative To-Do Hobbies,* Seahorse Press, 1952.

Flight Today and Tomorrow, illustrated by Clifford N. Geary, McGraw, 1953, revised edition, 1962.

Driving Today and Tomorrow, illustrated by Clifford N. Geary, McGraw, 1954, revised edition, 1965.

Atoms Today and Tomorrow, illustrated by Clifford N. Geary, McGraw, 1955, 4th edition, 1970.

(With husband, E. Y. Hyde, Jr.) *Where Speed Is King,* illustrated by Clifford N. Geary, McGraw, 1955, revised edition, 1961.

Medicine in Action: Today and Tomorrow, McGraw, 1956, revised edition, 1964.

Exploring Earth and Space: The Story of the I.G.Y., McGraw, 1957, 5th edition, illustrated by E. Winson, 1970.

From Submarines to Satellites: Science in Our Armed Forces, McGraw, 1958.

Off into Space! Science for Young Space Travelers, McGraw, 1959, 3rd edition, illustrated by B. Myers, 1969.

MARGARET O. HYDE

Plants Today and Tomorrow, illustrated by P. A. Hutchison, McGraw, 1960.

Animal Clocks and Compasses, illustrated by P. A. Hutchison, McGraw, 1960.

This Crowded Planet, illustrated by Mildred Waltrip, McGraw, 1961.

Animals in Science: Saving Lives through Research, McGraw, 1962.

Molecules Today and Tomorrow, illustrated by Mildred Waltrip, McGraw, 1963.

Your Brain, Master Computer, illustrated by P. A. Hutchison, McGraw, 1964.

(With Edward S. Marks) *Psychology in Action,* illustrated by Carolyn Cather, McGraw, 1967, 2nd edition, 1976.

(And editor) *Mind Drugs,* McGraw, 1968, fifth revised edition, Putnam, 1988.

The Earth in Action, McGraw, 1969.

The Great Deserts (adapted from the book by Folco Quilici), McGraw, 1969.

Your Skin, illustrated by Richard Jones, McGraw, 1970.

(With B. G. Hyde) *Know about Drugs,* illustrated by Bill Morrison, McGraw, 1971, revised edition, Walker & Co., 1990.

For Pollution Fighters Only, illustrated by Don Lynch, McGraw, 1971.

(With Edward S. Marks and James B. Wells) *Mysteries of the Mind,* McGraw, 1972.

VD: The Silent Epidemic, McGraw, 1972, 2nd edition published as *VD-STD: The Silent Epidemic,* 1983.

The New Genetics: Promises and Perils, F. Watts, 1974.

Alcohol: Drink or Drug?, McGraw, 1974.

Hotline!, McGraw, 1974.

(With Elizabeth H. Forsyth) *What Have You Been Eating? Do You Really Know?,* McGraw, 1975.

(With E. H. Forsyth) *Know Your Feelings,* F. Watts, 1976.

Speak Out on Rape, McGraw, 1976.

Juvenile Justice and Injustice, F. Watts, 1977.

Fears and Phobias, McGraw, 1977, revised edition (with E. H. Forsyth) published as *Horror, Fright and Panic,* Walker & Co., 1987.

Brainwashing and Other Forms of Mind Control, McGraw, 1977.

Know about Alcohol, foreword by Morris E. Chafetz, illustrated by Bill Morrison, McGraw, 1978.

Addictions: Smoking, Gambling, Cocaine Use and Others, McGraw, 1978.

(With E. H. Forsyth) *Suicide: The Hidden Epidemic,* F. Watts, 1978, 3rd revised edition, 1991.

(With B. G. Hyde) *Everyone's Trash Problem: Nuclear Wastes,* McGraw, 1979.

My Friend Wants to Run Away, McGraw, 1979.

Crime and Justice in Our Time, F. Watts, 1980.

Cry Softly: The Story of Child Abuse, Westminster, 1980, revised and enlarged edition, 1986.

Is the Cat Dreaming Your Dream?, McGraw, 1980.

My Friend Has Four Parents, McGraw, 1981, revised edition (with E. H. Forsyth) published as *Parents Divided, Parents Multiplied,* Westminster, 1989.

Energy: The New Look, McGraw, 1981.

Foster Care and Adoption, F. Watts, 1982.

Computers That Think? The Search for Artificial Intelligence, Enslow, 1982, revised edition published as *Artificial Intelligence,* 1986.
The Rights of the Victim, F. Watts, 1983.
Know about Smoking, illustrated by Dennis Kendrick, McGraw, 1983, revised edition, Walker & Co., 1990.
Is This Kid "Crazy"? Understanding Unusual Behavior, Westminster, 1983.
(With son, Lawrence E. Hyde) *Cloning and the New Genetics,* Enslow, 1984.
Sexual Abuse: Let's Talk about It, Westminster, 1984, revised and enlarged edition, 1987.
(With L. E. Hyde) *Cancer in the Young: A Sense of Hope,* Westminster, 1985.
(With L. E. Hyde) *Missing Children,* F. Watts, 1985.
(With E. H. Forsyth) *AIDS: What Does It Mean to You?,* Walker & Co., 1986, fourth revised edition, 1992.
(With E. H. Forsyth) *Terrorism: A Special Kind of Violence,* Putnam, 1987.
(With E. H. Forsyth) *Know about AIDS,* illustrated by Debora Weber, Walker & Co., 1987, revised edition, 1990.
Teen Sex, Westminster, 1988.
Alcohol: Uses and Abuses, Enslow, 1988.
The Homeless: Profiling the Problem, Enslow, 1989.
(With L. E. Hyde) *Meeting Death,* Walker & Co., 1989.
(With E. H. Forsyth) *Medical Dilemmas,* Putnam, 1990.
Drug Wars, Walker & Co., 1990.
(With E. H. Forsyth) *The Violent Mind,* F. Watts, 1991.
Know about Abuse, Walker & Co., 1992.
Peace and Friendship: Russian and American Teens Meet, Cobblehill Books, Dutton, 1992.
Know about Gays and Lesbians, Millbrook Press, in press.
(With E. H. Forsyth) *Kids with Asthma,* Walker, in press.
Kids In and Out of Trouble, Cobblehill Books, Dutton, in press.

Also author of two television scripts, "How the Mind Begins," and "Can Human Nature Be Changed?," for *Animal Secrets,* NBC-TV, 1967.

■ Sidelights

Margaret O. Hyde is one of the most prolific and respected of today's writers on science for young readers. "For over thirty years," writes Patty Campbell in *Wilson Library Bulletin,* "Hyde has used her scientific training, her skill at organization, and her meticulous research to produce a stream of excellent books for junior high readers on the social and biological sciences. Her subjects are as current as the evening news, and she goes straight to the cutting edge by garnering much of her material from the experts and organizations who are making that news." "She has the gift," Campbell concludes, "of making complex matters easy to understand."

As a young girl, Hyde's ambition was to become a doctor. She states in her *Something about the Author Autobiography Series* (*SAAS*) entry that she was proba-

bly inspired by a distant relative, with whom she stayed during the summer, who practiced medicine in a rural Pennsylvania town. "In addition to the novelty of shopping at the country store and playing with friends who remained the same summer after summer, I enjoyed driving through country roads in the doctor's car when he took me on calls to see patients." Occasionally Hyde was allowed to witness simple operations, "a tonsillectomy, the removal of a small growth on an arm or leg, or some other procedure that was considered simple enough to perform in the office."

"Although I was not a tomboy," Hyde writes, "I liked subjects that, in those days, appealed most to boys. Perhaps I liked math and science because they were the subjects that were easiest for me. My parents were very tolerant of my collections of insects, earthworms, and other animals, although I remember my mother sounding disgusted when she emptied some worms from my pockets." However, "when I was growing up," Hyde continues, "women became nurses, secretaries, teachers, librarians, or had other ladylike careers. Many of my friends were totally consumed with the idea of getting married and raising children. My mother, who had always wanted to be a teacher herself, decided I should

Many of Hyde's nonfiction works are designed to educate young people on difficult topics such as drugs, smoking, sex, and AIDS. (Cover illustration by Russell & Hinrichs Associates.)

teach. Although I had many ideas about what I wanted to be when I grew up, a teacher was not one of them."

In college, Hyde specialized in science, intending to enter medical school. However, "when it came near the time to apply for admission to medical school," she writes, "my parents balked at the idea. According to them, medicine should be left to men; women should be teachers, etc. They were willing to pay for graduate school, providing I considered becoming a teacher. Research was an acceptable option, but they still hoped I would change my mind and enter the teaching profession." Hyde attended graduate school in zoology at Columbia University, and began looking for work as a researcher. "In those days, women were usually relegated to inferior jobs in the field of science, and even those jobs were scarce." She enrolled at Columbia University Teachers College to prepare for a career as a public school teacher.

Science Textbook Launches Writing Career

It was while at Columbia University Teachers College that Hyde first met Dr. Gerald Craig. "Dr. Craig apparently liked my way of teaching, for when there was an opening at Lincoln School of Teachers College, he recommended me for that position," Hyde writes. Some time later, Craig invited her to rewrite a science textbook he had originally written for sixth-graders. "My response to Dr. Craig's suggestion was a hasty no," Hyde recalls, "and I explained that I had no writing ability. He felt that I could do the job based on my science background and he finally persuaded me to accept the offer." The resulting book, *New Ideas in Science,* was published in 1947. "From the time I began to work on *New Ideas in Science* until now," Hyde comments in *Third Book of Junior Authors,* " . . . science has become increasingly exciting and still challenges me to explore further." Due to the technical nature of science, many of Hyde's topics are complex. "I like the challenge of explaining something complicated," she reveals in her *SAAS* entry. Her subjects include atoms and molecules, plants, space, suicide, pollution control, sexually transmitted diseases, AIDS, and genetics, as well as other topics.

In addition to writing biological science books, Hyde also writes about the social sciences, or the study of how people relate and function in society. Her titles focus on a wide range of issues which are of interest to teenagers, such as drug abuse, running away, child abuse, divorce, and phobias. Two of her recent works are *Peace and Friendship: Russian and American Teens Meet* and *The Violent Mind.* Student exchange programs, pen pals, and international relationships are all topics covered in *Peace and Friendship.* The book encourages students and teachers to communicate through writing projects, visits, and working together for a common cause. In *The Violent Mind,* Hyde teamed up with E. H. Forsyth, a psychiatrist, to explore the reasons why violent acts are committed by and against young people today. The authors describe theories on the causes of violence and

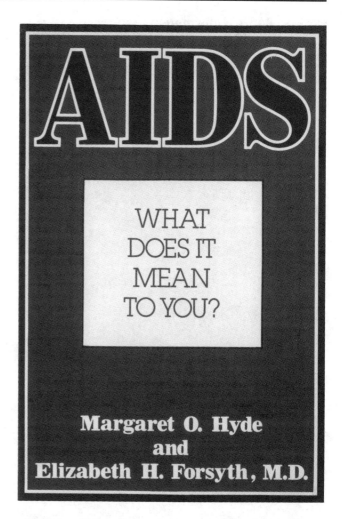

In this collaboration with Dr. Elizabeth H. Forsyth, Hyde presents a scientific and historical look at the AIDS virus and what people can do to prevent it from spreading.

offer summaries of many strategies used to control violent behaviors.

Hyde commented: "Writing is a wonderful way to learn more about the exciting world of science, for today one must contact people who are active in research to find out what is happening. Such people are most cooperative in talking about their projects and in checking material for accuracy. I gather material for several years from many sources and sometimes work on as many as four books at once."

■ Works Cited

de Montreville, Doris, and Donna Hill, *Third Book of Junior Authors,* H. W. Wilson, 1972, pp. 143-45.
Something about the Author Autobiography Series, Volume 8, Gale, 1989.
Wilson Library Bulletin, April, 1988, pp. 74-75.

■ For More Information See

BOOKS

Contemporary Literary Criticism, Volume 21, Gale, 1982.

PERIODICALS

Booklist, December 1, 1991, p. 688; July, 1992, p. 1930.
School Library Journal, October, 1992, p. 129.
Voice Of Youth Advocates, December, 1991, p. 337.*

I–J

IGUS, Toyomi 1953-

■ Personal

Born October 10, 1953, in Iowa City, IA; daughter of Will (an attorney) and Kazumi (a homemaker; maiden name, Tamori) Gibson; married Darrow Igus (an actor); children: Kazumi, Kenji. *Education:* Barnard College, B.A., 1974. *Politics:* Liberal Democrat.

■ Addresses

Office—P.O. Box 10421, Marina Del Rey, CA 90295.

■ Career

L.A. Style, Los Angeles, CA, associate managing editor, 1986-89; University of California at Los Angeles Center for Afro-American Studies Publications, managing editor, 1990—. *Member:* American Black Book Writers Association, Society of Scholarly Publishing.

■ Writings

(With Veronica Freeman Ellis, Diane Patrick, and Valerie Wilson Wesley; and editor) *Book of Black Heroes, Volume II: Great Women in the Struggle,* Just Us Books, 1992.

(Editor with Charles Roland) *Life in a Day of Black L.A.: The Way We See It,* Center for Afro-American Studies, 1992.

When I Was Little, Just Us Books, 1992.

Contributor of articles and reviews to the *American Black Bookwriters Association Journal.* Co-author of several plays and screenplays, including *Zeke: History of Blacks in the Movies. American Black Book Writers Association Journal,* executive editor, 1986-1992.

■ Sidelights

Toyomi Igus, a woman of Japanese and African-American descent and a graduate of Barnard College, has spent fifteen years in the West Coast publishing indus-
try. During these years, she has written for various trade and consumer magazines, co-authored several plays and scripts, and edited periodicals such as *L.A. Style.* Since 1992 she has been the managing editor of CAAS Publications, an academic press at UCLA's Center for Afro-American Studies; Igus coordinated and edited a project for them entitled *Life in a Day of Black L.A.,* a collection of photographic essays produced by black Los Angeles photographers; *Life in a Day of Black L.A.* has since been reproduced as a traveling exhibition.

It was not until the birth of her daughter, Kazumi, and her son, Kenji, that Igus was motivated to write books for children. The first to be published was the product of a project that Igus coordinated, edited, and co-wrote, *Book of Black Women, Volume II: Great Women in the Struggle.* This work spotlights more than eighty historical and contemporary women of African descent. The writer's second book for children, 1992's *When I Was Little,* was written solely by Igus. In this picture book, a little boy visiting his grandfather imagines life without televisions, VCRs, and video games, and also learns that the need for love and sharing is one thing that will not change with time.

■ For More Information See

PERIODICALS

Horn Book, fall, 1992, p. 331.
School Library Journal, August, 1992, p. 166.

* * *

JAMES, Philip
See del REY, Lester

JOHNSON, Scott 1952-

■ Personal

Born November 23, 1952, in Chicago, IL; son of Roy and Gladys (Hurt) Johnson; married Susan Newton, September 28, 1985; children: Ethan Lucas, Jordan Guthrie. *Education:* Indiana University, B.A. (with honors), 1974; University of Massachusetts, M.F.A., 1978. *Hobbies and other interests:* Backpacking, hiking, bicycling, acoustic music (guitar and mandolin).

■ Addresses

Home—25 Wright Ave., Mahopac, NY 10541. *Office*—c/o Pleasantville High School, Romer Ave., Pleasantville, NY 10570. *Agent*—Richard Parks Agency, 138 East 16th St., New York, NY 10003.

■ Career

Pleasantville High School, Pleasantville, NY, teacher of English and creative writing, 1978—. *Member:* National Conference of Teachers of English, New York State English Council, Sierra Club, Nature Conservancy.

■ Awards, Honors

Fulbright exchange teacher, 1983; National Endowment for the Humanities independent study fellowship, 1987; *One of the Boys* was selected as one of the "Best Book for Young Adults" by the American Library Association, 1993.

■ Writings

One of the Boys (young adult novel), Atheneum, 1992. *Overnight Sensation* (young adult novel), Atheneum, 1994.

Contributor of articles and short stories to *English Journal, TriQuarterly,* and *Ploughshares.*

■ Sidelights

Scott Johnson told *SATA:* "There aren't too many second chances in life, and writing for young people, for me, is a way to get back and live through some of those choices and decisions I had to make—and often didn't make too wisely. When I write I get to watch some character, some boy or girl I've come to feel close to over the course of a book, struggle with choices that he or she must now face."

In *One of the Boys,* Johnson has created a character who faces some rough choices. Eric is a "nice" kid who, out of the desire to fit in, joins up with the wrong crowd. Randy Meyer wrote in *Booklist:* "Johnson has written a tough, quickly paced story about the irony and complexity of peer pressure.... The pain and promise of friendship come clear in a story that demonstrates that there are no easy choices."

SCOTT JOHNSON

Johnson's ability to empathize with adolescents comes from his continuing contact with them in his position as a high school teacher. He first discovered young adult novels as a teacher; his favorites, he recalls for *SATA,* provided him "with a direct line to my past, to those adolescent sensations that haunted and tortured all of us, and other times left us soaring with glee. That teenager from long ago is still inside, still seeing the world as unjust and overly complicated, still crying out for understanding, some guidance and maybe a little bit of attention. We need to listen to that teenager, and [young adult] books help to put us in touch."

Growing up, Johnson never really considered himself a writer. "I was destined to be a zoologist," he explained to *SATA.* "It only took a couple of semesters memorizing the arterial circulation in reptilian hearts, or hunting the pituitary gland of fetal pigs, and before I knew it, I was trading in my Developmental Anatomy text at the college bookstore for used paperbacks of Dickens, Fitzgerald, and Twain.

"A short time after that I admitted to myself, cautiously, at first, nervous for the consequences—I was a writer. At least I wanted to be. Even back then I knew the best writers only made it look easy. But I wanted to take my turn. There was something in fiction that reminded me of the tales told around the fire on my old Boy Scout camping trips. Tales swapped, with everyone hoping the next one would be even better—scarier, wilder, more real than life. And as we lay there, each snap of a twig or rustle of a leaf outside our tent was surely the telltale sign of some creature we had thrilled to around the fire, drawing near, long after the last story was spoken. That's how fiction works, I think. 'Good story,' we say, when the storyteller reaches the end, but that's not the half of it. The true measure of fiction is how much it grows inside you, how much the tale still burns after the campfire is only embers."

■ Works Cited

Meyer, Randy, review of *One of the Boys, Booklist,* April 1, 1992.

*   *   *

JONES, John R(obert) 1926-
(John Dalmas)

■ Personal

Born September 3, 1926, in Chicago, IL; son of John Robert (a marine engineer) and Harriett Evelyn (a librarian; maiden name, Engstrom) Jones; married Neva Gail Hill (a secretary), September 15, 1954; children: Judith Lynn, Jack Allen. *Education:* Michigan State College (now University), B.S. (with honors), 1954; University of Minnesota, M. Forestry, 1955; Colorado State University, Ph.D., 1967; attended Purdue University, 1958-60.

■ Addresses

Home—1425 West Glass Ave., Spokane, WA 99205.

■ Career

Novelist, 1984—. U.S. Forest Service, Chequeamegon National Forest, WI, assistant district ranger and administrative forester, 1956-58; research ecologist, Rocky Mountain Experiment Station, 1960-77. *Military service:* U.S. Army, parachute infantryman and medic, 1944-46. *Member:* Science Fiction Writers of America, Swedish-American Order of Vasa, Los Angeles Science Fantasy Society, Sigma Xi, Xi Sigma Pi, Phi Kappa Phi.

■ Writings

Homecoming (science fiction; also see below), Tor Books, 1984.
(With others) *Aspen: Its Ecology and Management in the Western United States,* U.S. Forest Service, 1985.
The Walkaway Clause (science fiction), Tor Books, 1985.

Author or co-author of numerous government publications.

SCIENCE FICTION UNDER PSEUDONYM JOHN DALMAS

The Yngling (originally serialized in *Analog;* also see below), Pyramid Press, 1971, Tor Books, 1984.
The Varkaus Conspiracy, Tor Books, 1983.

JOHN R. JONES

(With Carl Martin) *Touch the Stars: Emergence,* Tor Books, 1983.
Fanglith, Baen Books, 1985.
The Scroll of Man, Tor Books, 1985.
The Reality Matrix, Baen Books, 1986.
Return to Fanglith, Baen Books, 1987.
The Regiment, Baen Books, 1987.
(With Rod Martin) *The Playmasters,* Baen Books, 1987.
The General's President, Baen Books, 1988.
The Lizard War, Baen Books, 1989.
The Lantern of God, Baen Books, 1989.
The White Regiment, Baen Books, 1990.
The Kalif's War, Baen Books, 1991.
The Yngling and the Circle of Power, Baen Books, 1992.
The Orc Wars (contains *The Yngling* and *Homecoming*), Baen Books, 1992.
The Regiment's War, Baen Books, 1993.

Contributor Baen Books' *War World* series, edited by Jerry Pournelle; contributor of short fiction to periodicals, including *Analog, Magazine of Fantasy & Science Fiction, Far Frontiers, World's Best SF, Science Fiction Yearbook,* "The Saint" *Mystery Magazine, Pulphouse,* and *New Destinies.*

■ Work in Progress

The Yngling in the Land of Yamato; The Last of the 70,000 (a historical novel of the Great Northern War).

■ Sidelights

John R. Jones told *SATA:* "My life has been a learning process. As a child I lived with several families and twice in boarding houses. As a young man, I mostly went where I wanted, did what I wanted, and enjoyed the experiences. I served as a parachute infantryman, smoke-jumped, worked as a merchant seaman and in logging camps and on the docks, and rode freights. Eventually I began college on the GI Bill and had a ball. After graduating with honors I worked two years as a forester, discovering professional responsibility. I especially enjoyed two winters spent on snowshoes cruising timber.

"Intrigued by ecological problems in forestry, I began work on my doctorate in ecology, and was hired by the Forest Service as a research ecologist. While earning a reputation in my field, I learned about the gap between theory and reality. At the same time I discovered an ability to write—both technical papers and science fiction. I sold some stories, notably *The Yngling.*

"Finally I quit my secure government job and went to Hollywood to make my fortune as a film writer. Meanwhile I made a scant living as a casual laborer, mostly working for moving companies, and as a freelance editor, all the while hustling screenplay treatments. I never made it as a film writer, but those were extremely interesting and enjoyable years."

"I have used two separate personas in two separate careers," Jones once commented. "I was John R. Jones as a researcher and author for the U.S. Department of Agriculture's Forest Service. I am now John Dalmas as an author of science fiction novels and occasional mysteries. I will not be returning to research, but will continue to write fiction as John Dalmas for the rest of my active life."

Jones has penned a number of science fiction series, the most popular being the "Yngling" books and the "Regiment" series. The former introduces a group of telepathic neo-Vikings who populate the wasteland of post-Apocalyptic Earth; the latter, an ongoing war on a distant planet. Kelly Flynn, writing in *Voice of Youth Advocates,* calls Jones's style "straightforward prose" with "no archaic shilly-shally," while a reviewer for *Booklist* describes the "Regiment" series as a "fast-moving adventure tale, featuring workmanlike prose, an abundance of ingenious concepts, and extensive description of things military." While some critics have found Jones's books too preachy—*The General's President* and *The Kalif's War,* in particular—he is generally considered to be a no-nonsense author of entertaining and accessible fantasies.

■ Works Cited

Booklist, January 15, 1987, p. 753.

Flynn, Kellie, review of *The Yngling and the Circle of Power, Voice of Youth Advocates,* June, 1992, p. 108.

■ For More Information See

PERIODICALS

Analog, April, 1984, p. 164; February, 1985, p. 180; August, 1988, p. 137; October, 1989, p. 177; December, 1991, p. 161.

Booklist, December 1, 1984, p. 481; December 1, 1985, p. 534; December 1, 1986, p. 549; January 15, 1988, p. 830.

Fantasy Review, November, 1984, p. 30; October, 1986, p. 23.

Kliatt, spring, 1986, p. 19.

Locus, October, 1989, p. 29; January, 1990, p. 50; July, 1990, p. 53; July, 1991, p. 45; March, 1992, p. 56.

Publishers Weekly, December 5, 1986, p. 67; January 8, 1988, p. 76.

Voice of Youth Advocates, December, 1983, p. 26; April, 1986, p. 39; February, 1987, p. 291; April, 1987, p. 36; June, 1987, p. 92; February, 1988, p. 286.

West Coast Review of Books, number 5, 1989, p. 37.

K

KAEMPFERT, Wade
See del REY, Lester

*   *   *

KELLER, Holly 1942-

■ Personal

Born February 11, 1942, in New York, NY; married Barry Keller (a pediatrician), June, 1963; children: Corey (daughter), Jesse (son). *Education:* Sarah Lawrence College, A.B., 1963; Columbia University, M.A., 1964; studied printmaking at Manhattanville College; studied illustration at Parsons School of Design. *Hobbies and other interests:* Tennis.

■ Addresses

Home—West Redding, CT.

■ Career

Writer. Redding Board of Education, member and vice chair, 1975-85.

■ Awards, Honors

Ten Sleepy Sheep was voted a Library of Congress Children's Book of the Year, 1983; *Geraldine's Blanket* was named a *School Library Journal* best book of the year, 1984; *Goodbye Max* was named a Children's Choice and was a Child Study Association Children's Book of the Year, both 1987; *The Best Present* received a Notable Children's Trade Book in the Field of Social Studies designation, 1989.

■ Writings

SELF-ILLUSTRATED CHILDREN'S BOOKS

Cromwell's Glasses, Greenwillow, 1982.
Ten Sleepy Sheep, Greenwillow, 1983.
Too Big, Greenwillow, 1983.

HOLLY KELLER

Geraldine's Blanket, Greenwillow, 1984.
Will It Rain?, Greenwillow, 1984.
Henry's Fourth of July, Greenwillow, 1985.
When Francie Was Sick, Greenwillow, 1985.
A Bear for Christmas, Greenwillow, 1986.
Lizzie's Invitation, Greenwillow, 1987.
Goodbye Max, Greenwillow, 1987.
Geraldine's Big Snow, Greenwillow, 1988.
Maxine in the Middle, Greenwillow, 1989.
The Best Present, Greenwillow, 1989.
Henry's Happy Birthday, Greenwillow, 1990.
What Alvin Wanted, Greenwillow, 1990.
Horace, Greenwillow, 1991.
The New Boy, Greenwillow, 1991.
Furry, Greenwillow, 1992.
Island Baby, Greenwillow, 1992.
Harry and Tuck, Greenwillow, 1993.

ILLUSTRATOR OF CHILDREN'S BOOKS

Jane Thayer, *Clever Raccoon,* Morrow, 1981.
Melvin Berger, *Why I Cough, Sneeze, Shiver, Hiccup, and Yawn,* Crowell, 1983.
Roma Gans, *Rock Collecting,* Crowell, 1984.
Franklyn M. Branley, *Snow Is Falling,* revised edition, Crowell, 1986.
Branley, *Air Is All around You,* revised edition, Crowell, 1986.
Patricia Lauber, *Snakes Are Hunters,* Crowell, 1988.
Branley, *Shooting Stars,* Crowell, 1989.
Lauber, *An Octopus Is Amazing,* Crowell, 1990.
Paul Showers, *Ears Are for Hearing,* Crowell, 1990.
Lauber, *Be a Friend to Trees,* HarperCollins, 1994.
Barbara Esbensen, *Sponges Are Skeletons,* HarperCollins, 1994.

■ Work in Progress

Grandfather's Dream, publication expected in 1994; a story about Vietnam.

■ Sidelights

An author and illustrator of more than twenty books for children, Holly Keller creates characters and stories that entertain as well as educate. Many of her protagonists are faced with moral dilemmas that they ultimately overcome with the help of friends, family, or inner reflection. From tales like *Horace,* which depicts the difficulty a boy has coping with his adoption, to stories like *Geraldine's Blanket,* which describes the problems a girl has giving up her security blanket, Keller often uses animal protagonists and a bit of humor to explore real childhood concerns. "Keller portrays the feelings of adopted children honestly and within the context of a lively, enjoyable tale," wrote *Horn Book* contributor Nancy Vasilakis in a review of *Horace.* Assessing Keller's body of work in a *School Library Journal* article, Lauralyn Persson declared: "Keller has a knack for creating appealing picture books about real problems that ... children encounter."

Keller was born and raised in New York City. Her family lived in a big apartment house, and she rarely socialized with other children, except at school. "I was very happy to spend my time by myself because I was an avid reader," Keller told *Something about the Author* (*SATA*) in an interview. "I also liked to draw a lot. My childhood project was copying all of [American artist John James] Audubon's birds from a book that my parents had. I would spend hours doing that. Then I went into a horse stage, like so many other young girls, and I drew horses endlessly."

Describing her youth as "a pretty ordinary, middle-class childhood," Keller related that she took piano and ballet lessons and spent summers vacationing with her family or at camp. She admits that she was not a very discriminating reader. "I would really and truly read anything that I could find," she recalled. "I was a tremendous Nancy Drew fan. My parents could get me to do anything by promising me another Nancy Drew

Milton overcomes his naughty behavior when another student arrives to take his place as "new boy" in the class. (Illustration by the author from *The New Boy.*)

book. But then, the next day, I might take a copy of [William Shakespeare's] *Romeo and Juliet* off the bookshelf and read that." She added: "We really didn't have an enormous number of books in our house, but my mother was a great library goer and our trips were always great adventures." Among her most favorite stories was William H. Hudson's *The Green Mansions.*

Although she attended schools for the gifted, Keller considers herself "a pretty good, but not great" student. "I think I was basically just as undisciplined in my schoolwork as I was in my reading, until I got to about my junior year in high school," she confessed. "Then it suddenly dawned on me that I really needed to perform better if I wanted to go to college." As Keller began improving her grades and study habits, she attempted to better her mark in a required Latin course by doing an extra credit project. As she worked on this assignment—translating *Little Red Riding Hood* into Latin—she began developing a talent for what would later become her career. Not only did she complete the translation, but she prepared pictures for the work as well. "I remember enjoying that project so much that I should have known then that children's books were really what I wanted to do," Keller acknowledged. "It just took me a whole lot longer to figure that out."

Merges Interests in Art and Writing

Keller concedes that she did not realize a career as a children's author and illustrator until she was forty years old. She admits having a conflict of interests in her life between academic and artistic pursuits. "My whole life is checkered with a movement back and forth between those two kinds of activities," she said. She began her college career by attending Sarah Lawrence College to study art and ended up getting a degree in history. "I went to graduate school to study American history and afterward, when I was married and working, I was always taking art classes." While enrolled in a printmaking class she was encouraged by the instructor to become involved in children's book illustrations. "I decided to work on a portfolio of art samples for children's book illustrations. That was about fifteen years ago when my children were quite small." In 1981 she visited Greenwillow Books to show her illustrations and was given one week to create a story to accompany one of her drawings. Since that test of her talents, she has gone on to write and illustrate more than twenty books for Greenwillow.

When asked about who has influenced her art and writing, Keller responds that her styles are constantly evolving. "I wouldn't say any one person had influenced it, but really many people," she explained. "My art style has changed and developed over the last decade in so many different ways. I think the influence has come from an increased awareness of the work of other illustrators and also from feelings about the art world in

general." She credits editor Susan Hirschman of Greenwillow Books with guiding her writing style. "Susan actually got me to the point of believing that I could write and then to the point where I can't imagine not writing."

Describing her art as "water colors, usually with a pen outline," Keller called her style minimalist. "My work tends to include flat shapes. It's sometimes cartoon-like, and when it's not cartoon-like, it's still not really realistic work." In her books, Keller frequently uses animals as her protagonists. The title character of *Geraldine's Blanket* and *Geraldine's Big Snow* is a piglet, while *Horace* features a spotted cat, *Too Big* and *Henry's Happy Birthday* concern a family of opossums, *What Alvin Wanted* and *The New Boy* are populated with mice, and *Cromwell's Glasses* and *Maxine in the Middle* involve rabbits.

"I never had any pets when I was a child," Keller stated. "But, my reasons for using animal protagonists are

Simon enjoys helping Pops take care of injured birds like Baby, but finds it difficult to part with his flamingo friend when it is well enough to leave. (Illustration by the author from *Island Baby*.)

many and varied. There are just some books where it seems more natural, more comfortable, to use an animal than a person. I'm not sure that I could always tell you why. For me, personally, it's more fun to draw animals because they are whimsical, and I don't have to be so concerned about anatomical accuracy and things like that. And animals just seem very well suited to children's stories. I always enjoy doing those more. It's really just sort of a gut feeling that, as I write a story, the character begins to emerge in my mind and it either takes a human or an animal form."

Although she provided the art for Jane Thayer's *Clever Raccoon* in 1981, Keller waited another year to see publication of her first solo book as an author and illustrator. That work, *Cromwell's Glasses,* describes a young rabbit's anxiety as he gets his first pair of spectacles. Next, Keller wrote *Ten Sleepy Sheep,* which tells of a boy who, finding he cannot fall asleep, decides to count sheep to make himself drowsy. His insomnia continues, however, as he is kept awake when the sheep appear in his room and throw a party. *Too Big,* published in 1983, introduced the character Henry, a possum who has problems adjusting to his new baby sibling. Keller continued to inform readers of Henry's antics and adventures in books like *Henry's Fourth of July* and *Henry's Happy Birthday.*

Stories Based on Family Experiences

As Keller's career progressed, she found ideas for stories came from various sources, including her pediatrician husband and their son and daughter. "I have a habit of always listening when children are speaking," she told *SATA.* "I try to pay very close attention and to put myself in that situation as often as possible because children's lives are just full of stories. So, sometimes I

A little leopard begins to worry when he realizes he looks different from the other members of his tiger-striped family in Keller's self-illustrated book *Horace.*

get the ideas just from listening to children. Occasionally, my husband will bring home some good things."

Geraldine's Blanket portrays an experience that her husband described. In the book, a piglet counters the loss of her security blanket by using the fabric to make clothes for a new doll. Keller's 1992 story *Furry* was inspired by her daughter's allergy to animals. The book delineates a girl's frustrations as she realizes she cannot own a pet with fur. Her sadness is reversed, however, when her brother brings home an unusual pet—a chameleon—to which she is not allergic.

"*Horace* came from a personal experience of mine," the author told *SATA.* "I had once met an adopted child who clearly knew she was adopted but had not been told and was troubled by that, as one would be." Keller claims *Geraldine's Big Snow,* the narrative of a child who long awaits a big snowfall so she can go sledding, as her own story. "A lot of times I will take a personal experience or observation and dress it in different clothing and turn it into a book," she added.

Among Keller's other popular titles are *Goodbye Max, The New Boy, Island Baby,* and *Harry and Tuck.* In *Goodbye Max,* readers get acquainted with Ben, a boy who is struggling to cope with the death of his dog. Through friendship, happy memories, and a little help from a new puppy, Ben overcomes his grief. *The New Boy* again uses an animal protagonist to talk about a realistic childhood issue. Here, Milton the Mouse has trouble fitting in with the other students at his new school. Because he is new, Milton is considered weird by his classmates and attempts to be overly nice to gain their acceptance. When his actions are misconstrued, he decides to act weird, sticking out his tongue, singing during naptime, and putting a caterpillar in a girl's lunchbox. Scolded for his antics, Milton improves his behavior and finally begins to fit in once another new, "weird" kid starts school.

Island Baby combines human and animal protagonists. The book concerns a bird hospital owner and his young assistant who try to help an injured baby bird. The story is based on an experience that Keller's husband and son had while scuba diving in the Caribbean. *Harry and Tuck* is the story of two best friends who find their relationship changes as they enter school and are assigned to different classes.

Characters Capture Children's Emotions

"I think *Horace* and *Geraldine's Blanket* are my two favorites," Keller told *SATA.* "I like *Geraldine* because she's really me, and *Horace* because it's a gentle and nice story, one of the better ones I've done." When asked to describe her recurring protagonists Geraldine and Henry, Keller explained: "Geraldine is a character who is wise beyond her years, or at least beyond the adults in her life. She is strong-minded and defiant, but never destructive. She always manages to have things come out in her favor, but she's never naughty about it. She's just clever. The children who read the Geraldine stories

Laura learns the redeeming qualities of the family's non-furry pet, a chameleon, in Keller's humorous book *Furry*. (Illustration by the author.)

identify with her somewhat mischievous behavior, but it's all perfectly safe because she never does anything that is really wrong. I wrote a couple of books about Henry. He's just fun. He doesn't have any special meaning, except that he is always somewhat beleaguered somehow, which, in a funny way, was how my son, Jesse, was when he was very little. He always had this feeling that things weren't working out for him and that somehow he had been singled out for that misfortune. That's why *Henry's Happy Birthday* is dedicated to Jesse."

Keller is uncertain why her books are so popular with young readers. "It's a constant miracle to me," she exclaimed. "Sometimes when a child comes up to me and says in a completely earnest voice, 'This is my favorite book,' or 'I love this story,' it almost moves me to tears. That's the most wonderful thing. And the children can never tell you exactly why, and they really shouldn't have to. Adults tell me that my books really hit the target with children's feelings—that I somehow seem to speak directly to the children's experiences and things that they care about. I hope that's true."

While Keller loves writing and illustrating her own stories, she also enjoys creating art for other authors' books. "There are challenges to both," she said. "When you write and illustrate the same book, you conceive it as a whole. It's really wonderful to make the pictures complement the words and vice versa. When you're given somebody else's text, there are other possibilities—to interpret that text in a way that's visually appealing and in a way that's accurate, interesting, and informative."

As the author continues her work with children's books, she has no plans to write for older readers. "Creating children's stories is the most wonderful job in the world; I never think of it as being work." Keller's current project is a book about Vietnam. Describing it as her most difficult work to prepare to date, she explained that she and her husband visited the country in 1992 as they worked on a wildlife conservation project. "For my book I did a little research beyond what I brought back myself in terms of data. But it is an entirely different kind of book for me—different from anything I've ever done."

While Keller believes that her books do not contain an overall message, people have told her that her stories seem to have morals to them. However, she asserts that she does not set out to craft books with particular meanings. "It just happens," she related. "I don't think that children's books have an obligation to teach a lesson or have a message. It's enough that they be fun to read."

■ Works Cited

Keller, Holly, telephone interview for *Something about the Author* conducted by Kathleen J. Edgar, May 4, 1993.

Persson, Lauralyn, review of *Furry, School Library Journal*, April, 1992, p. 94.

Vasilakis, Nancy, review of *Horace, Horn Book*, May-June, 1991, pp. 314-315.

■ For More Information See

PERIODICALS

Booklist, April 15, 1983, p. 1095; March 15, 1992, p. 1388.

Bulletin of the Center for Children's Books, June, 1987, pp. 190-191; March, 1989, pp. 173-174; July, 1990, p. 269.

Horn Book, May-June, 1987, p. 332; May-June, 1990, p. 326.

Kirkus Reviews, February 1, 1983; September 1, 1983; March 1, 1984.

New York Times Book Review, May 17, 1987, p. 40.

Publishers Weekly, April 5, 1991, p. 145.

School Library Journal, March, 1982, p. 136; February, 1984, p. 59; October, 1986; February, 1989, p. 72; September, 1989, p. 228; August, 1990, pp. 143-144; November, 1991, p. 100; November, 1992, p. 72.

Tribune Books (Chicago), May 3, 1987, p. 8; June 18, 1989, p. 10; September 13, 1992, p. 7.

—Sketch by Kathleen J. Edgar

KING, Colin 1943-

■ Personal

Born November 11, 1943, in Great Tey, Essex, England; son of F. (a blacksmith) and Joslin King; married Valerie Anne (an author, teacher, and embroiderer) Waight, 1976; children: Andrew, Vanessa, Tom, Ben. *Education:* Colchester School of Art, National Diploma in Art and Design, 1965; Royal College of Art, M.Art., 1968. *Politics:* "Left, Right, & Centre!" *Religion:* Christian. *Hobbies and other interests:* Listening to music—"still a Dylan, Van Morrison, and Beethoven freak!"

■ Addresses

Home—Saddlers Cottage, Well Lane, Clare, Sudbury, Suffolk CO10 8NH. *Agent*—Linda Rogers Associates, P.O. Box 330, 1 Bloomsbury House, 9 Guilford St., London WC1N 1PX, England.

■ Career

Free-lance illustrator, 1968—. Worked in advertising and editorial areas; notable commissions include *Fortune* magazine, *Sunday Times,* Shell UK, *Economist,* London Science Museum, Dunlop, and others. Part-time instructor at Harrow, Wimbledon, and Cambridge Art Schools.

■ Illustrator

"KNOW HOW" SERIES

Annabelle Curtis and Judy Hindley, *The Know How Book of Paper Fun,* Peter Usborne, 1975.

Judy Hindley, *The Know How Book of Spycraft,* Peter Usborne, 1975.

Judy Hindley, *The Know How Book of Flying Models,* Peter Usborne, 1975.

Mary Jean McNeil, *How Things Began,* Peter Usborne, 1975.

Judy Hindley, *How Your Body Works,* Peter Usborne, 1975.

Christopher Rawson, *Machines,* Peter Usborne, 1976.

Anne Civardi, *Fishing,* Peter Usborne, 1976.

Heather Amery and others, *The Know How Make and Do Encyclopedia,* compiled by Christopher Rawson, Peter Usborne, 1976.

Heather Amery, *The Know How Book of Jokes & Tricks,* Peter Usborne, 1977.

Judy Hindley, *Detection,* Peter Usborne, 1978.

Angela Wilkes, *Letters,* Peter Usborne, 1979.

Angela Wilkes, *Numbers,* Peter Usborne, 1979.

Angela Wilkes, *Colours,* Peter Usborne, 1979.

Carol Watson, *The House,* Peter Usborne, 1980.

Carol Watson, *The Shop,* Peter Usborne, 1980.

Carol Watson, *The Town,* Peter Usborne, 1980.

Johnson, Ward, and McPherson, *Science Fun,* Peter Usborne, 1981.

Heather Amery, *Word Detective,* Peter Usborne, 1982.

"SPY GUIDES" SERIES

Judy Hindley, *Secret Messages,* Peter Usborne, 1978.

COLIN KING

R. Thomson, *Tracking and Trailing,* Peter Usborne, 1978.

Christopher Rawson, *Disguises,* Peter Usborne, 1978.

"DETECTIVE GUIDES" SERIES

Anne Civardi, *Catching Crooks,* Peter Usborne, 1979.

Judy Hindley, *Fakes and Forgeries,* Peter Usborne, 1979.

Angela Wilkes, *Clues and Suspects,* Peter Usborne, 1979.

"ALFIE ALLIGATOR" SERIES

Judy Hindley, *Animal Parade,* Collins, 1985.

Judy Hindley, *Alphabet Game,* Collins, 1985.

Judy Hindley, *How Big? How Tall?,* Collins, 1985.

Judy Hindley, *Isn't It Time?,* Collins, 1986.

OTHER

Althea, *Building a House,* Dinosaur Publications, 1974.

J. R. C. Yglesias and L. E. Snellgrove, *Mainstream English,* Longman, 1975.

M. G. Graham-Cameron, *Playing Football,* Dinosaur Publications, 1975.

W. Richardson, *Work Study: Time and Motion,* Longman, 1975.

M. G. Graham-Cameron, *The Cambridge Scene,* Dinosaur Publications, 1977.

Heather Amery, *The Alphabet Book,* Peter Usborne, 1979.

Anne Civardi and others, *Detective's Handbook,* Peter Usborne, 1979.

Angela Wilkes, *Picture Dictionary,* Peter Usborne, 1984.

Heather Amery, *The Usborne Children's Wordfinder,* Peter Usborne, 1984.

J. Elliott, *Children's Encyclopedia,* Peter Usborne, 1986.

Heather Amery, *Black Knight's Victory,* Peter Usborne, 1987.

Heather Amery, *Mammoth Hunt,* Peter Usborne, 1987.

Heather Amery, *Ships, Sailors, and the Sea,* Peter Usborne, 1988.

Mother Goose Nursery Rhymes, Octopus/Hamlyn, 1988.

Caroline Young, *Castles, Pyramids, and Palaces,* Peter Usborne, 1988.

J. Wood, compiler, *Amazing Jokes,* Conran, 1989.

J. Wood, compiler, *Amazing Puzzles and Tricks,* Conran, 1989.

Lizzie Swanson, *Hunt the Tiger,* Ginn, 1989.

Kate Petty, *Illustrated Atlas,* Conran, 1990.

Caroline Young, *Railways and Trains,* Peter Usborne, 1991.

Valerie King, *Old Smokey,* Collins, 1991.

Valerie King, *Horatio Whale,* Collins, 1991.

Angela Royston, *Car: See How It Works,* F. Lincoln, 1991.

Susan Mayles, *How Do Animals Talk?,* Peter Usborne, 1991.

Susan Meredith, *What's Inside You?,* Peter Usborne, 1991.

Sophy Tahta, *First Book of Britain,* Peter Usborne, 1992.

Louise Jervis, *Picture Dictionary,* Grisewood & Dempsey, 1992.

Angela Royston, *Plane: See How It Works,* F. Lincoln, 1992.

Harriet Griffey, *It's My Birthday,* Ladybird, 1992.

Sophy Tahta, *Where Does Rubbish Go?,* Peter Usborne, 1993.

■ Sidelights

Colin King told *SATA* that he wanted to be an artist from a very early age. He says that he was always drawing at school, and was fascinated by how machines worked. After training in both graphic design and fine art at the Colchester School of Art, he attended the Royal College of Art, where his instructors included notables such as Edward Bawden, John Nash, Quentin Blake, and Paul Hogarth. There he developed a style that combines humor with detailed description.

After graduation, King began working as a free-lance illustrator and graphic designer. He also held part-time teaching posts at the Harrow, Wimbledon, and Cambridge art schools. It was while teaching at Wimbledon in the mid-1970s that he was contacted to work for a new children's publisher, Peter Usborne. "His philosophy, 'combine fun, colour, and information—make learning fun!' suited my style," King told *SATA.* He was their first published illustrator, and he worked extensively on their hugely successful "Know How," "Spy Guides" and "Detective Guides" series. He has gone on to illustrate for other publishers, including two books by his wife, Valerie, for Collins.

King states that he works from his home in Clare, Suffolk, in a 14th-century timber-framed cottage, which he shares with three dogs and a cat: "They often get featured in my illustrations." The books he has illustrated have been translated into many different languages, including French, Italian, German, Japanese, Irish, Welsh, and Hebrew. "I am still doing what I wanted to do in primary school," King declares. "Advice to would-be illustrators sounds obvious—learn to draw and develop an unshakeable commitment!"

* * *

KLEVEN, Elisa 1958-
(Elisa Schneider)

■ Personal

Name is pronounced "clay-ven"; born October 14, 1958, in Los Angeles, CA; daughter of Stanley (a doctor) and Lorraine Art (an artist) Schneider; married Paul Kleven, July, 1984; children: Mia. *Education:* University of California, Berkeley, B.A., 1981, teaching credentials, 1983.

■ Addresses

Home—1028 Peralta Ave., Albany, CA 94706.

■ Career

Berkeley Hills Nursery School, Berkeley, CA, nursery school teacher, 1978-80; weaver and toy maker, 1980-84; Prospect School, El Cerrito, CA, fourth-grade and art teacher, 1984-86; writer and illustrator. *Member:* Society of Children's Book Writers and Illustrators,

ELISA KLEVEN

Amnesty International, World Wildlife Fund, Humane Society of the United States, Phi Beta Kappa.

■ Awards, Honors

Parent's Choice award for illustration for *Abuela*; *Abuela* was also named a notable book by the American Library Association and a "Fanfare" book by *Horn Book*.

■ Writings

(Under name Elisa Schneider) *The Merry-Go-Round Dog*, Knopf, 1988.
Ernst, Dutton Children's Books, 1989.
The Lion and the Little Red Bird, Dutton, 1992.
(And illustrator) *The Paper Princess*, Dutton, 1994.

Ernst was translated into Japanese and Chinese.

ILLUSTRATOR

Isabel Wilner, *B Is For Bethlehem*, Dutton, 1990.
Arthur Dorros, *Abuela*, Dutton, 1991.
Tricia Brown, *The City by the Bay*, Chronicle, 1993.
Karen Lotz, *Snow Song Whistling*, Dutton, 1993.

■ Sidelights

Elisa Kleven told *SATA:* "A comment I hear often about my work is, 'It looks like you were having fun when you made this!' I never know exactly how to respond. I agonize a lot over my stories and my pictures: Is this a stupid idea? Is this a cluttered illustration?

"Yet once the flow and excitement of creation carries me safely beyond the internal critical voices, picture-book-making is indeed fun—so much fun I can't imagine not doing it. Creating the little make-believe world of a book—bringing characters to life, 'dressing' them, naming them, worrying over and loving them, giving them landscapes to roam in and skies to fly through—gives me the same deep joy and satisfaction that playing with beloved dolls and toys gave me in childhood.

"The very way in which I create my illustrations is akin to child's play. I work in mixed-media collage, a malleable, forgiving medium which allows me great freedom to experiment, arrange, rearrange, and discover joyful surprises. In addition to watercolor, gouache, ink, crayons, pastels, felt-tipped pens, and colored pencils, I incorporate found objects into my pictures. I love to snip and glue scraps of this and that into new shapes: a doily cut to bits becomes a snowstorm, a scrap of lace becomes a curtain, a patterned piece cut out of a quilt calendar becomes a skyscraper, a snippet of lamb's wool becomes a lion's mane. I usually draw my characters first, then cut them out like paper dolls and glue them into their 'worlds,' the larger scenes of which they're part.

"My advice to aspiring writers/illustrators of picture books would be to value and love your imaginations.

Try not to forget that you're creating books for *children*—try to remember what you were thrilled and intrigued by, and what you loved, as a child. Don't be slick or gimmicky; while creating, try not to think about 'the market'—just the children."

■ For More Information See

PERIODICALS

Booklist, October 15, 1991.
Children's Book Review Service, January, 1990, p. 51.
Horn Book, November/December, 1991, p. 726; May/June, 1992, p. 321.
Kirkus Reviews, May 15, 1992, p. 672.
Los Angeles Times Book Review, November 26, 1989, p. 27.
Newsweek, December 16, 1992, p. 68.
New York Times Book Review, June 21, 1992, p. 27.
Publishers Weekly, May 18, 1992, p. 68; October 4, 1993, p. 78.
School Library Journal, December, 1989, p. 84; July, 1992, p. 60.

* * *

KNOX, James
See BRITTAIN, William (E.)

* * *

KNOX, Jolyne 1937-

■ Personal

Born November 2, 1937, in Cheshire, England; daughter of Robert Edgar Helm (a company director) and Elizabeth Georgina (Hunter) Kennedy; married Julian James Knox (an anthropologist), September 3, 1960 (died October 30, 1987); children: Alexander Julian, Benedict James. *Education:* University of London, Goldsmith College School of Art, B.A., 1974.

■ Addresses

Agent—c/o Publicity Director, A. & C. Black, Ltd., 35 Bedford Row, London WC1R 4JH, England.

■ Career

Freelance illustrator and writer, 1974—. *Member:* British Association of Illustrators, British Society of Authors.

■ Awards, Honors

Short list, Smarties Prize (Great Britain), 1988, for *Desperate for a Dog; No-Name Dog* was selected as a Children's Book of the Year by the Children's Book Committee at Bank Street College, 1991.

JOLYNE KNOX

■ Writings

(And illustrator) *Mr. String,* Hamish Hamilton, 1988, Puffin Books, 1992.

ILLUSTRATOR

Jacynth Hope Simpson, *Always on the Move,* Heinemann, 1975.

The Gingerbread Boy, Traditional Folk Tale, Macdonald, 1975.

Ian Weekly, *The Secret Hide,* Hamish Hamilton, 1977.

Frank Walker, *Pop go the Vipers,* Macmillan, 1979.

William Geldard, *The Day the Clocks Stopped,* Readers Digest, 1980.

Jean Morris, *Twist of Eight,* Chatto & Windus, 1981.

Ruth Thompson, *The Hedgerow Circus,* Readers Digest, 1982.

Thompson, *In the Park,* Readers Digest, 1982.

David Malouf, *12 Edmonston Street,* Chatto & Windus, 1985.

Ann Pilling, *No Guns No Oranges,* Heinemann, 1986.

Jennifer Zabel, *Cobwebs and Creepers,* Macdonald, 1988.

Pilling, *The Beast in the Basement,* Heinemann, 1988.

Shirley Isherwood, *Alice Alone,* Macdonald, 1988.

Rose Impey, *Desperate for a Dog,* A. & C. Black, 1988.

Impey, *Houdini Dog,* A. & C. Black, 1988, published as *No-Name Dog,* Dutton, 1990.

Anne Mangan, *The School Cat,* Hodder & Stoughton, 1990.

Jill Paton Walsh, *Farmer Farmer,* Bodley Head, 1990.

Walsh, *Queenie,* Random Century, 1990.

Walsh, *Jenny Jones,* Random Century, 1990.

Walsh, *Wolf,* Random Century, 1990.

Marian Swinger, *Guess What?,* Harper, 1992.

Swinger, *Riddle Me Re, What Can It Be?,* Harper, 1992.

■ Work in Progress

A picture book as author and illustrator; a design project for Royal Worcester, Ltd.

■ Sidelights

Jolyne Knox has worked as a professional illustrator of children's books since 1974. "I cannot remember when I first started to draw," she told *SATA.* "Drawing is something I have always *had* to do, a daily draw is as important as a daily meal. Withdrawal symptoms take over if pencil and paper are not readily available." Knox's passion for drawing is apparent in her work. Two books she illustrated have won prizes: *Desperate for a Dog,* written by Rose Impey, made the short list for the Smarties Prize in the United Kingdom in 1988, and *No-Name Dog,* (published as *Houdini Dog* in the U.K.) was selected as a Children's Books of the Year in 1991 by the Child Study Children's Book Committee at Bank Street College in the United States.

Knox explained to *SATA* her approach to illustrating a story: "I try to respond visually to the text in a way that works at different levels both for a child and for the adult who may be reading it, so each will feel interested, amused, involved and the boredom threshold kept at bay. I want my work to convey the fun and excitement of taking a line for a walk and also to reflect the freshness and vitality of the watercolour medium I most frequently use."

In 1988, Knox published the first book that she wrote as well as illustrated, *Mr. String.* The book, Knox related to *SATA,* "grew from the frustration of being the one non-playing member of a house full of musicians. At one time both my husband and two sons had the following collection of instruments in use: two violins, one viola, a piano, bassoon and flute. In case anyone thinks I must have been living with a family of contortionists, they were not all played at once. However the constant practicing, the 'Oh dear what if . . . ?' nerves just before a concert, the endless worries about strings, reeds, bows, humidity and heaven knows what else led to my story of the little problems of *Mr. String.*

"I believe passionately in attracting the young to discover, early in life, the joy of books and reading and the marvelous world unlocked by this skill. I want all my future work to encourage this in every way possible."

KOLODNY, Nancy J. 1946-

■ Personal

Born March 18, 1946, in New York, NY; daughter of Lawrence M. (a doctor) and Estelle (Srebnik) Shapiro; married Robert Charles Kolodny (a doctor, researcher and writer), June 6, 1966; children: Linda Hillary, Lora Elizabeth, Lisa Michelle. *Education:* Barnard College, B.A., 1967; Washington University, M.A., 1969, M.S.W., 1980.

■ Addresses

Office—Behavioral Medicine Institute, 885 Oenoke Ridge Rd., New Canaan, CT 06840.

■ Career

University City High School, University City, MO, English teacher, 1967-69; South Boston High School, South Boston, MA, English teacher, 1970-71; Clayton High School, Clayton, MO, English teacher, 1971-72; Bulimia Anorexia Self Help, St. Louis, MO, psychiatric social worker and eating disorder therapist, 1981-83; Behavioral Medicine Institute, New Canaan, CT, psychiatric social worker and eating disorder therapist, 1983—. Class correspondent, Barnard College, New York City, 1982-87; board member, Saxe Middle School, New Canaan, CT, 1985-88; board member, Fairfield County Seven Sisters Alumnae seminars, 1985-92; creator/facilitator of "Closing the Gap," a high school parent-student communication program, New Canaan High School, 1987-89. Consultant to University of Bridgeport, Home Box Office and Allegra Films; public speaker on eating disorders, adolescence and parenting. *Member:* National Association of Social Workers, American Association of University Women (board member, 1987-89; member of committee on women, 1989), Kappa Delta Pi.

■ Awards, Honors

Editor's Choice Award, *Booklist,* 1987, and Best Book Award nomination, *Voice of Youth Advocates,* 1988, both for *When Food's a Foe; Smart Choices* was named a Young Adult's Choice book by the International Reading Association, 1988.

■ Writings

(With Mark Schwartz) *Instructor's Manual for "Human Sexuality" by Masters, Johnson, Kolodny,* Little, Brown, 1982; revised edition, 1988.

(With Felix E. F. Larocca) *Anorexia and Bulimia Facilitator's Training Manual: A Primer, the BASH Approach,* Midwest Medical Publications, 1983.

(With Robert C. Kolodny, Thomas E. Bratter, and Cheryl Deep) *How to Survive Your Adolescent's Adolescence,* Little, Brown, 1984.

(With R. C. Kolodny and Bratter) *Smart Choices: A Guide to Surviving at Home and in School, Dating and Sex, Dealing with Crises, Applying to College, and More,* Little, Brown, 1986.

When Food's a Foe: How to Confront and Conquer Eating Disorders, Little, Brown, 1987, revised edition, 1992.

Contributor to *New Directions Quarterly Sourcebook's* mental health series, Jossey-Bass, 1984.

■ Sidelights

As a psychiatric social worker and an eating disorder therapist, Nancy J. Kolodny writes about the types of problems she treats in the Behavioral Medical Institute. These problems are faced by today's adolescents, and Kolodny's books help them to face such challenges effectively. Patty Campbell, writing about self-help books for the *Wilson Library Bulletin,* reports: "Although self-help for adults has proliferated, such books for teenagers have been relatively scarce."

Campbell describes Kolodny's *Smart Choices* as "an encyclopedia of advice for every conceivable social problem of adolescence, [covering] not only parents, sex, school, and emotions, but drugs and alcohol, eating disorders, divorce, pregnancy, loneliness, depression, suicide, death, and how to persuade your friends not to break the law." Also included in *Smart Choices* are some relatively new problems today's teenagers may face, including bulimia, contraception, tattoos, attending one's first funeral, and how to handle the persistence of military recruiters. Problems experienced in everyday conflicts within families and among friends are also discussed, thereby giving teenagers a chance to help understand their family dynamics as well as their relationships with friends. A *Publishers Weekly* reviewer writes: "An up to date, extensive bibliography and a tone of respect make *Smart Choices* a 'smart choice' to have on hand."

NANCY J. KOLODNY

Kolodny's *When Food's a Foe: How to Confront and Conquer Eating Disorders* not only describes anorexia and bulimia but also helps to guide teenagers who are afflicted with these disorders. The information on self-image, eating disorder symptoms, how to get help and how to help others, makes the book appropriate for many adolescent readers. Kolodny uses teen-related analogies and quotes from adolescent anorexics and bulimics to appeal to her youthful audience. Kolodny also incorporates questions, suggestions, and words of encouragement to the readers. Information on how to face the problem and change the behavior which leads to eating disorders is detailed using quizzes designed to help the reader examine their self-image and self-esteem. With the number of such cases on the rise, Shirley Carmony, writing for *Voice of Youth Advocates,* calls *When Food's a Foe* "an excellent addition to a school library. It is both readable and timely."

■ Works Cited

Campbell, Patty, "The Young Adult Perplex," *Wilson Library Bulletin,* December, 1986, pp. 50-51.
Carmony, Shirley, review of *When Food's a Foe, Voice of Youth Advocates,* February, 1988, p. 296.
Publishers Weekly, December 26, 1986, p. 62.

■ For More Information See

PERIODICALS

Bulletin of the Center for Children's Books, February, 1988, p. 119.
Children's Book Review Service, April, 1987, p. 100.
Publishers Weekly, December 11, 1987, p. 67.
School Library Journal, January, 1987, p. 84; March, 1988, p. 221.
Voice of Youth Advocates, August, 1988, p. 118.

*   *   *

KROLL, Virginia L(ouise) 1948-
(Melrose Cooper)

■ Personal

Born April 28, 1948, in Buffalo, NY; daughter of Lester H. (a United States immigration inspector) and Helen (a registered nurse and model; maiden name, Szewczyk) Kroll; married David Haeick (in construction); children: Sara, Seth, Joshua, Hannah, Katya, Noah. *Education:* Attended State University of New York at Buffalo and Canisius College. *Religion:* Roman Catholic. *Hobbies and other interests:* reading, crafts, friends.

■ Addresses

Home—214 Maple Avenue, Hamburg, NY 14075.
Office—c/o Publicity Director, Four Winds Press, 866 Third Avenue, New York, NY 10022.

VIRGINIA L. KROLL

■ Career

Fifth grade teacher in the Buffalo, NY area, 1968-69 and 1980-81; Hamburg Memorial Youth Center, Hamburg, NY, recreation assistant, 1978-80. Medaille College, Buffalo, college instructor for Writing for Children course, 1993.

■ Writings

PICTURE BOOKS

Helen the Fish, illustrated by Teri Weidner, Albert Whitman and Co., 1992.
My Sister, Then and Now, illustrated by Mary Worcester, Carolrhoda Books, 1992.
Masai and I, illustrated by Nancy Carpenter, Four Winds Press/Macmillan, 1992.
Naomi Knows It's Springtime, illustrated by Jill Kastner, Boyds Mills Press, 1993.
Woodhoopoe Willie, illustrated by Katherine Roundtree, Charlesbridge Publishing, 1993.
Africa Brothers and Sisters, illustrated by Vanessa French, Four Winds Press/Macmillan, 1993.
(Under pseudonym Melrose Cooper) *I Got a Family,* illustrated by Dale Gottlieb, Henry Holt, 1993.
A Carp for Kimiko, illustrated by Roundtree, Charlesbridge Publishing, 1993.
I Wanted to Know All about God, illustrated by Debra Reid Jenkins, William B. Eerdmans Publishing, 1994.

An American schoolgirl daydreams about what life would be like as one of the Masai people of East Africa in Kroll's picture book, *Masai and I*. (Illustration by Nancy Carpenter.)

Beginnings, illustrated by Stacey Schuett, Albert Whitman and Co., 1994.

Pink Paper Swans, illustrated by Nancy Clouse, William B. Eerdmans Publishing, 1994.

Sweet Magnolia, illustrated by Laura Jakes, Charlesbridge Publishing, 1994.

The Seasons and Someone, illustrated by Tatsuro Kiuchi, Harcourt Brace Jovanovich, 1994.

Faraway Drums, illustrated by Floyd Cooper, Little, Brown, in press.

Hands Fit, Boyds Mills Press, in press.

OTHER

When Will We Be Sisters?, Scholastic, 1993.

Jaha and Jamil Went down the Hill, illustrated by Roundtree, Charlesbridge Publishing, 1994.

Handy Hairstyles and Dandy Do's, illustrated by Kay Life, Charlesbridge Publishing, 1994.

I Saw a Whale, Seacoast Publications, 1994.

Butterfly Boy, Boyds Mills Press, in press.

UNDER PSEUDONYM MELROSE COOPER

Life Riddles (chapter book), Henry Holt, 1994.

I Got Community, illustrated by Gottlieb, Henry Holt, in press.

Contributor to periodicals.

■ Sidelights

Kroll told *SATA:* "All I ever wanted to be is an author. And now that I am one, all I ever want to be is an author. In between the desire and the realized dream, I became a mother. Good thing. My six children and one grandchild give me stories every day. So do the children I visit in schools. There is a story in everyone I meet, everything I encounter, because they induce wonder.

"*Masai and I* began as a discussion with my former fifth graders about each other's heritage. *Helen the Fish* involves the experiences of three of my children and a pet goldfish. *My Sister, Then and Now* deals with the struggles of mental illness, which I have seen in two families who are close to me. *Life Riddles* includes many true incidents of my personal struggle with poverty. My brother, 'Donald the drummer,' gave me the idea for the musical percussionist in *Woodhoopoe Willie* and my sister, Nancy, a wildlife rehabilitator, for *Sweet Magnolia.* The list goes on . . . . "

Kroll might be considered an inspiration for many writers since most of her books were accepted from the "slush pile." Despite the positive response from editors, Kroll has had several negative responses which bothered her. One was a prejudice some editors had against a white author writing about other cultures. Kroll feels it's foolish to believe a white person is not capable of writing "black material." She doesn't want to write about a suburban middle-class white woman's world. So she writes whatever she has a desire to write.

Masai and I is about a young African American girl who is learning about the Masai culture in school. Each day she goes home and compares herself to an East African child she is studying. She wonders where a Masai girl would sleep, what she would do in her free time, what she would wear, eat, etc. Readers learn that while the everyday lives of Americans are different than the everyday lives of the Masai, children are still children, no matter where they live. Martha Topol in the *School Library Journal* calls *Masai and I* "an interesting, richly blended book that connects two different worlds . . . pointing out similarities and differences."

Another type of prejudice which Kroll has had to deal with is that some felt she was writing too many books too fast. She addressed this criticism by using a pseudonym. She chose one which neither reveals her sex nor hints at her race. The first time she submitted a manuscript under the new name, it was immediately accepted.

Kroll has had a lot of people tell her how wonderful it is that she has a gift that she can get paid for. Her comment is, "This is true, but talent needs work. A gift can sit there and look beautiful, but it is worth nothing at all until is it unwrapped and used properly."

■ Works Cited

Topol, Martha, review of *Masai and I, School Library Journal,* October, 1992, p. 91.

■ For More Information See

PERIODICALS

Children's Book Review Service, spring, 1992, p. 135.
Kirkus Reviews, September 1, 1992, p. 1131.
Publishers Weekly, June 29, 1992, p. 62; December 28, 1992, p. 26.
School Library Journal, June 6, 1992, p. 96; November, 1992, p. 94.

KURTZ, Katherine (Irene) 1944-

■ Personal

Born October 18, 1944, in Coral Gables, FL; daughter of Fredrick Harry Kurtz (an electronics technician) and Margaret Frances Carter (a paralegal); married Scott Roderick MacMillan (an author and producer), March 9, 1983; children: Cameron Alexander Stewart. *Education:* University of Miami, B.S., 1966; University of California, Los Angeles, M.A., 1971. *Religion:* "Nominally Church of Ireland (Anglican)."

■ Addresses

Home and office—Holybrooke Hall, Bray, County Wicklow, Ireland. *Agent*—Russell Galen, Scott Meredith Literary Agency, 845 Third Ave, New York, NY 10022.

■ Career

Writer. Los Angeles Police Department, Los Angeles, CA, instructional technologist, 1969-81. *Member:* Authors Guild, SFFWA.

■ Awards, Honors

Edmund Hamilton Memorial Award, 1977, for *Camber of Culdi;* Balrog Award, 1982, for *Camber the Heretic; The Legacy of the Lair* was cited as a "Best Science Fiction Title of 1986" by *Voice of Youth Advocates;* Dame of the Military and Hospitaller Order of St. Lazarus of Jerusalem; Dame Grand Officer of the Supreme Military Order of the Temple of Jerusalem; Dame of Honour of the Hospitaller Order of St. John of Jerusalem; Dame of the Noble Company of the Rose;

KATHERINE KURTZ

Companion of the Royal House of O'Conor; Augustan Society fellow; Octavian Society fellow.

■ Writings

"DERYNI" SERIES

The Chronicles of the Deryni, Volume 1: *Deryni Rising,* Ballantine, 1970, hardcover edition, Century, 1985, Volume 2: *Deryni Checkmate,* Ballantine, 1972, hardcover edition, Century, 1985, Volume III: *High Deryni,* Ballantine, 1973, hardcover edition, Century, 1985; all three books published in one volume as *The Chronicles of the Deryni,* Science Fiction Book Club, 1985.

The Legends of Saint Camber, Volume I: *Camber of Culdi,* Ballantine, 1976, hardcover edition, Del Rey, 1979, Volume II: *Saint Camber,* Del Rey, 1978, Volume III: *Camber the Heretic,* Del Rey, 1981, hardcover edition, Science Fiction Book Club, 1981.

The Histories of King Kelson, Del Rey, Volume I: *The Bishop's Heir,* 1984, Volume II: *The King's Justice,* 1985, Volume III: *The Quest for Saint Camber,* 1986.

The Heirs of Saint Camber, Del Rey, Volume I: *The Harrowing of Gwynedd,* 1989, Volume II: *King Javan's Year,* 1992, Volume III: *The Bastard Prince,* in press.

"ADEPT" SERIES; WITH DEBORAH TURNER HARRIS

The Adept, Ace, 1991.
Adept II: The Lodge of the Lynx, Ace, 1992.
Adept III: The Templar Treasure, Ace, 1993.
Adept IV: Dagger Magic, Ace, in press.

OTHER

Lammas Night (novel), Ballantine, 1983, hardcover edition, Severn, 1986.
The Deryni Archives (stories), Del Rey, 1986, hardcover edition, Science Fiction Book Club, 1987.
The Legacy of Lehr (science fiction novel), Walker, 1986.
Deryni Magic: A Grimoire, Del Rey, 1991.
Two Crowns for American, Bantam, in press.

Contributor of stories to anthologies, including *Flashing Swords #4,* edited by Lin Carter, Dell, 1977; *Hecate's Cauldron,* edited by Susan Shwartz, DAW, 1982; *Nine Visions,* edited by Andrea LaSonde Melrose, Seabury Press, 1983; *Moonsinger's Friends,* edited by Shwartz, Bluejay, 1985; *Once upon a Time,* edited by Lester del Rey and Risa Kessler, Del Rey, 1991; *Crafter I,* edited by Bill Fawcett and Christopher Stasheff, Ace, 1991; *Gods of War,* edited by Fawcett, Baen, 1992; and *Battlestation II,* edited by Fawcett and Stasheff, Ace, 1992. Contributor of stories to periodicals, including *Fantasy Book.*

Kurtz's works have been translated into Dutch, German, Italian, Polish, Swedish, Japanese, Spanish, and Romanian.

■ Work in Progress

Two Crowns for America.

■ Sidelights

Katherine Kurtz's love of history has helped to shape the medieval worlds of her fantasy novels, as well as her books set in twentieth-century England and Scotland. Her "Deryni" series, composed of four trilogies, focuses on the land of Gwynedd in the Eleven Kingdoms, a world based on medieval Wales. There the Deryni, a race of beings with unusual psychic powers, struggle against persecution by humans and attempt to preserve their powers and their culture. In her review of *The Quest for Saint Camber* in *Publishers Weekly,* Genevieve Stuttaford stated, "Kurtz is queen of the proliferating fantasy subgenre that adds a magical element to dynastic historical romances." Kurtz's ability to weave historical detail with themes of magic and sorcery has made her books popular with both adults and young

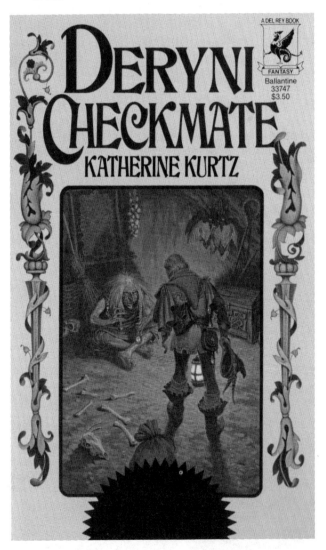

The history of medieval Wales provided the inspiration for the fantasy world of the Eleven Kingdoms, the setting for Kurtz's "Deryni" series. (Cover illustration by Darrell K. Sweet.)

adults; Barbara A. Bannon in *Publishers Weekly* declared Kurtz "a master of epic fantasy." Kurtz has also produced the thriller *Lammas Night* and, with Deborah Turner Harris, has written the "Adept" series of contemporary mysteries.

Kurtz told *SATA:* "I was born in Coral Gables, Florida, during a hurricane—a whirlwind entry into the world which I like to think was a portent of exciting things to come. I can only barely remember a time when I couldn't read. None of elementary school was particularly challenging for me, so I used to take library books to school and hide them in my lift-top desk or under the book I was supposed to be reading. I also read under the covers at night by flashlight.

"Early in fourth grade, I read my first science fiction novel, a juvenile called *Lodestar.* After that, no science fiction book in any library was safe from eye-tracking by 'The Kurtz.' Even though I was to become a science major in late high school and college, and take a bachelor of science degree in chemistry, my tastes always leaned toward humanities rather than hard science. It was during my undergraduate years at the University of Miami that I consciously fell in love with history, and it was to history that I returned when I decided, after one year of medical school, that I would rather write about medicine than practice it. My graduate studies at the University of California, Los Angeles, led to a masters degree in English history, but more important than the piece of paper was the formal knowledge of the medieval and renaissance world that I gained and the sharpening of research skills which would stand me in good stead as I continued writing medievally-set fantasy.

"I became a full-time writer in 1980, after more than ten years as a technical writer and curriculum designer for the Los Angeles Police Department—all the time the first six Deryni novels were being written—and can't imagine a more satisfying life than to be making a living doing what I love. Far too few people get the opportunity to do that, and especially at a relatively young age.

"I have made several literary forays outside the medieval world of the Eleven Kingdoms. The first was a historical adventure-thriller called *Lammas Night,* which takes place in England during World War II. British folk tradition has it that England has been saved from invasion more than once by the magical intervention of those appointed to guard her, Napoleonic and Armada times being cited as two specific examples. Less well-known tradition has it that similar measures were employed to keep Hitler from invading Britain during that fateful summer of 1940, with its sagas of Dunkirk and the Battle of Britain. Whether or not what was done actually had any effect we will never know for certain, but the fact remains that Hitler never did invade, even though he was poised to do so for many months. *Lammas Night* is the story of how and why that might have been. I have also written a science fiction novel called *The Legacy of Lehr,* and I am working on a major historical novel set during the American Revolutionary

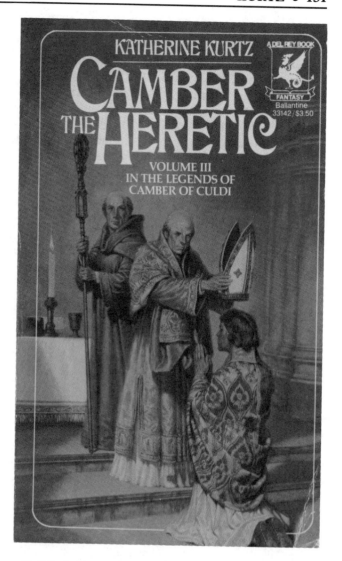

Political intrigue and conflicts between church and crown characterize this volume of Kurtz's "Legends of Saint Camber" trilogy. (Cover illustration by Sweet.)

War. Also in progress is a series of modern Scottish detective novels with an occult twist, coauthored with Deborah Turner Harris.

"I have a number of interests besides writing, though most of them do tend to relate to my writing or medieval background in some way. I read voraciously, of course—whatever I need for research, plus straight history, religion, and the occasional Brother Cadfael mystery for fun. I delight in counted cross-stitch embroidery and needlepoint, will occasionally crochet, but am totally indifferent to knitting. I can sew just about anything, including medieval costumes and horse bardings. For nearly twenty years I was an active member of the Society for Creative Anachronism (SCA)—an educational recreation and research organization which attempts to recreate the Middle Ages as they should have been, not necessarily as they were, by staging tournaments, banquets, and the like. In that context, I've been able to pursue most of my interests, plus a few others like heraldry, court protocol and ceremonial, calligraphy, and manuscript illumination. The SCA has also given me valuable insights into medieval fighting, monarchy, and chivalry, the latter of which interest I continue to indulge in the form of several chivalric orders to which my husband and I belong. He's a MacMillan, and we're also involved in various clan activities; aptly enough, we met at a Scottish country dance in Santa Monica, California. In 1986, our love of celtic heritage and tradition led us to move to Ireland, where we are slowly restoring a historic country house in County Wicklow."

■ Works Cited

Bannon, Barbara, review of *Saint Camber, Publishers Weekly,* September 11, 1978, p. 77.

Stuttaford, Genevieve, review of *The Quest for Saint Camber, Publishers Weekly,* August 8, 1986.

■ For More Information See

BOOKS

Clarke, Boden, and Mary A. Burgess, *The Work of Katherine Kurtz: An Annotated Bibliography and Guide,* Borgo Press, 1993.

PERIODICALS

Publisher Weekly, April 10, 1972, p. 60; July 9, 1973, p. 48; May 31, 1976, p. 197; September 25, 1981, p. 87; September 21, 1984, p. 92; July 5, 1985, p. 66; September 26, 1986, p. 69; December 2, 1988, p. 48; December 21, 1990, p. 50; February 8, 1991, p. 54.

School Library Journal, January, 1985, p. 92; February, 1986, p. 103; November, 1986, p. 116; December, 1986, p. 126; September, 1991, p. 298; September, 1992, p. 29.

Voice of Youth Advocates, December, 1986, p. 238; April, 1987, p. 38; August, 1989, p. 166.

L

LANCE, Kathryn 1943-
(Lynn Beach)

■ Personal

Born November 26, 1943, in El Paso, TX; daughter of John F. (a paleontologist) and Kathryn (a homemaker; maiden name, Haisley) Lance. *Education:* University of Arizona, B.A., 1966, M.A., 1969; also attended Ohio State University and New York University. *Politics:* "McCarthy campaign, 1968." *Religion:* Unitarian. *Hobbies and other interests:* Gardening, hiking, yoga, opera.

■ Addresses

Home and office—3272 North Glen Creek Drive, Tucson, AZ 85712. *Agent*—(for adult books) Jeff Herman, Jeff Herman Literary Agency, 500 Greenwich Street, Suite 501-C, New York, NY 10013.

■ Career

Writer, 1971—. Scholastic, Inc., associate editor, 1972-77; New York University, teacher, 1981-89; teacher of writing workshop for senior citizens, 1991—. *Member:* American Society of Journalists and Authors, Science Fiction Writers of America, Mystery Writers of America, Society of Children's Book Writers and Illustrators, Society of Southwest Authors.

■ Awards, Honors

Best new science fiction novel, *Romantic Times,* 1985, and recommended list, *Locus,* 1986, both for *Pandora's Genes.*

■ Writings

YOUNG ADULT FICTION

Going to See Grassy Ella, Lothrop, 1993.

UNDER PSEUDONYM LYNN BEACH

Attack of the Insecticons, Ballantine, 1985.
The Haunted Castle of Ravencurse, Avon, 1985.
Secrets of the Lost Island, Scholastic, 1985.
Conquest of the Time Master, Avon, 1986.
Invasion from Darkland, Avon, 1986.
Operation Jungle Doom, Random House, 1987.
Operation Time Machine, Random House, 1987.

Tamara's photographs of a mysterious Native American hold the answer to the disappearance of mountain lions from the hills around Phantom Valley in this suspenseful work Kathryn Lance wrote as Lynn Beach. (Cover illustration by Lisa Falkenstern.)

Invisibility Island, Parachute Press, 1988.

Also ghostwriter of four young adult mystery novels, 1990-91.

"PHANTOM VALLEY" SERIES; UNDER PSEUDONYM LYNN BEACH

The Evil One, Minstrel Books, 1991.
The Dark, Minstrel Books, 1991.
Scream of the Cat, Minstrel Books, 1992.
Stranger in the Mirror, Minstrel Books, 1992.
The Spell, Minstrel Books, 1992.
Dead Man's Secret, Minstrel Books, 1992.
In the Mummy's Tomb, Minstrel Books, 1992.
The Headless Ghost, Minstrel Books, 1992.
Curse of the Claw, Minstrel Books, 1993.

NONFICTION FOR CHILDREN; UNDER PSEUDONYM LYNN BEACH

Contributor of articles on science, health, nutrition, consumerism, technology, and lifestyles to periodicals, including *Scholastic Voice, Future Tech, Fast Track, Bananas,* and *Creative Classroom.* Author of booklets on such topics as space exploration, scientific experiments, and libraries, for Macmillan and other publishers.

FICTION FOR ADULTS

Pandora's Genes, Questar, 1985.
Pandora's Children, Questar, 1986.

NONFICTION FOR ADULTS

Running for Health and Beauty, Bobbs-Merrill, 1977; Bantam, 1978.
Getting Strong, Bobbs-Merrill, 1978; Bantam, 1979.
(With Maria Agardy) *Total Sexual Fitness for Women,* Rawson, Wade, 1981.
Sportsbeauty, Avon, 1984.
Low-Impact Aerobics, Crown, 1988.

Also ghostwriter for *The Setpoint Diet,* by Gilbert Leveille, Ballantine, 1985, *The Princeton Plan,* by Edwin Heleniak and Barbara Aston, St. Martin's, 1990, and *Heart and Soul,* by Bruno Cortis, Villard, 1994. Contributor of articles on topics including diet, sports, fitness, sexuality, and biotechnology to periodicals, including *Family Circle, Parade, Self, Town and Country, Ladies Home Journal,* and *Medical Tribune.*

Lance's works have been translated into Italian, German, and Spanish.

FOR TELEVISION

Writer for television series *All My Children, One Life to Live, Another World,* and *Somerset,* 1970-73.

■ Work in Progress

A ghostwritten book on home remedies for pet ailments; the sequel to *Going to See Grassy Ella.*

■ Sidelights

Kathryn Lance told *SATA:* "Although I write both fiction and nonfiction, there is something especially satisfying about writing fiction for children and teens. Of all my books, *Going to See Grassy Ella* is the one that means the most to me. Beyond all the adventures and the question of whether or not Peej will be cured, it is the story of the love between two sisters. I dedicated the book to the memory of my sister, Margaret, who died of leukemia in 1964. She was the person I have loved the most in my life, and though Margaret wasn't really like Peej, the character of Peej is inspired by her.

"Many books have influenced me; it is probably telling that I knew I wanted to be a writer from the time I could first read. Among the children's books that made the biggest impression on me were the *Oz* books, *Anne of Green Gables,* and Edward Eager's modern fantasies, which my sister and I used to read together."

Kathryn Lance's writings cover a wide gamut which includes fiction and nonfiction for both children and adults. *Pandora's Genes* is the first of Lance's two adult fiction books. The story is set in a world of the future

A young girl with cancer overcomes a number of obstacles in order to visit a faith healer whom she hopes will cure her. (Cover illustration by Guy Porfirio.)

which has been destroyed by the effect of recombinant deoxyribonucleic acid (DNA) research. This world struggles to overcome the effects of the disaster—mainly genetic diseases and mutants roaming the countryside. Taking advantage of the catastrophic situation, religious fanatics spread the fear and hatred of science, which they hold responsible for causing the problem. Meanwhile a group of committed women scientists conduct research in the hopes of saving the race. A *Publishers Weekly* contributor commented, "This first novel ... displays solid talents in its characterization and storytelling. Enjoyable and promising." *Pandora's Genes* ends suddenly, as if there might be a sequel—and there is.

Pandora's Children continues the story set in the futuristic world. Women scientists continue to try to find a cure for a genetic illness killing off the women. The religious group, called The Traders, are still set on destroying science. Both plots revolve around Evvy, a scientist; the Principal; and his brother, Zach. In *Fantasy Review*, Debbie Ledesma reported that Lance's "work is smooth and flowing, with a solid balance of theme, action, and romance. Readers will enjoy this book."

For junior high-age readers, under the name Lynn Beach, Lance wrote the fictional novel, *Conquest of the Time Master*. In this book the reader decides where the story line will go. Choices are made throughout the story. Paths are chosen by the toss of a coin or by the day of the week, and patterns devised by the reader select the skill. These choices form the basis for the outcome of the adventure. Since the choices vary each time the book is read, it can be read over and over again, with a different outcome each time. Under the pseudonym Lynn Beach, Lance has also written the fictional "Phantom Valley" series of mysteries for young adults.

■ Works Cited

Ledesma, Debbie, review of *Pandora's Children, Fantasy Review,* September, 1986, p. 25.
Review of *Pandora's Genes, Publishers Weekly,* March 1, 1985, p. 78.

■ For More Information See

PERIODICALS

Fantasy Review, May 5, 1985, p. 15; October, 1985, p. 28.
Locus, January, 1992, p. 54.
School Library Journal, January 1, 1986, p. 82.
Science Fiction for Children, April, 1986, p. 43.
Voices of Young Adults, February 2, 1986, p. 400.

*   *   *

LEESON, R. A.
See LEESON, Robert (Arthur)

LEESON, Robert (Arthur) 1928-
(R. A. Leeson)

■ Personal

Born March 31, 1928, in Barnton, Cheshire, England; son of William George (a chemical worker) and Nellie Louisa (a domestic servant; maiden name, Tester) Leeson; married Gunvor Hagen (a teacher, biologist, and geologist), May 25, 1954; children: Frederick Alan, Christine Ann. *Education:* University of London, B.A. (honors), 1972.

■ Addresses

Home—18 McKenzie Rd., Broxbourne, Hertfordshire, England.

■ Career

Worked on local newspapers and magazines in England and Europe, 1944-56; *Morning Star,* London, England, reporter, 1956-58, parliamentary correspondent, 1958-61, feature writer, 1961-69, literary editor, 1961-80, children's editor, 1969-84; free-lance writer and editor, 1969—. Founding member of Other Award Panel, 1975—. Member of British section of the International Board on Books for Young People (treasurer, 1979—). *Military service:* British Army, 1946-48; served in Egypt. *Member:* National Union of Journalists, Writers Guild (chair, 1985-86).

■ Awards, Honors

Eleanor Farjeon Award, 1985, for services to children's literature.

■ Writings

FOR CHILDREN

Beyond the Dragon Prow, illustrated by Ian Ribbons, Collins, 1973.
'Maroon Boy (historical), illustrated by Michael Jackson, Collins, 1974.
Bess (sequel to *'Maroon Boy*), illustrated by Christine Nolan, Collins, 1975.
The Third Class Genie (also see below), Collins, 1975.
The Demon Bike Rider, illustrated by Jim Russell, Collins, 1976.
The White Horse, Collins, 1977.
Challenge in the Dark, illustrated by Russell, Collins, 1978.
The Cimaroons (nonfiction), Collins, 1978.
Silver's Revenge, Collins, 1978, Philomel, 1979.
Grange Hill Goes Wild (based on the British Broadcasting Corp. [BBC] television series *Grange Hill* by Phil Redmond), Fontana Books, 1980.
Grange Hill Rules, O.K.?, BBC Publications, 1980.
It's My Life, Collins, 1980.
Harold and Bella, Jammy and Me (short stories), Fontana Books, 1980.
Grange Hill for Sale, Fontana Books, 1981.
Grange Hill Home and Away, Fontana Books, 1982.

ROBERT LEESON

The People's Dream, pictures by Ken Sprague, Cooperative Union, 1982.

Mum and Dad's Big Business, pictures by Sprague, Cooperative Union, 1982.

Forty Days of Tucker J (based on the BBC television series *Tucker's Luck* by Redmond), Fontana Books, 1983.

Candy for King, Collins, 1983.

Genie on the Loose, Fontana Books/Hamish Hamilton, 1984.

Time Rope, Volume 1: *Time Rope,* Volume 2: *Three against the World,* Volume 3: *At War with Tomorrow,* Volume 4: *The Metro Gangs Attack,* Longman, 1986.

Wheel of Danger, illustrated by Anthony Kerins, Collins, 1986.

The Reversible Giant, illustrated by Chris Smedley, A. & C. Black, 1986.

Slambash Wangs of a Compo Gormer, Collins, 1987.

The Third-Class Genie (play; adapted from the author's book of the same title), produced in Leicester, England, 1987.

Never Kiss Frogs!, illustrated by David Simonds, Hamish Hamilton, 1988.

Hey Robin!, A. & C. Black, 1989.

How Alice Saved Captain Miracle, Heinemann, 1989.

Jan Alone, Collins, 1989.

Burper, illustrated by Caroline Crossland, Heinemann, 1989.

Right Royal Kidnap, illustrated by Chris Smedley, A. & C. Black, 1989.

Coming Home, Collins, 1990.

One Frog Too Many, illustrated by Simonds, Hamish Hamilton, 1991.

Pancake Pickle, illustrated by Crossland, Hamish Hamilton, 1991.

April Fool at Hob Lane School, illustrated by Crossland, Hamish Hamilton, 1992.

No Sleep for Hob Lane, illustrated by Crossland, Hamish Hamilton, 1992.

Ghosts at Hob Lane, illustrated by Crossland, Hamish Hamilton, 1993.

The Zarnia Experiment, Volume 1: *Landing,* Volume 2: *Fire,* Volume 3: *Deadline,* Volume 4: *Danger Trail,* Volume 5: *Hide and Seek,* Volume 6: *Blast Off,* Reeds Childrens Books, 1993.

Karla's Tale, illustrated by Hilda Offen, Collins, 1993.

The Last Genie, Collins, 1993.

Smart Girls, Walker Books, 1993.

FOR ADULTS

(Under name R. A. Leeson) *United We Stand: An Illustrated Account of Trade Union Emblems,* Adams & Dart, 1971.

(Under name R. A. Leeson) *Strike: A Live History, 1887-1971,* Allen & Unwin, 1973.

Children's Books and Class Society: Past and Present, edited by Children's Rights Workshop, Writers and Readers Publishing Cooperative, 1977.

(Under name R. A. Leeson) *Travelling Brothers: The Six Centuries Road from Craft Fellowship to Trade Unionism,* Allen & Unwin, 1978.

Reading and Righting: The Past, Present, and Future of Fiction for the Young, Collins, 1985.

■ Sidelights

British author Robert Leeson has been writing for children since the 1970s. He is perhaps best known for his books about the characters of the British Broadcasting Corporation (BBC) television series *Grange Hill,* but he has also done noteworthy original work such as the science fiction *Time Rope* series, the historical '*Maroon Boy,* and the controversial young-adult novel *It's My Life.* In all of Leeson's books, he shifts the emphasis from what he feels is a predominantly upper-middle-class point of view to more working-class characters. Leeson complained to *SATA* of "the relative failure of all branches of literature to reflect the vitality, variety, and importance of working class life." He further explained: "My historical novels for children explore such areas as the Puritan side of Elizabethan and Stuart history, or the exploits of groups like the Cimaroons or escaped slaves. My children's books with a contemporary setting center on the lives of those at day school rather than the traditional boarding school of most literature."

Leeson was born March 31, 1928, in Barnton, Cheshire, England. He began working on local newspapers and magazines while he was still a teenager; he interrupted this early career with a stint in the British Army from 1946 to 1948. In 1956 Leeson landed a job as a reporter with the London newspaper *Morning Star.* He stayed with the *Morning Star* through various positions, including correspondent to the British Parliament, literary editor, and children's editor. He began working as a free-lance writer and editor in 1969, though he continued as children's editor for the *Morning Star* until 1984. In the early 1970s, Leeson also obtained a bachelor's degree from the University of London.

Although Leeson's first published volume was for adults, he soon went on to the children's works for which he became best known. *Beyond the Dragon Prow,* the author's first children's book, is a historical tale about Viking life, but it focuses on outcasts from that society, including a crippled boy, who has pacifistic, tolerant views about humanity. *'Maroon Boy* is the story of a young boy growing up in Elizabethan England. Through the adventures of the protagonist, Matthew, the reader is led through the poverty-stricken and disease-ridden streets of the past to a realization of the harsh realities of living in that world. His next two books for youngsters were also historical, but *The Third-Class Genie* brought the typical tale of finding a wish-granting genie to modern times and gave it a working-class twist. This story of Alec and the third-class genie was followed, almost ten years later, by Alec's adventures with Abdul, the son of the third-class genie, in a sequel titled *Genie on the Loose.* Unlike his father, Abdul is inexperienced and unqualified to be a genie, and the book follows the adventures of Alec and Abdul from trips on flying mats to rescuing people in mob fights. 1993 saw the trilogy completed with *The Last Genie* in which the hero flies through time and space to rescue the genie.

Leeson finished out the 1970s with a nonfiction book for children about the Cimaroons and with a sequel to Robert Louis Stevenson's *Treasure Island* entitled *Silver's Revenge. Silver's Revenge* is set in the past and has a number of black characters at its center. These people are slaves, but they are equal to, if not better than, their masters. The book also features Betsy, Long John Silver's daughter by his Jamaican wife.

Series Portrays Working-Class Children

In the 1980s Leeson began one of his most successful series, the Grange Hill books, based on the *Grange Hill* television series on BBC. He used characters created by Phil Redmond, but he only agreed to do the books if he could make up his own stories rather than adapting text from the television scripts. The series, about the adventures of working-class students, has proved very popular with readers. Leeson also followed one of the Grange Hill characters after graduation in *Forty Days of Tucker J.*

At about the same time Leeson began the Grange Hill series, he also wrote a young-adult novel called *It's My Life.* The story of a teenage girl, Jan, whose mother leaves home, it deals frankly with her developing sexuality and even contains a scene in which she attempts to perform an abortion on herself. As Mary Hoffman asserted in *Twentieth-Century Children's Writers,* "this novel has always been immensely popular with

teenage girls and, after much urging from this readership, Leeson has written a sequel, *Jan Alone."* A third book, *Coming Home,* completes the saga. *Jan Alone* continues the story of Jan, who has now dropped out of school to work in the factory where her mother had once worked. The book portrays modern everyday life, and Leeson has been praised for his adept portrayal of Jan's situation.

In later works for young readers, Leeson has branched into the fields of science fiction and fantasy with the "Time Rope" books and *Slambash Wangs of a Compo Gormer.* The former is a four-volume series involving time travel experiments and class warfare; in the latter Leeson invents his own future slang for a tale about an alternate universe. These have now been joined by the six volume *Zarnia Experiment* which features a robot from space on a mystery mission involving four Earth children.

Leeson has carried his interest in and philosophy of children's literature to his work for adults, including *Children's Books and Class Society: Past and Present* and *Reading and Righting: The Past, Present, and Future of Fiction for the Young.* In *Reading and Righting* he surveys children's books in the past and present and argues that, in the past, books written for children served ruling-class interests by perpetuating mostly upper- and middle-class images of childhood rather than the reality of working-class children. Leeson says that this exclusion was partly due to the fact that working-class children did not have any political power. He feels that literature needs to reflect reality and thus initiate social change for the better.

In addition to his writing, Leeson does public speaking engagements, especially in schools. He told *SATA:* "Along with concern about the alienation of literature from the potential reader goes a concern with the isolation of the writer. I do a good deal of work in schools, helping children develop their own creative writing style and conducting storytelling sessions for children and adults in libraries, schools, and community centers."

■ Works Cited

Hoffman, Mary, entry on Leeson in *Twentieth-Century Children's Writers,* 3rd edition, St. James Press, 1989, pp. 566-67.

■ For More Information See

PERIODICALS

Junior Bookshelf, June, 1977; February, 1979; December, 1980; August, 1982; August, 1983; June, 1985; October, 1988.
School Librarian, June, 1985.
School Library Journal, January, 1980; January, 1985.
Times Literary Supplement, April 6, 1973; July, 1974; March 29, 1985; January 31, 1986; October 17, 1986.

LEWIN, Ted 1935-

■ Personal

Born May 6, 1935, in Buffalo, NY; son of Sidney (a retail jeweler) and Berenece (Klenn) Lewin; married Betsy Reilly (an artist). *Education:* Pratt Institute of Art, B.F.A., 1956. *Hobbies and other interests:* Photographing, painting, and watching birds.

■ Addresses

Home and office—152 Willoughby Ave., Brooklyn, NY 11205.

■ Career

Professional wrestler, 1952-65; artist and free-lance illustrator, 1956—. *Exhibitions:* One man show, Laboratory of Ornithology, Cornell University, 1978. *Military service:* U.S. Army, 1958.

■ Writings

SELF-ILLUSTRATED

World within a World—Everglades, introduction by Don R. Eckelberry, Dodd, 1976.
World within a World—Baja, Dodd, 1978.
World within a World—Pribilofs, Dodd, 1980.
Tiger Trek, Macmillan, 1990.
When the Rivers Go Home, Macmillan, 1992.
Amazon Boy, Macmillan, 1993.
I Was a Teenage Professional Wrestler (memoir), Orchard Books, 1993.

ILLUSTRATOR

Jack McClellan, Millard Black, and Sid Norris, *A Blind Man Can!,* Houghton, 1968.
Wyatt Blassingame, *The Look-It-Up Book of Presidents,* Random House, 1968.
Jack McClellan, Millard Black, and Sheila Flume Taylor, *Up, out, and Over!,* Houghton, 1969.
George S. Trow, *Meet Robert E. Lee,* Random House, 1969.
Margaret T. Burroughs, *Jasper, the Drummin' Boy,* Follett, 1970.
Janet H. Ervin, *More Than Half Way There,* Follett, 1970.
Donald W. Cox, *Pioneers of Ecology,* Hammond, 1971.
Nellie Burchardt, *A Surprise for Carlotta,* Watts, 1971.
Darrell A. Rolerson, *Mr. Big Britches,* Dodd, 1971.
Gene Smith, *The Visitor,* Cowles, 1971.
Betty Horvath, *Not Enough Indians,* Watts, 1971.
Maurine H. Gee, *Chicano, Amigo,* Morrow, 1972.
Rose Blue, *Grandma Didn't Wave Back,* Watts, 1972.
Michael Capizzi, *Getting It All Together,* Delacorte, 1972.
Rose Blue, *A Month of Sundays,* Watts, 1972.
Rita Micklish, *Sugar Bee,* Delacorte, 1972.
Darrell A. Rolerson, *In Sheep's Clothing,* Dodd, 1972.
Rose Blue, *Nikki 108,* Watts, 1972.
Charlotte Gantz, *Boy with Three Names,* Houghton, 1973.

William MacKellar, *The Ghost of Grannoch Moor,* Dodd, 1973.
Marjorie M. Prince, *The Cheese Stands Alone,* Houghton, 1973.
Marian Rumsey, *Lion on the Run,* Morrow, 1973.
Darrell A. Rolerson, *A Boy Called Plum,* Dodd, 1974.
Jean Slaughter Doty, *Gabriel,* Macmillan, 1974.
Gene Smith, *The Hayburners,* Delacorte, 1974.
Matt Christopher, *Earthquake,* Little, Brown, 1975.
Patricia Beatty, *Rufus, Red Rufus,* Morrow, 1975.
Charles Ferry, *Up in Sister Bay,* Houghton, 1975.
Jean Slaughter Doty, *Winter Pony,* Macmillan, 1975.
S. T. Tung, *One Small Dog,* Dodd, 1975.
Rose Blue, *The Preacher's Kid,* Watts, 1975.
Scott O'Dell, *Zia,* Houghton, 1976.
Lynne Martin, *Puffin, Bird of the Open Seas,* Morrow, 1976.
Laurence Pringle, *Listen to the Crows,* Crowell, 1976.
Patricia Edwards Clyne, *Ghostly Animals of America,* Dodd, 1977.
Mildred Teal, *Bird of Passage,* Little, Brown, 1977.
Marian Rumsey, *Carolina Hurricane,* Morrow, 1977.
Nigel Gray, *The Deserter,* Harper, 1977.
Robert Newton Peck, *Patooie,* Knopf, 1977.
Philippa Pearce, *The Shadow-Cage, and Other Tales of the Supernatural,* Crowell, 1977.
Helen Hill, Agnes Perkins, and Alethea Helbig, editors, *Straight on Till Morning: Poems of the Imaginary World,* Crowell, 1977.
Rose Blue, *The Thirteenth Year: A Bar Mitzvah Story,* Watts, 1977.
Leslie Norris, *Merlin and the Snake's Egg: Poems,* Viking, 1978.

TED LEWIN

William MacKellar, *The Silent Bells,* Dodd, 1978.

Robert Newton Peck, *Soup for President,* Knopf, 1978.

William MacKellar, *The Witch of Glen Gowrie,* Dodd, 1978.

Anne E. Crompton, *A Woman's Place,* Little, Brown, 1978.

Margaret Goff Clark, *Barney and the UFO,* Dodd, 1979.

Patricia Edwards Clyne, *Strange and Supernatural Animals,* Dodd, 1979.

Robert Newton Peck, *Hub,* Knopf, 1979.

David Stemple, *High Ridge Gobbler: A Story of the American Wild Turkey,* Collins, 1979.

Jean Slaughter Doty, *Can I Get There by Candlelight?,* Macmillan, 1980.

Rose Blue, *My Mother, the Witch,* McGraw, 1980.

Margaret Goff Clark, *Barney in Space,* Dodd, 1981.

Francine Jacobs, *Bermuda Petrel: The Bird that Would Not Die,* Morrow, 1981.

Mark Twain, *The Adventures of Tom Sawyer,* Wanderer Books, 1982.

Margaret Goff Clark, *Barney on Mars,* Dodd, 1983.

Eleanor Clymer, *The Horse in the Attic,* Bradbury Press, 1983.

Priscilla Homola, *The Willow Whistle,* Dodd, 1983.

Enid Bagnold, *"National Velvet,"* Morrow, 1985.

R. R. Knudson, *Babe Didrikson, Athlete of the Century,* Viking Kestrel, 1985.

Mary Francis Shura, *The Search for Grissi,* Dodd, 1985.

Frances Wosmek, *A Brown Bird Singing,* Lothrop, Lee, 1986.

Patricia Reilly Giff, *Mother Teresa, Sister to the Poor,* Viking Kestrel, 1986.

Elizabeth Simpson Smith, *A Dolphin Goes to School: The Story of Squirt, a Trained Dolphin,* Morrow, 1986.

Scott O'Dell, *The Serpent Never Sleeps: A Novel of Jamestown and Pocahontas,* Houghton, 1987.

Susan Saunders, *Margaret Mead: The World Was Her Family,* Viking Kestrel, 1987.

Kathleen V. Kudlinski, *Rachel Carson: Pioneer of Ecology,* Viking Kestrel, 1988.

Yukio Tsuchiya, *Faithful Elephants: A True Story of Animals, People, and War,* translated by Tomoko Tsuchiya Dykes, Houghton, 1988.

Lynne Reid Banks, *The Secret of the Indian,* Doubleday, 1989.

Bruce Coville, editor, *Herds of Thunder, Manes of Gold: A Collection of Horse Stories and Poems,* Doubleday, 1989.

Leon Garfield, *Young Nick and Jubilee,* Delacorte, 1989.

Florence Parry Heide and Judith Heide Gilliland, *The Day of Ahmed's Secret,* Lothrop, Lee, 1990.

Scott O'Dell, *Island of the Blue Dolphins,* Houghton, 1990.

Gregory Patent, *Shanghai Passage,* Clarion, 1990.

Brenda Seabrooke, *Judy Scuppernong,* Cobblehill Books, 1990.

Jane Yolen, *Bird Watch: A Book of Poetry,* Philomel, 1990.

Margaret Hodges, *Brother Francis and the Friendly Beasts,* Scribner, 1991.

Lewin's illustrations capture the light of old-fashioned street lamps in this story of a young immigrant in America. (Illustration from *Peppe the Lamplighter,* written by Elisa Bartone.)

Megan McDonald, *The Potato Man,* Orchard Books, 1991.

Frances Ward Weller, *I Wonder If I'll See a Whale,* Philomel, 1991.

Corinne Demas Bliss, *Matthew's Meadow,* Harcourt, 1992.

Florence Parry Heide and Judith Heide Gilliland, *Sami and the Time of the Troubles,* Clarion, 1992.

Megan McDonald, *The Great Pumpkin Switch,* Orchard Books, 1992.

Frances Ward Weller, *Matthew Wheelock's Wall,* Macmillan, 1992.

Elisa Bartone, *Peppe the Lamplighter,* Lothrop, Lee, 1993.

Ann Herbert Scott, *Cowboy Country,* Clarion, 1993.

Illustrations have also appeared in periodicals, including *Boy's Life, Ladies' Home Journal, Seventeen,* and *Reader's Digest.*

■ Work in Progress

Illustrating *Months: A Book of Poems for Children,* by Charlotte Otten, and *Ali, Child of the Desert,* by Jonathan London, both for Lothrop, Lee, 1995.

■ Sidelights

Ted Lewin once told *SATA:* "I am primarily an artist-illustrator, and my writing has grown out of an interest in the natural world which, until my first book, I confined to graphic form only. I am a deeply concerned environmentalist and conservationist and travel to wilderness areas around the world for both graphic and literary material." Lewin has written and illustrated a large number of books for children and young adults, often relying on his knowledge of and concern for wildlife and their habitats throughout the world. His paintings are characterized by their detail and realism, and his writings have been praised for their poetic quality.

As a young boy growing up in upstate New York, Lewin always had dreams of becoming an artist. "Not a policeman, fireman, or doctor—an artist," he recalled in *I Was a Teenage Professional Wrestler.* "I remember working first with a metal-armed copying toy I got for Christmas, then the Magic-Pad, on which you could pull up a flap and make whatever you'd drawn disappear." With the encouragement of his family, Lewin practiced drawing by copying photographs, illustrations from children's books, and even a portrait of President Harry S Truman, for which he received a personal letter from the White House.

By the time Lewin graduated from high school, he had made plans to study art at the Pratt Institute in Brooklyn. Paying for school and living expenses would be expensive, however, so Lewin started on a secondary career that would help support him for almost fifteen years: professional wrestling. Lewin had attended professional matches with his family for many years, and his older brother Donn had become a wrestler after serving in the marines during World War II. With the aid of his brother and the many contacts his family had made over the years, Lewin began wrestling at age seventeen during summers and at night during the school year. In his autobiography, Lewin recalled his dual life, alternating between art classes and wrestling matches: "Every day I had classes in two-dimensional design, three-dimensional design, and figure drawing. Around me, the light-filled, high-ceilinged studio would be electric with concentrated effort.... I would see a great play of light and shadow—in a sense, not so different from what I'd seen in the charged, dramatic atmosphere of a wrestling arena. The medium was different, that's all."

After earning his bachelor of fine arts degree, Lewin continued wrestling as he slowly built a career as a freelance artist. He begun with magazine work, and by the late 1960s obtained work illustrating children's books. In 1976 Lewin debuted his series, *World within a World,* which focuses on wildlife in several regions visited by the author; the series has received high praise for both Lewin's text and the illustrations. The first volume in the series, concerning the Everglades, is based on observations of the plant and animal life in the area made by Lewin over a five-year period. The volume on Baja, California, describes elephant seals and details the annual migration of the California gray whales. Of the volume on the Pribilof Islands, which highlights the precarious fate of the seals who bear and raise their young on these Alaskan coastal islands, a reviewer from

Booklist called the prose "elegant and uncompromising," adding that "the evocation of this small corner of the world is strong."

Lewin depicts a trip made on the back of an elephant through one of India's national parks in *Tiger Trek.* Joan McGrath, reviewing the book for *School Library Journal,* found it "gorgeous" and "far above the ordinary." *When the Rivers Go Home* describes a similar journey, this time through a large swamp in central Brazil called the Pantanal. This book also received praise for its watercolor paintings, with a *Kirkus Reviews* writer describing Lewin's work as "lovely" and "evocative." And in 1993's *Amazon Boy* Lewin's "light-filled pictures, dense with detail, reinforce the theme that the riches of the rain forest must be protected," according to *School Library Journal* contributor Kathleen Odean.

Lewin turned from nature to his own past in *I Was a Teenage Professional Wrestler.* "More a series of vignettes than an autobiography," as *Bulletin of the Center for Children's Books* writer Deborah Stevenson describes it, *I Was a Teenage Professional Wrestler* details Lewin's involvement with the sport and provides portraits—written and painted—of the many wrestlers he met during his career. "It is a fascinating story that leaves the reader wanting to learn more about both Lewin and the other wrestlers," notes Patrick Jones in the *Voice of Youth Advocates.* In recreating a different era, Lewin describes the wrestlers "quite masterfully in

Lewin used his talents as an artist to capture another side of his life—the world of the professional wrestler—in this 1993 book.

words, then he brings them to life with old black and white photographs, drawings and paintings." *School Library Journal* contributor Todd Morning likewise praises Lewin's "surprisingly funny and affectionate" remembrances, as well as the author's combination of "vivid" artwork and human stories. "The artist's sensibility and eye for detail are always in evidence," the critic concludes. "His talent in this realm is truly formidable."

■ Works Cited

Jones, Patrick, review of *I Was a Teenage Profesisonal Wrestler, Voice of Youth Advocates,* October, 1993, p. 247.

Lewin, Ted, *I Was a Teenage Professional Wrestler,* Orchard Books, 1993.

McGrath, Joan, review of *Tiger Trek, School Library Journal,* March, 1990, p. 208.

Morning, Todd, review of *I Was a Teenage Professional Wrestler, School Library Journal,* July, 1993, p. 108.

Odean, Kathleen, review of *Amazon Boy, School Library Journal,* June, 1993, pp. 80, 83.

Stevenson, Deborah, review of *I Was a Teenage Profesional Wrestler, Bulletin of the Center for Children's Books,* June, 1993, pp. 321-322.

Review of *When the Rivers Go Home, Kirkus Reviews,* February 15, 1992, pp. 257-58.

Review of *World within a World: Pribilofs, Booklist,* January 1, 1981, p. 625.

■ For More Information See

PERIODICALS

Booklist, November 15, 1976; February 1, 1979, p. 866; March 15, 1992.

Family Circle, September 16, 1982, pp. 22, 26.

Horn Book, August, 1977.

Publishers Weekly, January 15, 1979, p. 132.

School Library Journal, October, 1976, p. 118; March, 1981, p. 148; April, 1992, p. 107.*

*   *   *

LEWIS, Naomi

■ Personal

Born in Norfolk, England. *Education:* Attended a women's college in London, England.

■ Addresses

Home—3 Halsey House, 13 Red Lion Square, London WC1 R4QF, England.

■ Career

Worked variously as a teacher in Switzerland and England and as an advertising copywriter; *New Statesman,* London, England, reviewer; British Broadcasting Corporation (BBC-Radio), England, broadcaster; writer,

editor, and translator. *Member:* Royal Society of Literature (fellow).

■ Writings

A Visit to Mrs. Wilcox (essays), Cresset Press, 1957.

(Author of English text) *Leaves,* illustrated by Fulvio Testa, Andersen, 1980, Peter Bedrick, 1983.

Once upon a Rainbow, illustrated by Gabriele Eichenauer, Cape, 1981.

(With Tony Ross) *Hare and Badger Go to Town,* illustrations by Ross, Andersen, 1981.

Come with Us (poems), illustrations by Leo Lionni, Andersen, 1982.

(With Janice Thompson) *Marco Polo and Wellington: Search for Solomon,* Cape, 1982.

Puffin, illustrated by Deborah King, Lothrop, 1984.

Swan, illustrated by Deborah King, Lothrop, 1985.

A School Bewitched (based on Edith Nesbit's *Fortunatus Rex, or The Mystery of the Disappearing Schoolgirls*), illustrated by Errol Le Cain, Blackie, 1985.

(With James Kruess) *Johnny Longnose* (picture book with poetry), illustrated by Stasys Eidrigevicius, North-South, 1989.

The Mardi Gras Cat (poetry), Heinemann, 1993.

RETELLER

The Story of Aladdin, illustrated by Barry Wilkinson, H. Z. Walck, 1970.

The Three Golden Hairs: A Story from the Brothers Grimm, illustrated by Francoise Tresy, Hutchinson, 1983.

Wayne Anderson and Leonard Price, *A Mouse's Tale,* illustrated by Wayne Anderson, Cape, 1983, Harper, 1984.

Jutta Ash, *Jorinda and Joringel* (based on *Jorinde und Joringel* by the Brothers Grimm), Andersen Press, 1984.

Hans Christian Andersen, *The Flying Trunk and Other Stories from Hans Andersen,* Prentice-Hall, 1986.

The Stepsister, illustrated by Allison Reed, Dial Books, 1987.

Stories from the Arabian Nights, illustrated by Anton Pieck, Holt, 1987.

Cry Wolf and Other Aesop Fables, illustrated by Barry Castle, Oxford University Press, 1988.

ADAPTOR

Andersen, *The Snow Queen,* illustrated by Toma Bogdanovic, Scroll Press, 1968, new adapted version with illustrations by Le Cain, Viking, 1979, with an introduction by Lewis and illustrated by Andrea Barrett, Holt, 1988.

The Butterfly Collector, illustrated by Fulvio Testa, Prentice-Hall, 1979.

TRANSLATOR

(And author of notes and introduction) Andersen, *Hans Andersen's Fairy Tales,* illustrated by Philip Gough, Puffin, 1981.

Andersen, *The Wild Swans,* illustrated by Angela Barrett, Peter Bedrick, 1984.

Heide Helene Beisert, *My Magic Cloth: A Story for a Whole Week,* illustrated by Beisert, North-South, 1986.

Jutta Ash, *Wedding Birds* (adapted from a traditional German song), Andersen, 1986.

Andersen, *The Swineherd,* illustrated by Dorothee Duntze, North-South, 1987.

(And adaptor) *Proud Knight, Fair Lady: The Twelve Lais of Marie de France,* illustrated by Andrea Barrett, Viking, 1989.

Jacob Grimm, *The Frog Prince,* illustrated by Binette Schroeder, North-South, 1989.

Siegfried P. Rupprecht, *The Tale of the Vanishing Rainbow,* illustrated by Jozef Wilkon, North-South, 1989.

(And author of introduction) Andersen, *The Nightingale,* illustrated by Josef Palecek, North-South, 1990.

Kurt Baumann, *Three Kings,* illustrated by Ivan Gantschev, North-South, 1990.

Andersen, *Thumbelina,* North-South, 1990.

(And editor) Andersen, *The Steadfast Tin Soldier,* illustrated by P. J. Lynch, Harcourt, 1992.

(And adaptor) Kurt Baumann, *The Hungry One: A Poem,* illustrated by Stasys Eidrigevicius, North-South, 1993.

EDITOR

Christina Rossetti, *Christina Rossetti* (poems), E. Hulton, 1959.

The Best Children's Books of . . . , six annual volumes, Hamish Hamilton, 1964-69.

(And annotator and author of introduction) Emily Bronte, *A Peculiar Music: Poems for Young Readers,* Macmillan, 1971.

(And annotator) *Fantasy Books for Children,* National Book League, 1975, new edition, 1977.

Edith Nesbit, *Fairy Stories,* illustrated by Brian Robb, E. Benn, 1977.

(And author of introduction) *The Silent Playmate: A Collection of Doll Stories,* illustrated by Harold Jones, Gollancz, 1979, Macmillan, 1981, abridged

Naomi Lewis has received praise for her superior translations of many of the classic tales of Danish author Hans Christian Andersen, including *The Wild Swans.* (Illustration by Angela Barrett.)

edition published as *The Magic Doll: A Collection of Doll Stories*, Magnet, 1983.

A Footprint on the Air: An Anthology of Nature Verse, illustrated by Liz Graham-Yool, Hutchinson, 1983, published as *A Footprint in the Air: A Collection of Nature Verse*, Knight, 1984.

Messages: A Book of Poems, Faber & Faber, 1985.

Grimms' Fairy Tales, illustrated by Lidia Postma, Hutchinson, 1985.

Jacob Grimm, *The Twelve Dancing Princesses and Other Tales from Grimm*, illustrated by Postma, Dial Books, 1986.

William Shakespeare, *A Midsummer Night's Dream*, illustrated by Sylvie Monti, Hutchinson, 1988.

OTHER

Also author of the preface to *Twentieth-Century Children's Writers*, 3rd edition, St. James Press, 1989. Contributor to periodicals, including London *Observer, New Statesman, Listener, New York Times, Times Literary Supplement*, and *Times Educational Supplement*.

■ Sidelights

Naomi Lewis is a respected critic and anthologist who is also much-admired as a children's book author, poet, translator, and adaptor. Of her work as a commentator, anthologist and editor, a reviewer for *Junior Bookshelf* remarked: "What sets Naomi Lewis in a class apart from the general run of critics today is her breadth of sympathies and her ability to see the course of literature whole, so that each new book can be set into its proper slot in the grand structure." In addition, Lewis is the author of several original stories and collections of poetry, including 1993's *The Mardi Gras Cat*.

Lewis has received acclaim for the numerous books that she has edited, adapted, retold, and translated, scholarly work that she continues to perform on a regular basis. She came to prominence as a literary critic for the *New Statesman*, a eminent British periodical, and has also shared her knowledge on radio for the BBC. One of her first publications was the *The Best Children's Books* series, a British annual bibliography. A review of the 1965 edition which appeared in the *Times Literary Supplement* found that Lewis "applies to children's books the standards of adult criticism that the best of them deserve."

She continues to uphold these standards in bringing the work of other writers to the attention of modern audiences; in editing, adapting, and translating these works she provides her readers not only with accessible versions, but critical essays that detail the background of each story. Reviewers have noted that Lewis's books, such as *A Peculiar Music, Proud Knight, Fair Lady*, and *Stories from the Arabian Nights*, have made these unique works available to young readers for the first time.

■ Works Cited

Review of *The Best Children's Books of 1965, Times Literary Supplement*, June 9, 1966, p. 519.

Review of *Messages: A Book of Poems, Junior Bookshelf*, February, 1986, pp. 35-36.

■ For More Information See

PERIODICALS

Books for Keeps, November, 1990, pp. 14-15.

Bulletin of the Center for Children's Books, February, 1984.

Growing Point, January, 1980; November, 1985, p. 4538; January, 1989, pp. 5081-82.

Horn Book, February, 1982.

Junior Bookshelf, October, 1981, p. 199; August, 1982, pp. 133-34; June, 1989, pp. 132-33.

Kirkus Reviews, June 15, 1986, pp. 937-38; January 15, 1987, p. 136; August 1, 1987, pp. 1159-60; September 1, 1987, p. 1322.

Listener, December 30, 1971, p. 911; November 6, 1980.

Los Angeles Times Book Review, October 23, 1988.

New York Times Book Review, November 11, 1979, pp. 58, 64; July 9, 1989.

Observer, December 23, 1979, p. 36.

Publishers Weekly, April 10, 1972, p. 58; July 9, 1979, p. 106; August 13, 1979, p. 66; June 27, 1986, p. 86.

School Library Journal, January, 1980, p. 64; October, 1982, p. 142; May, 1987, p. 85.

Times Educational Supplement, November 20, 1981, p. 31; November 2, 1984, p. 26; June 7, 1985, p. 55; February 13, 1987, p. 48.

Times Literary Supplement, July 2, 1970, p. 714; December 14, 1979; July 24, 1981, p. 841; November 9, 1984; November 29, 1985, p. 1361.

*   *   *

LIVO, Norma J. 1929-

■ Personal

Born July 31, 1929, in Tarentum, PA; daughter of David John, Sr. (a chemist) and Della Mae (a teacher; maiden name, Kline) Jackson; married George O. Livo (a geophysicist), January 29, 1951; children: Lauren, Keith Eric, Kim B., Robert. *Education:* University of Pittsburgh, B.S., 1962, M.Ed., 1963, Ed.D., 1969; postdoctoral study at University of Utah, 1969, 1971, and 1973, and University of Colorado, 1976 and 1980. *Hobbies and other interests:* Hiking, photography, licensed private pilot.

■ Addresses

Home—11960 West 22nd Place, Lakewood, CO 80215.

■ Career

Geophysical assistant, Gulf Research Laboratory, Harmarville, PA, 1950-51; Falk Laboratory School, University of Pittsburgh, Pittsburgh, PA, demonstration teacher, 1962-65, lecturer in elementary education, 1965-67; University of Denver, Denver, CO, visiting professor of reading, 1968; University of Colorado, Denver, assistant professor, 1968-71, associate professor, 1971-77, professor of education, and children's and young adult literature, storytelling, folklore, and language arts, 1977-92. Oklahoma State University, visiting professor of education, 1972; Lesley College, Cambridge, MA, visiting professor of storytelling, 1979-81. *Member:* National Association for the Preservation and Perpetuation of Storytelling (board of directors, 1991-93), Colorado Council International Reading Association (president, 1976; state coordinator, 1977-81).

■ Awards, Honors

Meritorious Professional Achievement citation, University of Pittsburgh, 1981; service recognition award for outstanding public service, and teacher recognition award finalist, both University of Colorado at Denver, both 1981; distinguished service award, Colorado Council of the International Reading Association, 1981; Fannie Stabenow Award for outstanding contribution, Colorado Council of the International Reading Association, 1984; outstanding service award for Project Wild, Colorado Division of Wildlife, 1985; excellence in research and creative endeavor award, University of Colorado at Denver, 1987; C. K. Jefferson Memorial Competition winner for outstanding achievement for

NORMA J. LIVO

Newspapers in Education, American Newspapers Publishers Association, 1990.

■ Writings

(With Robert Ruddell) *Free Rein,* Allyn Bacon, 1981.
(With Sandra A. Rietz) *Storytelling: Process and Practice,* Libraries Unlimited, 1986.
(With Rietz) *Storytelling Activities,* Libraries Unlimited, 1987.
(With Dia Cha) *Folk Stories of the Hmong: Peoples of Laos, Cambodia, and Vietnam,* Libraries Unlimited, 1991.
(With Rietz) *Storytelling Folklore Sourcebook,* Libraries Unlimited, 1991.
(With Glenn McGlathery) *Who's Endangered on Noah's Ark?,* Libraries Unlimited, 1992.
Who's Afraid of the Big Bad . . . : Coping with Children's Fears through Literature, Libraries Unlimited, 1992.

Also author of *The Hmong, Hmong at Peace and War,* and *Hmong Folkstories,* slide/tape presentations, Colorado Endowment for the Humanities, 1989. Columnist for *Rocky Mountain News.*

EDITOR

(With Anne Pellowski) *Joining In: An Anthology of Audience Participation Stories and How to Tell Them,* Yellow Moon Press, 1988.
Hmong Textile Design, Stemmer House, 1990.

■ Work in Progress

Short stories, and possibly picture books.

■ Sidelights

"Norma Livo is truly the grande dame of storytelling in the Rocky Mountain region," asserts the executive director of the National Association for the Preservation and Perpetuation of Storytelling, Jimmy Neil Smith, to M. S. Mason of the *Christian Science Monitor.* Born July 31, 1929, and raised in Appalachia, Livo grew up in a household full of music and storytelling: "Mother's stories were folklorish kinds of things and they always had a moral to them . . . . Then from my father's side [the stories] were full of the blarney, leg-pullers, tall tales, music, and ballads full of mischief . . . . So no matter what side of the family got together, music and storytelling were important," Livo relates to Mason.

It was not until after Livo married and had children that she decided to go back to school, primarily because one of her sons had a learning disability. Since education programs dealing with disabilities were as yet nonexistent, Livo wanted to be able to help him herself. Livo used both her own and her children's stories to teach her son to read and greatly enhanced what all of her children learned. When Livo earned her doctorate in education in 1969, she began to incorporate storytelling into her curriculum at the University of Colorado at Denver, School of Education, and in 1976, as professor of education. Eventually she restructured her education courses for her graduate students and included one on storytelling. Elaborating on the importance of storytelling, Livo once noted that "storyteller and listening to stories stimulates interest, emotional and language development, and the imagination."

Beginning in 1981, Livo, who stresses that any subject can be taught with a story, started writing books about the storytelling process. In addition, Livo has assisted in recording the folklore and storytelling traditions of other cultures. In particular, Livo worked with Dia Cha, a Hmong immigrant, to write *Folk Stories of the Hmong Peoples of Laos, Cambodia, and Vietnam.* The Hmongs are an ancient and distinctive Asian people who managed to retain their cultural uniqueness without benefit of a written language and despite living among other major groups of Asians with differing and sometimes more technically advanced cultures. The instability of Southeast Asia and the resulting emigration of many Hmong, however, disrupted the Hmong's storytelling tradition and threatened to disintegrate this tradition. In response to that threat, Cha and Livo recorded the stories of Hmong friends and relations. One story collected relates how it happens that farmers must work so hard. According to the myth, when the vegetables the farmer planted were ready for harvest, they pulled themselves out of the ground and walked to the farmer's door. The farmer, being lazy, told them to wait; the offended vegetables never walked again and from then on the farmer was forced to work hard for his harvest. *Booklist*'s Donna Seaman describes the collection as containing "lively tales." And Mary K. Chelton states in *Voice of Youth Advocates* that this "striking" book is "helpful to storytellers and ... a beautiful book and a real labor of love."

■ Works Cited

Chelton, Mary K., review of *Folk Stories of the Hmong: Peoples of Laos, Cambodia, and Vietnam, Voice of Youth Advocates,* June, 1992, p. 129.

Mason, M. S., "Teaching Tale-Tellers to Tell Tales," *Christian Science Monitor,* December 24, 1990, p. 14.

Seaman, Donna, review of *Folk Stories of the Hmong: Peoples of Laos, Cambodia, and Vietnam, Booklist,* October 1, 1991, p. 224.

*   *   *

LOW, Alice 1926-

■ Personal

Born June 5, 1926, in New York, NY; daughter of Harold (in textiles) and Anna (a children's book author under pseudonym Ann Todd; maiden name, Epstein) Bernstein; married Martin Low (a film studio owner), March 25, 1949; children: Andrew, Katherine, David (died, 1978). *Education:* Smith College, B.A., 1947; attended Columbia University, 1956-58. *Hobbies and other interests:* "Painting and ceramics were my first

ALICE LOW

interests. I still sing in a local chorus. Travel stimulates, and many a line has come to me on a tennis court."

■ Addresses

Home—441 Sleepy Hollow Rd., Briarcliff Manor, NY 10510. *Agent*—(Attorney) Cowan & Gold, 40 West 57th St., New York, NY 10019.

■ Career

Warren Schloat Productions, Tarrytown, NY, writer and producer of educational filmstrips, 1968-72; Birch Wathen School, New York City, teacher of creative writing, 1972-73; free-lance reading program editor, Random House and Harcourt Brace, both New York City, both 1975—; Scholastic Book Services, New York City, editorial consultant to Children's Choice Book Club, 1978-85, became co-editor, then editor. Volunteer at Metropolitan Museum of Art. *Member:* Authors Guild, Authors League of America, American Society of Composers, Authors, and Publishers (ASCAP), PEN, Society of Children's Book Writers and Illustrators.

■ Awards, Honors

The Macmillan Book of Greek Gods and Heroes and *Herbert's Treasure* were named Literary Guild selections; Notable Children's Trade Book in the Field of

Social Studies selection, Children's Book Council, 1985, and Washington Irving Children's Book Choice Award, Westchester Library Association, 1988, both for *The Macmillan Book of Greek Gods and Heroes*.

■ Writings

Open up My Suitcase, Simon & Schuster, 1954.
Grandmas and Grandpas, Random House, 1962.
Out of My Window, Random House, 1962.
Summer, Random House, 1963.
Taro and the Bamboo Shoot (adaptation of a folk tale), Pantheon, 1964.
A Day of Your Own, Your Birthday, Random House, 1964.
What's in Mommy's Pocketbook?, Golden Press, 1965.
Kallie's Corner, illustrated by David Stone Martin, Pantheon, 1966.
At Jasper's House and Other Stories, Pantheon, 1968.
Herbert's Treasure, illustrated by Victoria de Larrea, Putnam, 1971.
Witches's Holiday, illustrated by Tony Walton, Pantheon, 1971.
David's Windows, illustrated by Tomie de Paola, Putnam, 1974.
The Witch Who Was Afraid of Witches (also see below), illustrated by Karen Gundersheimer, Pantheon, 1978.
(With Bernard Stone) *The Charge of the Mouse Brigade*, illustrated by Tony Ross, Pantheon, 1980.
(Adaptor of verses by Colin McNaughton) *If Dinosaurs Were Cats and Dogs*, illustrated by McNaughton, Four Winds Press, 1981.
Genie and the Witch's Spells, illustrated by Lady McCrady, Knopf, 1982.
All around the Farm, illustrated by Maggie Swanson, Random House, 1984.
All through the Town, illustrated by Denise Fleming, Random House, 1984.
The Macmillan Book of Greek Gods and Heroes, illustrated by Arvis Stewart, Macmillan, 1985.
Who Lives in the Sea?, illustrated by Rowan Barnes-Murphy, Fisher-Price, 1987.
The Family Read-Aloud Christmas Treasury, illustrated by Marc Brown, Little, Brown, 1989.
Zena and the Witch Circus, illustrated by Laura Cornell, Dial, 1990.
The Family Read-Aloud Holiday Treasury, illustrated by Brown, Little, Brown, 1991.
The Quilted Elephant and the Green Velvet Dragon, illustrated by Christopher Santoro, Simon & Schuster, 1991.
(With Zheng Zhensun) *A Young Painter: The Life and Paintings of Wang Yani—China's Extraordinary Young Artist*, illustrated with photographs by Zheng Zhensun, Scholastic, 1991.
The Popcorn Shop, illustrated by Patricia Hammel, Scholastic, 1993.
(Author of script and lyrics) *The Witch Who Was Afraid of Witches* (play; based on Low's book of same title, with music by Jacob Stern), first produced in New York City, 1993.

Also contributor to anthologies, including *Captain Kangaroo's Read Aloud Book*, Random House, 1962, and *Captain Kangaroo's Sleepytime Book*, Random House, 1963. Author of scripts for filmstrips, including "Folk Songs and the American Flag," "Folk Songs and the Declaration of Independence," "Folk Songs and Abraham Lincoln," "Folk Songs and Frederick Douglas," all for Warren Schloat Productions, 1968-70; "First Things, Social Reasoning" (series of eight filmstrips), Guidance Associates, 1973-74; "You Can Be Anything," Teaching Resource Films, 1975; and "Bringing Home the Beach," Guidance Associates, 1975. Author of filmstrip scripts and producer of "Folk Songs and the Railroad," "Cowboys," and "Whaling," all for Warren Schloat Productions, 1970-72; and "History of the City," Warren Schloat Productions, 1972.

Author of operetta for elementary school children and of material for UNICEF. Contributor of stories to young adult magazines, including *Ingenue* and *Seventeen*. Reviewer of children's books for the *New York Times*.

Several of Low's works have been translated into French and Japanese.

■ Adaptations

The Witch Who Was Afraid of Witches was made into an animated film by the Learning Corporation of America.

■ Sidelights

Alice Low is the author of fiction, nonfiction, and poetry books for children and young adults. Her writings, especially those for younger readers, are known for their humorous plots and fanciful characters. In addition, Low has compiled selections of short stories and verse for some highly-regarded anthologies.

One of Low's earliest successes came with *Kallie's Corner*, the story of a new girl at a private school who doesn't fit in with the popular group. When Jane, one of girls in the group, tentatively befriends Kallie, they discover they don't need the group's arbitrary approval. The book garnered praise for its lively prose, engaging setting and characters, and its satisfying conclusion.

Low scored another success with *At Jasper's House*, a collection of short stories for young adults. "Candy for Oriana" tells the story of a young black girl at camp who encounters racism but gets her needs met by a counselor. The title story was commended for its tender depiction of a thirteen-year-old girl's transition from child to young adult. Max Steele, reviewing the collection in the *New York Times Book Review*, stated that "the reader wishes some of these stories, such as 'A Real Country Christmas,' had been the first chapters of novels. Others, such as 'The Naked Spot,' are complete in themselves—and completely amusing."

Turning her attention to younger readers, Low penned *Herbert's Treasure*, the story of a boy who collects junk, much to his mother's dismay. One day he finds a key that fits a lock and builds himself a shack out of all the "useless" things he had been collecting. While some reviewers found this work lacking the exaggeration necessary for a truly tall tale, Susanne Gilles in *School Library Journal* remarked: "A fantasy without a moral ... [*Herbert's Treasure*] will be especially enjoyed by other young treasure collectors." Low later adapted the poems of Colin McNaughton for *If Dinosaurs Were Cats and Dogs,* a simple rhyming tale of a boy who straps a balloon to his head and flies off to a land where small animals are the size of dinosaurs. And in *The Quilted Elephant and the Green Velvet Dragon,* Low examines jealousy and sibling rivalry between two stuffed animals brought along on a sleepover.

Unusual Witches Star in Several Books

The adventures (and misadventures) of witches have been featured in several of Low's works. *Witches' Holiday* is another rhyming tale for young children that depicts a group of witches who pop out of a closet on Halloween night to fingerpaint on the ceiling, rollerskate through the house, and eat up all the Halloween candy before flying away. *The Witch Who Was Afraid of Witches* tells the story of Wendy, whose older, more powerful sisters make her stay at home on Halloween. When a young boy comes trick-or-treating and invites Wendy along, the young witch gains self-confidence and finds her own witch power during their adventures. A *Publishers Weekly* reviewer called this parable of sibling rivalry "an irresistible way to add joy to the scarey fall holiday."

In a later work, *Genie and the Witch's Spells,* two little girls having trouble in school strike a bargain to help each other out, only to find the improvement in their grades was due to their own efforts rather than magical spells. A *Booklist* critic remarked: "The pat ending is telegraphed far too early, but Genie and her magical counterpart are engaging enough to lure some into the mixture of magic and reality." *Zena and the Witch Circus* is the humorous tale of a young witch who is prevented from participating in the witch circus because she can't perform magic. Zena gains self-confidence and self-esteem when she saves the witch circus from disaster with the help of a friendly cat she rescues in the woods. While some reviewers found the plot a bit confusing, Julie Corsaro, writing in *Booklist,* called the work "an entertaining and challenging romp."

Low adapted the myths and legends of ancient Greece for *The Macmillan Book of Greek Gods and Heroes,* a highly praised introduction to this topic for young readers. While some reviewers found that these shortened, simplified versions lacked animation, many agreed that this attractive collection is ideal for presenting complex ancient myths to a young audience. Reviewing *Greek Gods,* a *Booklist* critic complimented the volume's "broad scope" and "useful index," noting as well that the tales are "clearly told."

Low selected works for two well-received anthologies, *The Family Read-Aloud Christmas Treasury,* and *The Family Read-Aloud Holiday Treasury.* The anthologies mix well-known with lesser-known pieces and were commended for their inclusion of tales and poems from other cultures. A reviewer in *Publishers Weekly* called the *Holiday Treasury* "richly diverse" and "exuberant;" another contributor to the same periodical applauded the "well-chosen collection" of "cheery stories, songs, and poems" found in the *Christmas Treasury.*

■ Works Cited

Corsaro, Julie, review of *Zena and the Witch Circus, Booklist,* September 15, 1990, p. 177.

Gilles, Susanne, review of *Herbert's Treasure, Library Journal,* May 15, 1971, p. 1798.

Review of *The Family Read-Aloud Christmas Treasury, Publishers Weekly,* December 8, 1989, p. 53.

Review of *The Family Read-Aloud Holiday Treasury, Publishers Weekly,* October 18, 1991, p. 60.

Review of *Genie and the Witch's Spells, Booklist,* April 1, 1982, p. 1019.

Review of *The Macmillan Book of Greek Gods and Heroes, Booklist,* November 15, 1985, p. 497.

Steele, Max, "Teen-Age Fiction," *New York Times Book Review,* November 3, 1968, p. 10.

Review of *The Witch Who Was Afraid of Witches, Publishers Weekly,* September 4, 1978, p. 114.

■ For More Information See

PERIODICALS

Bulletin of the Center for Children's Books, February, 1967, p. 94; May, 1971, p. 140; October, 1974, p. 32.

Kirkus Reviews, November 1, 1968, p. 1226; May 1, 1974, p. 475.

Library Journal, January 15, 1972, p. 275.

Saturday Review, November 12, 1966, p. 51.

School Library Journal, December, 1978, p. 45; November, 1981, p. 80; May, 1991, p. 81; December, 1991, p. 96; January, 1992, p. 92.*

* * *

LUCAS, Eileen 1956-

■ Personal

Born July 23, 1956, in Chicago, IL; daughter of Robert (a commercial artist) and Patricia (a homemaker; maiden name, Costello) O'Donnell; married Joseph Lucas (a shipping/receiving/assembly manager), April 4, 1981; children: Travis, Brendan. *Education:* Attended School of Irish Studies (Dublin, Ireland), 1976; Western Illinois University, B.A. (with honors), 1977.

■ Addresses

Home—167 Fontana Avenue, P.O. Box 89, Fontana, WI 53125.

EILEEN LUCAS

■ Career

Writer of juvenile nonfiction books. *Member:* Society of Children's Book Writers and Illustrators, Council for Wisconsin Writers.

■ Writings

Vincent Van Gogh, Franklin Watts, 1991.
Peace on the Playground, Franklin Watts, 1991.
Acid Rain, Children's Press, 1991.
Water: A Resource in Crisis, Children's Press, 1991.
Jane Goodall, Millbrook Press, 1992.
The Cherokees, Millbrook Press, 1993.
The Mind at Work, Millbrook Press, 1993.
The Ojibwas, Millbrook Press, 1994.

American Conservationists, Naturalists and Environmentalists, Facts on File, 1994.
The Everglades, Steck Vaughn, 1994.

■ Sidelights

"I feel I am very lucky to have been able to make a career out of two of the things I really enjoy doing—reading and writing," Eileen Lucas told *SATA.* "I enjoy communicating about things I read and think about through the written word. I think that these are valuable skills for anyone, regardless of the career they choose.

"Being a mother is a very important part of who I am and it just feels right for me to write for and about kids," she says. Lucas wrote *Vincent Van Gogh* in order to share with children the story of the artist's life, how he struggled to create beauty and how he remained true to himself despite many personal problems. She wrote *Peace on the Playground* so that children would know that there are other alternatives to problem solving besides violence.

Lucas writes about subjects that concern her deeply, and tries to share her information with children at all different age levels. "As I read and I write I am learning all the time," says Lucas. "I learn about the subjects I am working on, and I learn about writing. I think learning is very exciting, and so I am always excited about what I do."

■ For More Information See

PERIODICALS

Booklist, May 1, 1991, p. 1710; January 1, 1992, p. 827; March 1, 1992, p. 1269; May 1, 1992, p. 1596; May 15, 1992, pp. 1679-80.
Kirkus Review, October 1, 1991, p. 1289.
School Library Journal, July, 1991, p. 83; December, 1991, p. 112.

M

MacDONALD, Amy 1951-
(Del Tremens)

■ Personal

Born June 14, 1951, in Beverly, MA; daughter of
Alexander S. (a doctor) and Mary (a psychotherapist;
maiden name, Wright) MacDonald; married Thomas A.
Urquhart (a conservationist), June 26, 1976; children:
Emily, Alexander, Jeremy. *Education:* University of
Pennsylvania, B.A., 1973; Centre de Formation des
Journalistes, 1982-83, fellow. *Politics:* Democrat. *Religion:* Unitarian.

■ Addresses

Home—10 Winslow Rd., Falmouth, ME 04105.

■ Career

Harvard Post, Harvard, MA, editor, 1979-82; *Highwire
Magazine,* Lowell, MA, senior editor, 1983-84; Cambridge University Press, Cambridge, England, copyeditor, 1984-88; freelance journalist, editor and children's
book author, 1984—. Harvard University, summer
writing instructor, 1988; Stonecoast Writers' Conference, instructor, 1991, 1992, 1993. *Member:* Figure of
Speech Theater (board member, 1990—), Society of
Children's Book Writers and Illustrators, Maine Writers
and Publishers Alliance (board member, 1993—), numerous environmental groups.

■ Awards, Honors

Silver Stylus Award for best children's book, Collectieve
Propaganda van her Nederlandse Boek (Dutch Book
Association), 1990, for *Little Beaver and the Echo,*
which was named one of the ten best children's books by
New York Times, Horn Book, and *Fanfare,* and a Book-
of-the-Month-Club selection, as well as to the short list
for the Children's Book Award, U.K.

■ Writings

(Compiler) *The Whale Show* (play), first produced at
Proposition Theatre, Cambridge, MA, 1975; produced in New York City, 1977.
(Under pseudonym Del Tremens) *A Very Young House-
wife* (parody of children's books), Harvard Common Press, 1979.
Little Beaver and the Echo, illustrated by Sarah Fox-
Davies, Putnam, 1990.
Rachel Fister's Blister, illustrated by Marjorie Priceman,
Houghton, 1990.
Let's Do It, Candlewick Press, 1991.
Let's Make a Noise, Candlewick Press, 1991.
Let's Play, Candlewick Press, 1991.
Let's Try, Candlewick Press, 1991.
Let's Pretend, Candlewick Press, 1993.
Let's Go, Candlewick Press, 1993.

AMY MacDONALD

The Spider Who Created the World, Orchard Books, 1994.

Little Beaver and the Echo has been published in eight languages.

■ Work in Progress

A screenplay.

■ Sidelights

Amy MacDonald's first picture book, *Little Beaver and the Echo,* tells the story of a lonely little beaver who calls out his need for a friend and hears the exact same plea echoing from across the pond. He goes in search of this voice to befriend it, and comes across a duck, an otter, and a turtle, also in need of friends. When the group reaches the other side of the pond, the mystery of the echo is explained by a wise old beaver. At the book's end, the pond echoes with the gleeful noises made by the four new friends. While one reviewer found this story somewhat predictable, many considered it a gentle and satisfying parable for young children. Carolyn Phelan, writing in *Booklist,* described *Little Beaver and the Echo* as "a simple, satisfying picture book ... there's a bit of Little Beaver in every kid."

MacDonald explained to *SATA* the genesis of *Little Beaver and the Echo:* "I have always loved children's books, but I never intended to write one. [*Little Beaver and the Echo*] came about entirely by accident. I was staying at a beautiful lake and playing with the echo there when my one-year-old son asked me what an echo was. Instead of answering, I wrote a story. The setting, of course, was the lake where I had spent so many happy summers as a child. And the main character was a

A lonely little beaver follows the sound of crying and makes a pleasant discovery in MacDonald's first picture book. (Illustration by Sarah Fox-Davies.)

beaver—like the ones who lived on the lake. The resulting book combines my love of a simple story with my love of the outdoors."

Rachel Fister's Blister is the humorous, rhyming story of Rachel, who has a blister on her toe, and all the people in her town, from the fireman to the priest and rabbi, who offer silly solutions to her problem. A reviewer for *Publisher's Weekly* commented: "MacDonald's sparkling tale has the exceptional virtue of making her verse seem effortless," while Kathy Piehl remarked in *School Library Journal:* "This book's infectious rhythm and rhyme demand that it be read aloud."

MacDonald has also written the text for several board books in the "Let's Explore" series from Candlewick Press. The books combine simple ideas and bright, colorful drawings that together introduce the youngest children to activities and objects around them. Phelan remarked of the series: "Simple, bright, and appealing, this set of board books offers a pleasant introduction to the world of reading."

■ Works Cited

Phelan, Carolyn, review of *Little Beaver and Echo, Booklist,* January 1, 1991, p. 938.
Phelan, Carolyn, review of *Let's Do It* and *Let's Make a Noise, Booklist,* March 15, 1992, p. 1385.
Piehl, Kathy, review of *Rachel Fister's Blister, School Library Journal,* November, 1990, p. 96.
Review of *Rachel Fister's Blister, Publishers Weekly,* August 31, 1990, p. 63.

■ For More Information See

PERIODICALS

Children's Book Review Service, winter, 1991, p. 64; January, 1991, p. 52.
Horn Book, November/December, 1990, p. 731; July/August, 1992, p. 457.
Publishers Weekly, June 29, 1990, p. 100.
School Library Journal, March, 1991, p. 175; August, 1992, p. 143.

* * *

MAHONY, Elizabeth Winthrop
See WINTHROP, Elizabeth

* * *

MALLETT, Jerry J. 1939-

■ Personal

Born March 27, 1939, in Toledo, OH; son of George (a tool/die maker) and Myrtle (a homemaker/florist, maiden name, Brown) Mallett; married Karen Pettibone (executive director of a hospice); children: David and Christopher (twins), Michael. *Education:* Ohio University, B.S., 1961; University of Toledo, M.E., 1963, Ph.D., 1972. *Politics:* Independent. *Religion:* Unitarian.

■ Addresses

Home—15232 Amanda TR 190, Arlington, OH 45814. *Office*—c/o The University of Findlay, 1000 N. Main St., Findlay, OH 45840.

■ Career

Washington Local Schools, Toledo, OH, teacher, 1961-64, principal, 1964-68; University of Findlay, Findlay, OH, professor, 1968—. Educational consultant; director of the Mazza Collection Gallery. *Member:* International Reading Association, Society of Children's Book Writers and Illustrators, National Council for Teachers of English, American Association of University Professors, Phi Delta Kappa.

■ Awards, Honors

Distinguished Educator Award, Ohio Chamber of Commerce, 1983; outstanding teacher award, Ohio Independent Colleges and Universities, 1987.

■ Writings

"ERNIE" SERIES; WITH MARIAN BARTCH

Good Old Ernie, Perma-Bound, 1983.
Poor Old Ernie, Perma-Bound, 1988.
Just Old Ernie, Perma-Bound, 1988.
Clearly Old Ernie, Perma-Bound, 1989.

"TUMTWIT" SERIES

(With Bartch) *The First & Last Gravelsburg School Spelling Bee,* illustrated by Mark Smith, Perma-Bound, 1986.
(With Bartch) *A Bellyful of Ballet!,* illustrated by M. Smith, Perma-Bound, 1986.
(With Bartch) *Close the Curtains,* illustrated by M. Smith, Perma-Bound, 1986.
(With Bartch) *Goodbye to Camp Crumb,* illustrated by M. Smith, Perma-Bound, 1986.
(With Bartch) *On Your Mark, Get Set, HELP!,* illustrated by M. Smith, Perma-Bound, 1986.
(With Timothy S. Ervin) *Elevator,* illustrated by Clinton Johnston, Perma-Bound, 1992.
(With Ervin) *Good Day, Blue Goose!,* illustrated by Kathy Feraris, Perma-Bound, 1992.

JUVENILE MYSTERIES; WITH MARIAN BARTCH

The Mystery at Chung's Chinese Restaurant, Perma-Bound, 1987.
The Mystery at Madame Darkle's Wax Museum, Perma-Bound, 1987.
The Mystery at the Hollender Hotel, Perma-Bound, 1987.
The Mystery at the Laff-A-Lott Amusement Park, Perma-Bound, 1987.
The Mystery at the Seesaw Cinema Company, Perma-Bound, 1987.

JERRY J. MALLETT

OTHER

Also author of texts and activity packets for the Center for Applied Research in Education, Perma-Bound, Scott, Foresman and Co., and Alleyside Press.

■ Work in Progress

A series of seven picture books which are predictable in nature; a series of three books containing a variety of folk-tales from around the world.

■ Sidelights

Jerry J. Mallett was born in Toledo, Ohio and grew up in the surrounding rural area, which had a great influence on his becoming a storyteller. He told *SATA:* "Mine was a childhood of forest adventures, tree houses, and berry picking. More significantly, it was a childhood of stories. Not only did I create a wonderful group of characters with whom to play and some very interesting plots, but story-telling was also the mode of entertainment at my grandparent's home. And what stories! Even a Saturday at the movies couldn't compare with my Grandmother's tales of her childhood in her beloved Dallas, Texas. I can still vividly recall her telling of the flooding of the 'treacherous Trinity River' and the horrible day the Fort Worth stockyards burned to the ground. I could almost smell the burning flesh of the poor livestock.

"By high school, I had decided on a career in teaching and writing ... a career that would allow me to share my love of story telling. Other than marrying the neighbor girl down the block, it was the most important and best decision of my life. It has been a career I have loved and one in which I have found deep satisfaction. Indeed, many of the ideas for my stories have come from my teaching experiences. Other ideas have, of course, come from my family.

"My wife and three sons have provided ample material for my books. We lived in a one-hundred-and-sixty-year-old brick farm house all the while our sons grew up. It was in this setting that many of the episodes in the 'Ernie Books' took place. For instance, in one of my books, Claude, the cat, runs up the Tubbs' Christmas tree causing it to come crashing to the floor. Well, that same thing happened many years ago when my three sons were very young. Our cat, Midnight, made a mad dash up our eleven foot tree just after we finished decorating it. There we stood in silent shock as our tree came crashing to the floor, breaking many of the lights and ornaments. I made a late night visit to Bargain City to purchase new decorations to replace all of the broken ones. I would have liked to replace Midnight!"

Although Claude the cat was based on a real-life feline, he is the only "real" character in Mallett's fiction. "I am often asked if any of my characters are based on a real person," he told SATA. "Well, not entirely, but I do use bits and pieces of many persons I have known in order to create 'original' characters. For example, one of my favorite characters in my 'Tumtwit Series' is Bernice Batsdaffy. When asked if I have ever had Bernice in any of my classes, I explain that I have had many Bernices in my classes over the thirty-some years I have been a teacher."

All of Mallett's books look at the humorous side of life, although that was not always his intention. "One of my first mystery stories was intended to be a very serious murder mystery," he says. "What it turned out to be was similar to the 'Pink Panther' movie series I loved so much. My detective, Malcolm P. Muddle, simply muddles through each case in a similar manner to Peter Sellers in the movie series. My favorite character is not Detective Muddle, though, it is Mildred. I fell in love with Mildred in *The Mystery at the Hollender Hotel* even though she had a minor role as the elevator operator. I enjoyed writing about her so much that I devised a logical way in which to include her as a 'main' character in another of the Muddle books, *The Mystery at the Laff-A-Lott Amusement Park.*

"Today, I divide my time between teaching, writing, speaking throughout the country, directing the Mazza collection Gallery, a gallery of original art from children's books, and family life ... admittedly a schedule with a pace that verges on hectic, if not downright impossible! And I love every minute of it!"

MARBACH, Ethel
See POCHOCKI, Ethel Frances

*   *   *

MARION, Henry
See del REY, Lester

*   *   *

MARKER, Sherry 1941-
(Alice Whitman)

■ **Personal**

Born August 10, 1941, in Evanston, IL; daughter of Tom Marker and Mary McSherry (a writer); children: Jessica Alice Nenner, Sarah Whitman Nenner. *Education:* Attended Smith College, 1959-61; Radcliffe College, B.A. (cum laude), 1964; attended American School of Classical Studies, 1964-65, and University College—London, 1965-66; University of California at Berkeley, M.A., 1970. *Politics:* Democrat. *Religion:* Catholic.

■ **Addresses**

Home and office—25 Tyler Ct., Northampton, MA 01060.

■ **Career**

Freelance writer. Smith College, Northampton, MA, lecturer, 1992—. *Member:* Melanoma Foundation, American Cancer Society.

SHERRY MARKER

■ Awards, Honors

Sword of Hope, Massachusetts American Cancer Society 1987, for the best first-person newspaper piece on cancer published in 1987; Support of Education Medal, Council for Advancement and Support of Education, 1988, for an article published in an alumni magazine.

■ Writings

BOOKS FOR YOUNG ADULTS

London, Black Birch, 1990.
Cooperation, Black Birch, 1991.

TRAVEL BOOKS

The Meteora, Efstathiadis, 1984.
The Peloponnese, Efstathiadis, 1984.
Athens, Attica, and the Islands of the Argo-Saronic Gulf, Efstathiadis, 1985.
Macedonia, Thessaly, and Epirus, Efstathiadis, 1987.
Athens, Efstathiadis, 1988.
Philip of Macedon and the Royal Sites of Macedonia, Efstathiadis, 1989.
Athens and Attica, Kedros, 1990.
The Peloponnese, Kedros, 1990.

BIOGRAPHIES AND AMERICAN HISTORY

Illustrated History of the United States, Bison-Crown, 1988.
Norman Rockwell, Bison-Crown, 1989.
Edward Hopper, Bison-Crown, 1990.

Contributor to *Great Generals of the American Civil War and Their Battles,* 1986, *World Almanac of the American West,* 1986, *Treasures of Ancient Greece,* 1987, *Facts on File Scientific Yearbook,* 1987, *Chronology of Twentieth Century History,* 1992, and *Cambridge Dictionary of American Biography,* 1993. Also contributor to *Penguin/Berlitz Travellers Guides.*

OTHER

Contributor, sometimes under the pseudonym Alice Whitman, of articles and reviews to periodicals, including *New York Times, Hampshire Life, San Juan Star, Travel and Leisure, Horizon, Museum Insights, Smith College Alumnae Quarterly,* and *Journal of the American Academy of Religion.*

■ Work in Progress

Research on United States history.

■ Sidelights

Sherry Marker has written several travel guides and many historical books. Although the majority of her work is designed for adult audiences, Marker has written two books for young adults. The first, 1990's *London,* describes the city of London, its history, and its people. *Cooperation,* published in 1992, is a discussion of the need for cooperation in every situation.

Marker explained for *SATA* her emergence as a writer: "A few years ago, my dear octogenarian friend Vivian Anagnostaki, remarked that 'getting older is very interesting. Everything starts to pull together.' Even in my 50's, I can see that she's right. When I first began to study Ancient Greek as an undergraduate, how could I have known that long after I'd stopped seriously reading Ancient Greek, I'd be passably fluent in modern Greek? In 1976, I bought a small house in the Peloponnese where I have yet to miss a summer. While avoiding working on my Ph.D. thesis in Ancient History, I wrote an article on buying the house which was published in the *New York Times.* One thing led to another and I began to do articles on Greece, England, and New England for the *Times* travel section. At the same time, I cranked out a series of guides to Greece for two Greek publishers. These were not 'serious' guides, but rather the sort of thing weary travellers buy in airports and skim in their hotel rooms. Happily, since 1990, I have been writing for two guides that are serious: the Berlitz guides to Greece and Turkey.

"What lies ahead? More of all of the above, I hope. Something I hope doesn't lie ahead: any repetition or resumption of the two bouts of cancer I've had since 1980. That experience has made me a firm believer in the philosophy which Horace expressed as 'Carpe Diem' and the Shakers' Mother Anne stated as 'Do all your work, as though you had a thousand years to live, and as you would if you knew you must die tomorrow.'"

*   *   *

MARTIN, Claire 1933-

■ Personal

Born December 6, 1933, in San Francisco, CA; daughter of Clair Devere (a geologist) and Mary (a homemaker; maiden name, McGowan) Jones; married Chet Martin (a radio news correspondent), February 12, 1955; children: Claire, Craig, Stephen, David, Philip, Eileen Gottlieb, Richard. *Education:* Mount St. Mary's College, B.A.; Immaculate Heart College, M.L.S. *Hobbies and other interests:* Tennis, skiing, scuba diving, reading and knitting.

■ Addresses

Home—96 Benthaven Ct., Boulder, CO 80303. *Agent*—Pesha Rubinstein, 37 Overlook Terrace, Apt. 10, New York, NY 10033.

■ Career

Los Angeles Public Library, Los Angeles, CA, children's librarian, 1971-75; children's librarian in Rahway, NJ, and Fanwood, NJ, 1976-83; County College of Morris, Randolph, NJ, reference librarian, 1986-88. *Member:* Society of Children's Book Writers and Illustrators, Author's Guild.

CLAIRE MARTIN

■ Awards, Honors

Honor book, Society of Illustrators, 1991, for *The Race of the Golden Apples,* illustrated by Leo and Diane Dillon; Gold Medal, Society of Illustrators, 1992, for *Boots and the Glass Mountain,* illustrated by Gennady Spirin; Martin was commended by City of Los Angeles as a contributor of outstanding children's programs.

■ Writings

I Can Be a Weather Forecaster, Children's Press, 1987.
My Best Book: A Year-Round Journal of Personal Bests, Black Birch Books, 1989.
The Race of the Golden Apples, illustrated by Leo and Diane Dillon, Dial, 1991.
Boots and the Glass Mountain, illustrated by Gennady Spirin, Dial, 1992.

Contributor to *Wonders and Winners,* Scott, Foresman, 1985.

■ Adaptations

The Race of the Golden Apples was featured on "Mrs. Bush's Story Time," ABC Radio Network.

■ Work in Progress

"Other retellings and original picture books."

■ Sidelights

Claire Martin told *SATA:* "I was raised in the city of San Francisco, in the shadow of St. Anne's Church and School, but my family moved for a few years to the 'mother lode' country of California, where my father owned and worked a gold mine (this was during World War II). We lived on a farm in a town called Rescue. Those childhood years gave me a taste for the freedom of country living. They also instilled in me a love of animals. What they did not provide was much schooling. When we returned to San Francisco and I went back to the parochial school, I was totally out of step with the rest of the class.

"During that period of isolation, I drowned myself in books. I remember reading *Lorna Doone,* one of my father's favorites. My reading also included *The Idylls of the King* and other versions of the Arthurian Cycle. My all-time favorite book still remains *The Once and Future King.* I loved noble narrative poems like 'Horatius at the Bridge,' and devoured the poems of Gerard Manley Hopkins.

"The seed for my writing was planted when, as a children's librarian, the book *Sir Gawain and the Loathly Damsel* by Joanna Throughton crossed my desk. What a wonderful way to introduce children to a rather obscure medieval tale, I thought. And then I thought, maybe I can do that! It wasn't until many years later, after my seven children were adults, that I tried to retell tales that I had loved. My only regret is that I did not start sooner."

A reviewer for *Publishers Weekly* calls Martin's first picture book, *The Race of the Golden Apples,* "a stylish, lucid retelling of the myth of Atalanta," a girl who was raised from a baby by the goddess Diana after she was abandoned by her father, who only wanted sons. As a young woman, Atalanta reluctantly returns to the kingdom of her father and agrees to marry in order to give him an heir, but insists she will only accept a man who can outrun her. The young man in love with her, Hippomenes, is aided by Venus in his quest to win her hand. Ann Welton writes in the *School Library Journal:* "Martin's retelling is clear and romantic, maintaining suspense until the finish line."

In *Boots and the Glass Mountain,* Martin retells a Norwegian fairy tale depicting a young farmboy who tames the wild horses owned by the fearful trolls who descend from the mountain every Midsummer's Night. In this reverse Cinderella-tale, the boy, Boots, rides the horses in a competition for the princess's hand in marriage and is transformed into a prince. A *Publishers Weekly* reviewer described Martin's narration in *Boots and the Glass Mountain* as "tinged with romance, mystery and drama," making it "well suited to read-aloud enjoyments."

Martin told *SATA:* "There are so many stories and tales that exist in formats that are daunting to children.

Perhaps, if they are introduced to them in beautifully illustrated books, then they'll hunger for more."

■ Works Cited

Review of *Boots and the Glass Mountain, Publishers Weekly,* July 13, 1992, p. 54.
Review of *The Race of the Golden Apples, Publishers Weekly,* June 28, 1991.
Welton, Ann, review of *The Race of the Golden Apples, School Library Journal,* October, 1991, p. 111.

■ For More Information See

PERIODICALS

American Bookseller, March, 1992, p. 19.
Booklist, November 15, 1987, p. 570; September, 1991; August, 1992, p. 2015.
Bulletin of the Center for Children's Books, November, 1991, p. 69.
Children's Book Review Service, September, 1991.
Horn Book, July/August, 1992, pp. 457-58.
Kirkus Reviews, July 15, 1991.
School Library Journal, July, 1992, p. 70.

* * *

McCANN, Edson
See del REY, Lester

* * *

McCULLY, Emily Arnold
See ARNOLD, Emily

* * *

McDERMOTT, Michael 1962-

■ Personal

Born February 14, 1962, in Baltimore, MD; son of Frank J. (in sales) and Joan Catherine (a psychologist; maiden name, Kunz) McDermott; married Elizabeth L. Alessi (a store manager), October 10, 1987 (separated). *Education:* Attended Maryland Institute College of Art. *Politics:* None. *Religion:* Catholic. *Hobbies and other interests:* Chess, basketball, "restoring my old house."

■ Addresses

Home and office—P.O. Box 343, 12 South Main St., Stewartstown, PA 17363. *Agent*—Dilys Evans Fine Illustration, P.O. Box 400, Norfolk, CT 06058.

■ Career

Freelance illustrator, 1986—. *Member:* Illustrators' Club of Maryland, Illustrators' Club of Virginia, Illustrators' Club of Washington, D.C., York Chess Club.

■ Awards, Honors

Starr Foundation Award, Society of Illustrators, 1986, for *Three Good Blankets; The Truth about Unicorns* was selected as one of *Booklist*'s top 50 titles of 1990.

■ Illustrator

Willow Finds a Baby, Random House/Lucas Films, 1988.
Mary K. Whittington, *Carmina, Come Dance,* Atheneum, 1989.
Ida Luttrell, *Three Good Blankets,* Atheneum, 1990.
Bruce Colville, *The Prehistoric People,* Doubleday, 1991.
James Cross Giblin, *The Truth about Unicorns,* Harper, 1991.

■ Sidelights

Michael McDermott, the winner of a 1986 Starr Foundation Award from the Society of Illustrators for his work on *Three Good Blankets,* related to *SATA* his motivation to illustrate books: "I have always admired the work of many book illustrators, too numerous to mention. To look at an illustration that is so perfectly drawn, so well crafted, so well painted and just so perfect that it makes you ask, 'How did someone do that by hand?' That is what gets me and makes me want to try to do work that will elicit the same response."

McDermott explained that his career developed with practice, training, and education. He liked to draw and practiced to "gain a certain command" of the craft. He then took some high school art classes and continued to practice. At the Maryland Institute College of Art, McDermott said, he was "exposed to some great professional illustrators' work" and was "inspired to do similar work." He then became an illustrator for advertisers and publishers.

McDermott continues to illustrate book jackets as well as advertisements. He stated that he is "striving to become as good or hopefully better than my heroes first and foremost [for] the love of the pictures" and the "love of illustration itself."

* * *

McKENNA, Colleen O'Shaughnessy 1948-

■ Personal

Born May 31, 1948, in Springfield, IL; daughter of Joseph F. (a civil engineer) and Ruth Short (an office manager) O'Shaughnessy; married J. Frank McKenna III (an attorney), March 25, 1972; children: Collette, Jeff, Laura, Steve. *Education:* Slippery Rock University, B.S., 1970; post-graduate studies at Carnegie Mellon University and Pitt University. *Religion:* Roman Catholic.

■ Addresses

Home—101 Fox Ridge Farms, Pittsburgh, PA 15215.

■ Career

Third and fourth grade teacher in Bethel Park, PA, 1970-1973; writer. Member of St. Lucy's Auxillary. *Member:* Society of Children's Book Writers and Illustrators.

■ Awards, Honors

Award of Excellence, Slippery Rock University, 1992.

■ Writings

"MURPHY" SERIES

Too Many Murphys, Scholastic, 1988.
Fourth Grade Is a Jinx, Scholastic, 1989.
Fifth Grade: Here Comes Trouble, Scholastic, 1989.
Eenie, Meanie, Murphy, No, Scholastic, 1990.
Murphy's Island, Scholastic, 1991.
The Truth about Sixth Grade, Scholastic, 1991.
Mother Murphy, Scholastic, 1992.
Camp Murphy, Scholastic, 1993.

JUVENILE

Merry Christmas, Miss McConnell!, Scholastic, 1990.

COLLEEN O'SHAUGHNESSY McKENNA

Good Grief, Third Grade, Scholastic, 1993.
Roger Friday: Live from the Fifth Grade, Scholastic, in press.

"COUSINS" SERIES

Not Quite Sisters, Scholastic, 1993.
Stuck in the Middle, Scholastic, 1993.

YOUNG ADULT

The Brightest Light, Scholastic, 1993.

■ Work in Progress

Scout's Honor; also sequels to *The Brightest Light, Murphy's Island,* and *Eenie, Meanie, Murphy, No.*

■ Sidelights

To many young readers the name Colleen O'Shaughnessy McKenna means a fun read. The kids in her stories think and talk like kids and are people other children can identify with. Reviewers have called her books warm, funny, and insightful, and have noted the way her "Murphy" books capture the chaos, struggles and joys of a loving, boisterous family. Since *Too Many Murphys* was first published in 1988, McKenna's books have become popular with children between the ages of eight and twelve.

McKenna began serious attempts at writing while in the eighth grade. Because she loved the character of Little Joe from the television series *Bonanza,* she began to write her own scripts for the show. "I wanted him to notice me. The best way to do that was to make myself the main character," she recalls. In all, McKenna wrote twenty-seven scripts, mailing the best three to *Bonanza.* "It was a good experience because I learned about the opening, middle, and end of a story."

After graduating from Slippery Rock University with a degree in elementary/special education, McKenna taught third and fourth grades in Bethel Park, Pennsylvania. While there, she began writing plays for her classes. Noting that her students enjoyed working on the plays, McKenna did not hesitate to use them to gain control of her classroom. "I guess we can't have rehearsal today because someone is throwing spitballs," she would say. The kids disciplined each other in order to rehearse.

In 1972 she married J. Frank McKenna III, and when they started their family she stopped teaching. Within six years their family had grown to include children Collette, Jeff, Laura, and Steve. It was a time for absorbing facts and learning experiences about life in a growing family and the individuals that are part of it. When her husband, an attorney, announced that he would be away from home for about fourteen weeks trying a case, he encouraged McKenna to find something to do that she would really love. "You'll go crazy being alone with four children for more than three months," he told her. She began to think, "If I could do *anything,* what would it be?" The one thing she really

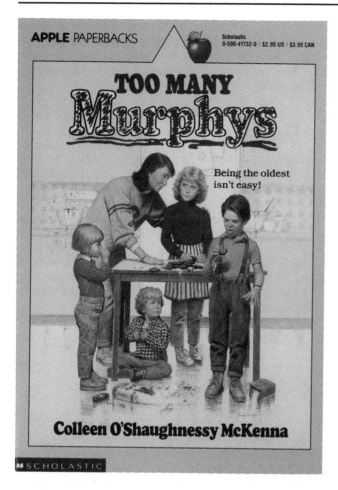

Oldest sister Collette's wish to be an only child for Christmas doesn't turn out as she planned in McKenna's first novel.

An invitation to a skating party—with BOYS—spells trouble for Collette in this "Murphy" story.

missed was writing, so she signed up for a course in children's literature.

Home Experience Leads to "Murphy" Books

One important piece of advice McKenna gained from the class was "write about what you know." She realized that being a full-time mother, it would be natural to write about her own children. "One day, my oldest daughter, Collette, came up to me and said, 'None of my friends want to come to our crazy house. No offense, Mom, but you have too many babies. Sometimes I just wish I could be an only child.'" McKenna thought that sounded like a good story idea and she began work on her first book, *Too Many Murphys*. The story became the first in a series of books depicting the often disastrously humorous antics of the Murphy family, based on the experiences of McKenna's own children and their friends.

Too Many Murphys focuses on Collette, a third-grader who is the oldest child in her family. She feels the weight of being the one who is always responsible, setting a good example for the other three children: Jeff, Laura, and Stevie. Collette describes herself as a "midget mother" and often wishes she had more time with her parents all to herself. In her review in *School Library*

Journal, Carolyn Jenks states that "the outstanding quality" of *Too Many Murphys* is realism. "The characters and the things that happen to them will be familiar to many young readers," she observes.

In the "Murphy" books Collette deals with all the pains and joys of growing up. *Fourth Grade Is a Jinx, Fifth Grade: Here Comes Trouble,* and *The Truth about Sixth Grade* all focus on learning how to relate to parents, teachers, and classmates in school. Nancy P. Reeder, reviewing *The Truth about Sixth Grade* for *School Library Journal,* comments that "all of the characters may be found in any sixth grade classroom," where "students live in the moment ... and every event is a crisis." Making friends in new situations such as camp and a new school are explored in *Eenie, Meanie, Murphy, No* and *Murphy's Island.* Collette also learns to adjust to big changes, such as her mother's pregnancy in *Mother Murphy.* Of her own writing, McKenna says: "In my 'Murphy' books I deliberately stretch out the awfulness and I make Collette wade through it all, not just to get the laugh, but to force her to react. It is her reactions that draw readers to her, giving them a chance to identify with her because she really is a lot like them."

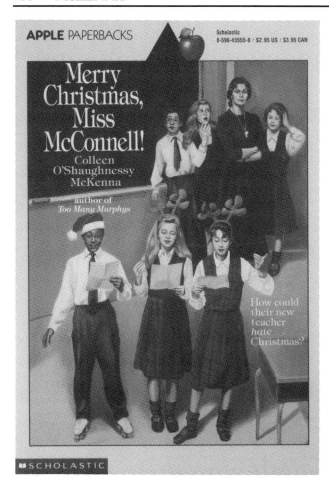

APPLE PAPERBACKS

Merry Christmas, Miss McConnell!

Colleen O'Shaughnessy McKenna

author of *Too Many Murphys*

How could their new teacher hate Christmas?

SCHOLASTIC

In McKenna's first non-Murphy book, a severe new teacher threatens to spoil Meg's holiday.

School Trials Come to Life in McKenna's Novels

Another of McKenna's books for middle-grade readers is *Merry Christmas, Miss McConnell!*, in which fifth-grader Meg Stafford and her family discover that Christmas need not be filled with expensive decorations, dinners and presents to be celebrated. McKenna balances the serious story of a family with financial difficulties with the humorous antics of Meg's friend, Raymond. In her *School Library Journal* assessment of *Merry Christmas, Miss McConnell!*, Susan Hepler declares that "McKenna has a good ear and eye for sketching fifth graders in a Catholic school."

McKenna has also penned a young adult novel, *The Brightest Light.* The book follows the trials of Kitty Lee, a sixteen year old who grows as she confronts a number of new and confusing issues, including her best friend's mysterious romance and elopement with an older man. She also experiences new feelings for her old friend Cody, who asks her out on a date, and for the man whose children she babysits while his wife battles alcoholism. Although Carol A. Edwards in *School Library Journal* finds *The Brightest Light* a fairly predictable teenage romance novel, she also lauds McKenna's refusal to happily resolve all difficult issues: "To give McKenna credit, anything that couldn't be fixed in the

last ten pages is realistically left hanging." A *Bulletin of the Center for Children's Books* reviewer praises the "subtle strength" of McKenna's heroine and suggests that *The Brightest Light* is "steadily told, entirely contemporary, and deeply romantic."

Colleen McKenna enjoys making presentations about herself and her writing to young readers. She wants her love of reading and writing to help inspire children to succeed in these fields. "The first thing you have to do is entertain them," she says. "I start by acting out scenes from *Bonanza* to show them what I was like in the eighth grade. Basically I show them I'm an ordinary person who chose writing as a career." She also explains to these groups how a story is written, using *The Three Little Pigs* to illustrate what makes a story work. She talks to the children about the importance of being a reader and gives them writing tips. "I want to represent a persistent kid who loved books so much I decided to write some of my own."

■ Works Cited

Review of *The Brightest Light, Bulletin of the Center for Children's Books,* October, 1990, p. 183-84.

Edwards, Carol A., review of *The Brightest Light, School Library Journal,* December, 1992, p. 133.

Hepler, Susan, review of *Merry Christmas, Miss McConnell!, School Library Journal,* October, 1990, p. 38.

Jenks, Carolyn, review of *Too Many Murphys, School Library Journal,* December, 1988, p. 109.

Reeder, Nancy P., review of *The Truth about Sixth Grade, School Library Journal,* April, 1991, p. 121.

■ For More Information See

PERIODICALS

Booklist, September 15, 1992, p. 138.

Bulletin of the Center for Children's Books, October, 1988, p. 47; February, 1989, p. 152; October, 1989, p. 39; October, 1990, p. 38; February, 1992, p. 163.

Kirkus Reviews, September 1, 1988, p. 1325; February 1, 1989, p. 211; January 1, 1992, p. 54.

Publishers Weekly, August 26, 1988, p. 90; April 27, 1992, p. 272.

School Library Journal, March, 1989, p. 178; September, 1989, p. 254; March, 1990, p. 219; December, 1990, p. 105; February, 1992, p. 87.

Wilson Library Bulletin, January, 1991, p. 6.

—*Sketch by Mary Lois Sanders*

*   *   *

MILLER, Louise (Rolfe) 1940-

■ Personal

Born May 9, 1940, in Chicago, IL; daughter of George Rolfe (in insurance sales) and Catherine (a teacher; maiden name, Walsh) Miller. *Education:* Attended University of Vienna, 1959-60; St. Xavier College, B.A.,

1961; University of Kansas, M.A., 1965. *Politics:* Independent.

■ Addresses

Home—626 West Waveland 1E, Chicago, IL 60613. *Office*—Catherine College, 2 North LaSalle St., Chicago, IL 60602.

■ Career

Researcher and publicist for various firms in Los Angeles, CA, 1975-77; Rand McNally, Skokie, IL, editorial director, 1977-81; free-lance writer, Chicago, IL, 1981-82; Jenner and Block (law firm), Chicago, proofreader, recruiter, and trainer, 1982-85; Catherine College, Chicago, instructor of English and office skills, 1985—. Instructor of German at University of Kansas, University of Missouri, University of Illinois, Harold Washington College, and Rosary College. Writing consultant for individuals and nonprofit organizations. Member of Citizens Action Program; member of Women Employed. *Member:* American Society for Training and Development, National Business Education Association, Chicago Women in Publishing.

■ Writings

Careers for Animal Lovers and Other Zoological Types, NTC Publishing, 1991.
Careers for Nature Lovers and Other Outdoor Types, NTC Publishing, 1992.

LOUISE MILLER

Wildlife columnist, *Sentinel* newspaper, Woodstock, IL, 1981.

■ Work in Progress

A book on cats; a German book with tapes; a follow-up book on animal lovers for younger people (10-14); career book for night owls; short stories.

■ Sidelights

Louise Miller told *SATA:* "I was born and reared in Chicago, Illinois, but have lived in Kansas, Missouri, California, Germany, and Austria. As a young girl, I was fascinated with geography, travel, and language. I grew up during World War II and was especially interested in Germany, probably because I have a German heritage and Germany was so much in the news at that time (and not for good reasons). Only five years after the end of the war (1950), I knew I was going to spend some time in Europe, maybe even as a glamorous foreign correspondent for a major newspaper!

"Although that was not to be my fate, I did study in Vienna, Austria, and Bonn, Germany, in my late teens and early twenties. I went on to become a German instructor at several universities and colleges. But in the process of learning the spelling, grammar, and beautiful new sounds of this wondrous language, I was not neglecting my English—not with my grandmother (a stickler for spelling) and the sisters in the Catholic schools that I attended. I was also quite intrigued by the flexibility, rich vocabulary, and literary tradition of English and loved to compare words and sounds of both languages.

"In the late sixties, when many foreign languages were being dropped from college and university programs, I decided to try my hand at commercial writing and editing for publishing houses in Chicago. I started out as a copy editor and writer for a brand-new, from-scratch encyclopedia on aviation and aerospace. During the seventies, I worked full time and free-lanced writing articles and brochures in the fields of real estate, economics, and anything else that would give me some experience. For several years, I was research director for *Compton's Encyclopedia.* During that time, I was sent to Hollywood to set up a research facility for a new TV quiz show called *Gambit.* I was also a senior editor for the *Mobil Travel Guide,* which entailed research, travel writing, and supervising. I have also worked as a legal proofreader and am currently teaching English and German and conducting writing workshops. So when the publisher approached me about actually writing a book of my own, I felt I was ready.

Author's First Pet Led to Concern for Animal Welfare

"My concern for the lives and well-being of our animal friends came rather late in life, actually while I was living in Los Angeles in 1975. Since I am (happily) single, I always wanted to be free to move whenever and wherever I wanted, which meant not having any pets. We always had a cat, a dog, a hamster, or a bird when I was growing up, but I never had a pet of my own.

"Things changed when I took in my first cat on a two-week probationary period. Her name was Susie and she was with me for fourteen years! I had really thought that I was a 'dog person.' In about two days, I was hopelessly in love and foolishly thought, 'Why not get a companion for Susie?' Within the month, Susie had three companions—Eloise, Mugwump, and Natty Bumpo. Who can resist kittens in a shelter? These four new friends opened doors of compassion, affection, and understanding that I had never felt with other humans. They have since died, and after a brief period of mourning, my need for feline companionship was rewarded with the arrival of Baby and Buster—two bouncing tiger tabbies who fill every nook and cranny of my life and house.

"Having all these fascinating, bright, and beautiful friends in my life has really brought me to a vegetarian lifestyle, memberships in many animal-rights organizations, and a deep appreciation for the distinctive qualities of other species.

"So writing a book on careers with animals seemed very natural to me and my publisher. I have since written a book in the same series called *Careers for Nature Lovers and Other Outdoor Types*. Both of these books are research based, that is, they did not come from my imagination. I was glad that I had had such a good grounding in research methodology and in the use of the library. I found many people who were very helpful in providing me with the information that I needed to write these books because I sent out letters of inquiry, talked on the phone with sources, and interviewed people in person who worked with or for animals for a living. I also made some good friends in the process.

"The important thing for me now is to write every day, to keep some quiet time to think, and always be alert to a new story idea, research project, human experience, or special interest. Then I just hope the muse will be with me when I'm near my new computer!"

*   *   *

MITGUTSCH, Ali 1935-

■ Personal

Born August 21, 1935; son of Ludwig and Paula Mitgutsch; married Karin Ramm, February 4, 1960; children: Oliver, Florian, Katrin. *Religion:* Catholic.

■ Addresses

Home—Tuerkenstrasse 54, 8000 Muenchen 40, Germany. *Office*—Schraudolphstrasse 26, 8000 Muenchen 40, Germany.

■ Career

Publishing art designer. Children's book author and illustrator.

■ Awards, Honors

Received Germany's most important children's book prize, for *Rundherum in meiner Stadt* (title means *All around My Town*).

■ Writings

"START TO FINISH" SERIES; SELF-ILLUSTRATED

From Beet to Sugar, Carolrhoda, 1981 (originally published as *Von der Ruebe zum Zucker*).
From Blossom to Honey, Carolrhoda, 1981 (originally published as *Von der Blute zum Honig*).
From Cacao Bean to Chocolate, Carolrhoda, 1981 (originally published as *Vom Kakao zur Schokolade*).
From Cement to Bridge, Carolrhoda, 1981 (originally published as *Vom Zement zur Brucke*).
From Clay to Bricks, Carolrhoda, 1981 (originally published as *Vom Lehn zum Ziegel*).
From Cotton to Pants, Carolrhoda, 1981 (originally published as *Von der Baumwolle zur Hose*).
From Cow to Shoe, Carolrhoda, 1981 (originally published as *Von der Kuh zum Schuh*).

ALI MITGUTSCH

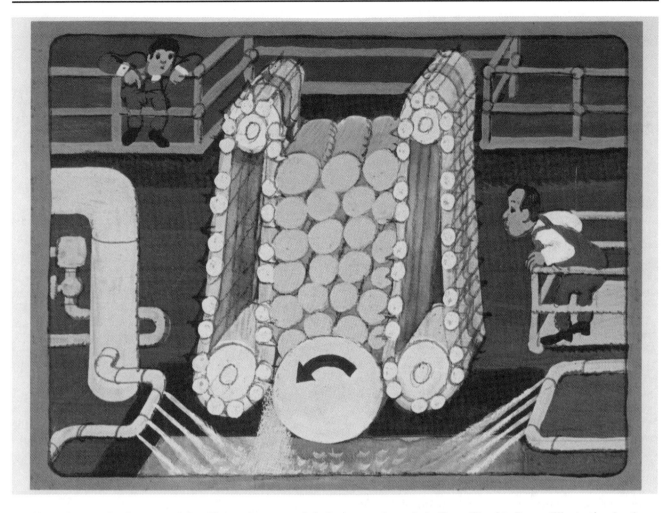

Mitgusch uses simple, entertaining illustrations to explain how paper is made in *From Wood to Paper*. (Illustration by the author.)

From Fruit to Jam, Carolrhoda, 1981 (originally published as *Vom Obst zur Marmelade*).

From Grain to Bread, Carolrhoda, 1981 (originally published as *Vom Korn zum Brot*).

From Grass to Butter, Carolrhoda, 1981 (originally published as *Vom Gras zur Butter*).

From Milk to Ice Cream, Carolrhoda, 1981 (originally published as *Von der Milch zum Speiseeis*).

From Oil to Gasoline, Carolrhoda, 1981 (originally published as *Vom Erdol zum Benzin*).

From Ore to Spoon, Carolrhoda, 1981 (originally published as *Vom Erz zum Loffel*).

From Sand to Glass, Carolrhoda, 1981 (originally published as *Vom Sand zum Glas*).

From Seed to Pear, Carolrhoda, 1981 (originally published as *Vom Kern zur Birne*).

From Sheep to Scarf, Carolrhoda, 1981 (originally published as *Vom Schaf zum Schal*).

From Tree to Table, Carolrhoda, 1981 (originally published as *Vom Baum zum Tisch*).

From Gold to Money, Carolrhoda, 1985 (originally published as *Vom Gold zum Geld*).

From Graphite to Pencil, Carolrhoda, 1985 (originally published as *Vom Graphit zum Bleistift*).

From Sea to Salt, Carolrhoda, 1985 (originally published as *Vom Meer zum Salz*).

From Swamp to Coal, Carolrhoda, 1985 (originally published as *Vom Urwald zur Kohle*).

From Lemon to Lemonade, Carolrhoda, 1986 (originally published as *Von der Zitrone zur Limonade*).

From Rubber Tree to Tire, Carolrhoda, 1986 (originally published as *Vom Kautschuksaft zum Reifen*).

From Wood to Paper, Carolrhoda, 1986 (originally published as *Vom Holz zum Papier*).

From Idea to Toy, Carolrhoda, 1988 (originally published as *Vom Bar zum Teddy*).

From Picture to Picture Book, Carolrhoda, 1988 (originally published as *Vom Maler zum Bilderbuch*).

IN ENGLISH TRANSLATION; SELF-ILLUSTRATED

World on Wheels, translated and adapted by Alice Popper, Golden Press, 1975, (published in England as *All about Wheels*, Dent).

The Busy Book, Golden Press, 1976.

A Knight's Book, translated by Elizabeth D. Crawford, Clarion Books, 1991 (originally published as *Ali Mitgutsch Ritterbuch*).

OTHER

(With Irmgard Haller) *Die Hexe und die sieben Fexe,* Ravensburg, 1970.

Also author of *All around My Town,* Western Publishing (originally published as *Rundherum in meiner Stadt,* Ravensburger), and *Nico Finds a Treasure,* Blackie. Author of untranslated published works, including *Unsere grosse Stadt, Bei uns im Dorf, Komm' mit ans Wasser, Wir spielen Abenteuer, In den Bergen, Rund um's Rad, Rund um's Schiff, Pirateninsel,* and *Von der Skizze zum Buch.*

■ Sidelights

Ali Mitgutsch is best known as an illustrator whose colorful, engaging paintings often carry the humorous element in science-oriented books for young children. His first book translated into English, *World on Wheels,* uses bright, busy illustrations to present the evolution of the wheel and the many uses to which this important invention has been put. This work was followed by an extensive science-oriented series of books for young children called "Start to Finish" books, published in the United States by Carolrhoda. Including such works as *From Beet to Sugar, From Grass to Butter, From Tree to Table,* and *From Picture to Picture Book,* the series breaks down both natural and technological processes into simple terms and processes for the young reader or preschooler curious about the origin of common objects. While some reviewers have observed that the series oversimplifies some processes, many find the series effective in explaining complex topics to young children.

Mitgutsch's next work to appear in English, *A Knight's Book,* tells the story of a young squire who learns to joust from a poor but valiant knight and then stays on at his castle to help prepare for an impending attack. The book has been praised for its informative text and colorful, detailed illustrations of medieval life. A contributor to *Kirkus Reviews* comments that the story's "greatest strength is its informational value." Another work to appear in English, *Nico Finds a Treasure,* presents the story of a shy boy who proves his worth to the relatives he is visiting by finding a fantastic treasure. Again, Mitgutsch's colorful illustrations were singled out for critical praise.

■ Works Cited

Review of *A Knight's Book, Kirkus Reviews,* August 15, 1991, p. 1092.

■ For More Information See

PERIODICALS

Booklist, October 15, 1981, pp. 300-301.
Junior Bookshelf, December, 1976, pp. 316-17; February, 1986, p. 27.
School Library Journal, January, 1982, p. 63; October, 1991, p. 125.

MOSS, Miriam 1955-

■ Personal

Born September 2, 1955, in Aldershot, England; daughter of John Kennedy (a lecturer) and Myra (a teacher; maiden name, Hunt) Moss; married Stephen White-Thomson (a publisher), July 28, 1984; children: Imogen, Morwenna, Finn. *Education:* Oxford University, B.Ed., 1977. *Religion:* Church of England.

■ Addresses

Home and office—37 Hampstead Rd., Brighton, East Sussex, England.

■ Career

King's School, Canterbury, Kent, England, teacher, 1977-82; Imani School, Thika, Kenya, teacher, 1982-83; Windlesham House School, Findon, Sussex, England, teacher, 1983-85; writer. Creative writing teacher, 1993. Volunteer teacher of adult literacy. *Member:* Society of Authors (London), Amnesty International.

■ Awards, Honors

Street Fashion and *Fashion Design* were listed by the American Library Association as recommended books for reluctant adult readers, 1992.

■ Writings

In the Pond, Macdonald, 1988.
The Fashion Industry, Wayland, 1989.
Women and Business, Wayland, 1989.
Castles, Andromeda, 1993.

"HOW THEY LIVED" SERIES

A Slave in Ancient Greece, Wayland, 1986.
A Norman Baron, Wayland, 1987.
A Schoolchild in World War II, Wayland, 1988.

"LIVING HISTORY" SERIES

The Victorians, Wayland, 1986.
The American West, Wayland, 1986.
Great Explorers, Wayland, 1986.
The Crusades, Wayland, 1986.
Ancient China, Wayland, 1987.

"TOPICS" SERIES

Language and Writing, Wayland, 1987.
Fairs and Circuses, Wayland, 1987.
Zoos, Wayland, 1987.

"COSTUMES AND CLOTHES" SERIES

Uniforms, Wayland, 1988.
Working Clothes, Wayland, 1988.
Clothes in Hot Weather, Wayland, 1988.
Clothes in Cold Weather, Wayland, 1988.
Fashionable Clothes, Wayland, 1988.
Children's Clothes, Wayland, 1988.
Traditional Costumes, Wayland, 1988.

MIRIAM MOSS

"MY SCHOOL" SERIES

The Schools' Librarian, Wayland, 1988.
Easter, Wayland, 1988.
The School Nurse, Wayland, 1988.

"FASHION WORLD" SERIES

Fashion Model, Wayland, 1990.
Fashion Photographer, Wayland, 1990.
Fashion Designer, Wayland, 1990.
Street Fashion, Wayland, 1990.

"THREADS" SERIES

Eggs, A & C Black, 1990.
Fruit, A & C Black, 1990.

"STAY HEALTHY" SERIES

Keep Fit, Wayland, 1992.
Eat Well, Wayland, 1992.
Be Positive, Wayland, 1992.

■ Work in Progress

Stories for young children; the "Weather Watch!" series of four books on the seasons, for Wayland, 1994.

■ Sidelights

When Miriam Moss became pregnant with her first child, she left teaching after eight years and began looking for work which she could combine with motherhood. By chance, an editor friend asked her to write a children's information book on a subject she had taught. "Three children and over forty books later, it has proved to be a wonderful rhythm of life which suits me," Moss told *SATA.* "I work every morning and feel full of energy and excitement at the prospect of the afternoons with my children. They have proved to be a source of inspiration for my stories too. I listen to the

remarkable way in which young children use language, combining unusual words to create powerful images, and I am inspired." The author is now also running creative writing workshops in schools.

■ For More Information See

PERIODICALS

Appraisal, summer, 1988, p. 63.
Booklist, April 15, 1988, pp. 1431-32; May 15, 1991, pp. 1790-91.
Books for Your Children, autumn, 1988, p. 30; spring, 1989, p. 16.
Bulletin of the Center for Children's Books, May, 1988.
Kirkus Reviews, May 1, 1991, p. 607.
School Library Journal, July, 1991, p. 84.

*   *   *

MURPHY, Claire Rudolf 1951-

■ Personal

Born March 9, 1951, in Spokane, WA; daughter of Kermit (a lawyer) and Frances Claire (a librarian; maiden name, Collins) Rudolf; married Robert Patrick Murphy (a teacher and principal), June 9, 1979; children: Conor Liam, Megan Frances. *Education:* Santa Clara University, B.A., 1973; University of California—Berkeley, secondary teaching credentials, 1974; University of Alaska—Fairbanks, M.F.A. in creative writing, 1987. *Politics:* Democrat. *Religion:* Catholic. *Hobbies and other interests:* Family outdoor activities, "such as biking, swimming, hiking, and cross-country skiing," running, and tennis; music (piano and voice) and community theater.

■ Addresses

Home—221 Well St., Fairbanks, AK 99701. *Agent*—Liza Voges, c/o Kirchoff/Wohlberg, 866 United Nations Plaza, New York, NY 10017.

■ Career

St. Mary's Mission High School, St. Mary's, AK, teacher of English and drama, 1974-77; Fairbanks Borough School District, Fairbanks, AK, secondary school teacher of English and drama, 1977-83; Fairbanks Correctional Center, Fairbanks, writing instructor, 1984-89; University of Alaska—Fairbanks, instructor in composition, 1990-91; free-lance writer, 1991—. Alaska State Writing Consortium teacher consultant, 1984—. Member, Fairbanks Light Opera, Immaculate Conception Church, Running Club North, and Nordale School Parent-Teacher Association. *Member:* Alaska Society of Children's Book Writers (co-chair and presenter at 1992 convention), Fairbanks Drama Association.

CLAIRE RUDOLF MURPHY

■ Writings

Friendship across Arctic Waters: Alaskan Cub Scouts Meet Their Soviet Neighbors, photographs by Charles Mason, Lodestar/Penguin, 1991.
To the Summit (young adult novel), Lodestar/Penguin, 1992.
The Prince and the Salmon People, illustrated by Dwayne Pasco, Rizzoli Children's Library, 1993.
We Are Alaska, photographs by Charles Mason, Alaska Northwest Books, 1994.
Gold Star Sister, Lodestar, 1994.

■ Work in Progress

A series of sports biographies; another Alaskan native legend; a young adult novel about Alaska in World War II.

■ Sidelights

Claire Rudolf Murphy told *SATA,* "My first book, *Friendship across Arctic Waters: Alaskan Cub Scouts Meet Their Soviet Neighbors,* came about in a very

unusual way. While I was working on my MFA degree I thought I wanted to write for young adults, but I wasn't quite sure. So my thesis ended up being a collection of short stories, half for young adults and half for adult readers. Afterwards I got sidetracked for a while writing newspaper and magazine articles. At one point I was trying to sell my short story 'To the Summit' to the Boy Scout magazine *Boys' Life* because I thought they would print an adventure story. I contacted the local director of the Boy Scouts in town here to talk about what kinds of articles and stories *Boys' Life* accepted. He said, 'You know, you really should write a story about the Nome Cub Scouts, this great group of boys that do all sorts of community service projects. Besides, they need some articles about Alaska.' So I wrote a query letter to *Boys' Life* about it and they said, 'Yes, write the article.' So I interviewed several Scouts, leaders and parents in Nome about their pack and wrote an article. In the article I mentioned that their dream was to take a field trip to Provideniya, Soviet Far East.

"As it turned out *Boys' Life* didn't publish my article or short story, but the local Fairbanks newspaper did and it got reprinted around the state. So news about the Cub Scouts and their dream got around. The Nome Cub Scouts used my article to help convince American government officials to let them visit Provideniya in the summer of 1989. The trip was the opportunity of a lifetime. Here I had grown up thinking of the Russians as enemies. In fact, in school during the Fifties we used to have air raid drills and many people in my neighborhood built bomb shelters to protect their families from the terrible Russians. They were our enemies. They didn't believe in God and they wanted to control the earth. Now I had the chance to get to know them for myself. During the visit I found them to be the friendliest, most articulate and most generous people in the world (next to the Irish, of course!) Many of them spoke English because English is taught in the schools from the first grade on. They all wanted to know about life in America, our government, what Russian books I had read and movies I had seen. The scouts and the young pioneers were like long-lost buddies. They knew the same games, told the same jokes and just had fun together.

Great Mountain Inspires First Novel

"Ever since I first saw Denali (the Athabaskan Indian name for Mount McKinley, meaning 'high one,' a term commonly used by Alaskans) in 1974 it has reached out for me, as it has to many Alaskans. It is the mighty symbol of our state, a magnificent statement about the beauty of our world. Fairbanks is only 120 miles from Denali National Park and on a clear day I can see Denali, jutting out, white and mighty. It is one of the wonders of the modern world, so I felt it deserved a novel about climbing it. I wrote *To the Summit* because I believe it speaks to the idea of how much a physical challenge such as climbing Denali can help strengthen a person's inner self. People, teens particularly, can often feel powerless today, and having confidence in one's abilities can help overcome that. Though I am athletic and have been a serious competitor at different times in my life, I have to admit that I do not at this time have the drive or discipline to climb Denali's mighty peak. However, I have great admiration for those who attempt it and feel that researching and writing this book, I have climbed Denali in spirit. And, interviewing as many climbers and guides as I did, I feel the story is as accurate as it could be without my actually climbing it.

"My third book, *The Prince and the Salmon People,* is very special to me. The salmon is my favorite wild animal, and I am concerned with how endangered they have become today. At the University of Alaska— Fairbanks library, I came upon a set of Tsimshian legends, and included in one volume was the story of the Prince and the Salmon People. After that I found other Tsimshian and Tlingit versions of the same story. I began my own retelling of the story, using the original story along with what I was learning about the Tsimshian culture. I contacted a traditional Tsimshian artist, Jack Hudson, who lives in Metlakatla, the only Tsimshian community in Alaska. He read my story and gave me important feedback. He also validated my desire to retell this story. He said he was glad I was trying to get this Tsimshian legend out to more children. As always, I wanted to make sure it was accurate because there are so many things written about Alaska, especially the native peoples, that are not accurate.

"I really wanted a Tsimshian artist to illustrate the story. After some checking around, Dwayne Pasco, from Poulsbo, Washington was recommended as an outstanding Northwest Coast Indian artist. Though Dwayne is not Indian himself, he has spent the last forty years studying and practicing the Northwest Coast Indian art form. I hope that children around the world will enjoy and learn more about the Tsimshian people from our book, also. The Tsimshian learned how to respect and take care of the salmon, so that they would return to them every spring. My hope is that we today can take better care of the salmon so that they will continue to return to us every year, instead of dying out. The book is dedicated to my brother Matt because in 1988 he and I fought the mighty king salmon one July day and it was then that I first said aloud that I wanted to write a book about the salmon.

"I care so much about our incredible state and hopefully this book conveys that love and warmth for younger readers everywhere. We have many natural resources up here, as well as a diversity of cultural groups and wild animals, and our job as Alaskans now is to protect all we have for future generations."

N–O

NEAL, Harry Edward 1906-1993

OBITUARY NOTICE—See index for *SATA* sketch: Born May 4, 1906, in Pittsfield, MA; died of a stroke, June 14, 1993, in Culpeper, VA. Secret Service agent and author. Neal, a Secret Service agent-turned writer, began his career with the U.S. agency in 1926 as a stenographer. He was promoted to agent after assisting in a raid on counterfeiters in 1931 and was later given an assignment to write articles on how to detect counterfeit money. He subsequently enrolled in a night course on writing articles, which led to the pursuit of writing fiction and short stories in the evenings and on weekends. He began to publish books beginning in 1949 with his first title, *Writing and Selling Fact and Fiction.* Neal retired from the Service as assistant chief in 1957 to become a full-time writer, concentrating on such nonfiction topics as effective writing and the history of the kite. He also penned a series of career books for young people, focusing on conservation, aviation, engineering, banking, and medical research, among other fields. The author of more than thirty books, Neal has seen his work sell in the hundreds of thousands. Among Neal's other titles are *The Story of the Secret Service, The Hallelujah Army: The Salvation Army in Action, From Spinning Wheel to Spacecraft: The Story of the Industrial Revolution,* and his most recent publication, 1981's *Before Columbus: Who Discovered America?*

OBITUARIES AND OTHER SOURCES:

PERIODICALS

New York Times, June 16, 1993, p. D24.
Washington Post, June 15, 1993, p. C8.
The Writers Directory: 1990-1992, St. James Press, 1990.

NIGHTINGALE, Sandy 1953-

■ Personal

Born September 23, 1953, in Farnbough, Kent, England; daughter of Robert (a civil engineer) and Katherine Margret (a florist; maiden name, Larner) Nightingale; married Gary Day-Ellison (an art director), September 21, 1991. *Education:* Attended Croydon College of Art and Design, 1971-75. *Politics:* "Disillusioned socialist." *Religion:* Church of England. *Hobbies and other interests:* History, herbalism, literature, art history.

■ Addresses

Home and office—London, England.

■ Career

Free-lance writer, illustrator, and artist of varying media, including books, magazines, packaging, ceramics, and three-dimensional greeting cards.

■ Writings

(Illustrator) Patricia Daniels, *Rumpelstiltskin,* Raintree Children's Books, 1980.
(Illustrator) Tony Nightingale, *Hamnet and the Pig Afloat,* J.M. Dent, 1983.
Hansel and Gretel, Random House, 1985.
A Giraffe on the Moon, Harcourt, 1991.
Pink Pigs Aplenty, Harcourt, 1992.
Cat's Knees and Bee's Whiskers, Harcourt, 1993.

■ Work in Progress

A book on Egyptian history, using wall paintings and hieroglyphics, for Andersen Press.

SANDY NIGHTINGALE

■ Sidelights

After years of illustrating other people's stories, Sandy Nightingale decided that she would rather concentrate on her own work. Nightingale told *SATA:* "Other authors of children's picture books don't always consider the finished book visually. So many stories take place all in the same setting and often using only one or two characters who must appear constantly throughout the book. This can sometimes have the effect of making every page look similar to the last and can be very tedious for the poor illustrator!

"When I wrote *Giraffe on the Moon,* I was determined that every page would look vastly different from the last. The result is, I think, that the child's interest is re-engaged with every turn of the page, and surely that's the object of the game.

"I have always wanted to illustrate picture books for children. It gives one the freedom to draw wild, crazy, magical, and impossible things which just shouldn't exist but do because you have decided so."

■ For More Information See

PERIODICALS

Booklist, February 15, 1992, p. 1107.
Growing Point, November, 1983, p. 4170.

Junior Bookshelf, October, 1983, p. 201; December, 1991, pp. 244-45.
School Library Journal, March, 1992, p. 223.
Times Educational Supplement, September 30, 1983, p. 42.

* * *

OUGHTON, Jerrie 1937-

■ Personal

Born April 13, 1937, in Atlanta, GA; daughter of Edwin (a college president) and Mary Frances (an educational director and author; maiden name, Johnson) Preston; married William Paul Oughton (a business owner), November 28, 1963; children: Cher, Lisa, Shannon, Sean, Preston. *Education:* Meredith College, B.A. *Religion:* Southern Baptist.

■ Addresses

Office—c/o Publicity Director, Houghton Mifflin Co., 222 Berkely St., Boston, MA 02116-3764.

■ Career

Teacher, Raleigh, NC, 1963-64; substitute teacher and teaching assistant, Washington, NC, 1974-85; secretary with Fayette County Public Schools, 1989—.

■ Writings

How the Stars Fell into the Sky: A Navajo Legend, illustrated by Lisa Dessami, Houghton, 1992.

Contributor to periodicals, including *Catholic Digest* and denominational magazines.

■ Work in Progress

Another Navajo legend, about the Navajo God Spider Woman and how she taught the People to weave.

■ Sidelights

Jerrie Oughton's career began when she was eight years old and a magazine asked her to write a review of a book for them. In high school in Raleigh, NC, she studied under the creative writing teacher, Mrs. Phyllis Peacock, who also taught the well-known Southern writer, Reynolds Price, who, in turn, taught Anne Tyler.

For twenty years, Oughton wrote articles and short stories and received encouraging letters from some of the most prominent (and caring) editors in children's publishing. But she had written no book. Then, as Oughton told *SATA,* "There came a point which I really believe is a milestone most writers have to pass. I knew that I would be writing whether or not I ever had a book published. It is part of my make-up and if I tried to turn it off it would be as futile as stemming a flood.

"It was at this point that I sent Houghton Mifflin Co. two manuscripts. One I discussed in the cover letter. A 'P.S.' stated that I was also enclosing a manuscript for a Navajo legend called *How the Stars Fell into the Sky.* This is the book they bought. My editor linked me up with Lisa Dessami who is an extraordinary artist. When the first copy of the book came to me, I felt that I had written the words to a song and Lisa had written the music. I was astounded.

"Sometimes people ask me how I got interested in Native American lore. I admire the Navajo greatly and feel any honor and recognition that can be channeled their way is certainly richly deserved. So much of their literary heritage is oral history from their Medicine Men and others who told the stories. I was just fortunate enough to find mention of two oral legends and to be able to pass them on through my mind and soul."

P

PATRON, Susan 1948-

■ Personal

Born March 18, 1948, in San Gabriel, CA; daughter of George Thomas (a business owner) and Rubye (a homemaker; maiden name, Brewer) Hall; married Rene Albert Patron (a rare book restorer), July 27, 1969. *Education:* Pitzer College, B.A., 1969; Immaculate Heart College, School of Library Science, M.L.S., 1972.

■ Addresses

Office—Los Angeles Public Library, Children's Services, 630 W. 5th St., Los Angeles, CA 90071.

■ Career

Los Angeles Public Library, children's librarian, 1972-79, senior children's librarian, 1979—. Served on Caldecott Committee of the American Library Association; taught courses in children's literature. Member of the board of advisors, KCET public television's *Storytime. Member:* Society of Children's Book Writers and Illustrators, Author's Guild, American Library Association, California Library Association.

■ Writings

Burgoo Stew, illustrated by Mike Shenon, Orchard Books, 1991.
Five Bad Boys, Billy Que, and the Dustdobbin, illustrated by Shenon, Orchard Books, 1992.
Bobbin Dustdobbin, illustrated by Shenon, Orchard Books, 1993.
Maybe Yes, Maybe No, Maybe Maybe, illustrated by Dorothy Donahue, Orchard Books, 1993.
Dark Cloud Strong Breeze, illustrated by Peter Catalanotto, Orchard Books, 1994.

Contributor to *Expectations,* an anthology for blind children published in Braille, 1992. Children's book reviewer, *School Library Journal* and *Five Owls.* Member of the board of advisors, *L.A. Parent* magazine.

SUSAN PATRON

■ Work in Progress

A sequel to *Maybe Yes, Maybe No, Maybe Maybe.*

■ Sidelights

Susan Patron grew up in Los Angeles, California, the middle of three sisters, and, as she told *SATA,* "a reader, dreamer, eavesdropper, washer of cars, shiner of shoes, mower of lawns, director of elaborate neighborhood plays, and teller of stories" who knew by the time she

by Susan Patron

Maybe Yes,
Maybe No,
Maybe Maybe

pictures by
Dorothy Donahue

Growing up and a family move means middle sister PK must deal with some confusing feelings in this story. (Cover illustration by Dorothy Donahue.)

was eight that she wanted to be a writer. "Confiding this ambition to my father," said Patron, "I received both encouragement (go ahead: if you want to be a writer, write) and excellent advice (learn how to type). He also told me I wouldn't have to go far to find story ideas; all I had to do was keep my ears open. He was right. I began eavesdropping and hearing stories everywhere."

Patron spent her junior year of college in independent study at Trinity College, Dublin, listening to the "gowned professors as well as the cab drivers, the children, and the pub orators—the best extemporaneous talkers in the world." Back in the states, Patron was offered a job as children's librarian at the Los Angeles Public Library, where she voraciously read children's literature, learned how to tell stories to preschoolers and elementary school children, and created a project in which older adults were recruited and taught storytelling techniques.

Beginning in 1989, Patron wrote a series of stories about Billy Que, some bad boys who are friends of his, and two "dustdobbins" (Hob and Bobbin) who live in the dust under Billy Que's bed. "I hear in my mind the voices of my Mississippi grandparents, Baby R. Della and Homer, as these stories spin out. They are meant to be told or read aloud like stories from the folk tradition.

I only recently met the illustrator of these books, Mike Shenon, who draws and paints with the same wit, verve, and inventiveness as the great Irish storytellers. And by an extraordinary coincidence, his Billy Que resembles—in the kindness of his face—my husband.

"The text of *Dark Cloud Strong Breeze,* a rhythmic, circular tale for very young children, moves back and forth between the fanciful and the mundane, the wish-world and the everyday one. I had long admired the way that the artist Peter Catalanotto paints both qualities into his beautiful illustrations, so I asked my editor, Richard Jackson—a man of great vision—whether he thought Mr. Catalanotto might be interested in working on my story. To my great happiness, he was.

"I hope that by sharing vividly remembered feelings from childhood in my stories, I will be giving readers or listeners a way of recognizing and articulating their own."

■ For More Information See

PERIODICALS

Booklist, September 15, 1991, p. 153; November 1, 1992; March 15, 1993.
Horn Book, September, 1991, p. 606; January/February, 1992; July/August, 1993.
Kirkus Reviews, July 15, 1991, p. 939; September 1, 1992, p. 1133; March 3, 1993.
Publishers Weekly, August 23, 1991, p. 61; August 31, 1992, p. 77; April 5, 1993.
School Library Journal, October, 1991, pp. 111-112; December, 1992; March, 1993; October, 1993, p. 107.

*   *   *

PAUL, Ann Whitford 1941-

■ Personal

Born February, 1, 1941, in Evanston, IL; daughter of George (a business executive) and Genevieve (a home-maker and poet; maiden name, Smith) Whitford; married Ronald S. Paul (a surgeon), July 21, 1968; children: Henya, Jonathon, Alan, Sarah. *Education:* University of Wisconsin—Madison, B.A., 1963; Columbia University School of Social Work, M.S.W., 1965. *Hobbies and other interests:* Quilting, knitting, cooking, reading, and walking.

■ Addresses

Home and office—2531 North Catalina St., Los Angeles, CA 90027. *Agent*—Ginger Knowlton, Curtis Brown Ltd., Ten Astor Pl., New York, NY 10003.

■ Career

Writer; worked as a social worker in medical hospitals and adoption agencies, 1965-1970. *Member:* Society of Children's Book Writers and Illustrators, Southern

California Council on Literature for Children and Young People.

■ Awards, Honors

New York Times Notable Children's Book citation, and Notable Social Studies Book citation, both 1991, for *Eight Hands Round: A Patchwork Alphabet;* Outstanding Science Trade Book citation, and Junior Library Guild Selection, both 1992, for *Shadows Are About.*

■ Writings

Owl at Night, Putnam, 1985.
Eight Hands Round: A Patchwork Alphabet, HarperCollins, 1991.
Shadows Are About, Scholastic, 1992.

Also author of *The Seasons Sewn,* Harcourt-Brown Deer Press; and *In My Yard,* Scholastic.

■ Work in Progress

A book about life during the Colonial period; compiling a collection of poetry.

■ Sidelights

Ann Whitford Paul grew up in the midwest, the oldest of five children. Although she loved books, and would often stay up late into the night to read, she did not think about writing books until the birth of her third child. She was thirty-five and her inspiration came from her children. "Except for that time after supper when teeth were brushed and baths were done, it was rarely quiet in our crowded house," Paul told *SATA.* It was then that she would sit with each child in a rocker or in bed under the covers, and together they would read. This was the impetus. Paul decided to write books that

ANN WHITFORD PAUL

parents, grandparents, aunts and uncles, could share with the children special to them.

Between her decision to be a writer and actually becoming one there were many years of study. Paul cites three teachers as being particularly helpful: Sue Alexander, Sonia Levitin, and Myra Cohn Livingston. These three were true mentors, being both supportive and critical of her work, helping her to grow in her craft. The work began to pay off—in 1985 Putnam published her first book, *Owl at Night.* It is the simple story about two children and their family who settle down to sleep just as an owl begins his activities in the night. Susan Hepler, in her review for *School Library Journal,* called this story "a cozy catalog of nighttime activity that would make a good addition to the bedtime story collection." A *Publishers Weekly* reviewer found Paul's writing to contain "a gentle touch and a lyrical voice."

In 1991 HarperCollins published Paul's second book, *Eight Hands Round: A Patchwork Alphabet,* which was distinguished by being chosen one of the outstanding social studies books of the year. Aimed at children between the ages of 8 and 12, this work combines the alphabet-book idea with twenty-six patchwork quilt patterns, from A for Anvil to Z for Zigzag, and then presents the historical background of the past customs and events which inspired each design. Through it all "a fine history lesson emerges," states Denise Wilms in her review for *Booklist.* "A novel way to introduce patchwork's economic, social, and artistic role while relating it to history," writes a *Kirkus Reviews* critic.

Paul's next book, *Shadows Are About,* was published by Scholastic in 1992, and is also written for younger children. The rhyming text is gently flowing as it follows the shadow explorations of a brother and sister. It has a "simple, lyrical text," writes Stephanie Loer of the *Boston Globe.* Deborah Abbott, in her *Booklist* review, says that "shadows, which are about light and movement and new perspectives, take on a life of their own in this beautifully crafted picture book."

"Now that my oldest child has graduated from college," Paul told *SATA,* "I finally have an office." Paul says that in her work the first draft is always "painful," but the fun part is the revision. "I liken these to making a puzzle and trying to get all the pieces (or words) to fit in their right places." Paul encourages other aspiring writers to follow the well-known advice to "Write about what you know." She adds: "Trying to jump on the bandwagon or write to the demands of the market does not make good books. Stories that tug at a reader's emotions have to come out of the writer's strong emotions. Don't worry if your life isn't a roller coaster of grand adventure. I've never rescued a drowning person, or climbed the Himalaya Mountains, or driven a race car, but I still find plenty of material in my own quiet world that I want to share with others. In fact, I'll probably need ten lifetimes to get everything I want to say down on paper."

■ Works Cited

Abbott, Deborah, review of *Shadows Are About, Booklist,* July, 1992, p. 1944.

Review of *Eight Hands Round: A Patchwork Alphabet, Kirkus Reviews,* February 1, 1991, p. 183.

Hepler, Susan, review of *Owl At Night, School Library Journal,* December, 1985, p. 80.

Loer, Stephanie, "Picture-book Winners," *Boston Globe,* May 31, 1992.

Review of *Owl At Night, Publishers Weekly,* October 18, 1985, p. 64.

Wilms, Denise, review of *Eight Hands Round: A Patchwork Alphabet, Booklist,* June 1, 1991, p. 1876.

■ For More Information See

PERIODICALS

Bulletin of the Center for Children's Books, July, 1991, p. 270.

New York Times Book Review, May 19, 1991, p. 29.

School Library Journal, July, 1991, p. 70; April, 1992, p. 98.

*   *   *

PENNEY, Ian 1960-

■ Personal

Born December 10, 1960, in Bromley, Kent, England; son of John (a personnel consultant) and Marion (a homemaker; maiden name, Sheehan) Penney; married Catherine Ann Weaver (a bank manager), June 2, 1990; children: Sarah Elizabeth. *Education:* Brighton Polytechnic, B.A. with Honors, 1984; Manchester Polytechnic, M.A., 1985. *Religion:* Agnostic.

■ Addresses

Home and office—Pine Bank, Main Street, Beckley, Near Rye, East Sussex TN31 6RR, England. *Agent*—Gina Pollinger, 222 Old Brompton Rd., London SW5 OB2, England.

■ Career

Freelance illustrator and part-time teacher of illustration.

■ Writings

(Self-illustrated) *A Shop Full of Kittens,* G. P. Putnam's Sons, 1990.

ILLUSTRATOR

John Seymour and Herbert Girardet, *Blueprint for a Green Planet,* Prentice-Hall, 1987.

William Shakespeare, *The Sonnets,* Barrie & Jenkins, 1988.

Kevin Crossley-Holland, *Under the Sun and over the Moon,* Putnam, 1989.

IAN PENNEY

Antony Lishak, *Clickety Clack Something to Pack,* Orchard Books, 1992.

■ Work in Progress

Changing picture books; a book of nursery rhymes; a book on formal English gardens concentrating on their magical and ephemeral aspects.

■ Sidelights

Ian Penney told *SATA:* "My work is heavily influenced by childhood holidays and days out, when my brother and I were taken to London every week in the long summer holidays to look at museums and art galleries. I was particularly fascinated by early Italian Renaissance art. Our family holiday would often take in visits to gardens, castles and grand houses. The combination of those beautiful paintings and wonderful gardens has formed the way I work today. My images ignore perspective or at least use it as a tool, not a rule, and I tend to do away with scale.

"I work alone from my own home in the Sussex countryside about six miles from the sea, fifty miles from London. Since leaving art college I have worked for myself and alone, and I listen to BBC Radio Four all day which is an all talk station with documentaries, soaps, dramas and news ... wonderful! I really don't get bored or lonely with the radio on while painting, but I find writing very difficult as it must be done in silence—and a blank sheet of writing paper is far more daunting than a white sheet of water-color board waiting for an image."

One of Penney's trademarks is that each of his picture's contain his wife's maiden name initials: C.A.W. "I hope to continue working on children's picture books," he says, "as I feel they are the very best expression of my work and the most exciting area of publishing in which to practice."

*   *   *

PERRET, Gene 1937-

■ Personal

Surname rhymes with "ferret"; born April 3, 1937, in Philadelphia, PA; son of Joseph H. (a shipping clerk) and Mary (a homemaker; maiden name, Martin) Perret; married Joanne Bonavitacola (a nurse), October 11, 1958; children: Joseph M., Terry, Carole, Linda. *Education:* Attended Drexel Institute of Technology, 1956-61.

■ Addresses

Home—San Marino, CA.

GENE PERRET

■ Career

Comedy writer for comedians and television programs, including *The Jim Nabors Hour,* 1969-70, *Laugh-In,* 1970, and *The Carol Burnett Show,* 1973-78; script supervisor, *The Bill Cosby Show,* 1972; television writer for Bob Hope, 1969-78, head writer, 1978—; producer for television programs, including *Welcome Back Kotter,* 1978, *Three's Company,* 1978, and *The Tim Conway Show,* 1979-80. Professional speaker, 1977—. *Member:* Writers Guild of America.

■ Awards, Honors

Emmy Awards for writing, National Association of Television Arts and Sciences, 1974, 1975, and 1978, and Writers Guild Award, 1974, all for *The Carol Burnett Show;* named outstanding discovery in the field of humor by the International Platform Association, 1983, for the speech "Laughing Matters."

■ Writings

FOR YOUNG READERS

How to Write and Sell Your Sense of Humor, Writer's Digest, 1982, published as *Comedy Writing Step by Step,* foreword by Carol Burnett, Samuel French, 1990.
Funny Comebacks to Rude Remarks, illustrated by Sanford Hoffman, Sterling, 1990.
Comedy Writing Workbook, Sterling, 1990.
Laugh-A-Minute Joke Book, illustrated by Hoffman, Sterling, 1991.
Super Funny School Jokes, illustrated by Hoffman, Sterling, 1991.
(With daughter, Terry Perret Martin) *Great One-liners,* illustrated by Myron Miller, Sterling, 1992.

OTHER

Hit or Miss Management: The World's First Organic, Natural, Holistic, Environmentally Sound Management Technique, Houghton, 1980.
How to Hold Your Audience with Humor: A Guide to More Effective Speaking, Writer's Digest, 1984.
Using Humor for Effective Business Speaking, Sterling, 1989.
(With daughter, Linda Perret) *Gene Perret's Funny Business: Speaker's Treasury of Business Humor for All Occasions,* Prentice-Hall, 1990.
(With L. Perret) *Bigshots, Pipsqueaks, and Windbags: Jokes, Stories, and One-liners about People, Power, and Politics,* Prentice-Hall, 1993.
Shift Your Writing Career into High Gear, Writer's Digest, 1993.

Contributor to *You Know You're a Workaholic If—,* by Mel Loftus, illustrations by Rick Penn-Kraus, Price, Stern, 1991.

■ Work in Progress

If Bob Hope Calls, Tell Him I'm Not Home, a reminiscence of working with Bob Hope; *Make Me Laugh or Else,* a novel.

■ Sidelights

Gene Perret told *SATA:* "My writing career was actually a hobby that got carried away. As a youngster in grade school, I was fascinated with comedy. I listened to Red Skelton on the radio, I enjoyed Abbot and Costello films, and I idolized Bob Hope, who was then both a radio and movie star. I loved to make people laugh. People now ask if I was the 'class clown.' I wasn't; that required courage. Getting in trouble with the teacher was too big a risk for me to take, so I behaved myself. However, I would sometimes tell the class clown what to say and do. As a professional comedy writer now, I suppose that's what I still do.

"Writing witty sayings became a hobby that I enjoyed through high school. I wrote a humorous column for the school paper. Even having to work for a living and go to night school at the same time didn't dampen my

Perret shares his sense of humor with a schoolage audience in this book of wisecracks. (Cover illustration by Sanford Hoffman.)

comedy spirits. My coworkers enjoyed books of cartoons about our office that I drew and collections of photographs that I captioned. That eventually led to my writing career.

"My first supervisor retired, and our office planned a going-away party for him. Because I dabbled with comedy writing, they asked me to emcee his banquet and write a short 'roast'—sort of like a Johnny Carson or Jay Leno monologue about the guest of honor. The roast went over well. Not only the audience enjoyed it, but also the guest of honor and his family. It was important to me to do humor about this gentleman that kidded him, but didn't offend.

"The people I worked with then asked if I would do another retirement a few weeks later, then another a few weeks after that. Soon I was writing and delivering a new monologue about two or three times a month. I became the Bob Hope of our office.

"After a few years of this, I gained such a local reputation that people began to call me and ask to see my material. That's how I began to write material for Phyllis Diller. She asked to see some of my comedy writing. I sent it, and she sent back a check. After that assignment, Jim Nabors hired me to do his variety show. Then I worked on *Laugh-In, The New Bill Cosby Show,* and *The Carol Burnett Show.* After that, I produced *Welcome Back Kotter, Three's Company,* and *The Tim Conway Show.*

Association with Bob Hope Leads to World Travel

"In 1969 Bob Hope also asked me to write monologue material for his television specials and personal appearances. That became my first free-time assignment, working for Bob Hope when I wasn't working on the various television shows. In 1982, I began working exclusively for Bob Hope and am presently his head writer. My television writing career has been exciting and fun. In working with Bob Hope, I've travelled around the world several times. We've entertained the military in Beirut, the Persian Gulf, and Saudi Arabia. We've visited the Berlin Wall when it was being dismantled, and even did a show in Moscow. I've had the privilege of meeting many of the legendary entertainers and sports figures of our time.

"However, there is one drawback in writing television comedy—someone is always telling you what to write. That's the reason why books have such an appeal. When a person writes a book, he or she communicates directly to the audience, the readers. Also, television shows disappear after being shown on the screen. They're gone. A book you can hold in your hands, put on your shelf. You can leaf through a book from time to time. It's much more permanent.

"The collections of children's humor that I've written are especially rewarding because young people have a glorious sense of humor. They enjoy laughing. I enjoy

As a professional comedy writer, Perret now creates jokes for his childhood idol, Bob Hope.

making them laugh. The first book I did for school children was *Snappy Comebacks to Rude Remarks*. Through that book I relived my school yard duels of wits. Someone would kid me about something, and I'd try to 'get even.' Unfortunately, I didn't think of the clever retort until much later. So, I published a collection of snappy responses. Of course, I warned the young readers that the 'insults' were purely there for fun. I still believe, and think the readers should realize, that humor shouldn't be offensive.

"*The Laugh-A-Minute Joke Book* also was inspired by my own childhood—my own brothers and sisters, uncles and aunts, and many of the other things that I laughed at through my childhood. Youngsters can still laugh at these today, I thought, and so I wrote about them. *Super Funny School Jokes* seemed a natural since youngsters spend a good portion of their day in the classroom. It's their workplace and funny things happen there. I tried to capture some of that fun in the pages of this book.

Books Preserve Classic Humor for Today's Kids

"My goal in writing these books was to introduce a more sophisticated type of comedy to the younger readers. I wanted to write jokes they could enjoy, but also jokes that would help them develop a sense of humor. In the book *Great One-liners,* I've coupled some of my jokes with classic one-liners from legendary comics. The young readers of today can enjoy the wit of some of the funniest people of the past.

"I believe, too, that many young adults can learn to write comedy and might even be inspired to make it their career. That's why I've written two books about the craft of comedy writing: *Comedy Writing Step by Step,* which explains the process of writing a funny monologue, sketch, or television show from start to finish, from the blank pages to the completed manuscript. And to help develop the skills they'll need, I've written *Comedy Writing Workbook,* which contains almost one-hundred writing workouts and exercises.

"Comedy is a valuable, and often overlooked, resource in our lives. It helps us to think straight, it relieves stress. Doctors even tell us now that it aids the healing process. Through my books and my occasional lectures on humor, I want people, and especially youngsters, to learn that appropriate laughter is a reward in itself. It needn't be justified. Humor is not only fun, it serves a valid purpose for all of us.

"Bob Hope says of his travels that he's been welcomed with 'aloha,' 'willkommen,' 'shalom,' and even a twenty-one gun salute, which, he says, luckily missed. He says also, 'The most universal welcome I've received is the sound of laughter. It needs no translation. It means happiness and joy. Most important, it means freedom. In any country where liberty has been banished, the next thing to disappear is laughter.' He adds, 'The best way to communicate is with a chuckle.' That's what I'm trying to do with my writing."

*   *   *

PERRY, Steve 1947-

■ Personal

Born August 31, 1947, in Baton Rouge, LA; married Dianne Waller (a political expert and newspaper publisher); children: Dal, Stephani.

■ Addresses

Agent—Jean V. Naggar Literary Agency, Inc., 216 East 75th St., New York, NY 10021.

■ Career

Writer. Taught writing classes in the Portland and Washington County public school systems; has taught adult writing classes at the University of Washington in Seattle; briefly held a position as a staff writer for Ruby-Spears Productions, Hollywood, CA; worked variously as a swimming instructor and lifeguard, toy assembler, hotel gift shop clerk, aluminum salesperson, kung fu instructor, private detective, Licensed Practical Nurse, and Certified Physician's Assistant.

■ Writings

The Tularemia Gambit (mystery), Fawcett, 1981.
Civil War Secret Agent (young adult), Bantam, 1984.

(With Michael Reaves) *Sword of the Samurai* (young adult), Bantam, 1984.
Conan the Fearless (fantasy), Tor, 1986.
Conan the Defiant (fantasy), Tor, 1987.
(With Reaves) *The Omega Cage,* Ace, 1988.
Conan the Indomitable (fantasy), Tor, 1989.
Conan the Free Lance (fantasy), Tor, 1990.
Conan the Formidable (fantasy), Tor, 1990.

SCIENCE FICTION

(With Reaves) *Hellstar,* Berkley, 1984.
The Man Who Never Missed, Ace, 1985.
Matadora, Ace, 1986.
The Machiavelli Interface, Ace, 1986.
(With Reaves) *Dome,* Berkley, 1987.
The 97th Step, Ace, 1989.
The Albino Knife, Ace, 1991.
Black Steel, Ace, 1992.
Brother Death, Ace, 1992.

Also the author of *Curlwave,* Bluejay.

"ALIENS" SERIES

Earth Hive, Dark Horse/Bantam, 1992.
Nightmare Asylum, Dark Horse/Bantam, 1993.
(With Stephani Perry) *The Female War,* Dark Horse/Bantam, 1993.

"STELLAR RANGERS" SERIES

Peacemaker, B. Fawcett, 1993.
Guns and Honor, B. Fawcett, 1993.

OTHER

Has written numerous television scripts for animated action programs, including *Centurions, The Real Ghostbusters, Chuck Norris/Karate Commandos, The Spiral Zone, U.S. Starcom,* and *Batman.* Contributor to short fiction anthologies; contributor of short fiction works to magazines, including *Asimov's* and *Pulphouse Monthly.*

■ Work in Progress

Eidetic, a mystery-suspense novel; *Spin,* science fiction for Ace; *The Forever Hormone,* science fiction for Ace.

■ Sidelights

Beginning in the late 1970s with contributions to numerous magazines and short fiction anthologies, Steve Perry has developed a style of fast-paced action scenes filled with expert knowledge about weapons and combat. He is best known for his science fiction/martial arts action series fiction for both young adults and adults, as well as for his "Conan" heroic fantasy novels.

Perry's "Conan" adventures, based on the Robert E. Howard fantasy character, are popular with young adult readers. These include *Conan the Formidable, Conan the Indomitable, Conan the Free Lance, Conan the Defiant,* and *Conan the Fearless. Conan the Defiant* tells a tale of a young Conan fighting an army of undead warriors. Barbara Evans, reviewing *Conan the Fearless* in *Voice of Youth Advocates,* states that "YA fans should

STEVE PERRY

enjoy this book.... It is a fast paced story with characters being good or evil."

Perry's "Matador" series targets more mature readers. This science fiction adventure series includes *The Man Who Never Missed, Matadora, The Machiavelli Interface, The 97th Step, The Albino Knife, Black Steel,* and *Brother Death.* Roland Green, in his *Booklist* review of *Black Steel,* states that "each Matador novel now stands pretty much independently, which is a tribute to Perry's emphasis on fast action and well-choreographed battle scenes." Another reviewer, Bonnie Kunzel, in *Voice of Youth Advocates,* states, "There's blood and gore galore in this ... entry in the Matador series."

Perry has also written for younger readers as part of the "Time Machine Series" with his *Civil War Secret Agent,* published in 1984. The premise of the series is to take the reader back in time, "armed with a data bank to give information on the age you are visiting," observes Drew Stevenson in *School Library Journal.* In this book readers are taken back in time to 1849 and asked to help Harriet Tubman and the Underground Railroad.

■ Works Cited

Evans, Barbara, review of *Conan the Fearless, Voice of Youth Advocates,* June, 1986, p. 90.

Green, Roland, review of *Black Steel, Booklist,* January 15, 1992, p. 916.

Kunzel, Bonnie, review of *Black Steel, Voice of Youth Advocates,* June, 1992, p. 113.

Stevenson, Drew, review of *Civil War Secret Agent, School Library Journal,* April, 1985, p. 103.

■ For More Information See

PERIODICALS

Booklist, December, 1989, p. 726; July, 1991, p. 2034.

Magazine of Fantasy and Science Fiction, July, 1987, p. 23.

Science Fiction Chronicle, July, 1986, p. 38; May, 1988, p. 44; December, 1989, p. 39.

Voice of Youth Advocates, February, 1986, pp. 396, 399.

*   *   *

PINKWATER, Daniel Manus 1941-
(Manus Pinkwater)

■ Personal

Born November 15, 1941, in Memphis, TN; son of Philip (a ragman) and Fay (Hoffman) Pinkwater (a chorus girl); married Jill Miriam Schutz (a writer and illustrator), October 12, 1969. *Education:* Bard College, B.A., 1964. *Politics:* "Taoist." *Religion:* "Republican." *Hobbies and other interests:* "Various."

■ Addresses

Home—111 Crum Elbow Rd., Hyde Park, NY 12538. *Agent*—Dorothy Markinko, McIntosh and Otis, 310 Madison Ave., New York, NY 10017.

■ Career

Writer and illustrator of children's books. Art instructor at various settlement houses around New York City. *All Things Considered,* National Public Radio, regular commentator, 1987—. *Exhibitions:* Various small galleries and university shows. *Member:* American Federation of Theater and Radio Artists.

■ Awards, Honors

New Jersey Institute of Technology award, 1975, for *Fat Elliot and the Gorilla;* American Library Association Notable Book award, 1976, for *Lizard Music;* Junior Literary Guild selection, 1977, for *Fat Men from Space; New York Times* Outstanding Book, 1978, for *The Last Guru;* Children's Choice book award from the International Reading Association and the Children's Book Council, 1981, for *The Wuggie Norple Story;* Parents' Choice award (literature), 1982, for *Roger's Umbrella.*

■ Writings

FOR CHILDREN

Alan Mendelsohn, the Boy from Mars, Dutton, 1979.

Yobgorgle: Mystery Monster of Lake Ontario, Clarion Books, 1979, revised edition, Bantam, 1981.

The Wuggie Norple Story, illustrated by Tomie de Paola, Four Winds, 1980.

The Worms of Kukumlima, Dutton, 1981.

Slaves of Spiegel: A Magic Moscow Story, Four Winds, 1982.

Young Adult Novel (also see below), Crowell, 1982.

Roger's Umbrella, illustrated by James Marshall, Dutton, 1982.

The Snarkout Boys and the Avocado of Death, Lothrop, 1982.

The Snarkout Boys and the Baconburg Horror, Lothrop, 1984.

Jolly Roger, a Dog of Hoboken, Lothrop, 1985.

Borgel, Macmillan, 1990.

Contributor to *Cricket.*

FOR CHILDREN; SELF-ILLUSTRATED

Wizard Crystal, Dodd, 1973.

Magic Camera, Dodd, 1974.

Lizard Music, Dodd, 1976.

The Blue Thing, Prentice-Hall, 1977.

DANIEL MANUS PINKWATER

A BANTAM-SKYLARK BOOK

An ALA Notable Children's Book

LIZARD MUSIC

D MANUS PINKWATER

author of THE MUFFIN FIEND

To help his readers feel "snarky," Pinkwater writes tales such as this story of musical reptiles who mysteriously appear on late-night television. (Cover illustration by Catherine Huerta.)

The Big Orange Splot, Hastings House, 1977.
Fat Men from Space, Dodd, 1977.
The Hoboken Chicken Emergency, Prentice-Hall, 1977.
The Last Guru, Dodd, 1978.
Return of the Moose, Dodd, 1979.
Pickle Creature, Four Winds, 1979.
The Magic Moscow, Four Winds, 1980.
Tooth-Gnasher Super Flash, Four Winds, 1981.
Attila the Pun: A Magic Moscow Book, Four Winds, 1981.
I Was a Second Grade Werewolf, Dutton, 1983.
Ducks!, Little, Brown, 1984.
Devil in the Drain, Dutton, 1984.
The Moosepire, Little, Brown, 1986.
The Muffin Fiend, Lothrop, 1986.
The Frankenbagel Monster, Dutton, 1986.
Aunt Lulu, Macmillan, 1988.
Guys from Space, Macmillan, 1989.
Uncle Melvin, Macmillan, 1989.
Doodle Flute, Macmillan, 1991.
Wempires, Macmillan, 1991.
The Phantom of the Lunch Wagon, Macmillan, 1992.
Author's Day, Macmillan, 1993.

FOR CHILDREN; UNDER NAME MANUS PINKWATER

The Terrible Roar, Knopf, 1970.
(Self-illustrated) *Bear's Picture,* Holt, 1972.
Fat Elliot and the Gorilla, Four Winds, 1974.
Three Big Hogs, Seabury, 1975.
(Self-illustrated) *Blue Moose,* Dodd, 1975.
(Self-illustrated) *Wingman,* Dodd, 1975.

FOR ADULTS

(With wife, Jill Pinkwater) *Superpuppy: How to Choose, Raise, and Train the Best Possible Dog for You,* illustrated by J. Pinkwater, Seabury, 1977.
Young Adults (three parts; first part based on *Young Adult Novel*), Tor, 1985.
Fish Whistle, Commentaries, Uncommentaries, and Vulgar Excesses, Addison-Wesley, 1990.
Chicago Days, Hoboken Nights, Addison-Wesley, 1991.

■ **Adaptations**

Wingman was made into a cassette by Listening Library, 1981; *Blue Moose* was produced as a videocassette by Positive Images, 1982; *The Hoboken Chicken Emergency* was adapted for television by Public Broadcasting System (PBS), 1984; *I Was a Second Grade Werewolf* was made into a cassette by Live Oak Media, 1986.

The legendary Northern tale of a famous moose is brought to life in Pinkwater's wacky *Moosepire*. (Illustration by the author.)

■ Work in Progress

"Much."

■ Sidelights

Were a blue moose to come striding into Daniel Manus Pinkwater's living room one day and ask for a cup of coffee, Pinkwater should not be at all surprised, for that is exactly the kind of situation he has been describing in his years of writing books for children. From his home in upstate New York, Pinkwater writes and illustrates books about the lives of such characters as Aunt Lulu, the Muffin Fiend, and the Frankenbagel Monster. Though Pinkwater's characters are absurd, his intent in writing is not, and he says in an interview for *Something about the Author* (*SATA*): "I want my readers to feel encouraged and *snarky,* because basically they are kids taking on a hostile and/or indifferent world. My books are about finding favoring signs in the world, about discovering riches—things which are not dead. My stories are about people prevailing."

Pinkwater was born in Memphis, Tennessee in 1941, but grew up in Chicago. He remembers the kids in his neighborhood acting out the stories that they had read in adventure books like *20,000 Leagues under the Sea* and *Three Musketeers,* and he told *SATA:* "We heard about books by word of mouth—the kid next door had an older brother who told me about the *Three Musketeers.* I got to read good books, although mainly adventure stories." Pinkwater was a self-described oddball as a child, much like the characters in his stories, but was lucky enough to find a group of boys who shared his interests, keeping him from feeling alienated.

During his time at Bard College in Annandale-on-Hudson, New York, Pinkwater decided to become a sculptor in order to become a good writer. By the time he finished college and a three-year apprenticeship with a sculptor, however, he had changed his mind. "I don't want to be a writer," he remembered thinking in *SATA*. "Writer's lives are disgusting, and writing is a horrible unhealthy activity. You get coffee nerves and a bad back, and eye strain. You smoke, and you sit ... it's terrible." When four years later he returned to writing, he realized he was a better writer for his sculpting experience. Pinkwater advises anyone who wants to write to first learn to do something other than writing.

Pinkwater told *SATA* that he "didn't decide to start doing children's books, [he] floated into it." He had produced a set of illustrations for the book that was to become *The Terrible Roar,* and didn't want to deal with someone else writing the text for the book. So he wrote it himself. Though his first few books were "just a giggle" for him, he soon found them more and more interesting and soon committed himself to writing full-time. "I thought after two or three books I would have saturated my audience, whom I imagined as fat, bespectacled, intellectual boys," he commented to *SATA*. "I often receive photographs from my readers, including good-looking blonde-haired kids, who are captains of

I howled at the moon. I had a pretty good time.

Lawrence wakes up to find himself covered with hair and sporting sharp teeth—that no one else notices—in Pinkwater's *I Was a Second Grade Werewolf.* (Illustration by the author.)

their soccer teams. It's not just the sweaty, spotty, stinky, pimply kids who do college physics in middle school who read my work, although, of course those are my favorites."

Pinkwater enjoys writing for children because he thinks they are more honest and more receptive to art than adults. "They are very matter of fact," he explained in *SATA.* "They like something, or they don't, they can use something or they can't. Adults feel an obligation to consider what reflection their artistic preferences will make upon them as people of cultural breeding and intelligence."

Books Combine Bizarre Events and Everyday Life

Pinkwater's books have been classified as fantasy and science fiction, but Janice Alberghene argues in *Twentieth-Century Children's Writers* that the author "is less interested in the creation of a separate secondary world or alternate universe (as in *Alan Mendelsohn: The Boy from Mars,* or *The Worms of Kukumlima*) than he is in the eruption of the fantastic into everyday reality." Pinkwater often introduces extraordinary events into rather ordinary situations, which has the effect of making the ordinary situations stand out. In *Blue*

Pinkwater's outrageous stories and absurd humor make tales such as those of the "Snarkout Boys" popular with readers. (Cover illustration by the author.)

Moose, the title character walks into a restaurant and is hired as a waiter, and later the kitchen floor turns into a spring meadow. In *The Moosepire,* a railroad boxcar operates as a time machine. Both books bring the mundane to life, showing that imagination can make any situation an exciting adventure.

Pinkwater's books are an adventure at least in part because they seem to go off in so many directions at once. Alberghene finds it "par for the course to find James Dean, *The Sorrows of Young Werewolf,* and a giant avocado capable of being modified into a thought-wave producing 'Alligatron' all within the covers of the same book," as happens in *The Snarkout Boys and the Avocado of Death.* Pinkwater admitted to *SATA* that he actually looks for a book to get out of hand: "The work is like a skateboard that suddenly gets away from me, and the anticipation is that somehow, miraculously, I will finish with the skateboard." It is this sense of play and absurdity that makes children laugh out loud when they read his books.

Some critics, however, think that the absurdity is overdone. John Cech, reviewing *Yobgorgle: Mystery Monster of Lake Ontario* for *Children's Book Review Service,* finds that the continual "weirdness" drains the patience of even the youngest readers, and suggests that

the story is "without substance." On the other hand, many reviewers find that Pinkwater's books "have all been notably imaginative and appealing," in the words of a *Publishers Weekly* reviewer of *Lizard Music.* As Michele Landsberg notes in the Toronto *Globe and Mail,* "My entire family, in fact, relishes Pinkwater's benign surrealism, his deadpan post-Python humor and rich allusiveness, and his hidden but unmistakable tenderness for underdogs and oddballs."

Though Pinkwater's stories are not serious, he is very serious about his work. "I think children's books are the most important thing you can do," Pinkwater told Joann Davis in *Publishers Weekly,* "because these are people who are learning about reading." He says that one of his goals as a writer is to celebrate dying cultural treasures such as beer gardens, used bookstores, old railroad cars, and other aspects of urban life. In addition, Pinkwater doesn't hesitate to mention the names of authors and artists in his works, hoping to encourage young readers to learn more about those people. Though teaching isn't the main focus of his books, Pinkwater says that "it *is* an intention of my books to present the sheer pleasure of the phenomena of civilized life."

Pinkwater told *SATA:* "I also believe it is impossible to make sense of life in this world except through art. That's always been so, but it's more true now than ever before. The only way we can deal with the proliferation of ideas and impetus is to make a story or a picture out of it. At present, there are things happening that I like, as well as things I don't like; by participating I'm able to put some weight on the side of the things I like."

■ Works Cited

Alberghene, Janice, essay in *Twentieth-Century Children's Writers,* 3rd edition, St. James Press, 1989, pp. 781-782.

Cech, John, review of *Yobgorgle: Mystery Monster of Lake Ontario, Children's Book Review Service,* winter, 1980, pp. 68-69.

Davis, Joann, "Spring Is a Season of Plenty for Children's Author Daniel Pinkwater," *Publishers Weekly,* May 7, 1982, pp. 53-54.

Landsberg, Michele, "A Loopily Sane Social Satirist," *Globe and Mail* (Toronto), April 18, 1987.

Review of *Lizard Music, Publishers Weekly,* October 18, 1976, p. 64.

Pinkwater, Daniel M., interview in *Something about the Author,* Volume 46, Gale, 1987, pp. 178-191.

■ For More Information See

BOOKS

Children's Literature Review, Volume 4, Gale, 1982.

Landsberg, Michele, *Reading for the Love of It,* Prentice-Hall, 1987.

Marquardt, Dorothy A., and Martha E. Ward, *Authors of Books for Young People,* supplement to the 2nd edition, Scarecrow, 1975.

Something about the Author Autobiography Series, Volume 3, Gale, 1987.

PERIODICALS

Booklist, April 1, 1974; June 1, 1979; April 1, 1982.
Christian Science Monitor, May 1, 1974; May 4, 1977.
Graphis 155, Volume 27, 1971-72.
Horn Book, April, 1977; August, 1977; April, 1983;
    September-October, 1984; May-June, 1986.
New York Times Book Review, April 29, 1979; February
    24, 1980.
People, December 21, 1981.
Publishers Weekly, June 9, 1975; July 18, 1977; August
    1, 1977; September 12, 1977; February 27, 1978;
    October 17, 1980; April 3, 1981; June 27, 1986.
Science Fiction and Fantasy Book Review, July-August,
    1982.
Voice of Youth Advocates, June, 1982; August, 1982;
    August, 1984.
Washington Post Book World, November 5, 1972; June
    10, 1984.

*   *   *

PINKWATER, Manus
See PINKWATER, Daniel Manus

*   *   *

POCHOCKI, Ethel (Frances) 1925-
(Ethel Marbach)

■ Personal

Name pronounced "po-chock-i"; born September 17,
1925, in Bayonne, NJ; daughter of Czeslaw Romuald (a
lawyer) and Ethel (a homemaker; maiden name, Szlobo-
da) Pochocki; married Francis Marbach, October 5,
1946 (divorced December 18, 1970); children: Therese,
Julia, Carol, Martin, Peter, Charles, Lucy, Rosemary.
Education: Attended Holy Family Academy High
School, and Katherine Gibbs Secretarial School, 1942-
44. *Politics:* Democrat/Independent. *Religion:* Roman
Catholic.

■ Addresses

Home and office—RR 1, Box 110, Brooks, ME 04921.

■ Career

Writer.

■ Awards, Honors

Lupine Award, Maine Library Association, 1992, for
Rosebud and Red Flannel.

■ Writings

UNDER NAME ETHEL MARBACH

Do It Yourself Guide to Holy Housewifery, Abbey Press,
    1965.
The Holy Housewifery Cookbook, Abbey Press, 1968.

ETHEL POCHOCKI

My Mother and Leopold Stokowski (adult fiction), Alba
House, 1970.

JUVENILES; UNDER NAME ETHEL MARBACH

Emily's Rainbow, Green Tiger Press, 1980.
The Cabbage Moth and the Shamrock, Green Tiger
    Press, 1981.
Soup Pot! and Christmas Tree for All Seasons, Green
    Tiger Press, 1981.
Once upon a Time Saints, Volume 1, St. Anthony
    Messenger Press, 1981.
Once upon a Time Saints, Volume 2, St. Anthony
    Messenger Press, 1982.
Saints in Waiting (also see below), St. Anthony Messen-
    ger Press, 1983.
Saints for the Journey (also see below), St. Anthony
    Messenger Press, c. 1984.
Saints for the Harvest (also see below), St. Anthony
    Messenger Press, c. 1985.
The White Rabbit, St. Anthony Messenger Press, 1985.
Dandelions, Fireflies and Rhubarb Pie, Upper Room
    Press, 1985.
Saints for the Seasons (also see below), St. Anthony
    Messenger Press, 1986.

Saints in Waiting, Saints for the Journey, Saints for the Harvest, Saints for the Seasons, were reprinted in one volume, St. Anthony Messenger Press, 1990.

JUVENILES; UNDER NAME ETHEL POCHOCKI

Grandma Bagley Leads the Way, Augsburg/Fortress, 1989.
Grandma Bagley to the Rescue, Augsburg/Fortress, 1989.
The Attic Mice, Holt, 1990.
The Fox Who Found Christmas, Ave Maria Press, 1990.
Rosebud and Red Flannel, Holt, 1991.
The Mushroom Man, Simon & Schuster, 1993.
Wildflower Tea, Simon & Schuster, 1993.
The Gypsies' Tale, Simon & Schuster, 1994.
Saints and Heroes for Today, St. Anthony Messenger Press, 1994.

Contributor to periodicals, including *Cricket* and *Pockets;* and to anthologies, including *Cabbages and Kings,* 1991. Also author of television scripts for program, *Saints Alive.*

■ Work in Progress

A sequel to *The Attic Mice;* a book about the adventures of Mrs. Persimmon, a red squirrel.

■ Sidelights

Ethel Pochocki told *SATA:* "I was born in Bayonne, New Jersey, to a first-generation Hungarian mother and a Polish-born father. He had been caught teaching the catechism, a crime in Russian-occupied Poland at the turn of the century, and sentenced to exile in Siberia at the age of 19. He escaped and somehow made his way to

Monsieur Philippe, a gourmet chef with a skill for snaring small animals, discovers the true meaning of Christmas in Pochocki's fable. (Cover illustration by Thomas P. Bell.)

the U.S. After studying for the priesthood in Michigan, he became a lawyer. He met my mother, a young widow, while visiting in New Jersey, and married her. I am the one and only remembrance of that union.

"I remember childhood as a wonderfully sunny and happy time, free of all shadows and insecurity. One of the happiest of memories is that of bringing armfuls of books home from the library and reading them in an old, stuffed, lumpy chair in the attic. There was a specific 'attic' smell—dust and honey and fresh ironing and talcum powder—that is still synonymous to me with sweet content. In the fall, there was a bushel of crisp apples beside me, with fingers of sun filtering through and tree limbs tapping at the window.

"I was taught by tough (but loving) Irish nuns who drilled the rules of grammar, punctuation, and diagramming into us, their motto being *Learn or Die.* I am eternally grateful to them. I went on to Katherine Gibbs Secretarial School in New York City, where I failed at shorthand and typing and got an A in Music Appreciation and Psychology. I worked as a 'Girl Friday' in the Music Room of the New York Public Library on 42nd Street until my marriage in 1946.

"I met my husband, who was in the Navy, at a USO dance at Annapolis. When the war was over, we married and lived with other ex-GIs in a housing project at Niagara University, New York. He became a teacher, first in high school, then in college, and we moved from New York state to Indiana to Pennsylvania in a succession of jobs, while the family grew to eight children.

Victory in Essay Contest Starts Writing Career

"I began writing in Franklinville, New York, when I had 5 children under the age of ten and needed something to keep my mind out of the diapers. I already had a typewriter so I settled on writing (I didn't have to buy equipment—a requirement since money was in short supply). I entered an essay contest held by the *New York Herald Tribune* for the hosts of Fresh Air children (New York City inner-city children who were given two weeks in the country with families in thirteen states). I told myself if I got an honorable mention, I would continue writing. I won it—*and* $25. This was definitely for me!

"I began submitting to Catholic magazines, since I was most familiar with them—essays on family life at first, then anything they asked me to do—fiction, reviews, poetry. It was a wonderful apprenticeship. And it gave me a centering, a certainty that I had something wonderfully secure and *mine.* I wrote when the older children were in school and when the younger children napped. I wrote during the night when they awoke. I wrote anytime, anyplace. The exhilaration and satisfaction sustained me through tough personal times. During this 'Catholic' time, I published a book of essays, a cookbook, a collection of adult fiction, a series of liturgical booklets and many magazine articles.

"When I obtained my divorce in 1970, I stopped writing for about four years, figuring that I couldn't with integrity continue to write about Catholic life. I moved to Maine in 1975, with four teenagers (the other four, the 'first batch' were either married or in college). This was the fulfillment of a childhood dream, since I first read *The Little Locksmith* by Katherine Butler Hathaway. By a lovely, serendipitous irony, our first home in Maine was on Penobscot Bay, where we could look directly across to the town of Castine and the house where Hathaway lived when she wrote this book.

"Coming to Maine was a rebirth of spirit as well as relocation of body. I began to emerge from a strict observance of Catholicism to a more relaxed one. I realize that much in my true nature was inclined to Zen and Celtic Spirituality, the connectedness of nature and animals and humans. Although I will always be a cultural Catholic and believe deeply in Christ and his gospel and the saints and angels, I feel now that there are as many ways to God as there are people, none of which is the *right* or *only* way. To each his own!

Traditional Tales Inspire Children's Books

"I decided also that I would write here what I had always wanted to write: fairy tales and poetry. My favorite writer and strongest influence was, is, Hans Christian Andersen. I still cannot read *The Little Match Girl* without tears rising. I would give my soul to have written that! So I began writing these for *Church World*, the diocesan paper of Maine; many have been published as books. One of these, 'The Attic Creche,' became the idea for a series of stories which eventually became *The Attic Mice.*

"I realize, after doing a variety of writing, that fairy tales and anthropomorphic stories are my first love. Yes, talking animals—*and* bugs, flowers, birds et al. At times I feel like a remnant of Victoriana, living in a time warp of nannies and nurseries, and finding it just my cup of tea. I think if I were living 100 years ago, I would have it made! I often wonder if the stories of Andersen and Grahame and Milne were submitted today, would they be accepted? Would they be considered too harsh or demanding of their young readers? They did not compromise with reality. They did not condescend. They used big words. They made no fuss over death. And their teddy bears and badgers and brave tin soldiers *talked!* I am at home and comfortable with them.

"Now the children have grown and flown, and I live with a menage of 7 cats (the number is always in a state of flux). I can write at any time I choose now. Winter is best, when I'm held willing captive by howling snowstorms, with nothing to lure or distract from the typewriter. Ideas come from anywhere and everywhere. Items in the daily paper are a great source—mystery flowers 'planted' by a hurricane, French gypsies gathering mistletoe for English Christmas festivities, turkeys being guests of a Thanksgiving dinner instead of the main course, a *Dear Abby* column on the friendship of two birds, one blind, the other crippled. A *Nova*

program on bower birds. A glance out the kitchen window to see a pair of frozen long johns dancing in the wind, or a red squirrel trying to carry off a piece of cake thrown out for the birds. My own experiences: the guilt felt over vacuuming up spiders and flies (alive), frustration over a proliferation of zucchinis, a ladybug settling into a bowl of forced hyacinths, the collection of oddities on a fireplace mantel. I have an infinity of worlds to write about without ever leaving home."

*   *   *

PORTER, Sue 1951-

■ Personal

Born October 18, 1951, in London, England; daughter of Derek Leslie (a mathematician), and Elizabeth Marjorie (a secretary) Keeble; married Roger Derrick Porter (an architect); children: David, Megan. *Education:* Leicester Polytechnic College, Honors Degree in art and design.

■ Addresses

Agent—Eunice McMullen, 38 Clewer Hill Rd., Windsor, Berkshire SL4 4BW, England.

■ Career

Writer and illustrator. *Member:* Society of Authors (England).

■ Awards, Honors

Runner-up for the Mother Goose Award (England), Children's Book Award from the Arts Council of Great Britain, Owl Award (Japan), and the Prix Verselle (France).

■ Writings

(Self-illustrated) *Baa, Baa, Black Sheep,* Harper, 1982.
One Potato, Macmillan, 1989.
Action Packed: 30 Ideas for Drama, Heinemann, 1990.
Play It Again: Suggestions for Drama, Heinemann, 1990.
(Self-illustrated) *Little Wolf and the Giant,* Simon & Schuster, 1990.

ILLUSTRATOR

Mathew Price, *Do You See What I See?,* Harper, 1986.
Michaela Morgan, *Edward Gets a Pet,* Dutton, 1987.
Morgan, *Visitors for Edward,* Dutton, 1987.
Morgan, *Edward Hurts His Knee,* Dutton, 1988.
Morgan, *Edward Loses His Teddy Bear,* Dutton, 1988.
Jana Novotny Hunter, *Ghost Games,* Doubleday, 1992.
Rose Impey, *Letter to Father Christmas,* Delacorte, 1989.
Rex Harley, *Mary's Tiger,* Harcourt, 1990.
Impey, *Joe's Cafe,* Orchard Books, 1990.

Also author and illustrator of *Chloe's Eggs*, Simon & Schuster. Illustrator of Morgan's *Monster is Coming*, and Impey's *Little Smasher, First Class*, and *The Baddies*.

■ Sidelights

Sue Porter has, she reported to *SATA*, "designed, illustrated and sometimes written" thirty-seven books for children. Among those children's books written and illustrated by Porter, the nursery rhyme press-out book *Baa, Baa, Black Sheep* and *Little Wolf and the Giant* stand out. Porter described her working philosophy: "I would like to think that my books all share one thing in common—a gentle humour. There should always be a feeling of warmth to draw the young reader close." This warmth has succeeded in charming readers and garnering Porter the title of "runner-up" for several prestigious prizes around the world.

Porter recalled her career path for *SATA:* "A wonderfully eccentric teacher, Mr. Lamb, surprised me with the idea that I was good in art. In his class, I became runner-up in a National Art Competition." After attending comprehensive school and working as a research assistant in a laboratory, Porter studied at art at Leicester Polytechnic College. "Apart from a brief period nursing," she explained, "I have worked as a designer, illustrator, and writer ever since."

Porter intends to continue creating children's books at her studio in Uppingham, England. She cautions readers of *SATA* who look forward to experiencing this future work: "I don't think it is always easy to pick out a book as being 'mine.' Although nowadays I often use watercolours, I love to use all kinds of media and methods, and I like to tailor the artwork to the age of the child and to the story itself."

* * *

PRIDEAUX, Tom 1908-1993

OBITUARY NOTICE—See index for *SATA* sketch: Born May 9, 1908, in Hillsdale, MI; died of heart failure, May 8, 1993, in New York. Editor, playwright, and author. An editor for *Life* magazine for more than three decades, Prideaux penned several books on the theater. After graduating from Yale University in 1930, Prideaux joined *Life* as its theater and amusements editor. He became entertainment editor and retired in the early 1970s. Prideaux is the author of several biographies, including the well-known *Love or Nothing: The Life and Times of Ellen Terry,* and, with the editors of Time-Life, *The World of Delacroix, 1798-1863* and *The World of Whistler, 1834-1903,* both written for young people. He also published *World Theater in Pictures: From Ancient Times to Modern Broadway,* and edited, with Josephine Mayer, *Never to Die: The Egyptians in Their Own Words.* In addition to his books, Prideaux wrote successful plays, including *Another Man's Poison, Gallivanting Lady,* and *The Milwaukee Rocket.*

OBITUARIES AND OTHER SOURCES:

PERIODICALS

New York Times, May 11, 1993, p. B7.

* * *

PULVER, Robin 1945-

■ Personal

Born August 14, 1945, in Geneva, NY; daughter of Willard B. (a biochemist) and Alice (Alden) Robinson; married Donald Pulver (a physician), June 12, 1971; children: Nina, David. *Education:* William Smith College, B.A., 1967; attended Syracuse University. *Politics:* Democrat. *Religion:* Protestant. *Hobbies and other interests:* Hiking, swimming, bird-watching, reading, journalkeeping.

■ Addresses

Home—19 Cricket Hill Dr., Pittsford, NY 14534.

■ Career

Has worked in public relations; writer. *Member:* Society of Children's Book Writers and Illustrators, National Coalition Against Censorship, Authors' Guild, Association for Retarded Citizens, World Wildlife Fund, Sierra Club.

ROBIN PULVER

■ Awards, Honors

"Pick of the Lists," American Booksellers Association, 1990, for *Mrs. Toggle's Zipper; The Holiday Handwriting School* was named a Children's Choice book, International Reading Association and the Children's Book Council, 1992.

■ Writings

Mrs. Toggle's Zipper, illustrated by R. W. Alley, Four Winds, 1990.
The Holiday Handwriting School, illustrated by G. Brian Karas, Four Winds, 1991.
Mrs. Toggle and the Dinosaur, illustrated by Alley, Four Winds, 1991.
Nobody's Mother Is in Second Grade, illustrated by Karas, Dial, 1992.

Contributor of articles and stories to periodicals, including *Highlights for Children, Jack and Jill, Pockets, Cricket,* and *Ranger Rick.*

■ Work in Progress

Mrs. Toggle's Beautiful Blue Shoe and *Homer and the House Next Door,* both for Four Winds, completion expected in 1994.

■ Sidelights

Robin Pulver told *SATA:* "I have always enjoyed writing and reading. As a child, I was shy about speaking and relied on writing to express what I knew and felt. I think I unwittingly served an apprenticeship in writing for children when I studied journalism in graduate school, then short story writing. Both forms require economy of language and respect for every word.

"My appreciation of children's books deepened when my own children were born. I remember carrying my newborn infant daughter into a children's bookstore in 1978 and being swept off my feet by the beautiful language and extraordinary art. Reading to my two children from their earliest days gave me a profound appreciation of the impact of literature on children and families. Sharing books with my bright, language-loving daughter has been a joy. Reading to my son, who is handicapped but also bright and language-loving in his own way, has been a salvation. It has brought us precious moments of calm and touchstones for moments of recognition and laughter.

"It came as a happy surprise when I found that I could write and sometimes publish stories for children. My first publications were in magazines, then I wrote a story called *Mrs. Toggle's Zipper,* which became my first picture book. My goal is to write well enough to move people and offer them a good story to share. I would like to give back to children's literature the kind of gifts I have received from it."

R

RA, Carol F. 1939-

■ Personal

Surname is pronounced "rah"; born October 29, 1939, in Newport, IN; daughter of Samuel Wilson (a mechanic) and Elsie Maxine (a township trustee; maiden name, Kinderman) Hawn; married J. O. Ra, June 30, 1962 (divorced, October 29, 1980); children: Stephanie, Alison. *Education:* Attended Hollins College; Indiana State University, B.S., 1961; University of Illinois, M.Ed., 1968. *Politics:* Democrat. *Religion:* Methodist.

■ Addresses

Home—P.O. Box 718, Cayuga, IN 47928-0718. *Agent*—Harriet Wasserman, 137 East 36th St., New York, NY 10016.

■ Career

Richmond City Schools, Richmond, IN, elementary school teacher, 1961-62; Vigo County Schools, Terre Haute, IN, elementary school teacher, 1962-64; Champaign Unit 4 Schools, Champaign, IN, teacher of gifted children, 1964-68; St. James Episcopal, Roanoke, VA, preschool director, 1973-74; Hollins College, Roanoke, lecturer in early childhood education and children's literature, 1974-87; *Herald News,* Cayuga, IN, editor/columnist, 1990—. *Member:* Delta Theta Tau, Kappa Delta Pi.

■ Awards, Honors

Awarded Mellon Research grant to study children's folk rhymes while teaching at Hollins College.

■ Writings

Trot, Trot to Boston: Play Rhymes for Baby, illustrated by Catherine Stock, Lothrop, 1987.
(With William Jay Smith) *Behind the King's Kitchen: A Roster of Rhyming Riddles,* illustrated by Jacques Hnizdovsky, Boyds Mills Press, 1992.

(With Smith) *The Sun is Up,* Boyds Mills Press, 1993.

Also author of weekly column, "Rambling," in *Herald News,* Cayuga, IN, 1990—. Contributor of adult poetry to periodicals, including *Artemis, Passages North, Roanoke Review, Wind,* and *Blue Unicorn.* Contributor to *Anthology of Magazine Verse,* 1986-88 edition.

CAROL F. RA

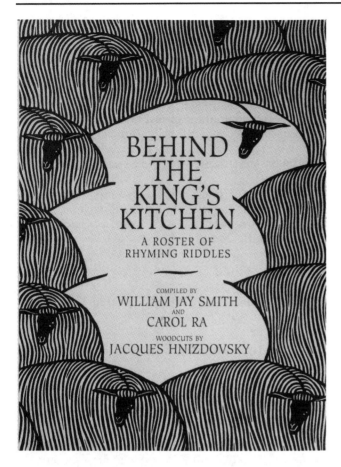

BEHIND THE KING'S KITCHEN
A ROSTER OF RHYMING RIDDLES

COMPILED BY
WILLIAM JAY SMITH
AND
CAROL RA

WOODCUTS BY
JACQUES HNIZDOVSKY

Ra and William J. Smith bring together rhyming riddles from many ages in this entertaining collection. (Illustration by Jacques Hnizdovsky.)

■ Work in Progress

A collection of poems for children; a collection of nonsense verse; a collection of rhyming riddles.

■ Sidelights

Carol F. Ra was born at home in rural Indiana on the eve of World War II, and grew up during hard times. "Our family's socializing centered around visiting, and being visited by, relatives," Ra told *SATA.* "Sunday afternoons were the favored times for getting together with aunts, uncles and cousins. The games we played were full of rhymes and rhythms. We wrote rhymes in each other's autograph albums. We chanted taunts and teases. We wrote rhyming graffiti in our textbooks (this was accepted as all children had to buy their books). In elementary school I received a book of folk rhymes and riddles for my birthday. I read and re-read it until I had memorized the collection."

Ra's undergraduate and graduate level coursework underscored for her the imperative of reading aloud to babies and children. As an elementary teacher for seven years, a preschool director for a year and a half, and as a mother of two, she spent much of her time at libraries selecting good books and then reading them aloud.

"While teaching at Hollins College, Virginia, I joined the Virginia Folklore Society," Ra said. "I was especially interested in folk rhymes. At the same time, I compiled a collection of folk rhymes from my childhood. I shared the collection with my sister, who helped me remember others. While teaching at Hollins, I received a Mellon research grant to study children's folk rhymes. I studied sources at the Library of Congress, the University of Virginia, the University of North Carolina, the University of Illinois, and in the rare books room at Hollins College. Subsequently I collected play rhymes that parents could do with their toddlers—for example, face-touching, toe-counting, and knee-riding rhymes. *Trot, Trot to Boston* is the result."

Living and teaching at Hollins College, with its emphasis on literature and writing, strongly influenced Ra's writing development. She told *SATA:* "At Hollins I attended Valery Nash's poetry workshops, and readings by W.H. Auden, Eudora Welty, James Dickey, Lee Smith, R.H.W. Dillard, Jeanne Larsen, and Richard Adams, among others. Many of these writers were Hollins faculty, products of the Hollins graduate program, or writers-in-residence there. The 1992 Nobel Prize winner in poetry, Derek Wolcott, was writer-in-residence at Hollins and a guest at my home on more than one occasion. The rich conversations with these writers over dinner, and the reading of their books expanded my knowledge and appreciation of literature. I love to read. My large library of literature, including a special collection of folklore, gathers very little dust."

*   *   *

RANSOME, James E. 1961-

■ Personal

Born September 25, 1961, in Rich Square, NC; married Lesa Cline (a teacher), September 2, 1989. *Education:* Pratt Institute, B.F.A.

■ Addresses

Home and office—94 North Street, No. 4N, Jersey City, NJ 07307.

■ Career

Illustrator. *Exhibitions:* Kimberly Gallery, New York; Artist's Proof, New England; Society of Illustrators, New York; Chowan College, North Carolina; Elizabeth Stone Gallery, Michigan; African-American Museum of Fine Art, California; Sterling Creations, Essex Community College, and Art for Living, all in New Jersey. Permanent children's book art collection, Charlotte Library, Charlotte, NC. *Member:* Society of Illustrators.

■ Awards, Honors

Parenting magazine Reading Magic Award, for *Do Like Kyla;* Parent's Choice Foundation's Annual Award, for *Aunt Flossie's Hats (and Crab Cakes Later).*

JAMES E. RANSOME

■ Illustrator

Elizabeth Fitzgerald Howard, *Aunt Flossie's Hats (and Crab Cakes Later),* Clarion, 1990.
Angela Johnson, *Do Like Kyla,* Orchard Books, 1990.
Arthur A. Levine, *All the Lights in the Night,* Tambourine Books, 1991.
Lenny Hort, *How Many Stars in the Sky?,* Tambourine Books, 1991.
Denise L. Patrick, *Red Dancing Shoes,* Morrow, 1993.
Johnson, *The Girl Who Wore Snakes,* Orchard Books, 1993.
Margaree King Mitchell, *Uncle Jed's Barbershop,* Simon & Schuster, 1993.
Christine Widman, *The Hummingbird Garden,* Macmillan, 1993.
Deborah Hopkinson, *Sweet Clara and the Freedom Quilt,* Knopf, 1993.
James Weldon Johnson, *The Creation,* Holiday House, 1994.
Marilee R. Burton, *My Best Shoes,* Morrow, 1994.
Michael Rose, *Bonesy and Isabel,* Harcourt, 1994.

Illustrator of book jackets for young adult works, including *The Middle of Somewhere, Winning Scheherazade, Children of the Fire, Down in the Piney Woods, The Cry of the Wolf,* and *Chevrolet Saturdays.*

■ Work in Progress

Illustrating *Freedom's Fruit,* by William H. Hooks, for Random House, 1995.

■ Sidelights

James E. Ransome's interest in art began at an early age, and was influenced by television cartoons, superhero comic books, and *Mad* magazine. In later years his influences included film and photography, the paintings of Mary Cassatt, John Singer Sargent, Winslow Homer, and Edgar Degas, and contemporary illustrators such as Bernie Fuchs, Robert Cunningham, Skip Leipke, and Jerry Pinkney.

"I am a visual storyteller," Ransome has said, "and because each book has a special voice, my approach is different as well. Whether it be through my choice of palette, design, or perspective, there is always a desire to experiment and explore what makes each book unique.

"By conveying to young readers the individual traits of characters I only hope that I am instilling an appreciation for all the wonderfully unique qualities and cultural and racial differences we all possess."

■ Works Cited

"James E. Ransome" (publicity release), Tambourine Books, c. 1993.

■ For More Information See

PERIODICALS

Horn Book, September-October, 1991, p. 584; January-February, 1992, p. 65.
New Yorker, November 25, 1991, p. 146.
New York Times Book Review, February 21, 1993, p. 22.
Publishers Weekly, March 16, 1990, p. 68; February 15, 1991, p. 88; April 5, 1991, p. 145; November 1, 1991, p. 80; December 7, 1992, p. 63.
School Library Journal, April, 1990, p. 92; May, 1991, p. 79; March, 1992, p. 216.

* * *

RATZ de TAGYOS, Paul 1958-

■ Personal

Born January 30, 1958, in New Rochelle, NY; son of Paul (a fine artist) and Helen Ratz de Tagyos. *Education:* Attended Parsons School of Design. *Politics:* "Cynical." *Religion:* None. *Hobbies and other interests:* Landscape painting, microtonal music, walking, bicycling, Indian food ("eating, not cooking").

■ Addresses

Home and office—30 Eastchester Rd., Apt. 6-A, New Rochelle, NY 10801.

■ Career

Commercial artist.

■ Awards, Honors

Certificate of Merit, Society of Illustrators; Certificate of Design Excellence, *Print* magazine.

■ **Writings**

(Self-illustrated) *A Coney Tale,* Clarion, 1992.

■ **Work in Progress**

Showdown in Lonesome Pellet (another coney story).

■ **Sidelights**

Paul Ratz de Tagyos has received favorable attention for his first book, *A Coney Tale.* In this work, a writer for *Kirkus Reviews* notes, the author-illustrator "creates an appealing coney (rabbit) society in 17th-century Flanders, with unique enterprises like a 'pad repair shop' and an 'ear care center' and respectable coney burghers eating salad in timbered houses." After it is discovered that a huge tree is actually an enormous carrot, the rabbits find a way to unearth it. They feast on it for months and transform the hole it created into a public fountain. "Skewed perspectives create an amiably offbeat effect in the clean, crisp artwork," proclaims a reviewer for *Publishers Weekly.*

Ratz de Tagyos explained to *SATA* that his father and grandfather were painters. While he was "neither encouraged nor discouraged to pursue" art, he decided to

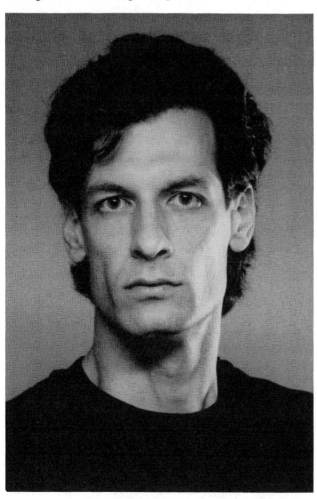

PAUL RATZ de TAGYOS

become what he calls an "unfine" artist, or a commercial artist. He attended Parsons School of Design and majored in illustration for four years. After leaving school he worked a series of odd jobs to make money. Ratz de Tagyos then began to pursue "comp work," creating "quick, mostly disposable, marker drawings of proposed ads used by ad agencies to show to their clients." Although he "hated those ugly comps," the "usage of marker and pencil became an available technique" and "a key factor in attempting to create a children's picture book."

Ratz de Tagyos told *SATA* that the "characters and their traits" in *A Coney Tale* are the "result of a longtime involvement I have with someone named Constance; I called her Coney. And it was, in fact, Coney who told me what a coney is. It's a bunny-rabbit, or dupe." *A Coney Tale* "is a direct adaptation from a bedtime story," he continues. "The prototype text [of the story] was verbose and endless (that's where editors come in, and I'm lucky with mine). I came to this project more as an illustrator with a story rather than an author with pictures. I feel much more comfortable with being the illustrator, it comes naturally."

■ **Works Cited**

Review of *A Coney Tale, Kirkus Reviews,* March 1, 1992.
Review of *A Coney Tale, Publishers Weekly,* March 30, 1992.

*   *   *

REES, David Bartlett 1936-1993

OBITUARY NOTICE—See index for *SATA* sketch: Born May 18, 1936, in London, England; died of an AIDS-related disease, May 22, 1993. Teacher and writer. Rees was perhaps best known for his books for young adults which explore feelings about growing up. Rees characteristically created fictional characters who experience many of the conflicts and emotions he experienced during his own childhood, and who often live in geographic settings similar to his own. For example, his best-known book, *The Exeter Blitz,* is an account of World War II Nazi bombing raids in suburban London, where Rees spent much of his childhood. The book won the prestigious Carnegie Medal in 1978 as the most distinguished children's book published in the United Kingdom that year. In 1979 Rees began incorporating a homosexual theme into his narratives, publishing *In the Tent, The Lighthouse,* and *The Milkman's on His Way,* a best-seller in 1982. After his 1958 graduation from Queen's College in Cambridge, Rees taught English and writing at secondary schools for eight years, then transferred to St. Luke's College in Exeter, where he lectured until the mid-1980s. Turning to free-lance writing in 1984, he concentrated on children's literature and research. Among Rees's other children's titles is *The Green Bough of Liberty,* a chronicle of Ireland in 1798 which received an award from the Children's Rights Workshop in 1980.

Rees also authored books for adults, including 1987's *Twos and Threes,* 1988's *Quince,* and 1992's *Dog Days, White Nights.* He published his autobiography, *Not for Your Hands,* in 1992.

OBITUARIES AND OTHER SOURCES:

BOOKS

The Writers Directory: 1992-1994, St. James Press, 1991, p. 816.

PERIODICALS

Times (London), May 26, 1993, p. 19.

*　　*　　*

REEVES, Faye Couch 1953-

■ Personal

Born June 17, 1953, in Seattle, WA; daughter of Joseph Douglas (in the military) and Helen (a homemaker; maiden name, Dunn) Couch; married Ronald G. Reeves (a systems analyst), November 24, 1979; children: Stephanie, Caitlin. *Education:* Moorhead State University, B.A. and B.S., both 1975. *Religion:* Presbyterian.

■ Addresses

Home and office—8101 Sprenger N.E., Albuquerque, NM 87109. *Agent*—Andrea Brown Literary Agent, 1081 Alameda, Suite 71, Belmont, CA 94002.

■ Career

KBHB Radio, Sturgis, SD, copywriter, 1975-77; Burroughs Corporation, Albuquerque, NM, account manager, 1977-79; Children's Day Out, Albuquerque, teacher, 1980-88; free-lance writer, 1988—. Member of Parent-

FAYE COUCH REEVES

Teacher Association and Art in the School. *Member:* International Reading Association.

■ Writings

My Witness, United Methodist Reporter, 1989.
Howie Merton and the Magic Dust, illustrated by Jon Buller, Random House, 1991.
What Really Happened to Annabelle Dupree, Toll Associates, in press.

■ Sidelights

Faye Couch Reeves told *SATA:* "My favorite authors—Elizabeth Enright, Beverly Cleary, Eleanor Estes—have one thing in common: they make me laugh. They also make me cry, think, and feel, but they *always* make me laugh. Humor is the saving grace of everyday life, and I feel it is the most important aspect of what I write.

"*Howie and the Magic Dust* is the first book that I have ever written. One of the main characters owns a dead cat—this came from an episode in my own childhood. The funny, real things from childhood make the best stories, especially when something important was learned along the way.

"Some may think that being published is the end of the journey. For me, being published has been the beginning. Working with editors, rewriting, and polishing my work has given me the same thing a good education gave me—the knowledge that I still have a lot to learn. Every time I sit down to write at my computer, I learn something new about myself and about writing.

"After my first book was published, I experienced the thrill of meeting my reading public—the children! They read my book and complete the communication circle. They tell *me* what my book was about. Their imaginations make my book bigger and better. I love to go into their classrooms and hear what they want to write about and what they like to read. They help me remember what it was like to be a child. What was scary? What was funny? I, in turn, encourage them to be *writers*—even if they have no desire to be *authors.*"

*　　*　　*

REISS, Kathryn 1957-

■ Personal

Surname is pronounced "reese"; born December 4, 1957, in Cambridge, MA; daughter of Edmund Alan Reiss and Dorothy Ann (Kauffman) Molnar; married Thomas Strychacz (a professor), October 2, 1981; children: Nicholas, Daniel. *Education:* Duke University, B.A., 1980; attended Rheinische-Friedrich-Wilhelms-Universitat-Bonn, 1980-81; University of Michigan, M.F.A., 1988. *Hobbies and other interests:* Traveling, reading, collecting old series books.

KATHRYN REISS

■ Addresses

Home—3 Faculty Village, Mills College, Oakland, CA 94613. *Agent*—Marilyn E. Marlow, Curtis Brown, Ltd., 10 Astor Pl., New York, NY 10003.

■ Career

Princeton Language Group, Princeton, NJ, instructor, 1981-82; Stuart Country Day School, Princeton, director of foreign exchange, 1981-82; Princeton Young Women's Christian Association (YWCA), Princeton, instructor, 1981-82 and 1984; Europa at Princeton (a bookshop), Princeton, manager, 1982-83; Princeton Public Library, Princeton, assistant to children's librarian, 1982-83; Trenton State College, Ewing, NJ, instructor, 1984-86; University of Michigan, Ann Arbor, instructor, 1986-88; Mills College, Oakland, CA, lecturer of English, 1989—. Princeton Arts Council, writer-in-residence, 1986. *Member:* Society of Children's Book Writers and Illustrators, Mystery Writers of America.

■ Awards, Honors

Scholarship, American Field Service, 1975; Fulbright-Hayes Scholar, 1980-81, to study contemporary German short fiction; grant, New Jersey State Council on the Arts, 1983-84; Cowden Memorial Prize for fiction, University of Michigan, 1987; Best Books for Young Adults citation, American Library Association, 1993, for *Time Windows.*

■ Writings

Time Windows (novel), Harcourt, 1991.
The Glass House People (novel), Harcourt, 1992.
Dreadful Sorry (novel), Harcourt, 1993.
Pale Phoenix (sequel to *Time Windows*), Harcourt, 1994.

Contributor of short stories to periodicals, including *The Archive.* Associate editor, *The Archive,* 1979-80.

■ Work in Progress

Research on earthquakes, triplets and multiple births, and life in working-class areas of nineteenth-century England.

■ Sidelights

Kathryn Reiss told *SATA:* "By the time I was six-years-old, I knew I wanted to be a writer. My mother would sometimes find me out of bed late at night, lying on the floor in the hallway (where the light was on), working on a story. I remember the first story I ever wrote was one page long and was about an owl. I called it 'The Owl's Order'—but I can't remember for the life of me what it was about! I began many stories, carried along on one exciting idea or another, but rarely managed to finish them. I credit my father with showing me how to push on to an ending. My usual practice was to write a great opening paragraph or two, then get all excited and rush off to show my family or friends. They'd be appreciative—and ask what was going to happen next. After I'd told them, however, I usually found that the pressing need to write down the story had vanished. When I was in sixth grade and took a story (about an Amish farm boy) to my father, he declined to read it *until it was finished,* not before then. I was crushed at the time (writing a whole story is, after all, a huge amount of work!), but I did go on to write the entire thing.

"There are certain stories that simply beg to be told. I feel a kind of urgency to write when I have a good plot in mind. But if I tell the tale verbally, much of the urgency disappears. It has become important for me to keep my plot to myself until I get it down at least in a rough form. If I share a story before it's written, the writing becomes a sort of re-run. Some of the energy is lost.

"I took creative writing classes in high school and college whenever I got the chance. Although I do not think it's possible to turn everybody into novelists, I do believe we all have stories to tell. The writers among us will benefit from taking writing courses where the focus is on transplanting stories from the imagination to the printed page. After graduating from Duke University in 1980, I went to Bonn, Germany, to study at the university there. At one point I was up to my ears in [the German poet Johann Wolfgang] Goethe's works, analyzing them, writing about them, preparing to give an oral report in class (a scary thought!)—and I decided to take a day off from work just to read something light, preferably in English—despite my promise to myself to avoid the English language as much as I possibly could. I had read all of my English novels already, and it was pouring rain outside, so a trip to the bookstore didn't seem so good. I thought to myself: 'This is your chance. You've been saying for years that you want to write a book, right? So, why not start now?' I got a pad of paper and my pen, and sat down and started writing a story. When the rain stopped, I was still engaged in my new story, and I went out to sit on my little balcony (I rented a room in a big, drafty house) and kept on writing far into the night. I continued to write in my free time until I had an entire first draft of a novel. I revised it over several years (taking breaks to get married, to go to graduate school, and to have two children) and so produced my first novel, *Time Windows.*

"I am currently a lecturer at Mills College, where I teach writing. I have a special interest in our various notions of time—memory, perception, history, time travel (as a child I was always looking for ways to travel in time; perhaps my writing is my own version of a time machine!). I have a special interest in writing for middle grade and young adult audiences, and write the sort of books now that I liked when I was the age of my readers—especially favoring books about magic or mystery. I have many other story ideas waiting on the back burner."

*   *   *

ROTNER, Shelley 1951-

■ Personal

Born January 1, 1951, in New York, NY; daughter of William and Babette (an author and guidance counselor) Rotner; married Stephen Calcagnino (an arts administrator), January 31, 1981; children: Emily. *Education:* Attended Syracuse University Extension Program, 1972; Syracuse University, B.A., 1972; post graduate work at Columbia University 1977; Bank Street College of Education, M.A., 1979.

■ Addresses

Home and office—35 Columbus Ave., Northampton, MA 01060.

■ Career

Free-lance photographer, 1975—. Aggasiz Community School District, Cambridge, MA, photography instructor, 1975; Learning Guild, Boston, MA, photography instructor, 1975-76; Lincoln Community School System, Cambridge, MA, photography instructor, 1975-76; International Center of Photography, New York City, assistant photography instructor, 1977; Bank Street School for Children, New York City, photography instructor, 1977-78; United Nations Photo Library, New York City, photo researcher, 1977-78; International Center of Photography, New York City, curatorial assistant, 1977-78; United Nations and UNICEF, New York City, photographer, 1979—; The American Museum of Natural History, New York City, photography instructor, 1979. *Exhibitions:* Exhibitor at galleries and museums in Holyoke, MA, Springfield, MA, Boston, New York, Seattle, and Portland, ME, including the American Museum of Natural History, and the International Center of Photography.

■ Awards, Honors

Grand Prize, *Natural History* magazine photo competition, 1979; Third Prize, World Photographic Society, 1983, for color photographs of children; Northampton, MA, Arts Lottery, funds to take portraits of the women of the Lathrop Home for their centennial celebration, 1984; Northampton, MA, Arts Lottery, Funds to exhibit community portraits, 1985; Grand Emmy Award in advertising for images used in Polaroid advertisements, The Polaroid Corporation, 1986; Parade/Kodak, Finalist, 1988, for a work to be published in *Parade* magazine, a book, and part of a traveling exhibit; First Prize, Zone Gallery, Springfield, MA, for color portraits.

■ Writings

Changes, Macmillan, 1991.
Nature Spy, Macmillan, 1992.
Action Alphabet, Picture Book Studio, 1993.
City Streets, Orchard Press, 1993.
Faces, Macmillan, 1993.

■ Sidelights

Shelley Rotner worked as a teacher, a photographer, and a curatorial assistant before she became involved in the creation of children's books. She told *SATA:* "After several years as an educator both in the classroom and in museum settings and after the birth of my daughter, I started to think about ideas for children's books. My daughter always loved to look at books and as she grew I started to think and write about the subjects that interested her."

*   *   *

RUOFF, A. LaVonne Brown 1930-

■ Personal

Born April 10, 1930, in Charleston, IL; daughter of Oscar (a farmer and factory worker) and Laura Alice Witters (a teacher and homemaker) Brown; married Milford A. Prasher, August 19, 1950 (divorced, 1964); married Gene W. Ruoff (a professor of English), June 10, 1967; children: Stephen C., Sharon L. *Education:* Attended University of Illinois, Chicago, 1948-50; Northwestern University, B.S., 1953, M.A., 1954, Ph.D., 1966.

■ Addresses

Home—300 Forest Ave., Oak Park, IL 60302. *Office*—Department of English (m/c 162), University of Illinois at Chicago, 601 South Morgan St., Chicago, IL 60607-7120.

■ Career

University of Illinois, Chicago, instructor in English, 1956-57; Roosevelt University, Chicago, instructor, 1961-62, assistant professor of English, 1962-66; University of Illinois, assistant professor, 1966-69, associate professor, 1969-81, professor of English, 1981—. National Endowment for the Humanities, director of Summer Seminar for College Teachers on American Indian Literature, 1979, 1983, and 1989; American Literature Committee for the Council for International Exchange of Scholars, member, 1987-90, chair, 1990. *Member:* Association for Study of American Indian Literature (president, 1980), Modern Language Association (chair of Discussion Group on American Indian Literature, 1978, 1991), Society for Study of Multiethnic Literature in the United States.

■ Awards, Honors

Fellowship, Dartmouth College, 1979, in the Native American studies program; grant, National Endowment for the Humanities Research Division, 1981; award for distinguished contributions to ethnic studies, Society for Study of Multiethnic Literature in the United States, 1986; fellowship, National Endowment for the Humanities, 1992-93.

■ Writings

(Editor) E. Pauline Johnson, *The Moccasin Maker* (young adult), University of Arizona, 1987.
American Indian Literatures, Modern Language Association, 1990.
Literatures of the American Indian (young adult), Chelsea House, 1990.
(Editor with Jerry W. Ward, Jr.) *Redefining American Literary History,* Modern Language Assocation, 1990.

Contributor to books, including *Old Indian Days,* by Charles Eastman, University of Nebraska Press, 1991. Editor of "American Indian Lives" series, University of Nebraska Press, 1985—. Consultant on Norton and Heath anthologies of American literature; member of advisory board for "Native American Bibliography" series, Scarecrow Press. Contributor to periodicals.

■ Work in Progress

Oxford Book of Native American Literature, completion expected in 1995; an edition of S. Alice Callahan's *Wynema,* which "may be the first novel written by an Indian woman," for University of Nebraska Press; researching a history of literature written by American Indians from 1772 to the present.

■ Sidelights

A. LaVonne Brown Ruoff told *SATA:* "The impetus to my research on American Indians is the fact that I was formerly married to an Indian, and one of my two adopted children is an Indian."

RYLANT, Cynthia 1954-

■ Personal

Surname is pronounced "rye-*lunt*"; born June 6, 1954, in Hopewell, VA; daughter of John Tune (an army sergeant) and Leatrel (a nurse; maiden name, Rylant) Smith; children: Nathaniel. *Education:* Morris Harvey College (now University of Charleston), B.A., 1975; Marshall University, M.A., 1976; Kent State University, M.L.S., 1982. *Politics:* Democrat. *Religion:* "Christian, no denomination."

■ Career

Writer. Marshall University, Huntington, WV, part-time English instructor, 1979-80; Akron Public Library, Akron, OH, children's librarian, 1983; University of Akron, Akron, part-time English lecturer, 1983-84; Northeast Ohio Universities College of Medicine, Rootstown, OH, part-time lecturer, 1991—.

■ Awards, Honors

Booklist reviewer's choice, 1982, Caldecott Honor Book (illustrations by Diane Goode), American Library Association (ALA) notable book, Reading Rainbow selection, and American Book Award nomination, all 1983,

CYNTHIA RYLANT

and English Speaking Union Book-across-the-Sea Ambassador of Honor Award, 1984, all for *When I Was Young in the Mountains;* ALA notable book, *School Library Journal* best book of 1984, National Council for Social Studies best book, 1984, and Society of Midland Authors best children's book, 1985, all for *Waiting to Waltz ... a Childhood; New York Times* best illustrated book, *Horn Book* honor book, and Children's book of the year, Child Study Association of America, all 1985, and Caldecott Honor Book (illustrations by Stephen Gammell), 1986, all for *The Relatives Came;* Children's book of the year, Child Study Association of America, 1985, for *A Blue-eyed Daisy; School Library Journal* best book citation, 1985, for *Every Living Thing; Parents' Choice* selection, 1986, *Horn Book* honor book, and Newbery Honor Book, ALA, both 1987, all for *A Fine White Dust;* ALA best book for young adults citation, 1988, for *A Kindness; Boston Globe/Horn Book* honor book for nonfiction, 1991, for *Appalachia: The Voices of Sleeping Birds;* Garden State Children's Book Award, Children's Services Section of the New Jersey Library Association, 1992, for *Henry and Mudge Get the Cold Shivers; Boston Globe-Horn Book* Award for children's fiction, 1992, and John Newbery Medal, 1993, for *Missing May;* ALA best book for young adults citation, for *A Couple of Kooks and Other Stories about Love; School Library Journal* best book of the year citation, for *Children of Christmas.*

■ Writings

PICTURE BOOKS

When I Was Young in the Mountains, illustrated by Diane Goode, Dutton, 1982.
Miss Maggie, illustrated by Thomas DiGrazia, Dutton, 1983.
This Year's Garden, illustrated by Mary Szilagyi, Bradbury, 1984.
The Relatives Came, illustrated by Stephen Gammell, Bradbury, 1985.
Night in the Country, illustrated by Szilagyi, Bradbury, 1986.
Birthday Presents, illustrated by Sucie Stevenson, Orchard Books, 1987.
All I See, illustrated by Peter Catalanotto, Orchard Books, 1988.
Mr. Griggs' Work, illustrated by Julie Downing, Orchard Books, 1989.
An Angel for Solomon Singer, illustrated by Catalanotto, Orchard Books, 1992.
The Dreamer, illustrated by Barry Moser, Scholastic Inc., 1993.

"THE EVERYDAY BOOKS" SERIES; SELF-ILLUSTRATED

The Everyday Children, Macmillan, 1993.
The Everyday Garden, Macmillan, 1993.
The Everyday House, Macmillan, 1993.
The Everyday School, Macmillan, 1993.
The Everyday Town, Macmillan, 1993.

Rylant's lyrical language brings to life the story of a lonely city man who makes a friend in an unlikely place. (Cover illustration by Peter Catalanotto.)

"HENRY AND MUDGE" SERIES; ILLUSTRATED BY SUCIE STEVENSON

Henry and Mudge: The First Book of Their Adventures, Macmillan, 1987.
Henry and Mudge in Puddle Trouble: The Second Book of Their Adventures, Macmillan, 1987.
Henry and Mudge in the Green Time: The Third Book of Their Adventures, Macmillan, 1987.
Henry and Mudge under the Yellow Moon: The Fourth Book of Their Adventures, Macmillan, 1987.
Henry and Mudge in the Sparkle Days: The Fifth Book of Their Adventures, Macmillan, 1988.
Henry and Mudge and the Forever Sea: The Sixth Book of Their Adventures, Macmillan, 1989.
Henry and Mudge Get the Cold Shivers: The Seventh Book of Their Adventures, Macmillan, 1989.
Henry and Mudge and the Happy Cat, Macmillan, 1990.
Henry and Mudge and the Bedtime Thumps, Macmillan, 1991.
Henry and Mudge Take the Big Test: The Tenth Book of Their Adventures, Macmillan, 1991.
Henry and Mudge and the Long Weekend, Macmillan, 1992.
Henry and Mudge and the Wild Wind, Macmillan, 1992.
Henry and Mudge and the Careful Cousin: The Thirteenth Book of Their Adventures, Macmillan, 1994.

OTHER

Waiting to Waltz ... a Childhood (poetry), illustrated by Stephen Gammell, Bradbury, 1984.

Rylant's childhood, spent in rural West Virginia with her grandparents, formed the basis of *When I Was Young in the Mountains*, her first book for children. (Illustration by Diane Goode.)

A Blue-eyed Daisy (novel), Bradbury, 1985 (published in England as *Some Year For Ellie*, illustrated by Kate Rogers, Viking Kestrel, 1986).

Every Living Thing (stories), Bradbury, 1985.

A Fine White Dust (novel), Bradbury, 1986.

Children of Christmas: Stories for the Season, illustrated by S. D. Schindler, Orchard Books, 1987 (published in England as *Silver Packages and Other Stories*, 1987).

A Kindness (novel), Orchard Books, 1989.

But I'll Be Back Again: An Album (autobiography), Orchard Books, 1989.

A Couple of Kooks: And Other Stories about Love, Orchard Books, 1990.

Soda Jerk (poetry), illustrated by Peter Catalanotto, Orchard Books, 1990.

Appalachia: The Voices of Sleeping Birds (nonfiction), illustrated by Barry Moser, Harcourt, 1991.

Missing May (novel), Orchard Books, 1992.

Best Wishes (autobiography), photographs by Carlo Ontal, Richard C. Owen, 1992.

I Had Seen Castles (novel), Harcourt Brace, 1993.

■ Adaptations

When I Was Young in the Mountains, 1983, *This Year's Garden*, 1983, and *The Relatives Came*, 1986, were adapted as filmstrips by Random House.

■ Work in Progress

"Mr. Putter and Tabby," a series for beginning readers, illustrated by Arthur Howard, for Harcourt, including *Mr. Putter and Tabby Pour the Tea* and *Mr. Putter and Tabby Walk the Dog;* "Blue Hill Meadows," a picture book series.

■ Sidelights

Cynthia Rylant is an award-winning children's and young adult author whose work includes picture books, poetry, short stories, and novels. With a writing style that has been described as unadorned, clear, and lyrical, the author presents young people's experiences with sensitivity and perceptiveness, branding her protagonists' concerns as legitimate and equally important as those of adults. Rylant's characters tend to be contemplative and set apart from their peers by their situations. Explaining her leaning toward such subjects, the author remarked in a *Horn Book* interview with Anita Silvey, "I get a lot of personal gratification thinking of those people who don't get any attention in the world and making them really valuable in my fiction—making them absolutely shine with their beauty." She continued, "I don't ever quite write really happy novels; I don't want to deal with the people who have what they want. I want to deal with people who don't have what they want, to show their lives too."

Critics suggest that Rylant appears sympathetic to her characters' plights because she also faced uncommon hardships as a child. In her autobiography *But I'll Be Back Again: An Album*, the author stated, "They say that to be a writer you must first have an unhappy childhood. I don't know if unhappiness is necessary, but I think maybe some children who have suffered a loss too

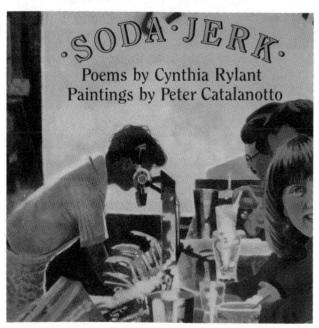

A broad spectrum of people come under the scrutiny of a fountain worker's eyes in this collection of poems. (Cover illustration by Catalanotto.)

great for words grow up into writers who are always trying to find those words, trying to find a meaning for the way they have lived."

Rylant's parents had a stormy marriage and separated when the author was four years old; she admits that she naively blamed herself for their troubles. The author and her mother moved to West Virginia where Rylant was left in her grandparents' care while her mother earned a nursing degree. Her father wrote occasionally when she first moved, but the letters eventually stopped. Because none of her relatives spoke about her father, she was afraid to ask questions about him. After years of silence, however, he contacted Rylant. The author dreamed of their reunion, but before it could take place her father, a Korean War veteran who suffered from hepatitis and alcoholism, succumbed to these diseases. He died when she was thirteen. In *But I'll Be Back Again,* the author stated, "I did not have a chance to know him or to say goodbye to him, and that is all the loss I needed to become a writer."

Unhappiness, however, did not dominate the author's childhood. Rylant enjoyed the rustic West Virginia environment while living with her grandparents in a mountain town where many houses had neither electricity nor running water. The lack of amenities did not bother young Rylant; she felt secure surrounded by equally poor yet friendly, church-going neighbors. When the author was eight years old, she and her mother moved to another West Virginia town named Beaver. Once, judging in retrospect, she called this new location "without a doubt a small, sparkling universe that gave me a lifetime's worth of material for my writing."

As an adolescent in this rural setting, though, Rylant began to recognize and become envious of the fact that other people had more material possessions than she and her mother did. In addition, Beaver—which had at first offered adventure—now appeared backward and dull compared to larger cities. Reflecting in her autobiography, *But I'll Be Back Again,* Rylant remarked, "As long as I stayed in Beaver, I felt I was somebody important . . . . But as soon as I left town to go anywhere else, my sense of being somebody special evaporated into nothing and I became dull and ugly and poor." She continued, "I wanted to be someone else, and that turned out to be the worst curse and the best gift of my life. I would finish out my childhood forgetting who I really was and what I really thought, and I would listen to other people and repeat their ideas instead of finding my own. That was the curse. The gift was that I would be willing to try to write books when I grew up."

Teenage Sensitivity Led to Writer's Sensibility

As an adolescent, Rylant claims she showed few signs of being a future writer. She was interested in boys, the Beatles, and *Archie* comic books. She remarked in the *Something about the Author Autobiography Series* (*SAAS*) that "it wasn't piles of poems or short stories which were the hints in my childhood that I might be a writer someday. The clues were much more subtle and

In Rylant's first novel, eleven-year-old Ellie begins to understand that growing up is a complicated business.

had something to do with the way I grieved over stray animals, the heroes I chose (a presidential candidate, a symphony orchestra conductor), and the love I had of solitude. It is called sensitivity, this quality which sets creative people apart. If they have too much of it, they can be miserable and miserable to be around. But if they possess only a little-more-than-reasonable amount, they can see into things more deeply than other people and can write or paint or sing what they saw in a way that moves people profoundly."

In her first English class in college Rylant found a part of herself that she had not recognized before. She told *SAAS* that "after taking one college English class, I was hooked on great writing . . . I didn't know about this part of me until I went to college—didn't know I loved beautiful stories." But, thinking that great writers only wrote in the manner of Charles Dickens and William Shakespeare, Rylant did not attempt to write creatively while in college. After getting her master's degree in English, she eventually got a job in the children's room of a public library. In this job Rylant, who had never been exposed to children's literature before, absorbed herself in reading children's books and finally recognized that she was going to become a children's author.

The first book Rylant produced was *When I Was Young in the Mountains,* a picture book reminiscing about life in West Virginia's Appalachian Mountains which was praised for its simple, yet evocative text and was named a Caldecott honor book. With subsequent picture books, including *The Relatives Came, This Year's Garden,* and her "Henry and Mudge" series, Rylant has received considerable recognition and awards. The author once commented: "I like writing picture books because that medium gives me a chance to capture in a brief space what I consider life's profound experiences—grandmother crying at a swimming hole baptism, a family planting a garden together, relatives coming for a visit. There is a poignancy and beauty in these events, and I don't want to write adult poetry about them because then I'll have to layer it with some adult disillusionment."

Rylant continued her use of poetry in books for older readers. In *Waiting to Waltz ... A Childhood,* the author offers an autobiographical collection of thirty free-verse poems which record her coming-of-age. These events include embarrassment because her mother was too busy to join school committees and reckoning with the deaths of both an absent father and a beloved pet. One passage documents the surprising transformation from child to young adult: "Forgetting when/ I was last time/ a child./ Never knowing/ when it/ ended." *Wait-*

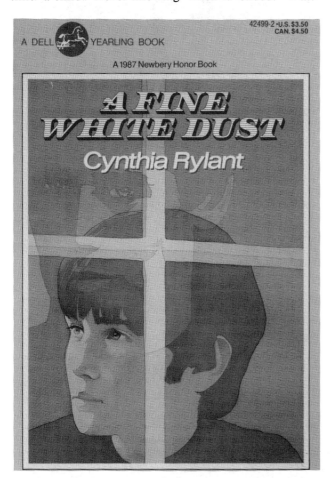

Rylant's story of a young boy's growing involvement with a traveling preacher provides lessons in love, life, and faith.

ing to Waltz also weaves in events and symbols of the 1960s to produce what critics deemed a vivid re-creation of the era.

Poetry Recreates Small-Town Life

Another book of verse, *Soda Jerk,* combines illustrations by Peter Catalanotto with twenty-eight related poems by Rylant to present the thoughts of a nameless protagonist who works as an attendant at a soda fountain. The title of this work is the slang term for the job. The jerk, as the narrator calls himself, offers commentary on issues ranging from his customers' lives to his fears about the future. Valerie Sayers, writing in *New York Times Book Review,* remarked that with her short poems, "Rylant manages to shape enough action to fill several short stories and to create a protagonist who is not only likable but charming and engaging." *Soda Jerk,* the critic concluded, "is full of respect for a boy's powers of observation, and its images, both written and painted, are striking."

In 1985 Rylant published her first novel, *A Blue-eyed Daisy.* Set in Appalachia, the episodic work is told by eleven-year-old Ellie Farley during the course of a year. The youngest of five daughters, Ellie contends with her apprehensions and conflicting emotions about growing up. For example, she overcomes her fear of contracting epilepsy after witnessing a classmate's seizure; copes with her unemployed, alcoholic father's imperfections and the possibility of his death after an accident; and battles the nervous anticipation of her first co-ed party. A reviewer for *Publishers Weekly* proclaimed *A Blue-eyed Daisy* an "exquisite novel, written with love."

Rylant's 1986 novel, *A Fine White Dust,* was named a Newbery Honor Book. In this work, a deeply religious seventh-grader named Pete believes he has found a human incarnation of God in a roving preacher named Carson. When attending a revival meeting, Pete is mesmerized by Carson's charismatic presence and, after being "saved," agrees to become his disciple. Despite his hesitance to leave his family and friends, Pete reasons that such a sacrifice is needed to fully embrace the holy life. Pete's mission is never fulfilled, however, because the preacher unexpectedly runs off with a young woman. Although he initially feels betrayed, Pete develops a more mature understanding of love and faith. *Wilson Library Bulletin* contributor Frances Bradburn proclaimed, "The careful crafting of delicate subjects is ... beautifully illustrated" in *A Fine White Dust.*

Another of Rylant's 1990 works, *A Couple of Kooks: And Other Stories about Love,* offers various examples of emotion. In "A Crush," a mentally handicapped man secretly leaves flowers for a female hardware store worker. An older woman finds love with a man ten years her junior in "Clematis." And in the title story, two teenagers use the nine months of the girl's pregnancy to try to instill their hopes, love, and food preferences on the baby that they will be forced to give up for adoption. Critics commended Rylant for her honest, compassionate portrayal of her subjects' feelings.

Tale of Loss and Acceptance Earns Newbery Medal

Missing May, the 1993 Newbery award winner, also deals with emotional and internal changes rather than physical action. Summer, the protagonist, is a six-year old orphan who has been passed from family to family, "treated like a homework assignment somebody was always having to do," Summer explains in *Missing May,* until Summer's elderly "Uncle Ob and Aunt May from West Virginia visited, and they knew an angel when they saw her and they took me on home." Summer lives happily with Ob and May for six years when May suddenly dies while gardening. Summer and Ob have difficulty adjusting to life without May. Summer fears Ob will die too if she does not find a way to help him overcome his grief. Ob eventually becomes convinced that he feels the spirit of May with him and needs to contact her somehow; this prompts an odyssey to a spiritualist. Ob, Summer, and Summer's school friend, Cletus, journey to find the medium who will connect them to May's spirit, but instead find that the medium is dead. Disappointed and dejected the trio began the journey back home, with Summer assuming that Ob does not want to live anymore. At some point during the return trip, however, Ob transforms and decides being alive—even without May—is important. When they arrive home, Summer is finally able to grieve for May with Ob's support and embrace.

Missing May elicited praise from many critics. "Ms. Rylant writes award-winning everything: picture books, humor, poetry, short stories and nonfiction. But it is in her novels for young adults that her spare language, sense of place and deceptively simple stories explode most effectively," asserted *New York Times Book Review*'s Karen Ray in her assessment of *Missing May.* Ray added that Rylant "brings insight and acceptance to an odd collection of characters we will come to love very much." "Cynthia Rylant gives substance to the abstract concept of love," wrote a contributor to *Horn Book.* A *Bulletin of the Center for Children's Books* reviewer similarly commented that "strong nuances of despair and hope create a suspense that forcefully replaces action and that will touch readers to tears." Commending Rylant's concise writing skills, *School Library Journal*'s Marcia Hupp also acknowledged Rylant's "natural grace of language, an earthly sense of humor, and a wellgrounded sense of the spiritual," that are brought together in *Missing May.* And even though *Missing May* deals with such a sensitive subject as death for middle school readers, Ray concluded that readers will find *Missing May* "not only comforting, but also complex and rewarding."

With her works for children and young adults, Rylant has earned a loyal readership as well as positive critical responses. Yet, when facing the future of her career, Rylant admits to insecurities. In *Horn Book* she explained, "I get afraid of what I am going to do for the next fifty years. Surely, I think to myself, I can't keep this up. I am just going to run dry—or worse, get boring and predictable." Nonetheless, the author does feel a

A simple, spare tale of a girl learning to accept her foster mother's death, *Missing May* earned Rylant the Newbery Medal. (Cover illustration by Rene Ade.)

sense of accomplishment beyond the recognition and awards her works have received. In *Horn Book* Rylant confided that writing "has given me a sense of self-worth that I didn't have my whole childhood. I am really proud of that. The [books] have carried me through some troubled times and have made me feel that I am worthy of having a place on this earth."

■ Works Cited

Bradburn, Frances, review of *A Fine White Dust, Wilson Library Bulletin,* April, 1987, p. 49.

Review of *A Blue-eyed Daisy, Publishers Weekly,* March 8, 1985, p. 91.

Hupp, Marcia, review of *Missing May, School Library Journal,* March, 1992, pp. 241-42.

Review of *Missing May, Bulletin of the Center for Children's Books,* March, 1992, p. 192.

Review of *Missing May, Horn Book,* March/April, 1992, p. 206.

Ray, Karen, review of *Missing May, New York Times Book Review,* p. 48.

Rylant, Cynthia, *Waiting to Waltz ... a Childhood,* Bradbury, 1984.

Rylant, Cynthia, *But I'll Be Back Again: An Album,* Orchard Books, 1989, pp. 7, 32-34.

Rylant, Cynthia, entry in *Something about the Author Autobiography Series,* Volume 13, Gale, 1991, pp. 155-163.

Rylant, Cynthia, *Missing May,* Orchard Books, 1992, pp. 5, 7.

Sayers, Valerie, review of *Soda Jerk, New York Times Book Review,* June 3, 1990, p. 24.

Silvey, Anita, "An Interview with Cynthia Rylant," *Horn Book,* November/December, 1987, pp. 695-703.

■ For More Information See

BOOKS

Children's Literature Review, Volume 15, Gale, 1988, pp. 167-174.

PERIODICALS

New York Times Book Review, November 10, 1985, p. 37; June 30, 1990, p. 24; January 26, 1993, p. C-16.

Publishers Weekly, March 1, 1991; February 3, 1992, p. 82.

School Library Journal, August, 1991, p. 152; March, 1992, p. 241; May, 1993, pp. 26-29.

Washington Post, December 24, 1990.

S

St. JOHN, Philip
See del REY, Lester

*   *   *

SALISBURY, Graham 1944-

■ Personal

Born April 11, 1944, in Philadelphia, PA; son of Henry
Forester Graham (an officer in the U.S. Navy) and
Barbara Twigg-Smith; married second wife, Robyn Kay
Cowan, October 26, 1988; children: Sandi Weston,
Miles, Ashley, Melanie, Alex, Keenan, Zachary. *Educa-
tion:* California State University at Northridge, B.A.
(magna cum laude), 1974; Vermont College of Norwich
University, M.F.A., 1990. *Politics:* "Middle of the
road."

■ Addresses

Office—319 Southwest Washington No. 320, Portland,
OR 97204. *Agent*—Emilie Jacobson, Curtis Brown Ltd.,
10 Astor Pl., New York, NY 10003.

■ Career

Writer. Worked variously as a deckhand, glass-bottom
boat skipper, singer-songwriter, graphic artist, and
teacher; manager of historic office buildings in down-
town Portland, OR. *Member:* Society of Children's
Book Writers and Illustrators, Women's National Book
Association, American Library Association, Hawaiian
Mission Children's Society.

■ Awards, Honors

Parents Choice Award, Bank Street College Child Study
Children's Book Award, Judy Lopez Memorial Award
for Children's Literature, Women's National Book Association, and citations as one of the best books for
young adults, American Library Association, and best
books of the year, *School Library Journal,* all 1992, for
Blue Skin of the Sea; PEN/Norma Klein Award, 1992;
John Unterecker Award for Fiction, Chaminade University and Hawaii Literary Arts Council.

■ Writings

Blue Skin of the Sea (novel), Delacorte, 1992.

Contributor to periodicals, including *Bamboo Ridge,
Chaminade Literary Review, Hawaii Pacific Review,
Journal of Youth Services in Libraries, Manoa: A Journal
of Pacific and International Writing,* and *Northwest.*

■ Work in Progress

Another novel, completion expected in 1994.

■ Sidelights

Graham Salisbury told *SATA:* "Embarrassing as it is to
admit, especially to fellow writers, I didn't read until I
was a little past thirty. Sure, I escaped with Edgar Rice
Burroughs and Louis L'Amour a couple of times, and I
read the required *Iliad* and *Odyssey* in high school, but I
didn't read of my own choice until my first son was
born. Then I read Alex Haley's *Roots,* which changed
my life forever. I don't have a clue as to *why* I picked
this book up, but I did, and I loved it so much that I
wanted to read another, and another . . . and another. I
surprised myself and quite suddenly became a voracious
reader.

"Because reading eventually grew into something as
large as life itself, I started feeling an urge to do some
writing of my own. Maybe that's how we all come to this
art—a desire to create those fantastic worlds and
passionate feelings we got when reading something
wonderful. I started writing memory pieces. Eventually I
found myself stretching my stories, bending the truth,
twisting the realities, and surprising myself by the ease
with which I could lie. Simply by stumbling in and
writing lies, I discovered that writing *fiction* was what I
enjoyed most.

GRAHAM SALISBURY

"'Write what you know' is good advice, but 'write what you *feel*' is better. I was raised in the Hawaiian Islands, a setting I know and a setting I love. I can *feel,* even now, the rocking of my stepfather's deep-sea charter fishing boat, the hot sun on my shoulders, salt itching under my T-shirt after swimming. I can hear the constant rumble of waves and smell the sweet aroma of steaks cooking at the hotels in the village of Kailua-Kona. I can even make myself shudder when I remember the time I got caught in quicksand in Kanehoe, Oahu, and had to wait, sinking slowly, while my friend ran for help.

Important Values Provide Material for Writing

"I was also raised—for the most part—without a father, and I have some big holes in my life because of it. I'm reminded of these holes constantly, nearly every day of my life. It's no surprise that I write a lot about relationships, especially family relationships, I guess because they're so important to me. If a writer can discover what is important to him or her, then that writer will have discovered the things he or she has to write about. That's why I say, write what you *feel.*

"There are so many things to learn about writing— about thought, about feelings and passions, about story-telling, about craft, about commitment, and about one's own personality and habits. But in my mind, one element is most important. Without it a writer will struggle endlessly. That element is discipline. Someone once said that a published writer is an amateur who didn't give up. There's so much truth in that. Discipline, to me, means consistent—almost habitual—writerly thinking, writing, rewriting, revising, and submitting.

"The important thing for me to understand as a writer for young readers is that though the world has changed, the basic needs of young people haven't. There are many, many kids out there with holes in their lives that they desperately want to fill. I can write about those holes. I can do this because I am human and have suffered and soared myself. Strange as it sounds to say, I—as a writer—consider myself lucky, indeed, to have all the holes I have in my own life. Because when I write, I remember, I understand, I empathize, and I feel a need to explore those holes and maybe even fill a couple of them—for myself and for any reader with a similar need who happens to stumble onto my work."

Blue Skin of the Sea is Salisbury's tale, told in a series of related stories, of a young boy growing up in Hawaii. Reviewing the book in *Five Owls,* Gary D. Schmidt called it "entertaining, moving, and poignant," and he praised the author's "ability to depict island life" and "the pressures and tensions and loves and fears of it." He felt that Salisbury "creates a compelling story of growth and change." A *Publishers Weekly* writer remarked upon the "extraordinary mood" of the work, in which Salisbury distills "the most powerful and universal experiences of adolescence."

■ Works Cited

Review of *Blue Skin of the Sea, Publishers Weekly,* June 15, 1992, p. 104.
Schmidt, Gary D., review of *Blue Skin of the Sea, Five Owls,* May/June, 1992.

■ For More Information See

PERIODICALS
Publishers Weekly, July 13, 1992, p. 22.

*   *   *

SATTERFIELD, Charles See del REY, Lester

*   *   *

SAVAGE, Deborah 1955-

■ Personal

Born December 15, 1955, in Northampton, MA. *Education:* University of Massachusetts, B.A., 1987.

■ Addresses

Home—147 Woodside Ave., Amherst, MA 01002.

■ Career

Alderkill Camp, Rhinebeck, NY, teacher of arts program, 1975; University of Massachusetts, Amherst, teaching assistant for creative writing course, 1977; Wildwood Elementary School, Amherst, teacher of

Deborah Savage's first novel details a girl's plans to leave home to search for a lake where otters live.

creative writing, 1978; The Hotchkiss School, Lakeville, CT, teacher of art, 1987; The Forman School, Litchfield, CT, teacher of English and art, 1988-91; writer, 1991—. Taught classes and workshops in wood-cut printmaking to young people and adults at various schools in Massachusetts and New Zealand, 1980-1985; guest author and workshop presenter in schools in New Zealand, Pennsylvania, New York, Massachusetts, Washington and Connecticut, 1985-91; served as guest author and workshop presenter for the Brookline Area Schools in Massachusetts, 1987-1988. Has also given presentations at the Northwest Corner Coalition for Nuclear Disarmament, the Massachusetts Association for Educational Media, the Boston Public Library Creative Writing Workshop, the International Federation of Teachers of English conference, and the American Association of University Women Book and Author luncheon. *Exhibitions:* Savage's wood-cut prints and watercolors have been exhibited at the Berkshire Museum, Pittsfield, MA; the Pratt Museum of Natural History, Amherst, MA; the Cape Cod Museum of Natural History, Brewster, MA; the Auckland Institute and Museum, Auckland, NZ; and the White Memorial Conservation Area Museum, Litchfield, CT.

■ Awards, Honors

Award of Merit, American Museum Association, 1984, for Cape Cod Museum of Natural History poster; Notable Children's Book citation, American Library Association, remarkable book of literature award, *Parents Choice Magazine,* and *School Library Journal* best books citation, all 1986, all for *A Rumour of Otters.*

■ Writings

YOUNG ADULT NOVELS

A Rumour of Otters, Houghton, 1986.
Flight of the Albatross, Houghton, 1988.
A Stranger Calls Me Home, Houghton, 1992.
To Race a Dream, Houghton, 1993.

OTHER

Contributor of poetry to periodicals, including *Dark Horse, Spectrum,* and *Cross Currents.* Also contributor of illustrations to periodicals, including *Planning Quarterly* and *Cross Currents. Flight of the Albatross* has appeared in French and German translations.

■ Adaptations

Flight of the Albatross has been optioned by film companies in Germany and New Zealand.

■ Work in Progress

Along a Path of Stars, a novel; *Approaching Sacred Places,* a collection of short stories.

■ Sidelights

Deborah Savage told *SATA,* "When I was a young girl I wrote story after story that I never finished; then, I thought it was because I grew bored with them—now I think it was because I was too young to know that stories never did end at all. I lived way out in the country surrounded by woods and hills and mountains, and I read a great deal.... I read so many stories at the same time they all became entwined within me like a great winding loop going forever through me. I loved to draw and paint, and often I would write stories about the things I liked to draw, just so I could draw them over and over as illustrations. My writing has remained visual like that; I write the story and illustrate it with word-pictures.

"Most of the people who came to my home when I was young were adults, and except for school, I knew very few children. Adults were bristling with stories, it seemed to me, and if they did not tell them to me I made them up. I think that is how I learned to traverse the divide between my experience of living and my writing, until now there is almost no division. Characters come from an infinite store of barely-known people who may no longer be in my life, but have left in their going a wake of richly-scented stories ... I have only to lift my head and sniff the air, and there I find them.

"I write stories and books about young people ... people just leaving childhood and coming into adulthood. The transformation is so intense it colors the world in a manner that never happens when they are older. I write books about people who each are discovering the entire universe for the very first time, identifying it, naming it, finding their place in it where they will live for the rest of their life. Everything they have learned about love they must now test out for themselves, for the first time. They have gained a voice and they discover they have something to say. They discover how alone they are. These are the people I write about in my stories. It would be a mistake to say I write *for* young adults, because I do not have any specific audience in mind when I write (at least, not an audience defined by terms of age or sex or nationality)."

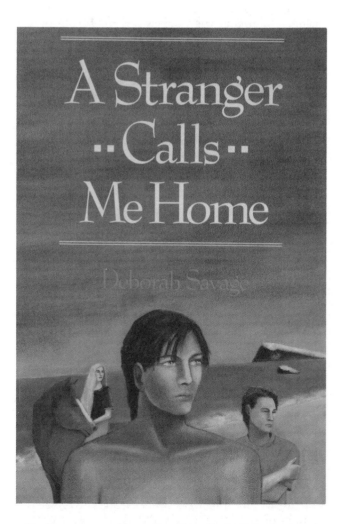

Paul's return to his native New Zealand leads to a journey with his half-Maori friend Simon and a love triangle with a mysterious girl. (Cover illustration by Joanne Pendola.)

SCHEFFRIN-FALK, Gladys 1928-

■ Personal

Born August 15, 1928, in Atlantic City, NJ; daughter of Michael (a tailor) and Eva (a seamstress; maiden name, Krawatsky) Scheffrin; married Herbert Falk (in public relations), December 16, 1977; children: Werner Alfredo Padilla, Eugenie Moody Weber, Charles Falk, Michael Bagley. *Education:* City College of the City University of New York, B.A., 1967; attended Rutgers University, Brooklyn College of the City University of New York, and New School for Social Research. *Politics:* Conservative liberal. *Religion:* Agnostic. *Hobbies and other interests:* Playing violin, hiking, travel, writing poetry, reading.

■ Addresses

Home—79 Choate Ln., Pleasantville, NY 10570.

■ Career

Secretary for Howard D. H. Brown, New York City, 1949-57; Kings County Hospital, Brooklyn, NY, medical caseworker, 1967-68; Bellevue Hospital, New York City, medical caseworker, 1968-87; Vantage Press, New York City, apprentice copy editor, 1988-90; New York Foundation for Senior Citizens, New York City, case manager, 1990-92; writer. Founded and led Ludlow St. Writers' Workshop, 1970-72; helped establish Washington Squares (writers' workshop), 1982.

■ Awards, Honors

Another Celebrated Dancing Bear was named one of the *New York Times* Ten Best Illustrated Books, 1991.

■ Writings

Another Celebrated Dancing Bear, illustrated by Barbara Garrison, Scribner, 1991.

Also author of *When the Wind Howls.* Work represented in anthologies. Contributor to periodicals, including *New Mexico Quarterly Review.*

■ Work in Progress

Riff-Raff: The Making of a Social Worker, a nonfiction book, completion expected in 1994; a novel, tentatively titled *Writer, Editor, Scholar, Murderer.*

■ Sidelights

Gladys Scheffrin-Falk told *SATA:* "When my eighth-grade English teacher said that I should publish my writings, she spawned my dream of writing a novel, making a fortune, and thereby rescuing my family from hardship.

"One of the younger members to be accepted into Hiram Haydn's novel workshop at the New School for

Social Research, I completed a seven-hundred-page first novel, began a second, and was referred to an agent. But when I finished the second novel, this one about three generations of women, she and two other agents turned it down. Discouraged, I put both aside and seemed at that point to have lost the belief I had that I could write novels and that I could write them well enough to sell them.

"Now that I have learned a little about the literary world, I have concluded that I should have continued to market both novels. An artist friend induced me to try my hand at a picture book, and an editor at Crown persuaded me to convert it into a full-length book. Since fantasy seems to have regained acceptance in the field of children's literature, *When the Wind Howls* is again making the rounds. I did finally sell a picture book, *Another Celebrated Dancing Bear.*

"I have retired and am writing other picture books, short stories, and novels. Even more importantly, I am enjoying sleeping later and visiting with my four children and my grandchild at a less hectic pace."

*   *   *

SCHMIDT, Lynette 1952-

■ Personal

Born July 26, 1952, in Britton, SD; daughter of Kenneth R. (a tool grinder) and Eileen (a bank clerk; maiden name, Hall) Schmidt; married Richard Arndt, June 5, 1971 (marriage ended, December, 1973); married Michael Yencho, September 9, 1993; children: (first marriage) Noel Grady. *Education:* Mankato Area Vocational Technical Institute, studied under Rodney Furan, graduated with honors, 1971; attended Minneapolis

LYNETTE SCHMIDT

College of Art and Design, 1975. *Politics:* Liberal Democrat.

■ Addresses

Home and office—931 Portland Ave., St. Paul, MN 55104.

■ Career

Artist and illustrator. Free-lance artist, 1970-72; Josten's, Red Wing, MN, staff artist, 1972-74; Commons House School, Minneapolis, MN, art instructor and free-lance artist, 1974-76; Llewellyn Publications, St. Paul, MN, art director, 1976-78; *Minneapolis Star,* Minneapolis, staff illustrator, 1978-82; free-lance illustrator, 1982—. Teacher of advanced commercial art, Duluth Art Institute, 1990-91. Costume and set designer for the Colder by the Lake comedy group (Duluth, MN) and the Duluth Ballet. Designer of sculpture and other products for "collectables" companies, such as Bradford, Goebel, Hamilton Group, Lance, Lenox, and Southpaw Productions. *Exhibitions:* One-artist shows include Owatonna Arts Council, 1975, 1983; Cornucopia Gallery, Minneapolis, 1976; St. Paul Gnostica Books, 1977; Buckley Gallery, 1978; patron Jeanne Campbell's private home, 1978, 1979; YWCA Urban Center, 1980; Duluth Depot Museum, 1986; Art Dock, 1988, 1990; Teachers Credit Union, 1989; Duluth Art Institute, 1989. *Member:* International Sculpture Center, American Lily Society, Minnesota Artist's Association, Minnesota Citizens for the Arts, Graphic Artist's Guild.

■ Awards, Honors

Lambda Award, Best Children's Book Illustrator, 1992.

■ Illustrator

Carole Garbuny Vogel and Kathryn Allen Golkner, *The Dangers of Strangers,* Dillon Press, 1983.
Johnny Valentine, *The Duke Who Outlawed Jelly Beans and Other Stories,* Alyson, 1991.
Daddy Machine, Alyson, 1992.
The Day They Put a Tax on Rainbows, Alyson, 1992.

■ Work in Progress

Illustrations for *Tangle Fairy,* by Margaret Davis, and *Peaches, the Dragon,* by Christopher Cook. Contributor to *Dragon Hunt,* a fundraising book for North Shore Theatre in Duluth.

■ Sidelights

Lynette Schmidt told *SATA:* "My career is always in the position of straddling survival work and more experimental work I consider my own. The latter always seemed to need support from the former, and for ten years I never expected the two could be the same. However, in 1979 I started working for the Minneapolis *Star* where I was given a story and expected to illustrate

Schmidt's intricate designs highlight Johnny Valentine's parable *The Duke Who Outlawed Jelly Beans.*

it in a way that appealed to the public. Now as a free-lancer I have received creative assignments from Alyson Publications.

"I have many interests and do a lot of things for 'the experience.' It adds to the character of my work when I can feel what something is like as well as see it. For example, I go to rock concerts in the rain and mud one day, and the next I might be at the Pittock mansion having tea with a friend while listening to chamber music. Like most people, I think that keeping oneself physically fit helps performance in any task. I work out on a regular basis and I study martial arts. I have a garden where I can watch the birds and animals, and the flowers often serve as a reference.

"My studio is on an acre of property on the north shore of Lake Superior. To have eight paintings and several sculptures in progress at the same time is normal. I live in the same space in which I work, and the studio seems to have split up into sections naturally. There is the sculpting area, the drawing board area where things get started and often finished, the larger painting area and airbrush area, office space, and kitchenette with a bed above it. That's all I need.

"These days the hardest part of being an artist is to remember myself. I think every artist will ask him- or

herself at some time or another, 'why am I doing this?' Is it for money and business? Or is one driven to live and understand, and, more importantly, contribute to our society? Sometimes it seems society does not care. As technology progresses, can we maintain an appreciation for what we have done? I think so, as long as there is still art of every kind."

*   *   *

SCHNEIDER, Elisa
See KLEVEN, Elisa

*   *   *

SCHWARZ, Adele Aron
See GREENSPUN, Adele Aron

*   *   *

SHANE, Harold Gray 1914-1993

OBITUARY NOTICE—See index for *SATA* sketch: Born August 11, 1914, in Milwaukee, WI; died July 12, 1993, in Bloomington, IN. Educator and author. The author of numerous books and hundreds of articles, Shane specialized in education, penning works on such subjects as administration, linguistics, child development, international education, and the evaluation of teaching curriculums. A graduate of the University of Wisconsin, Shane completed his master's and doctoral degrees at Ohio State University. He began his career in 1935, teaching elementary school for five years. He went on to work as a college professor for several years, a school superintendent, a professor of education, and, from 1959 to 1965, dean of the School of Education at Indiana University. He continued to teach at the university until his retirement in 1983 as professor emeritus. Shane began to write during his high school years and continued throughout his life, including during his four-year term in the U.S. Navy from 1943 to 1946, when he authored naval textbooks and manuals. Shane also wrote children's books, some of which were coauthored with his first wife, Ruth, and found success in the field: *The New Baby,* published in 1948, has sold more than twenty-five million copies, and *The Twins: The Story of Two Little Girls Who Look Alike,* was a popular book in 1955. Other books authored or edited by Shane include *Linguistics and the Classroom Teacher: Some Implications for Instruction in the Mother Tongue, Guiding Human Development: The Counselor and Teacher in the Elementary School, Learning for Tomorrow,* and *Microcomputers and Education.* For his work Shane received two Educational Press Association Awards for educational journalism, and twice won the Enoch Pratt Memorial Library Outstanding Education Book of the Year Award.

OBITUARIES AND OTHER SOURCES:

BOOKS

Who's Who in the Midwest, 23rd edition, Marquis, 1992.

PERIODICALS

Chicago Tribune, July 14, 1993, p. B11; July 18, 1993, section 6, p. 2.
Los Angeles Times, July 14, 1993, p. A14.
New York Times, July 16, 1993, p. D20.
Washington Post, July 14, 1993, p. C9.

*   *   *

SIROIS, Allen L. 1950-

■ Personal

Born March 14, 1950, in Bridgeport, CT; son of Louis A. (an industrial engineer) and Mildred (a homemaker; maiden name, Hoffman) Sirois; married Linda Katherine Jackson, June, 1977 (divorced); married Paula Robin Warsh (a medical editor), October 19, 1991; children: Daniel, Kira. *Education:* Attended University of Bridgeport, 1968-70. *Religion:* Pagan. *Hobbies and other interests:* Writing, reading, music, cooking, playing drums.

■ Addresses

Home—Hopewell Junction, NY. *Agent*—William Morris Agency, 1350 Avenue of the Americas, New York, NY 10019.

■ Career

Compu-Teach, Inc., New Haven, CT, art director, 1983-85; Prodigy Services, White Plains, NY, senior graphic artist, 1985—. *Member:* Science Fiction and Fantasy Writers of America (SFFWA), Author's Guild, Society of Children's Book Writers and Illustrators.

■ Writings

Dinosaur Dress Up, illustrated by Janet Sweet, William Morrow/Tambourine Books, 1992.

Also author of short stories; contributor of illustrations to magazines and journals.

■ Sidelights

In spite of the problems facing today's world and its people, Allen L. Sirois believes that writing fiction—story telling—is essential. Dreams are "awakened and energized" through story telling, and this, as Sirois told *SATA,* must happen at an early age. He concluded, "Writing needs no other justification than that fiction has the potential to illuminate at least one young mind, somewhere, and to help that mind develop the will and courage necessary to take the first tentative steps down the road to self-realization. What could be more honorable than to have helped someone to learn to think?"

*   *   *

SLAVIN, Bill 1959-

■ Personal

Born February 12, 1959, in Belleville, Ontario, Canada; son of William Joseph Vincent (an electrician and teacher) and Dorothy Barry (Rugg) Slavin; married Esperanca Melo (a book designer), June 2, 1990. *Education:* Attended Sheridan College, Oakville, Ontario, Canada.

■ Addresses

Home—Box 431, Millbrook, Ontario, Canada LOA 1GO.

■ Career

Tele-Direct, Toronto, Ontario, Canada, layout artist, 1978-81; General Store Publishing House, Burnstown, Ontario, art director, 1982-87; free-lance illustrator, 1988—. *Member:* Canadian Society of Children's Authors, Illustrators, and Performers.

■ Illustrator

PICTURE BOOKS

Paulette Bourgeois, *Too Many Chickens!,* Little, Brown, 1990.
Bob King, *Sitting on the Farm,* Orchard Books, 1991.
Ben Brooks, *Lemonade Parade,* Albert Whitman, 1991.
Ethan Miles, *Otto's Tricks,* Silver, Burdett & Ginn, 1991.

ALLEN L. SIROIS

BILL SLAVIN

Nathan Zimerman, *How the Second Grade Got $8,205.50 to Visit the Statue of Liberty,* Albert Whitman, 1992.

Kathleen Tucker (reteller), *The Cat Came Back,* Albert Whitman, 1992.

Amanda Lewis and Tim Wynne-Jones, *Rosie in Stratford,* Kids Can Press, 1994.

NONFICTION

Brian McFarlane, *Hockey: The Book for Kids,* Kids Can Press, 1990.

Catherine Ross, *Circles,* Addison-Wesley, 1992.

Linda Granfield, *Extra! Extra!,* Addison-Wesley, 1993.

■ Adaptations

The Cat Came Back and *Sitting on the Farm* were adapted as computer books by Literatek, 1993.

■ Sidelights

"I have been drawing since I can remember, and have wanted to illustrate books for just about as long," Bill Slavin told *SATA*. "Grade three was an important year, because it was when I produced my first illustrated book, 'Zok the Caveman.' This was such a success that I promptly followed it up with a sequel, 'The Adventures of Black Cloud, Son of Zok.' I continued to write and illustrate books throughout public school, as well as

draw profusely. I graduated to pen and ink at a fairly early age, a medium which is still my favorite. (Fortunately, my mother was a tolerant person and did not object too much to the many bottles of ink which I spilled on the living room carpet.) In high school I became interested in comic book art, and wrote and illustrated countless numbers of these, as well as producing a short-lived comic strip called *Rat Fink* for our local village weekly."

After graduating from high school Slavin attended Sheridan College, where he studied cartooning and graphic illustration. After two years of college Slavin began his career as a professional illustrator. He worked for several years as a commercial artist before illustrating *Too Many Chickens!,* and has since devoted most of his time to illustrating children's books. "It is work which I love," he stated, "and I consider myself one of the most fortunate people around to be working in this industry."

He continued: "Today I am living in paradise in an old farmhouse on the edge of the village of Millbrook. I live with my wife, Esperanca Melo, who is also an artist and is an integral part of all I do.... I tend to work quickly and impetuously at my art, but am trying to learn to slow down. Up until now I have had very little contact with the authors whose books I am illustrating, and I feel that that works well, allowing each party to have free reign on their creative vision. I put a lot of interpretation into the story that may be hindered if I found out what the author really intended!"

■ For More Information See

PERIODICALS

Booklist, September 15, 1992, p. 150.
Kirkus Reviews, December 1, 1992, p. 1509.

*   *   *

SMEE, Nicola 1948-

■ Personal

Born February 9, 1948, in Shrewesbury, Salop, England; daughter of Richard (a carpenter, antique restorer, and author) and Fara (a homemaker; maiden name, Bartlett) Gethin; married Michael Smee (an art lecturer), November 15, 1969; children: Oliver, Milo, Leo. *Education:* Attended Birmingham College of Arts. *Religion:* Roman Catholic.

■ Career

Author and illustrator. *Member:* Association of Illustrators.

■ Awards, Honors

Children's Book of the Year citations, Anderson Press/Children's Book Foundation, 1991, for *The Invitation,* and 1992, for *Finish the Story, Dad.*

NICOLA SMEE

■ Writings

SELF-ILLUSTRATED PICTURE BOOKS

Down in the Woods, Collins, 1985.
Beach Boy, Collins, 1987.
The Invitation, Collins, 1989, Little, Brown, 1991.
ABC, Collins, 1990.
Finish the Story, Dad, Simon & Schuster, 1991.
Teacher's Pet, HarperCollins, 1992.
Noah's Ark (six board books in "ark" box), Little, Brown, 1993.
The Tusk Fairy, Orchard Books, 1993.
Three Little Bunnies, Scholastic, in press.
Three Little Chicks, Scholastic, in press.

ILLUSTRATOR

Colin Stone, *The Legend of the Gnomes,* Chappell & Co., 1976.
Dorothea King, *Rex Q. C.,* Pavilion Books, 1983.
Diane Wilmer, *Benny: The Story of a Dog,* Collins, 1985.
Wilmer, *Benny and Football Match,* Collins, 1986.
Wilmer, *Benny and the Fair,* Collins, 1986.
Wilmer, *Benny and the Builders,* Collins, 1986.
Wilmer, *Benny and the Jumble Sale,* Collins, 1986.
Ruth Craft, *Wise Dog,* Collins, 1986.
Baby's First Year, Heinemann, 1987.
Craft, *Fancy Nancy,* Collins, 1988.
Wilmer, *Step by Step* (twelve book series), Albion Press/Macmillan, 1988.
Robert Robinson, *Going to the Dentist,* Conran Octopus/Mothercare, 1989.

Barbara Taylor Cork, *Going to School,* Conran Octopus/Mothercare, 1989.
My Birthday [and] *Animals* (includes activity book, wall chart, and story book), Carnival/Collins, 1989.
Judy Bastyra, *Busy Little Cook,* Conran Octopus, 1990.
Craft, *Something Old: Jets,* A. & C. Black, 1992.

■ Work in Progress

Three Little Elves and *Two Little Mice,* novelty puppet books for David Bennett Books; *A Christmas Story,* a novelty book for Orchard Books; illustrating *The Spangled Pandemonium,* an anthology of nonsense verse and stories for World International Publishing.

■ Sidelights

Nicola Smee is an illustrator and writer with many published picture and story books in her list of credits. A former student at the Birmingham College of Art, Smee began illustrating stories by other authors before trying her hand at writing. *Down in the Woods,* her first solo picture book, was commended by an *Observer* reviewer for the book's "admirable plot, pictures and text for [age] four to seven readers or listeners."

Two of Smee's books have been honored as Children's Books of the Year by the Children's Book Foundation: *The Invitation* in 1991, and *Finish the Story, Dad* in 1992. *The Invitation,* illustrated in cartoon style with balloons for dialogue, tells how Leo finds a surprise prize in his cereal box. It is an invitation to dine at the fanciest restaurant in town, which he and his parents quickly set out to enjoy. It is a lively look, from the child's perspective, of "what grown-ups do on Saturday night" with "brightly colored, motion-filled illustrations" of the eating and dancing, according to Ilene Cooper in her *Booklist* review.

In *Finish the Story, Dad,* Ruby wants her father to finish reading the bedtime story he has begun for her. When her father does not give in to her pleading, Ruby returns to her bed and dreams of animals in the jungle, asking each of them to tell her the ending to the interrupted story. "This is a charming little tale," commented a *Junior Bookshelf* reviewer. "The body language and facial expressions are so well observed, and the colours delightful." Like *The Invitation, Finish the Story, Dad* is illustrated in watercolor cartoons with stylized people and animals. Virginia E. Jeschelnig in *School Library Journal* observed that "[Smee's] colors are subdued with a sprinkling of pattern to add interest, but the soft hues make [*Finish the Story, Dad*] best for sharing one-on-one."

■ Works Cited

Cooper, Ilene, review of *The Invitation, Booklist,* March 15, 1990, p. 1459.
Review of *Down in the Woods, Observer,* April 7, 1985, p. 21.
Review of *Finish the Story, Dad, Junior Bookshelf,* December, 1991, p. 245.

Jeschelnig, Virginia E., review of *Finish the Story, Dad*, *School Library Journal*, December, 1991, p. 107.

■ For More Information See

PERIODICALS

Independent on Sunday, June 27, 1993.
Junior Bookshelf, October, 1990, p. 221.
Kirkus Reviews, September 1, 1991, p. 1169.
Practical Parenting, July, 1993.
School Library Journal, July, 1990, p. 64.

* * *

SMITH, Lane 1959-

■ Personal

Born August 25, 1959, in Tulsa, OK; son of Lewis (an accountant) and Mildred (Enlow) Smith. *Education:* California Art Center College of Design, B.F.A., 1983.

■ Addresses

Home—New York, NY. *Agent*—Edite Kroll, 12 Grayhurst Park, Portland, ME 04102.

■ Career

Illustrator and author. Free-lance illustrator, 1983—. Contributor of illustrations to periodicals, including *Rolling Stone, Time, Ms., Newsweek, New York Times, Atlantic*, and *Esquire*. *Exhibitions:* Works have been exhibited at Master Eagle Gallery, New York City; Brockton Children's Museum, Brockton, MA; Joseloff Gallery, Hartford, CT; and in the AIGA touring show.

■ Awards, Honors

New York Times Ten Best Illustrated Books of the Year citation, *School Library Journal* Best Book of the Year citation, *Horn Book* Honor List, American Library Association (ALA) Booklist/Editor's Choice List, and Silver Buckeye Award, all 1987, for *Halloween ABC;* Silver Medal, Society of Illustrators, *New York Times* Best Books of the Year citation, ALA Notable Children's Book citation, Maryland Black-Eyed Susan Picture Book Award, and *Parenting's* Reading Magic Award, all 1989, for *The True Story of the Three Little Pigs;* Golden Apple Award, Bratislava International Biennial of Illustrations, 1990, Silver Medal, Society of Illustrators, 1991, and first place, New York Book Show, all for *The Big Pets; Parent's Choice* Award for Illustration, *New York Times* Best Books of the Year citation, ALA Notable Children's Book citation, all 1991, for *Glasses—Who Needs 'Em?;* Caldecott Honor Book, *New York Times* Best Illustrated Books of the Year citation, *School Library Journal* Best Books of the Year citation, *Booklist* Children's Editors' "Top of the List" citation, and ALA Notable Children's Book citation, all 1992, for *The Stinky Cheese Man.*

LANE SMITH

■ Writings

SELF-ILLUSTRATED

Flying Jake, Macmillan, 1989.
The Big Pets, Viking, 1990.
Glasses—Who Needs 'Em?, Viking, 1991.
The Happy Hocky Family, Viking, 1993.

ILLUSTRATOR

Eve Merriam, *Halloween ABC*, Macmillan, 1987.
Jon Scieszka, *The True Story of the Three Little Pigs*, Viking, 1989.
Jon Scieszka, *The Stinky Cheese Man and Other Fairly Stupid Tales*, Viking, 1992.

ILLUSTRATOR; "TIME WARP TRIO" SERIES; WRITTEN BY JON SCIESZKA

Knights of the Kitchen Table, Viking, 1991.
The Not-So-Jolly Roger, Viking, 1991.
The Good, the Bad, and the Goofy, Viking, 1992.
Your Mother Was a Neanderthal, Viking, 1993.

■ Work in Progress

Illustrating *The Time Warp Trio Meet the XYZ Guys*, written by Jon Scieszka, the fifth installment in the "Time Warp Trio" series, for Viking.

■ Sidelights

Lane Smith's award-winning style of illustration captures a brand of irreverent humor that appeals to both school-aged children and adults. In both his self-illustrated works and his collaborations with author Jon Scieszka, Smith's work has been variously termed "goofy," "unconventional," and "dark," based on his exaggerated characters, unusual palette of colors, and visual jokes. The artist dismisses the idea that children cannot appreciate the parody and complex illustrations that fill his work, and also defends his use of "gross, elementary-school humor," saying in a *Horn Book* essay that "kids love it." Not only kids, but parents, teachers, and reviewers have come to love his illustrations; such success is evidenced in Smith's numerous awards, including a Caldecott Honor. Signe Wilkinson described Smith's appeal in her *New York Times Book Review* appraisal of his self-illustrated book, *Flying Jake:* "Smith's style offers a minor-key look at the world that is a welcome relief from the vast oversupply of C major art and morality found in many books for young children." Wilkinson further defended Smith's work in a review of *The Stinky Cheese Man and Other Fairly Stupid Tales* in *New York Times Book Review:* "While not conventionally beautiful, [Smith's illustrations] do what all good art must—create an alternate and believable universe."

Smith describes his childhood as a happy, stable one. He was born in Oklahoma, but he spent most of his childhood in the foothills of Corona, California with his parents and his brother Shane. "Shane and Lane. My mom thought this was funny," Smith told *SATA.* "Yeah, a real hoot. However, *her* brothers were named Dub, Cubby, Leo, and Billy-Joe! My dad's brothers were Tom and Jerry (this is the truth)!"

As a child, Smith developed a sense of both the fantastic and the absurd. During the summers, his family would travel back to Oklahoma. "Our family would take the old Route 66 highway," he recalled. "I think that's where my bizarre sense of design comes from. Once you've seen a 100-foot cement buffalo on top of a doughnut stand in the middle of nowhere, you're never the same."

Autumn Activities Spurred Imagination

Although such summers were memorable, Smith's favorite season as a child was autumn. He told *SATA:* "I *lived* for Halloween and I loved the old Universal Monster movies. Shane and I would watch them, then read each other horror stories with titles like 'Tales to Tremble By.' The foothills were full of dry bushes and desert trees, and in the fall we'd get a lot of creepy-looking tumbleweeds blowing through our backyard at night. I used to lay awake in bed at night and imagine what wild adventures might be happening in the hills."

Smith attended college at the California Art Center College of Design. To help pay for his tuition, he took a job as a janitor at Disneyland. "Only they didn't call it a janitor," he told *SATA,* "we were called 'custodial hosts.' One of my duties was to clean out the attractions at night. It was great to be left in the Haunted Mansion all alone. Another duty was to clean up after someone if they got sick on the Revolving Teacup ride. Like I said, it was great to be left in the Haunted Mansion all alone."

When he wasn't cleaning up the Haunted Mansion or the Revolving Teacup, Smith studied illustration, developing an interest in Pop Art and European illustration. "My instructors said, 'When you get out of school,

you're never going to find work in America,'" he recalled in an essay in *Horn Book.* "I was getting worried, but then the punk/new-wave movement came, and my work seemed to fit acceptably into that category."

A year after he graduated, Smith moved to New York City. He became a successful free-lance illustrator, and his work began to appear in magazines such as *Ms., Time,* and *Rolling Stone.* Shortly after he arrived in New York, Smith also made his first venture into children's books. In college, he had concentrated on drawing, and he decided to try to paint for a change. This new medium of oil painting was one that Smith would use successfully in all his children's books, even though reviewers have frequently misidentified his illustrations as watercolors or drawings. One of his first projects was a series of paintings depicting the letters of the alphabet, each inspired by his favorite holiday, Halloween. He eventually produced thirty paintings and submitted them to Macmillan.

The company was impressed with his work, and hired children's author Eve Merriam to write poems to accompany the illustrations. In *Horn Book,* Smith discussed his collaboration with Merriam: "I changed some of the artwork to fit some new poems she had written. I had *V* for 'Vampire,' and she came up with 'Viper,' which I liked a lot, because I could use the *V* for the viper's open mouth." The resulting book, *Halloween ABC,* was published in 1987. Reviewers enjoyed Smith's unique style of illustration. A *Horn Book* contributor declared that "Smith's illustrations are suitably mystical and surreal. They ... look as though they could have come from a witch's book of evil spells." And a *Publisher's Weekly* reviewer noted that Smith's "wickedly eerie paintings" perfectly complemented Merriam's text.

Partnership with Teacher Leads to Bestselling Book

In the mid-1980s, Smith met writer and teacher Jon Scieszka (pronounced "sheska"), with whom he has collaborated on several irreverent, satirical children's books. Their first work, 1989's *The True Story of the Three Little Pigs,* tells the traditional fairy tale from the wolf's point of view. In the Scieszka-Smith version of the story, Alexander T. Wolf, now imprisoned at the Pig Pen, tries to present himself as a victim of misunderstanding and media hype. He explains that he visited the pigs to borrow a cup of sugar. Unfortunately, he had a very bad cold, and the first two pigs' houses were very poorly built. Hence, whenever he sneezed, he blew their houses down. He also justified eating the pigs after he killed them, explaining that it would be foolish to let the meat go bad. In *Horn Book,* Smith described how his illustrations worked with Scieszka's story: "I think Jon thought of the wolf as a con artist trying to talk his way out of a situation. But I really believed the wolf, so I portrayed him with glasses and a little bow tie and tried to make him a sympathetic victim of circumstance."

Smith's illustrations help turn traditional fairy tales on their head; in his version of the story, a lonely couple makes a son out of smelly cheese before discovering they weren't *that* lonely. (Illustration by Smith from *The Stinky Cheese Man*, written by Jon Scieszka.)

Some reviewers, such as John Peters in *School Library Journal*, noted that the dark colors—and humor—of the book would make it a success with older children and adults. Peters particularly praised Smith's illustrations for the way the wolf's "juicy sneezes tear like thunderbolts through a dim, grainy world." Noting the "fetching and glib" tone of *The True Story of the Three Little Pigs*, a *Publishers Weekly* contributor commented that Smith's pictures "eschew realism," adding a modern flair to the tale. "Smith adds brilliant contemporary illustrations," declared Donnarae MacCann and Olga Richard in their *Wilson Library Journal* assessment. "Using minimal but subtly changing browns and ochers, he combines great variety of creative modes: fanciful, realist, surreal, cartoonish."

School-children and classroom teachers were especially receptive to *The True Story of the Three Little Pigs;* the book sold more than 600,000 copies. In a *Publishers Weekly* interview with Amanda Smith, the illustrator related how he was "stupefied when [the book] took off. We would go out on signings, and every other person there was a teacher, and they would talk about how they used the book for point-of-view writing. All of a sudden we were these young educators."

On their trips to schools, Scieszka and Smith began reading other fairy-tale satires that Scieszka had written prior to *The True Story of the Three Little Pigs*. The positive reception they received from students encouraged them to create a collection of such pieces in *The Stinky Cheese Man and Other Fairly Stupid Tales*. Scieszka discussed the origins of the duo's second book in an interview with Stephanie Zvirin in *Booklist:* "*The Stinky Cheese Man* was really a collaboration. I don't think there's any way to pick apart who did what. When Lane and I went out to visit schools ... I started reading the stories as fairy tales that *didn't* work. Lane would illustrate them as I spoke. Kids would really crack up."

Fractured Fairy Tales Earn Popularity and Caldecott Honors

A headline in *The New York Times Book Review* summed up *The Stinky Cheese Man:* "No Princes, No White Horses, No Happy Endings." One of the first stories in the book is about Chicken Licken, who runs around warning others that the sky is falling. Sure enough, animals are crushed when the not the sky, but the book's table of contents unexpectedly falls on them. Elsewhere other traditional tales are turned on their heads: the ugly duckling grows up to become an ugly duck, the frog prince turns out to be just a frog, and the story "The Princess and the Pea" is retitled "The Princess and the Bowling Ball." Smith's pictures carry characters in and out of each other's stories and even into such unexpected places as the endpapers and copyright notice, causing a *Publishers Weekly* reviewer to note that "the collaborators' hijinks are evident in every aspect of the book."

The Stinky Cheese Man was a hit with many reviewers and readers, receiving a prestigious Caldecott Honor for Smith's illustrations and appearing on several notable book lists. Wilkinson wrote: "Kids, who rejoice in anything stinky, will no doubt enjoy the blithe, mean-spirited anarchy of these wildly spinning stories." "Text and art work together for maximum comic impact," noted a *Publishers Weekly* critic. Claudia Logan in *Washington Post Book World* lauded Smith's work in both *The True Story of the Three Little Pigs* and *The Stinky Cheese Man:* "Observant readers will discover visual punnery in his small details, and he tries to make his pictures resemble 'small collections of things in a museum.' His characteristically dark [illustrations] are striking and distinctive." Logan also declared that *The Stinky Cheese Man* "is perhaps the best expression to date of the collaborative process between [Smith and Scieszka] and demonstrates how off-beat their humor can be."

Scieszka and Smith have also co-created the "Time Warp Trio" series, which is about three boys who, with the aid of a magical book, travel back in time and have assorted misadventures. The series includes the titles *Knights of the Kitchen Table, The Not-So-Jolly Roger, The Good, the Bad, and the Goofy,* and *Your Mother Was a Neanderthal.* Aimed at middle-grade readers, the books are designed to provide exciting and humorous stories for children who are looking for more than picture books, but are not yet ready for longer chapter books. The author and illustrator hoped that by basing their tales on traditional narratives or historical events, they would encourage kids to do further reading.

In *Knights of the Kitchen Table,* for example, the characters Joe, Sam, and Fred, are transported back to the medieval world of King Arthur's England. While there, the boys use their "magical" power to read and their quick-thinking to save the kingdom of Camelot by defeating an evil knight, a giant, and a dragon. The boys take a second time-journey in *The Not-So-Jolly Roger,* where they encounter the legendary pirate, Blackbeard. While *New York Times Book Review* contributor Elizabeth-Ann Sachs appreciated the "Time-Warp Trio" series, she felt that the first story was the strongest, stating that the sequel was "not nearly as much fun" as *Knights of the Kitchen Table.* Sachs also praised Smith's illustrations for the books, declaring the pictures to be "wonderfully menacing and appropriately silly." Trev Jones in *School Library Journal* enjoyed the first two books in the series, calling them "a true melding of word and pictures, and jolly good fun." Joe, Sam, and Fred travel to the wild west of the 19th-century United States in 1992's *The Good, the Bad, and the Goofy,* where they initially find themselves on a rather unexciting cattle drive. Soon, however, they must use their wits to survive various dangers, including cattle stampedes, an Indian attack, a cavalry charge, and a flash flood. Observing that the continuing "Time Warp Trio" series was sure to please readers, Gale W. Sherman in *School Library Journal* found that "Smith's typically zany pencil and charcoal drawings heighten the drama and enhance the wacky mood."

Smith's dark, collage-like oil paintings perfectly complement his tale of several children and their unusually large pets. (Illustration by the author from *The Big Pets*.)

Smith has also illustrated three of his own books: *Flying Jake, The Big Pets,* and *Glasses—Who Needs 'Em?* The first two books involve children's relationships with animals. In the wordless picture book *Flying Jake,* published in 1989, a boy tries to catch his pet bird after it escapes from its cage. He suddenly begins to fly, and before long, he finds himself frolicking among the birds. Some reviewers found the action of *Flying Jake* to be confusing, especially for younger readers. A *Publishers Weekly* contributor acknowledged that it takes some effort to follow the narrative, but felt that "the effort is amply repaid" in Smith's "jaunty, fanciful and energetic" pictures. Wilkinson expressed overall disappointment in the logic of the book, but admitted that Smith "has created a rich picture poem that gives readers of any age a certain feeling about flight among the birds."

Solo Projects Combine Humor and Fantasy

The Big Pets depicts a nighttime fantasy world in which children and gigantic animals happily co-exist. It begins with a little girl and her oversized cat playing in the Milk Pool, and goes on to present other enormous animals in such places as the Bone Gardens and the Hamster Holes. *Entertainment Weekly*'s Ken Tucker gave *The Big Pets* a glowing review: "*Pets* suggests that we all share the same sort of dreams and can delight in the spookiness and serenity of the night." A reviewer for *Publishers Weekly* wrote: "This fantastic story is enhanced with dark, jewel-like paintings that exhibit an almost phosphorescent glow."

As the title indicates, *Glasses—Who Needs 'Em?* is about a boy's reluctance to wear glasses—a theme Smith is very familiar with. He told *Publishers Weekly,* "I was fitted for glasses in the fifth grade, but I never really wore them—too geeky. My instructors thought I was pretty studious because I was in the front row all the time, but I was the only fifth grader with premature crow's feet—I couldn't see the board." In *Glasses,* the young patient's feeling that glasses are only for "dorks" disappears once his optometrist enlightens him about the multitude of remarkable spectacle-wearers in the world. Both the story and art for Smith's self-illustrated book were given praise by reviewers. "Smith demonstrates 20/20 vision for the sarcastic, zany humor that children adore," stated a *Publishers Weekly* contributor. Wendy Wasserstein, reviewing the book in *New York Times Book Review,* declared *Glasses* to be "one of those perfect children's books ... a breezy read toward an enlightened end and all the way there incredibly beautiful to look at."

In 1993, Smith published a fourth self-illustrated work, *The Happy Hocky Family,* which parodies the "Dick and Jane" stories familiar to beginning readers of the 1950s. "While poking fun at the genre, *The Happy Hocky Family* is actually an excellent choice for early readers," Steven Engelfried declared in *School Library Journal.* Smith told *SATA* that "*The Happy Hocky Family* is my favorite book to date. I am a big fan of 'hand separated' color books from the 1940s and 50s. I did this book in that style. Each of the colors was done on a separate plate by hand (as opposed to doing a color painting and then having it separated mechanically). I tried to emulate the look of those older books even more by printing the text and illustrations on recycled brown, aged-looking paper. The design was by Molly Leach, who has won acclaim for her innovative designs on *The Stinky Cheese Man, The Big Pets,* and *Glasses, Who Needs 'Em?,* among others."

Smith continues to divide his time between children's books and magazine work. "I don't consider myself a children's book illustrator, just an all-around illustrator," he stated in *Horn Book.* He added that his success in children's books has had an effect on his career. "I used to get all these assignments on murder and rape and the economy," he explained, "and now I get assigned topics such as childhood toys and children's phobias." When asked by Zvirin in *Booklist* whether he would continue to create works that use humor to turn traditional stories and ideas upside-down, Smith replied: "There are so many serious books out there and lots of people who do them really well. But there aren't many people who do really goofy work. It's so refreshing to see kids who really respond to funny stuff, and if that gets them to read ... "

The knowledge that he is getting kids to read is only one of the rewards that Smith receives by creating books for young readers. "I just love the print medium," Smith admitted in his *Horn Book* essay. "I always thought it would be kind of depressing to work for months on a painting and then just have it hang in somebody's house. I've sold some of the paintings from the books through children's art galleries, but I've decided not to do much of that, because I miss them too much. But I have a wonderful existence—I've been able to create the children's books that come naturally to me."

■ Works Cited

Review of *The Big Pets, Publishers Weekly,* December 21, 1990, p. 55.

Engelfried, Steven, review of *The Happy Hocky Family, School Library Journal,* August, 1993.

Review of *Flying Jake, Publishers Weekly,* February 12, 1988, p. 83.

Review of *Glasses—Who Needs 'Em?, Publishers Weekly,* August 9, 1991, p. 56.

Review of *Halloween ABC, Horn Book,* November/December, 1987, pp. 753-54.

Review of *Halloween ABC, Publishers Weekly,* July 24, 1987, p. 186.

Jones, Trev, review of *Knights of the Kitchen Table* and *The Not-So-Jolly Roger, School Library Journal,* August, 1991, p. 169.

Logan, Claudia, "Jingle Bells, Batman Smells," *Washington Post Book World,* December 6, 1992, p. 21.

MacCann, Donnarae, and Olga Richard, "Picture Books for Children," *Wilson Library Journal,* June, 1992, p. 118.

Peters, John, review of *The True Story of the Three Little Pigs, School Library Journal,* October, 1989, p. 108.

Sachs, Elizabeth-Ann, review of *Knights of the Kitchen Table* and *The Not-So-Jolly Roger, New York Times Book Review,* October 6, 1991, p. 23.

Sherman, Gale W., review of *The Good, the Bad, and the Goofy, School Library Journal,* July, 1992, p. 64.

Smith, Amanda, "Jon Scieszka and Lane Smith," *Publishers Weekly,* July 26, 1991, pp. 220-21.

Smith, Lane, "The Artist at Work," *Horn Book,* January-February, 1993, pp. 64-70.

Review of *The Stinky Cheese Man and Other Fairly Stupid Tales, Publishers Weekly,* September 28, 1992, pp. 79-80.

Review of *The True Story of the Three Little Pigs, Publishers Weekly,* July 28, 1989, p. 218.

Tucker, Ken, "Of Large Cats and Midnight Rambles," *Entertainment Weekly,* April 26, 1991, p. 71.

Wasserstein, Wendy, "One Spectacle after Another," *New York Times Book Review,* November 10, 1991, p. 54.

Wilkinson, Signe, review of *Flying Jake, New York Times Book Review,* June 12, 1988.

Wilkinson, Signe, "No Princes, No White Horses, No Happy Endings," *New York Times Book Review,* November 8, 1992, pp. 29, 59.

Zvirin, Stephanie, "Jon Scieszka and Lane Smith," *Booklist,* September 1, 1992, p. 57.

■ For More Information See

PERIODICALS

Bulletin of the Center for Children's Books, October, 1993, p. 58.

Horn Book, January/February, 1990, p. 58.

Kirkus Reviews, March 1, 1988, p. 369; August 1, 1991, pp. 1015-16.

New York Times Book Review, November 12, 1989, p. 27.

Publishers Weekly, May 17, 1991, p. 64; May 11, 1992, p. 72.

School Library Journal, June/July, 1988, p. 94; June, 1991, p. 91; August, 1991, p. 169; October, 1991, p. 105; October, 1993, p. 130.

*   *   *

SMOTHERS, Ethel Footman 1944-

■ Personal

Born April 5, 1944, in Camilla, GA; daughter of Ira Lee (a fruitpicker) and Ethel (a maid; maiden name, Jackson) Footman; married Ernest Lee Smothers (a shipping clerk), July 15, 1964; children: Delsey, Darla, Dana, Dion. *Education:* Grand Rapids Community College, A.A., 1981. *Politics:* Democrat. *Religion:* Seventh Day Adventist.

■ Addresses

Home—Grand Rapids, MI.

ETHEL FOOTMAN SMOTHERS

■ Career

Amway Corp., Ada, MI, telephone order clerk, 1980-85, service specialist, 1985-92; author and speaker, 1992—. *Member:* Society of Children's Book Writers and Illustrators, Friends of the Library.

■ Writings

Down in the Piney Woods, Knopf, 1992.

■ Work in Progress

Moriah's Pond, a sequel to *Down in the Piney Woods;* a children's historical fiction novel set in 1865.

■ Sidelights

Set in the rural South during the 1950s, *Down in the Piney Woods* is the story of Annie Rye, a ten-year-old sharecropper's daughter. During the course of the novel, Annie must confront not only the racism of a neighboring white sharecropper, but her own feelings of resentment and hostility when her three older half-sisters move in with her family. Critics praised Footman's work; a reviewer for *Publishers Weekly* stated, "This zesty first novel is chock-a-block with fresh, authentic language," and Hazel Rochman, writing in *Booklist,* added, "The pleasure is in the rhythm of the narrative voice, in the sense of place, and in the characters."

Ethel Footman Smothers told *SATA:* "*Down in the Piney Woods* is drawn from childhood memories and imagination. And when I decided to tell my story, I felt that Piney Woods rhythm in my head, with the black English and short, choppy sentences. That's the language of my childhood, and of my people. That uniqueness—that real flavor of our ancestry—must be preserved, or our children—all children—will be deprived of a rare richness that never can be recaptured. You see, it's not just black history. It's American history."

■ Works Cited

Review of *Down in the Piney Woods, Publishers Weekly,* November 29, 1991.
Rochman, Hazel, review of *Down in the Piney Woods, Booklist,* December 15, 1991.

■ For More Information See

PERIODICALS

Publishers Weekly, July 13, 1992.
School Library Journal, December 16, 1991.

*   *   *

SMUCKER, Barbara (Claassen) 1915-

■ Personal

Born September 1, 1915, in Newton, KS; daughter of Cornelius W. (a banker) and Addie (Lander) Claassen; married Donovan E. Smucker (a minister and professor of sociology and religion), January 21, 1939; children: Timothy Lester, Thomas Cornelius, Rebecca Mary. *Education:* Kansas State University, B.S., 1936; attended Rosary College, 1963-65, and University of Waterloo, 1975-77. *Politics:* Democrat. *Religion:* Mennonite.

■ Addresses

Home—20 Pinebrook Dr., Bluffton, OH 45817.

■ Career

Public high school teacher of English and journalism in Harper, KS, 1937-38; *Evening Kansas Republican,* Newton, KS, reporter, 1939-41; Ferry Hall School, Lake Forest, IL, teacher, 1960-63; Lake Forest Bookstore, Lake Forest, bookseller, 1963-67; Kitchener Public Library, Kitchener, Ontario, children's librarian, 1969-77; Renison College, Waterloo, Ontario, head librarian, 1977-82. Has also worked as an interviewer for Gallup Poll. *Member:* American Association of University Women, Canadian Association of University Women, Canadian Society of Children's Authors, Illustrators and Performers, Canadian Writers Union, Children's Reading Roundtable of Chicago.

■ Awards, Honors

Named one of the fifty best books of all time in Canada, Children's Book Center, 1978, Canadian Library Association award runner-up, 1979, Brotherhood Award, National Conference of Christians and Jews, 1980, and top honors from All-Japan Library Committee and from Catholic Teachers Association of West Germany, all for *Underground to Canada;* children's literary award, Canada Council, and Ruth Schwartz Foundation Award, both 1980, both for *Days of Terror;* distinguished service award for children's literature, Kansas State University, 1980; senior honorary fellow, Renison College, 1982; D.Litt., honoris causa, University of Waterloo, 1986; D.H.L., Bluffton College, Bluffton, Ohio, 1989; Municipal Chapter of Toronto IODE Book Award, 1991, for *Incredible Jumbo.*

■ Writings

CHILDREN'S BOOKS

Henry's Red Sea, illustrated by Allan Eitzen, Herald Press, 1955.
Cherokee Run, illustrated by Eitzen, Herald Press, 1957.
Wigwam in the City, illustrated by Gil Miret, Dutton, 1966, published as *Susan,* Scholastic Book Services, 1978.
Underground to Canada, illustrated by Tom McNeely, Clarke, Irwin, 1977, published as *Runaway to Freedom: A Story of the Underground Railway,* Harper, 1978.
Days of Terror, illustrated by Kim La Fave, Clarke, Irwin, 1979.
Amish Adventure, Clarke, Irwin, 1983.
White Mist, Clarke, Irwin, 1985.
Jacob's Little Giant, Viking, 1987.
Incredible Jumbo, Viking, 1989.
Garth and the Mermaid, Viking, 1992.

OTHER

Also author of oratorio *The Abiding Place,* music by Ester Wiebe, produced in Strasbourg, France, 1984. Contributor of articles to *American Educator Encyclopedia.* Smucker's manuscript collection is housed in the Kerlan Collection at the University of Minnesota and in the Doris Lewis Rare Book Room, University of Waterloo Library, Ontario. Her books have been published in sixteen countries and translated into French, German, Japanese, Swedish, Spanish, Dutch, and Danish.

■ Sidelights

Canadian author Barbara Smucker is best known for her well-researched historical fiction for young adults. She often writes about important events that have been overlooked by other authors, such as the underground railroad that led slaves to freedom in Canada in *Underground to Canada,* and the vast immigration of Russian Mennonites to the United States and Canada in *Days of Terror.* Many of her books have some kind of personal significance; for example, her grandfather was involved in the evacuation of Mennonites and the author herself was very involved in the civil rights

BARBARA SMUCKER

movement. With her careful research and strong character development, Smucker has been able to bring new dimensions of history alive, while showing that it is the strength of her characters' convictions that bring them through difficult times.

Smucker was born in Kansas in 1915, the granddaughter of a Mennonite family who had come to America from East Prussia. She grew up reading and loving books, including *Alice in Wonderland* and *Anne of Green Gables,* while hanging out at her local library. "I would never have dreamed that someday I would write children's books, live in Canada, and speak to schoolchildren in the Anne of Green Gables School on Prince Edward Island," Smucker related in her *Something about the Author Autobiography Series* (*SAAS*) essay.

Because her mother was having difficulty keeping up with four young children, the family hired Ella Underwood, a widowed black woman, to take care of them. Smucker would listen to the entrancing stories Underwood told her, many of them about the days of slavery. These tales were to prove important to Smucker in her career: "Years later, when I wrote my book *Underground to Canada,*" she commented in *SAAS*, "I could hear [Ella's] voice and the way she pronounced words."

In the sixth grade, Smucker decided she wanted to be a writer. This happened when her teacher gave the class an assignment to write an original fairy tale. Smucker's was considered to be one of the best. "From then on, I was hooked on writing," Smucker remarked in *SAAS.* The next year, Smucker's life was greatly changed when she became ill with rheumatic fever. After weeks of illness, her fever broke, but she was left with an enlarged heart and a heart murmur. An expert was called in to provide a cure and he suggested that Smucker be put to bed for a year. While this might have been a great tragedy for other children, Smucker used the time to read the classics—from Charles Dickens to Charlotte Bronte.

After finishing high school, Smucker attended the local Bethel College for a year, then went to Kansas State University to study journalism. A year after graduation, she obtained a job at the Newton *Evening Kansas Republican.* She was thrilled to actually have a position as a "real writer." Excitement came when she was granted interviews with movie stars who happened to be travelling by rail from coast to coast. One time, she interviewed a young man named Donovan Smucker, a Mennonite who had come to Kansas to work at Bethel College. Smitten with him, Smucker travelled on a university summer course to Russia, where he was one of the guides. The two were married in 1939.

The next few years of the young couple's life were busy—they moved many times and had three children. They ended up living semi-permanently near Chicago in an interracial cooperative community. While there, a neighbor told Smucker an incredible story about how a thousand Mennonite refugees had escaped from Russia to Paraguay after World War II. The story was so entrancing that Smucker's three small children didn't stir during the two-hour narrative. Realizing that this story should be captured for children, Smucker created a fictionalized account of it in her first book, *Henry's Red Sea.*

In 1967, Smucker's husband was asked to become president of an all-black Presbyterian college in Mississippi, while she was offered a position as the first white teacher in a nearby all-black high school. The couple decided to take on this challenge, despite the threat of racial unrest. Smucker learned a great deal from the students there, especially from one girl who told her that they could never understand each other because Smucker felt with a "white" heart. "I was to use this material many years later when I wrote my book, *Underground to Canada,*" Smucker pointed out in *SAAS.* The Smuckers left after tension increased following the assassination of Martin Luther King, Jr, in 1968.

In 1969, Smucker's husband accepted an offer to teach at Conrad Grebel College, a Mennonite school in Ontario, Canada. The couple was thrilled to be involved in a Mennonite community and to be living in a new country. Smucker took a job in a local public library and, disappointed with the lack of children's literature with Canadian content, as well as any literature on the

Canadian cause in fighting slavery, Smucker wrote *Underground to Canada.* This work recounts the story of Julilly, Liza, and Lester, three slaves who run away from their cruel master to find freedom in Canada. One of Smucker's most popular books, it has been translated into many languages, including French, German and Japanese. It was also the subject of an essay contest for Japanese junior high school age students.

"At that time," Smucker wrote in *SAAS,* "my mind became filled with historical stories clamoring to be unearthed and turned into fiction." The next book she researched hit close to home—it was about the exodus of twenty thousand Mennonites from Russia in the late 1900s and their subsequent lives in the United States and Canada. Smucker had vivid memories of her grandfather wanting to help these people. *Days of Terror* describes the tragedies suffered by the Mennonites in their homeland and their eventual journey to freedom. Cory Bieman Davies says in *Canadian Children's Literature* that the book represents "Smucker's attempt to keep strong within the larger Canadian community her own Mennonite heritage and faith, and to contribute

In her first novel, *Henry's Red Sea,* Smucker brings to life the historical journey of Russian Mennonites to Canada after World War II. (Cover illustration by Allan Eitzen.)

strengthening Mennonite strands to multicultural Canadian peoplehood."

After this book, Smucker took a look at life on an Amish farm in *Amish Adventure,* probed the story of Indians removed from their land in *White Mist,* chronicled the life of a boy who raises the endangered Giant Canada Geese in *Jacob's Little Giant,* and provided a fictionalized account of P. T. Barnum's famous elephant who was killed in a Canadian railway accident in *Incredible Jumbo.*

"I write for young people because I like their fresh response, buoyant enthusiasm, and honest frankness," Smucker wrote in *Twentieth Century Children's Writers.* With her ability to bring historical events to life through fictional, but believable characters, Smucker has become a well-known name in her field. She moved back to the United States in 1993, and retains dual Canadian-American citizenship. She adds modestly in *SAAS* that "hopefully my books will add positively to [a child's] act of growing."

■ Works Cited

Davies, Cory Bieman, "Remembrance and Celebration: Barbara Smucker's Days of Terror," *Canadian Children's Literature,* Number 25, 1982, pp. 18-25.

Smucker, Barbara Claassen, essay in *Something about the Author Autobiography Series,* Volume 11, Gale, 1991, pp. 321-335.

Twentieth-Century Children's Writers, 3rd edition, St. James Press, 1989, pp. 902-903.

■ For More Information See

BOOKS

Children's Literature Review, Volume 10, Gale, 1986.

Egoff, Sheila, and Judith Saltman, *New Republic of Childhood: A Critical Guide to Canadian Children's Literature in English,* Oxford University Press, 1990.

PERIODICALS

Canadian Children's Literature, Number 22, 1981; Number 56, 1989; Number 67, 1992.

Globe and Mail (Toronto), November 30, 1985.

In Review, fall, 1977.

Mennonite Quarterly Review, January, 1981.

New York Times, March 3, 1991.

Saturday Night, November, 1979.

*   *   *

SOBOL, Rose 1931-

■ Personal

Born October 25, 1931, in New York, NY; daughter of Maurice (a manufacturer) and Lillian (Himoff) Tiplitz; married Donald J. Sobol (a writer), August 14, 1953; children: Diane, Glenn (deceased), Eric, John. *Education:* Brandeis University, B.A., 1955. *Politics:* Democrat. *Hobbies and other interests:* Tennis, cycling, gardening, camping, travel.

■ Addresses

Home—Miami, FL.

■ Career

Bendix Aviation, Teterboro, NJ, engineer, 1953-56; Computer Usage, New York City, programmer, 1956-57; Beth Am Library, Miami, FL, librarian, 1970—; writer.

■ Writings

(With husband, Donald J. Sobol) *First Book of Stocks and Bonds,* Franklin Watts, 1963.
Woman Chief (fictionalized biography), Dial, 1976.
(With D. J. Sobol) *Encyclopedia Brown's Book of Strange but True Crimes,* Scholastic, 1991.

■ Work in Progress

A mystery novel.

■ Sidelights

Best known for *Woman Chief,* which, according to the *Bulletin of the Center for Children's Books,* is "sound as a biography, and ... gives a sympathetic and detailed picture of the Plains Indians," Rose Sobol is not a full-time writer. Sobol once confessed, "Writing is terribly painful for me, but research is my joy. I feel I can only indulge in research if I justify any intensive project by writing a book." She also remarked, "As a librarian, I find gaps in children's literature, yet these areas usually do not motivate me. My own interests are the prime movers in my writing." *Woman Chief,* published in 1976, explores the Crow Indian culture through an invented biography of a Crow warrior and chief.

Sobol "grew up with books." She told *SATA,* "I was a reader, an engineer, a wife, a frequent mother, and a librarian before I became a sometime writer. Of my three books for young readers, two were written with my husband, a professional author."

Sobol's interests include tennis, cycling, camping, and travel. She noted, "I have traveled extensively throughout the United States and Europe, and have discovered after three trips to England that I am, indeed, an anglophile."

The author explained to *SATA* in the fall of 1992, "A fourth manuscript has been delayed by Hurricane Andrew. We are still in the process of scrambling for roofers, carpenters, etc. Plotting and research have been put on hold."

■ Works Cited

Review of *Woman Chief, Bulletin of the Center for Children's Books,* April, 1977.

* * *

STINE, Jovial Bob
See STINE, R(obert) L(awrence)

* * *

STINE, R(obert) L(awrence) 1943-
(Jovial Bob Stine; pseudonyms: Eric Affabee, Zachary Blue)

■ Personal

Born October 8, 1943, in Columbus, OH; son of Lewis (a retired shipping manager) and Anne (Feinstein) Stine; married Jane Waldhorn, (owner/managing director of Parachute Press), June 22, 1969; children: Matthew Daniel. *Education:* Ohio State University, B.A. in English, 1965; graduate study at New York University, 1966-67. *Religion:* Jewish. *Hobbies and other interests:* Swimming, watching old movie classics from the 1930's and 1940's, reading, especially P.G. Wodehouse novels.

R. L. STINE

■ Addresses

Home—New York, NY.

■ Career

Social Studies teacher at a junior high school in Columbus, OH, 1965-66; writer for several magazines in New York City, 1966-1968; *Junior Scholastic* Magazine, New York City, assistant editor, 1968-71; Scholastic, Inc., New York City, editor of *Search* Magazine, 1972-75, editor/creator of *Bananas* (magazine), 1975-84, editor/creator of *Maniac* (magazine), 1984-85; freelance writer of books for children and young adults, 1982—; head writer for *Eureeka's Castle*, Nickelodeon cable television network. *Member:* Mystery Writers of America.

■ Awards, Honors

Childrens' Choice Awards for several novels, American Library Association.

■ Writings

JUVENILE

The Time Raider, illustrations by David Febland, Scholastic, Inc., 1982.
The Golden Sword of Dragonwalk, illustrations by Febland, Scholastic, Inc., 1983.
Horrors of the Haunted Museum, Scholastic, Inc., 1984.
Instant Millionaire, illustrations by Jowill Woodman, Scholastic, Inc., 1984.
Through the Forest of Twisted Dreams, Avon, 1984.
Indiana Jones and the Curse of Horror Island, Ballantine, 1984.
Indiana Jones and the Giants of the Silver Tower, Ballantine, 1984.
Indiana Jones and the Cult of the Mummy's Crypt, Ballantine, 1985.
The Badlands of Hark, illustrations by Bob Roper, Scholastic, Inc., 1985.
The Invaders of Hark, Scholastic, Inc., 1985.
Demons of the Deep, illustrations by Fred Carrillo, Golden Books, 1985.
Challenge of the Wolf Knight (Wizards and Warriors Series), Avon, 1985.
James Bond in Win, Place, or Die, Ballantine, 1985.
Cavern of the Phantoms, Avon, 1986.
Operation: Deadly Decoy, Ballantine, 1986.
Jungle Raid (G.I. Joe Series), Ballantine, 1988.

YOUNG ADULT NOVELS

Blind Date, Scholastic, Inc., 1986.
Twisted, Scholastic, Inc., 1987.
Broken Date (Crosswinds Series), Simon & Schuster, 1988.
The Baby-sitter, Scholastic, Inc., 1989.
Phone Calls, Archway, 1990.
How I Broke up with Ernie, Archway, 1990.
Curtains, Archway, 1990.
The Boyfriend, Scholastic, Inc., 1990.
Beach Party, Scholastic, Inc., 1990.

Stine turned from humor to horror with the creation of his "Fear Street" series for young adults. (Cover illustration by Bill Schmidt.)

Snowman, Scholastic, Inc., 1991.
The Girlfriend, Scholastic, Inc., 1991.
Baby-sitter II, Scholastic, Inc., 1991.
Beach House, Scholastic, Inc., 1992.
Hit and Run, Scholastic, Inc., 1992.
Hitchhiker, Scholastic, Inc., 1993.
Baby-sitter III, Scholastic, Inc., 1993.
The Dead Girl Friend, Scholastic, Inc., 1993.
Halloween Night, Scholastic, 1993.

"FEAR STREET" SERIES

The New Girl, Archway, 1989.
The Surprise Party, Archway, 1990.
The Stepsister, Archway, 1990.
Missing, Archway, 1990.
Halloween Party, Archway, 1990.
The Wrong Number, Archway, 1990.
The Sleepwalker, Archway, 1991.
Ski Weekend, Archway, 1991.
Silent Night, Archway, 1991.
The Secret Bedroom, Archway, 1991.
The Overnight, Archway, 1991.
Lights Out, Archway, 1991.
Haunted, Archway, 1991.
The Fire Game, Archway, 1991.

Prom Queen, Archway, 1992.
The Knife, Archway, 1992.
First Date, Archway, 1992.
The Best Friend, Archway, 1992.
Sunburn, Archway, 1993.
The Cheater, Archway, 1993.

"FEAR STREET: SUPER CHILLER" SERIES

Party Summer, Archway, 1991.
Goodnight Kiss, Archway, 1992.
Silent Night 2, Archway, 1992.
Broken Hearts, Archway, 1993.

"FEAR STREET: CHEERLEADERS" SERIES

The First Evil, Archway, 1992.
The Second Evil, Archway, 1992.
The Third Evil, Archway, 1992.

"FEAR STREET SAGA" SERIES

The Betrayal, Archway, 1993.
The Secret, Archway, 1993.
The Burning, Archway, 1993.

"SPACE CADETS" SERIES

Jerks-in-Training, Scholastic, Inc., 1991.
Losers in Space, Scholastic, Inc., 1991.
Bozos on Patrol, Scholastic, Inc., 1992.

"GOOSEBUMPS" SERIES

Welcome to Dead House, Scholastic, Inc., 1992.
Stay out of the Basement, Scholastic, Inc., 1992.
Monster Blood, Scholastic, Inc., 1992.
Say Cheese and Die, Scholastic, Inc., 1992.
The Curse of the Mummy's Tomb, Scholastic, Inc., 1993.
Let's Get Invisible, Scholastic, Inc., 1993.
Night of the Living Dummy, Scholastic, Inc., 1993.
The Girl Who Cried Monster, Scholastic, Inc., 1993.
Welcome to Camp Nightmare, Scholastic, Inc., 1993.
The Ghost Next Door, Scholastic, Inc., 1993.
The Haunted Mask, Scholastic, Inc., 1993.

JUVENILES; UNDER NAME JOVIAL BOB STINE

The Absurdly Silly Encyclopedia and Flyswatter, illustrations by Bob Taylor, Scholastic Book Services, 1978.
How to Be Funny: An Extremely Silly Guidebook, illustrations by Carol Nicklaus, Dutton, 1978.
The Complete Book of Nerds, illustrations by Sam Viviano, Scholastic Book Services, 1979.
The Dynamite Do-It-Yourself Pen Pal Kit, illustrations by Jared Lee, Scholastic Book Services, 1980.
Dynamite's Funny Book of the Sad Facts of Life, illustrations by Lee, Scholastic Book Services, 1980.
Going Out! Going Steady! Going Bananas!, photographs by Dan Nelken, Scholastic Book Services, 1980.
The Pigs' Book of World Records, illustrations by Peter Lippman, Random House, 1980.
(With wife, Jane Stine) *The Sick of Being Sick Book,* edited by Ann Durrell, illustrations by Nicklaus, Dutton, 1980.
Bananas Looks at TV, Scholastic Book Services, 1981.

The Beast Handbook, illustrations by Taylor, Scholastic Book Services, 1981.
(With J. Stine) *The Cool Kids' Guide to Summer Camp,* illustrations by Jerry Zimmerman, Scholastic Book Services, 1981.
Gnasty Gnomes, illustrations by Lippman, Random House, 1981.
Don't Stand in the Soup, illustrations by Nicklaus, Bantam, 1982.
(With J. Stine) *Bored with Being Bored!: How to Beat the Boredom Blahs,* illustrations by Zimmerman, Four Winds, 1982.
Blips!: The First Book of Video Game Funnies, illustrations by Bryan Hendrix, Scholastic, Inc., 1983.
(With J. Stine) *Everything You Need to Survive: Brothers and Sisters,* illustrated by Sal Murdocca, Random House, 1983.
(With J. Stine) *Everything You Need to Survive: First Dates,* illustrated by Murdocca, Random House, 1983.
(With J. Stine) *Everything You Need to Survive: Homework,* illustrated by Murdocca, Random House, 1983.
(With J. Stine) *Everything You Need to Survive: Money Problems,* illustrated by Murdocca, Random House, 1983.
Jovial Bob's Computer Joke Book, Scholastic, Inc., 1985.
Miami Mice, illustrations by Eric Gurney, Scholastic, Inc., 1986.
One Hundred and One Silly Monster Jokes, Scholastic, Inc., 1986.
The Doggone Dog Joke Book, Parachute Press, 1986.
Pork & Beans: Play Date, illustrations by Jose Aruego and Ariane Dewey, Scholastic, Inc., 1989.
Ghostbusters II Storybook, Scholastic, Inc., 1989.
One Hundred and One Vacation Jokes, illustrated by Rick Majica, Scholastic, Inc., 1990.
The Amazing Adventures of Me, Myself, and I, Bantam, 1991.

JUVENILES; UNDER PSEUDONYM ERIC AFFABEE

The Siege of the Dragonriders, (Wizards, Warriors and You Series), Avon, 1984.
G.I. Joe and the Everglades Swamp Terror, Ballantine, 1986.
Attack on the King, Avon, 1986.
G.I. Joe-Operation: Star Raider, Ballantine, 1986.
The Dragon Queen's Revenge, (Wizards, Warriors and You Series), Avon, 1986.

JUVENILES; UNDER PSEUDONYM ZACHARY BLUE

The Protectors: The Petrova Twist, Scholastic, Inc., 1987.
The Jet Fighter Trap, Scholastic, Inc., 1987.

■ Sidelights

"Somebody once called me the Jekyll and Hyde of children's publishing," R. L. Stine told *Something about the Author* (*SATA*) in a special interview. "My career has switched so much from personality to personality. For a long time I mainly wrote humor for kids ... joke books and other funny books. I was known as Jovial Bob Stine.

Now I don't do funny stuff any more. Now I'm scary all the time."

Teens around the United States would agree that R. L. Stine is not funny, at least not often, in his young adult novels. They seem to like him that way, because they buy his books in astonishing numbers. According to Paul Gray of *Time*, "adolescents now constitute a booming niche market for the peddling of published gore and violence." The thriller or teen-horror novel is the genre of the 1990s, and R. L. Stine is one of the most read authors in the field. But Stine didn't start out to write terror fiction for teens. He started out to be funny.

"I've had the most single minded life, I think, that anybody could have," Stine said in his interview. "When I was nine years old I found an old typewriter up in the attic. I brought it downstairs and started typing stories and little joke books and magazines. I've been doing that ever since. I think I knew when I was nine that I wanted to be a writer."

At an early age Stine listened to his mother read Golden books and story books and was hooked. "I liked fantasy stories and fairy tales," he told *SATA*. "I remember going into the school library, to the shelf of Grimm's fairy tales and Norse legends and reading every book." As he grew he began reading ghost stories, joke books, sports books, Matt Christopher books, and science fiction works, such as those by Ray Bradbury and Isaac Asimov. Although he wrote often, he didn't share his work with many people. "I was pretty shy at first," Stine remarked. "Mainly I loved writing and typing these stories." Later, he began publishing little magazines and passing them out at school. "I was the kind of student who didn't have to work hard to get Bs. I think every report card would say, 'Bob could do much better, he isn't really working up to the best of his ability.'" He was also the one who made jokes and broke the class up. "I remember being bored a lot in school, being more interested in things like radio shows, TV and writing." Stine enjoyed reading James Thurber and Max Shulman, a humorist from Minnesota who wrote the Dobie Gillis books. He was also an avid fan of such radio shows as *The Shadow, Suspense,* and *Innersanctum.* "When I was a little kid I remember being real scared, lying in bed listening to these scary things on the radio. I loved that," Stine said.

College Activities Inspired Wish for Writing Career

In college at Ohio State Stine spent three years as editor of the campus humor magazine. "That's mainly what I did at Ohio State. I'd hang out at the magazine office in the Student Union and put out this magazine every month." After graduation, with a BA in English, Stine taught social studies for one year in a junior high school, then headed for New York City. "I loved magazines and wanted to get some kind of magazine job," he said in his interview. "My ambition in life was to someday be editor of my own humor magazine."

An avid fan of radio suspense shows such as *The Shadow* and *Innersanctum,* Stine brings the same kinds of thrills and chills to his readers. (Cover illustration by Schmidt.)

Stine's first magazine job was with a publisher of fan and movie magazines. "The job was to make up interviews with celebrities, but we never met anyone," he remembers. "It was great training. In a way it was very creative work, because we had to make up everything. Sometimes we would do the same story two different ways. First as 'Those Whispers about Tom Jones, They're Not True,' then, 'Those Whispers about Tom Jones Are True.'" Stine's next job was with a trade magazine called *Soft Drink Industry.* "It was a horrible year, but the training helped me later as far as writing really fast," Stine said. "I would have to do twenty articles a day from stacks of news clippings on my desk. It taught me not to stop and think about it, just sit down and write."

In 1968 Stine became an assistant editor for *Junior Scholastic Magazine* in New York City. He was with Scholastic for sixteen years, working on four magazines, two of which he created. After four years on *Junior Scholastic,* Stine was made editor of a new magazine, *Search.* The goal was to create a social studies magazine that did not read or look like a social studies magazine. The challenge was to make learning material fun, thus helping kids who didn't read well to learn while they enjoyed reading.

Next came *Bananas,* a humor magazine for older kids. "My wife, Jane, was editing a magazine for kids called *Dynamite,* the biggest selling kids' magazine in the country," Stine said. "It was selling over 1.25 million copies every month, and Scholastic decided to do a funny magazine, too, but for older readers. *Bananas* was the result, a humor magazine for kids twelve years old and up. I was doing what I had always wanted to do," Stine added. He was thirty-two and had reached his life's ambition.

While editing *Bananas* he got a call from Ellen Rudin, an editor of children's books at Dutton. She had read *Bananas,* thought it really funny, and asked him to consider writing a humorous book for younger readers. Stine had never thought about writing children's books, but agreed to work up an idea. That first book was *How To Be Funny,* published in 1982. "It was how to be funny in the cafeteria, at the breakfast table, in bed at night," Stine told *SATA.* "You know, a really offensive book for parents."

Early Career Focuses on Funny Books

After that came many funny books, under the name Jovial Bob Stine, some co-authored by his wife, Jane. Other books from those years, under his name R. L. Stine, were "twist-a-plot" books, a form of "you choose the story line" book that was popular in the 1980s. These stories were often based on licensed characters from television and movies, such as G.I. Joe and Indiana Jones. Each book had about thirty endings, and many twists to the plot, great training for future novel writing.

At Scholastic, *Bananas* was beginning to lose readership, and it was time for a different kind of humor magazine, *Maniac,* with a 1980s title and content for kids 13 years and up. But financially Scholastic was having trouble, and in a reorganization Stine was let go. "I was fired!" he says, "but I was already doing all kinds of books for children for different publishers, so I came home and started writing more books." That was in 1985, and since then Stine has published over 100 books for young readers.

After humorous story and joke books, and action-adventure "choice plots" books, Stine was ready for the next step, novels. His opportunity came when Jean Feiwel, editorial director at Scholastic, asked if he would try writing a scary novel for young adults. She suggested a title, *Blind Date,* and Stine went home to figure out a plot. He spent a lot of time working on that first novel, and when it was published in the summer of 1986, he was amazed that his story, about a young man's memory lapse and involvement with a mysterious girl, was a big seller. The horror genre was new in the market for young adults, but growing fast due to authors such as Christopher Pike. After *Blind Date* Stine signed to do another book, *Twisted,* 1986, and then in 1989 *The Baby-sitter.*

Each novel, dealing in suspicious characters and life-threatening situations, promptly made the juvenile best sellers list. The teen-horror novel was in and Stine was becoming one of its most popular writers; his quick-paced stories and contemporary characters have led *Publishers Weekly* to note that "Stine's popularity with young people is well deserved."

"It occurred to my wife and me that maybe a series with novels that came more often would sell," the author noted in his interview. Jane, who runs her own company, Parachute Press, suggested that Stine try to think of a series of scary books that would come out every other month or so. She would package the series and sell it, through her company, to a publisher. "So I sat down and thought. I needed a good title, then I could figure out a way to do a series of scary books. When the words 'Fear Street' sort of magically appeared, I wrote it down, then came up with the concept."

"Fear Street" Series Revolutionizes Genre

"Fear Street" is a place where terrible things always happen to its residents. There are dark and mysterious legends and ominous happenings, with one street in

Every step she takes, he'll be watching.

One of Stine's first and most popular books, *The Baby-sitter* tells how Jenny's afterschool job turns sinister and threatening.

town linking the series. Jane and Parachute Press sold the idea to Pat MacDonald at Archway, a division of Pocket Books. That first contract was for six books, and the series debuted with *The New Girl,* in which Corey's girl problems involve figuring out if his new girlfriend, who lives on Fear Street, really exists. There are now more than thirty books in the "Fear Street" and "Fear Street: Super Chiller" Series; and two mini-series of three books each, "Fear Street: Cheerleaders," and "Fear Street Saga." The "Fear Street" novels, aimed at the 13 and up age group, are all written by Stine, which keeps him busy writing about one book each month.

Another series, aimed for the 8- to 11-year-old market, is "Goosebumps." With nine titles in two years published by Scholastic, this series is becoming very popular with younger readers. The key to the popularity of these novels seems to be surprise. Kids seem to like the books for their unpredictability; for the many plot twists; and the cliff-hanger chapter endings. "They like the fact that there is some kind of jolt at the end of every chapter," Stine said. "They know that if they read to the end of the chapter they're going to have some kind of funny surprise, something scary, something that's going to

happen right at the end of the chapter and force them to keep reading."

Stine works hard at making the kids in his novels as real as possible, using short phrases and sentences and "teenspeak." The teens in his books also dress like real teens. Readers identify with the teens in the novels, which makes for a scarier read—as do the "cheap thrills" which the author tries to put in each book. "I mean disgusting, gross things to put in the books that they'll like," Stine commented in *Time.* Stine's philosophy of writing is that kids should have some books to read that are not just for learning or uplifting their morals and social behavior, and not "good for them" like medicine. As he said in his interview, "In these days, with so many distractions, and so many reasons not to read, it's important that kids should be able to discover that they can turn to reading for entertainment, instead of television or Nintendo."

It's working. Letters from teens say, "I hate to read but I love your books," and "I never read any books because I don't like to read, but I buy every book you write." Teachers and librarians are telling about students who would never read a book, yet now they can't wait for the next Stine thriller. "It's rewarding for me," says Stine. "I feel so lucky that these books have become so popular."

■ **Works Cited**

Gray, Paul, "Carnage: An Open Book," *Time,* August 2, 1993, p. 54.
Review of *Phone Calls, Publishers Weekly,* June 8, 1990, p. 56.
Stine, R. L., interview with Mary Lois Sanders for *Something about the Author,* July, 1993.

■ **For More Information See**

BOOKS

Roginski, Jim, *Behind The Covers,* Libraries Unlimited, Inc., 1985, pp. 206-213.

PERIODICALS

Publishers Weekly, July 5, 1993, pp. 30-31.
School Library Journal, December, 1989, p. 49; September, 1990, p. 258; November, 1990, p. 142.
Voice of Youth Advocates, February, 1991, p. 368; April, 1992, pp. 36-37; June, 1992, p. 102.

—*Sketch by Mary Lois Sanders*

*   *   *

SUFRIN, Mark 1925-

■ **Personal**

Born July 21, 1925, in Brooklyn, NY; son of Arthur (a business executive) and Ann (a homemaker; maiden name, Putter) Sufrin. *Education:* New School for Social Research, B.A., 1950; Columbia University, M.A., 1951; attended University of California, Berkeley. *Poli-*

An innocent teen stumbling across an ominous secret is the starting point for terror in this installment of the "Fear Street" series. (Cover illustration by Schmidt.)

tics: Democrat. *Religion:* Jewish. *Hobbies and other interests:* Sports, photography, hiking, reading, sketching, music (classical and jazz of the 1920s-1950s).

■ Addresses

Home and office—300 West 12th St., New York, NY 10014.

■ Career

Free-lance writer. *Military service:* U.S. Army, 1942-46, served in the Pacific Theater; became first lieutenant. *Member:* Society of Military Writers.

■ Awards, Honors

Teaching fellow, Columbia University, 1950-51; British Academy of Film and Television Arts Best Short Film Award, Venice Film Festival Grand Prize—documentary, Edinburgh Film Festival Grand Prize—documentary, and Academy Award nomination, best documentary, all 1956, all for *On the Bowery.*

■ Writings

NONFICTION

To the Top of the World: Sir Edmund Hillary and the Conquest of Everest, Platt & Munk, 1966.
The Brave Men: Twelve Portraits of Courage, illustrated by Richard Smith, Platt & Munk, 1967.
Surfing: How to Improve Your Technique (part of "Concise Guide" series), F. Watts, 1973.

BIOGRAPHIES

Focus on America: Profiles of Nine Photographers, Scribner, 1987.
Payton, Scribner, 1988.
George Bush: The Story of the Forty-first President of the United States, Delacorte, 1989.
George Catlin: Painter of the Indian West, Atheneum, 1991.
Stephen Crane, Atheneum, 1992.
Palmyra, Knightsbridge, 1992.
F. Scott Fitzgerald, Atheneum, 1993.
Walt Whitman, Atheneum, 1994.

SCREENPLAYS

(And codirector) *On the Bowery,* Film Representations, 1956.

Also author of *Jerash.* Author and director of documentaries, *Acre* and *Home Front.*

OTHER

Raid at Matupai, Tower, 1981.
The Nightriders, Dell, 1982.
Operation Hoax (science fiction; part of "Golden Heroic Champions" series), illustrated by Dan Spiegle, Golden Book, 1985.
Defenders of the Earth: The Sun Stealers (science fiction; part of "Golden Super Adventure" series), illustrated by Fred Carrillo, Golden Book, 1986.

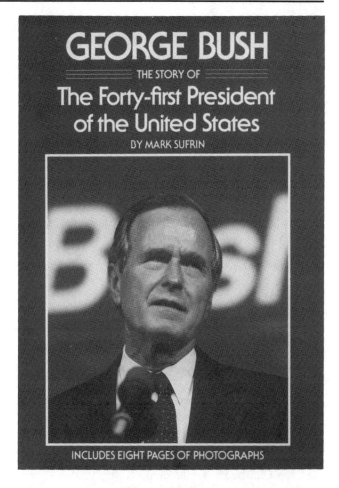

Mark Sufrin's nonfiction works for younger readers include this biography of former President Bush. (Cover photo by J. L. Atlan.)

Also author of *A Time of Heroes.* Contributor to periodicals, including the *New York Times, Chicago Tribune,* and *New Republic.* Contributor to anthologies.

■ Work in Progress

A novel about middle-class life between World Wars I and II; a nonfiction work on the development of New York City between 1890 and 1930, with emphasis on its artists, writers, architects, and photographers; a novel about the U.S. Marine who predicted the bombing of Pearl Harbor in 1921.

■ Sidelights

Mark Sufrin told *SATA:* "My consuming interest is social history and middle-class life between the two World Wars. 'The past,' said British author L. P. Hartley, 'is a foreign country. They do things differently there.' In my next novel I hope to illuminate the period—its crimps and pleasures, the charm and banality of its popular culture. The middle class of those years aspired and conformed with innocence, docility, and quiet courage—and barely understood how precarious its position was. My obsession is with the time author John Cheever said was 'a long lost world when the city of New York was still filled with river light, when you heard Benny Goodman quartets from a radio in a corner stationery store, and when almost everybody wore a hat.'"

*   *   *

SWANSON, June 1931-

■ Personal

Born June 22, 1931, in St. Louis, MO; daughter of George Joseph (an engineer) and Helen (an artist and homemaker; maiden name Bange) Charlier; married Stanley Swanson, June 4, 1954; children: Sandra, Laura, John, Steven. *Education:* University of Texas, B.A., 1952; Florida Atlantic University, M.A., 1986. *Hobbies and other interests:* Antiques, hiking, primitive rug hooking, gardening.

■ Addresses

Home—15 Lisa Dr., Nashua, NH 03062.

■ Career

Elementary school teacher, 1952-1954; free-lance writer, 1954—.

■ Awards, Honors

Notable Children's Trade Book in the field of social studies, National Council for Social Studies and Children's Book Council, 1983, for *The Spice of America.*

JUNE SWANSON

■ Writings

NONFICTION

The Spice of America, illustrated by Priscilla Kiedrowski, Carolrhoda, 1983.
I Pledge Allegiance, illustrated by Rick Hanson, Carolrhoda, 1990.
David Bushnell and His Turtle, illustrated by Mike Eagle, Atheneum, 1991.

OTHER

That's for Shore (riddles), Lerner, 1991.

Also author of over 200 articles, short stories, and poems in more than 30 different magazines, for children and adults.

■ Work in Progress

Two more riddle books to be published by Lerner.

■ Sidelights

Since the publication of her first book, *The Spice of America,* June Swanson has explored little-known aspects of American history. In *The Spice of America,* Swanson writes about such overlooked figures as Dolley Madison and Andrew Johnson, and discusses the origins of such commonplace items as blue jeans and doughnuts.

Swanson's second book, *I Pledge Allegiance,* was published on the 100th anniversary of the writing of the pledge and provides some historical background on its origin. Janie Schomberg wrote in the *School Library Journal* that programs involved with new immigrants, students with English as a second language, and social studies "will be enriched by this book; it will also be helpful in public library programs."

Swanson's *David Bushnell and His Turtle* is about the man who tried to invent the submarine in the late eighteenth century. Bushnell was a graduate of Yale University who proved that explosives could be set off underwater. His submarine (which resembled two turtle shells joined together; hence the title) was intended to attach mines to British ships. While his invention was unsuccessful, he paved the way for such inventors as Robert Fulton, who created the first successful steamboat. "A most informative sketch of the first working underwater craft and its inventor," asserted a contributor *School Library Journal.* A *Kirkus Reviews* contributor noted that the author's explanation of Bushnell's problem solving "make a fascinating story that illuminates both the technology and the society of his day."

■ Works Cited

Review of *David Bushnell and His Turtle, Kirkus Reviews,* August 15, 1991.
Review of *David Bushnell and His Turtle, School Library Journal,* December, 1991.

Janie Schomberg, review of *I Pledge Allegiance, School
    Library Journal,* July, 1990.

T

TANAKA, Beatrice 1932-

■ Personal

Vowels in surname are open, as in "father"; born March 1, 1932, in Cernauti, Romania; daughter of Paul (a lawyer and industrialist) and Clara (a homemaker; maiden name, Spitzer) Lauder; married Flavio-Shiro Tanaka (a painter under the name Flavio-Shiro), July 13, 1955; children: Josue, Noemi Kopp-Tanaka. *Education:* Attended Guignard School of Art, Belo Horizonte, Brazil, 1947-50, Ecole Paul Colin, Atelier d'Essai des Decorateurs-Maquettistes, 1951-54, and Universite du Theatre des Nations, Paris, 1961-62. *Politics:* "Trying to be a decent 'Earthling'; no party." *Religion:* "No fixed dogma." *Hobbies and other interests:* "Folktales, traditional arts and crafts (especially toys, textiles, theater), classical music (especially Balinese and Indian), Bible studies and mythologies (not only Greek!), poetry, non-European theater, puppetry, ecology, ethnography, anthropology, painting, sculpture, cooking (even worked on a Vietnamese cookbook!), and history (mostly the history of those who didn't write—or rewrite!—it: American Indians, African peoples, South-East Asians, women and children, and plain people instead of kings and generals)."

■ Addresses

Home—Paris, France.

■ Career

Set and costume designer for Brazilian and French theaters, 1954—, including work for Escola de Samba Portela in Rio de Janeiro, Brazil, University Theater of Bahia, Festival de Liege, Comedie de la Loire, and Festival de Hammamet; author-illustrator of children's books and for children's magazines; author of plays for children. Free-lance advertising designer in Brazil and France, 1959-61. Teacher of crafts classes for children and puppetry classes for the elderly; organizer of exhibits of drawings by children of Third World countries. *Member:* Sociedade Brasileira de Autores de Teatro

BEATRICE TANAKA

(Rio de Janeiro), Societe des Auteurs et Compositeurs Dramatiques (Paris, France), Societe des Auteurs Multimedia (Paris), Societe des Gens de Lettres (Paris), Compositeurs et Editeurs de Musique (Paris), La Charte des Auteurs (Paris).

■ Awards, Honors

Prize for best Brazilian costumes at Sao Paulo International Art Biennial, 1961, for *Threepenny Opera;* sets and costume awards, Universite du Theatre des Nations, 1962, for *Don Perlimplin;* best carnival costumes award (Rio de Janeiro), 1966, for *Memorias dum Sargento de Milicias;* Prix Leon Chancerel, Association Theatre Enfance Jeunesse, 1968, for *Equipee Bizarre au Cirque Basile;* Diplome Loisirs-Jeunes, 1971, for *Le Tresor de l'Homme,* 1972, for *La Savane Enchantee,* 1976, for *La Montagne aux Trois Questions,* and 1984, for *Kantjil et la Guerre de Tigres;* Best of the Best Award, International Jugendbibliothek, 1971, for *Le Tresor de l'Homme;* Fifty Best Books of the Year citation (Paris), 1971, for *Le Tresor de l'Homme,* and 1972, for *La Savane Enchantee;* silver medal at Novi Sad Triennial, 1972, for *Equipee Bizarre au Cirque Basile.*

■ Writings

JUVENILE CRAFT BOOKS IN ENGLISH TRANSLATION

(With Francoise Douvaines and Pierre Marchand) *Seaside Treasures,* translated by Halina Tunikowska, Mills and Boon, 1971 (originally published as *Tresors de la Plage,* Edicope, 1971).

(With Marie-Francoise Heron and Michele Rivol) *Fun with Paper,* Collins and World (London), 1975 (originally published as *Joyeux Papiers,* Gallimard, 1975).

Disguise Workshop, translated by Anthea Bell, Pepper Press, 1982 (originally published with *Build It Workshop* [also see below] in *Aktionsbuch,* Otto Maier, 1981).

Build It Workshop, translated by Anthea Bell, Pepper Press, 1983 (originally published with *Disguise Workshop* in *Aktionsbuch,* Otto Maier, 1981).

CHILDREN'S FOLKTALES IN ENGLISH TRANSLATION

(Adaptor; self-illustrated) *The Tortoise and the Sword: A Vietnamese Legend,* Lothrop, 1972.

The Chase: A Kutenai Indian Tale, illustrated by Michel Gay, Crown, 1991 (originally published as *La Course,* Kaleidoscope, 1990).

(Self-illustrated) *Green Tales,* Four Walls Eight Windows, in press.

OTHER WORK IN ENGLISH TRANSLATION

(Illustrator) Andree Clair and Boubou Hama, *The Enchanted Savannah: Tales from West Africa,* translated by Olive Jones, Methuen, 1974 (originally published as *La Savane Enchantee: Contes d'Afrique,* Editions La Farandole, 1972).

(Self-illustrated) *The History of the Ytch* (short story), translated by Doris Orgel in *Cricket,* 1977, published as *Ytch et les Choumoudoux,* Editions La Farandole, 1982.

UNTRANSLATED CRAFT BOOKS

Les Trois Coups (title means "Three Knocks [Before the Theater-Curtain Rises . . . .]"), Hachette, 1974.

Le Cirque, Jouets Animes (title means "Circus: Mobile Toys"), Editions La Farandole, 1974.

Fetes (title means "Festivals"), Francs and Franches Camarades, 1980.

Quand s'Anime le Jersey (title means "When Jersey Comes Alive"), Dessain-Tolra, 1981.

Marchenspiele (title means "Play Fairy-Tales"), Otto Maier, 1983.

Puppen Puppen Puppen (title means "Dolls, Dolls, Dolls"), Otto Maier, 1985.

UNTRANSLATED CHILDREN'S FOLKTALES; SELF-ILLUSTRATED (EXCEPT AS NOTED)

Le Tresor de l'Homme (title means "Humankind's Treasure"), Editions La Farandole, 1971.

La Fille du Grand Serpent (title means "The Great Serpent's Daughter"), Editions La Farandole, 1973.

La Montagne aux Trois Questions (title means "The Mountain of Three Questions"), Editions La Farandole, 1976.

Le Pinceau (title means "The [Painter's] Brush"), illustrated by M. Garnier, Bayard Presse, 1977.

Le Crapaud et la Pluie (title means "The Toad and the Rain"), illustrated by T. Bong and N. Duong, Editions La Farandole, 1978.

Le Tonneau Enchante (title means "The Enchanted Barrel"), Editions La Farandole, 1982.

Kantjil et la Guerre des Tigres (folktale/picture book with cassette; title means "Kantjil's Tigerwar"), Vif Argent, 1984.

Savitri la Vaillante (title means "Valliant Savitri"), Editions La Farandole, 1984.

Contes en F (title means "Tales in F"), Editions La Farandole, 1985.

La Princesse aux Deux Visages (title means "The Two-Faced Princess), Vif-Argent, 1985.

Les Contes du Ciel (title means "Sky Tales"), Syros, 1986.

Les Tresors (title means "The Treasures"), Syros, 1987.

La Legende de Chico-Rei (title means "The Legend of Chico-Rei"), Vif-Argent, 1987.

Trois Sorcieres (title means "Three Witches"), Syros, 1988.

La Quete du Prince de Koripan (title means "The Quest of the Prince of Koripan"), Syros, 1992.

Le Jaboti et les Fruits Inconnus (title means "The Jaboti [rain forest turtle] and the Unknown Fruit"), illustrated by B. Leclercq, Kaleidoscope, 1992.

Au Temps du Caiman (title means "The Alligator Days"), illustrated with clay figures made by Karaja women potters, Vif-Argent, 1993.

TRANSLATOR AND ILLUSTRATOR

M. Matsutani, *Taro du Dragon* (title means "Taro Dragon-Boy"), Magnard, 1976.

Nunes Pereira, *Le Sage Bahira* (title means "Wise Bahira"), Editions La Farandole, 1979.

OTHER UNTRANSLATED WORK; SELF-ILLUSTRATED (EXCEPT AS NOTED)

Maya ou la 53eme semaine de l'Annee (novel; title means "Maya or the Fifty-Third Week of the Year"), Editions La Farandole, 1975.

Des Quatre Vents (nursery rhymes; title means "From All Four Winds"), L'Ecole des Loisirs, 1975.

Venise Venise (nonfiction; title means "Venice, Venice"), illustrated with photographs and children's drawings, Unesco-La Noria, 1979.

Bali: Une Culture Differente vue par ses Enfants (nonfiction; title means "Bali: A Different Culture as Seen by Its Children"), illustrated with Balinese children's drawings, La Noria, 1979.

Boia, Boi e Bang (nonfiction picture book; title means "Beans, Beef, and Bang"), Antares, 1984.

(Adaptor) *Pour la Terre* (nonfiction; title means "For the Earth"), Vif-Argent, 1986.

Chen du Grand Large (short story; title means "Chen of the Wide Seas"), Editions La Farandole, 1987.

(Adaptor) *Contes des Charmeurs de Serpents* (title means "Snake Charmer Tales"), illustrated by Indian folk artists, Syros, 1987.

Les Manguiers d'Antigone (novel; title meas "Antigone's Mango Trees"), Pere Castor-Flammarion, 1993.

Author of the children's play *Equipee Bizarre au Cirque Basile*. Contributor to *Cricket's Choice*, edited by Marianne Carus and Clifton Fadiman, Open Court, 1974. Contributor to magazines, including *Jeunes Annees*, *Puffin Post*, and *Cricket*. Editor of children's magazines.

ILLUSTRATOR OF UNTRANSLATED WORKS

Clair and Hama, *Kangue Ize*, Editions la Farandole, 1974.

Hama, *Ize-Gani*, Presence Africaine, 1985.

Also illustrator of *Histoires de Tibbo*, *Founya le Vaurien*, *Safia et le Fleuve*, *Safia et le Puits*, *Safia et le Jardin*, *Farfelettis*, *Kangourourimes*, *Escargotiques*, *Marc et Nathalie*, *Bemba*, *Elefantaisies*, *Le Chant du Riz Pile*, *Jeux d'Etoiles et de Lune*, *Mandoline*, *I'Ile des Quatre Familles*, *Les Affreux Jojos*, and *Les Contes de Koutou es Samala*.

■ **Adaptations**

Equipee Bizarre au Cirque Basile was adapted for French television.

■ **Sidelights**

Beatrice Tanaka told *SATA:* "I was born on one continent, grew up on another, and got my present surname—by marriage—from a third. I passed from one to the other as I passed from drawing to writing to theater. I'm just as hard up to define my nationality as my profession; so, to simplify, I say that I'm an '*Earthling*' and a '*Fairy-Tale-Ferry-Woman*.'

"An *Earthling* is someone who loves our little planet, soil, water, and air as her (or his) endangered 'motherland,' and doesn't bother about 'fatherlands' with their changing and blood-soaked borders. *Fairy-Tale-Ferry-(Wo)man* is someone who—if obliged to choose between a self-invented story and a traditional 'speaking' tale threatened by oblivion (because of war, accelerated urbanization, breaking-up communities, or the eruption

of modern mass media)—prefers to get the latter published, so that this survivor of a culture labelled 'prelogical' by money grabbers may help us find the way toward a post-industrial, more convivial shore.

"I'm concerned with *Speaking Tales*—not necessarily a culture's best-known tales (sometimes emptied of all substance through over-repetition), but those that, under their at-first-sight strange (since foreign) images, raise fundamental questions that concern us here and now. These tales, even if only perceived as moving shadows, don't let me alone until I restore them to life in our culture. I do this by trying to share some of their original flavor, their smells of sea or primal forest, their rhythm and their timeless wisdom, with the children of the TV-asphalt jungles, of rock and clips.

"Through this introduction to another culture and different mode of thought, I try to give the reader a glimpse of the rainbow-coloured cloak of differences that covers the deep unity of mankind; to show that in our thousands of languages, we try to express the same dreams."

*   *   *

THAMER, Katie
See TREHERNE, Katie Thamer

*   *   *

THE Tjong Khing 1933-

■ **Personal**

Born August 4, 1933, in Purworejo, Indonesia; son of The Sien Tjing (in sales) and Kwee Lee Sie; married Monika Guhl (divorced); married Mino Wortel (a textile artist), 1970; children: Markus, Erik.

■ **Addresses**

Home and office—Duvenvoordestraat 110, 2013 AH Haarlem, the Netherlands.

■ **Career**

Martin Toonder Studios, Amsterdam, the Netherlands, comic strip draftsman, 1957-60; free-lance illustrator, 1960—.

■ **Awards, Honors**

Golden Brush Awards (the Netherlands), 1978, for *Wiele Wiele Stap*, and 1985, for *Little Sophie and Lanky Flop*; Youth Literature Prize (Germany), 1986, for *Little*

THE TJONG KHING

Sophie and Lanky Flop; Amsterdam Art Prize, 1988, for *City of Gold.*

■ Illustrator

Colin Dann, *Animals of Farthing Wood,* Querido, 1979.
Els Pelgrom, *Little Sophie and Lanky Flop,* J. Cape, 1987 (originally published as *Kleine Sofie en Lange Wapper*).
Peter Dickinson, *City of Gold,* Querido, 1987.
Joke Van Leeuwen, *Look, Listen and Play,* Exley, 1988.
Klaus Kordon, *The Big Fish,* Macmillan, 1992 (originally published as *Der Grosse Fisch Tin Lin,* Ravensburger, 1990).
Markus und der Schimpf-im-Sack, Nord-Sud Verlag, 1993.

Also illustrator of numerous other works published in the Netherlands, including *Wiele Wiele Stap,* written by Miep Diekmann.

■ Sidelights

The Tjong Khing told *SATA:* "I began as a comic-strip draftsman. After more than 10 years I wanted something else, and started illustrating children's books. I'm often asked what it is in illustrating that I like. I don't know really. All I know is I enjoy drawing and depicting situations, emotions, characters, moods. I like to search for a new way, a better way to achieve a particular mood I want. I like to find out what is vital in a certain illustration, so I can leave out the superfluous. I certainly don't succeed every time, and I have had to settle for less many, many times."

■ For More Information See

PERIODICALS

Times Educational Supplement (London), October 4, 1990, p. 27.

*   *   *

TOLLES, Martha 1921-

■ Personal

Born September 7, 1921, in Oklahoma City, OK; daughter of Willis and Mary Natalie (Dunbar) Gregory; married Edwin Leroy Tolles (an attorney), June 21, 1944; children: Stephen, Henry, Cynthia, Roy, James, Thomas. *Education:* Smith College, B.A., 1943. *Religion:* Presbyterian.

■ Addresses

Home—860 Oxford Rd., San Marino, CA 91108.

■ Career

Port Chester Daily Item, Port Chester, NY, reporter, 1943-44; *Publishers Weekly,* New York City, member of editorial staff, 1945; writer. Speaker at schools, libraries, and reading associations. *Member:* Society of Children's Book Writers and Illustrators, Authors Guild, Southern California Council on Literature for Children and Young People.

■ Awards, Honors

International Reading Association Children's Choices list, *Darci in Cabin 13* in 1990, and *Marrying Off Mom* in 1991; International Reading Association Children's Choice Award, for *Secret Sister.*

■ Writings

Too Many Boys, Thomas Nelson, 1965, reissued as *Katie and Those Boys,* Scholastic, 1974.
Katie for President, Scholastic, 1976.
Who's Reading Darci's Diary?, Lodestar, 1984.
Katie's Babysitting Job, Scholastic, 1985.
Darci and the Dance Contest, Lodestar, 1985.
Darci in Cabin 13, Scholastic, 1989.
Marrying off Mom, Scholastic, 1990.
Secret Sister, Scholastic, 1992.

Contributor to children's magazines.

■ Sidelights

The heroines of Martha Tolles's books are young girls approaching adolescence who must deal with issues typical of growing girls, such as making friends, going to dances, babysitting, and writing about dreams and experiences in a highly secretive journal. Tolles's novels have been compared to the works of Beverly Cleary and

MARTHA TOLLES

Carolyn Haywood, other authors whose stories of contemporary life are popular with young readers.

For her first book, *Too Many Boys,* later reissued as *Katie and Those Boys,* Tolles drew on her own family for inspiration. The author once told *SATA:* "When I decided to write my first book I cast about for an idea and soon realized I had one right before me. In our family we had a problem, created by the fact that there were five boys and only one girl. Our daughter, with two older brothers and three younger ones, constantly wanted another girl to play with and there were none at all in our neighborhood, only boys. Much of her time was spent on the front lawn, or in our playroom, or eating lunch with perhaps a dozen boys ... all her brothers and their many friends. And so her life was indeed filled with too many boys." Tolles added that since the book was published, "I have received letters from girls, some saying they sympathize with Katie because they have the same problem, others saying they wish they had it too!" In a *Library Journal* review, Beatrice M. Adam described the book as "a humorous, fast-moving story which will appeal to readers who enjoy the Beverly Cleary and Carolyn Haywood books."

Katie's adventures continue in *Katie for President* and *Katie's Babysitting Job.* The latter is about Katie's first babysitting job, which turns into a disaster after some jewelry is stolen from the house. Katie decides to solve the mystery with the aid of her friend Will Madison

(who makes his first appearance in *Too Many Boys*). A *Booklist* critic noted the author's sensitive treatment of the boy-girl relationship in the story, and concluded that "the clues are well placed, the pace is lively, and the characters nicely realized."

Tolles's next book, 1984's *Who's Reading Darci's Diary?,* follows the escapades of Darci Daniels, a sixth grader who has a crush on Travis, the cutest boy in her class. Her diary details her infatuation, when suddenly the diary disappears, and Darci is terrified to think of who might be reading it. A reviewer for *Children's Book Review Service* said, "Darci learns about taking responsibility, about making friends, and, above all, about not prejudging people." A *Booklist* reviewer maintained that young readers will be "interested to the end." *Darci and the Dance Contest* continues Darci's adventures as her family moves—in the middle of the school year—from California to New York. Darci is homesick for California, but still eager to make new friends. Among her new acquaintances are Lisa, a popular girl at school, and Nathan, a boy who asks Darci to enter a dance contest with him. "Darci's characterization shows compassion and kindness, although not without temptations to be 'one of the crowd,'" Beatrice Ebert Martinez wrote in *School Library Journal.* "Sixth-Graders here sound just like sixth-graders everywhere; even the teachers are familiar—so realistic and likable that we want Martha Tolles to plot more Darci adventures," enthused Kristiana Gregory in *Los Angeles Times Book Review.*

Tolles continued the adventures of Darci with *Darci in Cabin 13,* a summer camp story which revolves around the competition between the Cabin 10 girls, and Darci and her friends in Cabin 13. Another book, *Secret Sister,* finds Darci participating in a class project to make new friends. Darci draws the name of Crystal, the beautiful new girl, but someone very special has drawn Darci's name. Tolles creates suspense by focusing on whether Crystal and Darci will become friends, and whether Darci is ready to find out who her secret sister really is.

Tolles told *SATA:* "I am encouraged by my fan mail. Many readers write that they 'can't put the book down,' or that they had never liked reading before. Inspiring children to read is the greatest reward of all."

■ Works Cited

Adam, Beatrice M., review of *Too Many Boys, Library Journal,* May 15, 1965.

Gregory, Kristiana, review of *Darci and the Dance Contest, Los Angeles Times Book Review,* September 1, 1985.

Review of *Katie's Babysitting Job, Booklist,* February 15, 1986, p. 874.

Martinez, Beatrice Ebert, review of *Darci and the Dance Contest, School Library Journal,* May, 1985, p. 85.

Review of *Who's Reading Darci's Diary?, Booklist,* November 1, 1984, p. 376.

Review of *Who's Reading Darci's Diary?, Children's Book Review Service,* winter supplement, 1985.

TREHERNE, Katie Thamer 1955- (Katie Thamer)

■ Personal

Born March 27, 1955, in Los Angeles, CA; daughter of Donald Chapman (a lawyer) and Hillary (a real estate agent; maiden name, Fitzpatrick) Thamer; married Patrick John Treherne (an organic market gardener), March 8, 1986; children: Mary Agnes, Thomas Michael Justin, Joseph Patrick Ciaran, Peter Edmund Gabriel. *Education:* Attended University of California, Santa Barbara, 1973-75, Chapman College World Campus Afloat, 1975, and University of California, Berkeley, 1975-77. *Religion:* Roman Catholic.

■ Addresses

Home—England.

■ Career

Painter and illustrator. Formerly affiliated with Kathryn Markel Gallery, Galeria Elena, and Simard Halm Gallery.

■ Illustrator

George MacDonald, *The Light Princess* (adapted by Robin McKinley), Harcourt, 1988.
(And adapter) Hans Christian Andersen, *The Little Mermaid,* Harcourt, 1989.
Elizabeth Enright, *Tatsinda,* Harcourt, 1990.

UNDER NAME KATIE THAMER

Andersen, *The Red Shoes* (adapted from the translation by H. B. Paull), Green Tiger Press, 1982.
Marianna Mayer, *The Black Horse,* Dial Press, 1984.

Also illustrator of *Song of Songs* (adapted from the Bible), Green Tiger Press.

WITH N.M. BODECKER; ALL WRITTEN BY EDWARD EAGER

Seven-Day Magic, Harcourt, 1989.
Magic or Not?, Harcourt, 1989.
Magic by the Lake, Harcourt, 1989.
Knight's Castle, Harcourt, 1989.
Half Magic, Harcourt, 1989.
The Time Garden, Harcourt, 1990.
The Well Wishers, Harcourt, 1990.

■ Work in Progress

Writing two books.

■ Sidelights

Katie Thamer Treherne told *SATA:* "I have always loved to draw, and have credited this talent as a gift from God. Therefore I have always felt the need to dedicate my work to God and try to work on projects that are of a loving and spiritual nature. Hans Christian Andersen and George MacDonald in particular inspire me because this seems to be the nature of their work too—to illuminate the life of the Spirit and to try and inspire people, to encourage them, to increase their faith. I am thrilled that the first bit of luck I had in getting published was a piece from God's own book— the Bible. That in itself was a coincidental story!"

* * *

TREMENS, Del
See MacDONALD, AMY

* * *

TULLOCH, Richard (George) 1949-

■ Personal

Born September 1, 1949, in Melbourne, Australia; son of Ian Mitchell (a doctor) and Cecily Muriel (a social worker; maiden name, Dean) Tulloch; married Agnes Blaauw (a drug and alcohol counselor), October, 1977; children: Telma, Bram. *Education:* Melbourne University, 1968-73, received B.A., B.L., and diploma of education.

■ Addresses

Home—172 Cavendish, Stanmore, New South Wales 2048, Australia. *Agent*—Cameron's Management, 163 Brougham St., Woolloomooloo, New South Wales 2011, Australia.

■ Career

Free-lance actor and musician in Melbourne and Europe, 1975-78; National Theatre, Perth, Australia, associate director, 1979-80; Toe Truck Theatre, Sydney, Australia, artistic director, 1981-83; free-lance actor, theater director, and writer, 1984—. *Member:* International Theatre Institute (member of Australian committee, 1990-92), Australian Writers Guild (member of the management committee, 1990-92), Actors Equity (Australia).

■ Awards, Honors

Australian Writers Guild awards for *Hating Alison Ashley: The Play* and *Talking to Grandma While the World Goes By,* both 1988.

■ Writings

CHILDREN'S BOOKS

Stories from Our House, illustrated by Julie Vivas, Cambridge University Press, 1987.
Stories from Our Street, illustrated by Vivas, Cambridge University Press, 1989.
Rain for Christmas, illustrated by Wayne Harris, Cambridge University Press, 1989.

RICHARD TULLOCH

The Strongest Man in Gundiwallanup, illustrated by Sue
O'Loughlin, Cambridge University Press, 1990.
The Brown Felt Hat, illustrated by Craig Smith, Omni-
bus Books, 1990.
Danny in the Toybox, illustrated by Armin Greder,
Ashton Scholastic, 1990, Tambourine, 1991.
Being Bad for the Babysitter, illustrated by Coral Tul-
loch, Omnibus Books, 1991, Scholastic, 1992.
Barry the Burglar's Last Job, illustrated by C. Tulloch,
Omnibus Books, 1992.
Our New Old House, illustrated by O'Loughlin, Macmil-
lan, 1992.

PLAYS

Year 9 Are Animals, Heinemann, 1983.
If We Only Had A Cat, Currency Press, 1985.
Face to Face, Cambridge University Press, 1987.
Hating Alison Ashley: The Play, Penguin Books, 1988.
Space Demons: The Play, Omnibus Books, 1990.
The Cocky of Bungaree, illustrated by Peter Tierney,
Currency Press, 1991.
Could Do Better, Currency Press, 1992.

OTHER

Letter to Santa (screenplay), Nine Network, 1986.
The Miraculous Mellops (television series) Ten Network,
1991.
Bananas in Pyjamas (television series), Australian
Broadcasting Co., 1991—.

Also author of *Talking to Grandma While the World
Goes By.*

■ Work in Progress

Two children's books, *My Rotten Little Brother* and
Augustus and Dorothy; a play adaptation of Oscar
Wilde's *The Happy Prince;* and continuing work on the
Bananas in Pyjamas television series.

■ Sidelights

Richard Tulloch told *SATA:* "I became a writer by
accident. I grew up in the sports-mad city of Melbourne,
and although I was a fair student, my main ambition
was to play cricket for Australia. By the time I'd been
dropped to the school's B cricket team, I'd changed my
aim to something more reasonable—playing field hockey in the Olympic Games. I tried hard but never made
it.

"During my last couple years at university, I discovered
studying law was pretty boring and acting in plays was
fantastic fun. Soon after graduating, I found myself
working in a small professional theatre company, usually making up our own plays and performing them in
theatres, schools, and out on the street.

"Children's theatre and street performing became my
main interests, so in 1975, with a pack on my back and a
yellow fiddle under my arm, I headed off for a tour of
Europe. For a young Australian like me, going overseas
was like going to the moon—it seemed as if I were off to
a new world so far away. For the next two years I hung
around children's theater companies and did a lot of
busking on street corners in Holland and France, as well
as washing hire cars when the coins weren't falling fast
enough. I also did my own one-man children's show in
Dutch, a language which at that time I didn't really
speak. Friends helped me with the writing, and I learned
it more or less phonetically. I was young and stupid
enough to think I could do anything!

"A friend became director of the National Theatre in
Perth, Western Australia, and offered me a job as an
actor there. So I packed up again, this time with a Dutch
wife and daughter, as well as the yellow fiddle. Although
I loved acting, my writing and directing started to
develop during our two-and-a-half years in Perth. I
wrote six plays and became associate director of the
company.

"1980. Perth is beautiful but very isolated. It's on the
west coast of Australia, about two-thousand miles from
the nearest other city. So when I was offered work in
Sydney, I took it. The job lasted four months and then
ran out. I'd hoped to find work as an actor in Sydney's
theatre and film industry, but I now had two hungry
children and needed a job fast.

Children Inspire Radio Plays

"During my unemployed time I wrote some short
stories for very young children and submitted them to a

radio program called *Kindergarten.* Most of my stories were rejected but enough were accepted to give me some encouragement. My son, Bram, was then about a year old. I tried in these early stories to see things from his point of view. Things which an adult may take little interest in—a line of ants on the kitchen floor, the garbage a dog has pulled from a bin in the street, a broken mug—could be fascinating for a little boy, and gave me ideas for stories.

"A job came up as director of Toe Truck Theatre, one of Australia's best children's theatre companies. For the next three years I ran that company, writing and directing a number of plays which were well received and earned me enough offers of work to quit the business of running the company (I've always found the responsibilities of being a boss very tough) and go freelance.

"1984. Australia is a big country with quite a small population (about seventeen-million). So to make a living, a free-lancer needs to have a lot of strings to his or her bow. I kept up my acting, writing, and play directing, but also studied writing for film and television. During this time I started working with an aboriginal writer called Jack Davis. I directed his play *Honey Spot,* which during the next three years travelled all over Australia as well as to festivals in Europe and North America, and led indirectly to my own plays being produced in the U.S., New Zealand, and Thailand.

"1986. Another lucky break got me into writing children's books. My daughter told me that one of her friends at school had a mother who was an artist. That mum turned out to be Julie Vivas, who was already one of Australia's most successful illustrators. I was flattered when Julie asked to see the stories I'd written for *Kindergarten* and even more flattered when she said she'd like to illustrate them for what became my first children's book—*Stories from Our House.* I've now had nine children's books published and book work takes up nearly half my time.

Storytelling Career Aids Writing Process

"Soon after *Stories from Our House* was published, I was asked to go and talk about my writing at a school. The children had lots of questions about how I write (and the usual one about how much money I earned) but the most fun we all had was when I read them some of my stories. I discovered the joys of being a storyteller, and now I spend a day or two most weeks doing this work. I learn all my stories by heart, devise simple ways to act them out, and inflict them on audiences in schools, theatres, and libraries. It's a way to combine my twin loves of performing and writing. Perhaps one day I'll find a way to work playing Olympic hockey into the act too!

"As well as being great fun, performing my stories has been a great discipline for my writing. In trying to construct a good story to tell out loud, I'm made aware of the importance of the rhythms of the language, the build up of tension, and the timing of the humor. Stories for young children really need to be good performance pieces. So often they're being performed for the child by a parent or teacher. *Danny and the Toybox* is particularly good for these storytelling performances. I really wrote it to give the audience a chance to scream out loud in different funny voices as they chant along with Danny (who has a temper tantrum and shuts himself in a toybox), 'I'm never coming out for the rest of my life, never, never, never, so there!'

"Usually when I write a new story, my first aim is to be able to use it in my storytelling show (and maybe drop out one of the old stories which will drive me crazy if I have to repeat it one more time). Trying out the new stories in performance shows me which bits are boring and which bits are working well. I find I can think up better ideas on my feet than ever come to me sitting at a desk. The terror of standing up on your own and having to entertain an audience, especially an audience of young people who will not be polite if you are boring them, is a great motivator.

"I'm a very quick writer. Sometimes this is because I have to be. The television series that I now write for need a lot of material very fast. There are deadlines which have to be met. And I've often found myself getting up early to write scenes for a play which have to be rehearsed that morning. But I'm also quick because I'm afraid that if I slow down and look back I'll lose confidence in what I've just written. Stories which seemed really exciting when I wrote them can look terrible the next morning. So if I've got my teeth into something, I write it fast, edit it carefully but quickly,

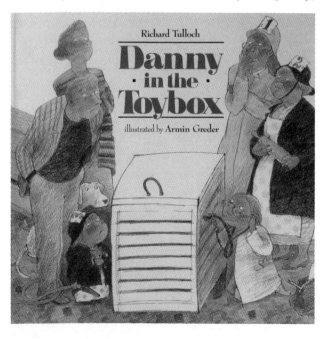

Danny stumps his family by throwing a temper tantrum and crawling into his toybox in Tulloch's picturebook. (Cover illustration by Armin Greder.)

and get it off to a publisher before I have time to change my mind.

"There's an old story about a man who rode across a frozen lake, not realizing how thin the ice was. He made it safely, but when he was told about the risk he'd just taken, he dropped dead from the shock. I know the feeling only too well. If I'd thought before doing a one-man show in Dutch or telling stories at an international festival in Northern Ireland or performing a play to non-English-speaking aboriginal communities in Central Australia or directing a play in a remote village in Northern Thailand—I'd probably have said it was too hard and I couldn't do it. I only managed to do those things because I didn't know what to expect. I did the jobs first and saved the worrying until later. As they say in the movies—'don't look down!'"

■ **For More Information See**

PERIODICALS

Horn Book, January, 1990, p. 238; July, 1990, pp. 42, 56; spring, 1992, p. 50.

Publishers Weekly, July 24, 1987, p. 186.

Quill & Quire, spring, 1989, p. 25.

School Library Journal, February, 1988, p. 66; February, 1992, p. 78.

Times Educational Supplement, May 13, 1988, p. B8; October 6, 1989, p. 32.

V

VAINIO, Pirkko 1957-
(Pirkko Hannele)

■ Personal

Born September 24, 1957, in Jamsankoski, Finland; daughter of Olavi and Annikki (Kettinen) Vainio; married Andrea Baldini (a printer), May 7, 1983; children: Irina Baldini. *Education:* Attended Academy of Fine Arts (Helsinki, Finland), 1978-81 and 1983. *Religion:* Lutheran.

■ Addresses

Home—via Metastasio, 19, 50124 Firenze, Italy.

■ Career

Writer and illustrator of children's books, 1984—. Participated in illustrators' exhibitions at Bologna Book Fair and Itabashi Art Museum (Tokyo, Japan), both 1991. *Member:* Icograda (International Council of Graphics), Grafia (Finnish graphic artists association), Nordiska Tecknare.

■ Writings

IN ENGLISH TRANSLATION

(Self-illustrated) *The Snow Goose,* translated by J. Alison James, North-South Books, 1993 (originally published as *Die Schneegans,* Nord-Sud Verlag, 1993).

SELF-ILLUSTRATED PICTURE BOOKS; UNTRANSLATED

Kuplamatka Kukkarantaan, Sanoma Book Publishing (Finland), 1988.
Kleiner Vogel flieg ganz hoch, Nord-Sud Verlag (Switzerland), 1990.
Tattivaaran Hattuvaras, Sanoma Book Publishing, 1992.

ILLUSTRATOR; IN ENGLISH TRANSLATION; "JOSIE SMITH" SERIES, WRITTEN BY MAGDALEN NABB

Josie Smith, HarperCollins, (Great Britain), 1988.

Josie Smith at the Seashore, M.K. McElderry Books, 1990.
Josie Smith and Eileen, M.K. McElderry Books, 1991.
Josie Smith at School, M.K. McElderry Books, 1991.
Josie Smith at Christmas, HarperCollins, 1992.

ILLUSTRATOR; UNTRANSLATED WORKS

I. Salo, *Junalla Arikspaaniin,* Sanoma Book Publishing, 1984.

PIRKKO VAINIO

A. Savisaari, *Hemppa,* Sanoma Book Publishing, 1989.

■ Work in Progress

Writing and illustrating *Keine Angst vor Fridolin* ("The Scarecrow") and *A Christmas Story* (tentative title), for Nord-Sud Verlag; writing and illustrating *Pieni Kaalimato,* for Sanoma Book Publishing; illustrating Nabb's *Josie Smith in Hospital,* for HarperCollins.

■ Sidelights

After attending the Academy of Fine Arts in Helsinki, Finland, Pirkko Vainio stopped painting and became interested in graphic art, especially black and white expression. She told *SATA* that she felt the simplicity of black and white to be "more near to the world of dreams and our subconscious life."

Now an accomplished illustrator, Vainio described for *SATA* her early attempts at illustration: "I saw that every etching I made had a story around it and this brought me to invent stories around the pictures. This is still the way I work on the illustrations of fairy tales. I first make one picture—which later will be the central 'high point' of the story—the picture I receive like a vision or like a dream. Then I look for the reasons for this impression, the things that have led into such a feeling—this will be the beginning of the story. After, I try to work in my mind to get a good solution for the central expression (aiming at a happy end). This will be the final part of the book.

"I believe that all kinds of art are keys to our subconscious," Vainio concluded. Her musical inspirations include Mozart, Bach, Mahler, Bizet, and Puccini. "With my illustrations I pretend that they move something in the children's minds—for I consider illustration work as any other form of art; maybe it is only the most fortunate one to have such a pure and innocent public as the children are."

* * *

van LHIN, Erik
See del REY, Lester

* * *

verDORN, Bethea (Stewart) 1952-

■ Personal

Born November 2, 1952, in Des Moines, IA; daughter of Robert (an electrician) and Virginia (a homemaker; maiden name, Wheat) Stewart; married Jerry verDorn (a television and film actor), June 4, 1977; children: Jacob, Peter. *Education:* Moorhead State University, B.S., 1975; Hunter College, M.A., 1982; attended Institute of Children's Literature, 1986-92. *Hobbies and other interests:* Reading, computers, travel, theater-going, gardening.

■ Addresses

Home—Sparta, NJ. *Office*—c/o Arcade Publishing, 141 Fifth Ave., New York, NY 10010.

■ Career

Brookings Harbor High School, Brookings, OR, high school teacher, 1975-77; Moorhead State University, Moorhead, MN, managing director, summer theater, 1975-78, 1987—; Manhattan Theatre Club, New York City, associate business manager, 1978-80; Nyack Public Schools, Nyack, NY, teacher of English as a second language, 1988-92; freelance writer, 1987—. Member, Parent-Teacher Association. *Member:* Authors Guild, Society of Children's Books Writers and Illustrators.

■ Awards, Honors

Children's Book Council Notable Children's Trade Book in Social Studies, 1991, for *Moon Glows; Highlights for Children* Author of the Month Award, 1991, for "The Half-a-Chance Lad."

■ Writings

Moon Glows, illustrated by Thomas Graham, Arcade Publishing, 1990.
Day Breaks, illustrated by Graham, Arcade Publishing, 1992.

Contributor to periodicals, including *Highlights for Children.*

"BABY JAY" SERIES

Daytime With Baby Jay, Modern Publishing, 1987.
Playtime With Baby Jay, Modern Publishing, 1987.
Naptime With Baby Jay, Modern Publishing, 1987.
Rhymetime With Baby Jay, Modern Publishing, 1987.

■ Work in Progress

Various short stories; a series of four preschool board books; a chapter book; a picture book.

■ Sidelights

Bethea verDorn told *SATA:* "I began writing for children after my two sons were born, and their insatiable appetite for books led me to rediscover children's literature. At that time, there was not the number of preschool board books available today, so I entered the field with ideas for some toddler board books." Modern Publishing, a mass market children's book publisher, offered to publish verDorn's *Baby Jay* board book series, provided that she supply the artwork and do the typesetting herself. "I enlisted the help of an artist friend to do the illustrations," she recalled, "and we spent weeks working on the design layouts and preparing the mechanicals. The process gave me real hands-on experience and appreciation for the steps involved in creating a picture book."

In 1990, *Moon Glows* was published, followed a year later by a companion book, *Day Breaks.* VerDorn said, "*Moon Glows* ... came about after my older son and I discovered that on full moon nights, we could put away his night light and open the window shade. The moon's glow was enough to chase away his fears of the dark, and the thought that it shone on creatures everywhere somehow comforted him .... Extending the images of *Moon Glows* to their daytime counterparts seemed to be a logical step."

VerDorn explained: "The ideas for my books and magazine stories usually come from experiences with my children or from memories of my own childhood, although one story, 'The Half-a-Chance Lad,' was based on the real-life adventures of my Scottish uncle.

"My favorite children's books are those with simple language that evokes vivid mental images, even when read without looking at the illustrations. Then, with pictures added to the pages, the book becomes doubly exciting. I try to create that kind of mental imagery when I write and to be sensitive to how well the words read aloud (this from a background in theater and oral interpretation!)

"For me, the most rewarding thing about writing for children is having personal contact with kids who have read my books and talking with them about reading and writing. Several elementary school appearances have taught me never to underestimate the effect a book can have on a child. What a thrill it is to see children so fascinated by the power of words and pictures that they clamor for the chance to create their own books, to tell their own stories! That, I think, is what writing for children is all about."

WALDHERR, Kris 1963-

■ Personal

Born May 17, 1963, in West Haverstraw, NY; daughter of Irene (Prince) Cahill. *Education:* School of Visual Arts, B.F.A. (with honors), 1985. *Hobbies and other interests:* Opera, travel, women's studies, playing the cello and flute.

■ Addresses

Home—Brooklyn, NY. *Office*—c/o Dial Books, 375 Hudson St., Brooklyn, NY 10014.

■ Career

Free-lance children's book author and illustrator, 1987—; book designer, 1988—. Shows and sells the artwork from her books at galleries in the U.S. and Great Britain. Makes author appearances at schools and libraries. *Member:* Children's Book Illustrators Guild (steering committee member, 1991-93).

■ Writings

(Self-illustrated) *Persephone and the Pomegranate,* Dial, 1993.

ILLUSTRATOR

Amy Ehrlich, *Rapunzel,* Dial, 1989.
Robert San Souci, *The Firebird,* Dial, 1992.

■ Work in Progress

The Lion's Bride, a picture book retelling of "Beauty and the Beast" set in Venice, Italy; an adult collection of oral histories of women who grew up without fathers.

■ Sidelights

Kris Waldherr told *SATA:* "There is something about picture books that offers endless challenges and delights for an artist and author. For me, the form is as rich and transporting to the senses as an opera, which is one of the main inspirations for my work. In my books, I would love to achieve as seamless a union of words and pictures and good book design as there is of pageantry and music in some of my favorite operas, such as Wolfgang Amadeus Mozart's *The Magic Flute.* Richness of color, archetypal resonance, and beauty—all these I yearn to incorporate and master.

"One of my earliest memories is of being given an elaborately illustrated edition of *King Arthur.* I spent hours looking at the pictures and trying to dress up like Guinevere! I didn't understand what the stories were about, but those mysterious pictures woke something in me, this feeling of yearning melancholy for a long-ago time that I wasn't sure existed. I especially loved the illustration of the Lady of Shalott, so pale upon her death-barge ferried by a fierce, protective monk in

KRIS WALDHERR

black. I didn't know what was going on, or how healthy it was for a five-year-old child, but I wanted it!

"From there on, all I drew was princesses. I also became fixated with the idea that I was perhaps royalty in disguise and would one day be rescued by my 'true' family—not an unusual sentiment for a child whose parents divorced when I was eleven. My fantasies were encouraged by my maternal grandfather's tall stories of our English royal heritage, which he claimed to have given up to move to America. Even at an early age, I spent most of my time alone drawing, and later, writing stories, rather than playing with my younger sister, who was more athletic. The stories I wrote became more and more gothic, influenced by Charlotte Bronte's *Jane Eyre* and Mary Wollstonecraft Shelley's *Frankenstein,* favorite books of mine. My mother encouraged me to interact more with the outside world—one time she even locked me outside to play—but it was to no avail. I now tease her that I got my revenge by becoming a children's book illustrator and author, for despite all her efforts, I now make my living spending days inside, painting and writing.

"Growing up in suburban Ridgefield Park, New Jersey, I prized summers when I could draw and read uninterrupted. I loved the library there and still dream about the treasures that seemed to be in that building. Every year the library had a contest in which children would draw a poster for their favorite book. I entered and won, to my surprise, for L. Frank Baum's *The Wizard of Oz,* and thereafter looked forward to the contest and planned elaborate designs for my entry. I suppose that could be considered my introduction to being a book illustrator! My mother indulged me by borrowing adult books for me to read, despite the librarians' disapproval of her not censoring some of my choices. I loved Louisa May Alcott's *Little Women,* any books on the supernatural, and biographies of strong women—especially fifteenth-century saint Joan of Arc. I would love to do a book about Joan of Arc one day! But my tastes also ran to the pedestrian, such as the *Alfred Hitchcock and the Three Investigators* books and Carolyn Keene's *Nancy Drew* series. When I was in fourth grade, I even had an investigative service like Nancy; I spent a lot of time searching for lost pencils instead of anything meatier.

"Eventually my interests turned back to art and writing as a career, and when I realized that it was actually possible to make a living as an artist by becoming a graphic designer, I decided to make that my choice. I received a full scholarship to the School of Visual Arts (SVA), where I intended to major in advertising, but after first year foundation decided that I really wanted to illustrate books and instead majored in that. It was at the end of my first year there that I discovered a book of paintings by the English Victorian pre-Raphaelite painter Burne-Jones and felt a strong connection to his work. Now that I look at it, it was similar to that King Arthur book that resonated within me so strongly, so there was no surprise; aren't most people drawn to their earliest experiences in some form or another? Later I discovered the work of Burne-Jones's contemporaries, Dante Ros-

setti and William Morris, who strived to incorporate book design and illustration together, and whose Arts and Crafts Movement and ideals influenced my work as both an illustrator and children's book designer.

English Sojourn Inspires First Book

"After my graduation from SVA, I traveled to England to see the works of these artists and the place where they lived their romantic lives. While there, I also met the book illustrator Alan Lee, whose work with Brian Froud in *Faeries* was so popular in the early 1980s. Seeing an illustrator successfully and so beautifully creating such books inspired me even further to create the books that I really wanted to illustrate, and after I returned from my trip to England, I began to illustrate my first book, *Rapunzel,* while between free-lance jobs.

"In early 1987 I finally sold *Rapunzel* to Dial Books, and an idea for another book, which became *The Firebird.* Tired of living in New York, I took the advance money and moved to England for a year to work full time on the books. Chagford, Devon, the village I moved to, was the home of Alan Lee, my mentor, and other artists, and also the most beautiful place I have ever seen that I've wanted to call home. The landscapes of the moors around Devon served as a major inspiration for *Rapunzel,* along with the book design of the *Kelmscott Chaucer,* William Morris's masterpiece book. I consider the year in Chagford one of the most magical in my life. I lived in a small cottage which I rented from two potters who loved music like I did and became my friends. I made many wonderful friends and discovered my English relatives. I helped restore the cottage when in between stages on *Rapunzel,* took long walks over the mysterious Devon moors and woods, feeling very 'Brontesque,' and became healthy after years of New York City stress and art school poverty. I was very sad to leave when my visa expired and the money ran out.

"When I returned to New York, I started work on *The Firebird,* which took me a very long time to finish, perhaps because I was working larger than I normally did and was painting in oils instead of watercolors, since I wanted the colors to be more intense than they had been in *Rapunzel.* I had also seen the Italian artist Bellini's paintings in Venice, and was so impressed with his use of color to create emotion and intensity that I wanted to give my work some of that feeling. In many ways I feel that *The Firebird* was a transitional book, moving from an earlier, perhaps simpler style and use of composition, to something more substantial but not quite fully developed yet. I suppose, though, that that's how many artists feel about their work—that the next book will always be better than whatever they're working on now.

"In New York I turned back to my writing, neglected for so long except for the occasional poem or journal entry. From a drawing I did for a Christmas card came the inspiration for my next book, *Persephone and the Pomegranate,* a feminist retelling of the Greek nature myth. In this book I've tried to combine my love for landscape with my love for intense mood and mystery. Working with characters who are Greek gods and goddesses also presented attractions and difficulties; while painting *Persephone,* I often thought of nineteenth-century German composer Richard Wagner's 'Ring' cycle of operas, in which he has managed to give mythic characters from Norse mythology strong personalities and human qualities while also retaining their innate divinity and symbolism.

"There are so many directions I'd like to explore in my artwork and writing. I'm hopeful that my writing will become as important to me in a creative sense as painting has been. A friend who is also a children's book editor suggested that I work on more humorous stories, so that is another aspect of my work that I would like to expand upon; I feel I've done enough ethereal heroines for a while! I would also like to create books which promote women's issues and their stories, like *Persephone* does for goddess/feminist mythology. I feel very fortunate to be able to work with the rich mother lode of material contained in myths and fairy tales. I hope I can create books that will move both children and adults toward that still, ancient place which folklore comes from."

* * *

WATSON, Amy Zakrzewski 1965-

■ Personal

Born August 4, 1965; daughter of Edward (a self-employed painter) and Justine (Bingham) Zakrzewski; married Neill Pat Watson III (a psychologist), December 1, 1990; children: Adam Zachary; (stepchildren) Anna Ruth Cory-Watson, Damon Thayer Cory-Watson. *Education:* Bloomsburg University, B.A., 1987; College of William and Mary, M.A., 1992. *Religion:* Catholic. *Hobbies and other interests:* Percussion, swimming, tennis.

■ Addresses

Home and office—117 Chestnut Dr., Williamsburg, VA 23185.

■ Career

Learning and Evaluation Center, Bloomsburg, PA, writer and editor, 1987-1990; Colonial Williamsburg Foundation, Williamsburg, VA, associate editor, 1989-1992; Child Development Resource Center, Lightfoot, VA, editor, 1989—. *Member:* Sigma Tau Delta, Phi Kappa Pi.

■ Writings

The Folk Art Counting Book, Colonial Williamsburg Foundation, 1992.
Colonial Williamsburg from A to Z, Colonial Williamsburg Foundation, 1993.

Counting With the Cooper, Colonial Williamsburg Foundation, 1993.
Colonial Animals, Colonial Williamsburg Foundation, 1993.
Colonial Colors, Colonial Williamsburg Foundation, 1993.

■ Sidelights

"I have always had an interest in children's literature," Amy Zakrzewski Watson told *SATA.* "How do you get and hold a child's attention? How do you instruct while you entertain? What appeals to the child at different ages?" In 1992, Watson became the parent of a baby boy, Adam. "As a new mother," she explained, "my interest [in children's literature] has intensified as I try out new books on my four-month-old and see which he responds to. As a young writer, I am realizing that this is an important part of writing—researching the audience.

"Who the audience is and how they respond won't change the content, but it should dictate the delivery. It's like the mother playing airplane as she feeds the child. The food gets to the tummy almost without the child realizing it."

* * *

WEIR, Bob 1947-

■ Personal

Born October 16, 1947, in San Francisco, CA; son of Frederick U. (an electrical engineer) and Eleanor (a giftware importer; maiden name, Cramer) Weir.

■ Addresses

Office—c/o Hyperion, 114 Fifth Ave., New York, NY 10011. *Agent*—Sarah Lazin, 126 Fifth Ave., Suite 300, New York, NY 10010.

■ Career

Rhythm guitarist and singer for The Grateful Dead, 1965—. *Member:* Seva Foundation, Creating Your Future, Rainforest Action Network.

■ Awards, Honors

Children's Book Council Notable Children's Trade Book in Social Studies, 1991, for *Panther Dream: A Story of the African Rainforest;* multiple gold and platinum record albums; honorariums.

■ Writings

(With sister, Wendy Weir, and soundtrack producer, performer, and narrator of audio cassette tape) *Panther Dream: A Story of the African Rainforest,* illustrated by W. Weir, Hyperion, 1991.

BOB AND WENDY WEIR

■ Work in Progress

Children's book and tape about life under the ocean on the Great Barrier Reef, Australia, 1994.

■ Sidelights

Bob Weir told *SATA:* "A children's book can influence a child toward looking at life and natural order with respect and admiration by making it fun, as well as intriguing. If this happens enough, the world could be a better place in years to come. And maybe their innocent vision can bring adults a greater respect for our planet."

WEIR, Wendy 1949-

■ Personal

Born October 2, 1949, in San Francisco, CA; daughter of Frederick U. (an electrical engineer) and Eleanor (a giftware importer; maiden name, Cramer) Weir. *Education:* University of California, Berkeley, B.A., 1970.

■ Addresses

Office—c/o Hyperion, 114 Fifth Ave., New York, NY 10011. *Agent*—Sarah Lazin, 126 Fifth Ave., Suite 300, New York, NY 10010.

■ Career

Senior bank executive positions in savings and loans and banks, 1973-1985; financial consultant in the banking and insurance industries, 1985—. Director of The Mountain School, 1991—, and Coral Forest (non-profit coral reef conservation organization). *Member:* Rainforest Action Network.

■ Awards, Honors

Children's Book Council Award Notable Children's Trade Book in Social Studies, 1991, for *Panther Dream: A Story of the African Rainforest.*

■ Writings

(With brother, Bob Weir, and illustrator) *Panther Dream: A Story of the African Rainforest,* Hyperion, 1991.

■ Work in Progress

Children's book and tape about life under the ocean on the Great Barrier Reef, Australia, 1994.

■ Sidelights

Wendy Weir told *SATA:* "I have always wanted to do something with my artistic talents, but was so heavily involved in making a living in the financial industry that I never took the time. Then, in my late thirties, I decided to do something that was totally *me.* I enjoy working with children, and decided to combine this interest with my art through the illustration of children's books."

Weir co-wrote *Panther Dream* with her older brother Bob, who is the singer and rhythm guitarist for the legendary San Francisco rock band The Grateful Dead. Like his sister, Bob Weir is also involved in rainforest preservation and other environmental causes. In September, 1988, the Dead played a rainforest benefit concert at Madison Square Garden in New York City. Wendy then approached him about the possibility of collaborating on a children's book.

"I talked to my brother Bob ... and asked if he wanted to continue educating people about the environment by producing a children's book and tape about the rainforest," she said. "We would write it together; I would illustrate it, and he would do the music and narration. He thought it was a great idea, and we started work on it immediately."

Weir explained that eighteen percent of the world's tropical rainforests are located in Africa. "We did extensive research on the animals ... and the interrelationship of the Bantu farmers and the Mbuti pygmies who reside in this region.... The book and tape were designed not only to entertain, but to educate, and they were created in a manner that would appeal to the imagination of both normal and learning disabled children. This latter aspect is extremely important to us since Bob is severely dyslexic, and he wanted to teach children about the beauty and diversity of life in a way that would reach them on many levels.

"Bob and I are now working on our second children's book and tape about life in and around the coral reefs. There is a natural connection here of which most people are unaware. There is as much, if not more, biodiversity in a coral reef as there is in a rainforest. Plus, the reefs are being destroyed in part through siltation resulting from deforestation and erosion. All life is interconnected, and, in helping to preserve our environment, we help to preserve our lives."

Weir told *SATA* that a portion of the proceeds from *Panther Dream* will be donated to Rainforest Action Network in San Francisco, California, Cultural Survival in Cambridge, Massachusetts, and the Africa NGO Environment Network in Nairobi, Kenya. She added: "We also have a section in our contract which states that the publisher will replant a tree for every one used in the production of this book."

*   *   *

WEISS, Harvey 1922-

■ Personal

Born April 10, 1922, in New York NY; son of Louis and Bertha (Stern) Weiss; married Miriam Schlein (a writer), 1954 (divorced, 1970); married Margaret I. McKinnickinnick, 1981; children: (first marriage) Elizabeth, John.

HARVEY WEISS

Education: Attended University of Missouri, New York University, Rutgers University, Art Students League, and National Academy School of Fine Arts; studied sculpture in Paris under Ossipe Zadkine.

■ Addresses

Home—42 Maple Ln., Green Farms, CT 06463.

■ Career

Freelance writer, illustrator, and sculptor. Adelphi University, Garden City, NY, professor of sculpture. Formerly worked in advertising industry as a production manager. *Exhibitions:* Sculptures exhibited in one-man shows at Paul Rosenberg Gallery, New York City, Fairfield University, Fairfield, CT, Silvermine Guild Arts Center, New Canaan, CT, American Institute of Arts and Letters, and elsewhere; group shows at Sculpture Center Gallery, New York City, Sculptors Guild, New York City, Albright Knox Gallery, Buffalo, NY, and elsewhere. Work represented in permanent collections of Nelson Rockefeller, Joseph Hirschhorn, Kranert Museum, the Ford Foundation, and others. *Military service:* U.S. Air Force. *Member:* Authors Guild, Authors League of America, Sculptors Guild (president, 1969-71), National Academy of Design, Silvermine Guild.

■ Awards, Honors

New York Herald Tribune Spring Book Festival Honor Book awards, 1957, for *A Gondola for Fun,* 1958, for *Paul's Horse, Herman,* and 1961, for *Pencil, Pen, and Brush: Drawing for Beginners;* Ford Foundation purchase awards, 1960 and 1961; Olivetti Award, New England Annual Exhibition, 1969; National Institute of Arts and Letters grant, 1970; National Sculpture Society grant, 1993.

■ Writings

"BEGINNING ARTISTS LIBRARY" SERIES; SELF-ILLUSTRATED

Clay, Wood, and Wire: A How-to-Do-It Book of Sculpture, Addison-Wesley, 1956.
Paper, Ink, and Roller: Print-Making for Beginners, Addison-Wesley, 1958, published in England as *The Young Printmaker: Printing with Paper, Ink, and Roller,* Kaye & Ward, 1969.
Pen, Pencil, and Brush Drawing for Beginners, Addison-Wesley, 1961.
Sticks, Spools, and Feathers, Addison-Wesley, 1962.
Ceramics: From Clay to Kiln, Addison-Wesley, 1964.
Paint, Brush, and Palette, Addison-Wesley, 1966.
Collage and Construction, Addison-Wesley, 1970.
Lens and Shutter: An Introduction to Photography, Addison-Wesley, 1971.
How to Make Your Own Movies: An Introduction to Filmmaking, Addison-Wesley, 1973.
Carving: How to Carve Wood and Stone, Addison-Wesley, 1976.

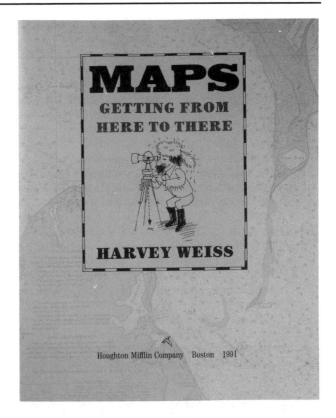

Houghton Mifflin Company   Boston   1991

Weiss provides descriptions of various types of maps, details their history, and gives simple, clear explanations of map features in this guide for children. (Cover illustration by the author.)

Working with Cardboard and Paper, Addison-Wesley, 1978.

SELF-ILLUSTRATED; JUVENILE

Twenty-four and Stanley, Putnam, 1956.
A Gondola for Fun, Putnam, 1957.
Paul's Horse, Herman, Putnam, 1958.
The Sooner Hound, Putnam, 1960.
The Expeditions of Willis Partridge, Abelard, 1960, reprinted as *The Adventures of Willis Partridge,* Young Readers Press, 1966.
How to Ooze, and Other Ways of Travelling, Abelard, 1961.
Horse in No Hurry, Putnam, 1961.
My Closet Full of Hats, Abelard, 1962.
Very Private Treehouse, Abelard, 1964.
Rocks and Gemstones, Crowell, 1967.
Sailing Small Boats, Addison-Wesley, 1967, published in England as *Better Sailing,* edited by John Chamier, Kaye & Ward, 1969.
The Big Cleanup, Abelard, 1967.
How to Be a Hero, Parents Magazine Press, 1968.
Motors and Engines and How They Work, Crowell, 1969.
The Gadget Book, Crowell, 1971.
Ship Models and How to Build Them, Crowell, 1973.
How to Make Your Own Books, Crowell, 1973.
Model Cars and Trucks and How to Build Them, Crowell, 1974.
Model Airplanes and How to Build Them, Crowell, 1975.

Games & Puzzles You Can Make Yourself, Crowell, 1976.

How to Run a Railroad: Everything You Need to Know about Model Trains, Crowell, 1977.

What Holds It Together, Little-Brown, 1977.

Model Buildings and How to Make Them, Crowell, 1979.

How to Be an Inventor, Crowell, 1980.

Hammer and Saw, Crowell, 1981.

Machines and How They Work, Crowell, 1983.

Shelters: From Tepee to Igloo, Crowell, 1988.

Cartoons and Cartooning, Houghton, 1990.

Submarines and Other Underwater Craft, Harper/Collins, 1990.

Maps: Getting from Here to There, Houghton, 1991.

Strange and Wonderful Aircraft, Houghton, 1994.

ILLUSTRATOR; JUVENILE

Miriam Schlein, *Here Comes Night,* Albert Whitman, 1957.

David C. DeJong, *The Happy Birthday Umbrella,* Little, Brown, 1959.

Schlein, *The Raggle Taggle Fellow,* Abelard, 1959.

Beth Y. Gleick, *Time Is When,* Rand, 1960.

Schlein, *My Family,* Abelard, 1960.

Alice Marriott, *First Comers: Indians of America's Dream,* McKay, 1960.

Norma Simon, *My Family Seder,* United Synagogue Books, 1961.

Simon, *Tu Bishvat,* United Synagogue Books, 1961.

Joan M. Lexau, *Olaf Reads,* Dial, 1961.

DeJong, *The Happy Birthday Egg,* Little, Brown, 1962.

Schlein, *The Pile of Junk,* Abelard, 1962.

Lexau, *Olaf Is Late,* Dial, 1963.

DeJong, *Looking for Alexander,* Little, Brown, 1963.

Schlein, *Who,* Walck, 1963.

Daniel Goldwater, *Bridges and How They Are Built,* Hale, 1965.

DeJong, *Alexander the Money-Sitter,* Little-Brown, 1965.

Marriott, *Black Stone Knife,* Archway, 1968.

Leonore Klein, *Silly Sam,* Scholastic, 1971.

Mel Cebulash, *Willie's Pet,* Scholastic, 1972.

Robert Froman, *Rubber Bands, Baseballs & Doughnuts: A Book about Topology,* Crowell, 1972.

David A. Adler, *3D, 2D, 1D,* Crowell, 1975.

Also illustrator of numerous other children's books, including *Every Friday Night,* by Norma Simon, United Synagogue Books.

■ Sidelights

Harvey Weiss was born in New York City and has lived there all his life, with the exception of three years he spent in the Air Force, some travel abroad, and a year of study at the University of Missouri. The broad cultural panorama surrounding him in the city environment exposed young Weiss to many different forms of creative endeavor. The deep enthusiasm for art that resulted has remained with Weiss throughout his life, prompting his exploration into such artistic mediums as sculpture, writing, and drawing. Weiss's varied interests have led

him to seek artistic outlets through the many jobs he held in the field of advertising and also to make a series of successful exhibitions as a sculptor. His creative talents have led him finally to a career as the author of a diverse series of nonfiction books for children. Weiss has made a name for himself as an author who can be counted on to inspire and inform young would-be artists and hobbyists with the same enthusiasm that he brings to his own work as a writer and artist.

Weiss discovered the world of books within the doors of the New York Public Library when he was around eleven years old, and he has been an avid reader ever since. "Books have always been very special to me," he once commented in *SATA,* "as sources of knowledge, as enlargers of experience, and as means of entertainment. Many of the books I bought and read and treasured as a youngster in school still rest in one of the many bookcases that are scattered through my home and which line the walls of the room where I work. One of the special shelves contains books that I have made myself, strictly for my own amusement. They are sketch books and photo albums, unfinished books of poetry, books full of doodles and random thoughts. Some have only a few pages. Others are fairly thick. The bindings are simple and were quickly done. Most of these books are dog-eared and worn from much use, and some, which were experimental, are crude and rather makeshift. But they were all great fun to make and to use. It is nice to have them close at hand where they can be thumbed through at idle moments or shown to friends."

Despite a great love for books and illustration, Weiss came to be an author himself in a round-about fashion. "It wasn't until I had met and married Miriam Schlein in 1954 that I first became aware of the fascination of

Weiss's *How to Be an Inventor* includes information on how famous inventors came up with their ideas. (Illustration by the author.)

CARTOONS and Cartooning

Harvey Weiss

Many of Weiss's books provide kids with practical information about creating things, as in this book, *Cartoons and Cartooning*. (Cover illustration by the author.)

children's books," he told *SATA*. "I succumbed to the irrepressible urge to write one myself when I began to realize that there was an audience of perceptive, fresh, honest, unspoiled people—children. I had never realized this before. It seemed to me that this was an opportunity for direct and honest art—writing and illustrating—that is rarely found in the commercial world of today. And it had a very close relationship in spirit with the sculpture I had been doing most of my life."

Weiss's other interest-turned-vocation is that of sculpture, which was inspired by the enjoyment of model building as a child. Many of his books for children have been inspired by this hobby, such as *Ship Models and How to Build Them*, and *How to Run a Railroad*. Weiss comments in *Model Cars and Trucks and How to Build Them*, "I find [models] interesting and pleasing by themselves, and I don't really care if they are very accurate or not. They are fun to make. They are fun to have around.... I find that my models end up on window sills, the kitchen counter, the coffee table in the living room—in fact, they look fine anywhere at all."

The understanding that the "creative process"—art, ceramics, photography, model making—is of greater importance than the resulting artwork underlies Weiss's "Beginning Artists Library" series. Young artists are given room for experimentation within the technique involved in their new medium, whether it be pencil,

paintbrush, pen-and-ink, or print-making, and Weiss's relaxed style allows them time to build confidence in their ability. Whatever subject he chooses, Weiss's books have been consistently commended for their clearly written and well-illustrated texts. As Margaret Sherwood Libby writes in the *New York Herald Tribune*, "Among the many books planned to aid and inspire children [in the arts], our favorites are those by Mr. Weiss."

■ Works Cited

Libby, Margaret Sherwood, *New York Herald Tribune*, October 7, 1962, p. 14.
Something about the Author, Volume 27, Gale, 1982, pp. 225-227.
Weiss, Harvey, *Model Cars and Trucks and How to Build Them*, Crowell, 1974.

■ For More Information See

BOOKS

Children's Literature Review, Volume 4, Gale, 1982.
Contemporary American Painting and Sculpture, University of Illinois Press, 1961.
de Montreville, Doris, and Donna Hill, *Third Book of Junior Authors*, H. W. Wilson, 1972.
Kingman, Lee, and others, compilers, *Illustrators of Children's Books, 1957-1966*, Horn Book, 1968.
Viguers, Ruth Hill, and others, compilers, *Illustrators of Children's Books, 1946-1956*, Horn Book, 1958.

PERIODICALS

Booklist, October 15, 1984, p. 316; March 1, 1986, p. 1024; June 1, 1988, p. 1680; March 15, 1990, p. 1460; July, 1990, p. 2096.
School Library Journal, September, 1988, p. 196; April, 1990, p. 138; May, 1990, p. 121.

*   *   *

WEKESSER, Carol A. 1963-

■ Personal

Born April 10, 1963, in Omaha, NE; daughter of Owen Vincent (an insurance analyst) and Hazel Leona (a bookkeeper; maiden name, Kirchenwitz) Winchell; married Michael Lee Wekesser (an architect), December 28, 1985; children: Grant Michael. *Education:* University of Nebraska-Lincoln, Bachelor of Journalism, 1985. *Politics:* Democrat. *Religion:* Lutheran.

■ Addresses

Home—4861 Glenwood, #7, Mission, KS 66202.

■ Career

Curriculum Concepts, San Diego, CA, book editor, 1988-1990; Greenhaven Press, San Diego, senior editor, 1990-93; free-lance writer and editor, 1993—.

CAROL A. WEKESSER

■ Writings

EDITOR

America's Children, Greenhaven Press, 1991.
The Death Penalty, Greenhaven Press, 1991.
America's Defense, Greenhaven Press, 1991.
Africa, Greenhaven Press, 1991.
(With others) Sexual Harassment, Greenhaven Press, 1992.
(With others) Europe, Greenhaven Press, 1992.
American Foreign Policy, Greenhaven Press, 1993.
(With others) The Breakup of the Soviet Union, Greenhaven Press, 1993.
Alcoholism, Greenhaven Press, 1993.

■ Work in Progress

The Supreme Court, Lucent Press.

■ Sidelights

Carol Wekesser has a real interest in history and political science and likes working on books which focus on these subjects. At one time she even thought about becoming an historian, but the opportunities in publishing for research and writing drew her to that field. Wekesser now works on books as diverse as children's welfare and the United States military. "I would like to work on books for younger children to help bring history alive to them," she told SATA.

WHITELAW, Nancy 1933-

■ Personal

Born August 29, 1933, in New Bedford, MA; daughter of Joseph Eaton (a furniture store manager) and Mildred (a furniture store manager; maiden name, Pehrson) Eaton; married David Whitelaw (a farmer), 1955; children: Katherine Whitelaw-Barrett, Patricia Whitelaw-Hurley. Education: Tufts University, B.A., 1954; University of Buffalo, M.Ed., 1968. Hobbies and other interests: Grass-roots politics, volunteering in local mayor's office.

■ Addresses

Home—3212 Salisbury Rd., Jamestown, NY 14701.

■ Career

Malden Schools, Malden, MA, teacher, 1954-55; Amerikan Kiz Koleji, Izmir, Turkey, teacher, 1955-58; Amherst public school system, Amherst, NY, teacher, 1968-88; instructor, Institute of Children's Literature, 1988—. Member: American Society of Journalists and Authors, Society of Children's Book Writers and Illustrators.

■ Writings

A Beautiful Pearl, Whitman, 1990.
Charles de Gaulle, Dillon/Macmillan, 1991.
Theodore Roosevelt Takes Charge, Whitman, 1992.
Joseph Stalin, Dillon/Macmillan, 1992.

Also contributor to newspapers and periodicals, including Christian Science Monitor, USA Today, and Sail.

■ Work in Progress

A biography of Margaret Sanger; researching the life of Grace Murray Hopper, a computer "genius" and the first female rear admiral in the U.S. Navy.

■ Sidelights

Nancy Whitelaw was inspired to begin writing when she visited a school to observe its reading program. As a reading teacher she was astonished to find that the children were not reading books. She watched as the children read brief stories and articles printed on little cardboard cards. When they finished they turned the cards over to answer the questions on the back. After checking their answers, they took another card and continued. "They reminded me of supermarket cashiers who read prices, record numbers, make change, and then greet the next customer," Whitelaw told SATA. "My disgust exploded in short angry bursts which became lines of a poem."

Whitelaw published that first poem in an educational journal and became hooked when she saw the words "by Nancy Whitelaw" in print. Quickly she "threw togeth-

NANCY WHITELAW

er" articles based on ideas which she had gathered during her years of teaching experiences and sent them to educational magazines. Thirty rejections later she decided to get help and signed up for several writing courses in adult education school. "I soaked up all the information I could get from other writers," she stated. Soon she began to sell articles not only to the educational magazines, but also to other magazine markets, such as *Christian Science Monitor, USA Today,* and *Sail.*

Spurred by her love of reading to children, Whitelaw then began writing for children. Because of her love for learning about people she is concentrating on writing biographies. "I am hooked on writing for young people," she concluded.

*   *   *

WHITMAN, Alice
See MARKER, Sherry

*   *   *

WINTHROP, Elizabeth 1948-

■ Personal

Born Elizabeth Winthrop Alsop, September 14, 1948, in Washington, DC; daughter of Stewart Johonnot Oliver (a writer) and Patricia (a medical technologist; maiden name, Hankey) Alsop; married Walter B. Mahony III, June, 1970 (divorced, 1993); children: Eliza G., Andrew A. *Education:* Sarah Lawrence College, B.A., 1970. *Politics:* Democrat. *Hobbies and other interests:* Tennis, swimming, hiking.

■ Addresses

Home—250 West 90th St., No. 6A, New York, NY 10024. *Office*—Editors Ink, P.O. Box 878, Planetarium Station, New York, NY 10024-0878.

■ Career

Berkshire Eagle, Pittsfield, MA, reporter, 1969; Harper & Row, New York City, assistant editor of Harper Junior Books, 1971-73; Editors Ink (manuscript evaluation service), New York City, founding partner, 1987—; writer. Has lectured at schools and universities and taught at writers' conferences. *Member:* PEN, Authors Guild, Society of Children's Book Writers and Illustrators.

■ Awards, Honors

School Library Journal's Best of the Best, 1966-1978, and American Library Association (ALA) Best Book for Young Adults, 1978, both for *A Little Demonstration of Affection;* ALA Best Book for Young Adults, 1980, for *Knock, Knock, Who's There?;* Children's Choice Award list, 1985, Utah State Book Award Honor Book, 1986, Dorothy Canfield Fisher Award, 1987, California Young Reader Award, 1989, West Virginia Book Award Honor Book, 1989, and Wyoming Young Adult Honor Book, 1991, all for *The Castle in the Attic;* PEN Syndicated Fiction Awards, 1985 and 1990, and Open Voice Award, 1987, for short stories; Texas Bluebonnet Award nomination, 1986, for *Belinda's Hurricane;* Children's Choice Award list, 1987, for *Lizzie and Harold;* Children's Choice Award list and Teacher's Choice Award list, both 1992, for *Vasilissa the Beautiful.* Several of Winthrop's books have been Junior Literary Guild, Book of the Month Club, and Weekly Reader Book Club selections.

■ Writings

PICTURE BOOKS

Bunk Beds, illustrated by Ronald Himler, Harper, 1972.
That's Mine!, illustrated by Emily McCully, Holiday House, 1976.
Potbellied Possums, illustrated by Barbara McClintock, Holiday House, 1977.
Are You Sad, Mama?, illustrated by Donna Diamond, Harper, 1979.
Journey to the Bright Kingdom, illustrated by Charles Mikolaycak, Holiday House, 1979.
Sloppy Kisses, illustrated by Ann Burgess, Macmillan, 1980.
I Think He Likes Me, illustrated by Denise Saldutti, Harper, 1980.
Katharine's Doll, illustrated by Marylin Hafner, Dutton, 1983.
A Child Is Born: The Christmas Story, illustrated by Mikolaycak, Holiday House, 1983.
Tough Eddie, illustrated by Lillian Hoban, Dutton, 1984.
He Is Risen: The Easter Story, illustrated by Mikolaycak, Holiday House, 1985.

Lizzie and Harold, illustrated by Martha Weston, Lothrop, 1986.

Shoes, illustrated by William Joyce, Harper, 1986.

Maggie and the Monster, illustrated by Tomie dePaola, Holiday House, 1987.

Bear and Mrs. Duck, illustrated by Patience Brewster, Holiday House, 1988.

The Best Friends Club: A Lizzie and Harold Story, illustrated by Weston, Lothrop, 1989.

Sledding, illustrated by Sarah Wilson, Harper, 1989.

Bear's Christmas Surprise, illustrated by Brewster, Holiday House, 1991.

A Very Noisy Girl, illustrated by Ellen Weiss, Holiday House, 1991.

Asleep in a Heap, illustrated by Mary Morgan, Holiday House, 1993.

I'm the Boss, illustrated by Morgan, Holiday House, 1994.

Nobody Ever Listens to Me, illustrated by Hoban, HarperCollins, in press.

CHAPTER BOOKS

Belinda's Hurricane, illustrated by Wendy Watson, Dutton, 1984.

Luke's Bully, illustrated by Pat Grant Porter, Viking, 1990.

YOUNG ADULT NOVELS

Walking Away, illustrated by Noelle Massena, Harper, 1973.

A Little Demonstration of Affection, Harper, 1975.

Knock, Knock, Who's There?, Holiday House, 1978.

Marathon Miranda, Holiday House, 1979.

Miranda in the Middle, Holiday House, 1980.

The Castle in the Attic, illustrated by Trina Schart Hyman, Holiday House, 1985.

The Battle for the Castle, Holiday House, 1993.

OTHER

In My Mother's House (adult novel), Doubleday, 1988.

(Adapter) *Vasilissa the Beautiful: A Russian Folktale,* illustrated by Alexander Koshkin, HarperCollins, 1991.

Contributor of story, "The Golden Darters," to *Best American Short Stories,* edited by Robert Stone, Houghton, 1992; contributor to *New England Review* and *American Short Fiction.*

Winthrop's works have been translated into French, Spanish, German, Danish, and Chinese.

■ Adaptations

Film rights for *The Castle in the Attic* have been sold to an independent producer. *Shoes* was recorded on cassette for Live Oak Media, 1988.

■ Work in Progress

The Little Humpback Horse (an adaptation), illustrated by Alexander Koshkin, for Clarion, 1995; *Silver Lightning,* a storybook; an adult novel; short stories.

ELIZABETH WINTHROP

■ Sidelights

"If I am ever remembered after I go, I would like to be remembered as a storyteller. That she told a good story." Elizabeth Winthrop has written books in numerous genres for every age group over the course of her twenty-year career. Many of the works concern family relationships and are closely linked to the author's experience as a child or a mother. In addition to her many picture books, including *Bunk Beds, Sloppy Kisses,* and *Bear and Mrs. Duck,* Winthrop has penned chapter books and novels for older children, and her critically acclaimed young adult novel *A Little Demonstration of Affection* was selected by *School Library Journal* as one of the best books for children published between 1966 and 1978. The author more recently published two well-received fantasy novels, *The Castle in the Attic* and its sequel, *The Battle for the Castle,* as well as a novel for adults and an adaptation of a Russian folktale.

In an interview with *Something about the Author* (*SATA*), Winthrop spoke of her early life in Washington, D.C., as a major inspiration for her writing. The author described her childhood home as "a large, ramshackle, sort of falling-down house. Although we were in the city itself, it was as if we were in the country. There was an acre of woods around our house. There was a stream at the bottom of the house where you could fish for crayfish. We had a rope-swing hanging from one of the trees." In this setting Winthrop enjoyed "a very imaginative, fantasy-like childhood" in a family atmosphere that encouraged creativity. "I had five brothers," she explained, "so that we were sort of a built-in play group. It was very adventuresome. We had no television in the house until I was twelve, so there was a lot of inventing going on. The house had a lot of secret, hidden places." A favorite among these spots was the basement, "because it was where the most space was and where we could be away from the parents and have secret, inventive, crazy games." Winthrop and her brothers divided up the basement space so that each had his or her own area in which to pursue hobbies and projects.

Winthrop's father was a journalist, and both parents shared a love of reading with their children. "We were surrounded in our house by books, absolutely surrounded," she told *SATA*. "My father and mother were both very big readers. My father read aloud from Shakespeare—he made us take parts and read from plays in the evenings sometimes. There were books everywhere in the house, so reading was like breathing." Seeing her father doing his work at home made it easy for Winthrop to take writing seriously from a young age. "I would come home from school at three o'clock in the afternoon, and I would hear the keys of his old Underwood typewriter—BANG, BANG, BANG, BANG. And I saw him published and I saw that we had food on the table and shoes on our feet, and so it really dignified the profession of a writer." Her father's brother, also a writer, had a charge account at a local bookstore, and Winthrop and her brothers were each permitted to choose one book every week and charge it to him. The author called this "a wonderful present." She enjoyed reading fantasy series such as P. L. Travers's *Mary Poppins* and C. S. Lewis's *Chronicles of Narnia,* both of which influenced her own works for children, as well as Charles Dickens's tales and Laura Ingalls Wilder's autobiographical works. For a time she latched on to her brothers' interest in the *Hardy Boys* mystery series, enjoying the opportunity to trade books.

Unlike her home life, the Catholic convent school that Winthrop attended during these years did not advocate imaginative play. She recalled: "There was a prayer before and after every class, and you went to mass every morning, and I think that I chafed under that. You had to open the doors for nuns, and you had to bow when they went through, and it was all very rigid and old-fashioned." But the author managed to use the rule prohibiting talking between classes to her advantage. She explained that "all that silence certainly let a lot of voices go on in my head, and I had a lot of imaginative time," however, "it was hard to form friendships and it was hard to have a normal school life."

Family of Writers Provided Support

Although her school did not encourage creative writing, Winthrop developed an early interest in it and devoted her after-school hours to composing stories and keeping a journal. She also spent a month each summer at her grandmother's house with her young cousin, an aspiring painter. Together they wrote and illustrated stories and put on plays. The author described the experience to *SATA* as "a lot of creative, yeasty words. A lot of dignity given to the concept of being a writer." One of the reasons her family members were so supportive of Winthrop's interest in writing was that it runs in her family: "My father was a published writer, my uncle was a published writer, my aunt is a published writer, my

grandmother wrote diaries and journals, her mother was a published poet, and my grandmother's uncle was Theodore Roosevelt. [In addition to being president] he wrote thirty-seven books. So the writing just comes right down through my blood." The author added, "I'm always slightly nervous about telling kids that, because then they think they can't be a writer unless they have all these relatives who are writers. But it just happens to be my story."

At the age of twelve Winthrop completed her first book. "I remember I got one of those composition books and I thought, 'I'm going to write a book now.' I thought to write a book you had to begin on the beginning page and finish right at the end of the last page. It was a very long book, and I think I was far more interested in length than I was in character development. So I have no real memory of the story except that it went on and on and it was called 'The Mice Who Lived in the White House,' because we lived near the White House and had been to visit it." Unfortunately, the author's first attempt was never read by anyone else. "I was taking it to school to show my teacher and I left it on the school bus and never found it again. I had spent weeks writing it and I remember saying, 'Maybe I won't become a writer. It's too hard to hang on to the books you write.'"

But her discouraged outlook was reversed a few years later, when, as a tenth grader, Winthrop began attending a Connecticut boarding school. She found a creative writing teacher who "was an incredible influence on my belief that I could do it, that I could be a writer and I could publish." From there, the author chose Sarah Lawrence College with the intention of majoring in creative writing. She recalled that each student at Sarah Lawrence was assigned to a teacher, or "don," with whom he or she worked independently. When Winthrop discovered that her don was a French teacher, she "raised holy hell, because the whole reason I went there was to write. So I managed to move out of that and switch into a fiction writing course with a man named Joe Papaleo. And he was a remarkable teacher for me." Papaleo pushed Winthrop to be prolific—resulting in her completing 250 short stories while at college—and also stressed rewriting, which was not something she had concentrated on previously. The author explained to *SATA* that before she studied with Papaleo, "I had this concept that you had to do it perfectly the first time. And now I've either written or have under contract something like forty-three books, and there is only one that I never had to rewrite. That was *Shoes,* a picture book that just fell out of my brain and onto the computer one day and I never had to change it. But other than that, I am always rewriting. And I learned that it isn't that I'm doing something wrong, that it's the process for me."

Winthrop also studied short story writing with noted author Grace Paley. But Paley was heavily involved in the Vietnam War protest movement, and was forced to teach from prison much of the time, instructing her students to send their work to her cell. For that reason, Winthrop conceded, "it was a difficult year in Grace's class." However, the author added, "I loved her, and she and I still fall in each other's arms when we cross at writers' meetings. But she was not as much of an influence on me as Jane Cooper was." Cooper, a poet who taught fiction writing, recognized Winthrop's gift for handling young characters and directed her toward children's literature. Following Cooper's advice, Winthrop went on to take a course in children's book writing in her senior year, and after graduation, sought a position in children's book publishing.

Harper an Inspirational Environment

Winthrop explained that previous to her interview at Harper and Row in 1971, she had been sending out manuscripts to publishers for some time. Charlotte Zolotow, a children's book author and editor at Harper, recognized Winthrop as a talented writer and hired her with the hope that she would continue submitting her work. The author refers to the early 1970s as "the golden age of children's books" and considers herself privileged to have witnessed it first-hand: "You would be sitting at your desk and Maurice Sendak would walk by. You'd pick up the phone and E. B. White would be on the other end. You'd look up and Arnold Lobel would be carrying his *Frog and Toad* stuff. Harper and Row had, to my mind, the best people working in children's books, and it was because of Ursula Nordstrom, a legendary, brilliant, quixotic lady. I worked there under her, and that taught me more than I'd ever have been able to learn anywhere else." Winthrop was the assistant to an editor who read incoming manuscripts, and she used the situation to her full advantage. She told *SATA,* "I would clean up her desk—she had a terribly messy desk—and I would put my manuscripts on it. I was constantly shuffling things around so that my manuscript was right on top of her pile. And they read some and turned some down, and then they read *Bunk Beds* and they liked it and they took it."

Bunk Beds, the author's first published work, is a picture book celebrating the power of the imagination. Each night as they are tucked into bed, a brother and sister imagine that their beds become other places, such as a ship and a race course. Ronald Himler's illustrations depict the real-life bedroom in black and white and the children's visions in color. *Bunk Beds* is based on some of Winthrop's earliest memories: "My family originally lived in Georgetown, in a small three-story house," she told *SATA.* "There were four children and there was no room for all of us. We were all in one big nursery room and I had to share bunk beds with my brothers. My brother Ian and I were always fighting over who slept on the top, who slept on the bottom. And we played those games. We turned those bunk beds into imaginative places—a house, a garage."

Bunk Beds also incorporates other details from Winthrop's bedtime memories. "I remember the sound of other children playing on the street, because my mother was very strict and English and she put us to bed very early—before it was dark in the summer. I remember wondering why we had to be in bed when they still got to

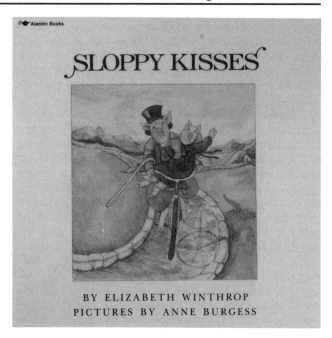

After a friend tells her that goodnight kisses are "for babies," Emmy Lou worries her parents by refusing their bedtime kisses. (Cover illustration by Anne Burgess.)

play. And I remember the look of the street lights through the green leaves. I think I put both those images in the book. That came right out of very early memories because we moved from that house when I was six. Those kinds of memories never leave you."

The author frequently tells school groups that most of her fiction is based on "things that happened to myself or to my children before the age of twelve. So that by the time you hit the sixth grade you have enough stories in you to write a hundred books." She related to *SATA,* "A child asked me once about that. I was talking about how you have all the stories you need, and you just have to be a witness to your own life, be an aware person, and notice your life as you're living it. And he put up his hand and said, 'How do you hold on to the right memories?' I thought that was the most beautiful question. And I said, 'Don't worry, the right ones will come when you need them.' Because I had no idea that I remembered those leaves and that light on the underside of those leaves until I was writing *Bunk Beds,* and it came right out of the well of memory."

Daughter's Words Frame *Bear and Mrs. Duck*

While Winthrop's first book was based on her own childhood experience, many of her picture books were inspired by things her son and daughter did or said as young children. For example, she explained to *SATA,* "I walked by my daughter's bedroom when she was four years old and I heard her say, 'Bear, I am going out. You will stay with Mrs. Duck.' Then she said, 'And stop that terrible crying, you *like* Mrs. Duck.' And I took those four lines and wrote them in my journal. And then I put them on an index card in a little box that says 'ideas.' Eight years later, I was going through that little box and

I pulled out the card and thought that I should write about this. And I wrote *Bear and Mrs. Duck,* and then I wrote *Bear's Christmas Surprise,* which is a story about a child who peeks at the Christmas presents in the closet and feels terrible about it. And that story came from the fact that I came home one day and said to my son, Andrew, who was about six, 'You look just terrible.' And finally he said, 'I peeked.' He felt Christmas had been ruined. In each of those books it's like a little germ hits me. With the picture books it's really hearing children talk and hearing what their concerns are. They are so open about them in their conversation and their play."

Winthrop has gone on to write more than twenty picture books, some of which deal in a concise manner with the same themes of family relationships, gender, and communication that are further explored in the author's novels. Winthrop's 1976 work, *That's Mine!,* concerns a boy and girl who are playing side by side, using separate blocks to build separate castles, each claiming his or hers will be biggest, tallest, and thickest. When only one block remains, they fight over it until they destroy both castles. Now the two sets of blocks are indistinguishable, and the girl and boy decide to build a single castle, twice as big as either of them could build alone. *Sloppy Kisses,* a 1980 book, concerns a family of pigs who dress, talk, and act like people. The story begins, "Emmy Lou's family loved to kiss." The conflict arises when Rosemary, one of Emmy Lou's school friends, sees Emmy Lou's father kissing her and remarks, "EEEE-YEW," explaining that kissing "is just for babies." Emmy Lou then announces to her family that she does not wish to be kissed any more. However, when she is unable to fall asleep because she has not had her good-night kiss, Emmy Lou decides that kissing is for everyone, and proves it by pecking Rosemary on the cheek before school the next morning.

In 1984 Winthrop published *Tough Eddie,* a picture book exploring gender issues. At school Eddie wears cowboy boots and builds spaceships to the moon with his friends. When he goes home for lunch, Eddie takes out his dollhouse. Later his friends come over, so he hides the dollhouse and they play with toy guns. But Eddie's sister reveals his secret to his friends. The next day Eddie plays by himself at school, but when the class visits the park and a bee lands on Eddie's nose, the other children admire his display of courage. This makes Eddie feel that his classmates will still accept him if he brings his dollhouse to school for show-and-tell.

Because Winthrop's children have grown older, she spends time with her friends' children to develop new picture book ideas. She told *SATA,* "My daughter was born in 1974 and my son in 1977, and that was a productive period from 1975 to about 1985 for my picture book writing. And I know it's because I was living with these young children who were coming up with their ideas all the time." Soon after completing *Bunk Beds,* Winthrop wrote a short story titled "Virginia's Grandfather," which began, "I never thought my grandfather would fit into a coffin." "The point of it," Winthrop told *SATA,* "was that he was tall and he was bigger than life. In other words, he would never die. It was a four- or five-page short story and I turned it in to Charlotte Zolotow and I said, 'What do you think I should do with this?' And she said, 'Make a novel out of it.' And so I did. Every afternoon at five o'clock when the office cleared, I would put aside my editorial work and I would pick up my novel and write for an hour."

The result, *Walking Away,* concerns Emily and her yearly visit to her grandparents' farm. Although her grandfather is growing older, he and Emily still have a special relationship, working together and fishing from inner tubes on the pond. But this year Emily has invited her friend Nina to join them. Emily's enthusiasm for the place has created an attractive picture in Nina's mind, and she is disappointed by the farm and the surrounding neighbors. Unable to enjoy the things Emily likes to do there, Nina instead devises ways to make trouble and convinces Emily to join her. Surprised at this new rift between herself and her friend, Emily is even more distressed by the loss of her grandfather's trust and companionship since Nina arrived. *Kirkus Reviews* called the novel "a muted, moving view of age, death, change, and incompatibility." The author told *SATA,* "*Walking Away* is very much my father. Particularly the early novels—*A Little Demonstration of Affection* and *Walking Away*—are right out of my childhood."

A Little Demonstration of Affection, Winthrop's 1975 novel, is a more subtle work about a family in which the parents have never hugged or kissed the children, and the children have behaved similarly toward each other. The plot concerns thirteen-year-old Jenny, who, with her two older brothers, decides to dig a giant hole—big enough to use as a room—in their backyard. When Jenny's oldest brother John and her best friend Lucy both go away for the summer, she and her brother Charlie, a sensitive writer, immerse themselves in the project and develop a new closeness which builds steadily as the summer progresses. Their relationship taps into their mutual longings for affection, and when they share their excitement over completing the hole, they also share a forbidden hug. Charlie responds by withdrawing from Jenny and becoming interested in Lucy when she returns. But Jenny misinterprets the hug as a sexual act, wanting more and hating herself for these feelings. A *Booklist* contributor found the story "most involving and immediate." A reviewer for the *Bulletin of the Center for Children's Books* noted that the characters and plot "are matched in strength and dignity by [Winthrop's] sympathetic percipience."

A Little Demonstration Breaks New Ground

Although contemporary young adults are accustomed to novels which turn on subtle nuance, Winthrop pointed out that psychologically-oriented novels for adolescents were rare at the time *A Little Demonstration of Affection* was published. "It's really a story of pre-adolescent love," she explained to *SATA.* "It's not about sexual abuse, it's not about incest really. It's just about those yearnings, and how when parents don't demonstrate

A brother and sister grow very close over the course of a summer project, which eventually leads to pain and confusion.

affection to their children, the children have to look for it elsewhere." The author views this message as central to her body of writing as a whole: "I think if there's been one theme throughout all of my books, it has been communication. It has been, 'Tell somebody about it. Don't be silent. Don't hold in your feelings.' Jenny never talks about how she feels and so she builds it up to something that's out of control."

In crafting this story, Winthrop drew on her imagination as well as her experience growing up. The activity that frames the plot—the digging of a giant hole in the backyard—was an actual event in the author's childhood. "My oldest brother, Joe, organized it. He set up a pulley system so the bucket would go downhill. All the neighborhood kids wanted to use the bucket, so my brother said, 'You can dig the hole and use the bucket system, but you have to pay me a quarter each time.' So not only did the hole get dug, but we made money in the process." The relationship between Jenny and Charlie, however, was invented: "I don't actually ever remember this happening with my brother, but I just imagined what it would be like to work very closely on a project the way they did, and then have the triumph of achieving it, and then the girl misconstruing what that

moment meant between them. And then her having to readjust and pick up her life again."

A Little Demonstration of Affection attracted a great deal of attention, and Winthrop left Harper and Row to concentrate on writing. The author told *SATA* that she has a better understanding of the book now than she had when she wrote it, adding, "It was in some ways, I think, a book before its time. I didn't realize how many layers there were. I was very proud of it, and I think Charlotte and Harper were very pleased with it."

In 1979 and 1980 Winthrop published two young adult novels which, unlike her previous novels, are narrated by a character. The author explained, "My earlier books are less visual and more intellectual. And then my editor at Holiday House said to me, 'I want you to try a novel in the first person. It will loosen you up.' And I wrote *Marathon Miranda* and *Miranda in the Middle,* and she was absolutely right. It made my writing looser and funnier and, for some reason that I'm not quite able to nail down, more visual." In *Marathon Miranda,* the title character, who suffers from asthma, meets Phoebe, a girl of Miranda's age who is training for a marathon. Phoebe convinces Miranda to take up running, and her participation in the marathon brings Miranda a sense of triumph. Phoebe has her own problems, however; her parents have just informed her that she was adopted, and her confused feelings lead her to run away from home. She is eventually reunited with her parents by Miranda's older friend Margaret. In *Miranda in the Middle,* thirteen-year-old Miranda is engaged in a struggle within her New York City community. Miranda, her father, her new friend Michael Oliver, and Margaret are attempting to save the old church building next door, which is soon to be demolished and replaced by a high rise which will block Miranda's family's view of the river. But a bigger problem for Miranda is Phoebe, who has fallen hopelessly in love with Philip, an older boy and avid runner. Afraid to tell her strict parents about Philip, Phoebe expects Miranda to lie to cover Phoebe's actions. Zena Sutherland lauded the work's "warmth, humor, [and] strong characters" in the *Bulletin of the Center for Children's Books.*

While Winthrop's early novels are rooted in her own childhood in terms of characters, settings, and situations, with *Marathon Miranda* and *Miranda in the Middle,* the author's adult life and her children's experiences began playing a more pronounced role. She commented that "the *Miranda* books have the feelings of my childhood, but they are placed in an apartment that I lived in as an adult for about sixteen, seventeen years. And my daughter went to private school in New York, so the concept of going across town on the bus and trying to save a building that's in danger, those are all very New York-based." The author added, "My later novels spring more from my imagination, although I think autobiographical novels also spring from your imagination. But the later ones are more invented."

Fantasy Novels Bridge Past and Present

Winthrop's first fantasy novel was her 1985 publication, *The Castle in the Attic,* in which ten-year-old William's nanny, Mrs. Phillips, has decided that it is time for her to move back to England. William is inconsolable at the thought of losing his lifelong care-giver and friend. As a gymnast, he depends on Mrs. Phillips to act as his spotter, symbolizing his need for protection and support. But when William's plan to force his nanny to stay with him backfires, he journeys to a medieval world, where he discovers that he is ready to let go of Mrs. Phillips and become his own spotter.

William's decision to try to stop Mrs. Phillips from leaving coincides with her giving him a good-bye present—a model castle and miniature silver knight that have been in her family for generations. The knight comes to life at William's touch, introduces himself as Sir Simon, and informs William that he hails from a tiny medieval world. He goes on to explain that an evil wizard, Alastor, has taken over the kingdom and turned its subjects—including himself—to lead. The knight carries part of a medallion that can shrink people and objects, and William takes advantage of this rare opportunity to overpower his nanny. He reduces Mrs. Phillips to Sir Simon's size and keeps her in the castle so that she cannot return to England. But now William is faced with a tiny Mrs. Phillips who is overcome with rage and grief, and he soon realizes that he must find a way to restore her to her original size. He uses the medallion on himself and travels with Sir Simon to the knight's kingdom, where William's intelligence, bravery, strength of character, and tumbling skills help him outwit and defeat Alastor and free both the leaden subjects and Mrs. Phillips. Writing in *School Library Journal,* Louise L. Sherman called *The Castle in the Attic* "a satisfying quest fantasy with a strong element of modern realism which will appeal to a wide range of readers." Although a *Booklist* contributor noted "a slight mechanical feel" to the story's ending, the reviewer added that this does not hinder the "light but involving piece of imagining."

Winthrop explained the source of the story to *SATA:* "We had a lady who worked for us, named Mrs. Miller, who took care of my children until my son, Andrew, was five. And when she left, Andrew was very sad and wanted her to stay." While this suggests that the character of William is based on the author's son, Winthrop stressed that all her characters largely stem from inside herself: "When I'm writing about characters there must be some part of them that I relate to. Even though a book may be based on an event in my children's lives, somewhere I have to be able to understand the feelings behind the major characters. I actually think that I was sadder about Mrs. Miller leaving than Andrew was, because Andrew still had a mother, and Mrs. Miller was somebody who had really helped me bring this child up, and she was leaving me. What was I to do then? I had to be a full-grown mother. So I think that sense of loss and that desire to hold on to her were more my feeling than Andrew's."

A realistic-looking model of a castle comes to life and leads William into fantastic adventures in Winthrop's popular novel.

Response to *The Castle in the Attic* was extremely positive, and Winthrop was pressured to write a sequel. She resisted for a long time, feeling that William's story was complete. But then the author began to think about the new problems the character might encounter as a twelve year old. "I realized he had a whole new set of challenges to face and I wanted to take him back across the drawbridge to find out how he handled them," she related. *The Battle for the Castle,* Winthrop's 1993 sequel to *The Castle in the Attic,* finds William and his biker friend Jason under pressure to "jump the trains." This test of courage, which in William's town separates the men from the boys, involves climbing the side of a moving train, crossing the top, and then jumping off the other side. When Jason succeeds at jumping the trains and William fails, William must find another way to prove himself. He tells Jason of the magic token and his triumph over the evil wizard. Jason is enthralled by the tale, and the two decide to shrink themselves and their bicycles and return to the kingdom. There a new problem awaits them: an army of man-eating rats led by a giant rat that walks on two legs. While Jason trains on his bicycle and plans to defeat the rats using armor and brute strength, William befriends Gudrin, an earthy twelve-year-old girl who teaches William to ride a horse and brings out his intuitive side. When it comes time to face the enemy, Jason's swords and muscles prove ineffective, but William, in partnership with Gudrin, destroys the rats using his intellect and imagination.

Mythical Elements in *Battle for the Castle*

The author views *The Battle for the Castle* as a strong example of her role as storyteller. She commented, "Jason goes over the top in a very old-fashioned male way, achieving something physically. William goes within. William does the work within. I'm very interested in the psychologist Carl Jung and his ideas, and this symbolism of William shrinking down and taking them into the dungeon of the castle is very archetypal." Winthrop added, "I almost think this book is a little bit like a myth. There are things there that children connect to, that have been in our storytelling consciousness for as long as human beings have been alive."

The author identifies the absence of traditional rites of passage in modern society as one of the major themes of *The Battle for the Castle*. She views dangerous tests such as jumping the trains as rituals invented by boys to compensate for the loss of formal rites of passage. Winthrop noted, "In New Guinea they take boys away from their mothers in a ritualistic way and leave them in the forest for three days. They have specific initiation rites which every primitive society has had. And the

Winthrop conducted extensive research in preparing the sequel to *The Castle in the Attic,* in which William faces challenges in the present and the past. (Cover illustration by Robert Sauber.)

knights in armor had them, and we had them in confirmation and bar mitzvah, but those are really so faint now. And I really believe that's why boys go out and drink and drive. Or take drugs to prove themselves. Or they go and find a gang to re-establish a family for themselves."

On the other side of the coin, the author stated, "I very much wanted a girl in this book, and I love the character of Gudrin. She's very important to me. I love the little wild witch girl. I think there's a little wild witch girl in me; I know how to dress properly and act properly, but some part of me wants to run down the middle of the street blowing a trumpet. There's a wild side of me that comes out in my writing and in my journal and when I'm alone, but I needed to put that character on paper."

In a project that utilized her storytelling skills, but was otherwise different from any she had undertaken before, Winthrop adapted the Russian folktale *Vasilissa the Beautiful,* in collaboration with Russian illustrator Alexander Koshkin, in 1991. Famous in its native land, this story is a cross between the well-known tales of "Cinderella" and "Hansel and Gretel." On her deathbed, young Vasilissa's mother gives her a magic doll, explaining that if she feeds the doll whenever she is sad or in danger, it will protect her from harm. After her mother's death, Vasilissa's father marries a cruel widow with two daughters. While Vasilissa's father travels, his new wife moves with the three girls to a house at the edge of the woods where he will not be able to find them. Vasilissa's stepmother then sends her into the forest to borrow fire from the evil witch Babayaga.

When Vasilissa arrives at Babayaga's house, the witch threatens to eat her if she does not complete a series of seemingly impossible tasks. However, the doll helps Vasilissa finish the work, and Babayaga gives her a skull containing fire. But when Vasilissa takes the skull home and places it in the middle of the room, it stares at her stepmother and stepsisters until they are burned to ashes. A kindly old woman then adopts Vasilissa and gives her flax to spin into thread. With the help of the doll, Vasilissa weaves beautiful fabric that the old woman presents to the tsar as a gift. The tsar is so impressed with Vasilissa's handiwork that he asks to meet her. The two fall instantly in love and are married. A *Bulletin of the Center for Children's Books* reviewer admired the ways in which "the stages of a child's passage into adulthood through grief, tests, and tempering" are incorporated into the story.

Winthrop was interested in the numerous female characters in this story and their symbolic meaning. "I loved all the women in the book," she told *SATA*. "They are all the sides of a woman; you've got the doll who's helpful, the mother who dies, the evil stepmother, the evil stepsisters, and Babayaga who is a wild witch woman and very powerful. And Vasilissa borrows Babayaga's fire, which is really a very good mythical kind of symbol; she needs to borrow the fire of a strong witch woman to go back and defeat her enemy, who is her own stepmother. I love to read those myths, and I love to read knights in armor stories, because there's so much going on behind what's up front. We reverberate so strongly, we resonate to the mythical elements of those stories."

Focus on Language

In terms of the process of adapting the story, Winthrop told *SATA:* "For me the adaptation of a fairy tale is really about language. What I do is I work from a very wooden translation. I want the most clumsy, basic translation of the fairy tale that I can find—usually the earliest one. What I'm trying to do is introduce the rhythm of our language to it so that children will hear the rhythm and love the story. I am very, very conscious of keeping all the basic elements of the story intact. The mythical elements are there and I don't touch them. I may highlight them by the way I write it, but I don't mess with them."

Considering her body of work as a whole, Winthrop told *SATA* that her books, while not intended to be educational per se, provide characters and scenarios intended to help her readers make positive choices. "I believe that readers want to see their own feelings reflected in the mirror of a book," she noted. "Mirrors don't tell you what to do or think, they just show you what is there. The more honest the mirror, the better the book." Winthrop points to William as a character with whom readers can relate, and whose adventures symbolize universal events: "William knows at the end of *The Battle for the Castle* that he doesn't have to jump the train and he doesn't have to go and do what his peers tell him to do, because he has an innate sense that he has defeated that rat by both his bravery and his intelligence." The author added that a man who read *The Battle for the Castle* as an adult once said to her, "I wish that I had gone to the castle when I was William's age, because then I would not have become an alcoholic."

Winthrop acknowledges that her readers' concerns have changed over the course of her career, but emphasizes that her work speaks to the aspects of humanity that remain unchanged: "I started writing in the early 1970s and that's now twenty years ago—twenty years of rising divorce rates, loss of money for education, and terrible inner-city drug problems. All of those issues are twenty years more prevalent than they were then, but there are still children and adults who have the basic needs: to be loved, to be cherished, to be validated, to be honored for what they think and feel. Those issues will always be, and I try to write about those things."

It is not surprising that Winthrop was one of the first young people's novelists to deal with the subtler nuances of relationships. Her success with her readers stems from her keen understanding of young people's issues and her respect for the challenges involved in growing up. "I always try to write from inside the child's head," Winthrop told *SATA.* "My books always have a theme and always have a deeper kind of focus, but I try to write right from inside those twelve-year-old boys' heads and not talk down to them or patronize them. I'm just

walking with them through what they have to go through."

■ Works Cited

Review of *The Castle in the Attic, Booklist,* January 15, 1986, p. 761.
Review of *A Little Demonstration of Affection, Booklist,* April 15, 1975, p. 869.
Review of *A Little Demonstration of Affection, Bulletin of the Center for Children's Books,* July, 1975, p. 188.
Sherman, Louise L., review of *The Castle in the Attic, School Library Journal,* February, 1986.
Sutherland, Zena, review of *Miranda in the Middle, Bulletin of the Center for Children's Books,* January, 1981, p. 103.
Review of *Vasilissa the Beautiful, Bulletin of the Center for Children's Books,* June, 1991, p. 254.
Review of *Walking Away, Kirkus Reviews,* April 1, 1973, pp. 386-387.
Winthrop, Elizabeth, *Sloppy Kisses,* Macmillan, 1980.
Winthrop, Elizabeth, telephone interview with Joanna Brod for *Something about the Author,* April 14, 1993.

■ For More Information See

PERIODICALS

Bulletin of the Center for Children's Books, February, 1978, p. 104; October, 1979, p. 40; March, 1985, p. 137.
Kirkus Reviews, June 15, 1979, p. 686; January 15, 1981, p. 76; February 15, 1991, p. 253.
New York Times Book Review, November 9, 1980, p. 71.
Publishers Weekly, August 7, 1972, p. 49; June 11, 1973, p. 155.
School Library Journal, December, 1977, p. 61; September, 1979, p. 151; November, 1980, p. 81; December, 1980, p. 57; May, 1985, p. 85; June, 1991.
Voice of Youth Advocates, April, 1986, p. 37.
Washington Post Book World, November 5, 1972, p. 3.

—Sketch by Joanna Brod

*   *   *

WINTON, Ian (Kenneth) 1960-

■ Personal

Born November 10, 1960, in Hastings, England; son of Joseph Kenneth (a marine and hospital engineer) and Joan (a nurse) Winton; married Jane Mary Harvey (an illustrator), August, 1986. *Education:* Attended Barnetart College, 1980-81; Middlesex University, B.A. (with honors), 1984. *Politics:* Green Party. *Hobbies and other interests:* Walking, mountain bike riding, going to the cinema, aerobics, gardening, reading science fiction.

■ Addresses

Home—Middle Aston Farmhouse, Montgomery, Powys, Wales SY15 6TA, United Kingdom.

■ Career

Free-lance illustrator, graphic designer, and paper engineer, 1984-85 and 1988—; Octopus Books, Ltd., London, England, in-house designer, 1985-88; Dorling Kindersley, London, in-house designer, 1988. Worked as a trainee manager in a department store, 1979-80.

■ Awards, Honors

Junior Information Award, *Times Educational Supplement,* and Sir Peter Kent Conservation Book Prize, both 1991, and Die Eule des Monats, 1992, all for *Ian and Fred's Big Green Book,* which was also shortlisted for the Science Book Prize sponsored by Copus, Rhone-Poulenc, and the London Science Museum, and for the Earthworm Award, Friends of the Earth, both 1992.

■ Illustrator

Liz Marks, *The Pirate Ship Pop-up Book,* Octopus Books, 1985.
Rupert Matthews, *The Great Dinosaur Pop-up Book,* Octopus Books, 1987.
Three Little Pigs, Parent-Child, 1989.
The Untidy Mole, Parent-Child, 1989.
(And originator) Fred Pearce, *Ian and Fred's Big Green Book,* Bennett/Kingfisher, 1991, published as *The Big Green Book,* Grosset and Dunlap, 1991.
Sue and Jim Finnie, *The Young Puffin Book of Trains,* Penguin, 1992.
My First Book of 123, Teeney Books, 1993.
My First Book of ABC, Teeney Books, 1993.
My First Book of Colours and Shapes, Teeney Books, 1993.
My First Book of Telling the Time, Teeney Books, 1993.

Ian and Fred's Big Green Book has been translated into seven languages.

■ Work in Progress

Illustrating and paper engineering the *Dinosaur Activity Book* for Walker Books and an interactive book about the senses; co-designing a series of one hundred books that will cover a wide range of subjects; designing a set of books "about the Great Explorers" and two books "about the world's hidden places."

■ Sidelights

Ian Winton told *SATA:* "I can never remember not drawing or making something or other, even beyond the amount most young children do. I know I inherited any creative aptitude I have from my father, who could draw well from memory and make model yachts from scratch or working model steam engines from chunks of solid metal. He certainly kindled my interest in the visual arts and taught me to be observant; to see the world, as I think all creative people do, in a slightly different way; and to always look at things a bit deeper.

"I almost did not pursue a career in art or design (although I would have come to it somehow sooner or later) because after finishing school I went to work full time in a department store as a trainee manager. In hindsight, I can look back to an almost subconscious dream I had then, and even in my last three or four years at school, of sitting in a design studio and working at a drawing board overlooking some part of central London. It did come true! Anyway, the department store did the trick! There's nothing like doing a job you hate for focusing the mind on what job you would like to do. I think it took me just a few weeks!

"I suppose I had not gone straight to art college basically through ignorance, as I was unaware of the massive range of career possibilities an art degree provided, and because of the inevitable outside pressures saying that I should get a 'proper job.' So, after chatting with a friend's father, who was a graphic designer, I applied and got a place in a local art college to do a one-year foundation course. After that, I went to Middlesex University and did a three-year degree in graphic design. It was a very broad course, which I liked, covering illustration, design, animation, photography, 3-D design, etc. My very first day at college told me I'd done the right thing and everything just fell into place. It was a fantastic discovery to be amongst like-minded people doing what I had done just as a hobby. It certainly confirmed my desire for a job in art or design, a desire that was really just an extension of what I'd always felt and the knowledge that I couldn't possibly do a job for the rest of my life that I didn't love and enjoy.

"In my final year at college I was all set to go into advertising as a creative team with a friend. However, a children's book publisher saw my work and offered me my first free-lance job, *The Pirate Ship Pop-up Book,* and from that moment my course has been set.

"I would say that aspiring illustrators don't need much advice other than a list of college courses to apply for and, subsequently, a list of publishers or agents to go and see with their portfolios when they've graduated. Direct feedback from publishers is invaluable. Meanwhile, keep drawing, keep a sketchbook for book ideas, and *never* give up.

First Big Break Key to Illustrating Career

"To me, illustration is very akin to the acting profession. You need that first couple of jobs to get yourself known and to give you experience. Finding someone to give you that first chance can be the most difficult step. Going to a publisher with your own idea can be a way in. When I was a designer at Octopus Books I saw many illustrators each week who came in with their portfolios looking for work. For every one brilliant or suitable illustrator who came in, there were usually five who still had a way to go, often those who had not been to college.

If you've got a creative ability, the training and general environment at college—especially one that offers a year's placement with a publisher or design studio halfway through the course—can help bring it out and develop it.

"I think the illustrator who was my greatest influence, when I was about fifteen or sixteen, was [the American illustrator] Frank Franzetta. Not because I wanted to emulate his style but because his was the most exciting drawing and painting I had ever seen both in terms of subject and style. It was mind-blowing. I then came across others like him, such as Bernie Wrightson, Jeff Jones, and Boris Vallejo.

"Obviously I do want to bring pleasure and enjoyment to the children who may see my books, and I hope this happens to a certain extent automatically, but I find that I only have time to really consider a specific achievement or goal through working on a book when it's my own project, such as *Ian and Fred's Big Green Book*. Like many other authors and illustrators, I have a very self-indulgent attitude when working on my own ideas and I really design or illustrate these books for my own enjoyment or amusement. If other people like them too, then that's a real thrill.

"I live in a very rural and almost isolated part of England and Wales (I am only into Wales by fifty yards). It's nice not to have to go down to London so often, which is a bind and a bit of a culture shock even though I lived on the outskirts of the city for twenty-three years. Living in the country with no neighbors in sight changes your outlook. Going back to a town or even a village would be a prison sentence.

"My wife Jane and I have quite a few animals, which we're both mad about. We have six cats and two dogs, and I know that number will increase over the years. When we go walking in the hills around our house with the dogs, most of the cats come, too, so you can probably imagine this procession of me and Jane followed by two dogs, chasing rabbits and each other, and then four or five of the cats, all in a long line!"

*   *   *

WOLFE, Art 1952-

■ Personal

Born September 12, 1952, in Seattle, WA; son of Richard (a photographer and printer) and Elinor (a printer) Wolfe. *Education:* University of Washington, Seattle, degrees in art education and painting, 1975.

■ Addresses

Agent—Bruce McGaw Graphics, 230 Fifth Ave., New York, NY, 10001.

■ Career

Photographer and painter. *Exhibitions:* Frye Art Museum, Seattle, WA, 1981 and 1982 (photographs and paintings), 1988 (photographs only); Silver Image Gallery, Seattle, 1991 (photographs only).

■ Writings

The Imagery of Art Wolfe (monograph), Arpel Graphics, 1985.

The Sierra Club Alaska Postcard Collection: A Portfolio, Sierra Club Books, 1989.

Light on the Land (part of "Earthsong Collection" series), edited by Art Davidson, Beyond Words Publishing, 1991.

The Art of Nature Photography, text by Martha Hill, Crown, 1993.

PHOTOGRAPHER; CHILDREN'S NONFICTION

James Martin, *Chameleons: Dragons in the Trees,* Crown, 1990.

Martin, *Hiding Out: Camouflage in the Wild,* Crown, 1993.

PHOTOGRAPHER; ADULT NONFICTION

Allan Lobb, *Indian Baskets of the Northwest Coast,* drawings by Barbara Paxson, Graphic Arts Center Publishing, 1978.

(With Wilbur Mills) T. H. Watkins, *Vanishing Arctic: Alaska's National Wildlife Refuge,* introduction by Edward Hoagland, Aperture Foundation/Wilderness Society, 1988.

Art Davidson, *Alakshak, The Great Country,* foreword by Galen Rowell, Sierra Club Books, 1989.

Douglas H. Chadwick, *The Kingdom: Wildlife in North America,* Sierra Club Books, 1990.

Owls, Their Life and Behavior: A Photographic Study of the North American Species, text by Julio de la Torre, foreword by Roger Tory Peterson, Crown, 1990.

Chadwick, *Kingdom: Wildlife in North America,* Sierra Club Books, 1990.

Gary Kowalski, *The Souls of Animals,* Stillpoint Publishing, 1991.

Martin, *Masters of Disguise: A Natural History of Chameleons,* foreword by Ron Tremper, Facts on File, 1992.

Bears, Their Life and Behavior: A Photographic Study of the North American Species, text by William Ashworth, Crown, 1992.

Penguins, Puffins, and Auks, Their Lives and Behavior: A Photographic Study of the North American and Antarctic Species, text by Ashworth, Crown, 1993.

Contributor of photographs to periodicals, including *National Geographic, Smithsonian, Natural History, Time, Newsweek,* and *Outdoor Photographer.* Contributor of photographs to books, including *Mountains of North America,* Sierra Club Books; *America's Wildlife Sampler,* National Wildlife Federation; *The Wonder of Birds,* National Geographic Society; *America, Land of*

Wildlife, National Wildlife Federation; and *Nature's Wonderlands,* National Geographic Society.

■ Work in Progress

"A comprehensive look at bio-diversity in the animal kingdom."

■ Sidelights

Young readers may know Art Wolfe best for the photographs in James Martin's *Chameleons: Dragons in the Trees.* Adults, however, may be more familiar with Wolfe's nature photographs, which have made countless appearances in books and periodicals. Whatever the audience, Wolfe's "photos jar the senses and awaken the imagination.... While capturing the sheer beauty and wonderment of Earth's far-distant corners, Art is also documenting for future generations many of the wild animals and places that may not remain in the future."

Wolfe was the third child of a U.S. Navy photographer and a commercial artist. He dreamed of becoming a painter and majored in fine arts and art education at the University of Washington in Seattle. While in college, he began to experiment with a used camera. He quickly taught himself how to use it and soon became a master of the mechanics of photography. In 1981 his photographs, as well as his monochromatic watercolor landscape paintings, were exhibited in a solo show in Seattle, Washington. Wolfe soon developed a strong reputation as a wildlife photographer. He has been featured in Kodak's instructional program series, *Techniques of the Masters,* and is the subject of an instructional and adventure video entitled *On Location with Art Wolfe.*

■ Works Cited

"Art Wolfe" (publicity profile), Bruce McGaw Graphics, c. 1992.

■ For More Information See

PERIODICALS

American Photographer, October, 1986.

* * *

WOODMAN, Allen 1954-

■ Personal

Born December 21, 1954, in Montgomery, AL; son of Frank Angelo (a designer) and Inez (a nurse and artist, maiden name, Holman) Woodman; married Jane Armstrong (a writer and teacher). *Education:* Huntingdon College, B.A., 1976; Florida State University, M.A., 1983, Ph.D., 1986.

■ Addresses

Home—P.O. Box 22310, Flagstaff, AZ 86002. *Office*—Box 6032, English Department, Northern Arizona University, Flagstaff, AZ 86011.

■ Career

Northern Arizona University, Flagstaff, AZ, associate professor of English, 1986—. *Member:* Authors Guild, Society of Children's Book Writers and Illustrators, PEN West, Associated Writing Programs, Poets & Writers.

■ Awards, Honors

Creative writing fellowship in fiction, Arizona Commission on the Arts, 1992; stories have been cited in *Best American Short Stories* and *The Pushcart Prize* series.

■ Writings

JUVENILE

(With David Kirby) *The Cows Are Going To Paris,* Boyds Mills/St. Martin's Press, 1991.
(With Kirby) *The Bear Who Came To Stay,* Bradbury Press, 1994.

ALLEN WOODMAN

ADULT

The Shoebox of Desire and Other Tales, Swallow's Tale Press, 1987, revised edition, Livingston University Press, 1994.
All-You-Can-Eat, Alabama (novel), Apalachee Press, 1994.

Also contributor to anthologies and periodicals, including *The North American Review, Pennywhistle Press, Flash Fiction, Epoch, Carolina Quarterly, Apalachee Quarterly,* and *The California Quarterly.*

■ Work in Progress

A collection of stories, *The Appliances of Loss,* Livingston University Press, 1994; two children's books; a novel; a screenplay.

■ Sidelights

Allen Woodman told *SATA* that he met his co-author, David Kirby, when he joined a literary bowling league at Florida State University, where the poets bowled against the fiction writers. "We both quickly found out that neither of us were very good bowlers but we both had the same sense of humor." Woodman, who is a fiction writer, combined his talent with Kirby, who is an award-winning poet. "It's probably the best combination for picture book writers," Woodman said. "The poet brings that sense of compression and image to the work, and the fiction writer never forgets that it's got to have a great story line. I guess David and I are fast becoming the post-modern Grimm Brothers."

When asked where their ideas come from the two will say that they are a result of what writers do naturally. They make connections between things. As Woodman described it: "Say you're driving along, thinking of your days at summer camp. You pass a field of cows and, as cows always seem to do, they turn in unison and stare at you in a kind of mythic way. Camp. Cows. All of a sudden, the writer's mind makes a connection. A summer camp for cows. What would that be like? You imagine the cows sitting around a campfire telling bovine ghost stories about the time the farmer came in the field with the hatchet." According to Woodman, this process also "explains why writers make such bad drivers."

*   *   *

WRIGHT, Cliff 1963-

■ Personal

Born October 24, 1963, in Newhaven, England; son of Ron (a construction site manager) and Nora (a homemaker; maiden name, Eager) Wright. *Education:* University of Brighton, B.A. (honors), 1986.

■ Addresses

Home and office—"Greenways," Pevensey Rd., Newhaven, East Sussex BN9 9TU, England.

■ Career

Children's book writer and illustrator. *Member:* Greenpeace.

■ Writings

(Self-illustrated) *When the World Sleeps,* Hutchinson, 1989.
(Self-illustrated) *Crumbs!,* Hutchinson, 1990.
(Self-illustrated) *The Tangleweed Troll,* Gollancz, 1993.

■ Work in Progress

Researching English and American badgers for a fourth picture book, as yet untitled, completion expected in 1993.

■ Sidelights

Cliff Wright told *SATA:* "I began writing seriously whilst at college, studying illustration. I have always been most enthusiastic about developing my own ideas rather than illustrating someone else's—so the college

CLIFF WRIGHT

projects which encompassed writing with pictures interested me most. Therefore, on leaving college I had a very generalized portfolio with no particular direction, although it did contain some ideas and wasn't just a collection of artwork. From that and the response from some publishers I quickly decided that writing/illustration for children was made for me."

Wright told *SATA* that his first book, *When the World Sleeps,* "started its life with too many words. It was obviously necessary to edit severely, and eventually I came to the conclusion that the story could be told with just pictures, encouraging kids to make up their own stories—although a great many publishers were concerned at this idea of a wordless picture book. As part of my own learning process, however, I have come to realize that it is essential to 'go with what you believe in,' and at last, two and a half years after it was conceived, *When the World Sleeps* was accepted for publication.

"I think it's important to develop and stretch your own capabilities, so with each successive project I have tried to introduce something different. With *Crumbs!* I hope this can be seen with the introduction of onomatopoeic words and a greater emphasis on my figurative drawing. In the third picture book, *The Tangleweed Troll,* I have tried to further the drawing still with regard to expression and movement and to develop a stronger story line—in this case every kid's desire to venture beyond his own backyard."

*   *   *

WRIGHT, Kenneth
See del REY, Lester